Fundamentals of Investing

Fundamentals of Investing

Lawrence J. Gitman
San Diego State University

Michael D. Joehnk
Arizona State University

Published for LOMA Education and Training Programs

Information in this text may have been changed or updated since its publication date.
For current updates, visit www.loma.org

LOMA
Information That Works®

PEARSON
Addison Wesley

Boston San Francisco New York
London Toronto Sydney Tokyo Singapore Madrid
Mexico City Munich Paris Cape Town Hong Kong Montreal

Cover art by Kathleen Ryan, FLMI, PCS, AIRC, AIAA, ARA, PAHM.

Taken from:
Fundamentals of Investing, Eighth Edition
by Lawrence J. Gitman and Michael D. Joehnk

Published by Addison Wesley, Inc.
A Pearson Education Company
Boston, Massachusetts 02116

This special edition published in cooperation with Pearson Custom Publishing.

Please visit our web site at *www.pearsoned.com*

ISBN 0-536-75427-6

BA 999228

JC

Printed in the United States of America

3 4 5 07

BRIEF CONTENTS

CONTENTS

PART ONE THE INVESTMENT ENVIRONMENT 1

INVESTING in action

CHAPTER 10 BOND VALUATION AND ANALYSIS 321

PART FIVE PORTFOLIO MANAGEMENT 353

CHAPTER 11 MUTUAL FUNDS: PROFESSIONALLY MANAGED INVESTMENT PORTFOLIOS 354

APPENDIX A FINANCIAL TABLES A-1

FOREWORD

LOMA is happy to introduce a new text, *Fundamentals of Investing*. This textbook is a special edition of *Fundamentals of Investing,* Eighth Edition, by Lawrence J. Gitman and Michael D. Joehnk, published by Addison Wesley, a Pearson Education company.

In addition to studying the material in *Fundamentals of Investing,* students who are preparing for the examination for LOMA 356 will study assigned material from *Introduction to Institutional Investing* (Atlanta: LOMA, 2004), a textbook in CD-ROM format.

LOMA selected *Fundamentals of Investing* from among several commercially published textbooks because it best meets LOMA 356 course objectives, presents the material in a clear and engaging fashion, and provides a sound overview of the fundamentals of investing. In producing this customized version, we have removed material unnecessary to meeting course objectives. In places where the authors express opinions, it should be noted that those opinions may or may not represent the views of LOMA.

The LOMA 356 examination is based exclusively on the assigned reading materials in *Fundamentals of Investing,* including information in the body of the text and in the chapter features (such as Investing in Action), figures, and tables; and *Introduction to Institutional Investing.* In addition to *Fundamentals of Investing* and *Introduction to Institutional Investing,* LOMA's *Test Preparation Guide for LOMA 356* (Atlanta: LOMA, 2004) is assigned for students preparing for the LOMA 356 exam. Used along with the assigned reading materials, the Test Preparation Guide will help you master the course material. Included in the Guide are practice exam questions, a full-scale sample examination in both paper and electronic form, and answers to all of the questions.

LOMA recommends that you use the Test Preparation Guide for this course. **Studies indicate that students who use LOMA study aids consistently perform significantly better on LOMA examinations than other students.**

Acknowledgments

As is the case with all projects at LOMA, development of *Fundamentals of Investing* depended upon the contributions and combined efforts of many individuals. First, we would like to thank the authors, Lawrence J. Gitman and Michael D. Joehnk, for writing such an excellent text and allowing LOMA to adapt it into this special edition. We would also like to thank Hal Hawkins, Senior Managing Editor, Pearson Custom Publishing; Donna M. Hendrickson, Special Sales Account Manager, Addison Wesley/Benjamin Cummings; and Sharon Stevens, Acquisitions Editor, Pearson Custom Publishing for their hard work and diligence and for making the arrangements for the adaptation.

In addition, a panel of external reviewers deserves LOMA's gratitude for their willingness to read through the text and offer their comments to guide us in our adaptation:

- Jac Amerell, Director of Investment Accounting, Northwestern Mutual Insurance Company

- Douglas DeMay, CFA, VP, Investment Technology, Times Square Capital Management, CIGNA Corp.
- Joseph Hanosek, Manager, Office of Investments, Nationwide Insurance
- Daniel C. Leimbach, CFA, Vice President, Private Placements, Hartford Investment Management Company
- Stephanie L. Riva, CFA, CCIM, FLMI/M, Managing Director, Principal Real Estate Investors
- Srinath Sampath, CFA, Manager, Public Bonds, Office of Investments, Nationwide
- Barbara E. Seith, FLMI, Managing Director, MONY Capital Management

Many LOMA staff members contributed to the project as well. Jena L. Kennedy, FLMI, ALHC, ACS, PAHM, CLU, Assistant Vice President, has worked tirelessly to help get this text and LOMA's Fellow, Financial Services Institute program off the ground. Special thanks go to Susan Conant, FLMI, HIA, CEBS, PAHM, Senior Associate, and Gene Stone, FLMI, ACS, CLU, Senior Associate, who carefully read through several commercial texts to help choose this text. Susan was also a constant source of wisdom and good humor. Susan, along with David A. Lewis, FLMI, ACS, Senior Associate, made invaluable contributions regarding the customization of the textbook. As always, Joyce R. Abrams, J.D., FLMI, PCS, AIRC, AIAA, AAPA, ARA, ALHC, PAHM, HIA, MHP, Assistant Vice President, provided good advice and moral support.

Members of the Examinations Department, including Robert H. Hartley, FLMI, ACS, ALHC, CLU, ChFC, RHU, PAHM, Manager; Sean Schaeffer Gilley, FLMI, ACS, AIAA, HIA, CEBS, PAHM, MHP, AIRC, AAPA, ARA, FLHC, Senior Associate; Vivian Heeden, FLMI, CLU, FLHC, ACS, AIAA, PAHM, AIRC, ARA, Senior Associate; Lisa Kozlowski, FLMI, CLU, ALHC, ACS, AIAA, PAHM, AIRC, ARA, FLHC, AAPA, Senior Associate; and David A. Lewis, FLMI, ACS, Senior Associate; all made valuable contributions to the project.

Aurelia K. Hemphill, Administrative Assistant III; Mary Rusch, Administrative Assistant; and Natalie Cape Sanders, Administrative Specialist, provided administrative support. Special thanks to Natalie for her good sense in resolving any and all problems. In LOMA's Production Department, Kathleen Ryan, FLMI, PCS, AIRC, AIAA, ARA, PAHM, Production Coordinator I, designed the cover; Amy Souwan, Production Coordinator II/Scheduling Coordinator, cheerfully coordinated the printing of the text; and Stephen J. Bollinger, ACS, Manager, guided the project through production. Audrey H. Gregory, ACS, Inventory Manager, provided outstanding business support for the project and helped keep us all on an even keel.

Finally, thanks to William H. Rabel, Ph.D., FLMI, CLU, Senior Vice President, Education Division, and Katherine C. Milligan, FLMI, ACS, ALHC, Vice President, Education & Training, for their ongoing encouragement and support.

Kristen L. Falk, FLMI, AAPA, ACS, AIAA, AIRC, ARA
Senior Associate and Project Coordinator
Education & Training Division, LOMA

PREFACE

"It was the best of times. It was the worst of times." No, you haven't stumbled into an English course. But that opening line from *A Tale of Two Cities* really does describe the behavior of the stock market over the past couple of years. It applies especially to the Nasdaq market, which is home to most of the technology stocks—of both large and small technology companies. Consider, for example, that between January 1999 and March 2000, the Nasdaq Composite Index, a popular measure of market performance, rose an eye-popping 130%. But in the next twelve months, from March 2000 to March 2001, the index fell 57%. During that decline, four out of every ten stocks listed on the Nasdaq—about 1,700 stocks—lost 50% or more of their value. Among the losers were a number of well-known technology companies, including Sun Microsystems, Oracle Corporation, Cisco Systems, and Yahoo!

After nearly two decades of unprecedented growth in the stock market, the events of 1999 and 2000 are a reminder that economic recessions and falling markets really aren't a thing of the past after all. They do happen every now and then, and investors have to be prepared to deal with them. Fortunately, far more often than not, the investor is faced with the pleasant task of trying to make the most of a good ("bull") market. In the midst of market euphoria on one hand and the prospect of serious market decline on the other, stands the investor, wondering what to do with his or her investment capital. This book offers guidance in today's investment environment.

Focusing on both individual securities and portfolios, *Fundamentals of Investing* explains how to implement investment goals in light of risk-return tradeoffs. A conversational tone and liberal use of examples guide students through the material and demonstrate important points.

Key Features of the Eighth Edition

Using information gathered from both academicians and practicing investment professionals, plus feedback from adopters, the eighth edition reflects the realities of today's investment environment. At the same time, it provides a structured framework for successful teaching and learning.

Comprehensive yet Flexible Organization

The text provides a firm foundation for learning by first describing the overall investment environment. Next it presents conceptual tools needed by investors—the concepts of risk and return and the basics of portfolio construction. It then examines each of the popular investment vehicles—common stocks, bonds, and mutual funds. Following this series of chapters on investment vehicles comes a chapter on how to administer one's own portfolio.

We organized each chapter according to a decision-making perspective, and we have been careful always to point out the pros and cons of the various vehicles and strategies that we present. With this information, individual investors can select the investment actions that are most consistent with their objectives. In addition, we've illustrated investment vehicles and strategies in such a way that students learn the decision-making implications and consequences of each investment action they contemplate.

Timely Topics

Various issues and developments constantly reshape financial markets and investment vehicles. Virtually all topics in this book take into account changes in the investment environment. For example, sources of investment information, as well as the process of online investing, are covered in Chapter 3. Similarly, coverage of tech stocks (in Chapters 6 and 8) presents timely information needed for a thorough understanding of today's investment opportunities.

Globalization

One issue that is reshaping investing is the growing globalization of securities markets. As a result, *Fundamentals of Investing* continues to stress the global aspects of investing. We initially look at the growing importance of international markets, investing in foreign securities (indirectly or directly), international investment performance, and the risks of investing internationally. In later chapters, popular international investment opportunities and strategies are described as part of the coverage of each specific type of investment vehicle. This integration of international topics helps students understand the importance of maintaining a global focus when planning, building, and managing an investment portfolio. Global topics are highlighted by inclusion of a globe icon.

Pedagogical Features

This textbook has long been recognized for its numerous pedagogical features, designed to help students focus their study of investments. Among the useful features it includes are Learning Goals, Investing in Action boxed essays, Investor Facts, Internet linkages, and a marginal glossary.

LG 1 Learning Goals

Each chapter begins with Learning Goals, labeled with numbered icons (noted at left of head), that clearly state the concepts and materials to be covered. The Learning Goal icons are tied to first-level headings and are reviewed point by point at the chapter's end.

Alongside the chapter's Learning Goals at the beginning of each chapter is a brief story (opening vignette). It features an investment situation involving a real company or event and ties it to the chapter topics, to help motivate student interest in the chapter.

Investing in Action

Each chapter features two boxed essays, called *Investing in Action,* that also describe real-life investing situations or events. Although we have revised and retained a few of the most popular boxes from the previous edition, the majority are new. These high-interest boxes, which have been written specifically for this textbook, demonstrate concepts introduced in the text and enliven the students' reading at a level consistent with their abilities.

Investor Facts

Each chapter also contains two to three Investor Facts—brief sidebar items that give an interesting statistic or cite an unusual investment experience. The facts and figures in these boxes are intended to stimulate student interest and motivate further thought. For example, the Investor Facts box on page 167 (Chapter 6) discusses the differences between a routine market decline, a market correction, and a bear market. The Investor Facts on page 213 (Chapter 7) compares GDP rates of various countries.

Internet Linkages

The growth of the Internet and its increasing use in college coursework has impelled us to add Internet linkages. *Hot Links* boxes are interspersed throughout. These inserts refer students to Web sites related to the topic being covered in the text.

Marginal Glossary

New terms are set in boldface type and defined when first introduced in the text. In addition, each term appears with its definition in the text margin, to facilitate student learning and review. The page numbers on which these entries appear within the text are noted in boldface in the book's index, to make it easy to find these definitions.

Summary

Each summary lists the chapter's key concepts and ideas, which correspond directly to the numbered Learning Goals presented at the beginning of the chapter. The Learning Goal icons precede each summary item, which begins with a boldfaced restatement of the learning goal.

Acknowledgments

Many people gave their generous assistance during the initial development and revisions of *Fundamentals of Investing.* The expertise, classroom experience, and general advice of both colleagues and practitioners have been invaluable. Reactions and suggestions from students throughout the country—comments we especially enjoy receiving—sustained our belief in the need for a fresh, informative, and teachable investments text.

A few individuals provided significant subject matter expertise in the initial development of the book. They are Terry S. Maness of Baylor University, Arthur L. Schwartz, Jr., of the University of South Florida at St. Petersburg, and Gary W. Eldred. Their contributions are greatly appreciated. In addition, Addison-Wesley obtained the advice of a large group of experienced reviewers. We appreciate their many suggestions and criticisms, which have had a strong influence on various aspects of this volume. Our special thanks go to the following people, who reviewed all or part of the manuscript for the previous seven editions of the book.

M. Fall Ainina
Gary Baker
Harisha Batra
Richard B. Bellinfante
Cecil C. Bigelow
Paul Bolster
A. David Brummett
Gary P. Cain
Gary Carman
Daniel J. Cartell
P. R. Chandy
David M. Cordell
Timothy Cowling
Robert M. Crowe
Richard F. DeMong
Clifford A. Diebold
James Dunn
Betty Marie Dyatt
Steven J. Elbert
Thomas Eyssell
Frank J. Fabozzi
Robert A. Ford
Albert J. Fredman
Chaim Ginsberg
Joel Gold
Frank Griggs
Brian Grinder
Harry P. Guenther
Mahboubul Hassan
Gay Hatfield
Robert D. Hollinger
Sue Beck Howard
Roland Hudson, Jr.
Donald W. Johnson
Ravindra R. Kamath
Bill Kane
Daniel J. Kaufmann, Jr.
Nancy Kegelman
Phillip T. Kolbe
Sheri Kole
Christopher M. Korth
Thomas M. Krueger
George Kutner
Robert T. LeClair
Chun I. Lee
Larry A. Lynch
Weston A. McCormac
David J. McLaughlin
Keith Manko
Timothy Manuel
Kathy Milligan
Warren E. Moeller
Homer Mohr
Majed R. Muhtaseb
Joseph Newhouse
Joseph F. Ollivier
John Park
Thomas Patrick
Ronald S. Pretekin
Stephen W. Pruitt
William A. Richard
Linda R. Richardson
William A. Rini
Roy A. Roberson
Edward Rozalewicz
William J. Ruckstuhl
David Russo
Keith V. Smith
Pat R. Stout
Nancy E. Strickler
Glenn T. Sweeney
Amir Tavakkol
Phillip D. Taylor
Wenyuh Tsay
Robert C. Tueting
Howard E. Van Auken
John R. Weigel
Peter M. Wichert
John C. Woods
Richard H. Yanow

The following people provided extremely useful reviews and input to the eighth edition:

Ping Hsiao, *San Francisco State University*

Larry Lynch, *Roanoke College*

John Palffy, *Wayne State University*

Michael Polakoff, *University of Maryland at College Park*

Barbara Poole, *Central Connecticut State University*

S. P. Umamaheswar Rao, *University of Louisiana at Lafayette*

Arthur L. Schwartz, Jr., *University of South Florida at St. Petersburg*

Howard Van Auken, *Iowa State University*

Because of the wide variety of topics covered in the book, we called upon many experts for advice. We thank them and their firms for allowing us to draw on their insights and awareness of recent developments, to ensure that the text is as current as possible. In particular, we want to mention Jeff Buetow, CFA, BFRC Services, Charlottesville, VA; John Markese, President, American Association of Individual Investors, Chicago, IL; George Ebenhack, Oppenheimer & Co., Los Angeles, CA; Mark D. Erwin, Northwestern Mutual Financial Network, San Diego, CA; Richard Esposito, Prana Investments, Inc., New York; Dennis P. Hickman, La Jolla, CA; Andrew Temte, CFA, Schweser Study Program, La Crosse, WI; Martin P. Klitzer, Sunrise Capital Partners, Del Mar, CA; David M. Love, C.P. Eaton and Associates, Rancho Santa Fe, CA; David H. McLaughlin, Chase Investment Counsel Corp., Charlottesville, VA; Michael R. Murphy, Sceptre Investment Counsel, Toronto, Ontario, Canada; Mark S. Nussbaum, PaineWebber, La Jolla, CA; John Richardson, Northern Trust Bank of Arizona, Phoenix, AZ; Pat Rupp, IDS, Inc., Dayton, OH; Richard Russell, Dow Theory Letters, La Jolla, CA; Mike Smith, Economic Analysis Corporation, Los Angeles, CA; Fred Weaver, Washington Mutual, Phoenix, AZ; and Lynn Yturri, BancOne Arizona, Phoenix, AZ.

We greatly appreciate the support of our colleagues at San Diego State University and Arizona State University. Special thanks to attorney Robert J. Wright of Wright & Wrights, CPAs, San Diego, for his help in revising and updating the many tax discussions, and to Professor Edward Nelling of Drexel University for his help in preparing the material on tech stocks and tech-stock valuation. We also thank S. P. Umamaheswar Rao ("Spuma") of the University of Louisiana for his work on the Hot Links and Karin Bonding of the University of Virginia for her useful feedback. Special thanks to Marlene Bellamy of Writeline Associates, La Jolla, California, for her work in updating certain chapters and preparing chapter vignettes, *Investing in Action* boxes, and *Investor Facts*.

The staff at Addison-Wesley, particularly Donna Battista and Denise Clinton, contributed their creativity, enthusiasm, and commitment to this textbook. Freelance development editor Ann Torbert, senior project manager Mary Clare McEwing of Addison-Wesley, Nancy Freihofer of Thompson Steele Production Services, senior production supervisor Nancy Fenton of Addison-Wesley, senior designer Regina Hagen of Addison-Wesley, and media producer Jennifer Pelland of Addison-Wesley warrant special thanks for shepherding the project through the development, production, and Web site construction stages. Without their care and concern, this text would not have evolved into the teachable and interesting text we believe it to be.

Finally, our wives, Robin and Charlene, and our children, Jessica and Zachary, and Chris and Terry and his wife, Sara, played important roles by providing support and understanding during the book's development, revision, and production. We are forever grateful to them, and we hope that this edition will justify the sacrifices required during the many hours we were away from them working on this book.

Lawrence J. Gitman

Michael D. Joehnk

Part One
THE INVESTMENT ENVIRONMENT

CHAPTER 1

THE ROLE AND SCOPE OF INVESTMENTS

LEARNING GOALS

After studying this chapter, you should be able to:

LG 1 **Understand the meaning of the term *investment* and the factors commonly used to differentiate among types of investments.**

LG 2 **Describe the investment process and types of investors.**

LG 3 **Discuss the principal types of investment vehicles.**

LG 4 **Describe the steps in investing, particularly establishing investment goals, and cite fundamental personal tax considerations.**

LG 5 **Discuss investing over the life cycle and investing in different economic environments.**

LG 6 **Understand the popular types of short-term investment vehicles.**

In just a few years, the world of investments has moved to center stage in American life. Twenty years ago, most people's only exposure to investment news was a 10-second announcement on the evening news about the change in the Dow Jones Industrial Average that day.

Today, about half of all Americans own stocks, and 20% of them only began investing after 1996. Cable TV stations such as CNNfn and CNBC specialize in business and financial news. You can't pass a newsstand without seeing headlines that scream, "Ten Stocks to Buy Now!" or "The Hottest Mutual Funds." Besides the *Wall Street Journal*, you can subscribe to *Investor's Business Daily, Financial Times, Barron's, Kiplinger's Personal Finance Magazine, Money, Smart Money*, and dozens more publications that focus on investing.

The Internet has played a large role in opening the world of investing to individual investors. By giving them access to tools formerly restricted to investment professionals, it creates a more level playing field. The Internet also places enormous amounts of information and a means of trading securities just a few mouse clicks away. In short, technology makes investing much easier, but it can also increase the risks for inexperienced investors.

Regardless of whether you make transactions online or use a traditional broker, the same investment fundamentals presented in this textbook apply. The first chapter introduces you to the types of investments, the investment process, key investment vehicles, the role of investment plans, and the importance of meeting liquidity needs. Becoming familiar with investment alternatives and developing realistic investment plans should greatly increase your chance of financial success.

Investments and the Investment Process

LG 1 LG 2

Note: The Learning Goals shown at the beginning of the chapter are keyed to text discussions using these icons.

If you have money in a savings account, you already have at least one investment to your name. An **investment** is simply any vehicle into which funds can be placed with the expectation that it will generate positive income and/or that its value will be preserved or increased. The rewards, or **returns,** from investing are received in two basic forms: current income and increased value. For example, money invested in a savings account provides current income in the form of periodic interest payments. A share of common stock purchased as an investment is expected to increase in value between the time it is purchased and the time it is sold.

Is cash placed in a simple (no-interest) checking account an investment? No, because it fails both tests of the definition. It does not provide added income, nor does its value increase. (In fact, the value of the cash in a checking account is likely to decrease, because it is eroded over time by inflation.)

We begin our study of investments by looking at types of investments and at the structure of the investment process.

investment
any vehicle into which funds can be placed with the expectation that it will generate positive income and/or preserve or increase its value.

returns
the rewards from investing, received as current income and/or increased value.

Types of Investments

When you invest, the organization in which you invest—whether it is a company or a government entity—offers you an expected future benefit in exchange for the current use of your funds. Organizations compete for the use of your funds. The one that will get your investment dollars is the one that offers a benefit you judge to be better than any competitor offers. But, different investors judge benefits differently. As a result, investments of every type are available, from "sure things" such as earning 3% interest on your bank savings account, to the possibility of tripling your money fast by investing in a newly issued dot-com stock. The investments you choose will depend on your resources, your goals, and your personality. We can differentiate types of investments on the basis of a number of factors.

securities
investments that represent evidence of debt or ownership or the legal right to acquire or sell an ownership interest.

property
investments in real property or in tangible personal property.

Securities or Property Investments that represent debt or ownership or the legal right to acquire or sell an ownership interest are called **securities.** The most common types of securities are stocks, bonds, and options. The focus of this book is primarily on securities.

Property, on the other hand, consists of investments in real property or tangible personal property. *Real property* is land, buildings, and that which is permanently affixed to the land. *Tangible personal property* includes items such as gold, artwork, antiques, and other collectibles.

direct investment
investment in which an investor directly acquires a claim on a security or property.

indirect investment
investment made in a *portfolio,* or collection of securities or properties.

portfolio
collection of securities or properties, typically constructed to meet one or more investment goals.

Direct or Indirect A **direct investment** is one in which an investor directly acquires a claim on a security or property. If you buy a stock or bond in order to earn income or preserve value, you have made a direct investment.

An **indirect investment** is an investment made in a **portfolio,** or collection of securities or properties, typically constructed to meet one or more investment goals. For example, you may purchase a share of a *mutual fund.* This share gives you a claim on a fraction of the entire portfolio rather than on the security of a single firm.

debt
funds lent in exchange for interest income and the promised repayment of the loan at a given future date.

Debt, Equity, or Derivative Securities Usually, an investment represents either a debt or an equity interest. **Debt** represents funds lent in exchange for interest income and the promised repayment of the loan at a given future date.

When you buy a debt instrument like a *bond,* in effect you lend money to the issuer. The issuer agrees to pay you a stated rate of interest over a specified period of time, at the end of which the original sum will be returned.

equity
ongoing ownership in a business or property.

derivative securities
securities that are structured to exhibit characteristics similar to those of an underlying security or asset and that derive their value from the underlying security or asset.

Equity represents ongoing ownership in a business or property. An equity investment may be held as a security or by title to a specific property. The most popular type of equity security is *common stock.*

Derivative securities are neither debt nor equity. They derive their value from, and have characteristics similar to those of, an underlying security or asset. *Options* are an example: An investor essentially buys the opportunity to sell or buy another security or asset at a specified price during a given period of time. Options and other derivative security investments, though not so common as debt and equity investments, have grown rapidly in popularity in recent years.

risk
the chance that actual investment returns will differ from those expected.

Low- or High-Risk Investments are sometimes differentiated on the basis of risk. As used in finance, **risk** is the chance that actual investment returns will differ from those expected. The broader the range of possible values or returns associated with an investment, the greater its risk.

Investors are confronted with a continuum of investments that range from low to high risk. Although each type of investment vehicle has a basic risk characteristic, the actual level of risk depends on the specific vehicle. For example, stocks are generally believed to be more risky than bonds. However, it is not difficult to find high-risk bonds that are more risky than the stock of a financially sound firm such as IBM or McDonald's.

speculation
the purchase of high-risk investment vehicles that offer highly uncertain returns and future value.

Low-risk investments are those considered safe with regard to the receipt of a positive return. *High-risk investments* are considered speculative: Their levels of return are highly uncertain. **Speculation** offers highly uncertain returns and future value, so it is high-risk investment. Because of this greater risk, the returns associated with speculation are expected to be greater. Both investment and speculation differ from gambling, which involves playing games of chance. In this book we will use the term *investment* for both investment and speculation.

short-term investments
investments that typically mature within one year.

long-term investments
investments with maturities of longer than a year or with no maturity at all.

Short- or Long-Term The life of an investment can be described as either short- or long-term. **Short-term investments** typically mature within one year. **Long-term investments** are those with longer maturities or, like common stock, with no maturity at all. It is not unusual to find investors matching the maturity of an investment to the period of time over which they wish to invest their funds.

Note: Discussions of international investing are highlighted by this icon.

domestic investments
debt, equity, and derivative securities of U.S.-based companies.

foreign investments
debt, equity, and derivative securities of foreign-based companies.

Domestic or Foreign As recently as 10 to 15 years ago, individuals invested almost exclusively in purely **domestic investments**: the debt, equity, and derivative securities of U.S.-based companies. Today, these same investors routinely also look for **foreign investments** (both direct and indirect) that might offer more attractive returns or lower risk than purely domestic investments. Information on foreign companies is now readily available, and it is now relatively easy to make foreign investments. As a result, many individuals now actively invest in foreign securities. All aspects of foreign investing are therefore routinely considered throughout this book.

The Structure of the Investment Process

financial institutions
organizations that channel the savings of governments, businesses, and individuals into loans or investments.

financial markets
forums in which suppliers and demanders of funds make financial transactions.

The investment process brings together *suppliers* of extra funds with *demanders* who need funds. Suppliers and demanders of funds are most often brought together through a financial institution or a financial market. (Occasionally, especially in property transactions, buyers and sellers deal directly with one another.) **Financial institutions** are organizations that channel the savings of governments, businesses, and individuals into loans or investments. Banks and insurance companies are financial institutions. **Financial markets** are forums in which suppliers and demanders of funds make financial transactions, often through intermediaries. They include securities, commodities, and foreign exchange markets.

The dominant financial market in the United States is the *securities market*. It includes stock markets, bond markets, and options markets. Similar markets exist in most major economies throughout the world. Their common feature is that the price of an investment vehicle at any point in time results from an equilibrium between the forces of supply and demand. As new information about returns and risk becomes available, the changes in supply and demand may result in a new equilibrium or *market price*. Financial markets streamline the process of bringing together suppliers and demanders of funds, and they allow transactions to be made quickly and at a fair price. They also publicize security prices.

Figure 1.1 diagrams the investment process. Note that the suppliers of funds may transfer their resources to the demanders through financial institutions, through financial markets, or in direct transactions. As the broken lines show, financial institutions can participate in financial markets as either suppliers or demanders of funds.

Participants in the Investment Process Government, business, and individuals are the three key participants in the investment process. Each may act as a supplier and a demander of funds. For the economy to grow and prosper, funds must be available to qualified individuals and to government and business. If

FIGURE 1.1

The Investment Process

Note that financial institutions participate in the financial markets as well as transfer funds between suppliers and demanders. Although the arrows go only from suppliers to demanders, for some transactions (e.g., the sale of a bond), the principal amount borrowed by the demander from the supplier (the lender) is eventually returned.

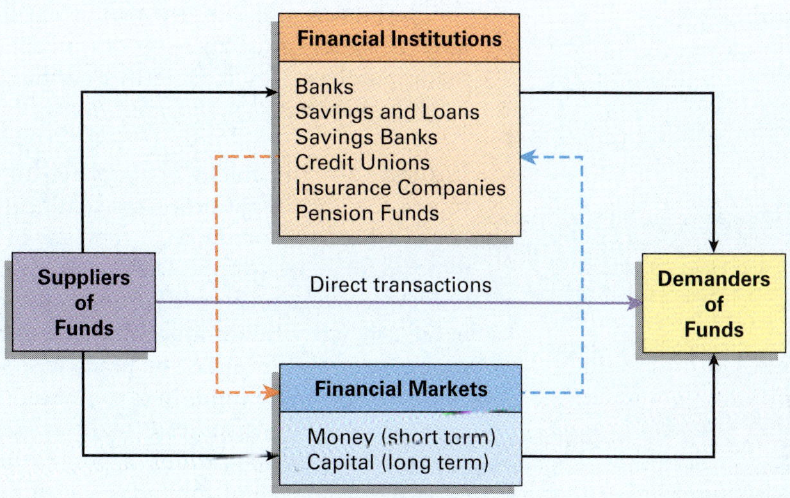

Note: Investor Facts offer interesting or entertaining tidbits of information.

INVESTOR FACTS

AMERICANS LOVE STOCKS— A recent survey showed that 48% of Americans now own stocks or stock mutual funds, compared to just 19% in 1983. Stocks and stock mutual funds account for about 36% of total household financial assets, up from 28% in 1995. As the rising equity markets made stocks more popular, holdings of other financial assets—particularly checking, savings, and money market accounts; money market mutual funds; and bonds—declined.

Source: Arthur B. Kennickell, Martha Starr-McCluer, and Brian J. Surette, "Recent Changes in U.S. Family Finances: Results from the 1998 Survey of Consumer Finances," *Federal Reserve Bulletin,* Board of Governors of the Federal Reserve System, Washington, DC, January 2000, pp. 8–9.

individuals began suddenly hiding their excess funds under floorboards rather than putting them in financial institutions or investing them in the financial markets, then government, business, and individuals in need of funds would have difficulty obtaining them. As a result, government spending, business expansion, and consumer purchases would decline, and economic activity would slow.

Government All levels of government—federal, state, and local—require vast sums of money. Some goes to finance *capital expenditures:* long-term projects related to the construction of public facilities such as schools, hospitals, public housing, and highways. Usually the financing for such projects is obtained by issuing various types of long-term debt securities. Another demand for funds comes from *operating needs*—the money required to keep the government running. At the federal level, for example, these funds are used to pay employee and other costs associated with national defense, education, public works, welfare, Social Security, Medicare, and so on, as well as interest on the national debt. These operating costs are usually paid from tax revenue and fee collections. However, when operating expenditures exceed government revenues or when there is a timing mismatch between government receipts and payments, the government borrows funds—typically by issuing short-term debt securities.

Occasionally, governments are also suppliers of funds. If a state has temporarily idle cash, it may make a short-term investment to earn a positive return. In general, though, government is a *net demander of funds.* That is, it demands more funds than it supplies. The financial activities of governments, both as demanders and suppliers of funds, significantly affect the behavior of financial institutions and financial markets.

Business Most business firms require large sums of money to support operations. Like government, business has both long- and short-term financial needs. On the long-term side, businesses seek funds to build plants, acquire equipment and facilities, and develop products. Their short-term needs center on obtaining funds to finance inventory and accounts receivable and to meet other operating costs. Businesses issue a wide variety of debt and equity securities to finance these needs.

Businesses also supply funds when they have excess cash. In fact, many large business firms have sophisticated cash-management operations and are major purchasers of short-term securities. But like government, business firms in general are *net demanders of funds.*

Individuals You might be surprised to learn that the individual investor's role in the investment process is significant. Most individuals are more aware of their need to borrow than they are of the ways in which they put money into the financial system. They frequently demand funds in the form of loans to finance the acquisition of property—typically automobiles and houses. Yet, in fact, the activities of individual investors help to satisfy the net demands of government and business for funds in a variety of ways: Individual investors place funds in savings accounts, buy debt or equity instruments, buy insurance, make retirement plan contributions, and purchase various types of property. Although the individual demand for funds seems great, individuals as a group are *net suppliers of funds:* They put more funds into the financial system than they take out.

Note: Addresses of additional information sources that can be found on the Internet are interspersed throughout the chapter.

HOTLINKS

An Investing in Action box at the text's Web site discusses the saving and investing habits of "Generation Xers."

www.awl.com/gitman_joehnk

HOTLINKS

Getting investment information is now only a few "mouse clicks" away. Everythlng from stock quotations, to news articles, to Wall Street research is available on the Web. There are many Web sites that provide tutorials on financial information.

CyberInvest.com contains contains free investing guides. Check out [Guides]. Guides compare resources and features at hundreds of the best investing sites on the Web. The guides can save you time—and thus money—by revealing at a glance how investing Web sites stack up against each other. Then you can jump to the site of your choice by clicking on its name. Especially check the *Investing 101* guide under [Education Center].

www.cyberinvest.com

Note: Two *Investing in Action* boxes per chapter describe real-life investing situations or elaborate on innovative investment vehicles. These high-interest boxes have been written for this textbook, with student readers in mind. Some of the concept review questions in the chapter are related to material in these boxes.

individual investors
investors who manage their own funds.

institutional investors
investment professionals paid to manage other people's money.

Types of Investors When we refer to individuals in the investment process, we do so to differentiate households from government and business. We can further characterize the participation of individuals in the investment process in terms of who manages the funds. **Individual investors** manage their personal funds in order to achieve their financial goals. The individual investor usually concentrates on earning a return on idle funds, building a source of retirement income, and providing security for his or her family. The accompanying *Investing in Action* box offers a quiz to determine a baseline on your investing "know-how."

Individuals who lack the time or expertise to make investment decisions often employ **institutional investors**—investment professionals who are paid to manage other people's money. These professionals trade large volumes of securities for individuals, businesses, and governments. Institutional investors include financial institutions (banks, life insurance companies, mutual funds, and pension funds). Financial institutions invest large sums in order to earn a significant return for their customers. For example, a life insurance company invests its premium receipts to earn returns that will permit payments to policyholders or beneficiaries.

Both individual and institutional investors apply similar fundamental principles. However, institutional investors generally invest larger sums of money on behalf of others and therefore are often more sophisticated in investment knowledge and methods. The information presented in this textbook is aimed primarily at individual investors; it represents only the first step toward developing the expertise needed to qualify as an institutional investor.

INVESTING in action

Test Your Investment IQ

How much do you know about investing? Take this investor literacy quiz, developed by *Money* magazine and the Vanguard Group to test the investment savvy of 1,500 mutual fund investors.

The average score (for the full 20-question quiz) was only 37%. But don't despair if you, too, don't score well. You'll learn the answers to these and many other questions from this book.

1. Which type of investment has offered the best protection against inflation over long periods of time?
   a. Money market funds and bank accounts.
   b. Government National Mortgage Association securities (also known as Ginnie Maes or GNMAs).
   c. Stocks.
   d. Corporate bonds.
2. Common stocks always provide higher returns than bonds or money market investments.
   a. True.
   b. False.
3. Interest earned by municipal bonds is exempt from federal income tax.
   a. True.
   b. False.
4. If interest rates declined, the price of a bond or bond fund generally would:
   a. Increase.
   b. Decrease.
   c. Stay about the same.
   d. It is impossible to predict.
5. If you own only U.S. stocks in your investment portfolio, you will reduce your overall risk by adding international stocks.
   a. True.
   b. False.
6. Which market benchmark or stock exchange is the best gauge of the performance of the entire U.S. stock market?
   a. S&P 500 Index.
   b. Wilshire 5000 Total Market Index.
   c. Dow Jones Industrial Average.
   d. Nasdaq Composite Index.
7. If you invest in a 401(k) plan at work, you are not eligible to contribute to an IRA.
   a. True.
   b. False.
8. From 1926 to 1999, the return on U.S. stocks has averaged:
   a. 5% per year.
   b. 11% per year.
   c. 19% per year.
   d. 28% per year.
9. Which of the following is not an attribute of mutual funds?
   a. Diversification.
   b. Professional management.
   c. Guaranteed return.
   d. None of the above.
10. If your investment returned 10% last year and inflation was 3%, your "real" (i.e., adjusted for inflation) return was:
    a. 3.3%.
    b. 7%.
    c. 13%.
    d. 30%.
11. A mutual fund that invests in government securities is guaranteed not to lose money.
    a. True.
    b. False.

Answers: 1 (c); 2 (b); 3 (a); 4 (a); 5 (a); 6 (b); 7 (b); 8 (b); 9 (c); 10 (b); 11 (b).

Sources: Laura Lallos, "What's Your Investing IQ?" *Money,* August 2000, pp. 91–92; quiz downloaded from **cgi.money.com/cgi-bin/money/polls/vanguard/vanguard.plx**

Investment Vehicles

LG 3

A wide variety of investment vehicles are available to individual investors. Vehicles differ in terms of maturities or lives, costs, return and risk characteristics, and tax considerations. We devote the bulk of this book—Chapters 6 through 11—to describing the characteristics, special features, returns and risks, and possible investment strategies that can be used with vehicles available to the individual investor. Here we will introduce these investment vehicles. Table 1.1 summarizes the investment vehicles covered in this book.

Short-Term Vehicles

short-term vehicles
savings instruments that usually have lives of 1 year or less.

liquidity
the ability of an investment to be converted into cash quickly and with little or no loss in value.

Short-term vehicles include savings instruments that usually have lives of 1 year or less. Short-term vehicles generally carry little or no risk. Often such instruments are used to "warehouse" idle funds and earn a return while long-term vehicles are being evaluated. They are also popular among conservative investors, who may use short-term vehicles as a primary investment outlet. Short-term vehicles also provide **liquidity.** That is, they can be converted into cash quickly and with little or no loss in value. Provision for liquidity is an important part of any financial plan. The role of short-term vehicles in financial planning and the key features of the most popular short-term vehicles are discussed later in this chapter.

Common Stock

common stock
equity investment that represents ownership in a corporation; each share represents a fractional ownership interest in the firm.

Common stock is an equity investment that represents ownership in a corporation. Each share of common stock represents a fractional ownership interest in the firm. For example, one share of common stock in a corporation that has 10,000 shares outstanding would represent 1/10,000 ownership interest. Next to short-term vehicles and home ownership, common stock is the most popular form of investment vehicle.

TABLE 1.1 Overview of Investment Vehicles

Type	Description	Examples	Where Covered in This Book
Short-term vehicles	Savings instruments with lives of 1 year or less. Used to warehouse idle funds and to provide liquidity.	Deposit accounts	Ch. 1
		Series EE savings bonds	Ch. 1
		U.S. Treasury bills (T-bills)	Ch. 1
		Certificates of deposit (CDs)	Ch. 1
		Commercial paper	Ch. 1
		Banker's acceptances	Ch. 1
		Money market mutual funds	Ch. 1
Common stock	Equity investment vehicles that represent ownership in a corporation.		Chs. 6–8
Fixed-income securities	Investment vehicles that offer a fixed periodic return.	Bonds	Chs. 9, 10
Mutual funds	Companies that raise money from sale of shares and invest in and professionally manage a diversified portfolio of securities.		Ch. 11

dividends
periodic payments made by firms to their shareholders.

capital gains
the amount by which the sale price of an asset *exceeds* its original purchase price.

The return on investment in common stock comes from either of two sources: dividends or capital gains. **Dividends** are periodic payments made by the corporation to its shareholders from its current and past earnings. **Capital gains** result from selling the stock (or any asset) at a price that *exceeds* its original purchase price. For example, say you purchased a single share of One Tech Industries common stock for \$40 per share. During the first year you owned it, you received \$2.50 per share in cash dividends. At the end of the year, you sold the stock for \$44 per share. If we ignore the costs associated with buying and selling the stock, you earned \$2.50 in dividends and \$4 in capital gains (\$44 sale price—\$40 purchase price).

Fixed-Income Securities

fixed-income securities
investment vehicles that offer a fixed periodic return.

Fixed-income securities are investment vehicles that offer a fixed periodic return. Some forms offer contractually guaranteed returns. Others have specified, but not guaranteed, returns. Because of their fixed returns, fixed-income securities tend to be popular during periods of high interest rates, when investors seek to "lock in" high returns. The key forms of fixed-income securities are bonds, preferred stock, and convertible securities.

bonds
long-term debt instruments (IOUs), issued by corporations and governments, that offer a known interest return plus return of the bond's *face value* at maturity.

preferred stock
ownership interest in a corporation; has a stated dividend rate, payment of which is given preference over common stock dividends of the same firm.

convertible security
a fixed-income obligation (bond or preferred stock) with a feature permitting conversion into a specified number of shares of common stock.

Bonds **Bonds** are the long-term debt instruments (IOUs) issued by corporations and governments. A bondholder has a contractual right to receive a known interest return, plus return of the bond's *face value* (the stated value given on the certificate) at maturity (typically 20 to 40 years). If you purchased a \$1,000 bond paying 9% interest in semiannual installments, you would expect to be paid \$45 (9% × ½ year × \$1,000) every 6 months. At maturity you would receive the \$1,000 face value of the bond. An investor may be able to buy or sell a bond prior to maturity.

Preferred Stock Like common stock, **preferred stock** represents an ownership interest in a corporation. Unlike common stock, preferred stock has a stated dividend rate. Payment of this dividend is given preference over common stock dividends of the same firm. Preferred stock has no maturity date. Investors typically purchase it for the dividends it pays, but it may also provide capital gains.

HOT LINKS

Successful investing can be surprisingly simple and straightforward. There are many baseline investing sites. Log on to SmartMoney.com. Scroll down the homepage to Smart Money University and read the sections on Investing 101 and Strategic Investing that explain the fundamentals of stocks, bonds, and mutual funds.

www.smartmoney.com

Convertible Securities A **convertible security** is a special type of fixed-income obligation (bond or preferred stock). It has a feature permitting the investor to convert it into a specified number of shares of common stock. Convertible bonds and convertible preferreds provide the fixed-income benefit of a bond (interest) or preferred stock (dividends) while offering the price-appreciation (capital gain) potential of common stock.

Mutual Funds

A company that raises money from sale of its shares and invests in and professionally manages a diversified portfolio of securities is called a **mutual fund.** Investors in the fund own an interest in the fund's portfolio of securities. All mutual funds issue and repurchase shares of the fund at a price that reflects the value of the portfolio at the time the transaction is made. **Money market mutual funds** are mutual funds that invest solely in short-term investment vehicles.

INVESTOR FACTS

THE FEELING'S MUTUAL!—Investors have put more than $7.1 trillion of investment assets into the almost 8,000 mutual funds in the United States. The 4,140 stock funds led the way with $4.2 trillion (60%) of the total, followed by 700 taxable money market funds with $1.5 trillion (21%).

Source: "Trends in Mutual Fund Investing, July 2000," Investment Company Institute, Washington, DC, August 30, 2000, downloaded from www.ici.org

Derivative Securities

As noted earlier, *derivative securities* derive their value from that of an underlying security or asset. They typically possess high levels of risk, because they usually have uncertain returns or unstable market values. But, because of their above-average risk, these vehicles also have high levels of expected return. The key derivative securities are options and futures.

Options **Options** are securities that give the investor an opportunity to sell or buy another security at a specified price over a given period of time. Most often, options are purchased in order to take advantage of an anticipated change in the price of common stock. However, the purchaser of an option is not guaranteed any return and could even lose the entire amount invested because the option does not become attractive enough to use. Aside from their speculative use, options are sometimes used to protect existing investment positions against losses. Three common types of options are *puts, calls,* and *warrants.*

Futures **Futures** are legally binding obligations stipulating that the sellers of such contracts will make delivery and the buyers of the contracts will take delivery of a specified commodity or financial instrument at some specific date, at a price agreed on at the time the contract is sold. Examples of commodities sold by contract include soybeans, pork bellies, platinum, and cocoa. Examples of financial futures are contracts for Japanese yen, U.S. Treasury securities, interest rates, and stock indexes. Trading in commodity and financial futures is generally a highly specialized, high-risk proposition.

Other Popular Investment Vehicles

Various other investment vehicles are also used by investors. The most common are real estate, tangibles, and tax-advantaged investments.

Real estate consists of entities such as residential homes, raw land, and a variety of forms of income property, including warehouses, office and apartment buildings, and condominiums. The appeal of real estate investment is the potential returns in the form of rental income, tax write-offs, and capital gains. **Tangibles** are investment assets, other than real estate, that can be seen

mutual fund
a company that raises money from sale of its shares and invests in and professionally manages a diversified portfolio of securities.

money market mutual funds
mutual funds that invest solely in short-term investment vehicles.

options
securities that give the investor an opportunity to sell or buy another security at a specified price over a given period of time.

futures
legally binding obligations stipulating that the sellers of such contracts will make delivery and the buyers of the contracts will take delivery of a specified commodity or financial instrument at some specific date, at a price agreed on at the time the contract is sold.

real estate
entities such as residential homes, raw land, and income property.

tangibles
investment assets, other than real estate, that can be seen or touched.

HOTLINKS

Real estate, tangibles, and tax-advantaged investments are discussed on the text's Web site. Click on the Web chapter titled Real Estate and Other Tangible Investments.

www.awl.com/gitman_joehnk

or touched. They include gold and other precious metals, gemstones, and collectibles such as coins, stamps, artwork, and antiques. These assets are purchased as investments in anticipation of price increases. Because the federal income tax rate for an individual can be as high as 39.6%, many investors look for **tax-advantaged investments.** These are investment vehicles and strategies for legally reducing one's tax liability. With them, investors find that their after-tax rates of return can be far higher than with conventional investments.

tax-advantaged investments
investment vehicles and strategies for legally reducing one's tax liability.

Making Investment Plans

The process of investing can be carried out by following a logical progression of steps. It is important that your investment plans take into account the impact of taxes. Your plans also should be responsive to your stage in the life cycle and to the changing economic environment.

LG 4 LG 5

Steps in Investing

Investing can be conducted on a strictly intuitive basis or on the basis of plans carefully developed to achieve specific goals. Evidence favors the more logical approach that begins with establishing a set of overall financial goals and then developing and executing an investment program consistent with those goals. The following brief overview of the steps in investing provides a framework for discussion of the concepts, tools, and techniques presented throughout the book.

Step 1: Meeting Investment Prerequisites Before investing, you must make certain that the *necessities of life* are adequately provided for. This category includes funds for housing, food, transportation, taxes, and clothing. In addition, a pool of easily accessible funds should be established for meeting emergency cash needs. (Meeting liquidity needs is discussed later in this chapter.)

Another prerequisite is adequate protection against the losses that could result from death, illness or disability, damage to property, or a negligent act. Protection against such risks can be acquired through life, health, property, and liability insurance.

HOTLINKS

Detailed information on meeting life insurance needs is available on this text's Web site. Click on the Web chapter titled Tax-Advantaged Investments and then on Deferred Annuities and Single-Premium Life Insurance.

www.awl.com/gitman_joehnk

Step 2: Establishing Investment Goals Once you have satisfied the prerequisites and set clearly defined financial goals, the next step is to establish *investment goals.* **Investment goals** are the financial objectives you wish to achieve by investing. Clearly, your investment goals will determine the types of investments you will make. Common investment goals include:

investment goals
the financial objectives that one wishes to achieve by investing.

1. *Accumulating Retirement Funds.* Accumulating funds for retirement is the *single most important reason for investing.* Too often, people tend to rely heavily on Social Security and employers for retirement funds. It is of the utmost importance to review the amounts that can realistically be expected from these sources. You can then decide, on the basis of your retirement goals, *whether they will be adequate to meet your needs.* If they are not, they must be supplemented through your own investment program. The earlier in life

you assess your retirement needs, the greater your chance of accumulating sufficient funds to meet them.

2. *Enhancing Current Income.* Investments enhance current income by earning dividends or interest. Retirees frequently choose investments offering *high current income at low risk.* The idea of a retired person "clipping coupons"—collecting interest—from high-grade bonds is a fair description of what most senior citizens should be doing at that point in their lives.

HOTLINKS

Tax-advantaged investments are discussed on the text's Web site. Click on the Web chapter titled Tax-Advantaged Investments.

www.awl.com/gitman_joehnk

3. *Saving for Major Expenditures.* Families often put aside money over the years to accumulate the funds needed to make major expenditures. The most common of these are the down payment on a home, education, vacation travel, and capital to start a business. The appropriate types of investment vehicles depend on the purpose and the amount of money needed. For purposes such as the down payment on a home or a child's education, for example, much less risk should be tolerated than for other goals. The attainment of such basic goals should not, if possible, be placed in jeopardy.

4. *Sheltering Income from Taxes.* Federal income tax law allows certain noncash charges to be deducted from specified sources of income. Such deductions reduce the amount of final taxable income. Obviously, if a person can avoid (or defer) paying taxes on the income from an investment, he or she will have more funds left for reinvestment.

investment plan
a written document describing how funds will be invested and specifying the target date for achieving each investment goal and the amount of tolerable risk.

Step 3: Adopting an Investment Plan Once your general goals have been established, you should adopt an **investment plan**—a written document describing how funds will be invested. A series of supporting investment goals can be developed for each long-term goal. For each goal, specify the target date for achieving it and the amount of tolerable risk.

Generally, the more important the financial objective, the lower the risk that should be assumed. Suppose, for example, one long-run goal is to accumulate \$80,000 in cash by the end of 10 years. That goal could be spelled out as a plan to accumulate \$80,000 in cash by investing in a portfolio evenly divided between low-risk and speculative stocks providing a total return of 10% per year. The more specific you can be in your statement of investment goals, the easier it will be to establish an investment plan consistent with your goals.

HOTLINKS

The *Investing in Action* box at the book's Web site describes the role of professional financial planners in helping their clients formulate investment goals and plans.

www.awl.com/gitman_joehnk

Step 4: Evaluating Investment Vehicles Once you have your investment goals and plan laid out, you will want to evaluate investment vehicles by assessing each vehicle's potential return and risk. This process typically involves *valuation,* the use of measures of return and risk to estimate the worth of an investment vehicle. (Chapter 4 offers a general discussion of the procedures for measuring these key dimensions of potential investments. Subsequent chapters focus on the valuation of specific vehicles.)

Step 5: Selecting Suitable Investments You now gather additional information and use it to select specific investment vehicles consistent with your goals. The best investments may not be those that simply maximize return.

Other factors, such as risk and tax considerations, may also be crucial. For example, to receive maximum annual dividends, you might purchase the common stock of a firm expected to pay high dividends. However, if the firm whose stock you purchased goes bankrupt, you could lose the money. The stock of a firm that pays lower dividends but with less risk of bankruptcy might have been a better choice. Careful selection of investment vehicles is essential to successful investing. Vehicles should be consistent with established goals and offer acceptable levels of return, risk, and value.

Step 6: Constructing a Diversified Portfolio Selecting suitable investments involves choosing vehicles that enable you to achieve investment goals and that optimize return, risk, and investment values. To do this, you will assemble an investment *portfolio* that meets one or more investment goals. For example, your portfolio might contain common stock, government bonds, and short-term investments. **Diversification** is the inclusion of a number of different investment vehicles in a portfolio to increase returns or reduce risk. By *diversifying* in this way, investors are able to earn higher returns or be exposed to less risk than if they limit their investments to just one or two vehicles. Diversification is the financial term for the age-old advice "Don't put all your eggs in one basket." (Chapter 5 includes discussions of diversification and other modern portfolio concepts.)

diversification
the inclusion of a number of different investment vehicles in a portfolio to increase returns or reduce risk.

Step 7: Managing the Portfolio Once you have constructed your portfolio, you should measure its actual behavior in relation to expected performance. If the investment results are not consistent with your objectives, you may need to take corrective action. Such action usually involves selling certain investments and using the proceeds to acquire other vehicles for the portfolio. *Portfolio management* involves monitoring the portfolio and restructuring it as dictated by the actual behavior of the investments. (Portfolio management is discussed in detail in Chapter 11.)

The *Investing in Action* box summarizes some general tips for successful investing.

Considering Personal Taxes

HOTLINKS

Financial planning is too important to leave to luck. The Web is extremely useful in helping investors establish their investment plans. The Wall Street City Web site has an interactive program that helps investors develop these plans. Visit the following address to learn more about planning and choose [Other Features] and then [Financial Planning].

www.wallstreetcity.com

Besides developing plans for achieving your specific investment goals, it's also important to consider the tax consequences associated with various investments. A knowledge of the tax laws can help you reduce taxes. By doing so, you increase the amount of after-tax dollars available for achieving your investment goals. Because tax laws are complicated and subject to frequent revision, we present only the key concepts and how they apply to popular investment transactions.

Basic Sources of Taxation The two major types of taxes are those levied by the federal government and those levied by state and local governments. The federal *income tax* is the major form of personal taxation. Federal rates currently range from 10 to 35% of taxable income.

State and local taxes vary from area to area. Some states have income taxes that range as high as 15% or more of income. Some cities, especially large East Coast cities, also have local income taxes that typically range

INVESTING in action

Lessons for Investment Success

The stock market has taken investors on a roller coaster ride in recent years. Even in such volatile times, however, some basic rules still apply. Becoming a successful investor takes time and effort; there are no sure-fire schemes for beating the market. Here are some tips to help you get started on the road to financial security.

- **Harness the power of compounding.** With compounding, time is your biggest ally. The longer you invest your money, the faster it will grow. If you earn a 9% annual return on your investment and reinvest your yearly earnings at the same rate for a 20-year period, your overall return is 460%, an average annual return of 23% (460%/20). Start now; waiting will cost you money. If you invest $2,000 a year for 10 years ($20,000 total) at 8% per year, in 35 years you'll have $198,422. But wait 10 years and invest $2,000 a year for 25 years at 8% per year, and your (considerably greater) $50,000 investment will be only $146,212 at the end of that same 35-year period. You can start small. Invest just $200 at 10% and you'll have almost $20,000 in 25 years. Make investing a habit now.
- **Don't wait for the "right" time to invest.** There isn't one! The "best" time to invest is now. You can always find a reason to put off taking the plunge: It's an election year, the market is too high, there's a crisis somewhere in the world. Studies show that it's more important to invest than to pick the right time. In the short run, market activity is unpredictable, even for the experts. Don't make excuses, like you are too busy, investing is too hard, or you can't possibly save enough for college or retirement. Investing is one of the best uses of your time. Rethink your priorities: Is it more important to go to the movies or to plan for your financial future? And don't be intimidated by the investment process. Set realistic goals, learn the basics, and start with simple investments that you understand. Once you gain control of your finances, your confidence will increase.
- **Diversify your portfolio.** Spreading your money among different types of investments is less risky than putting all your eggs in one investment basket. If some of your holdings go down, others go up, and vice versa. Diversify your portfolio by investing in several types of securities: short-term vehicles such as money market funds, intermediate-term bonds or bond funds, and, for the long-term, growth stocks or growth mutual funds. You should also have some international stocks or mutual funds. Don't concentrate too heavily in one industry or buy just one or two stocks. No one knows which sector will be hot tomorrow.
- **Monitor your investments.** Don't just buy securities and hold them forever. Review your portfolio monthly to check your progress against your goals. Weed out your poor performers and evaluate current holdings relative to other investment opportunities. Don't be too quick to unload a stock or mutual fund or to chase after that hot stock tip, though. Do your homework and be sure you have a good reason to buy or sell.

Sources: Jonathan Clements, "Don't Ignore Luck's Role in Stock Picks," *Wall Street Journal*, September 26, 2000, p. C1; Jonathan Clements, "Lessons from the School of Hard Knocks, *Wall Street Journal*, March 14, 2000, p. C1; "Money 101: Basics of Investing," *Money.com*, downloaded from www.money.com/money/101; Peter Psaras, "Ten Tips for Successful Investing," *The Motley Fool*, September 13, 2000, downloaded from fool.com

between 1% and 5% of income. In addition to income taxes, state and local governments rely heavily on sales and property taxes, which vary from community to community, as a source of revenue.

Income taxes at the federal, state, and local levels have the greatest impact on security investments, whose returns are in the form of dividends, interest, and increases in value. Property taxes can have a sizable impact on real estate and other forms of property investment.

Types of Income The income of individuals is classified into one of *three basic categories* defined below.

1. *Active income* consists of everything from wages and salaries to bonuses, tips, pension income, and alimony. Active income is made up of income earned on the job as well as most other forms of *noninvestment* income.
2. *Portfolio income* is earnings generated from various types of investment holdings. This category of income covers most (but not all) types of investments, from savings accounts, stocks, bonds, and mutual funds to options and futures. For the most part, portfolio income consists of interest, dividends, and capital gains (the profit on the sale of an investment).
3. *Passive income* is a special category of income, composed chiefly of income derived from real estate, limited partnerships, and other forms of tax-advantaged investments.

The key feature of these categories is that they limit the amount of deductions (write-offs) that can be taken, particularly for portfolio and passive income. The amount of allowable deductions for portfolio and passive income is *limited to the amount of income derived from these two sources.* For example, if you had a total of $380 in portfolio income for the year, you could deduct no more than $380 in investment-related interest expense. For deduction purposes, the portfolio and passive income categories cannot be mixed or combined with each other or with active income. *Investment-related expenses can be used only to offset portfolio income,* and (with a few exceptions) *passive investment expenses can be used only to offset the income from passive investments.*

Ordinary Income Regardless of whether it's classified as active, portfolio, or passive, ordinary income is taxed at one of six rates: 10, 15, 25, 28, 33, or 35%. There is one structure of tax rates for taxpayers who file *individual* returns and another for those who file *joint* returns with a spouse. Table 1.2 shows the tax rates and income brackets for these two categories. Note that the rates are *progressive.* That is, taxpayers with taxable income above a specified amount are taxed at a higher rate.

An example will demonstrate how ordinary income is taxed. Consider the Ellis sisters, Joni and Cara. Both are single. Joni's taxable income is $18,000. Cara's is $36,000. Using Table 1.2, we can calculate their taxes as follows:

TABLE 1.2 **Tax Rates and Income Brackets for Individual and Joint Returns (2003)**

	Taxable Income	
Tax Rates	Individual Returns	Joint Returns
10%	$0 to $7,000	$0 to $14,000
15%	Over $7,000 to $28,400	Over $14,000 to $56,800
25%	Over $28,400 to $68,800	Over $56,800 to $114,650
28%	Over $68,800 to $143,500	Over $114,650 to $174,700
33%	Over $143,500 to $311,950	Over $174,700 to $311,950
35%	Over $311,950	Over $311,950

Joni:

(0.15 × $18,000) = $2,700

Cara:

(0.15 × $28,400) + [0.25 × ($36,000 − $28,400)]
= $4,260 + $1,900 = $6,160

The progressive nature of the federal income tax structure can be seen by the fact that although Cara's taxable income is twice that of Joni, her income tax is about 2.5 times Joni's.

Capital Gains and Losses A *capital asset* is property owned and used by the taxpayer for personal reasons, pleasure, or investment. The most common types are securities and real estate, including one's home. A *capital gain* represents the amount by which the proceeds from the sale of a capital asset *exceed* its original purchase price. Capital gains are taxed at two different rates depending on the holding period.

The capital gains tax rate is 15% if the asset is held for more than 12 months. This 15% capital gains tax rate assumes that you're in the 25%, 28%, 33%, or 35% tax bracket. If you're in the 15% tax bracket or below, then the capital gains tax rate on an asset held for more than 12 months is just 5%. If the asset is held for less than 12 months, then the amount of any capital gain realized is added to other sources of income, and the total is taxed at the rates given in Table 1.2.

For example, imagine that James McFail, a single person who has other taxable income totaling $45,000, sold 500 shares of stock at $12 per share. He originally purchased this stock at $10 per share. The total capital gain on this transaction was $1,000 [500 shares × ($12/share − $10/share)]. Thus James's taxable income would total $46,000, which puts him in the 25% tax bracket (see Table 1.2).

If the $1,000 capital gain resulted from an asset that was held for more than 12 months, and because James is in the 25% tax bracket, the capital gain would be taxed at the maximum rate of 15%. His total tax would be calculated as follows:

Ordinary income ($45,000)		
(0.15 × $28,400) + (0.25 × [$45,000 − $28,400])		
= $4,260 + $4,150 =		$8,410
Capital gain ($1,000)		
(0.15 × $1,000) =		150.00
	Total tax	$8,560.00

James's total tax would be $8,560.00. Had his other taxable income been below $28,400 (i.e., in the 15% bracket), the $1,000 capital gain would have been taxed at 5% rather than 15%. Had James held the asset for less than 12 months, his $1,000 capital gain would have been taxed as ordinary income, which in James's case would result in a 25% rate.

Capital gains are appealing to investors because they are not taxed until actually realized. For example, if you own a stock originally purchased for $50 per share that at the end of the tax year has a market price of $60 per share, you have a "paper gain" of $10 per share. This *paper (unrealized) gain* is not taxable, because you still own the stock. *Only realized gains are taxed.* If you sold the stock for $60 per share during the tax year, you would have a realized—and therefore taxable—gain of $10 per share.

capital loss
the amount by which the proceeds from the sale of a capital asset are *less than* its original purchase price.

net losses
the amount by which capital losses exceed capital gains; up to $3,000 of net losses can be applied against ordinary income in any year.

tax planning
the development of strategies that will defer and minimize an individual's level of taxes over the long run.

A **capital loss** results when a capital asset is sold for *less than* its original purchase price. Before taxes are calculated, all gains and losses must be netted out. Up to $3,000 of **net losses** can be applied against ordinary income in any year. Losses that cannot be applied in the current year may be carried forward and used to offset future income, subject to certain conditions.

Investments and Taxes The opportunities created by the tax laws make tax planning important in the investment process. **Tax planning** involves looking at your earnings, both current and projected, and developing strategies that will defer and minimize the level of taxes. The tax plan should guide your investment activities so that over the long run you will achieve maximum after-tax returns for an acceptable level of risk. For example, the fact that capital gains are not taxed until actually realized allows you to defer tax payments on them as well as control the timing of these payments. However, investments that are likely to lead to capital gains income generally have higher risk than those that provide only current investment income. Therefore, the choice of investment vehicles cannot be made solely on the basis of the possible reduction of tax payments. The levels of both return and risk need to be viewed in light of their tax effects. *It is the after-tax return and associated risk that matter.*

HOTLINKS

The material on tax strategies and tax-advantaged investments available on this text's Web site provides more detailed information on this topic. Click on Chapter 17.

www.awl.com/gitman_joehnk

Tax plans should also reflect the (1) form of returns—current income, capital gains, or tax-advantaged income—and (2) the timing of loss recognition and profit taking. One common strategy is to claim losses as soon as they occur and to delay profit taking. Such an approach allows you to benefit from the tax deductibility of a loss and to delay having to claim income from gains. Tax planning, which is usually done in coordination with an accountant, tax expert, or tax attorney, is most common among individuals with high levels of income ($200,000 or more annually). Yet sizable savings can result for investors with lower incomes as well.

INVESTOR FACTS

TAX BITE—If you invest just $2,000 a year in taxable accounts and investments for the next 30 years and earn an 8% average compounded annual rate of return, you'll accumulate about $227,000—until you pay Uncle Sam his share. Then you will have only $175,230, assuming that an average federal income tax rate of 31% is applied to your earnings above the total investment of $60,000 ($2,000 × 30 years). Taxes will reduce your earnings from the investment by nearly one-third!

Investing Over the Life Cycle

Investors tend to follow different investment philosophies as they move through different stages of the life cycle. Generally speaking, most investors tend to be more aggressive when they're young and more conservative as they grow older. Typically, investors move through the following investment stages.

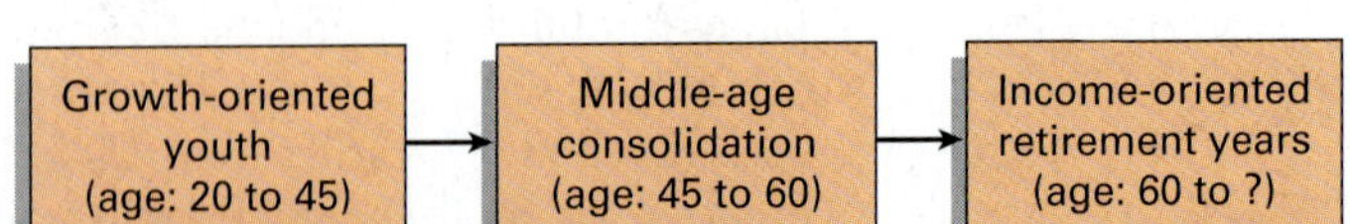

Most young investors, in their twenties and thirties, tend to prefer growth-oriented investments that stress *capital gains* rather than current income. Often young investors don't have much in the way of investable funds, so capital gains are viewed as the quickest (if not necessarily the surest) way to build capital. Young investors tend to favor growth-oriented and speculative vehicles, particularly high-risk common stocks, options, and futures.

As investors approach the middle-age consolidation stage of life (the mid-forties), family demands and responsibilities such as educational expenses and retirement contributions become more important. The whole portfolio goes through a transition to *higher-quality securities*. Low-risk growth and income stocks, preferred stocks, convertibles, high-grade bonds, and mutual funds are all widely used at this stage.

Finally, investors approach their retirement years. Preservation of capital and current income become the principal concerns. A secure, high level of income is paramount. Capital gains are viewed as merely a pleasant, occasional by-product of investing. The investment portfolio now becomes *highly conservative*. It now consists of low-risk income stocks, high-yielding government bonds, quality corporate bonds, bank certificates of deposit (CDs), and other short-term vehicles. At this stage, investors reap the rewards of a lifetime of saving and investing.

Investing in Different Economic Environments

Despite the government's arsenal of weapons for moderating economic swings, numerous changes are sure to occur in the economy during your lifetime of investing. At all stages of the life cycle, your investment program must be flexible enough to allow you to recognize and react to changing economic conditions. The first rule of investing is to know *where* to put your money. The second is to know *when* to make your moves.

The first question is easier to deal with, because it involves matching the risk and return objectives of your investment plan with the available investment alternatives. For example, if you're a seasoned investor who can tolerate the risk, then speculative stocks may be right for you. If you're a novice who wants a fair return on your capital, perhaps you should consider a good growth-oriented mutual fund. Unfortunately, although stocks and growth funds may do well when the economy is expanding, they can turn out to be disasters at other times. This leads to the second, and more difficult, question: What effect do economic and market conditions have on investment returns?

The question of when to invest is difficult because it deals with *market timing*. The fact is that most economists and most professional money managers—not to mention most investors—cannot consistently predict the peaks and troughs in the economy or stock market. It's a lot easier to get a handle on the *current state* of the economy/market. That is, knowing whether the economy/market is in a state of expansion or decline is considerably different from being able to pinpoint when it's about to change course. Thus, for our purposes, we can define **market timing** as the process of identifying the current state of the economy/market and assessing the likelihood of its continuing on its present course.

market timing
the process of identifying the current state of the economy/market and assessing the likelihood of its continuing on its present course.

As an investor, it's best to confine your assessment of the economy to three distinct conditions: (1) a state of recovery or expansion, (2) a state of decline or recession, or (3) uncertainty as to the direction of its movement. These different stages are illustrated in Figure 1.2. It's easy to see when things are moving up (recovery/expansion) and when they're moving down (decline/recession). The difficulty comes with the peaks and troughs. At those points, you don't know whether the economy will continue in its current direction, up or down, or whether it will change direction. That is why these areas in the figure are shaded, depicting *uncertainty*. How you will respond to these

FIGURE 1.2

Different Stages of an Economic/Market Cycle

The economic/market cycle shows three different conditions: (1) a state of recovery/expansion, (2) a state of decline/recession, and (3) uncertainty as to the direction in which the economy/market is going to move (shown by the shaded areas).

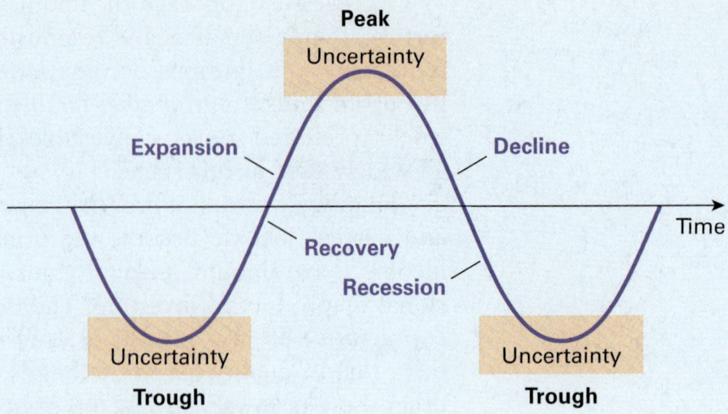

conditions depends on the types of investment vehicles you hold (for example, stocks or bonds).

Stocks and the Business Cycle Common stocks and other equity-related securities (convertible securities, stock mutual funds, stock options, and stock index futures) are highly responsive to conditions in the economy. Economic conditions are described generically as the *business cycle.* The business cycle reflects the current status of a variety of economic variables, including GDP (gross domestic product), industrial production, personal disposable income, the unemployment rate, and more.

A strong economy is reflected in an expanding business cycle. When business is good and profits are up, stocks react by increasing in value and return. Growth-oriented and speculative stocks tend to do especially well in strong markets. To a lesser extent, so do low-risk and income-oriented stocks. In contrast, when economic activity is declining, the values and returns on common stocks tend to be off as well.

Bonds and Interest Rates Bonds and other forms of fixed-income securities (preferred stocks and bond funds) are highly sensitive to movements in interest rates. In fact, interest rates are the single most important variable in determining bond price behavior and returns to investors. Interest rates and bond prices move in opposite directions (as will be explained in Chapters 9 and 10). Therefore, rising interest rates are unfavorable for bonds already held in an investor's portfolio. Of course, high interest rates enhance the attractiveness of new bonds because these bonds must offer high returns to attract investors.

Meeting Liquidity Needs: Investing in Short-Term Vehicles

LG 6

As discussed earlier, you should ensure that you have adequate liquidity. This provision is a prerequisite to implementing long-term investment goals. *Liquidity* is the ability to convert an investment into cash quickly and with little or no loss in value. A checking account is highly liquid. Stocks and bonds are not liquid, because there is no definite assurance that you will be able to quickly sell them at a price equal to or greater than their purchase price.

The Role of Short-Term Vehicles

Short-term vehicles are an important part of most savings and investment programs. They generate income—which can be quite high during periods of high interest rates. However, their primary function is to provide a pool of reserves that can be used for emergencies or simply to accumulate funds for some specific purpose. As a rule of thumb, financial planners often suggest that anywhere from 3 to 6 months' worth of after-tax income should be held in short-term vehicles to meet unexpected needs or to take advantage of attractive opportunities.

Investors usually hold short-term vehicles in their investment portfolios as a *temporary,* highly liquid investment until something better comes along. Some individuals choose to hold short-term vehicles because they simply are more comfortable with them. In fact, this approach has considerable merit during periods of economic and investment instability. Regardless of your motives for holding short-term vehicles, you should evaluate them in terms of their risk and return, just as you would longer-term investments.

Interest on Short-Term Investments Short-term investments earn interest in one of two ways. Some investments, such as savings accounts, pay a *stated rate of interest.* In this case, you can easily find the interest rate—it's the stated rate on the account.

Alternatively, interest is earned on short-term investments on a **discount basis.** This means that the security is purchased at a price below its redemption value, and the difference is the interest earned. U.S. Treasury bills (T-bills), for example, are issued on a discount basis.

discount basis
a method of earning interest on a security by purchasing it at a price below its redemption value; the difference is the interest earned.

Risk Characteristics Short-term investments are generally considered low in risk. Their primary risk results from the *loss of potential purchasing power* that occurs when the rate of return on these investments falls short of the inflation rate. This has often been the case with such vehicles as *passbook savings accounts,* the traditional bank savings accounts that generally pay a low rate of interest and have no minimum balance. Over long periods of time most other short-term investments have rates of return that are about equal to, or maybe slightly higher than, the average inflation rate.

HOTLINKS

A relatively simple formula can be applied when interest is earned on a discount basis in order to compare returns with vehicles earning a stated rate of interest. See this text's Web site for discussion of the formula.

www.awl.com/gitman_joehnk

The *risk of default*—nonpayment—is virtually nonexistent with short-term investment vehicles. The principal reason is that the primary issuers of most short-term vehicles are highly reputable institutions, such as the U.S. Treasury, large banks, and major corporations. Deposits in commercial banks, savings and loans, savings banks, and credit unions also are insured for up to $100,000 per account by government agencies. Finally, because the value of short-term investments does not change much in response to changing interest rates, exposure to capital loss is correspondingly low.

Advantages and Disadvantages of Short-Term Investments As noted, the major advantages of short-term investments are their high liquidity and low risk. Most are available from local financial institutions and can be readily converted to cash with minimal inconvenience. Finally, because the returns on most short-term investments vary with inflation and market interest rates, investors can readily capture higher returns as rates move up. On the negative side, when interest rates go down, returns drop as well.

Although a decline in market rates has undesirable effects on most short-term vehicles, perhaps their biggest disadvantage is their relatively low return. Because these securities are generally so low in risk, you can expect the returns on short-term investments to average less than the returns on long-term investments.

Popular Short-Term Investment Vehicles

Over the past 25 years or so, the number of short-term investment vehicles being offered has greatly expanded. Investing in short-term securities is no longer the easy task it once was, when the decision for most people amounted to whether to place funds in a passbook savings account or in U.S. savings bonds. Today, even some checking accounts pay interest on idle balances. Along with the increase in investment alternatives has come greater sophistication in short-term investment management. Investors now know they can use short-term vehicles as secure investment outlets for the long haul or as a place to hold cash until they find a longer-term outlet for the funds.

In the material that follows, we will first examine the best-known short-term investment vehicles—deposit accounts, Series EE savings bonds, and U.S. Treasury bills. Next we will describe some of the most popular nongovernment short-term securities. Finally, we will look at several ways to use these deposits/securities in an investment portfolio.

passbook savings account
a savings account, offered by banks, that generally pays a low rate of interest and has no minimum balance.

NOW (negotiated order of withdrawal) account
a bank checking account that pays interest; has no legal minimum balance, but many banks impose their own.

money market deposit accounts (MMDAs)
a bank deposit account with limited check-writing privileges; has no legal minimum balance, but many banks impose their own.

Deposit Accounts Banks offer investors several forms of deposit accounts that pay interest on account balances. (*Note:* We use the term *bank* to refer to commercial banks, savings and loans (S&Ls), savings banks, and credit unions—all of which issue deposit accounts.) Four such accounts are **passbook savings accounts, NOW (negotiated order of withdrawal) accounts, money market deposit accounts** (**MMDAs**), and **asset management accounts.** The distinguishing features of these accounts are summarized in Table 1.3. The first two—passbook savings accounts and NOW accounts—are primarily used as savings vehicles. They provide the individual investor with a highly liquid pool of funds that can be accessed easily to meet scheduled as well as unexpected expenditures. The second two—MMDAs and asset management accounts—are more likely to be used for investment purposes. For this use, they earn a reasonably competitive short-term return while maintaining sufficient liquidity to meet unexpected needs and seize attractive investment opportunities.

Series EE Savings Bonds **Series EE savings bonds** are the well-known savings bonds that have been available for decades. You may have been given some by thrifty or patriotic relatives on birthdays or other special occasions. (First issued in 1941, these savings bonds used to be called Series E bonds.)

asset management account a comprehensive deposit account that combines checking, investing, and borrowing activities; it automatically "sweeps" excess balances into short-term investments and borrows to meet shortages.

Series EE savings bonds savings bonds issued by the U.S. Treasury and sold at banks and through payroll deduction plans, in varying denominations, at 50% of face value; pay a variable rate of interest tied to U.S. Treasury security market yields and calculated every six months in May and November.

accrual-type securities securities for which interest is paid when the bond is cashed, on or before maturity, rather than periodically over the life of the bond.

Series EE bonds are **accrual-type securities.** This means that interest is paid when the bond is cashed, on or before maturity, rather than periodically over the life of the bond. They are sold at a discount—the purchase price of all denominations is 50% of the face value. Thus a $100 bond costs $50 and will be worth $100 at maturity. Series EE bonds are backed by the full faith and credit of the U.S. government. They can be replaced without charge in case of loss, theft, or destruction. They can be purchased at banks or other thrift institutions or through payroll deduction plans. They are issued in denominations of $50 through $10,000. A person is limited to maximum annual Series EE bond purchases of $15,000 (i.e., $30,000 face value).

The actual maturity date on EE bonds is unspecified because they pay a variable rate of interest. The higher the rate of interest being paid, the shorter the period of time it takes for the bond to *accrue* from its discounted purchase price to its face value. The rate of interest paid on EE bonds is 90% of the average 5-year Treasury security market yields for the preceding 6 months. Bonds can be redeemed any time after the first 6 months. All EE bonds held from 6 months to 5 years are penalized by forfeiting the last 3 months of interest earned. The U.S. Treasury calculates interest rates every 6 months (in May and November). Interest rates change in accordance with prevailing Treasury security market yields. You can obtain current rates on Series EE bonds from your bank or simply by calling 800-487-2663. (*Note:* For bonds purchased after May 1, 1997, the rate for the 6-month period ending October 31, 2001, was 4.50%.) Interest is credited every 6 months and compounds semiannually.

TABLE 1.3 Distinguishing Features of Interest-Paying Deposit Accounts

Type of Account	Brief Description	Minimum Balance	Interest Rate	Federal Insurance
Passbook savings account	Savings accounts offered by banks.* Used primarily for convenience or if investors lack sufficient funds for other short-term vehicles.	Typically none	2%–6% depending on economy	Yes, up to $100,000 per deposit.
NOW (negotiated order of withdrawal) account	Bank checking account that pays interest on balances.	No legal minimum, but often set at $500 to $1,000	At or near passbook rates	Yes, up to $100,000 per deposit.
Money market deposit account (MMDA)	Bank deposit account with limited check-writing privileges.	No legal minimum, but often set at about $2,500	Typically about 1% above passbook rate	Yes, up to $100,000 per deposit.
Asset management account	Deposit account at bank, brokerage house, mutual fund, or insurance company that combines checking, investing, and borrowing. Automatically "sweeps" excess balances into short-term investments and borrows to meet shortages.	Typically $5,000 to $20,000	Similar to MMDAs	Yes, up to $100,000 per deposit in banks. Varies in other institutions.

*The term *bank* refers to commercial banks, savings and loans (S&Ls), savings banks, and credit unions.

In addition to being exempt from state and local taxes, Series EE bonds provide an appealing tax twist: *Investors need not report the interest earned on their federal tax returns until the bonds are redeemed.* Interest *can* be reported annually. This might be done, for example, if the bonds are held in the name of a child who has limited interest income. But most investors choose to defer reporting the interest. In effect, this means the funds are being reinvested at an after-tax rate equal to the bond's current interest rate. Another attractive tax feature allows partial or complete tax avoidance of EE bond earnings when proceeds are used to pay education expenses (such as college tuition) for the bond purchaser, a spouse, or other IRS-defined dependent. To qualify the purchaser must be age 24 or older and must, after December 31, 1999, have adjusted gross income below $54,100 for single filers and $81,100 for married couples. (The maximum income levels are adjusted annually.)

The U.S. government also issues Series HH and Series I savings bonds. Both are issued at face value. The HH bonds pay interest twice a year. The I bonds, which are inflation-indexed, pay accrued interest at the bond's maturity, which is 30 years.

U.S. Treasury bills (T-bills) obligations of the U.S. Treasury, sold on a discount basis, and having varying short-term maturities; regarded as the safest of all investments.

U.S. Treasury Bills **U.S. Treasury bills (T-bills)** are obligations of the U.S. Treasury issued as part of its ongoing process of funding the national debt. T-bills are sold on a discount basis in minimum denominations of $1,000 and are issued with 3-month and 6-month maturities. The U.S. Treasury auctions off the 3- and 6-month bills every Monday.

Purchasing T-Bills You can purchase T-bills *directly,* through participation in the weekly Treasury auctions. Or you can purchase them *indirectly,* through local commercial banks, securities dealers, or brokers who buy bills for investors on a commission basis. You can directly purchase T-bills over the Internet (www.publicdebt.treas.gov) or by using a touch-tone phone (call Treasury Direct Electronic Services at 800-722-2678 and follow the interactive menu to complete transactions). You also can purchase outstanding Treasury bills in the resale market through banks or brokers. The biggest advantage of the resale market is that you have a much wider selection of maturities to choose from, ranging from less than a week to as long as 6 months.

It is relatively simple to buy T-bills directly. All you need to do is submit a tender offer to the nearest Federal Reserve Bank or branch, specifying both the amount and the maturity of T-bills desired. (Tender forms can be obtained by writing the Bureau of the Public Debt, Department N, Washington, DC 20239-1500, or by calling 202-622-2000.) The Treasury tries to accommodate individual investors through its noncompetitive bidding system, which most people use because of its simplicity. In essence, all noncompetitive tender offers (by mail, over the Internet, and by phone) are awarded T-bills at a price equal to the average of all the accepted competitive bids. Thus you are assured of buying bills in the quantity desired, while obtaining the benefits of an open auction system—all without going through the hassle of a competitive bid. Note, though, that T-bills bought directly through noncompetitive bidding are meant to be held to maturity. You should not purchase T-bills by noncompetitive bid if you want to trade them. It is difficult and time-consuming to sell these T-bills in the aftermarket.

Evaluating T-Bills A particularly attractive feature of T-bills is that they are *exempt from state and local income taxes,* which in some areas can be as high as 20%. Federal taxes are not due until the interest is actually received at maturity. Also, because they are issued by the U.S. Treasury, T-bills are regarded as the safest, though generally the lowest-yielding, of all investments. Furthermore, there is a highly active secondary market for Treasury bills (other than those bought through noncompetitive bidding), so you can easily sell them if you need the cash.

HOTLINKS

A specialized formula can be used to calculate the yields on T-bills. See this text's Web site for discussion of the formula.

www.awl.com/gitman_joehnk

Nongovernment Short-Term Securities We have seen that you can use deposit accounts, Series EE savings bonds, and U.S. Treasury bills to meet liquidity needs. You can also meet liquidity needs by using *nongovernment short-term securities.* These securities generally tend to have higher yields than deposit accounts, EE bonds, and T-bills with similar maturities due to the slightly higher risk associated with them. The principal nongovernment marketable securities include certificates of deposit, commercial paper, banker's acceptances, and money market mutual funds. Each is briefly described below.

certificates of deposit (CDs)
savings instruments in which funds must remain on deposit for a specified period; withdrawals prior to maturity incur interest penalties.

Certificates of Deposit **Certificates of deposit (CDs)** differ from the deposit accounts discussed above in that funds must remain on deposit for a specified period. This period can range from 7 days to a year or more. Although it is possible to withdraw funds prior to maturity, an interest penalty (equal to 31 to 90 days of interest) usually makes withdrawal costly. Banks today are free to offer any rate and maturity on these securities. The interest rate on CDs is fixed over their stated maturity.

CDs are convenient to buy and hold, and all offer attractive and highly competitive returns plus federal insurance protection (up to $100,000 per deposit). The decision whether to invest in a CD or in a more liquid short-term investment vehicle (such as a MMDA or a T-bill) generally depends on the length of the holding period and interest rate expectations. Uncertain holding periods and expected interest rate increases would favor MMDAs and T-bills; certain holding periods and expected interest rate declines would favor CDs.

brokered CDs
certificates of deposit sold by stockbrokers; offer slightly higher yields than other CDs and typically can be sold prior to maturity without incurring a penalty.

CDs can also be purchased from stockbrokers, in the form of **brokered CDs.** The brokerage house looks around the country for the highest yield it can get, buys these CDs, and then resells them to its clients. In essence, a bank issues the CDs, and the brokerage house places them with the investing public. There's usually no commission to pay, because the broker earns its commission from the issuing bank. The minimum denomination is usually $1,000. Brokered CDs are attractive for two reasons: (1) They can be sold prior to maturity without incurring a penalty. (2) They may provide higher yields—frequently ¼ to ¾ of a percent higher—than those available from a local bank.

commercial paper
short-term, unsecured promissory notes (IOUs) issued by corporations with very high credit standings.

Commercial Paper **Commercial paper** is short-term, unsecured promissory notes (IOUs) issued by corporations with very high credit standings. Most commercial paper is initially sold in multiples of $100,000. Typical maturities range from a few days up to 270 days, the maximum maturity that does not require registration with the Securities and Exchange Commission (SEC). Because the resale market for commercial paper is limited, most investors hold commercial paper to maturity. Its yield is comparable to the rate of return earned on large-denomination CDs. Most individual investors who obtain commercial paper do so from a bank or broker, who will "break down" the paper and sell the investor a small portion. However, returns on commercial paper are generally comparable to returns on CDs, which have a fixed maturity like commercial paper but in addition also have federal insurance protection.

banker's acceptances
short-term, low-risk investment vehicles arising from bank guarantees of business transactions; are sold at a discount from their face value and generally provide yields slightly below those of CDs and commercial paper.

Banker's Acceptances Banker's **acceptances** arise from short-term credit arrangements used by business firms to finance transactions. Most often these involve firms in foreign countries or with unknown credit capacities. Typically, an importer's bank agrees to pay its foreign supplier on behalf of the importer, who is contractually obligated to repay the bank within the 3 to 6 months it takes to receive and sell the merchandise involved in the transaction. The importer's bank may either hold the acceptance to maturity or sell it at a discount to obtain immediate cash. An investor who buys a banker's acceptance is therefore promised payment of its face value by the importer at the specified future date. As a result of its sale, the banker's acceptance becomes a marketable security.

The initial maturities of banker's acceptances are typically between 30 and 180 days, 90 days being most common. If the importer fails to pay the amount due at maturity, the bank is liable for the payment. Because of this, banker's acceptances, which typically have a minimum denomination of $100,000, are low-risk securities with good resale markets. The yields on banker's acceptances are generally slightly below those of CDs and commercial paper; they can usually be purchased through a bank or stockbroker.

money market mutual fund (MMMF)
a mutual fund that pools the capital of a large number of investors and uses it to invest exclusively in high-yielding, short-term securities.

Money Market Mutual Funds A **money market mutual fund** (MMMF) is a mutual fund that pools the capital of a large number of investors and uses it to invest exclusively in high-yielding, short-term securities, such as Treasury bills, large certificates of deposit, and commercial paper. Because such securities are sold in denominations of $1,000 to $1 million (or more), most small investors cannot purchase them individually. The MMMF makes these vehicles, which very often offer the highest short-term returns, available to even small investors. Shares of MMMFs can be purchased through brokers or directly from the fund in initial amounts as small as $500 to $1,000. MMMFs provide easy access to funds through check-writing privileges. You continue to earn interest while the check is being cleared through the banking system. Almost every major brokerage firm has a money fund of its own; hundreds more are unaffiliated with a specific brokerage firm.

The returns on money funds amount to what fund managers are able to earn from their investment activity in various short-term securities. Thus, the returns rise and fall with money market interest rates. Though they are not federally insured, MMMFs have very low risk because the securities they hold are very low in risk and diversification by the funds lowers risk even more. (More information about the features and types of MMMFs is included as part of the discussion of mutual funds in Chapter 12.)

Investment Suitability

Individual investors use short-term vehicles for both savings and investment. They use short-term vehicles to maintain a desired level of savings that will be readily available if the need arises—in essence, to provide *safety and security.* For this purpose, high yield is less important than safety, liquidity, and convenience. Passbook savings accounts, NOW accounts, and Series EE savings bonds are the most popular savings vehicles.

When short-term vehicles are used for *investment purposes*, yield is often just as important as liquidity. However, because the objective is different, the short-term vehicles tend to be used much more aggressively. Most investors will hold at least a part of their portfolio in short-term, highly liquid securities, if for no other reason than to be able to act on unanticipated investment opportunities. Some investors, in fact, devote all or most of their portfolios to such securities.

One of the most common uses of short-term securities as investment vehicles is as temporary outlets. In that use, investors buy short-term vehicles either to warehouse funds until an attractive permanent investment can be found or to sit on the sidelines in times of unsettled or undesirable market conditions. For example, if you have just sold some stock but do not have a suitable long-term investment alternative, you might place the proceeds in a money fund until you find a longer-term use for them. Or if you feel that interest rates are about to rise sharply, you might sell your long-term bonds and use the proceeds to buy T-bills. The high-yielding securities—like MMDAs, CDs, commercial paper, banker's acceptances, and money funds—are generally preferred for use as part of an investment program, as are asset management accounts at major brokerage firms.

To decide which securities are most appropriate for a particular situation, you need to consider such issue characteristics as availability, safety, liquidity, and yield. Though all the investments we have discussed satisfy the basic liquidity demand, they do so to varying degrees. A NOW account is unquestionably the most liquid of all. You can write as many checks on the account as you wish and for any amount. A certificate of deposit, on the other hand, is not so liquid, because early redemption involves an interest penalty.

TABLE 1.4 A Scorecard for Short-Term Accounts and Securities

Savings or Investment Vehicle	Availability	Safety	Liquidity	Yield (Average Rate)*
Passbook savings account	A+	A+	A	D (1.0%)
NOW account	A–	A+	A+	F (0.5%)
Money market deposit account (MMDA)	B	A+	A	B– (4.0%)
Asset management account	B–	A	A+	B (5.0%)
Series EE savings bond	A+	A++	C–	B+ (5.7%)
U.S. Treasury bill (91-day)	B–	A++	A–	A– (6.0%)
Certificate of deposit (3-month, large denomination)	B	A+	C	A (6.6%)
Commercial paper (90-day)	B–	A–	C	A– (6.5%)
Banker's acceptance (90-day)	D–	A	B	A– (6.5%)
Money market mutual fund (MMMF)	B	A/A+	B+	A– (6.0%)

*The average rates reflect representative or typical rates that existed in late 2000.

HOTLINKS

Get the latest Treasury securities data on 30-year bonds, 10-year notes, 5-year notes, and 13-week bills. Visit Yahoo! Finance, section U.S. Markets, [major U.S. Indices], to get the most current quote (last trade), the change from the previous trading day, the percent change, charts, news, and much more.

finance.yahoo.com

Table 1.4 summarizes the key characteristics for most of the short-term investments discussed here. The letter grade assigned for each characteristic reflects an estimate of the investment's quality in that area. For example, MMMFs rate only a B+ on liquidity, because withdrawals must usually be made in a minimum amount of $250 to $500. NOW accounts are somewhat better in this respect, because a withdrawal can be for any amount. Yields are self-explanatory. You should note, though, that if an investment scores lower on availability, safety, or liquidity, it will generally offer a higher yield.

Summary

Note: The end-of-chapter Summaries restate the chapter's Learning Goals and review the key points of information related to each goal.

LG 1 **Understand the meaning of the term *investment* and the factors commonly used to differentiate among types of investments.** An investment is any vehicle into which funds can be placed with the expectation that they will generate positive income and/or that their value will be preserved or will increase. The returns from investing are received either as current income or as increased value.

Some investment vehicles are securities; others are forms of property. Some investments are made directly, others indirectly. An investment can be a debt, an equity, or a derivative security such as an option. It can possess risk ranging from very low to extremely high. An individual can invest in either short-term or long-term vehicles. Today, individual investors have ready access to both domestic and foreign investments.

LG 2 **Describe the investment process and types of investors.** The investment process is structured around financial institutions and financial markets that bring together suppliers and demanders of funds. The dominant financial market in the United States is the securities markets for stocks, bonds, and options. The participants in the investment process are government, business, and individuals. Of these groups, only individuals are net suppliers of funds. Investors can be either individual investors or institutional investors.

LG 3 **Discuss the principal types of investment vehicles.** A broad range of investment vehicles is available. Short-term vehicles have low risk. They are used to earn a return on temporarily idle funds, to serve as a primary investment outlet of conservative investors, and to provide liquidity. Common stocks offer dividends and capital gains. Fixed-income securities—bonds, preferred stock, and convertible securities—offer fixed periodic returns with some potential for gain in value. Mutual funds allow investors conveniently to buy or sell interests in a professionally managed, diversified portfolio of securities.

Derivative securities are high-risk, high-expected-return vehicles. The key derivatives are options and futures. Options offer the investor an opportunity to buy or sell another security at a specified price over a given period of time. Futures are contracts between a seller and a buyer for delivery of a specified commodity or financial instrument, at a specified future date, at an agreed-on price. Other popular investment vehicles include real estate, tangibles, and tax-advantaged investments.

LG 4 **Describe the steps in investing, particularly establishing investment goals, and cite fundamental personal tax considerations.** Investing is a process that should be driven by well-developed plans established to achieve specific goals. It involves a logical set of steps: meeting investment prerequisites, establishing investment goals, adopting an investment plan, evaluating investment vehicles, selecting suitable investments, constructing a diversified portfolio, and managing the portfolio. Investment goals determine the types of investments made. Common investment goals include accumulating retirement funds, enhancing current income, saving for major expenditures, and sheltering income from taxes.

The tax consequences associated with various investment vehicles and strategies must also be considered. The key dimensions are ordinary income, capital gains and losses, and tax planning.

LG 5 **Discuss investing over the life cycle and investing in different economic environments.** The investment vehicles selected are affected by the investor's stage in the life cycle and by economic cycles. Younger investors tend to prefer growth-oriented investments that stress capital gains. As they age investors move to higher-quality securities. As they approach retirement they become even more conservative. The stage of the economy—(1) recovery or expansion, (2) decline or recession, or (3) uncertainty as to direction of movement—both current and expected, also affects investment choice.

LG 6 **Understand the popular types of short-term investment vehicles.** Investment plans must ensure adequate liquidity. Liquidity needs can be met by investing in various short-term vehicles, which can earn interest at a stated rate or on a discount basis. They typically have low risk. Numerous short-term investment vehicles are available from banks, the government, and brokerage firms. Their suitability depends on the investor's attitude toward availability, safety, liquidity, and yield.

CHAPTER 2

INVESTMENT MARKETS AND TRANSACTIONS

Learning Goals

After studying this chapter, you should be able to:

LG 1 **Identify the basic types of securities markets and describe the IPO process.**

LG 2 **Explain the characteristics of organized securities exchanges.**

LG 3 **Understand the over-the-counter markets, including Nasdaq and alternative trading systems, and the general conditions of securities markets.**

LG 4 **Review the importance of global securities markets, their performance, and the investment procedures and risks associated with foreign investments.**

LG 5 **Discuss trading hours and the regulation of securities markets.**

LG 6 **Explain long purchases and the motives, procedures, and calculations involved in making margin transactions and short sales.**

The Paris, Amsterdam, and Brussels stock exchanges merge to form Euronext, a larger cross-border stock exchange. The Scandinavian exchanges do the same, creating Norex. Competitive pressures bombard the venerable New York Stock Exchange (NYSE), whose cumbersome auction system has lost significant market share to Nasdaq's electronic trading system, home to most technology stocks. Upstart electronic communications networks (ECNs) that match buyers and sellers grab trades away from Nasdaq.

Welcome to the changing world of securities markets, where national boundaries are losing importance. Thanks to advances in telecommunications, networks of electronic screens replace the traditional stock exchange trading floor. Some industry observers envision the creation of a centralized "World Stock Exchange," an electronic marketplace that follows the sun, trading in issues listed on any recognized stock exchange. Others predict that three or four world markets will emerge. Opponents of such immense multinational exchanges call them unnecessary. Investors can already buy in London and sell in Hong Kong through online or traditional brokers. They worry that fewer securities markets will reduce competition. They also cite the very different national regulations as a major stumbling block to successful market consolidation.

In this chapter, we will study the markets, the exchanges, the regulations, and the transactions that enable companies to raise money in the capital markets and enable institutions and individuals to invest in these companies.

Securities Markets

Securities markets are forums that allow suppliers and demanders of *securities* to make financial transactions. They permit such transactions to be made quickly and at a fair price. In this section we will look at the various types of markets, their organization, and their general behavior.

LG 1 LG 2 LG 3

securities markets
forums that allow suppliers and demanders of *securities* to make financial transactions; they include both the *money market* and the *capital market.*

money market
market in which *short-term* securities are bought and sold.

capital market
market in which *long-term* securities such as stocks and bonds are bought and sold.

primary market
the market in which *new issues* of securities are sold to the public.

initial public offering (IPO)
the first public sale of a company's stock.

Securities and Exchange Commission (SEC)
federal agency that regulates securities offerings and markets.

public offering
the sale of a firm's securities to the general public.

rights offering
an offer of new shares of stock to existing stockholders on a pro rata basis.

private placement
the sale of new securities directly to selected groups of investors, without SEC registration.

Types of Securities Markets

Securities markets may be classified as either money markets or capital markets. The **money market** focuses on the purchase and sale of *short-term* securities. Investors turn to the **capital market** for transactions involving *long-term* securities such as stocks and bonds. In this book we will devote most of our attention to the capital market. There, investors can make stock, bond, mutual fund, options, and futures transactions. Capital markets can be classified as either *primary* or *secondary,* depending on whether securities are being sold initially by their issuing company or by intervening owners.

The Primary Market The market in which *new issues* of securities are sold to the public is the **primary market.** In the primary market, the issuer of the equity or debt securities receives the proceeds of sales. In 2000, 452 companies offered their stock for sale in the primary market. The main vehicle in the primary market is the **initial public offering (IPO)**, the first public sale of a company's stock. The primary markets also sell new securities, called *seasoned new issues,* for companies that are already public.

Before offering its securities for public sale, the issuer must register them with and obtain approval from the **Securities and Exchange Commission (SEC)**. This federal regulatory agency must confirm both the adequacy and the accuracy of the information provided to potential investors before a security is publicly offered for sale. In addition, the SEC regulates the securities markets.

To market its securities in the primary market, a firm has three choices. It may make (1) a **public offering**, in which the firm offers its securities for sale to the general public; (2) a **rights offering**, in which the firm offers new shares to existing stockholders on a pro rata basis; or (3) a **private placement**, in which the firm sells new securities directly, without SEC registration, to selected groups of investors such as insurance companies and pension funds.

Going Public: The IPO Process Most companies that go public are small, fast-growing companies that require additional capital to continue expanding. For example, biotechnology company Orchid Biosciences raised almost $48 million when it went public in May 2000 at $8 per share. In addition, large companies may decide to spin off a unit into a separate public corporation. AT&T did this when it spun off its wireless operations into AT&T Wireless in April 2000, raising over $10 billion at $29.50 per share.

When a company decides to go public, it first must obtain the approval of its current shareholders, the investors who own its privately issued stock. Next, the company's auditors and lawyers must certify that all documents for the company are legitimate. The company then finds an investment bank willing to *underwrite* the offering. This underwriter is responsible for promoting the stock and facilitating the sale of the company's IPO shares. The underwriter often brings in other investment banking firms as participants. We'll discuss the role of the investment banker in more detail in the next section.

HOTLINKS

The SEC site, in addition to providing corporate documents such as annual reports, offers basic information and warnings to new investors.

www.sec.gov

HOTLINKS

Read a four-part series on IPOs at the CBS site by scrolling down the page and clicking [more tools and data] and [IPO basics]. Also, to find an IPO index, go to the edgar site.

CBS.marketwatch.com
www.edgar-online.com/brand/quotecom/ipoexpress

The company files a registration statement with the SEC. One portion of the registration statement is called the **prospectus.** It describes the key aspects of the issue, the issuer, and its management and financial position. During the waiting period between the statement's filing and its approval, prospective investors can receive a preliminary prospectus. This preliminary version is called a **red herring,** because a notice printed in red on the front cover indicates the tentative nature of the offer. The cover of the preliminary prospectus describing the 2001 stock issue of Reliant Resources, Inc. is shown in Figure 2.1. Note the red herring printed vertically on its left edge.

prospectus
a portion of a security registration statement that describes the key aspects of the issue, the issuer, and its management and financial position.

red herring
a preliminary prospectus made available to prospective investors during the waiting period between the registration statement's filing with the SEC and its approval.

After the SEC approves the registration statement, the investment community can begin analyzing the company's prospects. However, from the time it files until at least one month after the IPO is complete, the company must observe a *quiet period,* during which there are restrictions on what company officials may say about the company. The purpose of the quiet period is to make sure that all potential investors have access to the same information about the company—that which is presented in the preliminary prospectus—and not to any unpublished data that might give them an unfair advantage.

The investment bankers and company executives promote the company's stock offering through a *road show,* a series of presentations to potential investors around the country and sometimes overseas. In addition to providing investors with information about the new issue, road show sessions help the investment bankers gauge the demand for the offering and set an expected pricing range. After the underwriter sets terms and prices the issue, the SEC must approve the offering.

INVESTOR FACTS

HOT IPO MARKETS—IPO markets have been really hot in recent years. In 2000, 452 newly public U.S. companies raised a record $80.6 billion through new equity offerings. In the last quarter of 2000, new issues tapered off to just 63 IPOs valued at $8.8 billion.

Table 2.1 shows the offering date and price, first-day gain, and return based on the price on August 31, 2000, for selected IPOs. Nuance Communications' offering price doubled on the first day and continued to rise. Often the investment banker adjusts the IPO offering price if demand seems very high or low. For example, the preliminary offering price range for the America Online Latin America IPO was $15–$17. Because of lukewarm investor reaction, the investment banker dropped the offering price to $8. The opposite may also be true. In recent years many IPO deals have been *underpriced,* resulting in huge first-day gains. Some industry experts question whether the underwriters misjudge demand for the issue or set the price artificially low to please their institutional clients, who buy at the offering price and then resell the shares. Sometimes companies themselves support undervaluation so that their stock will generate excitement and additional investor interest when the price zooms upward on opening day.

HOTLINKS

Log on to individualinvestor.com and click [education], [how to read], [A Prospectus].

www.individualinvestor.com

The IPO markets have been particularly active in recent years. Such activity has been a direct result of the strength of the public equity markets. However, investing in IPOs is risky business, particularly for individual investors who can't easily acquire shares at the offering price. Most of those shares go to institutional investors and brokerage firms' best clients. Although many news stories chronicle huge first-day gains, the stocks may not be good long-term investments. In the *Investing in Action* box on page 35 you will learn more about the perils and rewards of IPO investments.

investment banker
financial intermediary that specializes in selling new security issues and advising firms with regard to major financial transactions.

The Investment Banker's Role Most public offerings are made with the assistance of an **investment banker.** The investment banker is a financial

FIGURE 2.1

Cover of a Preliminary Prospectus for a Stock Issue

Some of the key factors related to the 2001 common stock issue by Reliant Resources, Inc. are summarized on the cover of the prospectus. The type printed vertically on the left edge is normally red, which explains its name "red herring."
(*Source:* Reliant Resources, Inc., April 16, 2001, p. 1.)

The information in this preliminary prospectus is not complete and may be changed. These securities may not be sold until the registration statement filed with the Securities and Exchange Commission is effective. This preliminary prospectus is not an offer to sell nor does it seek an offer to buy these securities in any jurisdiction where the offer or sale is not permitted.

Subject to Completion. Dated April 16, 2001.

52,000,000 Shares

Reliant Resources™

Reliant Resources, Inc.

Common Stock

This is an initial public offering of shares of common stock of Reliant Resources, Inc. All of the 52,000,000 shares of common stock are being sold by Reliant Resources.

Prior to this offering, there has been no public market for the common stock. It is currently estimated that the initial public offering price per share will be between $26.00 and $28.00. Our common stock has been approved for listing on the New York Stock Exchange under the trading symbol "RRI," subject to official notice of issuance.

See "Risk Factors" on page 11 to read about factors you should consider before buying shares of common stock.

Neither the Securities and Exchange Commission nor any other regulatory body has approved or disapproved of these securities or passed upon the accuracy or adequacy of this prospectus. Any representation to the contrary is a criminal offense.

	Per Share	Total
Initial public offering price	$	$
Underwriting discount	$	$
Proceeds, before expenses, to Reliant Resources	$	$

To the extent that the underwriters sell more than 52,000,000 shares of common stock, the underwriters have the option to purchase up to an additional 7,800,000 shares from Reliant Resources at the initial public offering price less the underwriting discount.

The underwriters expect to deliver the shares in New York, New York on , 2001.

Goldman, Sachs & Co. **Credit Suisse First Boston**
ABN AMRO Rothschild LLC
Banc of America Securities LLC
Deutsche Banc Alex. Brown
Merrill Lynch & Co.
UBS Warburg

Prospectus dated , 2001.

TABLE 2.1 **Performance of Selected IPOs**

Company Name	IPO Offering Date	IPO Offering Price	First-Day Gain	Current Price (8/31/00)	Return (IPO price to current price)
Vignette	2/18/99	$19.00	124.7%	$38.13	100.7%
FlashNet Communications	3/16/99	17.00	156.6	3.75	–77.9
Skechers USA	6/9/99	11.00	–3.4	17.81	61.9
Arriba	6/22/99	23.00	291.3	157.38	584.3
7/24 Solutions	1/27/00	26.00	176.2	46.88	80.3
Antigenics	2/3/00	18.00	241.0	15.56	–13.5
Buy.com	2/7/00	13.00	93.3	2.69	–79.3
Homegrocer.com	3/9/00	12.00	17.8	4.06	–66.2
Nuance Communications	4/12/00	17.00	99.6	131.63	674.3
Orchid Biosciences	5/4/00	8.00	36.8	43.00	437.5

Source: "Initial Public Offerings, Top to Bottom," *Wall Street Journal,* January 3, 2000, p. R4; and IPOhome www.TheIPOsite.com

FIGURE 2.2

The Selling Process for a Large Security Issue

The investment banker hired by the issuing corporation may form an underwriting syndicate. The underwriting syndicate buys the entire security issue from the issuing corporation at an agreed-on price. The underwriter then has the opportunity (and bears the risk) of reselling the issue to the public at a profit. Both the originating investment banker and the other syndicate members put together a selling group to sell the issue on a commission basis to investors.

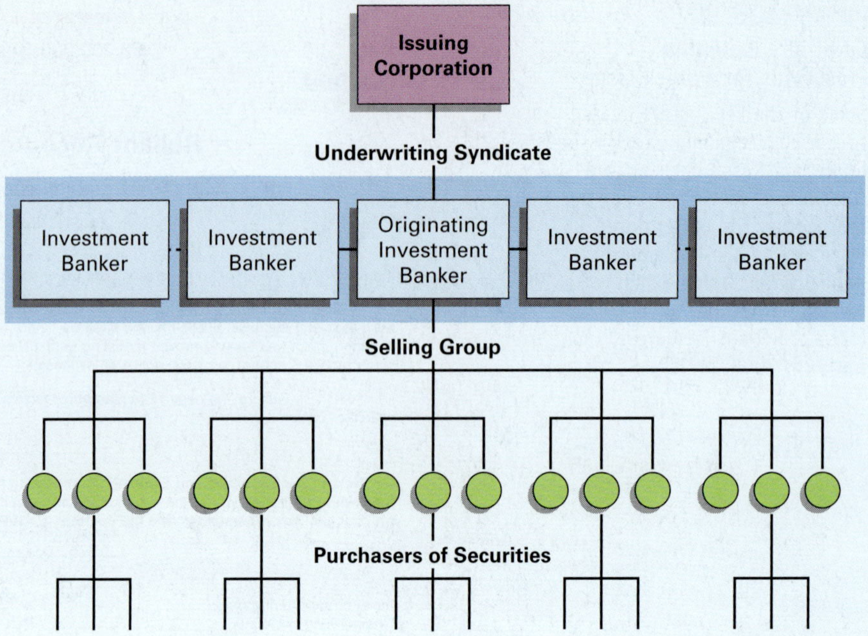

underwriting
the role of the *investment banker* in bearing the risk of reselling, at a profit, the securities purchased from an issuing corporation at an agreed-on price.

underwriting syndicate
a group formed by an investment banker to share the financial risk associated with *underwriting* new securities.

selling group
a large number of brokerage firms that join the originating investment banker(s); each accepts responsibility for selling a certain portion of a new security issue.

intermediary (such as Salomon Brothers or Goldman Sachs) that specializes in selling new security issues and advising firms with regard to major financial transactions. The main activity of the investment banker is **underwriting**. This process involves purchasing the security issue from the issuing corporation at an agreed-on price and bearing the risk of reselling it to the public at a profit. The investment banker also provides the issuer with advice about pricing and other important aspects of the issue.

In the case of very large security issues, the investment banker brings in other bankers as partners to form an **underwriting syndicate**. The syndicate shares the financial risk associated with buying the entire issue from the issuer and reselling the new securities to the public. The originating investment banker and the syndicate members put together a **selling group**, normally made up of themselves and a large number of brokerage firms. Each member of the selling group accepts the responsibility for selling a certain portion of the issue and is paid a commission on the securities it sells. The selling process for a large security issue is depicted in Figure 2.2.

The relationships among the participants in this process can also be seen in the so-called *tombstone* for the June 27, 2000, common stock offering for Community Health Systems, Inc. shown in Figure 6.4 (on page 177). This layout of the announcement indicates the roles of the various participating firms. Isolated firm names or a larger typeface differentiates the underwriter and the underwriting syndicate from the selling group. (In the figure, the key participants in the offering are labeled in the margin at the left.)

HOTLINKS

Check out some leading investment banks, such as:

www.salomonsmithbarney.com, www.gs.com, and www.morganstanley.com

Compensation for underwriting and selling services typically comes in the form of a discount on the sale price of the securities. For example, an investment banker may pay the issuing firm \$24 per share for stock that will be sold for \$26 per share. The investment banker may then sell the shares to members of the selling group for \$25.25 per share. In this case, the

INVESTING in action

Riding the IPO Roller Coaster

eToys comes to market at $20 and quadruples to $80 on its first day. Palm Inc., offered at $38, jumps to $95 on its first day and eventually reaches $160. Once reserved for institutional investors and high-net-worth individuals, IPO offerings like these are now available to average investors as well.

Start by visiting Web sites like IPOhome (www.ipohome.com), IPO.com (www.ipo .com), and IPO Central (www.hoovers.com /ipo) to find announcements of upcoming IPOs, market information, and research. (Also check www.iporesources.org, maintained by UCLA faculty members.) Then open an account with one of the online brokerage firms that deals in IPOs, such as DLJdirect, E*Trade/E*Offering, Charles Schwab, or Fidelity. Track IPO allocations on the broker's Web site or register for email alerts.

Once you find an interesting IPO, you have only a few days to review its preliminary prospectus and submit a conditional offer for a certain number of shares at a specified price. Because demand for IPO shares outstrips supply, your broker may not get shares. Even if it does, not all orders will be filled. If you are one of the lucky investors, you'll have only a very short time to confirm your purchase.

Brokers discourage investors from selling their shares quickly to profit from early price gains (this is called "flipping"). They request that you hold shares bought at the offering price for 15 to 60 days, depending on the broker's policy, after the IPO. This is not a binding rule, but don't expect to get more IPO shares from that broker if you don't comply.

Should you play the IPO game? Just as with other stock investments, do your homework. Understand the industry and its prospects. Study the prospectus and analyze the financial statements. You may have to trust your instincts and use some "guesstimates," too. "In a lot of ways, IPO investing is a shot in the dark or a leap of faith," says Tom Taulli, an analyst for EDGAR Online who specializes in IPOs. Not only is the company young and without a trading history, but its industry also may be new, as is the case with Internet firms. Market analysis becomes very important in IPO selection.

Taulli advises individuals not to buy an IPO on the first day of trading, however. "There is typically a tremendous amount of hype, and in some cases hysteria, that surrounds that first day," he says. You can often pick up good stocks at prices at or near their IPO price in the aftermarket, once things have settled down and you can gauge market acceptance of the issue. Besides, many of the best first-day performers turn out to be the worst over the longer term.

Sources: Cassell Bryan-Low, "Small Investors Wait Online for Hot IPOs," *Wall Street Journal*, July 28, 2000, pp. C1, C16; Dan McCarthy, "The Basics: How to Get in on IPOs," *IPO.com*, August 31, 2000, downloaded from www.ipo.com; Tom Taulli's IPO Tips and Tactics, *Business Week Online Daily Briefing*, May 17, 1999, downloaded from www.businessweek.com

original investment banker earns $1.25 per share ($25.25 sale price − $24 purchase price). The members of the selling group earn 75 cents for each share they sell ($26 sale price − $25.25 purchase price). Although some primary security offerings are directly placed by the issuer, the majority of new issues are sold through public offering via the mechanism just described.

secondary market
the market in which securities are traded *after they have been issued*.

Secondary Markets The market in which securities are traded *after they have been issued* is the **secondary market**, or the *aftermarket*. The secondary market provides a way for owners of securities that are already issued to sell them to others. In the secondary market, unlike the primary market, the transaction does not involve the corporation that issued the securities. Instead, money and securities are exchanged between investors; the seller exchanges securities for cash paid by the buyer. The secondary market gives security purchasers *liquidity*. It also provides a mechanism for continuous pricing of securities to reflect their value at each point in time, on the basis of the best information then available.

organized securities exchanges centralized institutions in which transactions are made in already outstanding securities.

over-the-counter (OTC) market widely scattered telecommunications network through which transactions are made in both *initial public offerings (IPOs)* and already outstanding securities.

The secondary markets include the various organized securities exchanges and the over-the-counter market. **Organized securities exchanges** are centralized institutions that bring together the forces of supply and demand for securities that are already outstanding. These exchanges are *auction markets* in which the flow of buy and sell orders determines the price. The **over-the-counter (OTC) market**, on the other hand, is a widely scattered telecommunications network through which transactions are made in both *initial public offerings (IPOs)* and securities that are already outstanding. The OTC markets use a quote system in which negotiation and dealer quotes determine the price. Because popular investment vehicles trade on the organized exchanges and in the over-the-counter market, individual investors are likely to make transactions in both of these markets.

Organized Securities Exchanges

Securities that trade on *organized securities exchanges* account for about 46% of the total *dollar volume* of domestic shares traded. Persons who are members of a given exchange (for example, the New York Stock Exchange on Wall Street) conduct all trading for that exchange in one place, under a broad set of rules. The best-known exchanges for stock and bond transactions are the New York Stock Exchange (NYSE) and the American Stock Exchange (AMEX), both located in New York City. They account for approximately 93% and 3%, respectively, of the total annual dollar volume of shares traded on *organized* U.S. exchanges. Other domestic exchanges include *regional exchanges*, such as the Chicago Stock Exchange and the Pacific Stock Exchange. Regional exchanges deal primarily in securities with regional or local appeal. Together, the regional exchanges account for about 4% of the annual dollar volume of shares traded on organized U.S. exchanges. In addition, foreign stock exchanges list and trade shares of firms in their own foreign markets. Separate domestic exchanges exist for options trading and for trading in futures. Here we will consider the basic structure, rules, and operations of each of these organized domestic securities exchanges. (We'll discuss foreign exchanges later.)

HOTLINKS

Go to the NYSE site and click on [Glossary] to find out the definition of a "growth stock," "American Depositary Receipt, ADR," and "S&P 500."

www.nyse.com

The New York Stock Exchange Most organized securities exchanges are modeled after the New York Stock Exchange (NYSE). It is the dominant organized exchange, often referred to as the "Big Board." To be a member, an individual or firm must own or lease a "seat" on the exchange. The word seat is used only figuratively, because its members trade securities standing up. The majority of seat holders are brokerage firms, and each typically owns more than one seat. The largest brokerage firm, Merrill Lynch Pierce Fenner & Smith, Inc., owns over 20 of the 1,366 seats on the NYSE.

Firms such as Merrill Lynch designate officers to occupy seats. Only such designated individuals can make transactions on the floor of the exchange. Although the majority of members make purchase and sale transactions on behalf of their customers, some members specialize in making transactions for other members or for their own account. For example, *commission brokers* are paid commissions by brokerage firms for executing their orders, and *floor brokers* are brokerage firm employees who execute orders for their firm.

Trading Activity Exchange members make all trades on the floor of the organized exchanges. The largest—the floor of the NYSE—is an area about the size of a football field. Its operation is typical of the various exchanges (though details vary). The NYSE floor has 18 trading posts. Certain stocks trade at each post. (Bonds and less active stocks are traded in an annex.) Around the perimeter are telephones and electronic equipment that transmit buy and sell orders from brokers' offices to the exchange floor and back again after members execute the orders.

All transactions on the floor of the exchange occur through an auction process. The goal is to fill all buy orders at the lowest price and to fill all sell orders at the highest price, with supply and demand determining the price. The actual auction takes place at the post where the particular security trades. Members interested in purchasing a given security publicly negotiate a transaction with members interested in selling that security. The job of the **specialist**—an exchange member who specializes in making transactions in one or more stocks—is to manage the auction process. The specialist buys or sells (at specified prices) to provide a continuous, fair, and orderly market in those securities assigned to her or him.

specialist
stock exchange member who specializes in making transactions in one or more stocks.

Listing Policies To list its shares on an organized stock exchange, a firm must file an application and meet certain listing requirements. Currently, over 3,025 firms list their securities on the NYSE; they account for about 3,300 stocks (common and preferred) and 1,750 bond issues. Of these firms, almost 400 are non-U.S. corporations. Some firms have **dual listing**, or listings on more than one exchange.

dual listing
listing of a firm's shares on more than one exchange.

The New York Stock Exchange has the strictest listing requirements. To be listed on the NYSE, a firm must have at least 2,000 stockholders owning 100 or more shares and a minimum of 1.1 million shares of publicly held stock; pretax earnings of at least $6.5 million over the previous 3 years, with no loss in the previous 2 years; and a minimum of $100 million in stockholders' equity. A foreign company must have pretax earnings of at least $100 million over the previous 3 years, with at least $25 million in each of the previous 2 years. The firm also must pay a listing fee. Once the NYSE accepts a firm's securities for listing, the company must continue to meet SEC requirements for exchange-listed securities. Listed firms that fail to meet specified requirements may be *de-listed* from the exchange.

The American Stock Exchange The American Stock Exchange (AMEX) is the second largest organized U.S. securities exchange in terms of number of listed companies. In terms of dollar volume of trading, the AMEX is actually smaller than the two largest regional exchanges—the Chicago and the Pacific. Its organization and its procedures are similar to those of the NYSE. Because its listing requirements are less stringent, many smaller and younger firms choose to list on the AMEX. In mid-1998 the AMEX merged with the National Association of Securities Dealers (NASD)—the backbone of the over-the-counter market—and, like the OTC, became a subsidiary of the NASD Market Holding Company. The AMEX has approximately 660 seats and about 770 listed stocks.

In recent years the AMEX has reinvented itself to focus on more specialized market instruments. Today about two-thirds of its daily volume comes from tradable index mutual funds, a security developed at the AMEX about 10 years ago. These

HOTLINKS

Read about index shares (Spiders and Diamonds) at the AMEX site:

www.amex.com/indexshares/index_shares_over.stm

funds track a published stock market benchmark. Trading in stock options accounts for another large segment of the AMEX's business.

Regional Stock Exchanges Each of the regional exchanges typically lists the securities of 100–500 companies. As a group, these exchanges handle about 4% of the dollar volume of all shares traded on organized U.S. exchanges. The best-known regional exchanges are the Chicago, Pacific (co-located in Los Angeles and San Francisco), Philadelphia, Boston, and Cincinnati exchanges. During 2001 the Pacific Exchange closed its Los Angeles and San Francisco trading floors and moved its equity trading operations to the Archipelago Exchange, the first fully electronic national stock market in the United States. At this writing the success of the Archipelago Exchange is unknown. Most other regional exchanges are modeled after the NYSE, but their membership and listing requirements are considerably more lenient. Trading costs are also lower.

The majority of securities listed on regional exchanges are also listed on the NYSE or the AMEX. About 100 million NYSE shares pass through one of the regional exchanges on a typical trading day. This dual listing may enhance a security's trading activity. In addition, the *Intermarket Trading System (ITS)* links nine markets—five regional exchanges, the NYSE, the AMEX, the over-the-counter market, and the Chicago Board Options Exchange—through an electronic communications network that allows brokers and other traders to make transactions at the best prices.

Like the AMEX, the regional exchanges are looking for ways to differentiate themselves to survive. In October 1999, the Chicago Stock Exchange became the first to offer extended floor-trading hours. The Pacific and Philadelphia exchanges trade heavily in stock options.

Options Exchanges *Options* allow their holders to sell or to buy another security at a specified price over a given period of time. The dominant options exchange is the Chicago Board Options Exchange (CBOE). Options are also traded on the AMEX, the NYSE, the Pacific Stock Exchange, and the Philadelphia Stock Exchange. Usually, an option to sell or buy a given security is listed on only one of the options exchanges, although dual listing sometimes occurs. Options exchanges deal only in security options. Other types of options (not discussed in this text) result from private transactions made directly between sellers and buyers.

Futures Exchanges *Futures* are contracts that guarantee the delivery of a specified commodity or financial instrument at a specific future date at an agreed-on price. The dominant exchange for trading commodity and financial futures is the Chicago Board of Trade (CBT). There are a number of other futures exchanges, some of which specialize in certain commodities and financial instruments rather than handling the broad spectrum listed on the CBT. The largest of these exchanges are the New York Mercantile Exchange, the Chicago Mercantile Exchange, the Deutsche Terminboerse, the London International Financial Futures Exchange, the New York Coffee, Sugar & Cocoa Exchange, the New York Cotton Exchange, the Kansas City Board of Trade, and the Minneapolis Grain Exchange.

The Over-the-Counter Market

The *over-the-counter (OTC) market* is not a specific institution. It represents another way of trading securities. The OTC market is the result of an intangible relationship among sellers and purchasers of securities, who are linked by a telecommunications network. Nasdaq, the leading OTC market, accounts for about 54% of the total dollar volume of domestic shares traded, compared to appproximately 43% for the NYSE, 1% for the AMEX, and 2% for regional exchanges. Instead of an auction system, the OTC market uses a quote system. This system relies on negotiation and dealer quotes to determine the prices at which securities trade in the OTC market. The actual process, which is described later, depends on the general activity of the security. Securities traded in this market are sometimes called *unlisted securities*.

About 35,000 stocks trade over the counter, as do most government and corporate bonds. The OTC market has three tiers. About 6,400 stocks have an active market in which transactions take place frequently, and another 5,000 trade on the OTC Bulletin Board. The rest are stocks of small, thinly traded companies. A majority of all corporate bonds, some of which are also listed on the NYSE, trade in the OTC market.

New Issues and Secondary Distributions To create a continuous market for unlisted securities, the OTC market also serves as a forum in which to sell both listed and unlisted *initial public offerings (IPOs)*. Subsequent transactions for listed securities then shift to the appropriate organized securities exchange; unlisted securities continue to trade in the OTC market. **Secondary distributions**—the public sales of large blocks of previously issued securities held by large investors—are also made in the OTC market to minimize the potentially negative effects of such transactions on the price of listed securities. These transactions are forms of third- or fourth-market trades, which we will describe in a moment.

secondary distributions
the public sales of large blocks of previously issued securities held by large investors.

The Role of Dealers The market price of OTC securities results from a matching of supply and demand for securities by traders known as **dealers**. Each dealer "makes markets" in certain securities by offering to buy or sell them at stated prices. Unlike the organized exchanges, where a *broker* brings together the buyer and seller of a security, the OTC market links a buyer or seller with a *dealer*. That is, the second party to an OTC transaction is always a dealer.

dealers
traders who "make markets" by offering to buy or sell certain over-the-counter securities at stated prices.

For example, a dealer making a market in Raco Enterprises might offer to buy shares from investors at $29.50 and sell shares to other investors at $31. The **bid price** is the highest price the dealer offers to purchase a given security. The **ask price** is the lowest price at which the dealer is willing to sell a given security. Because more than one dealer frequently makes a market in a given security, dealers compete. Buyers and sellers attempt to find and negotiate the best price—lowest buy price or highest sell price—when making OTC market transactions. The dealer makes a profit from the spread between the bid price and the ask price.

bid price
the highest price offered by a dealer to purchase a given security.

ask price
the lowest price at which a dealer is willing to sell a given security.

Nasdaq OTC dealers connect with the sellers and purchasers of securities through the **Nasdaq (National Association of Securities Dealers Automated Quotation) system.** Nasdaq is the first electronic communications network for securities trading. Its automated system provides up-to-date bid and ask prices on about 5,000 selected, highly active OTC securities. It enables buyers and sellers to locate one another easily. Not all OTC securities are listed on Nasdaq, however. To trade in securities not quoted on Nasdaq, buyers and sellers must find each other through references or through known dealers in the securities involved.

Nasdaq (National Association of Securities Dealers Automated Quotation) system
an automated system that provides up-to-date bid and ask prices on certain selected, highly active OTC securities.

HOTLINKS

Go to the Nasdaq site and scroll down the page and take a site tour by clicking [Tour].

www.nasdaq.com

Nasdaq National Market
a list of national or international Nasdaq stocks that meet certain qualification standards of financial size, performance, and trading activity.

The Nasdaq Stock Market includes about 6,400 stocks divided into two groups. Included in the **Nasdaq National Market** are about 5,000 companies with a national or international shareholder base. These stocks meet certain qualification standards of financial size, performance, and trading activity. To list initially, companies must have significant net tangible assets or operating income, a minimum public float of 1,100,000 shares, at least 400 shareholders, and a bid price of at least $5. Another 1,400 companies are part of the *Nasdaq SmallCap Market.* These companies too must also meet specified (but less stringent) requirements to list and trade their securities through Nasdaq's sophisticated electronic trading and surveillance system. Transactions in these two groups of stocks are reported quickly (immediately) and in detail similar to NYSE and AMEX trades in the financial press.

Alternative Trading Systems

third market
over-the-counter transactions made in securities listed on the NYSE, the AMEX, or one of the other organized exchanges.

Some individual and institutional traders now make direct transactions, without using brokers, securities exchanges, or Nasdaq, in the *third* and *fourth markets.* The **third market** consists of over-the-counter transactions made in securities listed on the NYSE, the AMEX, or one of the other organized exchanges. It allows large institutional investors, such as mutual funds, pension funds, and life insurance companies, to make large transactions at a reduced cost. These transactions are typically handled by firms or dealers that are not members of an organized securities exchange. Dealers charge lower commissions than the organized exchanges or Nasdaq would to bring together large buyers and sellers. Institutional investors are thus often able to realize sizable savings in brokerage commissions and to have minimal impact on the price of the transaction. Nasdaq also has third-market operations, called the Nasdaq InterMarket.

fourth market
transactions made directly between large institutional buyers and sellers of securities.

electronic communications networks (ECNs)
privately owned electronic trading networks that automatically match buy and sell orders that customers place electronically.

The **fourth market** consists of transactions made directly between large institutional buyers and sellers of securities. Unlike third-market transactions, fourth-market transactions bypass the dealer. The fourth market is a direct outgrowth of advanced computer technology. **Electronic communications networks (ECNs)** are at the heart of the fourth market. These privately owned electronic trading networks were formed in response to institutional investor frustration with the way organized exchanges handled large blocks of securities. Archipelago, Datek's Island, Reuter's Instinet, MarketXT, and Redibook are a few of the many ECNs that handle these trades.

The ECNs' trading volume already accounts for about a third of all Nasdaq transactions, as well as for an increasing share of New York Stock Exchange volume. They are most effective for high-volume, actively traded securities, and they play a key role in after-hours trading, discussed later in this chapter. They automatically match buy and sell orders that customers place electronically. If there is no immediate match, the ECN acts like a broker and posts its request on the Nasdaq under its own name. The trade will be executed if another trader is interested in making the transaction at the posted price.

ECNs can save customers money because they take only a transaction fee, either per share or based on order size. Money managers and institutions such as pension funds and mutual funds with large amounts of money to invest like ECNs for this reason. Many also use ECNs or trade directly with each other to find the best prices for their clients.

General Market Conditions: Bull or Bear

Conditions in the securities markets are commonly classified as "bull" or "bear," depending on whether securities prices are rising or falling over time. Changing market conditions generally stem from changes in investor attitudes, changes in economic activity, and government actions aimed at stimulating or slowing down economic activity. **Bull markets** are favorable markets normally associated with rising prices, investor optimism, economic recovery, and government stimulus. **Bear markets** are unfavorable markets normally associated with falling prices, investor pessimism, economic slowdown, and government restraint. Since late 1990, the stock market has been bullish primarily as a result of low inflation, improving trade balances, shrinking budget deficits, and economic recovery.

bull markets
favorable markets normally associated with rising prices, investor optimism, economic recovery, and government stimulus.

bear markets
unfavorable markets normally associated with falling prices, investor pessimism, economic slowdown, and government restraint.

In general, investors experience higher (or positive) returns on common stock investments during a bull market. However, some securities are bullish in a bear market or bearish in a bull market. During bear markets, many investors invest in vehicles other than securities to obtain higher and less risky returns. Market conditions are difficult to predict and usually can be identified only after they exist. Sources of information that can be used to assess market conditions are described in Chapter 3 and are applied to the analysis and valuation of common stock in Chapters 7 and 8.

Globalization of Securities Markets

LG 4

Today investors, issuers of securities, and securities firms look beyond the markets of their home countries to find the best returns, lowest costs, and best international business opportunities. The basic goal of most investors is to earn the highest return with the lowest risk. This outcome is achieved through **diversification**—the inclusion of a number of different investment vehicles in a portfolio to increase returns or reduce risk. The investor who includes foreign investments in a portfolio can greatly increase the potential for diversification by holding (1) a wider range of industries and securities, (2) securities traded in a larger number of markets, and (3) securities denominated in different currencies. The smaller and less diversified an investor's home market is, the greater the potential benefit from prudent international diversification. However, even investors from the United States and other highly developed markets can benefit from global diversification.

diversification
the inclusion of a number of different investment vehicles in a portfolio to increase returns or reduce risk.

Advances in technology and communications, together with the elimination of many political and regulatory barriers, allow investors to make cross-border securities transactions with relative ease. More and more financial markets are opening up and becoming integrated with the rest of the world's markets. Both investors and seekers of funds can view the world's markets as available to them. In short, globalization of the securities markets enables investors to seek out opportunities to profit from rapidly expanding economies throughout the world. Here we consider the growing importance of international markets, international investment performance, ways to invest in foreign securities, and the risks of investing internationally.

Growing Importance of International Markets

Securities exchanges now operate in over 100 countries worldwide. Both large (Tokyo) and small (Fiji), they are located not only in the major industrialized nations such as Japan, Great Britain, Canada, and Germany but also in emerging economies such as Brazil, Chile, India, South Korea, Malaysia, Mexico, Poland, Russia, and Thailand. The top four securities markets worldwide (based on dollar volume) are the Nasdaq, New York, London, and Tokyo stock exchanges. Other important foreign exchanges include Paris, Osaka, Toronto, Montreal, Sydney, Hong Kong, Zurich, and Taiwan.

HOTLINKS

This site links the world's stock exchanges and other major exchanges.

www.hougie.co.uk/exchange.htm

The economic integration of the European Union (EU), along with pressure from financial institutions that want an efficient process for trading shares across borders, is changing the European securities market environment. Instead of many small national exchanges, countries are banding together to create cross-border markets and compete more effectively in the pan-European equity-trading markets. The Paris, Amsterdam, and Brussels exchanges merged to form Euronext, and the Scandinavian markets formed Norex. Other stock exchanges are forming cooperative agreements—for example, Tokyo and Australia. The New York, Tokyo, Hong Kong, Australia, Mexico, Toronto, São Paulo, and Euronext exchanges are discussing the formation of a Global Equity Market (GEM). The exchanges would not merge but would form a 24-hour global market alliance, trading the stocks of selected large international companies via an electronic order-matching system. Nasdaq, with joint ventures in Japan, Hong Kong, Canada, and Australia, plans to expand into Latin America and the Middle East. As noted at the beginning of the chapter, these mergers and cooperative arrangements could be the first step toward a worldwide stock exchange.

INVESTOR FACTS

U.S. MARKET SHARE—Even though the U.S. securities markets lead the world in terms of market share, the United States accounts for only 36% of the over 30,000 companies in the worldwide equity markets.

Bond markets, too, have become global, and more investors than ever before regularly purchase government and corporate fixed-income securities in foreign markets. The United States dominates the international government bond market, followed by Japan, Germany, and Great Britain.

HOTLINKS

This site presents country credit ratings.

www.iimagazine.com/premium/rr
[Site requires free registration before you can view content.]

International Investment Performance

A primary motive for investing overseas is the lure of high returns. In fact, only once since 1980 did the United States finish first among the major stock markets of the world in terms of the rate of increase in its stock price index. For example, in 2000, a generally bad year, investors would have earned higher returns in some markets. During that year the stock price index in U.S. dollars for Denmark increased 22%; for France decreased 8%; for Germany decreased 16%; for Israel increased 2%; for Japan decreased 31%; for Mexico decreased 22%; for Russia decreased 33%; and for Thailand decreased 51%. By comparison, the U.S. stock price index decreased 10%. Of course, foreign securities markets tend to be more risky than U.S. markets. A market with high returns in one year may not do so well in the next.

Investors can compare activity on U.S. and foreign exchanges by following market indexes that track the performance of those exchanges. For instance, the Dow Jones averages and the Standard & Poor's indexes are popular measures of the U.S. markets, and indexes for more than 20 different stock markets are available. (We'll discuss indexes in more detail in

HOTLINKS

Go to the Yahoo site and check the World Finance section for investment performance.

quote.yahoo.com

Chapter 3.) The *Wall Street Journal* publishes daily reports on most major indexes, trading activity in selected stocks on major foreign exchanges, and currency exchange rates. Other financial publications also include regular reports. Also, the *Wall Street Journal*'s "World Stock Markets" in Section C frequently compares the performance of the U.S. exchanges with that of selected foreign markets.

Ways to Invest in Foreign Securities

Investors can make foreign security transactions either indirectly or directly. One form of *indirect* investment is purchasing shares of a U.S.-based multinational with substantial foreign operations. Many U.S.-based multinational firms, such as Exxon, IBM, Citicorp, Dow Chemical, Coca-Cola, Colgate-Palmolive, and Hewlett-Packard, receive more than 50% of their revenues from overseas operations. By investing in the securities of such firms, an investor can achieve a degree of international diversification. Purchasing shares in a mutual fund that invests primarily in foreign securities is another way to invest indirectly. Investors can make both of these indirect foreign securities investment transactions in a conventional fashion through a stockbroker, as explained in Chapter 3 and in Chapter 11 (which is devoted to mutual funds).

To make *direct* investments in foreign companies, investors have three options: They can purchase securities on foreign exchanges, buy securities of foreign companies that trade on U.S. exchanges, or buy *American depositary receipts (ADRs)*. The first way—purchasing securities on foreign exchanges—involves additional risks because the securities do not trade in U.S. dollars. This approach is not for the timid or inexperienced investor.

HOTLINKS

For a ranking of ADRs, see:

www.worldlyinvestor.com

Because each country's exchange has its own regulations and procedures, investors must cope with currency exchange (dollars to pesos, for example). They also must cope with different securities exchange rules, transaction procedures, accounting standards, tax laws, and with language barriers. Direct transactions are best handled either through brokers at major Wall Street firms with large international operations or through major banks, such as Chase Manhattan and Citicorp, that have special units to handle foreign securities transactions. Alternatively, investors can deal with foreign broker-dealers, but such an approach is more complicated and more risky.

The second form of direct investment is to buy the securities of foreign companies that trade on both organized and over-the-counter U.S. exchanges. Transactions in foreign securities that trade on U.S. exchanges are handled in the same way as exchange-traded domestic securities. These securities are issued by large, well-known foreign companies. Stocks of companies such as Alcan (Canada), Gucci (Netherlands), National Westminster Bank (U.K.), and Unilever (Netherlands) trade directly on U.S. exchanges. In addition, **Yankee bonds**, dollar-denominated debt securities issued by foreign governments or corporations and traded in U.S. securities markets, trade on organized exchanges and in the over-the-counter market in the United States.

Yankee bonds
dollar-denominated debt securities issued by foreign governments or corporations and traded in U.S. securities markets.

American depositary receipts (ADRs)
dollar-denominated negotiable receipts for the stocks of foreign companies that are held in the vaults of banks in the companies' home countries.

Finally, foreign stocks also trade on U.S. exchanges in the form of **American depositary receipts (ADRs)**. These are dollar-denominated negotiable receipts for the stocks of foreign companies that are held in the vaults of banks in the companies' home countries. Today, nearly 1,200 ADRs representing about 40 different home countries are traded on U.S. exchanges.

About one-fourth of them are actively traded. Included are ADRs of well-known companies such as Nippon, Nokia, Sony, Toyota, and Volvo. ADRs, which trade in the same way as standard domestic securities, are further discussed in Chapter 6.

Risks of Investing Internationally

Investing abroad is not without pitfalls. In addition to the usual risks involved in making any security transaction, investors must consider the risks associated with doing business in a particular foreign country. Changes in trade policies, labor laws, and taxation may affect operating conditions for the country's firms. The government itself may not be stable. When making investments in foreign markets, you must track similar environmental factors in each foreign country. This is clearly more difficult than following your home market, because you are less familiar with the foreign economic and political environments and may be following several countries.

U.S. securities markets are generally viewed as highly regulated and reliable. Foreign markets, on the other hand, may lag substantially behind the United States in both operations and regulation. Some countries place various restrictions on foreign investment. In Korea and Taiwan, for example, mutual funds are the only way for foreigners to invest. Mexico has a two-tier market, with some securities restricted to foreigners. Some countries make it difficult for foreigners to get their funds out, and many impose taxes on dividends. For example, Swiss taxes are about 20% on dividends paid to foreigners. In addition, accounting standards vary from country to country. Differences in accounting practices can affect a company's apparent profitability, conceal other attractive assets (such as the hidden reserves and undervalued assets that are permitted in many countries), and fail to disclose other risks. As a result, it is difficult to compare the financial performances and positions of firms operating in different foreign countries. Other difficulties include illiquid markets and an inability to obtain reliable investment information because of a lack of reporting requirements.

Furthermore, international investing involves securities denominated in foreign currencies. Trading profits and losses are affected not only by a security's price changes but also by changes in currency exchange rates. The values of the world's major currencies fluctuate with respect to each other on a daily basis. The relationship between two currencies at a specified date is called the **currency exchange rate**. On May 31, 2000, the currency exchange rate for the French franc (Ff) and the U.S. dollar (US$) was expressed as follows:

currency exchange rate
the relationship between two currencies on a specified date.

US$ 1.00 = Ff 6.99   Ff 1.00 = US$ 0.143

On that day, you would have received 6.99 French francs for every $1. Conversely, each French franc was worth $0.143.

Changes in the value of a particular foreign currency with respect to the U.S. dollar—or any other currency—are called *appreciation* and *depreciation*. For example, on August 29, 2000, the Ff/US$ exchange rate was 7.28. In the 3 months since May 31, 2000, the French franc had *depreciated* relative to the dollar (and the dollar had appreciated relative to the franc). On August 29, it took more francs to buy $1 (7.28 versus 6.99), so each franc was worth less in dollar terms ($0.137 versus $0.143). Had the French franc instead *appreciated* (and the dollar depreciated relative to the franc), each franc would have been worth more in dollar terms.

currency exchange risk
the risk caused by the varying exchange rates between the currencies of two countries.

Currency exchange risk is the risk caused by the varying exchange rates between the currencies of two countries. For example, assume that on May 31, 2000, you bought 100 shares of a French stock at 100 Ff per share, held it for about 3 months, and then sold it for its original purchase price of 100 French francs. The following table summarizes these transactions:

Date	Transaction	Number of Shares	Price in Ff	Value of Transaction Ff	Exchange Rate Ff/US$	Value in US$
5/31/00	Purchase	100	100	10,000	6.99	$1,430.62
8/29/00	Sell	100	100	10,000	7.28	$1,373.63

Although you realized the original purchase price in French francs, in dollar terms the transaction resulted in a loss of $56.99 ($1,430.62 − $1,373.63). The value of the stock in dollars decreased because the French franc was worth less—had depreciated—relative to the dollar. Investors in foreign securities must be aware that the value of the foreign currency in relation to the dollar can have a profound effect on returns from foreign security transactions.

Trading Hours and Regulation of Securities Markets

LG 5

Understanding the structure of domestic and international securities markets is an important foundation for developing a sound investment program. Now let's look at market trading hours and the regulation of U.S. securities markets.

Trading Hours of Securities Markets

The regular trading session for organized U.S. exchanges and Nasdaq runs from 9:30 A.M. to 4:00 P.M. Eastern time. However, trading is no longer limited to these hours. The exchanges, Nasdaq, and ECNs offer extended trading sessions before and after regular hours. These allow U.S. securities markets to compete more effectively with foreign securities markets, in which investors can execute trades when U.S. markets are closed. In mid-1991, the NYSE added two short electronic-trading sessions that begin after the 4:00 P.M. closing bell. One session, from 4:15 to 5:00 P.M., trades stocks at that day's closing prices via a computer matching system. Transactions occur only if a match can be made and are handled on a first-come, first-served basis. The other session lasts from 4:00 to 5:15 P.M. and allows institutional investors to trade large blocks of stock valued at $1 million or more. Since their inception, the NYSE has experienced growing interest in both sessions. From 1997 to 1999, both the average daily number and the dollar volume of shares traded in these two sessions more than doubled.

Nasdaq began its own extended-hours electronic-trading session in January 1992. Its Nasdaq International Market Session runs from 3:30 A.M. (when the London Exchange opens) to 9:00 A.M. Eastern Time, half an hour

INVESTING in action

Stock Around the Clock

Trading 24/7—the idea sounds great. Pick up the phone or go to your computer at any hour and buy or sell stocks and mutual funds. Such round-the-clock trading is not yet a reality, but individual investors can trade securities for several hours before and after the close of regular trading sessions.

What's the appeal of extended trading hours? Some investors don't have time to reflect on market news during the day. Investors in the Pacific time zone (3 hours behind New York) want a longer trading day; their regular trading day ends at 1 P.M. Pacific time. Others want to act on company news that is released after the markets close. For example, on January 19, 2000, IBM announced favorable year-end earnings about an hour after the New York Stock Exchange closed. After-hours traders were able to buy the stock at a discount from the next morning's opening price of $123.

But jumping in quickly may not be the right move. One day in February 2000, telephone equipment maker Lucent Technologies Inc. stock closed normal trading at $69.06 a share, down slightly. Sales by institutional night traders pushed the stock down to $51.75 by the opening bell, so that waiting to buy would have been a better strategy.

As these examples illustrate, after-hours investing brings greater risks for most individual investors. After-hours markets—especially the early-morning sessions—are very fragmented. Electronic communications networks (ECNs) handle after-hours trading. Each ECN serves only its client brokerages, and prices and volumes can differ from ECN to ECN. Currently there is no consolidated price reporting that lets investors compare prices, although some ECNs are working on agreements to share trading information. These sessions are also volatile and less liquid than regular trading sessions. Although interest is growing, fewer than a dozen stocks trade actively during most sessions. There are no market makers to create volume, so huge price swings are typical. Average bid-ask spreads on Nasdaq are often twice as high as during regular trading. Many in the investment community worry that knee-jerk reactions to earnings reports and other news will create havoc with market supply and demand.

To protect investors, most brokerages require limit orders (discussed further in Chapter 3) for after-hours trades. This type of order prevents investors from paying more than they intended or selling for less than they wished.

Sources: Bill Deener, "Timing the Market," *The Dallas Morning News,* April 13, 2000, p. 1D; James McNair, "Happy-Hours Trading," *The San Diego Union-Tribune,* July 2, 2000, pp. I-1, I-6; and Ruth Simon, "After-Hours Trading Carries Sizable Costs for Investors," *Wall Street Journal,* February 9, 2000, pp. C1, C17. For an index of articles about after-hours trading, see www.thestreet.com/basics/nightowl/777198.html

before the start of regular trading sessions in U.S. markets. Because it lists NYSE stocks as well as other U.S. equities and has less stringent disclosure requirements than other markets, Nasdaq International attracts traders from both the New York and the London exchanges. In addition, Nasdaq has an extended-hours session from 4:00 to 6:30 P.M. Eastern time, as well as two SelectNet trading sessions for large blocks of stock, from 8:00 to 9:30 A.M. Eastern time and from 4:00 to 5:15 P.M. Eastern time. Regional exchanges have also moved to after-hours trading sessions.

Until 1999, only large institutional investors could trade after hours. Most of this trading was through ECNs like Instinet, which facilitated fourth-market transactions in about 10,000 U.S. and European stocks. Now individual investors, too, can participate in after-hours trading activity. Many large brokerage firms, both traditional and online, offer after-hours trading services for their individual clients. For example, PaineWebber's extended-hours trading program runs from 8:00 to 9:00 A.M. and from 4:30 to 6:30 P.M. Eastern time. Charles Schwab's extended-hours trading sessions run from 7:45 to 9:15 A.M. and from 4:30 to 7:00 P.M. Eastern time.

ECNs handle after-hours trades for various brokerage firms, with each ECN executing transactions for its specific brokerage clients. Charles Schwab, Fidelity, and DLJ Direct use Redibook, for example. Most ECNs offer after-hours trading between 4 and 6:30 P.M. Eastern time. Is the increase in after-hours trading a positive trend? The *Investing in Action* box above discusses the pros and cons of extended trading hours.

Regulation of Securities Markets

Securities laws protect investors and participants in the financial marketplace. A number of state and federal laws require that investors receive adequate and accurate disclosure of information. Such laws also regulate the activities of participants in the securities markets. State laws that control the sale of securities within state borders are commonly called *blue sky laws* because they are intended to prevent investors from being sold nothing but "blue sky." These laws typically establish procedures for regulating both security issues and sellers of securities doing business within the state. Most states have a regulatory body, such as a state securities commission, that is charged with enforcing the related state statutes. However, the most important securities laws, briefly summarized below, are those enacted by the federal government.

Securities Act of 1933 Congress passed the *Securities Act of 1933* to ensure full disclosure of information about new security issues and to prevent a stock market collapse similar to that of 1929–1932. The act requires the issuer of a new security to file with the Securities and Exchange Commission (SEC) a registration statement containing information about the new issue. As discussed in the earlier section on IPOs, the firm cannot sell the security until the SEC approves the registration statement, which usually takes about 20 days. If the SEC approves the statement, the issuer can offer the new security issue for sale. If it determines that the registration statement is fraudulent, the SEC will reject the issue and may also sue the directors and others responsible for the misrepresentation.

As an investor, you should realize that approval of the registration statement by the SEC does not mean that the security is a good investment. It merely indicates that the facts presented in the statement appear to reflect the firm's true position.

Securities Exchange Act of 1934 The *Securities Exchange Act of 1934* formally established the SEC as the agency in charge of administering federal securities laws. The act gave the SEC the power to regulate the organized securities exchanges and the over-the-counter market by extending disclosure requirements to outstanding securities. It required the stock exchanges as well as the stocks traded on them to be registered with the SEC.

As a result of this act, the SEC covers the organized exchanges and the OTC market; their members, brokers, and dealers; and the securities traded in these markets. Each of these participants must file reports with the SEC and periodically update them. The act has been instrumental in providing adequate disclosure on issues that are traded in the secondary markets. The 1934 act has been amended several times over the years. It remains a key piece of legislation that protects participants in the securities markets.

Maloney Act of 1938 The *Maloney Act of 1938,* an amendment to the Securities Exchange Act of 1934, provided for the establishment of trade associations to self-regulate the securities industry. Since its passage, only one such trade association, the National Association of Securities Dealers (NASD), has been formed. NASD members include nearly all of the nation's securities firms that do business with the public. The NASD, operating under SEC supervision, establishes standardized procedures for securities trading and ethical behavior, monitors and enforces compliance with these procedures, and serves as the industry spokesperson. Membership in the NASD allows member firms to make transactions with other member firms at rates below those charged to nonmembers. Today, any securities firms that are not members of the NASD must agree to direct SEC supervision. Because the SEC can revoke the NASD's registration, it has the same power over this organization as over the exchanges. In addition to its self-regulatory role, the NASD greatly streamlined the functioning of the over-the-counter market by creating Nasdaq.

Investment Company Act of 1940 The *Investment Company Act of 1940* protects purchasers of investment company shares. An *investment company* is one that obtains funds by selling its shares to numerous investors and uses the proceeds to purchase securities. The dominant type of investment company is the *mutual fund* (discussed in detail in Chapter 11). The Investment Company Act of 1940 established rules and regulations for investment companies and formally authorized the SEC to regulate their practices and procedures. It required the investment companies to register with the SEC and to fulfill certain disclosure requirements. A 1970 amendment prohibits investment companies from paying excessive fees to their advisers and from charging excessive commissions to purchasers of company shares.

Investment Advisers Act of 1940 The *Investment Advisers Act of 1940* was passed to protect investors against potential abuses by *investment advisers*—persons hired by investors to advise them about security investments. It requires that advisers disclose all relevant information about their backgrounds, conflicts of interest, and so on, as well as about any investments they recommend. Advisers must register and file periodic reports with the SEC. A 1960 amendment extended the SEC's powers to permit inspection of the records of investment advisers and to revoke the registration of advisers who violate the act's provisions. *This act does not provide any guarantee of competence on the part of advisers.* It merely helps to protect the investor against *fraudulent and unethical practices by the adviser.*

Securities Acts Amendments of 1975 In 1975 Congress amended the securities acts to require the SEC and the securities industry to develop a competitive national system for trading securities. As a first step, the SEC abolished fixed-commission schedules, thereby providing for negotiated commissions. (Commissions are discussed in more detail in Chapter 3.) A second action was to establish the *Intermarket Trading System (ITS)*, an electronic communications network linking nine markets and trading over 4,000 eligible issues. This system allows trades to be made across these markets wherever the network shows a better price for a given issue.

Insider Trading and Fraud Act of 1988 The 1980s were a decade of general economic prosperity and rapidly rising stock prices. As typically happens during such periods in the financial markets, the decade also witnessed a takeover and buyout mania that spawned a host of speculators intent on profit. Many times these speculators operated without regard for the legality of their actions. Although the tactics varied, many of the illegal gains were achieved through insider-trading practices. **Insider trading** involves using nonpublic information to make profitable securities transactions. It is both illegal and unethical.

insider trading
the illegal use of *nonpublic* information about a company to make profitable securities transactions.

The *Insider Trading and Fraud Act of 1988* defined an insider as one who possesses material *nonpublic* information, and it established penalties for insider trading. Insiders are typically a company's directors, officers, major shareholders, bankers, investment bankers, accountants, or attorneys. Of course, insiders are not legally prohibited from trading the firm's shares once private information becomes public. To allow it to monitor insider trades, the SEC requires corporate insiders to file monthly reports detailing all transactions made in the company's stock. These reports are typically available at its Edgar Web site, www.sec.gov/edgarhp.htm, and large trades are frequently summarized and reported in various news media, including the *Wall Street Journal*.

The prosecution and conviction of a number of high-profile insiders during the 1980s and early 1990s created a body of case law that more clearly defines illegal and unethical acts. The definition of the term *insider*, which originally referred only to a company's employees, directors, and their relatives, was expanded to include anyone who obtains nonpublic information about a company. Recent legislation substantially increased the penalties for insider trading and gave the SEC greater power to investigate and prosecute claims of illegal insider-trading activity.

Clearly, the many insider-trading cases of the 1980s and early 1990s heightened the public's awareness of **ethics**—standards of conduct or moral judgment—in business. The financial community is continuing to develop and enforce ethical standards that will motivate market participants to adhere to laws and regulations. Although it is difficult to enforce ethical standards, it appears that opportunities for abuses in the financial markets are being reduced, thereby providing a more level playing field for all investors.

ethics
standards of conduct or moral judgment.

Basic Types of Securities Transactions

LG 6

An investor can make a number of basic types of security transactions. Each type is available to those who meet certain requirements established by various government agencies as well as by brokerage firms. Although investors can use the various types of transactions in a number of ways to meet investment objectives, we describe only the most popular use of each transaction here, as we consider the long purchase, margin trading, and short selling.

Long Purchase

long purchase
a transaction in which investors buy securities in the hope that they will increase in value and can be sold at a later date for profit.

The **long purchase** is a transaction in which investors buy securities in the hope that they will increase in value and can be sold at a later date for profit. The object, then, is to *buy low and sell high.* A long purchase is the most common type of transaction. Because investors generally expect the price of a security to rise over the period of time they plan to hold it, their return comes from any dividends or interest received during the ownership period, *plus* the difference (capital gain) between the price at which they sell the security and the price they paid to purchase it. This return, of course, is reduced by the transaction costs.

Ignoring any dividends (or interest) and transaction costs, we can illustrate the long purchase by a simple example. After studying various aspects of Varner Industries, you are convinced that its common stock, which currently sells for $20 per share, will increase in value over the next few years. On the basis of your analysis, you expect the stock price to rise to $30 per share within 2 years. You place an order and buy 100 shares of Varner for $20 per share. If the stock price rises to, say, $40 per share, you will profit from your long purchase. If it drops below $20 per share, you will experience a loss on the transaction. Obviously, one of the major motivating factors in making a long transaction is an expected rise in the price of the security.

Margin Trading

margin trading
the use of borrowed funds to purchase securities; magnifies returns by reducing the amount of equity that the investor must put up.

Security purchases do not have to be made on a cash basis; investors can use borrowed funds instead. This activity is referred to as **margin trading.** It is used for one basic reason: to magnify returns. As peculiar as it may sound, the term *margin* refers to the amount of equity (stated as a percentage) in an investment, or the amount that is *not* borrowed. If an investor uses 75% margin, for example, it means that 75% of the investment position is being financed with the person's own funds and the balance (25%) with borrowed money. Brokers must approve margin purchases. The brokerage firm then lends the purchaser the needed funds and retains the purchased securities as collateral. It is important to recognize that margin purchasers must pay a specified rate of interest on the amount they borrow.

margin requirement
the minimum amount of equity that must be a margin investor's own funds; set by the Federal Reserve Board (the "Fed").

The Federal Reserve Board (the "Fed"), which governs our banking system, sets the **margin requirement**, specifying the minimum amount of equity that must be the margin investor's own funds. The margin requirement for stocks has been at 50% for some time. By raising and lowering the margin requirement, the Fed can depress or stimulate activity in the securities markets.

A simple example will help to clarify the basic margin transaction. Assume that you wish to purchase 70 shares of common stock, which is currently selling for $63.50 per share. With the prevailing margin requirement of 50%, you need put up only $2,222.50 in cash ($63.50 per share × 70 shares × 0.50). The remaining $2,222.50 will be lent to you by your brokerage firm. You will, of course, have to pay interest on the amount you borrow, plus the applicable brokerage fees. With the use of margin, investors can purchase more securities than they could afford on a strictly cash basis. In this way, investors can magnify their returns (as demonstrated in a later section).

INVESTOR FACTS

BUYING TECH STOCKS ON MARGIN—Lured by the promise of high returns on technology stocks, individual investors are buying more stock on margin than ever before. In early 2000, margin debt reached $265 billion, the highest level since the government imposed margin regulations in 1934.

Source: Fred Vogelstein, Paul Sloan, and Anne Kates Smith, "In Hock for Stocks," *U.S. News & World Report*, April 17, 2000, p. 37.

Although margin trading can lead to increased returns, it also presents substantial risks. One of the biggest is that the issue may not perform as expected. If this occurs, no amount of margin trading can correct matters. Margin trading can only magnify returns, not produce them. And if the security's return is negative, margin trading magnifies the loss. Because the security being margined is always the ultimate source of return, choosing the right securities is critical to this trading strategy.

Essentials of Margin Trading Investors can use margin trading with most kinds of securities. It is regularly used, for example, with both common and preferred stocks, most types of bonds, mutual funds, options, warrants, and futures. It is not normally used with tax-exempt municipal bonds, because the interest paid on such margin loans is not deductible for income tax purposes. Since mid-1990, it has been possible to use margin on certain foreign stocks and bonds that meet prescribed criteria and appear on the Fed's "New List of Foreign Margin Stocks." For simplicity, we will use common stock as the vehicle in our discussion of margin trading.

HOTLINKS

Read about margin trading at:

www.vanguard.com/vbs/services/margins.html

financial leverage
the use of debt financing to magnify investment returns.

Magnified Profits and Losses With an investor's equity serving as a base, the idea of margin trading is to employ **financial leverage**—the use of debt financing to magnify investment returns. Here's how it works: Suppose you have $5,000 to invest and are considering the purchase of 100 shares of stock at $50 per share. If you do not margin, you can buy outright 100 shares of the stock (ignoring brokerage commissions). If you margin the transaction—for example, at 50%—you can acquire the same $5,000 position with only $2,500 of your own money. This leaves you with $2,500 to use for other investments or to buy on margin another 100 shares of the same stock. Either way, by margining you will reap greater benefits from the stock's price appreciation.

The concept of margin trading is more fully illustrated in Table 2.2. It shows an unmargined (100% equity) transaction, along with the same transaction using various margins. Remember that the margin rates (e.g., 65%) indicate the investor's equity in the investment. When the investment is unmargined and the price of the stock goes up by $30 per share (see Table 2.2, part A), the investor enjoys a very respectable 60% rate of return. However, observe what happens when margin is used: The rate of return shoots up as high as 120%, depending on the amount of equity in the investment. This occurs because the gain is the same ($3,000) *regardless of how the investor finances the transaction.* Clearly, as the investor's equity in the investment *declines* (with lower margins), the rate of return *increases* accordingly.

Three facets of margin trading become obvious from the table: (1) The price of the stock will move in whatever way it is going to, regardless of how the position is financed. (2) The lower the amount of the investor's equity in the position, the *greater the rate of return* the investor will enjoy when the price of the security rises. (3) The *loss is also magnified* (by the same rate) when the price of the security falls (see Table 2.2, part B).

Advantages and Disadvantages of Margin Trading A magnified return is the major advantage of margin trading. The size of the magnified return depends on both the price behavior of the security that is margined and the

TABLE 2.2 The Effect of Margin Trading on Security Returns

	Without Margin (100% Equity)	With Margins of 80%	65%	50%
Number of $50 shares purchased	100	100	100	100
Cost of investment	$5,000	$5,000	$5,000	$5,000
Less: borrowed money	0	1,000	1,750	2,500
Equity in investment	$5,000	$4,000	$3,250	$2,500
A. Investor's position if price rises by $30 to $80/share				
Value of stock	$8,000	$8,000	$8,000	$8,000
Less: cost of investment	5,000	5,000	5,000	5,000
Capital gain	$3,000	$3,000	$3,000	$3,000
Return on investor's equity (capital gain/ equity in investment)	60%	75%	92.3%	120%
B. Investor's position if price falls by $30 to $20/share				
Value of stock	$2,000	$2,000	$2,000	$2,000
Less: cost of investment	5,000	5,000	5,000	5,000
Capital loss	$3,000	$3,000	$3,000	$3,000
Return on investor's equity (capital loss/ equity in investment)*	(60%)	(75%)	(92.3%)	(120%)

*With a capital loss, return on investor's equity is *negative.*

amount of margin used. Another, more modest benefit of margin trading is that it allows for greater diversification of security holdings, because investors can spread their capital over a greater number of investments.

The major disadvantage of margin trading, of course, is the potential for magnified losses if the price of the security falls. Another disadvantage is the cost of the margin loans themselves. A **margin loan** is the official vehicle through which the borrowed funds are made available in a margin transaction. All margin loans are made at a stated interest rate, which depends on prevailing market rates and the amount of money being borrowed. This rate is usually 1% to 3% above the **prime rate**—the lowest interest rate charged the best business borrowers. For large accounts, it may be at the prime rate. The loan cost, which investors pay, will increase daily, reducing the level of profits (or increasing losses) accordingly.

margin loan
vehicle through which borrowed funds are made available, at a stated interest rate, in a margin transaction.

prime rate
the lowest interest rate charged the best business borrowers.

Making Margin Transactions To execute a margin transaction, an investor must establish a **margin account** with a minimum of $2,000 in equity, in the form of either cash or securities. The broker will retain any securities purchased on margin as collateral for the loan.

margin account
a brokerage account for which margin trading is authorized.

The margin requirement established by the Federal Reserve Board sets the minimum amount of equity for margin transactions. Investors need not execute all margin transactions by using exactly the minimum amount of margin; they can use more than the minimum if they wish. Moreover, it is not unusual for brokerage firms and the major exchanges to establish their own margin requirements, which are more restrictive than those of the Federal Reserve. In

TABLE 2.3 Initial Margin Requirements for Various Types of Securities

Security	Minimum Initial Margin (Equity) Required
Listed common and preferred stock	50%
OTC stocks traded on Nasdaq National Market	50%
Convertible bonds	50%
Corporate bonds	30%
U.S. Treasury bills, notes, and bonds	8% of principal
Other federal government issues	10% of principal
Federal-government-guaranteed issues	15% of principal
Options	Option premium plus 20% of market value of underlying stock
Futures	2% to 10% of the value of the contract

addition, brokerage firms may have their own lists of especially volatile stocks for which the margin requirements are higher. There are basically two types of margin requirements: initial margin and maintenance margin.

initial margin
the minimum amount of equity that must be provided by a margin investor *at the time of purchase*.

Initial Margin The minimum amount of equity that must be provided by the investor *at the time of purchase* is the **initial margin.** It prevents overtrading and excessive speculation. Generally, this is the margin requirement to which investors refer when discussing margin trading. All securities that can be margined have specific initial requirements, which the governing authorities can change at their discretion. Table 2.3 shows initial margin requirements for various types of securities. The more stable investment vehicles, such as U.S. Treasury issues, generally have substantially lower margin requirements and therefore offer greater opportunities to magnify returns. OTC stocks traded on the Nasdaq National Market can be margined like listed securities; all other OTC stocks are considered to have no collateral value and therefore cannot be margined.

restricted account
a margin account whose equity is less than the initial margin requirement; the investor may not make further margin purchases and must bring the margin back to the initial level when securities are sold.

As long as the margin in an account remains at a level equal to or greater than prevailing initial requirements, the investor may use the account in any way he or she wants. However, if the value of the investor's holdings declines, the margin in his or her account will also drop. In this case, the investor will have what is known as a **restricted account**, one whose equity is less than the initial margin requirement. It does not mean that the investor must put up additional cash or equity. But as long as the account is restricted, the investor may not make further margin purchases and must bring the margin back to the initial level when securities are sold.

maintenance margin
the absolute minimum amount of margin (equity) that an investor must maintain in the margin account at all times.

margin call
notification of the need to bring the equity of an account whose margin is below the maintenance level up to the initial margin level or to have enough margined holdings sold to reach this standard.

Maintenance Margin The absolute minimum amount of margin (equity) that an investor must maintain in the margin account at all times is the **maintenance margin.** When an insufficient amount of maintenance margin exists, an investor will receive a **margin call.** This call gives the investor a short period of time (perhaps 72 hours) to bring the equity up to the initial margin. If this doesn't happen, the broker is authorized to sell enough of the investor's margined holdings to bring the equity in the account up to this standard.

Margin investors can be in for a surprise if markets are volatile. When the Nasdaq stock market fell 14% in one day in early April 2000, brokerages made many more margin calls than usual. Investors rushed to sell shares, often at a loss, to cover their margin calls—only to watch the market bounce back a few days later.

The maintenance margin protects both the brokerage house and investors: Brokers avoid having to absorb excessive investor losses, and investors avoid being wiped out. The maintenance margin on equity securities is currently 25%. It rarely changes, although it is often set slightly higher by brokerage firms for the added protection of brokers and customers. For straight debt securities such as Treasury bonds, there is no official maintenance margin except that set by the brokerage firms themselves.

The Basic Margin Formula The amount of margin is always measured in terms of its relative amount of equity, which is considered the investor's collateral. A simple formula can be used with all types of long purchases to determine the amount of margin in the transaction at any given point. Basically, only two pieces of information are required: (1) the prevailing market value of the securities being margined and (2) the **debit balance,** which is the amount of money being borrowed in the margin loan. Given this information, we can compute margin according to Equation 2.1.

debit balance
the amount of money being borrowed in a margin loan.

Equation 2.1

$$\text{Margin} = \frac{\text{Value of securities} - \text{Debit balance}}{\text{Value of securities}}$$

Equation 2.1a

$$= \frac{V - D}{V}$$

To illustrate the use of this formula, consider the following example. Assume you want to purchase 100 shares of stock at $40 per share at a time when the initial margin requirement is 70%. Because 70% of the transaction must be financed with equity, the (30%) balance can be financed with a margin loan. Therefore, you will borrow 0.30 × $4,000, or $1,200. This amount, of course, is the *debit balance.* The remainder ($4,000 − $1,200 = $2,800) represents your equity in the transaction. In other words, equity is represented by the numerator ($V - D$) in the margin formula.

What happens to the margin as the value of the security changes? If over time the price of the stock moves to $65, the margin is then:

$$\text{Margin} = \frac{V - D}{V} = \frac{\$6{,}500 - \$1{,}200}{\$6{,}500} = 0.815 = \underline{\underline{81.5\%}}$$

Note that the margin (equity) in this investment position has risen from 70% to 81.5%. *When the price of the security goes up, the investor's margin also increases.*

On the other hand, *when the price of the security goes down, so does the amount of margin.* For instance, if the price of the stock in our illustration drops to $30 per share, the new margin is only 60% [($3,000 − $1,200) ÷ $3,000]. In that case, we would be dealing with a *restricted account,* because the margin level would have dropped below the prevailing initial margin of 70%.

Finally, note that although our discussion has been couched largely in terms of individual transactions, the same margin formula applies to margin accounts. The only difference is that we would be dealing with input that applies to the account as a whole—the value of all securities held in the account and the total amount of margin loans.

Return on Invested Capital When assessing the return on margin transactions, you must take into account the fact that you put up only part of the funds. Therefore, you are concerned with the *rate of return* earned on only the portion of the funds that you provided. Using both current income received from dividends or interest and total interest paid on the margin loan, we can apply Equation 2.2 to determine the return on invested capital from a margin transaction.

Equation 2.2

$$\text{Return on invested capital from a margin transaction} = \frac{\text{Total current income received} - \text{Total interest paid on margin loan} + \text{Market value of securities at sale} - \text{Market value of securities at purchase}}{\text{Amount of equity at purchase}}$$

This equation can be used to compute either the expected or the actual return from a margin transaction. To illustrate: Assume you want to buy 100 shares of stock at \$50 per share because you feel it will rise to \$75 within 6 months. The stock pays \$2 per share in annual dividends, and during your 6-month holding period you will be entitled to receive half of that amount, or \$1 per share. You are going to buy the stock with 50% margin and will pay 10% interest on the margin loan. Therefore, you are going to put up \$2,500 equity to buy \$5,000 worth of stock that you hope will increase to \$7,500 in 6 months. Because you will have a \$2,500 margin loan outstanding at 10% for 6 months, you will pay \$125 in total interest costs (\$2,500 × 0.10 × 6/12 = \$125). We can substitute this information into Equation 2.2 to find the expected return on invested capital from this margin transaction:

$$\text{Return on invested capital from a margin transaction} = \frac{\$100 - \$125 + \$7{,}500 - \$5{,}000}{\$2{,}500} = \frac{\$2{,}475}{\$2{,}500} = 0.99 = \underline{\underline{99\%}}$$

Keep in mind that the 99% figure represents the rate of return earned over a 6-month holding period. If you wanted to compare this rate of return to other investment opportunities, you could determine the transaction's annualized rate of return by multiplying by 2 (the number of 6-month periods in a year). This would amount to 198% (99% × 2 = 198%).

pyramiding
the technique of using paper profits in margin accounts to partly or fully finance the acquisition of additional securities.

Uses of Margin Trading Investors most often use margin trading in one of two ways. As we have seen, one of its uses is to magnify transaction returns. The other major margin tactic is called pyramiding, which takes the concept of magnified returns to its limits. **Pyramiding** uses the paper profits in margin accounts to partly or fully finance the acquisition of additional securities. This allows investors to make such transactions at margins below prevailing initial margin levels, and sometimes substantially so. In fact, with this technique it is even possible to buy securities with no new cash at all. Rather, they can all be financed entirely with margin loans. The reason is that the paper profits in the account lead to **excess margin**—more equity in the account than required. For instance, if a margin account holds $60,000 worth of securities and has a debit balance of $20,000, it is at a margin level of 66⅔% [($60,000 − $20,000) ÷ $60,000]. This account would hold a substantial amount of excess margin if the prevailing initial margin requirement were only 50%.

excess margin
more equity than is required in a margin account.

The principle of pyramiding is to use the excess margin in the account to purchase additional securities. The only constraint—and the key to pyramiding—is that when the additional securities are purchased, the investor's margin account must be at or above the prevailing required initial margin level. Remember that it is the *account,* not the individual transactions, that must meet the minimum standards. If the account has excess margin, the investor can use it to build up security holdings. Pyramiding can continue as long as there are additional paper profits in the margin account and as long as the margin level exceeds the initial requirement that prevails when purchases are made. The tactic is somewhat complex but is also profitable, especially because it minimizes the amount of new capital required in the investor's account.

In general, margin trading is simple, but it is also risky. Risk is primarily associated with potential price declines in the margined securities. A decline in prices can result in a *restricted account.* If prices fall enough to cause the actual margin to drop below the maintenance margin, the resulting margin call will force the investor to deposit additional equity into the account almost immediately. In addition, losses (resulting from the price decline) are magnified in a fashion similar to that demonstrated in Table 2.2, part B. Clearly, the chance of a margin call and the magnification of losses make margin trading more risky than nonmargined transactions. Margin should be used only by investors who fully understand its operation and appreciate its pitfalls.

Short Selling

In most cases, investors buy stock hoping that the price will rise. What if an investor expects the price of a particular security to fall? By using short selling, the investor may be able to profit from falling security prices. (Until 1997 investors could use short selling to *protect* themselves from falling security prices, a strategy called *shorting-against-the-box.*) Almost any type of security can be "shorted": common and preferred stocks, all types of bonds, convertible securities, listed mutual funds, options, and warrants. In practice, though, the short-selling activities of most investors are limited almost exclusively to common stocks and to options.

HOTLINKS

This site discusses the pros and cons of short selling.

www.fool.com/duelingfools/2001/duelingfools01060600.htm

Essentials of Short Selling

Short selling is generally defined as the practice of selling borrowed securities. Unusual as it may sound, selling borrowed securities is (in most cases) legal and quite common. Short sales start when securities that have been borrowed from a broker are sold in the marketplace. Later, when the price of the issue has declined, the short seller buys back the securities, which are then returned to the lender. A short seller must make an initial

short selling
the sale of borrowed securities, their eventual repurchase by the short seller, and their return to the lender.

TABLE 2.4 The Mechanics of a Short Sale

Step 1—Short sale initiated:	
100 shares of borrowed stock are *sold* at $50/share:	
Proceeds from sale to investor	$5,000
Step 2—Short sale covered:	
Later, 100 shares of the stock are *purchased* at $30/share and returned to broker from whom stock was borrowed:	
Cost to investor	3,000
Net profit	$2,000

equity deposit with the broker, subject to rules similar to those for margin trading. The deposit plus the proceeds from sale of the borrowed shares assure the broker that sufficient funds are available to buy back the shorted securities at a later date, even if their price increases. Short sales, like margin transactions, require investors to work through a broker.

Making Money When Prices Fall Making money when security prices fall is what short selling is all about. Like their colleagues in the rest of the investment world, short sellers are trying to make money by *buying low and selling high*. The only difference is that they reverse the investment process: *They start the transaction with a sale and end it with a purchase.*

Table 2.4 shows how a short sale works and how investors can profit from such transactions. (For simplicity, we ignore transaction costs.) The transaction results in a net profit of $2,000 as a result of an initial sale of 100 shares of stock at $50 per share (step 1) and subsequent covering (purchase) of the 100 shares for $30 per share (step 2). The amount of profit or loss generated in a short sale depends on the price at which the short seller can buy back the stock. Short sellers earn profit only when the proceeds from the sale of the stock are greater than the cost of buying it back.

Who Lends the Securities? Acting through their brokers, short sellers obtain securities from the brokerage firm or from other investors (brokers are the principal source of borrowed securities). As a service to their customers, they lend securities held in the brokers' portfolios or in *street name* accounts. It is important to recognize that when the brokerage firm lends street name securities, it is lending the short seller the securities of other investors. Individual investors typically do not pay fees to the broker for the privilege of borrowing the shares and, as a result, do not earn interest on the funds they leave on deposit with the broker.

Advantages and Disadvantages The major advantage of selling short is, of course, the chance to profit from a price decline. The key disadvantage of many short-sale transactions is that the investor faces limited return opportunities, along with high risk exposure. The price of a security can fall only so far (to a value of or near zero), yet there is really no limit to how far such securities can rise in price. (Remember, a short seller is hoping for a price decline; when a security goes up in price, a short seller loses.) For example, note in

Table 2.4 that the stock in question cannot possibly fall by more than $50, yet who is to say how high its price can go?

A less serious disadvantage is that short sellers never earn dividend (or interest) income. In fact, short sellers owe the lender of the shorted security any dividends (or interest) paid while the transaction is outstanding. That is, if a dividend is paid during the course of a short-sale transaction, the short seller must pay an equal amount to the lender of the stock. (The mechanics of these payments are taken care of automatically by the short seller's broker.)

Uses of Short Selling Investors short sell primarily to seek speculative profits when they expect the price of a security to drop. Because the short seller is betting against the market, this approach is subject to a considerable amount of risk. The actual procedure works as demonstrated in Table 2.4. Note that had you been able to sell the stock at $50 per share and later repurchase it at $30 per share, you would have generated a profit of $2,000 (ignoring dividends and brokerage commissions). However, if the market had instead moved against you, all or most of your $5,000 investment could have been lost.

Summary

LG 1 **Identify the basic types of securities markets and describe the IPO process.** Short-term investment vehicles trade in the money market; longer-term securities, such as stocks and bonds, trade in the capital market. New security issues are sold in the primary market. Once securities are outstanding, investors buy and sell them in the secondary markets. The first public issue of a company's common stock is called an initial public offering (IPO). The company selects an investment banker to advise it and sell the securities. The lead investment banker may form a selling syndicate with other investment bankers to sell the issue. The IPO process includes filing a registration statement with the Securities and Exchange Commission (SEC), getting SEC approval, promoting the offering to investors, pricing the issue, and selling the shares.

LG 2 **Explain the characteristics of organized securities exchanges.** The organized securities exchanges are auction markets. They include the New York Stock Exchange (NYSE), the American Stock Exchange (AMEX), regional stock exchanges, options exchanges, and futures exchanges. In these centralized markets, the forces of supply and demand determine prices. The organized exchanges act as secondary markets where existing securities trade.

LG 3 **Understand the over-the-counter markets, including Nasdaq and alternative trading systems, and the general conditions of securities markets.** The over-the-counter (OTC) market acts as a primary market in which initial public offerings are made. It also handles secondary trading in unlisted securities. It is a dealer market in which negotiation and dealer quotes, often obtained through its automated system, Nasdaq, determine price. Over-the-counter transactions in listed securities are made in the third market. Transactions directly between buyers and sellers are made in the fourth market. Electronic communications networks (ECNs) now offer an alternative to organized exchanges and Nasdaq. Market conditions are commonly classified as "bull" or "bear," depending on whether securities prices are generally rising or falling.

LG 4 **Review the importance of global securities markets, their performance, and the investment procedures and risks associated with foreign investments.** Today securities markets must be viewed globally. Securities exchanges operate in over 100 countries—both large and small. Foreign security investments can be made indirectly by buying shares of a U.S.-based multinational with substantial foreign operations or by purchasing shares of a mutual fund that invests primarily in foreign securities. Direct foreign investment can be achieved by purchasing securities on foreign exchanges, by buying securities of foreign companies that are traded on U.S. exchanges, or by buying American Depositary Receipts (ADRs). International investments can enhance returns, but they entail added risk, particularly currency exchange risk.

LG 5 **Discuss trading hours and the regulation of securities markets.** No longer are investors limited to trading securities during regular market hours (9:30 A.M. to 4:00 P.M., Eastern time). Pre- and post-market trading sessions are available to both individual and institutional investors. Trading activity during these sessions can be quite risky because of greater volatility and lack of centralized pricing data. The securities markets are regulated by the federal Securities and Exchange Commission (SEC) and by state commissions. The key federal laws regulating the securities industry are the Securities Act of 1933, the Securities Exchange Act of 1934, the Maloney Act of 1938, the Investment Company Act of 1940, the Investment Advisers Act of 1940, the Securities Acts Amendments of 1975, and the Insider Trading and Fraud Act of 1988.

LG 6 **Explain long purchases and the motives, procedures, and calculations involved in making margin transactions and short sales.** Most investors make long purchases—buy low, sell high—in expectation of price increases. Many investors establish margin accounts to use borrowed funds to enhance their buying power. The Federal Reserve Board establishes the margin requirement—the minimum investor equity in a margin transaction, both initially and during the margin transaction. The return on invested capital in a margin transaction is magnified; positive returns *and* negative returns are larger than in a comparable unmargined transaction. Paper profits can be used to pyramid a margin account by investing its excess margin. The risks of margin trading are the chance of a restricted account or margin call and the consequences of magnification of losses due to price declines.

Short selling is used when a decline in security prices is anticipated. It involves selling borrowed securities with the expectation of earning a profit by repurchasing them at a lower price in the future. To execute a short sale, the investor must make an initial equity deposit with the broker. The investor borrows the shares from the broker. The major advantage of selling short is the chance to profit from a price decline. The disadvantages of selling short are that the return opportunities are limited in spite of the unlimited potential for loss, and that short sellers never earn dividend (or interest) income. Short selling is used primarily to seek speculative profits from an anticipated decline in share price.

CHAPTER 3

INVESTMENT INFORMATION AND TRADING

Learning Goals

After studying this chapter, you should be able to:

LG 1 Identify the major types and sources of traditional and online investment information.

LG 2 Explain the characteristics, interpretation, and uses of the commonly cited stock and bond market averages and indexes.

LG 3 Review the roles of traditional and online stockbrokers, including the services they provide, selection of a stockbroker, opening an account, and transaction basics.

LG 4 Describe the basic types of orders (market, limit, and stop-loss), online transactions, transaction costs, and the legal aspects of investor protection.

In Elizabethan days, the motley fool was the court jester who wore multicolored garb. Fools were the only people who could get away with telling the king or queen the truth. The Motley Fool Web site (www.fool.com) was created by two English majors who studied more Shakespeare than investments when in college but are now in the business of offering investment advice. David and Tom Gardner talk to their readers in a straightforward yet humorous manner, referring to readers as "fools" in search of the truth about investing. They ask investors to think for themselves—and give them the tools to do so. The Motley Fool's strategy for beginners is (1) learn the rudiments of investment research, (2) pay down debt before beginning, (3) start with mutual funds that mimic the major stock indexes, and (4) invest in stocks you expect to hold for a long time. Meanwhile, their Motley Fool Rule Breaker and Rule Maker Portfolios consistently stack up well against market professionals. Through year-end 1999, these portfolios significantly outperformed the Standard & Poor's 500 Index.

Fool.com is one of many Web sites where investors can learn about, choose, and buy and sell securities. The Internet has revolutionized the financial services industry, empowering individual investors and simplifying the investing process. In this chapter, you'll learn how to use investment resources wisely and find the information to make and monitor investment decisions. We'll discuss the basics of making securities transactions through a traditional broker or online. Most of this material is serious and straightforward. But as the Motley Fool has shown, some aspects of investing can also be fun.

Types and Sources of Investment Information

LG 1

descriptive information factual data on the past behavior of the economy, the market, the industry, the company, or a given investment vehicle.

analytical information available current data in conjunction with projections and recommendations about potential investments.

As you learned in Chapter 1, becoming a successful investor starts with developing investment plans and meeting your liquidity needs. Once you have done this, you can search for the right investments to implement your investment plan and monitor your progress toward achieving your goals. Whether you use the Internet or print sources, you should examine various kinds of investment information to formulate expectations of the risk-return behaviors of potential investments and to monitor them once they are acquired. This section describes the key types and sources of investment information; the following section focuses on market averages and indexes.

Investment information can be either descriptive or analytical. **Descriptive information** presents factual data on the past behavior of the economy, the market, the industry, the company, or a given investment vehicle. **Analytical information** presents available current data in conjunction with projections and recommendations about potential investments. The sample page from *Value Line* included in Figure 3.1 provides both descriptive and analytical information on PepsiCo, Inc. Items that are primarily descriptive are marked with a D, analytical items with an A. Examples of descriptive information are the company's capital structure (7D) and monthly stock price ranges for the past 13 years (13D). Examples of analytical information are rank for timeliness (1A) and projected price range and associated annual total returns for the next 3 years (4A).

Some forms of investment information are free; others must be purchased individually or by annual subscription. You'll find free information on the Internet; in newspapers, magazines, and at brokerage firms; and at public, university, and brokerage firm libraries. Alternatively, you can subscribe to free and paid services that provide periodic reports summarizing the investment outlook and recommending certain actions. Many Internet sites now offer free e-mail newsletters and alerts. You can even set up your own personalized homepage at many financial Web sites so that stock quotes, portfolio tracking, current business news, and other information on stocks of interest to you appear whenever you visit the site. Other sites charge for premium content, such as brokerage research reports, whether in print or online form.

Although the Internet has increased the amount of free information, it may still make sense to pay for services that save you time and money by gathering material you need. But first consider the value of potential information: For example, paying $40 for information that increases your return by $27 would not be economically sound. The larger your investment portfolio, the easier it is to justify information purchases, because they are usually applicable to a number of investments.

Types of Information

Investment information can be divided into five types, each concerned with an important aspect of the investment process.

1. *Economic and current event information* includes background as well as forecast data related to economic, political, and social trends on a domestic as well as a global scale. Such information provides a basis for assessing the environment in which decisions are made.
2. *Industry and company information* includes background as well as forecast data on specific industries and companies. Investors use such information to assess the outlook in a given industry or a specific company.

FIGURE 3.1 **A Report Containing Descriptive and Analytical Information**

Value Line's full-page report on PepsiCo, Inc. from February 9, 2001, contains both descriptive (marked D) and analytical (marked A) information. (*Source:* Adapted from *The Value Line Investment Survey,* Ratings and Reports, Edition 10, February 9, 2001, p. 1542. © Value Line Publishing, Inc.)

PEPSICO, INC. NYSE-PEP | RECENT PRICE 44.07 | P/E RATIO 29.0 (Trailing: 31.5 Median: 22.0) | RELATIVE P/E RATIO 1.80 | DIV'D YLD 1.3% | VALUE LINE

1A → TIMELINESS 3 Lowered 12/15/00
2A → SAFETY 2 Lowered 11/13/98
3A → TECHNICAL 3 Raised 1/14/00
BETA .85 (1.00 = Market)

High:	11.0	13.9	17.8	21.7	21.8	20.6	29.4	35.9	41.3	44.8	42.6	49.9
Low:	6.3	9.0	11.8	15.3	17.3	14.6	16.9	27.3	28.3	27.6	30.1	29.7

Target Price Range 2003 2004 2005

4A **2003-05 PROJECTIONS**

	Price	Gain	Ann'l Total Return
High	65	(+45%)	11%
Low	45	(Nil)	2%

5D **Insider Decisions**

	M	A	M	J	J	A	S	O	N
to Buy	0	0	0	0	0	0	0	0	0
Options	0	0	0	0	0	0	0	0	0
to Sell	0	1	0	0	0	0	0	0	0

6D **Institutional Decisions**

	1Q2000	2Q2000	3Q2000
to Buy	375	390	422
to Sell	504	474	449
Hld's(000)	868472	898678	912486

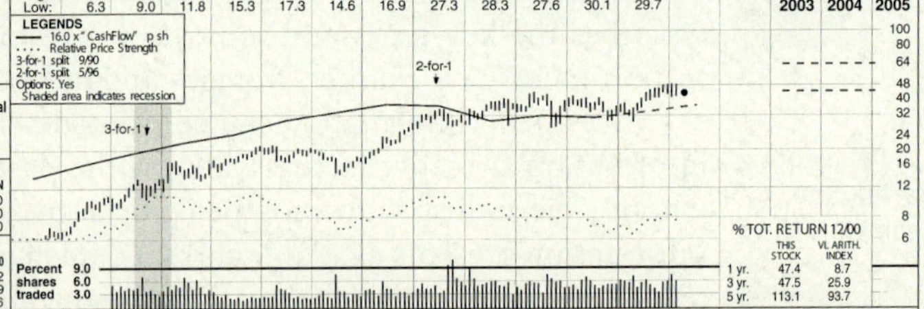

13D

2/16 14:46

1984	1985	1986	1987	1988	1989	1990	1991	1992	1993	1994	1995	1996	G1997	1998	G1999	2000	2001	© VALUE LINE PUB., INC.	03-05
4.55	5.10	5.95	7.35	8.25	9.63	11.29	12.42	13.75	15.66	18.02	19.30	20.48	13.93	15.19	14.00	14.00	14.75	Sales per sh	18.15
.35	.45	.55	.74	.88	1.05	1.23	1.42	1.58	1.90	2.13	2.37	2.32	1.89	2.04	1.98	2.15	2.35	"CashFlow" per sh	2.90
.19	.25	.29	.37	.48	.56	.66	.75	.81	.98	1.11	1.24	1.17	1.10	1.16	1.23	1.45	1.63	Earnings per sh B	2.15
.09	.10	.11	.11	.13	.16	.19	.23	.26	.31	.35	.39	.45	.49	.52	.54	.56	.60	Div'ds Decl'd per sh C ■	.80
.34	.50	.57	.50	.46	.60	.75	.92	.97	1.24	1.43	1.34	1.48	1.00	.96	.77	.65	.85	Cap'l Spending per sh	.90
1.10	1.16	1.32	1.61	2.00	2.46	3.11	3.51	3.35	3.97	4.34	4.64	4.29	4.62	4.35	4.73	4.95	5.75	Book Value per sh E	8.80
1690.3	1578.7	1561.9	1562.5	1576.9	1582.1	1576.8	1578.2	1597.6	1597.6	1579.8	1576.0	1545.0	1502.0	1471.0	1455.0	1435	1445	Common Shs Outst'g F	1445
11.8	12.6	16.3	15.5	12.6	15.7	17.8	20.4	22.8	20.0	15.9	18.5	26.5	32.5	32.4	29.8	28.3		Avg Ann'l P/E Ratio	26.0
1.10	1.02	1.11	1.04	1.05	1.19	1.32	1.30	1.38	1.18	1.04	1.24	1.66	1.87	1.69	1.70	1.88		Relative P/E Ratio	1.75
4.1%	3.1%	2.2%	1.9%	2.2%	1.8%	1.6%	1.5%	1.4%	1.6%	2.0%	1.7%	1.4%	1.4%	1.4%	1.5%	1.4%		Avg Ann'l Div'd Yield	1.4%

7D → **CAPITAL STRUCTURE as of 9/2/00**
Tot.Debt $2853.0 mill. **Due in 5 Yrs** $1856.0 mill.
LT Debt $2737.0 mill. **LT Interest** $185.0 mill.
(Total interest coverage: 8.5x) (28% of Cap'l)

8D → **Leases, Uncapitalized** Annual rentals $63.0 mill.

Pension Liability None
Pfd Stock None

Common Stock 1,443,597,000 shs. (72% of Cap'l) **at September 29, 2000**
MARKET CAP: $64 billion (Large Cap)

1990	1991	1992	1993	1994	1995	1996	1997	1998	1999	2000	2001		03-05
17803	19608	21970	25021	28472	30421	31645	20917	22348	20367	20100	21300	Sales ($mill) G	26200
16.6%	17.0%	16.3%	17.4%	16.8%	17.2%	16.1%	19.4%	18.4%	19.2%	20.5%	21.0%	Operating Margin	21.5%
884.0	1034.5	1214.9	1444.2	1576.5	1740.0	1719.0	1106.0	1234.0	1032.0	945	975	Depreciation ($mill)	1050
1050.0	1200.2	1301.7	1587.9	1784.0	1990.0	1865.0	1730.0	1760.0	1845.0	2120	2400	Net Profit ($mill)	3165
33.0%	34.8%	31.4%	34.5%	33.0%	32.6%	35.0%	33.4%	31.0%	32.2%	32.0%	32.0%	Income Tax Rate	33.0%
5.9%	6.1%	5.9%	6.3%	6.3%	6.5%	5.9%	8.3%	7.9%	9.1%	10.5%	11.3%	Net Profit Margin	12.1%
d689.1	844.0	517.9	d1411	d198.2	316.0	- -	1994.0	d3552	385.0	550	1250	Working Cap'l ($mill)	3350
5600.1	7806.2	7964.8	7442.6	8840.5	8509.0	8439.0	4946.0	4028.0	2812.0	2900	2800	Long-Term Debt ($mill)	2150
4904.2	5545.4	5355.7	6338.7	6856.1	7313.0	6623.0	6936.0	6401.0	6881.0	7000	8325	Shr. Equity ($mill)	12700
12.7%	11.3%	11.8%	12.9%	13.0%	14.3%	14.2%	16.6%	18.8%	19.9%	22.0%	22.5%	Return on Total Cap'l	22.0%
21.4%	21.6%	24.3%	25.1%	26.0%	27.2%	28.2%	24.9%	27.5%	26.8%	30.0%	29.0%	Return on Shr. Equity	25.0%
15.4%	15.5%	16.9%	17.8%	18.1%	19.0%	18.0%	14.3%	15.7%	15.5%	18.5%	18.5%	Retained to Com Eq	16.0%
28%	29%	30%	29%	30%	30%	36%	43%	43%	42%	38%	36%	All Div'ds to Net Prof	37%

14D

9D

CURRENT POSITION ($MILL.)	1998	1999	9/2/00
Cash Assets	394.0	1056.0	802.0
Receivables	2453.0	1704.0	1835.0
Inventory (FIFO)	1016.0	899.0	975.0
Other	499.0	514.0	588.0
Current Assets	4362.0	4173.0	4200.0
Accts Payable	- -	3399.0	3337.0
Debt Due	3921.0	233.0	116.0
Other	3993.0	156.0	168.0
Current Liab.	7914.0	3788.0	3621.0

10D

ANNUAL RATES of change (per sh)	Past 10 Yrs.	Past 5 Yrs.	Est'd '98 to '03-'05
Sales	5.5%	-2.0%	3.0%
"Cash Flow"	8.5%	1.0%	6.0%
Earnings	9.5%	4.0%	11.0%
Dividends	14.5%	11.0%	7.5%
Book Value	8.5%	3.5%	12.5%

11D

Calendar	QUARTERLY SALES ($ mill.) A G Mar.Per	Jun.Per	Sep.Per	Dec.Per	Full Year
1997	4213	5086	5362	6256	20917
1998	4353	5258	5544	7193	22348
1999	5114	4982	4591	5680	20367
2000	4191	4928	4909	6072	20100
2001	4450	5200	5200	6450	21300

Calendar	EARNINGS PER SHARE A B G Mar.Per	Jun.Per	Sep.Per	Dec.Per	Full Year
1997	.20	.26	.35	.29	1.10
1998	.24	.33	.37	.22	1.16
1999	.25	.31	.34	.33	1.23
2000	.29	.38	.40	.38	1.45
2001	.32	.42	.45	.44	1.63

Calendar	QUARTERLY DIVIDENDS PAID C ■ Mar.31	Jun.30	Sep.30	Dec.31	Full Year
1997	.23D	.125	.125	- -	.48
1998	.25D	.13	.13	- -	.51
1999	.26D	.135	.135	- -	.53
2000	.27D	.14	.14	- -	.55
2001	.28D				

BUSINESS: PepsiCo, Inc. operates three major businesses: Snack Foods, 64% of 1999 pro forma sales (ex bottling cos.) and 66% of operating profits; Soft Drinks, 24% and 28%; and Tropicana (acquired 9/98), 12% and 6%. International business, 32% of sales. Restaurants spun off, 10/97. Majority interest in Pepsi Bottling Group sold, 4/99. Major soft drink products: *Pepsi-Cola, Diet Pepsi,* and *Mountain Dew.* Specialty snack foods: Frito-Lay (major product offerings include *Doritos, Ruffles,* and *Lay's*), Walker Crisps, Smiths Crisps. Has about 118,000 employees, 207,000 stockholders. Insiders own less than 1% of common. Chrmn. & CEO: Roger A. Enrico. Pres. & COO: S. Reinemund. Inc.: NC. Add.: Purchase, NY 10577. Tel.: 914-253-2000. Internet: www.pepsico.com.

15D

PepsiCo is making another major move, this time agreeing to acquire Quaker Oats. This follows the spin-off of its restaurants in 1997, the purchase of Tropicana in 1998, and the sale of a majority interest in its bottling companies in 1999. Quaker's primary appeal is Gatorade, the largest selling and still fast growing sports drink. It also has attractive snack and convenience food lines in addition to its more mature cereal and food businesses. The all-stock acquisition is likely to close in the June quarter and is expected to help PepsiCo's earnings for the first full year after it is completed. (Our financial forecasts for Pepsi on this page will not include Quaker until after the acquisition has occurred.)

In the meantime, PepsiCo's current businesses are doing well, and we look for good sales and earnings growth this year. The most important product group, Frito-Lay North America, has close to 60% of the U.S. snack food market and is continuing to improve its position. Volume and prices should both be up this year. The Pepsi-Cola soft drink lineup has a strong #2 position in the U.S. and should continue to grow moderately. Mountain Dew and Aquafina are likely to continue to be particularly strong performers. Tropicana has been doing particularly well, and its strong growth should continue. We expect that Frito-Lay International will continue to provide above-average returns.

The core businesses are well positioned to achieve 10% or higher earnings growth. The Frito-Lay franchises, both at home and abroad, are extremely strong, and we expect that management will continue to build its current position. The same is true for the Pepsi-Cola and Tropicana brands in the U.S. Pepsi's soft drink operations outside North America are still relatively small, but the growth potential is large.

PepsiCo shares are now ranked to be average performers in the coming six to 12 months. An ongoing share-repurchase program has been discontinued because of the Quaker Oats acquisition. We expect that it will be reinstated sometime after the deal is completed and the two companies' operations have been integrated.

Stephen Sanborn, CFA February 9, 2001

16D

(A) Quarters are 12, 12, 12 and 16 weeks. (B) Prim. earns. thru 1996; diluted thereafter. Ex. nonrecur. gains (losses): '85, 22¢; '91, (7¢); '92, (65¢); '95, (24¢); '96, (45¢); '98, 15¢; '99, 14¢. Next earn. report due mid-Apr. (C) Next div. meeting about May. 3. Goes ex about Jun. 7. Pay. dates: about Jan. 2, March 31, June 30, Sept. 30. ■ Reinvest. plan avail. (D) Two divs. in qtr. (E) Incl. intang. In '99: $4.73 bil., $3.25/sh. (F) In millions., adj. for stock splits. (G) Reflects Restaurant spinoff in '97 and sale of majority of Pepsi Bottling Group in '99.

Company's Financial Strength	A+
Stock's Price Stability	80
Price Growth Persistence	75
Earnings Predictability	80

← 17A

18A

1. Rank for timeliness (price performance in next twelve months)—from 1 (highest) to 5 (lowest)
2. Rank for long-term safety—1 (highest) down to 5 (lowest)
3. Beta (the stock's sensitivity to market fluctuation—NYSE average = 1.00)
4. Projected price range and associated annual returns—3 years ahead
5. Insider decisions
6. Institutional decisions
7. Company's capital structure
8. Pension liability
9. Working capital
10. Growth rates
11. Quarterly sales, earnings, dividends—actual past, estimated future
12. Footnotes—including estimated constant dollar earnings, dividend payment dates
13. Monthly price ranges—past 15 years and value line (cash flow line)
14. Statistical milestones—on a per share basis and a company basis—historical past and estimated future
15. Brief summary of company's business
16. Critique—of recent developments and prospects
17. Company's financial strength
18. Important indices of quality

Because of its company orientation, it is most relevant to stock, bond, or options investments.

3. *Information on alternative investment vehicles* includes background and predictive data for securities other than stocks, bonds, and options, such as mutual funds and futures.
4. *Price information* includes current price quotations on certain investment vehicles, particularly securities. These quotations are commonly accompanied by statistics on the recent price behavior of the vehicle.
5. *Information on personal investment strategies* includes recommendations on investment strategies or specific purchase or sale actions. In general, this information tends to be educational or analytical rather than descriptive.

Sources of Information

A complete listing of the sources of each type of investment information is beyond the scope of this book. Our discussion focuses on the most common online and traditional sources of information on economic and current events, industries and companies, and prices, as well as other online sources.

Economic and Current Event Information Investors who are aware of current economic, political, and business events tend to make better investment decisions. Popular sources of economic and current event information include financial journals, general newspapers, institutional news, business periodicals, government publications, and special subscription services. These are available in print and online versions; often the online versions are free but may have limited content. Most offer free searchable article archives and charge a nominal fee for each article downloaded.

Wall Street Journal
a daily business newspaper, published regionally; the most popular source of financial news.

Financial Journals The ***Wall Street Journal*** is the most popular source of financial news. Published daily Monday through Friday in regional, European, and Asian editions, the *Journal* also has an online version called the *WSJ Interactive Edition* (www.wsj.com), which is updated frequently throughout the day and on the weekends. In addition to giving daily price quotations on thousands of investment vehicles, it reports world, national, regional, and corporate news. The first page of the third section of the *Journal* usually contains a column called "Heard on the Street" that focuses on specific market and company events. In addition, articles that address personal finance issues and topics are often included on that page. A print subscription to the *Wall Street Journal* costs $175 annually, compared to $59 per year for the online version; print subscribers pay $29 to add the online edition. *WSJ Interactive* includes features such as Briefing Books on individual companies and mutual funds; article searches; special online-only articles; and access to the Dow Jones Publications Library, a comprehensive database of articles from major general and business periodicals.

HOTLINKS

Federal Reserve Economic Data (FRED) has a historical database of economic and financial statistics.

www.stls.frb.org/fred

Barron's
a weekly business newspaper; a popular source of financial news.

A second popular source of financial news is ***Barron's***, which is published weekly. *Barron's* generally offers lengthier articles on a variety of topics of interest to individual investors. Probably the most popular column in *Barron's* is Alan Abelson's "Up & Down Wall Street," which provides a critical and often humorous assessment of major developments affecting the stock market and business. *Barron's* also includes current price quotations and a summary of statistics on a range of investment vehicles. Subscribers to *WSJ Interactive* also have access to *Barron's* online edition (www.barrons.com) because both are published by Dow Jones & Co.

Investor's Business Daily is a third national business newspaper published Monday through Friday. It is similar to the *Wall Street Journal* but contains more detailed price and market data. Its Web site (www.investors.com) has limited free content. Another source of financial news is the *Financial Times* (www.ft.com), with U.S., United Kingdom, and global editions.

General Newspapers Major metropolitan newspapers such as the *New York Times,* the *Washington Post,* and the *Los Angeles Times* provide investors with a wealth of financial information in their print and online editions. Most major newspapers contain stock price quotations for major exchanges, price quotations on stocks of local interest, and a summary of the major stock market averages and indexes. Local newspapers are another convenient source of financial news. In most large cities, the daily newspaper devotes at least a few pages to financial and business news. Another popular source of financial news is *USA Today,* the national newspaper published daily Monday through Friday. Each issue contains a "Money" section (Section B) devoted to business and personal financial news and to current security price quotations and summary statistics.

Institutional News The monthly economic letters of the nation's leading banks, such as Bank of America (based in Charlotte, North Carolina), Northern Trust (Chicago), and Wells Fargo (San Francisco), provide useful economic information. Wire services such as Dow Jones, Bloomberg Financial Services, AP (Associated Press), and UPI (United Press International) provide economic and business news feeds to brokerages, other financial institutions, and Web sites that subscribe to them. Bloomberg has its own comprehensive site (www.bloomberg.com). Business.com (www.business.com) offers industry-by-industry news, targeted business searches, and market coverage. Web sites specializing in financial news include CNNfn (money.cnn.com) and CBS MarketWatch (cbs.marketwatch.com).

Business Periodicals Business periodicals vary in scope. Some present general business and economic articles, others cover securities markets and related topics, and still others focus solely on specific industries. Regardless of the subject matter, most business periodicals present descriptive information, and some also include analytical information. They rarely offer recommendations.

The business sections of general-interest periodicals such as *Newsweek, Time,* and *U.S. News & World Report* cover business and economic news. Strictly business- and finance-oriented periodicals, including *Business Week, Fortune, Business Month,* and *Nation's Business,* provide more in-depth articles. These magazines also have investing and personal finance articles.

Some financial periodicals specialize in securities and marketplace articles. The most basic, commonsense articles appear in *Forbes, Kiplinger's Personal Finance Magazine, Money, Smart Money,* and *Worth. Forbes,* published every two weeks, is the most investment-oriented. Each January it publishes an

"Annual Report on American Industry" that compares the growth and performance of key industries over the past five years. In August of each year, *Forbes* also publishes a comparative evaluation of mutual funds. *Kiplinger's Personal Finance Magazine, Money, Smart Money,* and *Worth* are published monthly and contain articles on managing personal finances and on investments.

All these business and personal finance magazines have Web sites with free access to recent, if not all, content. Most include a number of other features. For example, *Smart Money* has interactive investment tools, including a color-coded "Map of the Market" that shows the current hot sectors.

Government Publications A number of government agencies publish economic data and reports useful to investors. The annual *Economic Report of the President* provides a broad view of the current and expected state of the economy. This document reviews and summarizes economic policy and conditions and includes data on important aspects of the economy. The *Federal Reserve Bulletin,* published monthly by the Board of Governors of the Federal Reserve System, and periodic reports published by each of the 12 Federal Reserve District Banks provide articles and data on various aspects of economic and business activity. (Visit www.federalreserve.gov to read many of these publications.) A useful Department of Commerce publication is the *Survey of Current Business.* Published monthly, it includes indicators and data related to economic and business conditions. A good source of financial statement information on all manufacturers, broken down by industry and asset size, is the *Quarterly Financial Report for Manufacturing Corporations,* published jointly by the Federal Trade Commission and the Securities and Exchange Commission. Most of these reports are now available at the Web sites of the issuing government agency; a good search engine such as Google (www.google.com) will quickly locate them for you.

Special Subscription Services Investors who want additional insights into business and economic conditions can subscribe to special services. These reports include business and economic forecasts and give notice of new government policies, union plans and tactics, taxes, prices, wages, and so on. One popular service is the *Kiplinger Washington Letter,* a weekly publication that provides a wealth of economic information and analyses.

Industry and Company Information Of special interest to investors is information on particular industries and companies. Often, after choosing an industry in which to invest, an investor will want to analyze specific companies. A recent change in disclosure rules, discussed below, gives individual investors access to more company information than before. General business periodicals such as *Business Week, Forbes,* the *Wall Street Journal,* and *Fortune* carry articles on the activities of specific industries and individual companies. Trade publications such as *Chemical Week, American Banker, Computerworld, Industry Week, Oil and Gas Journal,* and *Public Utilities Fortnightly* provide more focused industry and company information. *Red Herring, The Industry Standard, Business 2.0, Fast Company,* and *Upside* are magazines that can help you keep up with the high-tech world; all have good Web sites. Other specific popular sources are discussed in Table 3.1 on the next page.

TABLE 3.1 Online Sources for Industry and Company Information

Web Site	Description	Cost
Hoover's Online (www.hoovers.com)	Reports and news on public and private companies as well as 300 industries grouped into 28 sectors.	Considerable free information; $125 per year for in-depth reports and financial statements, advanced search, and stock screen.
CNET (www.news.com)	One of the best sites for high-tech news, analysis, breaking news, great search capabilities, links.	Free.
Company Sleuth (www.companysleuth.com)	Gathers "the inside scoop" on companies from around the Web: stock quotes, news, insider trades, and trademark and patent registrations; message boards; personalized daily e-mail reports.	Free; registration required.
News Alert (www.newsalert.com)	Latest company news from various wire services. Searchable by industry or company. Good for earnings announcements and tech news.	Free.

The Internet makes it easy to research specific industries and companies at the company's Web site, a publication's archive search, or database services such as the Dow Jones Publications Library. Table 3.1 presents several free and subscription resources that emphasize industry and company information.

Fair Disclosure Rules Until recently, executives at public companies could disclose market-moving information privately to investment professionals—analysts, money managers, and large institutional investors—before releasing it to the general public. This selective disclosure gave broker-dealers and their clients an unfair advantage. They could act on the information before the average investor could act. In August 2000, the SEC passed the **fair disclosure rule**, known as **Regulation FD**, a new rule requiring senior executives to disclose critical information such as earnings forecasts and news of mergers and new products simultaneously to investment professionals and the public via press releases or SEC filings. However, it does not apply to communications with journalists and securities ratings firms like Moody's Investor Services and Standard & Poor's. Violations of the rule carry injunctions and fines but are not considered fraud.

fair disclosure rule (Regulation FD)
rule requiring senior executives to disclose critical information simultaneously to investment professionals and the public via press releases or SEC filings.

The new regulations are not without controversy. The Securities Industry Association expressed concern that executives would be afraid to talk to anyone outside their companies, and that the rule would therefore curtail rather than increase the flow of information. Companies may limit contact with analysts if they are unsure whether the information requires a press release.

Stockholders' Reports An excellent source of data on an individual firm is the **stockholders' report,** or **annual report,** published yearly by publicly held corporations. These reports contain a wide range of information, including financial statements for the most recent period of operation, along with summarized statements for several prior years. These reports are free and may be obtained from the companies themselves or from brokers. A sample page from PepsiCo, Inc.'s 2000 stockholders' report is shown in Figure 3.2. Most

stockholders' (annual) report
a report published yearly by a publicly held corporation; contains a wide range of information, including financial statements for the most recent period of operation.

FIGURE 3.2 **A Page from a Stockholders' Report**

This page of the 2000 Annual Report of PepsiCo, Inc. quickly acquaints the investor with the key information on the firm's operations over the past year, in tabular and graphical form. The contents of the Annual Report are also shown on this page. (*Source:* PepsiCo, Inc. 2000 Annual Report; available at PepsiCo's Web site www.pepsico.com; PepsiCo, Inc. Investor Relations, 914-253-3055; PepsiCo, Inc., Purchase, NY 10577.)

Financial Highlights

PepsiCo, Inc. and Subsidiaries
($ in millions except per share amounts; all per share amounts assume dilution)

	As Reported			Pro Forma[b]		
	2000	1999	% Chg[a]	2000	1999	% Chg[a]
Summary of Operations						
Net sales	$20,438	$20,367	–	$20,144	$18,666	8
Segment operating profit	$ 3,550	$ 3,068	16	$ 3,482	$ 3,080	13
Net income	$ 2,183	$ 2,050	6	$ 2,139	$ 1,850	16
Net income per share	$ 1.48	$ 1.37	8	$ 1.45	$ 1.24	17
Other Data						
Net cash provided by operating activities	$ 3,911	$ 3,027	29			
Share repurchases	$ 1,430	$ 1,285	11			
Dividends paid	$ 796	$ 778	2			
Long-term debt	$ 2,346	$ 2,812	(17)			
Capital spending	$ 1,067	$ 1,118	(5)			

(a) Percentage changes are based on unrounded amounts.

(b) PepsiCo's fiscal year ends on the last Saturday in December and, as a result, a fifty-third week is added every 5 or 6 years. The fiscal year ended December 30, 2000 consisted of fifty-three weeks. For comparative purposes, the pro forma information for 2000 excludes the impact of the fifty-third week. The pro forma information for 1999 also gives effect to the bottling transactions described in Note 2 to the financial statements as if the transactions occurred at the beginning of PepsiCo's 1998 fiscal year. In addition, the 1999 pro forma results exclude the Frito-Lay impairment and restructuring pre-tax charge of $65 million ($40 million after-tax), the pre-tax gain on the sale of a chocolate business in Poland of $28 million ($25 million after-tax), the pre-tax net gain on the PBG and Whitman bottling transactions of $1 billion ($270 million after-tax) and the income tax provision of $25 million related to the PepCom transaction. The pro forma information does not purport to represent what PepsiCo's results of operations would have been had such transactions been completed as of the dates indicated nor does it give effect to any other events.

Pro Forma PepsiCo Net Sales
Total: $20,144
$ In Millions

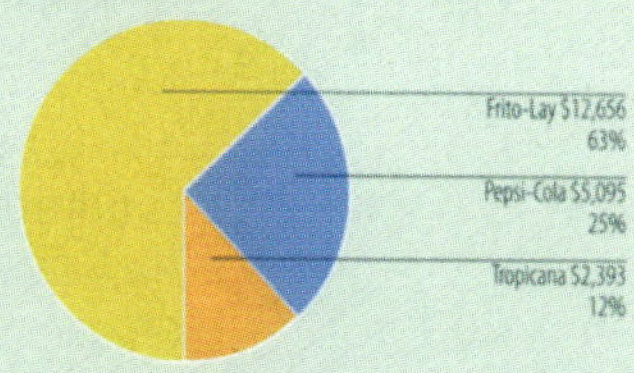

Pro Forma Segment Operating Profit
Total: $3,482
$ In Millions

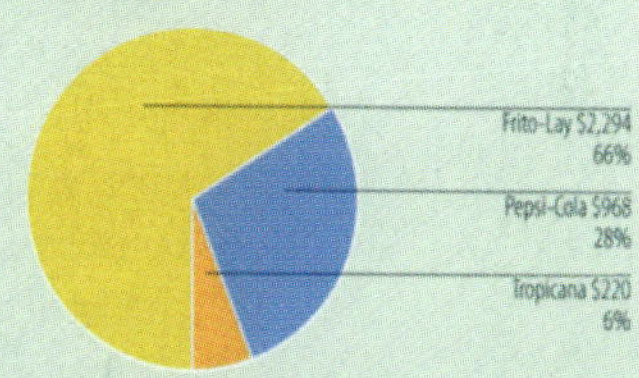

Contents

Michael Thomas
Shareholder since 2001.

To help us toast a great year, we invited several PepsiCo shareholders to pose for a few pictures eating, drinking and being merry. As you'll see, they very kindly obliged.

companies now place their annual reports on their Web sites. Annual Report Gallery (www.reportgallery.com) provides links to many company reports.

In addition to the stockholders' report, many serious investors review a company's **Form 10-K**. This is a statement that firms with securities listed on an organized exchange or traded in the Nasdaq market must file annually with the SEC. Finding 10-K and other SEC filings is now a simple task, thanks to SEC/Edgar (Electronic Data Gathering and Analysis Retrieval), which has reports filed by any company traded on a major exchange. You can read them free at EDGAR Online's FreeEdgar site (www.freeedgar.com).

Form 10-K
a statement that must be filed annually with the SEC by all firms having securities listed on an organized exchange or traded in the Nasdaq market.

Comparative Data Sources Sources of comparative data, typically broken down by industry and firm size, are a good tool for analyzing the financial condition of companies. Among these sources are Dun & Bradstreet's *Key Business Ratios,* Robert Morris and Associates' *Annual Statement Studies,* the *Quarterly Financial Report for Manufacturing Corporations* (cited above), and the *Almanac of Business and Industrial Financial Ratios.* These sources, which are typically available in public and university libraries, are a useful benchmark for evaluating a company's financial condition.

Subscription Services A variety of subscription services provide data on specific industries and companies. Today, many of these services are available on the Internet. (See the Investor's Resources section on the book's Web site.) Generally, a subscriber pays a basic fee to access the service's information and can purchase premium services for greater depth or range. The major subscription services provide both descriptive and analytical information, but they generally do not make recommendations. Most investors, rather than subscribing to these services, access them through their stockbrokers or a large public or university library. The Web sites for most services offer some free information and charge for the rest.

The dominant subscription services are those offered by Standard & Poor's Corporation, Moody's Investor Services, and Value Line. Table 3.2 summarizes the most popular services of these companies. **Standard & Poor's Corporation (S&P)** offers a large number of different financial reports and services. Its Personal Wealth Web site, owned by *Business Week* (www.businessweek.com/investor) is geared toward individual investors. Although basic news and market commentary is free, for just $100 a year subscribers get access to S&P stock reports on 4,600 companies and screening tools. **Moody's Investor Services** also publishes a variety of material, including its securities ratings, corporate research, and well-known reference manuals on eight industries. The ***Value Line Investment Survey*** is one of the most popular subscription services used by individual investors; it is available at most libraries and online (www.valueline.com).

Standard & Poor's Corporation (S&P)
publisher of a large number of financial reports and services, including *Corporation Records* and *Stock Reports.*

Moody's Investor Services
publisher of a variety of financial material, including *Moody's Manuals.*

Value Line Investment Survey
one of the most popular subscription services used by individual investors; subscribers receive three basic reports weekly.

Brokerage Reports Brokerage firms often make available to their clients reports from the various subscription services and research reports from their own securities analysts. They also provide clients with prospectuses for new security issues and *back-office research reports.* As noted in Chapter 2, a *prospectus* is a document that describes in detail the key aspects of the issue, the issuer, and its management and financial position. The cover of the prospectus describing the 2001 stock issue of Reliant Resources, Inc. was shown in Figure 2.1. **Back-office research reports** include the brokerage firm's analyses of and recommendations on prospects for the securities markets, specific industries, or

back-office research reports
a brokerage firm's analyses of and recommendations on investment prospects; available on request at no cost to existing and potential clients or for purchase at some Web sites.

TABLE 3.2 Popular Offerings of the Major Subscription Services

Subscription Service/ Offerings	Coverage	Frequency of Publication
Standard & Poor's Corporation		
Corporation Records	Detailed descriptions of publicly traded securities of over 10,000 public corporations.	Annually with updates throughout the year.
Stock Reports (sample shown in Figure 7.1, page 299)	Summary of financial history, current finances, and future prospects for thousands of companies.	Annually with updates throughout the year.
Stock Guide	Statistical data and analytical rankings of investment desirability for major stocks.	Monthly.
Bond Guide	Statistical data and analytical rankings of investment desirability for major bonds.	Monthly.
The Outlook	Analytical articles with investment advice on the market, industries, and securities.	Weekly magazine.
Moody's Investor Services		
Moody's Manuals	Eight reference manuals—*Bank and Finance, Industrial, International, Municipal and Government, OTC Industrial, OTC Unlisted, Public Utility,* and *Transportation*—with historical and current financial, organizational, and operational data on major firms.	Annually with biweekly updates.
Handbook of Common Stocks	Common stock data.	Quarterly.
Dividend Record	Recent dividend announcements and payments.	Twice weekly, with annual summary.
Bond Survey	Bond market conditions and new offerings.	Weekly.
Bond Record	Price and interest rate behavior of thousands of bonds.	Monthly.
Value Line Investment Survey		
Includes three reports:	Covers 1,700 of the most widely held stocks.	Weekly.
1. *Summary and Index*	Current ratings for each stock.	
2. *Ratings and Reports* (sample shown in Figure 3.5)	Full-page report including financial data, descriptions, analysis, and ratings for each of about 130 stocks.	
3. *Selection and Opinion*	Selected investment, business, and stock market prospects, and advice on investment strategy.	

specific securities. Usually a brokerage firm publishes lists of securities classified by its research staff as either "buy," "hold," or "sell." Brokerage research reports are available on request at no cost to existing and potential clients.

Securities analyst's reports are now available on the Web, either from brokerage sites or from sites that consolidate research from many brokerages. At Multex Investor (www.multexinvestor.com), a leading research site, reports from 500 brokerage and research firms cost from $4 to $150 each. Investors can use Zacks's (www.zacks.com) Brokerage Research Engine to find and purchase reports from 3,200 analysts on 7,500 companies for $10 to $150 per report or to read free brokerage report abstracts with earnings revisions and recommendations.

investment letters
newsletters that provide, on a subscription basis, the analyses, conclusions, and recommendations of experts in securities investment.

Investment Letters **Investment letters** provide, on a subscription basis, the analyses, conclusions, and recommendations of experts in securities investment. Some letters concentrate on specific types of securities; others are concerned solely with assessing the economy or securities markets. Among the more popular investment letters are *Bob Nurock's Advisory,* the *Dick Davis Digest, Dines Letter, Dow Theory Letters,* the *Growth Stock Outlook,*

Professional Tape Reader, the *Prudent Speculator*, and *Street Smart Investing*. Most newsletters come out weekly or monthly and cost from $75 to $400 a year. Advertisements for many of these investment letters can be found in *Barron's* and in various business periodicals.

The *Hulbert Financial Digest* (www.hulbertdigest.com) monitors the performance of investment letters. It is an excellent source of objective information on investment letters and a good place to check out those that interest you. Many newsletters now offer online subscriptions. Use a general search engine or the Newsletter Access (www.newsletteraccess.com), a searchable database of newsletters that lists over 1,600 stock-investing newsletters!

quotations
price information about various types of securities, including current price data and statistics on recent price behavior.

Price Information Price information about various types of securities is contained in their **quotations,** which include current price data and statistics on recent price behavior. The Web makes it easy to find price quotes for actively traded securities, and many financially oriented sites include a stock price look-up feature or a stock ticker running across the screen, much like the ones that used to be found only in brokerage offices. The ticker consolidates and reports stock transactions made on the NYSE, AMEX, regional exchanges, and Nasdaq National Market as they occur. Cable TV subscribers in many areas can watch the ticker at the bottom of the screen on certain channels, including CNNfn, CNN Headline News, and MSNBC. The ticker symbols for some well-known companies are listed in Table 3.3.

Investors can easily find the prior day's security price quotations in the published news media, both nonfinancial and financial. They also can find delayed or real-time quotations at numerous Web sites, including *financial portals* (described below), most business periodical Web sites, and brokerage sites. The Web sites for CNNfn and CNBC-TV have real-time stock quotes, as do sites that subscribe to their news feed. Stock quotes are usually free, but investors may have to pay for bond quotes. For example, Quote.com (www.quote.com) charges $9.95 a month for prices on Treasury securities.

TABLE 3.3 Symbols for Some Well-Known Companies

Company	Symbol	Company	Symbol
Amazon.com	AMZN	McDonald's Corp.	MCD
America Online	AOL	Microsoft	MSFT
Apple Computer	AAPL	Merrill Lynch	MER
AT&T	T	Nike	NKE
Cisco	CSCO	Oracle	ORCL
Dell Computer	DELL	PepsiCo, Inc.	PEP
Eastman Kodak	EK	Reebok	RBK
ExxonMobil	XOM	Sears, Roebuck	S
Genentech	DNA	Starbucks	SBUX
General Electric	GE	Sun Microsystems	SUNW
Hewlett-Packard	HWP	Texas Instruments	TXN
Intel	INTC	United Airlines	UAL
Int'l. Business Machines	IBM	Xerox Corporation	XRX
Lucent Technologies	LU	Yahoo!	YHOO

INVESTOR FACTS

PIRACY ON WALL STREET— The tradition of quoting stock prices in fractions based on eighths of a dollar is a holdover from the 17th century. To make change, pirates used to break coins into eight wedges. Hence the term "pieces of eight"!

The major published source of security price quotations is the *Wall Street Journal*, which presents quotations for each previous business day's activities in all major markets. (We'll explain how to read and interpret actual price quotations in later chapters.)

Prior to April 2000, stock prices were quoted in fractional form: eighths and, more recently, sixteenths. Starting in August 2000, some stocks began trading in decimals instead of this awkward pricing—⅛ of a point equals 12.5¢, 1/16 equals 6.25¢. Today all stocks are priced in decimals, a format that is much easier to read and understand.

Other Online Investment Information Sources Many other excellent Web sites provide information of all sorts to increase your investment skills and knowledge. Let's now look at financial portals, sites for bonds and mutual funds, international sites, and investment discussion forums. Table 3.4 lists some of the most popular financial portals, bond sites, and mutual fund sites. We'll look at online brokerage and investment adviser sites later in the chapter, and you'll find more specialized Web links in all chapters.

financial portals
supersites on the Web that bring together many investing features, including real-time quotes, stock and mutual fund screens, portfolio trackers, news, research, and transaction capabilities, along with other personal finance features.

Financial Portals **Financial portals** are supersites that bring together a wide range of investing features, such as real-time quotes, stock and mutual fund screens, portfolio trackers, news, research, and transaction capabilities, along with other personal finance features. These sites want to be your investing homepage. Some portals are general sites such as Yahoo! and Excite that offer a full range of investing features along with their other services, or they may be investing-oriented sites. You should check out several to see which best suits your needs, because their strengths and features vary greatly. *Investorama*, for example, is primarily a collection of links to other financial Web sites. Other portals want you to stay at their site and offer customization options so that your start page includes the data you want. Although finding one site where you can manage your investments is indeed appealing, you may not be able to find the best of what you need at one portal. You'll want to explore several sites to find the ones that meet your needs. Table 3.4 includes a summary of the features of several popular financial portals.

Although you can personalize financial portals, you generally have to visit several sites to manage your financial affairs. A new breed of financial portal aggregates all your financial information on one Web page: bank accounts, credit cards, brokerage and mutual fund accounts, retirement funds, and even frequent-flyer mileage! You provide the passwords, and the software gathers the financial information from other sites. With one click you can view summaries of all your personal accounts—finances, shopping, travel, e-mail, and more. You can even access your data from Web-enabled wireless devices. Figure 3.3 shows a sample of Yodlee's summary page. Although these sites can save you a lot of time, many consumers are hesitant to submit account numbers and passwords to one site. To counter these concerns, aggregators use multiple encryption techniques and limit employee access to client data. Banks and brokerage firms, already very security-conscious, are among the companies that offer these sites. Independent aggregation services include Yodlee (www.yodlee.com) and 1View Network (www.1viewnetwork.com).

HOTLINKS

Superstar Investor provides descriptive summaries and more than 21,000 links to the best investing sites on the Internet. The Investsearch Directory guide for Online investing provides basic contact information for over 60,000 service and products of interest to investors and traders.

www.superstarinvestor.com
investsearch.com

TABLE 3.4 Popular Investment Web Sites

The following Web sites are just a few of the thousands of sites that provide investing information. Unless otherwise mentioned, all are free.

Web Site	Description
Financial Portals	
America Online (www.aol.com)	Offers free Quicken analysis tools. Its Personal Finance channel for subscribers has 14 areas, including market and business news, research, education, tools, message boards, and a stock-trading simulation game. Ease of use is a big plus.
Investorama (www.investorama.com)	Links to 14,000 financial sites; personal homepage; stock power-search feature.
MSN MoneyCentral Investor (www.moneycentral.msn.com)	More editorial content than many sites; good research and interactive tools like Research Wizard; can consolidate accounts in portfolio tracker. (Many tools don't run on Macintosh.)
Motley Fool (www.fool.com)	Comprehensive and entertaining site with educational features, research, news, and message boards. Model portfolios cover a variety of investment strategies. Free but offers premium services such as Portfolio Trade Alerts for $25 a year.
Wall Street City (www.wallstreetcity.com)	For more experienced investors, with live Webcasts of company presentations and analysts' reports; advanced market analysis and stock-screening tools. ProSearch custom screening tool costs $9.95 per month.
Yahoo! Finance (finance.yahoo.com)	Simple design, content-rich; easy to find information quickly. Includes financial news, price quotes, portfolio trackers, bill paying, personalized homepage, and a directory of other major sites.
Yodlee (www.yodlee.com)	Aggregation site that collects financial account data from banking, credit card, brokerage, mutual fund, mileage, and other sites. One-click access saves time; offers e-mail accounts; easy to set up and track finances. Security issues concern potential users; few analytical tools.
Bond Sites	
Investing in Bonds (www.investinginbonds.com)	The Bond Market Association's Web site; good for novice investors. Investing guides, research reports, historical data, and links to other sites. Searchable database.
BondsOnline (www.bondsonline.com)	Comprehensive site for news, education, free research, ratings, and other bond information; strong emphasis on municipal bonds. Searchable database; Some charges for research.
CNNfn Bond Center (www.cnnfn.com/markets/bondcenter)	Individual investors can search for bond-related news, market data, and bond offerings.
Bureau of the Public Debt Online (www.publicdebt.treas.gov)	Run by U.S. Treasury Department; information about U.S. savings bonds and Treasury securities; can also buy Treasury securities online through Treasury Direct program.
Mutual Fund Sites	
Morningstar (www.morningstar.com)	Profiles of over 6,500 funds with ratings; screening tools, portfolio analysis and management; fund manager interviews, e-mail newsletters; educational sections. Advanced screening and analysis tools are $9.95 a month or $99 per year.
Mutual Fund Investor's Center (www.mfea.com)	Not-for-profit, easy-to-navigate site from the Mutual Fund Education Alliance with investor education, search feature, and links to profiles of funds, calculators for retirement, asset allocation, and college planning.
Fund Alarm (www.fundalarm.com)	Takes a different approach and identifies underperforming funds to help investors decide when to sell; alerts investors to fund manager changes. Lively commentary from the site founder, a CPA.
Findafund (www.maxfunds.com)	In addition to the basics, has a tool to compare funds based on stocks they own to build a diversified portfolio.
IndexFunds.com (www.indexfunds.com)	Comprehensive site covering only index funds.
Personal Fund (www.personalfund.com)	Especially popular for its fund expense calculator that shows the true cost of ownership, after fees, brokerage commissions, and taxes. Suggests lower-cost alternatives with similar investment objectives.

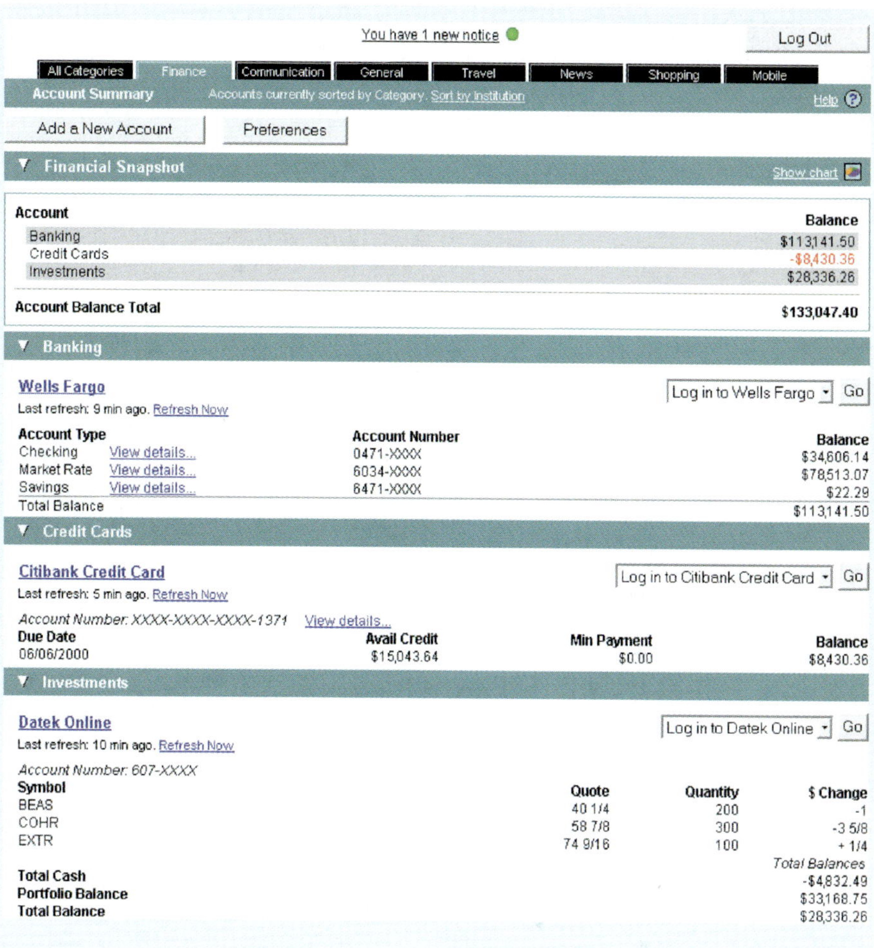

FIGURE 3.3

An Aggregation Site: Bringing It All Together

Yodlee offers users summaries and one-click access to personal account information—including bank balances, credit card balances, investments, travel reservations, e-commerce sites, e-mail, news, and more—from thousands of leading Web sites. (*Source:* www.yodlee.com/demo/demo.html Yodlee Inc., Redwood Shores, California; 650-980-3600; info@yodlee.com)

Bond Sites Although many general investment sites include bond and mutual fund information, you can also visit sites that specialize in these investments. Because Internet bond-trading activity is fairly limited at the present time, there are fewer online resources for individuals. Some brokerage firms are starting to allow clients access to bond information that formerly was restricted to investment professionals. In addition to the sites listed in Table 3.4, other good sites for bond and interest rate information include Briefing.com (www.briefing.com), TheStreet.com (www.thestreet.com), and WSJ.com (wsj.com).

The sites of the major bond ratings agencies—Moody's Investor Services (www.moodys.com), Standard & Poor's (www.standardpoor.com), and Fitch IBCA (www.fitchibca.com)—provide ratings lists, recent ratings changes, and information about how they determine ratings. Moody's free services also include a daily summary of the bond markets and some research reports.

Mutual Fund Sites With thousands of mutual funds, how do you find the ones that match your investment goals? The Internet makes this task much easier, offering many sites with screening tools and worksheets. Almost every major mutual fund family has its own Web site as well. Some allow visitors to

HOTLINKS

FundAlarm is a great source of information on poorly performing funds. The site maintains a list of "3-alarm" funds that have underperformed their benchmarks for the past 12 months, 3 years, and 5 years.

www.fundalarm.com

hear interviews or participate in chats with fund managers. Fidelity (www.fidelity.com) is one of the most comprehensive sites, with educational articles, fund selection tools, fund profiles, and more. Portals and brokerage sites also offer these tools. Table 3.4 includes some independent mutual fund sites that are worth checking out.

International Sites The international reach of the Internet makes it a natural resource to help investors sort out the complexity of global investing, from country research to foreign currency exchange. WorldlyInvestor (www.worldlyinvestor.com) is a comprehensive portal just for international investing. Free newsletters, articles, economic insights, and screening tools for mutual funds and ADRs are among this site's features. For more localized coverage, check out European Investor (www.europeaninvestor.com), UK-Invest (www.uk-invest.com), LatinFocus (www.latin-focus.com), and similar sites for other countries and regions. J.P. Morgan's ADR site (www.adr.com) is a good place to research American depositary receipts and includes analysts' recommendations. For global business news, the *Financial Times* site (www.ft.com) gets high marks. CBS Marketwatch (cbs.marketwatch.com) has good technology and telecommunications news, as well as coverage of international markets and an ADR report.

Investment Discussion Forums Investors can exchange opinions about their favorite stocks and investing strategies at the *online discussion forums* (message boards and chat rooms) found at most major financial Web sites. However, remember that the key word here is opinion. You don't really know much about the qualifications of the person posting the information. *Always do your own research before acting on any hot tips!* The Motley Fool's (www.fool.com) boards are among the most popular, and Fool employees monitor the discussions. Message boards at Yahoo! Finance (finance.yahoo .com) are among the largest online, although many feel that the quality is not so good as at other sites. The Raging Bull (www.ragingbull .com) includes commentary, news, and analysis along with its discussion groups. Technology investors flock to Silicon Investor (www.siliconinvestor .com), a portal site whose high-tech boards are considered among the best. You can read messages free, but to post you'll pay $120 a year or $200 for a lifetime membership.

If you want to check what people are saying about a stock on several different message boards, megasite Cnet (www.cnet.com) makes this easy. It compiles postings from six sites, including Motley Fool, Yahoo!, and Raging Bull. You'll get unlimited messages if you register at Eprobity; otherwise, you only get three per board.

Avoiding Online Scams Just as the Internet increases the amount of information available to all investors, it also makes it easier for scam artists and others to spread false news and manipulate information. Anyone can sound like an investment expert online, posting stock tips with no underlying substance. As mentioned earlier, you may not know the identity of the person touting or panning a stock on the message boards. The person panning a stock could be a disgruntled former employee or a short seller. For example, the ousted former chief executive of San Diego's Avanir Pharmaceuticals posted

INVESTING in action

Have I Got a Tip for You!

On the morning of Friday, August 25, 2000, a Web-based wire service called Internet Wire sent out a press release about Emulex, a Costa Mesa, California, fiber-optics company. The news was not good: The company was restating earnings, the CEO had resigned, and the SEC was launching an accounting investigation. This came as a shock to investors, because just three weeks earlier, Emulex had reported a doubling of revenues and 150% earnings increase. As the news spread to other news services such as Bloomberg, Dow Jones, and CNBC-TV, the company's stock plunged as much as 60% in Nasdaq trading.

Soon after, however, Emulex sent its own press releases to the major newswires, calling the prior news report a hoax and refuting its allegations. By the end of the trading day, Emulex had regained most of the losses.

A few days later the SEC and FBI cracked the case, arresting on securities-fraud charges a 23-year-old former community college student and ex-Internet Wire employee who sent the phony press release. His intent? To get out of a short sale of Emulex stock. He then repurchased the shares while they were down and profited as the price rebounded after the company proved the report false.

Emulex and its investors joined many other victims of phony press releases and false or overhyped message board postings. On Yahoo's boards the most outrageous posters are nicknamed "Yahooligans." Acting on a hot tip without researching a company leads to disaster, as investors who snapped up shares of Uniprime Capital learned. The company they thought was developing a successful cure for AIDS wasn't even a health-care company but a Las Vegas car dealership. Sometimes postings that appear to be from a company insider aren't. Callaway Golf brought court action against a man with 27 aliases who had posted 163 negative messages about Callaway. He turned out to be the chief executive of another golf club manufacturer.

Stock scams like these have increased because the Internet makes it easy to disseminate information rapidly. Fortunately, the SEC has stepped up the speed and level of its enforcement activities. To keep from being a victim yourself, follow the rules of good investing and *always* do your own research.

Sources: "E-Mail Trail Leads to Emulex Hoax Suspect," *Wall Street Journal,* September 21, 2000, pp. C1, C2; Amy Feldman, "The Seedy World of Online Stock Scams," *Money,* February 2000, pp. 143–148; Mike Freeman, "No-Name Critics Give Companies Chat-Room Fits," *San Diego Union Tribune,* April 2, 2000, pp. I-1, I-7; Michael Schroeder and John R. Ehmshwiller, "SEC Acts at Cyberspeed to Halt Suspect Trades," *Wall Street Journal,* August 7, 2000, pp. C1, C15.

negative remarks on stock message boards, adversely affecting share price. The company sued and won a court order prohibiting him from ever posting derogatory statements about the company on any Internet message boards.

In the fast-paced online environment, two types of scams turn up frequently: "pump-and-dump" schemes and get-rich-quick scams. In pump-and-dump schemes, promoters hype stocks, quickly send the prices sky-high, and then dump them at inflated prices. In get-rich-quick scams, promoters sell worthless investments to naïve buyers. One well-publicized pump-and-dump scheme demonstrates how easy it is to use the Internet to promote stocks. In September 2000, the SEC caught a 15-year-old boy who had made over $270,000 by promoting small-company stocks. The self-taught young investor would buy a block of a company's shares and then send out a barrage of false and/or misleading e-mail messages and message board postings singing the praises of that stock and the company's prospects. Once this misinformation pushed up the stock price, he sold and moved on to a new target company. His postings were so articulate that others at Silicon Investor's message boards thought he was a 40-year-old. The *Investing in Action* box on page 75 describes other online hoaxes and how they were shut down.

To crack down on cyber-fraud, the SEC created the Office of Internet Enforcement. The agency now has 15 staff members and several regional offices that quickly investigate reports of suspected hoaxes and prosecute the offenders. Former SEC Chairman Arthur Levitt cautions investors to remember that the Internet is basically another way to send and receive information, one that has no controls for accuracy or truthfulness. The SEC Web site (www.sec.gov/investor/online/scams.htm) includes tips to avoid investment scams. Three key questions that investors should ask are:

- *Is the stock registered?* Check the SEC's EDGAR database (www.sec.gov/edgar.shtml) and with your state securities regulator (www.nasaa.org).
- *Who is making the sales pitch?* Make sure the seller is licensed in your state. Check with the NASD for any record of complaints or fraud.
- *Is it too good to be true?* Then it probably is. Just being on the Web doesn't mean it's legitimate.

Another place to check on possible frauds is Stock Detective, a section of the Financial Web portal site (www.financialweb.com/skdindex.asp) that investigates suspicious stocks and reports on SEC activities against investment fraud.

Understanding Market Averages and Indexes

LG 2

The investment information we have discussed in this chapter helps investors understand when the economy is moving up or down and how individual investments have performed. Investors can use this and other information to formulate expectations about future investment performance. It is also important to know whether market behavior is favorable or unfavorable. The ability to interpret various market measures should help you to select and time investment actions.

A widely used way to assess the behavior of securities markets is to study the performance of market averages and indexes. These measures allow you conveniently to (1) gauge general market conditions, (2) compare your portfolio's performance to that of a large, diversified (market) portfolio, and (3) study market cycles, trends, and behaviors in order to forecast future market behavior. Here we discuss key measures of stock and bond market activity. In later chapters, we will discuss averages and indexes associated with other investment vehicles. Like price quotations, these measures of market performance are available at many Web sites.

Stock Market Averages and Indexes

averages
numbers used to measure the general behavior of stock prices by reflecting the arithmetic average price behavior of a representative group of stocks at a given point in time.

Stock market averages and indexes measure the general behavior of stock prices over time. Although the terms *average* and *index* tend to be used interchangeably when people discuss market behavior, technically they are different types of measures. **Averages** reflect the arithmetic average price

indexes
numbers used to measure the general behavior of stock prices by measuring the current price behavior of a representative group of stocks in relation to a base value set at an earlier point in time.

behavior of a representative group of stocks at a given point in time. **Indexes** measure the current price behavior of a representative group of stocks in relation to a base value set at an earlier point in time.

Averages and indexes provide a convenient method of capturing the general mood of the market. They also can be compared at different points in time to assess the relative strength or weakness of the market. Current and recent values of the key averages and indexes are quoted daily in the financial news, in most local newspapers, and on many radio and television news programs. Figure 3.4, a version of which is published daily in the *Wall Street Journal*, provides a summary and statistics on the major stock market averages and indexes. Let's look at the key averages and indexes listed there.

Dow Jones Industrial Average (DJIA)
a stock market average made up of 30 high-quality stocks selected for total market value and broad public ownership and believed to reflect overall market activity.

The Dow Jones Averages Dow Jones & Company, publisher of the *Wall Street Journal*, prepares five stock averages. The most popular is the **Dow Jones Industrial Average (DJIA)**. This average is made up of 30 stocks selected for total market value and broad public ownership. The group consists of high-quality stocks whose behaviors are believed to reflect overall market activity. The box within Figure 3.5 lists the stocks currently included in the DJIA.

Occasionally, a merger, bankruptcy, or extreme lack of activity causes a change in the makeup of the average. Citicorp's merger with Travelers moved it (Citigroup) to the DJIA. Changes to the 30 stocks also occur when Dow Jones believes that the average does not reflect the broader market. For example, in recent years technology companies such as Microsoft and Intel and financial services companies such as American Express replaced Allied Signal, Goodyear, and Union Carbide; Home Depot replaced Sears. When a new stock is added, the average is readjusted so that it continues to behave in a manner consistent with the immediate past.

The value of the DJIA is calculated each business day by substituting the *closing share prices* of each of the 30 stocks in the average into the following equation:

Equation 3.1

$$\text{DJIA} = \frac{\begin{matrix}\text{Closing share price} \\ \text{of stock 1}\end{matrix} + \begin{matrix}\text{Closing share price} \\ \text{of stock 2}\end{matrix} + \cdots + \begin{matrix}\text{Closing share price} \\ \text{of stock 30}\end{matrix}}{\text{DJIA divisor}}$$

The value of the DJIA is merely the sum of the closing share prices of the 30 stocks included in it, divided by a "divisor." The purpose of the divisor is to adjust for any stock splits, company changes, or other events that have occurred over time. Without the divisor, whose calculation is very complex, the DJIA value would be totally distorted. The divisor makes it possible to use the DJIA to make time-series comparisons. On September 28, 2000, the sum of the closing prices of the 30 industrials was 1829.27, which, when divided by the divisor of 0.169, resulted in a DJIA value of 10824.06. The current divisor is included in the *Wall Street Journal* table "Dow Jones Averages Hour by Hour," which is printed on the same page as the chart with the averages.

Because the DJIA results from summing the prices of the 30 stocks, higher-priced stocks tend to affect the index more than do lower-priced stocks. For example, a 5% change in the price of a \$50 stock (i.e., \$2.50) has less impact on the index than a 5% change in a \$100 stock (i.e., \$5.00). In spite of this and other criticisms leveled at the DJIA, it remains the most widely cited stock market indicator.

FIGURE 3.4

Major Stock Market Averages and Indexes

The "Stock Market Data Bank"summarizes the key stock market averages and indexes. It includes statistics showing the change from the previous day, the annual change, and the year-to-date change.
(*Source: Wall Street Journal,* September 29, 2000, p. C2. Reprinted by permission of the *Wall Street Journal.* © Dow Jones & Company, Inc. All rights reserved.)

STOCK MARKET DATA BANK 9/28/00

MAJOR INDEXES

†12-MO HIGH	†12-MO LOW		DAILY HIGH	DAILY LOW	CLOSE	NET CHG	% CHG	†12-MO CHG	% CHG	FROM 12/31	% CHG
DOW JONES AVERAGES											
11722.98	9796.03	**30 Industrials**	10856.25	10623.18	10824.06	+ 195.70	+ 1.84	+ 487.11	+ 4.71	− 673.06	− 5.85
3099.67	2263.59	**20 Transportation**	2577.73	2513.63	2572.32	+ 57.79	+ 2.30	− 336.84	− 11.58	− 404.88	− 13.60
397.04	269.20	**15 Utilities**	398.65	391.67	396.37	+ 5.24	+ 1.34	+ 98.11	+ 32.89	+ 113.01	+ 39.88
3305.46	2751.55	**65 Composite**	3216.10	3155.10	3211.63	+ 56.79	+ 1.80	+ 198.62	+ 6.59	− 2.75	− 0.09
364.71	285.95	**DJ US Total Mkt**	345.15	335.80	344.69	+ 7.88	+ 2.34	+ 53.14	+ 18.22	+ 3.13	+ 0.91
NEW YORK STOCK EXCHANGE											
677.58	576.17	**Composite**	669.08	655.94	667.75	+ 11.70	+ 1.78	+ 74.96	+ 12.65	+ 17.45	+ 2.68
851.94	728.87	**Industrials**	828.46	815.18	826.38	+ 10.73	+ 1.32	+ 80.07	+ 10.73	− 1.83	− 0.22
519.96	443.98	**Utilities**	467.73	451.61	467.34	+ 15.26	+ 3.38	− 14.64	− 3.04	− 43.81	− 8.57
493.03	353.51	**Transportation**	411.74	401.58	410.84	+ 8.47	+ 2.11	− 37.78	− 8.42	− 55.86	− 11.97
634.16	442.71	**Finance**	628.25	611.13	626.56	+ 15.43	+ 2.52	+ 147.62	+ 30.82	+ 109.95	+ 21.28
STANDARD & POOR'S INDEXES											
1527.46	1247.41	**500 Index**	1461.65	1425.79	1458.29	+ 31.72	+ 2.22	+ 175.58	+ 13.69	− 10.96	− 0.75
1917.64	1544.13	**Industrials**	1746.52	1704.33	1742.62	+ 36.96	+ 2.17	+ 161.31	+ 10.20	− 99.30	− 5.39
338.42	215.62	**Utilities**	337.30	333.51	336.99	+ 3.48	+ 1.04	+ 94.22	+ 38.81	+ 109.77	+ 48.31
548.60	369.50	**400 MidCap**	542.98	528.23	542.35	+ 13.31	+ 2.52	+ 161.76	+ 42.50	+ 97.68	+ 21.97
225.12	168.96	**600 SmallCap**	219.15	212.04	219.03	+ 6.86	+ 3.23	+ 42.83	+ 24.31	+ 21.24	+ 10.74
324.40	262.26	**1500 Index**	312.42	304.75	311.85	+ 6.92	+ 2.27	+ 42.40	+ 15.74	+ 2.96	+ 0.96
NASDAQ STOCK MARKET											
5048.62	2688.18	**Composite**	3778.38	3626.55	3778.32	+ 122.02	+ 3.34	+ 1032.16	+ 37.59	− 290.99	− 7.15
4704.73	2362.11	**Nasdaq 100**	3725.75	3556.34	3725.15	+ 153.25	+ 4.29	+ 1317.25	+ 54.71	+ 17.32	+ 0.47
2841.00	1549.93	**Industrials**	2084.53	2005.66	2084.53	+ 68.64	+ 3.40	+ 475.14	+ 29.52	− 154.44	− 6.90
2075.12	1602.08	**Insurance**	1881.65	1863.75	1879.85	+ 4.85	+ 0.26	− 153.15	− 7.53	− 16.43	− 0.87
1837.10	1340.36	**Banks**	1784.44	1739.05	1783.47	+ 41.88	+ 2.40	+ 100.32	+ 5.96	+ 92.18	+ 5.45
2964.66	1448.32	**Computer**	2217.78	2121.76	2217.38	+ 70.40	+ 3.28	+ 713.59	+ 47.45	− 108.02	− 4.65
1230.06	616.80	**Telecommunications**	731.80	689.85	731.73	+ 27.51	+ 3.91	+ 106.94	+ 17.12	− 283.67	− 27.94
OTHERS											
1036.40	774.49	**Amex Composite**	940.19	926.18	939.80	+ 11.37	+ 1.22	+ 151.57	+ 19.23	+ 62.83	+ 7.16
813.71	646.79	**Russell 1000**	785.46	765.38	784.09	+ 17.68	+ 2.31	+ 120.26	+ 18.12	+ 16.12	+ 2.10
606.12	408.90	**Russell 2000**	524.09	507.62	523.81	+ 15.68	+ 3.09	+ 96.51	+ 22.59	+ 19.06	+ 3.78
844.78	667.03	**Russell 3000**	811.99	791.30	811.03	+ 18.70	+ 2.36	+ 126.23	+ 18.43	+ 17.72	+ 2.23
439.78	394.35	**Value-Line** (geom.)	422.95	413.81	422.54	+ 8.51	+ 2.06	+ 4.89	+ 1.17	− 8.50	− 1.97
14751.64	11446.60	**Wilshire 5000**	....	....	13786.28	+ 321.01	+ 2.38	+ 2072.48	+ 17.69	− 26.39	− 0.19

†-Based on comparable trading day in preceding year.

The actual value of the DJIA is meaningful only when compared to earlier values. For example, the DJIA on September 28, 2000, closed at 10824. This value is meaningful only when compared to the previous day's closing value of 10629, a change of 1.84%. Many people mistakenly believe that one DJIA "point" equals $1 in the value of an average share. Actually, one point currently translates into about 0.56 cents in average share value. Figure 3.5 shows the DJIA over the 6-month period March 31, 2000, to September 29, 2000. During this 6-month period, the stock market remained generally bullish, although it experienced two significant dips. It started at 11200 and dropped to 10300 in mid-April. During the following 90 days, the market was somewhat sideways until it increased steadily from late July to early September, when it again began to slide.

The four other Dow Jones averages are the transportation, utilities, composite, and U.S. total market The *Dow Jones Transportation Average* is based on 20 stocks, including railroads, airlines, freight forwarders, and mixed transportation companies. The *Dow Jones Utilities Average* is computed using 15 public utility stocks. The *Dow Jones 65 Stocks Composite Average* is made up of the 30 industrials, the 20 transportations, and the 15 utilities. The *Dow Jones U.S. Total Market Index* is a market-weighted index. "Market-

FIGURE 3.5

The DJIA from March 31, 2000, to September 28, 2000

During this 6-month period, the stock market remained generally bullish but experienced two significant dips—one in April and one in September. (*Source: Wall Street Journal,* September 29, 2000, p. C3. Reprinted by permission of the *Wall Street Journal.* © Dow Jones & Company, Inc. All rights reserved.)

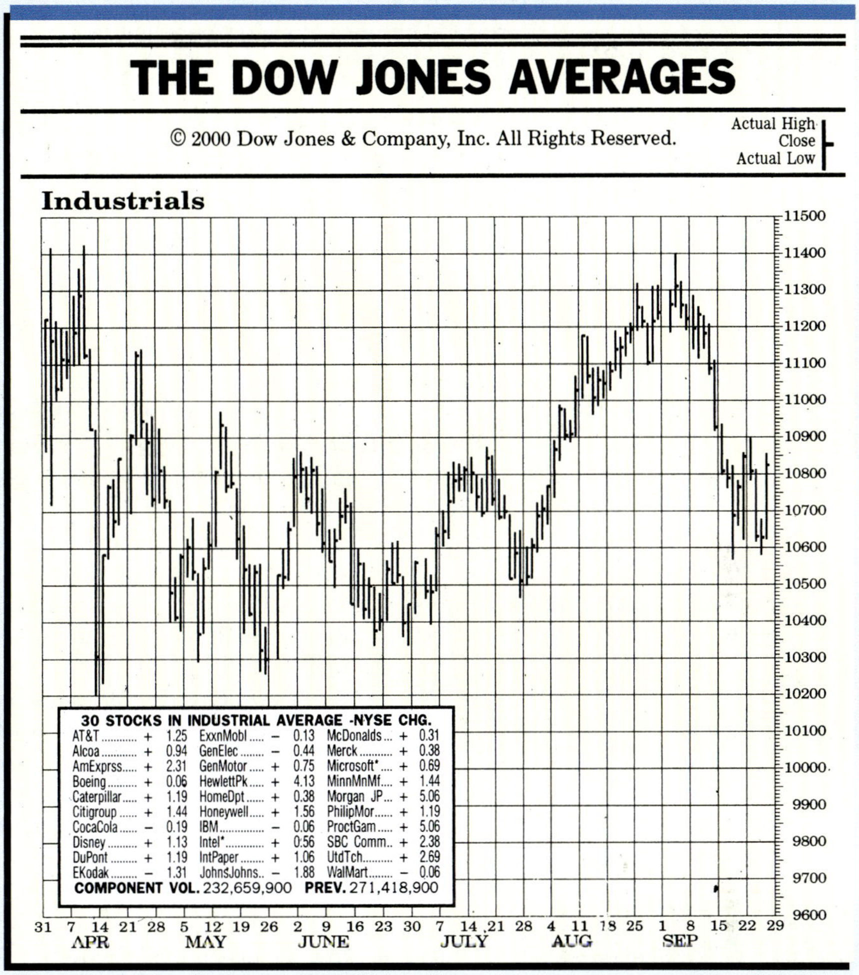

weighted" means that companies with large total market values have the most effect on the index's movement. The Dow Jones U.S. Total Market Index reflects 95% of the total market value for large-sized, medium-sized, and small-sized companies. The base value of the index is 100, which represents its value on June 30, 1997. Like the DJIA, each of the other Dow Jones averages is calculated using a divisor to allow for continuity of the average over time. The transportation, utilities, and 65-stocks composite are often cited in the financial news along with the DJIA, as shown in Figure 3.4.

In early 1999, Dow Jones introduced a new measure to monitor performance of U.S. Internet stocks. The *Dow Jones Internet Index (DJII)*, a 40-stock benchmark, includes only companies that generate a minimum of 50 percent of their revenues from the Internet. It has two component indexes, "Internet Commerce" and "Internet Services."

Standard & Poor's indexes true indexes that measure the current price of a group of stocks relative to a base (set in the 1941–1943 period) having an index value of 10.

Standard & Poor's Indexes Standard & Poor's Corporation, another leading financial publisher, publishes six major common stock indexes. One oft-cited S&P index is the 500-stock composite index. Unlike the Dow Jones averages, **Standard & Poor's indexes** are true indexes. They are calculated each business day by substituting the *closing market value of each stock* (closing price × number of shares outstanding) into the following equation:

Equation 3.2

$$\text{S\&P Index} = \frac{\begin{matrix}\text{Current closing}\\ \text{market value}\\ \text{of stock 1}\end{matrix} + \begin{matrix}\text{Current closing}\\ \text{market value}\\ \text{of stock 2}\end{matrix} + \cdots + \begin{matrix}\text{Current closing}\\ \text{market value}\\ \text{of last stock}\end{matrix}}{\begin{matrix}\text{Base period}\\ \text{closing market}\\ \text{value of stock 1}\end{matrix} + \begin{matrix}\text{Base period}\\ \text{closing market}\\ \text{value of stock 2}\end{matrix} + \cdots + \begin{matrix}\text{Base period}\\ \text{closing market}\\ \text{value of last stock}\end{matrix}} \times 10$$

The value of the S&P index is found by dividing the sum of the market values of all stocks included in the index by the market value of the stocks in the base period and then multiplying the resulting quotient by 10, the base value of the S&P indexes. Most S&P indexes are calculated in a similar fashion. The main differences lie in the stocks included in the index, the base period, and the base value of the index. For example, on September 28, 2000, the ratio of the closing market values of the S&P 500 composite stocks to the 1941–1943 base-period closing market values was 145.829, which, when multiplied by the base value of the S&P index of 10, results in an index value of 1458.29 (as shown in Figure 3.4).

HOT LINKS

The Barra site contains the S&P/BARRA family of indexes. These include returns over various periods plus fundamental characteristics and sector weights for any date, back to the index inception.

www.barra.com/research_library

Certain of the S&P indexes contain many more shares than the Dow averages do, and all of them are based on *market values* rather than *share prices*. Therefore, many investors feel that the S&P indexes provide a more broad-based and representative measure of general market conditions than do the Dow averages. Although some technical computational problems exist with these indexes, they are widely used—frequently as a basis for estimating the "market return," an important concept that will be introduced in Chapter 4.

Like the Dow averages, the S&P indexes are meaningful only when compared to values in other time periods or to the 1941–1943 base-period value of 10. For example, the September 28, 2000, value of the S&P 500 Stock Composite Index of 1458.29 means that the market values of the stocks in the index increased by a factor of 145.829 (1458.29 ÷ 10) since the 1941–1943 period. The September 28, 2000, market value of the stocks in the index was 1.17 times the lowest index value of 1247.41 in the preceding 365-day period (1458.29 ÷ 1247.41), and hence represented an increase of 17%.

INVESTOR FACTS

ELECTION RETURNS—During election years, the stock market tends to rise substantially more than the average annual increase. Look at the market returns for U.S. presidential elections since 1976: In every year except 2000—a unique election in every way!—the market rose substantially more than the average.

Year and Election Winner	S&P 500 Return for the Year
2000–George W. Bush	−10.1%
1996–Bill Clinton	+16.0%
1992–Bill Clinton	+17.7%
1988–George H. Bush	+12.4%
1984–Ronald Reagan	+25.8%
1980–Ronald Reagan	+19.1%
1976–Jimmy Carter	+15.6%

The eight major common stock indexes published by Standard & Poor's are

- The *industrials index,* made up of the common stock of 400 industrial firms.
- The *transportation index,* which includes the stock of 20 transportation companies.
- The *utilities index,* made up of 40 public utility stocks.
- The *financials index,* which contains 40 financial stocks.
- The *composite index* (described above), which consists of the total of 500 stocks that make up the industrials, transportation, utilities, and financials indexes.

- The *midcap index,* made up of the stocks of 400 medium-sized companies.
- The *smallcap index,* made up of 600 small-sized companies.
- The *1500 index,* which includes all stocks in the composite, midcap, and smallcap indexes.

The S&P midcap, smallcap, and 1500 indexes are the newest. Their popularity results from strong investor interest in the stocks of medium-sized and small companies. Like the Dow averages, many of the S&P indexes are frequently quoted in the financial news, as shown in Figure 3.4.

Although the Dow Jones averages and S&P indexes tend to behave in a similar fashion over time, their day-to-day magnitude and even direction (up or down) can differ significantly because the Dows are averages and the S&Ps are indexes.

NYSE, AMEX, and Nasdaq Indexes Three indexes measure the daily results of the New York Stock Exchange (NYSE), the American Stock Exchange (AMEX), and the National Association of Securities Dealers Automated Quotation (Nasdaq) system. Each reflects the movement of stocks listed on its exchange. The **NYSE composite index** includes all of the 3,000 or so stocks listed on the "Big Board." The index's base of 50 reflects the December 31, 1965, value of stocks listed on the NYSE. In addition to the composite index, the NYSE publishes indexes for industrials, utilities, transportation, and finance subgroups. The behavior of the NYSE industrial index is normally similar to that of the DJIA and the S&P 500 indexes.

NYSE composite index
measure of the current price behavior of the stocks listed on the NYSE, relative to a base of 50 set at December 31, 1965.

The **AMEX composite index** reflects the price of all shares traded on the American Stock Exchange, relative to a base of 100 set at August 31, 1973. Although it does not always closely follow the S&P and NYSE indexes, the AMEX index tends to move in the general direction they do.

AMEX composite index
measure of the current price behavior of the stocks listed on the AMEX, relative to a base of 100 set at August 31, 1973.

The **Nasdaq indexes** reflect over-the-counter market activity. They are based on a value of 100 set at February 5, 1971. The most comprehensive of the Nasdaq indexes is the OTC *composite index,* which is calculated using the 6,400 or so domestic common stocks traded on the Nasdaq system. Also important is the *Nasdaq 100,* which includes the top 100 nonfinancial companies listed on Nasdaq. The other five commonly quoted Nasdaq indexes are the *industrials,* the *insurance,* the *banks,* the *computer,* and the *telecommunications indexes.* Although their degrees of responsiveness may vary, the Nasdaq indexes tend to move in the same direction at the same time as the other major indexes.

Nasdaq indexes
measures of current price behavior of securities sold OTC, relative to a base of 100 set at February 5, 1971.

Value Line Indexes Value Line publishes a number of stock indexes constructed by equally weighting the price of each stock included. This is accomplished by considering only the percentage changes in stock prices. This approach eliminates the effects of differing market price and total market value on the relative importance of each stock in the index. The **Value Line composite index** includes the approximately 1,700 stocks in the *Value Line Investment Survey* that are traded on the NYSE, AMEX, and OTC markets. The base of 100 reflects the stock prices on June 30, 1961. In addition to its composite index, Value Line publishes indexes for *industrials, rails,* and *utilities.*

Value Line composite index
stock index that reflects the percentage changes in share price of about 1,700 stocks, relative to a base of 100 set at June 30, 1961.

Other Averages and Indexes A number of other indexes are available. The **Wilshire 5000 index,** published by Wilshire Associates, Inc., is reported daily in the *Wall Street Journal.* It represents the total dollar value (in billions of dollars) of 5,000 actively traded stocks, including all those on the NYSE and the AMEX in addition to active OTC stocks. Frank Russell Company, a pension advisory firm, publishes three primary indexes. The *Russell 1000* includes the 1,000 largest companies, the *Russell 2000* includes 2,000 small companies, and the *Russell 3000* includes the 3,000 largest U.S. companies. *Barron's* publishes a 50-stock average. The *New York Times* publishes its own average, which is similar to the Dow Jones averages. Moody's Investor Services prepares market indicators for a variety of groupings of common stock.

Wilshire 5000 index
measure of the total dollar value (in billions of dollars) of 5,000 actively traded stocks, including all those on the NYSE and the AMEX in addition to active OTC stocks.

In addition, the *Wall Street Journal* publishes a number of global and foreign stock market indexes in Section C. These indexes are summarized in the "International Stocks" section on the first page and are listed in greater detail in "World Stock Markets." Included are Dow Jones indexes for countries in the Americas, Latin America, Europe, South Africa, and the Asia-Pacific region that are based on a value of 100 set at December 31, 1991. More than 20 foreign stock market indexes and the Morgan Stanley Indexes are also given for major countries, including a *World Index* and the *Europe/Australia/Far East (EAFE) Index*. Each of the Morgan Stanley Indexes is calculated in local currencies and based on a value of 100 set at December 31, 1969. Like the purely domestic averages and indexes, these international averages and indexes measure the general price behavior of the stocks that are listed and traded in the given market. Useful comparisons of the market averages and indexes over time and across markets are often made to assess both trends and relative strengths of foreign markets throughout the world.

Bond Market Indicators

A number of indicators are available for assessing the general behavior of the bond markets. A "Bond Market Data Bank" that includes a wealth of return and price index data for various types of bonds and various domestic and foreign markets is published daily in the *Wall Street Journal*. However, there are fewer indicators of overall bond market behavior than of stock market behavior. The key measures of overall U.S. bond market behavior are bond yields, the Dow Jones bond averages, and the New York Stock Exchange bond diary.

Bond Yields A **bond yield** is a summary measure of the total return an investor would receive on a bond if it were purchased at its current price and held to maturity. Bond yields are reported as annual rates of return. For example, a bond with a yield of 8.50% would provide its owner with a total return from periodic interest and capital gain (or loss) that would be equivalent to an 8.50% annual rate of earnings on the amount invested, if the bond were purchased at its current price and held to maturity.

bond yield
summary measure of the total return an investor would receive on a bond if it were purchased at its current price and held to maturity; reported as an annual rate of return.

Typically, bond yields are quoted for a group of bonds that are similar with respect to type and quality. For example, *Barron's* quotes the yields on the Dow Jones bond averages of 10 utilities, 10 industrials, and 20 bond composites, as well as for specified grades of corporate bonds. In addition, like the *Wall Street Journal,* it quotes numerous other bond indexes and yields, including those for Treasury and municipal bonds. Similar bond yield data are available from S&P, Moody's, and the Federal Reserve. Like stock market averages and indexes, bond yield data are especially useful when viewed over time.

Dow Jones bond averages mathematical averages of the *closing prices* for groups of utility, industrial, and composite bonds.

Dow Jones Bond Averages The **Dow Jones bond averages** include a utility, an industrial, and a composite bond average. Each average reflects the simple mathematical average of the *closing prices*, rather than yields, for each group of bonds included. The utility bond average is based on the closing prices of 10 utility bonds; the industrial bond average is based on the closing prices of 10 industrial bonds; and the composite bond average is based on the closing prices of 10 utility and 10 industrial bonds.

Like bond price quotations, the bond averages are presented in terms of the percentage of face value at which the bond sells. For example, the September 28, 2000, Dow Jones 20-bond composite average of 95.97 indicated that, on average, bonds were on the day reported selling for 95.97 percent of their par or face value. For a $1,000 bond, the average price of an issue would equal about $959.70. The Dow Jones bond averages are published daily in the *Wall Street Journal* and summarized weekly in *Barron's*. Similar bond market indexes, prepared primarily by leading investment bankers such as Lehman Brothers and Merrill Lynch, are also published daily in the *Wall Street Journal* and summarized weekly in *Barron's*.

NYSE Bond Diary The New York Stock Exchange is the dominant organized exchange on which bonds are traded. Thus certain summary statistics on daily bond-trading activity on the NYSE provide useful insight into the behavior of the bond markets in general. These statistics include the number of issues traded and the number that advanced, declined, or remained unchanged. On September 28, 2000, 136 domestic issues were traded; 64 advanced, 53 declined, and 19 remained unchanged. Of the issues traded, 6 achieved a new price high for the year, and 4 fell to new price lows. Total sales volume was $7,489,000. The NYSE bond diary is published daily in the *Wall Street Journal* and summarized weekly in *Barron's*.

Making Securities Transactions

LG 3 LG 4

Now that you know how to find information to help you locate attractive security investments, you should understand how to make securities transactions. Whether you decide to start a self-directed online investment program or to use a traditional stockbroker, you must first open an account with a stockbroker to buy and sell securities. In this section we will look at the role stockbrokers play and how that role has changed with the growth in online investing. We will also explain the basic types of orders you can place, the procedures required to make regular and online securities transactions, the costs of investment transactions, and investor protection.

The Role of Stockbrokers

stockbrokers individuals licensed by both the SEC and the securities exchanges to facilitate transactions between buyers and sellers of securities.

Stockbrokers—also called *account executives, investment executives,* and *financial consultants*—act as intermediaries between buyers and sellers of securities. They typically charge a commission to facilitate these securities transactions. Stockbrokers must be licensed by both the SEC and the securities exchanges on which they place orders and must follow the ethical guidelines of those bodies.

Although the procedure for executing orders on organized exchanges may differ from that in the OTC market, it starts the same way: An investor places an order with his or her stockbroker. The broker works for a brokerage firm that owns seats on the organized securities exchanges, and members of the securities exchange execute orders that the brokers in the firm's various sales offices transmit to them. For example, the largest U.S. brokerage firm, Merrill Lynch, transmits orders for listed securities from its offices in most major cities throughout the country to the main office of Merrill Lynch and then to the floor of the stock exchanges (NYSE and AMEX), where Merrill Lynch exchange members execute them. Confirmation of the order goes back to the broker placing the order, who relays it to the customer. This process can take a matter of seconds with the use of sophisticated telecommunications networks and Internet trading.

For an over-the-counter securities transaction, brokerage firms transmit orders to market makers, who are dealers in the OTC market specializing in that security. As we learned in Chapter 2, the Nasdaq system, along with the available information on who makes markets in certain securities, enables brokers to execute orders in OTC securities. Normally, OTC transactions are executed rapidly, because market makers maintain inventories of the securities in which they deal.

INVESTOR FACTS

TOO MUCH PAPERWORK— Wasn't the computer supposed to cut down on paperwork? Tell that to the stock brokerage firms and mutual fund companies that send you monthly and year-end statements, confirmations of buy and sell orders, newsletters, and so on. What can you throw away? Keep your most recent brokerage statements and the year-end documents (which you'll need to prepare your tax returns). Check over the monthly statements to make sure they're correct—and then toss them when the next month's statements arrive.

street name
stock certificates issued in the brokerage firm's name but held in trust for its client, who actually owns them.

Brokerage Services The primary activity of stockbrokers is to execute clients' purchase and sale transactions at the best possible price. Brokerage firms will hold the client's security certificates for safekeeping; the stocks kept by the firm in this manner are said to be held in **street name**. Because the brokerage house issues the securities in its own name and holds them in trust for the client (rather than issuing them in the client's name), the firm can transfer the securities at the time of sale without the client's signature. Street name is actually a common way of buying securities, because many investors do not want to be bothered with the handling and safekeeping of stock certificates. In such cases, the brokerage firm records the details of the client's transaction and keeps track of his or her investments through a series of bookkeeping entries. Dividends and notices received by the broker are forwarded to the client who owns the securities.

Stockbrokers also offer clients a variety of other services. For example, the brokerage firm normally provides free information about investments. Quite often, the firm has a research staff that periodically issues analyses of economic, market, industry, or company behavior and makes recommendations to buy or sell certain securities. As a client of a large brokerage firm, you can expect to receive regular bulletins on market activity and possibly a recommended investment list. You will also receive a statement describing your transactions for the month and showing commission and interest charges, dividends and interest received, and detailed listings of your current holdings.

Today, most brokerage firms will invest surplus cash left in a customer's account in a money market mutual fund, allowing the customer to earn a reasonable rate of interest on these balances. Such arrangements help the investor earn as much as possible on temporarily idle funds.

Types of Brokerage Firms Just a few years ago, there were three distinct types of brokerage firms: full-service, discount, and online. No longer are the lines between these categories clear-cut. Most brokerage firms, even the most traditional ones, now offer online services to compete with the increasingly popular online firms. And many discount brokers now offer services, like research reports for clients, that were once available only from a full-service broker.

full-service broker
broker who, in addition to executing clients' transactions, provides them with a full array of brokerage services.

The traditional broker, or so-called **full-service broker**, in addition to executing clients' transactions, offers investors a full array of brokerage services: providing investment advice and information, holding securities in street name, offering online brokerage services, and extending margin loans. Investors who wish merely to make transactions and are not interested in taking advantage of other services should consider either a discount broker or an online broker.

discount broker
broker who charges low commissions to make transactions for customers but provides little or no free research information or investment advice.

Discount brokers focus primarily on making transactions for customers. They charge low commissions and provide little or no free research information or investment advice. The investor calls a toll-free number or visits the broker's Web site to initiate a transaction, and the discount broker confirms the transaction by phone, e-mail, or regular mail. Discount brokers that charge the lowest commissions and provide virtually no services are commonly referred to as *deep discounters*. However, brokers like Charles Schwab, the first discount broker, now offer many of the same services that you'd find at a full-commission broker. Other discounters still focus on transactions.

online broker
typically a deep-discount broker through which investors can execute trades electronically online via a commercial service or on the Internet.

Online brokers, also called *Internet brokers* and *electronic brokers*, are typically deep-discount brokers through which investors can execute trades electronically online via a commercial service or on the Internet. The investor accesses the online broker's Web site to open an account, review the commission schedule, or see a demonstration of the available transactional services and procedures. Confirmation of electronic trades can take as little as 10 seconds, and most trades occur within 1 minute. Some firms, such as Ameritrade, E*Trade, and Datek Online, operate only online. In response to the rapid growth of online investors, particularly among affluent young investors who enjoy surfing the Web, most brokerage firms now offer online trading.

The rapidly growing volume of business done by discount and online brokers attests to their success. Today, many banks and savings institutions are making discount and online brokerage services available to their depositors who wish to buy stocks, bonds, mutual funds, and other investment vehicles. Some of the major full-service, discount, and online brokers are listed in Table 3.5.

Selecting a Stockbroker If you decide to start your investing activities with the assistance of either a full-service or discount stockbroker, select the person you believe best understands your investment goals. Choosing a broker whose disposition toward investing is similar to yours is the best way to establish a solid working relationship. Your broker should also make you aware of investment possibilities that are consistent with your objectives and attitude toward risk.

TABLE 3.5 Major Full-Service, Discount, and Online Brokers

Type of Broker		
Full Service	Discount	Online-Only
Charles Schwab	Fidelity Brokerage Services	Ameritrade
Merrill Lynch	Jack White & Company	Datek Online
Morgan Stanley Dean Witter	Kennedy, Cabot & Co.	DLJ Direct
Prudential Securities	Muriel Siebert & Co.	E*Trade
Salomon Smith Barney	Quick & Reilly	National Discount Brokers
UBS PaineWebber	TD Waterhouse	Scottrade

You should also consider the cost and types of services available from the firm with which the broker is affiliated, to receive the best service at the lowest possible cost to you. The basic discount brokerage service is primarily transactional, and the online brokerage service is *purely* transactional. Contact with a broker, advice, and research assistance generally are available only at a higher price. Investors must weigh the added commissions they pay a full-service broker against the value of the advice they receive, because the amount of available advice is the only major difference among online, discount, and full-service brokers.

Referrals from friends or business associates are a good way to begin your search for a stockbroker. Don't forget to consider the investing style and goals of the person making the recommendation. However, it is not important—and often not even advisable—to know your stockbroker personally. And in this age of online brokers, you may never meet your broker face to face! A strictly business relationship eliminates the possibility that social concerns will interfere with the achievement of your investment goals. This does not mean that your broker's sole interest should be commissions. Responsible brokers do not engage in **churning**—that is, causing excessive trading of their clients' accounts to increase commissions. Churning is both illegal and unethical under SEC and exchange rules. However, it is often difficult to prove.

churning
an illegal and unethical practice engaged in by a broker to increase commissions by causing excessive trading of clients' accounts.

Opening an Account To open an account, the customer fills out various documents that establish a legal relationship between the customer and the brokerage firm. A signature card and a personal data card provide the information needed to identify the client's account. The stockbroker must also have a reasonable understanding of a client's personal financial situation to assess his or her investment goals—and to be sure that the client can pay for the securities purchased. The client also provides the broker with instructions regarding the transfer and custody of securities. Customers who wish to borrow money to make transactions must establish a margin account (described below). If the customer is acting as a custodian, trustee, or executor or is a corporation, the brokerage firm will require additional documents.

Investors may have accounts with more than one stockbroker. Many investors establish accounts at different types of firms to obtain the benefit and opinions of a diverse group of brokers and to reduce their overall cost of making purchase and sale transactions. You can even open an account online at some brokerage firms.

Next you must select the type of account best suited to your needs. We will briefly consider several of the more popular types.

Single or Joint A brokerage account may be either single or joint. Joint accounts are most common between husband and wife or parent and child. The account of a minor (a person less than 18 years of age) is a **custodial account**, in which a parent or guardian must be part of all transactions. Regardless of the form of the account, the name(s) of the account holder(s) and an account number are used to identify it.

custodial account
the brokerage account of a minor; requires a parent or guardian to be part of all transactions.

Cash or Margin A **cash account**, the more common type, is one in which the customer can make only cash transactions. Customers can initiate cash transactions via phone or online and are given 3 business days in which to transmit the cash to the brokerage firm. The firm is likewise given 3 business days in

cash account
a brokerage account in which a customer can make only cash transactions.

which to deposit the proceeds from the sale of securities in the customer's cash account.

margin account
a brokerage account in which the customer has been extended borrowing privileges by the brokerage firm.

A **margin account** is an account in which the brokerage firm extends borrowing privileges to a creditworthy customer. By leaving securities with the firm as collateral, the customer can borrow a prespecified proportion of the securities' purchase price. The brokerage firm will, of course, charge the customer a stated rate of interest on borrowings. (The mechanics of margin trading are covered in Chapter 2.)

wrap account
a brokerage account in which customers with large portfolios pay a flat annual fee that covers the cost of a money manager's services and the commissions on all trades.

Wrap The **wrap account** allows brokerage customers with large portfolios (generally $100,000 or more) to shift stock selection decisions conveniently to a professional money manager, either in-house or independent. In return for a flat annual fee equal to between 1% and 3% of the portfolio's total asset value, the brokerage firm helps the investor select a money manager, pays the manager's fee, and executes the money manager's trades. Initially the investor and manager discuss the client's overall goals. Wrap accounts are appealing for a number of reasons other than convenience. The annual fee in most cases covers commissions on all trades, virtually eliminating the chance of the broker churning the account. In addition, the broker monitors the manager's performance and provides the investor with detailed reports, typically quarterly.

odd lot
less than 100 shares of stock.

round lot
100-share units of stock or multiples thereof.

Odd-Lot or Round-Lot Transactions Investors can buy stock in either odd or round lots. An **odd lot** consists of less than 100 shares of a stock. A **round lot** is a 100-share unit or a multiple thereof. You would be dealing in an odd lot if you bought, say, 25 shares of stock but in a round lot if you bought 200 shares. A trade of 225 shares would be a combination of an odd lot and two round lots.

Transactions in odd lots require either additional processing by the brokerage firm or the assistance of a specialist. For odd lots, an added fee—known as an *odd-lot differential*—is tacked on to the normal commission charge, driving up the costs of these small trades. Small investors in the early stages of their investment programs are primarily responsible for odd-lot transactions.

Basic Types of Orders

Investors can use different types of orders to make security transactions. The type placed normally depends on the investor's goals and expectations. The three basic types of orders are the market order, the limit order, and the stop-loss order.

market order
an order to buy or sell stock at the best price available when the order is placed.

Market Order An order to buy or sell stock at the best price available when the investor places the order is a **market order**. It is generally the quickest way to fill orders, because market orders are usually executed as soon as they reach the exchange floor or are received by the dealer. Because of the speed with which market orders are executed, the buyer or seller of a security can be sure that the price at which the order is transacted will be very close to the market price prevailing at the time the order was placed.

limit order
an order to buy at or below a specified price or to sell at or above a specified price.

Limit Order A **limit order** is an order to buy at or below a specified price or to sell at or above a specified price. When the investor places a limit order, the broker transmits it to a specialist dealing in the security. The specialist notes the number of shares and price of the limit order in his or her book and executes the order as soon as the specified market price (or better) exists. The specialist must first satisfy all other orders with precedence—similar orders received earlier, buy orders at a higher specified price, or sell orders at a lower specified price. Investors can place the limit order in one of the following forms:

1. A *fill-or-kill order,* which is canceled if not immediately executed.
2. A *day order,* which if not executed is automatically canceled at the end of the day.
3. A *good-'til-canceled (GTC) order,* which generally remains in effect for 6 months unless executed, canceled, or renewed.

Assume, for example, that you place a limit order to buy, at a limit price of $30, 100 shares of a stock currently selling at $30.50. Once the specialist clears all similar orders received before yours, and once the market price of the stock falls to $30 or less, he or she executes your order. It is possible, of course, that your order might expire (if it is not a GTC order) before the stock price drops to $30.

Although a limit order can be quite effective, it can also keep you from making a transaction. If, for instance, you wish to buy at $30 or less and the stock price moves from its current $30.50 price to $42 while you are waiting, you have missed the opportunity to make a profit of $11.50 per share ($42 − $30.50). If you had placed a *market order* to buy at the best available price ($30.50), the profit of $11.50 would have been yours. Limit orders for the sale of a stock are also disadvantageous when the stock price closely approaches, but does not attain, the minimum sale price limit before dropping substantially. Generally speaking, limit orders are most effective when the price of a stock fluctuates greatly, because there is then a better chance that the order will be executed.

stop-loss (stop) order
an order to sell a stock when its market price reaches or drops below a specified level; can also be used to buy stock when its market price reaches or rises above a specified level.

Stop-Loss Order When an investor places a **stop-loss order** or **stop order,** the broker tells the specialist to sell a stock when its market price reaches or drops below a specified level. Stop-loss orders are *suspended orders* placed on stocks; they are activated when and if the stock reaches a certain price. The stop-loss order is placed on the specialist's book and becomes active once the stock reaches the stop price. Like limit orders, stop-loss orders are typically day or GTC orders. When activated, the stop order becomes a *market order* to sell the security at the best price available. Thus it is possible for the actual price at which the sale is made to be well below the price at which the stop was initiated. Investors use these orders to protect themselves against the adverse effects of a rapid decline in share price.

For example, assume you own 100 shares of Ballard Industries, which is currently selling for $35 per share. Because you believe the stock price could decline rapidly at any time, you place a stop order to sell at $30. If the stock price does in fact drop to $30, the specialist will sell the 100 shares at the best price available at that time. If the market price declines to $28 by the time your stop-loss order comes up, you will receive less than $30 per share. Of course, if the market price stays above $30 per share, you will have lost nothing as a result of placing the order, because the stop order will never be initiated. Often investors raise the level of the stop as the price of the stock rises. Such action helps to lock in a higher profit when the price is increasing.

Investors can also place stop orders to buy a stock, although buy orders are far less common than sell orders. For example, an investor may place a stop order to buy 100 shares of MJ Enterprises, currently selling for $70 per share, once its price rises to, say, $75 (the stop price). These orders are commonly used either to limit losses on short sales (discussed in Chapter 2) or to buy a stock just as its price begins to rise.

To avoid the risk of the market moving against you when your stop order becomes a market order, you can place a *stop-limit order,* rather than a plain stop order. This is an order to buy or sell stock at a given price, or better, once a stipulated stop price has been met. For example, in the Ballard Industries example, had a stop-limit order been in effect, then when the market price of Ballard dropped to $30, the broker would have entered a limit order to sell your 100 shares at $30 a share or *better*. Thus you would have run no risk of getting less than $30 a share for your stock—unless the price of the stock kept right on falling. In that case, as is true for any limit order, you might miss the market altogether and end up with stock worth much less than $30. Even though the stop order to sell was triggered (at $30), the stock will *not* be sold, with a stop-limit order, if it keeps falling in price.

Online Transactions

The competition for your online business increases daily as more players enter an already crowded arena. Brokerage firms are encouraging customers to trade online and offering a variety of incentives to get their business, including free trades! However, low cost is not the only reason to choose a brokerage firm. As with any financial decision, you must consider your needs and find the firm that best matches them. One investor may want timely information, research, and quick, reliable trades from a firm like Fidelity or Merrill Lynch. Another, who is an active trader, will focus on cost and fast trades rather than research and so will sign up with Ameritrade or Datek. Ease of site navigation is a major factor in finding an online broker. Table 3.6 compares the costs and services of a number of leading brokerage firms, all of which offer online trading of stocks. Some also offer online trading of bonds and mutual funds as well. A good site for objective, in-depth reviews of firms with online brokerage divisions is Gómez Advisors (www.gomez.com). It rates brokers on numerous factors, including response time, ease of use, online resources, and availability of 24-hour customer service.

Stocks If you decide that do-it-yourself investing is for you, choose an online broker and open an account. In most cases, you can fill out the application forms online, print and sign them, and mail them with a check to fund your account initially. As soon as you receive confirmation that the funds are in your account, you can start trading. You can place the same types of orders as with a traditional broker.

Here are the steps in making an online stock purchase transaction at Ameritrade's Web site. The specifics may vary slightly at other brokerage sites but will follow a similar pattern.

TABLE 3.6 Comparison of Costs and Services: Leading Brokerage Firms Offering Online Trading

Firm/Web Site	Online Products	Minimum Balance[1]	Base Stock Commission[2]	Other Services
Ameritrade (ameritrade.com)	Stocks, mutual funds, options, bonds (phone only)	$2,000	Online, $8 for market orders, $13 for limit orders; more for phone and broker trades	ATM/debit card, check writing; after-hours trading; alerts; fee for real-time quotes
Charles Schwab (www.schwab.com)	Stocks, mutual funds, options, bonds (phone only)	$5,000	$29.95 per online trade, less for active traders; minimum of $39.95 for broker trades	Check writing, ATM/debit card, electronic bill paying; access to stockbrokers; referrals to 3rd-party investment adviser
Datek (datek.com)	Stocks, mutual funds	none	Online, $9.99; Broker-assisted, $25	Check writing; 60-second execution guarantee
E*Trade (www.etrade.com)	Stocks, mutual funds, options, bonds (phone only)	$1,000	$14.95 for market orders, $19.95 for Nasdaq stocks, limit orders; more for phone and broker trades	Internet banking, online bill paying, ATM/debit cards; partnership with DirectAdvice.com
Fidelity (www.fidelity.com)	Stocks, mutual funds, options, bonds	$2,500	$25 per online trade, less for active traders; considerably more for phone and broker trades	Check writing, charge/debit card, electronic bill paying; free real-time quotes; access to stockbrokers and Fidelity consultants
Merrill Lynch (www.ml.com)	Stocks, mutual funds, options (phone only), bonds (phone only)	$2,000	Online, $29.95 per trade; also offers unlimited trades for a flat annual fee	Check writing, ATM/credit/debit card, electronic bill paying; access to stockbrokers and Merrill Lynch consultants
National Discount Brokers (www.ndb.com)	Stocks, mutual funds, options, bonds (phone only)	none	$14.75 for market orders, $19.75 for limit orders for multiple same-day same side (buy or sell) trades on same stock; more for phone and broker trades	Check writing, debit card, credit card
TD Waterhouse (www.tdwaterhouse.com)	Stocks, mutual funds, options, bonds (phone only)	$1,000	$12 for market orders, $15 for limit orders	Check writing, ATM/debit card, electronic bill paying and account transfers; Advisor Direct referral service for large accounts

[1]For cash account; may be different for retirement account and higher for margin account. These commissions are, of course, subject to change; also, some brokers/dealers may charge more than the indicated commission, others less.
[2]Some firms add a per-share surcharge after the first 1,000 or 5,000 shares.

Sources: Brokerage firm Web sites and "Discount Brokerage Comparison Table," *The Motley Fool*, downloaded from www.fool.com/dbc/tables/compare, October 1, 2000; "Full Service on the Net," *Business Week*, May 22, 2000, p. 152; "The Online Lineup," *Wall Street Journal*, June 12, 2000, p. 10.

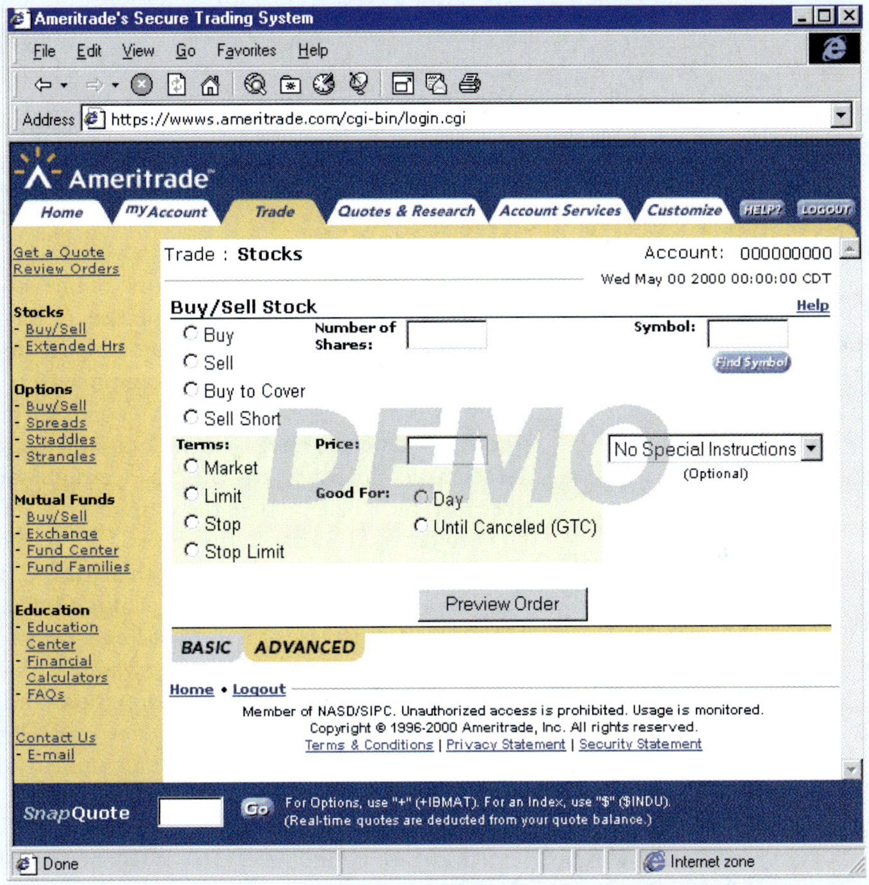

FIGURE 3.6

Order Ticket for an Online Broker

Ameritrade's advanced order ticket makes it easy to place a long or short order and to specify the order type (market, limit, stop, or stop-limit). (*Source:* Trading demo, Ameritrade.com, downloaded from **https://wwws.ameritrade.com/cgi-bin/logins.cgi**. Ameritrade Holding Corporation, 4211 S. 102nd St. Omaha, Nebraska 68127. Phone: 800-237-8692.)

1. Go to your brokerage firm's Web site and log in with your account number and personal identification number (PIN) to access your account. This takes you to your personal trading homepage.
2. At your personal trading page, you'll have access to your account information, trade screens, market news, daily market summaries, stock quotes, research, and more. If you have already done your research and know what stock you wish to buy, you move on to the order page.
3. Using the brokerage site's order form, place your order. Ameritrade has two order tickets: a basic ticket for market, limit, and stop orders and an advanced stock order ticket, shown in Figure 3.10. The advanced order ticket also includes selling short, stop-limit orders, and a place to enter special instructions to set the terms of your trade.
4. After placing your securities order, click to see a preview or confirmation page to review your order before submitting it. If everything is correct, click "Place Order." Otherwise click "Do Not Place Order" to delete the order information.
5. Clicking on the "Place Order" button takes you to the order-sent page that confirms Ameritrade's receipt of your order. You can check the status of your order at the "Review Orders" link.

Now you can even invest in non-U.S. stocks online at global trading sites Globeshare.com (www.globeshare.com) and IntlTrader.com (www.intltrader.com). IntlTrader.com charges $29.99 per trade; Globeshare commissions vary depending on the country.

See how easy it is? In fact, the ease of Internet investing has created a new type of investor: the compulsive investor, who can't get enough of investing. The *Investing in Action* box on page 93 describes the dilemmas of these investment addicts.

day trader
an investor who buys and sells stocks quickly throughout the day in hopes of making quick profits.

Day Trading For some investors, online stock trading is so compelling that they become day traders. The opposite of buy-and-hold investors with a long-term perspective, **day traders** buy and sell stocks quickly throughout the day. They hope that their stocks will continue to rise in value for the very short time they own them—sometimes just seconds or minutes—so they can make quick profits. Some also sell short, looking for small price decreases. True day traders do not own any stocks overnight—hence the term "day trader"—because they believe that the extreme risk of prices changing radically from day to day will lead to large losses. Day trading is not illegal or unethical, but it is highly risky. To compound their risk, day traders usually buy on margin to use leverage to earn higher profits. But as we saw in Chapter 2, margin trading also increases the risk of large losses.

Until recently, day trading was a little-known activity. Now that the Internet makes investment information and transactions accessible to the masses, it is a dangerously popular one. Day traders watch their computer screens continuously, trying to track numerous ticker quotes and price data to identify market trends. It's a very difficult task—essentially a very stressful, full-time job. Yet pitches for day trading make it seem like an easy route to quick riches. Quite the reverse is true. Day traders typically incur major financial losses when they start trading. Some never achieve profitability. Day traders also have high expenses for brokerage commissions, training, and computer equipment. By some estimates, they must make a 56% profit annually to break even on fees and commissions alone.

Technical and Service Problems As the number of online investors increases, so do the problems that beset brokerage firms and their customers. The number of complaints about online brokerage services doubled from 1998 to 1999, with technical difficulties the biggest category. Investors who report trading problems are also upset about the lack of response from brokers. And they claim that brokers do not get the best prices for stock orders.

Many online brokerage firms were not prepared for the heavy volume at their Web sites. Victims of their own successful marketing campaigns, the firms had inadequate computer systems and capacity. Software problems have also been to blame in some service outages. The resulting online traffic jams have left customers locked out of brokerage Web sites, unable to view their account information or place trades. Most firms have upgraded their systems to reduce the number of service outages.

The problems go beyond the brokerage sites, though. Once an investor places a trade at a firm's Web site, it goes through several other parties to be executed. Most online brokers don't have their own trading desks and have agreements with other trading firms to execute their orders on the *New York Stock Exchange* or *Nasdaq Stock Market*. Slowdowns at any point in the

INVESTING in action

Investing as Gambling

It's a common story: Howard, a young investor, watched his friends strike it rich and stepped gingerly into the waters of online investing. He made $4,000 in a matter of minutes on his first trade, and soon he was deep into *day trading*—buying and selling stocks very quickly to make a profit of a few cents per share. He sat, eyes glued to his computer screen, all day in search of a quick profit. As he met with some success, he opened a margin account to leverage his profits. Before long he was a confirmed "investaholic." Not until the market tanked and he was deep in debt did reality hit. "It all happened so unbelievably fast. I got sucked into believing," he laments.

Howard is not alone. The number of people who are addicted to investing is growing at an alarming rate. As long as the markets were up and paper profits climbed, naive investors rode the wave to profits. When the market became more volatile, investors began losing money. "As the markets get more treacherous, these people begin to see that they really were gambling," says Paul Good, a San Francisco psychologist specializing in stock market addiction.

Investing as gambling? Hard to accept, but at some Gamblers Anonymous meetings, stock traders now account for about half the participants. Investment addicts get a rush from watching stock prices move across the computer screen and quick satisfaction from point-and-click stock trading. Although the speed and simplicity of online investing are beneficial to many investors, for addicts they lead to increased impulse buying—as well as the chance to do it secretly. David G. admits that there are parallels between trading and gambling. "All the thrills are there when you make the right trade. There is absolutely no difference."

Nasdaq's spring 2000 plunge was a wake-up call for many investors, including 24-year-old Ryan G. He was making as many as 50 trades a day. "Fortunately, as the market went down, I lost my addiction," he says. Most of his funds are now in money market accounts, which he calls his "nicotine patch."

Sources: Ruth Simon and E. S. Browning, "Some Online Investors Can't Say No to Playing the Market," *Wall Street Journal*, August 4, 2000, pp. A1, A4; and Paul Sloan, "Can't Stop Checking Your Quotes?" *U.S. News & World Report*, July 10, 2000, p. 40.

process can create problems confirming trades. Investors, thinking that their trades had not gone through, might place the order again—only to discover later that they have bought the same stock twice. Online investors who don't get immediate trade execution and confirmation use the telephone when they can't get through online or to solve other problems with their accounts, and they often face long waiting times on hold.

Tips for Successful Online Trades Successful online investors take additional precautions before submitting their orders. Here are some tips to protect yourself from common problems:

- *Know how to place and confirm your order before you begin trading.* This simple step can keep you from having problems later.
- *Verify the stock symbol of the security you wish to buy.* Two very different companies can have similar symbols. Some investors have bought the wrong stock because they didn't check before placing their order.

- *Use limit orders.* The order you see on your computer screen may not be the one you get. With a limit order, you avoid getting burned in fast-moving markets. Although limit orders cost more, they can save you thousands of dollars. For example, customers eager to get shares of a hot IPO stock placed market orders. Instead of buying the stock near the offering price of $9, some were shocked to find that their orders were filled at prices as high as $90 during the stock's first trading day. Investors who were aware of the price run-up tried to cancel orders but couldn't get through to brokers. Charles Schwab and E*Trade accept only limit orders for online IPO purchases on the first day of trading.
- *Don't ignore the online reminders that ask you to check and recheck.* It's easy to make a typo that adds an extra digit to a purchase amount.
- *Don't get carried away.* It's easy to churn your own account. In fact, new online investors trade about twice as much as they did before they went online. To control impulse trading, have a strategy and stick to it.
- *Open accounts with two brokers.* This protects you if your online brokerage's computer system crashes. It also gives you an alternative if one brokerage is blocked with heavy trading volume.
- *Double-check orders for accuracy.* Make sure each trade was completed according to your instructions. It's very easy to make typos or use the wrong stock symbol, so review the confirmation notice to verify that the right number of shares was bought or sold and that the price and commissions or fees are as quoted. Check your account for "unauthorized" trades.

Bonds Electronic bond trading accounts for about 6% of the overall trading volume, and only 1% is from individual investors. Few fully automated online bond transactions systems are available to individual investors. Typically, you must find the information at Web sites like the ones mentioned earlier in the chapter and then phone your broker to fill the order. At E*Trade's Bond Center, investors can research various types of bonds to learn the price, yield, and maturity dates, although they must still place their orders by telephone. Some firms let customers place e-mail orders but then execute the order in the traditional way. TradeWeb (www.tradeweb.com) is one site where individuals can trade U.S. government securities.

HOTLINKS

Also check two popular sites that are used: The Bond Market Association and Bonds Online at:

www.investinginbonds.com
www.bonds-online.com

It won't be long, however, before individual investors can trade bonds online much as they do stocks. Many firms are developing online bond-trading capabilities in response to customer demand for full-service online investing. W.R. Hambrecht's OpenBook (www.openbook.com) offers online auctions of corporate bonds to investors. Dow Chemical and Ford Motor Credit have already auctioned bonds through OpenBook. A group of leading international investment banks established Market Axess (www.marketaxess.com) to offer institutional investors trading in investment grade corporate, Eurobond, high yield, emerging market, and convertible bonds.

Mutual Funds As we noted earlier in this chapter, the Internet is a big time-saver when it comes to sorting through thousands of mutual funds. Many sites offer descriptions of funds, what they invest in, and their track records, as well as screening tools to find funds that meet specific needs or goals.

You can buy and sell funds online at fund company or brokerage firm Web sites. You can also transfer your investment from one fund to another. As with stocks, you must first open an account and have a signature on file. You may be able to download and print a sign-up form and mail in a check either to the fund itself for direct transactions or to the brokerage firm. Once you fund your account, making online transactions is fairly easy.

Brokerage sites like Charles Schwab offer fund supermarkets where investors can buy funds from many different fund companies, instead of having to go from fund family site to fund family site to compare and then purchase them. However, some brokerage firms charge commissions on purchases of funds that you can buy without an initial sales charge if you purchase them directly from the fund family. Availability and commissions differ from one brokerage firm to another, so be sure you understand the fee structure before executing an order. Fund transactions are made through a major stock exchange or Nasdaq; there is no open public market for traditional mutual funds although, as explained in Chapter 11, *exchange-traded funds* are a new type of publicly traded fund.

Transaction Costs

Making transactions through brokers or dealers is considerably easier for investors than it would be to negotiate directly, trying to find someone who wants to buy that which they want to sell (or vice versa). To compensate the broker for executing the transaction, investors pay transaction costs, which are usually levied on both the purchase and the sale of securities. When making investment decisions, you must consider the structure and magnitude of transaction costs, because they affect returns.

Since the passage of the Securities Acts Amendments of 1975, brokers have been permitted to charge whatever brokerage commissions they deem appropriate. Most firms have established **fixed-commission schedules** that apply to small transactions, the ones most often made by individual investors. On large institutional transactions, the client and broker may arrange a **negotiated commission**—commissions to which both parties agree. Negotiated commissions are also available to individual investors who maintain large accounts, typically above $50,000.

fixed-commission schedules
fixed brokerage commissions that typically apply to the small transactions usually made by individual investors.

negotiated commissions
brokerage commissions agreed to by the client and the broker as a result of their negotiations; typically apply on large institutional transactions and to individual investors who maintain large accounts.

The commission structure varies with the type of security and the type of broker. We'll describe the basic commission structures for various types of securities in subsequent chapters. Because of the way brokerage firms charge commissions on stock trades, it is difficult to compare prices precisely. Traditional brokers generally charge on the basis of number of shares and the price of the stock at the time of the transaction. Internet brokers usually charge flat rates, often for transactions up to 1,000 shares, with additional fees for larger or more complicated orders. However, many traditional brokerage firms have reduced their commissions on broker-assisted trades and have instituted annual flat fees set as a specified percentage of the value of the assets in the account. Unless you are a very active trader, you will probably be better off paying commissions on a per-transaction basis.

Obviously, discount and online brokers charge substantially less than full-service brokers for the same transaction. However, most discounters charge a minimum fee to discourage small orders. For example, Charles Schwab, the largest online broker, charges a minimum fee of about $40 for a broker-assisted order and $30 for an online stock transaction. The savings from the discounter are substantial: Depending on the size and type of transaction, discount and online brokers can typically save investors between 30% and 80% of the commission charged by the full-service broker.

Investor Protection: SIPC and Arbitration

Securities Investor Protection Corporation (SIPC)
a nonprofit membership corporation, authorized by the federal government, that insures each brokerage customer's account for up to $500,000, with claims for cash limited to $100,000 per customer.

Although most investment transactions take place safely, it is important for you to know what protection you have if things *don't* go smoothly. As a client, you are protected against the loss of the securities or cash held by your broker. The **Securities Investor Protection Corporation** (**SIPC**), a nonprofit membership corporation, was authorized by the *Securities Investor Protection Act of 1970* to protect customer accounts against the consequences of financial failure of the brokerage firm. The SIPC currently insures each customer's account for up to $500,000, with claims for cash limited to $100,000 per customer. Note that SIPC insurance does not guarantee that the investor will recover the dollar value of the securities; it guarantees only that the securities themselves will be returned. Some brokerage firms also insure certain customer accounts for amounts in excess of $500,000. Certainly, in light of the diversity and quality of services available among brokerage firms, this may be an additional service you should consider when you select a firm and an individual broker.

HOTLINKS

The Securities Investor Protection Corporation (SIPC) protects customers of broker-dealers registered with the U.S. Securities and Exchange Commission.

www.sipc.org

The SIPC provides protection in case your brokerage firm fails. But what happens if your broker gave you bad advice and, as a result, you lost a lot of money on an investment? Or what if you feel your broker is *churning* your account, the illegal but difficult-to-prove practice of causing excessive trading to increase commissions? In either case, the SIPC won't help. It's not intended to insure you against bad investment advice or churning. Instead, if you have a dispute with your broker, the first thing you should do is discuss the situation with the managing officer at the branch where you do business. If that doesn't do any good, then contact the firm's compliance officer and the securities regulator in your home state.

mediation
an informal, voluntary dispute resolution process in which a customer and a broker agree to a mediator, who facilitates negotiations between them to resolve the case.

arbitration
a formal dispute resolution process in which a customer and a broker present their argument before a panel, which then decides the case.

If you still don't get any satisfaction, you can use litigation (judicial methods in the courts) to resolve the dispute. Alternative dispute resolution processes that may avoid litigation include *mediation* and *arbitration*. **Mediation** is an informal, voluntary approach in which you and the broker agree to a mediator, who facilitates negotiations between the two of you to resolve the case. The mediator does not impose a solution on you and the broker. The NASD and securities-related organizations encourage investors to mediate disputes rather than arbitrate them, because mediation can reduce costs and time for both investors and brokers.

If mediation is not pursued or if it fails, you may have no choice but to take the case to **arbitration**, a formal process whereby you and your broker present the two sides of the argument before an arbitration panel. The panel then decides the case. Many brokerage firms require you to resolve disputes by *binding arbitration;* in this case, you don't have the option to sue. You must accept the arbitrator's decision, and in most cases you cannot go to court to review your case. Before you open an account, check whether the brokerage agreement contains a binding-arbitration clause.

Settling securities disputes through mediation or arbitration rather than litigation has advantages and disadvantages. Mediation and arbitration proceedings typically cost less and are resolved more quickly than litigation. Recent legislation has given many investors the option of using either securities industry panels or independent arbitration panels such as those sponsored by the American Arbitration Association (AAA). Independent panels are considered more sympathetic toward investors. In addition, only one of the three arbitrators on a panel can be connected with the securities industry. However, the average arbitration award is about 60% of the original investment, before deducting any fees.

Probably the best thing you can do to avoid the need to mediate, arbitrate, or litigate with your broker is to select him or her carefully, understand the financial risks involved in the broker's recommendations, thoroughly evaluate the advice he or she offers, and continuously monitor the volume of transactions that he or she recommends and executes. Clearly, it is much less costly to choose the right broker initially than to incur later the financial and emotional costs of having chosen a bad one.

If you have a problem with an online trade, immediately file a written—not e-mail—complaint with the broker. Cite dates, times, and amounts of trades, and include all supporting documentation. File a copy with the NASD regulatory arm Web site (www.nasdr.com) and with your state securities regulator. If you can't resolve the problems with the broker, you can try mediation and then resort to arbitration, litigation being the last resort.

Summary

LG 1

Identify the major types and sources of traditional and online investment information. Investment information, descriptive or analytical, includes information about the economy and current events, industries and companies, and alternative investment vehicles, as well as price information and personal investment strategies. It can be obtained from financial journals, general newspapers, institutional news, business periodicals, government publications, special subscription services, stockholders' reports, comparative data sources, subscription services, brokerage reports, investment letters, price quotations, and electronic and online sources. Most print publications also have Web sites with access to all or part of their content. Financial portals bring together a variety of financial information online. Investors will also find specialized sites for bond, mutual fund, and international information, as well as message boards that discuss individual securities and investment strategies. Because it is hard to know the qualifications of those who make postings on message boards, participants must do their own homework before acting on an online tip.

LG 2

Explain the characteristics, interpretation, and uses of the commonly cited stock and bond market averages and indexes. Investors commonly rely on stock market averages and indexes to stay abreast of market behavior. The most often cited are the Dow Jones averages, which include the Dow Jones Industrial Average (DJIA). Also widely followed are the Standard & Poor's indexes, the NYSE composite index, the AMEX composite index, the Nasdaq indexes, and the Value Line indexes. Numerous other averages and indexes, including a number of global and foreign market indexes, are regularly reported in financial publications.

Bond market indicators are most often reported in terms of average bond yields and average prices. The Dow Jones bond averages are among the most popular. A wealth of return and price index data is also available for various types of bonds and various domestic and foreign markets. Both stock and bond market statistics are published daily in the *Wall Street Journal* and summarized weekly in *Barron's*.

LG 3 **Review the roles of traditional and online stockbrokers, including the services they provide, selection of a stockbroker, opening an account, and transaction basics.** Stockbrokers facilitate transactions among buyers and sellers of securities, and they provide a variety of other client services. An investor should select a stockbroker who has a compatible disposition toward investing and whose firm offers the desired services at competitive costs. Today the distinctions among traditional, discount, and online brokers is blurring. Most brokers now offer online trading capabilities, and many no-frills brokers are expanding their services to include research and advice. Investors can open a variety of types of brokerage accounts, such as single, joint, custodial, cash, margin, and wrap. An investor can make odd-lot transactions (less than 100 shares) or round-lot transactions (100 shares or multiples thereof). An added fee is typically charged on odd-lot transactions.

LG 4 **Describe the basic types of orders (market, limit, and stop-loss), online transactions, transaction costs, and the legal aspects of investor protection.** A market order is an order to buy or sell stock at the best price available. A limit order is an order to buy at a specified price or below or to sell at a specified price or above. Stop-loss orders become market orders as soon as the minimum sell price or the maximum buy price is hit. Limit and stop-loss orders can be placed as fill-or-kill orders, day orders, or good-'til-canceled (GTC) orders.

On small transactions, most brokers have fixed-commission schedules; on larger transactions, they will negotiate commissions. Commissions also vary by type of security and type of broker: full-service, discount, or online broker. The Securities Investor Protection Corporation (SIPC) insures customers' accounts against the brokerage firm's failure. To avoid litigation, mediation and arbitration procedures are frequently employed to resolve disputes between investor and broker. These disputes typically concern the investor's belief that the broker either gave bad advice or churned the account.

PART TWO

IMPORTANT CONCEPTUAL TOOLS

CHAPTER 4
INVESTMENT RETURN AND RISK

CHAPTER 5
MODERN PORTFOLIO CONCEPTS

CHAPTER 4

INVESTMENT RETURN AND RISK

LEARNING GOALS

After studying this chapter, you should be able to:

LG 1 Review the concept of return, its components, and the forces that affect the investor's level of return.

LG 2 Discuss the time value of money and the calculations involved in finding the future value of various types of cash flows.

LG 3 Explain the concept of present value, the procedures for calculating present values, and the use of present value in determining whether an investment is satisfactory.

LG 4 Describe real, risk-free, and required returns and the computation and application of holding period return, yield (internal rate of return), and growth rates.

LG 5 Discuss the key sources of risk and how they might affect potential investment vehicles.

LG 6 Understand the risk of a single asset, risk assessment, and the steps that combine return and risk.

When you go shopping for a computer, stereo system, or clothes, you go to a store, a catalog, or a Web site to examine the merchandise. When you invest in the stock of a company, what can you sample? For one thing, you can visit the company's Web site to find corporate information and financial data. Let's say you did that for Microsoft by going to **www. microsoft.com.** You would learn that the company was in great financial shape at September 30, 2000, the end of its fiscal year. Revenue was up 16% and net income 21%, compared to 1999, and earnings per share rose almost 20%. Microsoft also had substantial cash on hand and no long-term debt.

It is harder to discover the risks associated with owning the stock. Searching the business press and online investment sites for articles and investment research about Microsoft would provide insight into the various risks the company faces. In the case of Microsoft, your research would reveal that Microsoft is appealing a U.S. Justice Department ruling that the firm had violated U.S. antitrust laws and must be broken up. In addition, you would learn that Microsoft continues to look for ways to expand its technological base beyond personal computer software, where it has a dominant position, into television, games, wireless, and personal information appliances, where it faces greater competition. The stock is trading at about $69 per share, about 40 times earnings. Although this is high for the general market, it is not out of line for technology stocks. Microsoft exceeded analysts' earnings estimates in fiscal-year 1999, and most analysts have the stock on their "strong buy" or "moderate buy" lists. Its 25% return on equity is about five times the software industry average.

To use this information wisely, you need to understand the concepts of return and risk, which are at the heart of any investment decision. In this chapter we'll explain what factors affect the level of investment return and how to assess the different types of risk.

The Concept of Return

LG 1

return
the level of profit from an investment—that is, the reward for investing.

Investors are motivated to invest in a given vehicle by its expected return. The **return** is the level of profit from an investment—that is, the reward for investing. Suppose you have $1,000 in an insured savings account paying 5% annual interest, and a business associate asks you to lend her that much money. If you lend her the money for 1 year, at the end of which she pays you back, your return will depend on the amount of interest you charge. If you make an interest-free loan, your return will be zero. If you charge 5% interest, your return will be $50 (0.05 × $1,000). Because you are already earning a safe 5% on the $1,000, it seems clear that to equal that return you should charge your associate a minimum of 5% interest.

Some investment vehicles guarantee a return; others do not. The $1,000 deposited in an insured savings account at a large bank can be viewed as a certain return. The $1,000 loan to your business associate might be less certain. What is your return if she runs into financial difficulty? If she can repay you only $850, your return will be minus $150 ($850 − $1,000), or minus 15% (−$150 ÷ $1,000). Thus the size of the expected return is one important factor in choosing a suitable investment.

Components of Return

The return on an investment may come from more than one source. The most common source is periodic payments, such as dividends or interest. The other source of return is appreciation in value, the gain from selling an investment vehicle for more than its original purchase price. We call these two sources of return *current income* and *capital gains* (or *capital losses*), respectively.

current income
usually cash or near-cash that is periodically received as a result of owning an investment.

Current Income Current income may take the form of dividends from stocks, interest received on bonds, or dividends received from mutual funds. To be considered income, it must be in the form of cash or be readily convertible into cash. For our purposes, **current income** is usually cash or near-cash that is periodically received as a result of owning an investment.

Using the data in Table 4.1, we can calculate the current income from investments A and B, both purchased for $1,000, over a 1-year period of ownership. Investment A would provide current income of $80, investment B $120. Solely on the basis of the current income received over the 1-year period, investment B seems preferable.

Capital Gains (or Losses) The second dimension of return is concerned with the change, if any, in the market value of an investment. As noted in Chapter 1, the amount by which the proceeds from the sale of an investment exceed its original purchase price is called a *capital gain*. If an investment is sold for less than its original purchase price, a *capital loss* results.

total return
the sum of the current income and the capital gain (or loss) earned on an investment over a specified period of time.

We can calculate the capital gain or loss of the investments as shown in Table 4.1. For investment A, a capital gain of $100 ($1,100 sale price − $1,000 purchase price) is realized over the 1-year period. For investment B, a $40 capital loss results ($960 sale price − $1,000 purchase price).

Combining the capital gain (or loss) with the current income (calculated in the preceding section) gives the **total return** on each investment shown in

TABLE 4.1 Profiles of Two Investments

	Investment A	Investment B
Purchase price (beginning of year)	$1,000	$1,000
Cash received		
1st quarter	$ 10	$ 0
2nd quarter	20	0
3rd quarter	20	0
4th quarter	30	120
Total current income (for year)	$ 80	$ 120
Sale price (end of year)	$1,100	$ 960

TABLE 4.2 Total Returns of Two Investments

Return	Investment A	Investment B
Current income	$ 80	$120
Capital gain (loss)	100	(40)
Total return	$180	$ 80

Table 4.2. In terms of the total return earned on the $1,000 investment over the 1-year period, investment A is superior to investment B.

The use of *percentage returns* is generally preferred to the use of dollar returns. Percentages allow direct comparison of different sizes and types of investments. Investment A earned an 18% return ($180 ÷ $1,000), whereas B yielded only an 8% return ($80 ÷ $1,000). At this point investment A appears preferable, but differences in risk might cause some investors to prefer B. (We will see why later in this chapter.)

INVESTOR FACTS

WHAT A DIFFERENCE THE TIME PERIOD MAKES—Don't get too caught up in the historical rates of return, especially when dealing with technology stocks. Judging on the basis of data through November 7, 2000, the 3-year return for the online information industry was 134%. Change the time horizon to 1 year, however, and the return drops to −22.88%; for 3 months, it's about 7%. Clearly, in this case, the 3-year return is not the best indicator of future performance.

Source: "Stock Returns," *Morningstar.com*, November 9, 2000, downloaded from www.morningstar.com

Why Return Is Important

Return is a key variable in the investment decision: It allows us to compare the actual or expected gains of various investments with the levels of return we need. For example, you would be satisfied with an investment that earns 12% if you needed it to earn only 10%. You would not be satisfied with a 10% return if you needed a 14% return. Return can be measured historically, or it can be used to formulate future expectations.

Historical Performance Although most people recognize that future performance is not guaranteed by past performance, they would agree that past data often provide a meaningful basis for future expectations. A common practice in the investment world is to look closely at the historical performance of a given vehicle when formulating expectations about its future.

Interest rates and other measures of financial return are most often cited on an annual basis. Evaluation of past investment returns is typically done on the same basis. Consider the data for a hypothetical investment presented in Table 4.3. Two aspects of these data are important. First, we can determine the

TABLE 4.3 Historical Investment Data for a Hypothetical Investment

		Market Value (Price)			Total Return	
Year	(1) Income	(2) Beginning of Year	(3) End of Year	(4) (3) − (2) Capital Gain	(5) (1) + (4) ($)	(6) (5) ÷ (2) (%)*
1993	$4.00	$100	$ 95	−$ 5.00	−$ 1.00	− 1.00%
1994	3.00	95	99	4.00	7.00	7.37
1995	4.00	99	105	6.00	10.00	10.10
1996	5.00	105	115	10.00	15.00	14.29
1997	5.00	115	125	10.00	15.00	12.00
1998	3.00	125	120	− 5.00	− 2.00	− 1.60
1999	3.00	120	122	2.00	5.00	4.17
2000	4.00	122	130	8.00	12.00	9.84
2001	5.00	130	140	10.00	15.00	11.54
2002	5.00	140	155	15.00	20.00	14.29
Average	$4.10			$ 5.50	$ 9.60	8.10%

*Percent return on beginning-of-year market value of investment.

average level of return generated by this investment over the past 10 years. Second, we can analyze the trend in this return. As a percentage, the average total return (column 6) over the past 10 years was 8.10%. Looking at the yearly returns, we can see that after the negative return in 1993, 4 years of positive and generally increasing returns occurred before the negative return was repeated in 1998. From 1999 through 2002, positive and increasing returns were again realized.

expected return
the return an investor thinks an investment will earn in the future.

Expected Return In the final analysis, it's the future that matters when we make investment decisions. Therefore, **expected return** is a vital measure of performance. It's what you think the investment will earn in the future that determines what you should be willing to pay for it.

To see how, let's return to the data in Table 4.3. Looking at the historical return figures in the table, an investor would note the increasing trend in returns from 1999 through 2002. But to project future returns, we need insights into the investment's prospects. If the trend in returns seems likely to continue, an expected return in the range of 12% to 15% for 2003 or 2004 would seem reasonable. On the other hand, if future prospects seem poor, or if the investment is subject to cycles, an expected return of 8% to 9% may be a more reasonable estimate. Over the past 10 years, the investment's returns have cycled from a poor year (1993 and 1998) to 4 years of increasing returns (1994–1997 and 1999–2002). We might therefore expect low returns in 2003 to be followed by increasing returns in the 2004–2007 period.

Level of Return

The level of return achieved or expected from an investment will depend on a variety of factors. The key factors are internal characteristics and external forces.

Internal Characteristics Certain characteristics of an investment affect its level of return. Examples include the type of investment vehicle, the quality of management, how the investment is financed, and the customer base of the issuer. For example, the common stock of a large, well-managed, completely equity-financed plastics manufacturer whose major customer is IBM would be expected to provide a level of return different from that of a small, poorly managed, largely debt-financed clothing manufacturer whose customers are small specialty stores. As we will see in later chapters, assessing internal factors and their impact on return is one important step in analyzing potential investments.

HOTLINKS

An *Investing in Action* box on the book's Web site demonstrates that moderate deflation positively affects consumers and investors, but greater deflation poses some threat to them.

www.awl.com/gitman_joehnk

External Forces External forces such as Federal Reserve actions, shortages, war, price controls, and political events may also affect the level of return. None of these are under the control of the issuer of the investment vehicle. Investment vehicles are affected differently by these forces. It is not unusual to find two vehicles with similar internal characteristics offering significantly different returns. As a result of the same external force, the expected return from one vehicle may increase, while that of another decreases. Likewise, the economies of various countries respond to external forces in different ways.

inflation
a period of generally rising prices.

deflation
a period of generally declining prices.

Another external force is the *general level of price changes,* either up—**inflation**—or down—**deflation.** Inflation tends to have a positive impact on investment vehicles such as real estate, and a negative impact on vehicles such as stocks and fixed-income securities. Rising interest rates, which normally accompany increasing rates of inflation, can significantly affect returns. The actions, if any, the federal government takes to control inflation can increase, decrease, or have no effect on investment returns. Furthermore, the return on each type of investment vehicle exhibits its own unique response to inflation. The *Investing in Action* box on page 105 looks at the returns in the stock market in recent years, and considers whether such returns are likely to continue and what to do if they do not.

The Time Value of Money*

LG 2 LG 3

time value of money
the fact that as long as an opportunity exists to earn interest, the value of money is affected by the point in time when the money is received.

Imagine that at age 25 you begin making annual cash deposits of $1,000 into a savings account that pays 5% annual interest. After 40 years, at age 65, you will have made deposits totaling $40,000 (40 years × $1,000 per year). Assuming you made no withdrawals, what do you think your account balance will be—$50,000? $75,000? $100,000? The answer is none of the above. Your $40,000 will have grown to nearly $121,000! Why? Because the time value of money allows the deposits to earn interest, and that interest also earns interest over the 40 years. **Time value of money** refers to the fact that as long as an opportunity exists to earn interest, the value of money is affected by the point in time when the money is received.

* This section presents the fundamental concepts and techniques of time value of money. Those already familiar with these important ideas may wish to skip this discussion and continue at the heading "Determining a Satisfactory Investment" on page 113.

INVESTING in action

Many Happy Returns . . . Maybe

In recent years it's been fairly easy to make money in the stock market. From April 1991 through December 2000, the economy had been expanding—a record 117 months, compared to an average expansion of 35 months. Even novice investors enjoyed stellar returns. From 1990 through 1999, the average annual return on the S&P 500 stocks was 18.2%, and it climbed to a whopping 28.6% from 1995 to 1999. That annual return is considerably above the 1926–1999 average annual return of 11.4% on large-company stocks and 12.6% for small companies reported by market researcher Ibbotson Associates.

This seems like great news for today's investors, many of whom started buying stocks only in the past few years. These newcomers now *expect* average returns of 15% to 30%. Many of them ignore the market's brief bear-like periods, saying, "It's just a minor correction. Stocks will bounce back." And they did in the late 1990s on through the middle of 2000. But the recent stock market pattern of sudden crashes and quick "corrections" is not the norm. More often the recovery is extremely slow.

"We laugh about this, but it's really getting scary," says California financial planner Judith Martindale. "More and more investors think they are competent rather than lucky. When their luck runs out, they'll lose their money."

There's another hidden danger in expecting high returns: poor financial decisions. Investors who expect to earn 20% or more on their portfolio may spend more and allocate less to saving, counting on high returns to increase their nest eggs. Novice investors, many of whom have never experienced a bear market, may invest too heavily in equities or focus on the current hot sector. They won't be so happy when that industry falls from favor and normal return levels are restored.

When this will happen is anyone's guess. Market pundits have been predicting the end of the bull market for years, only to be proved wrong as the market repeatedly stumbles and then recovers. Even though uncertainty is a given in both the economy and the securities markets, economists and financial experts agree that the situation in mid-2000 was unlike any other. Both unemployment and inflation were low. No one was quite sure why the economy continued to grow or why stocks with no earnings traded at 100 times revenues.

History appears to be repeating itself; in 2000 a market downturn began and continues through mid-2001. In the bull markets of the 1920s and the 1950s–1960s, a period of above-average returns was followed by a period of lower-than-average returns. Such may be the case now in mid-2001. If this occurs when you plan to retire, you could find yourself unable to afford the lifestyle you envisioned.

What can you do to ride out the market's twists and turns? Plan to invest for the long term, because you can't predict stock market gains in advance. They come in sudden clumps—a big month or two, followed by flat or down months. If you try to time the market, selling when a price drop scares you and buying when prices are rising, you won't benefit from the market's successful long-term record. Invest as much as you can now to let compounding work for you. Don't be dazzled by companies with rapid revenue growth but no profits. Finally, diversify your portfolio among asset classes (more on this in Chapter 5).

Sources: Geoffrey Colvin, "From Here to Uncertainty," *Fortune,* October 2, 2000, downloaded from Electric Library, Business Edition, business.elibrary.com; Kathy Kristof, "Bull Run Shouldn't Lead Expectations Astray," *Dallas Morning News,* May 5, 2000, p. 5H; and Jane Bryant Quinn, "Challenging the Gospel of Buy and Hold," *Washington Post,* May 7, 2000, p. H2.

As a general rule, *the sooner you receive a return on a given investment, the better.* For example, two investments each requiring a $1,000 outlay and each expected to return $100 interest over a 2-year holding period are *not necessarily* equally desirable. If the first investment returns $100 at the end of the first year and the second investment returns the $100 at the end of the second year, the first investment is preferable (assuming that the base value of each remains at $1,000). Investment 1 is preferable because the $100 interest it earns could be *reinvested to earn more interest* while the $100 in interest from investment 2 is still accruing at the end of the first year. You should not fail to consider time-value concepts when making investment decisions.

Interest: The Basic Return to Savers

interest
the "rent" paid by a borrower for use of the lender's money.

A savings account at a bank is one of the most basic forms of investment. The saver receives interest in exchange for placing idle funds in an account. **Interest** can be viewed as the "rent" paid by a borrower for use of the lender's money. The saver will experience neither a capital gain nor a capital loss, because the value of the investment (the initial deposit) will change only by the amount of interest earned. For the saver, the interest earned over a given time frame is that period's current income.

simple interest
interest paid only on the initial deposit for the amount of time it is held.

Simple Interest The income paid on investment vehicles that pay interest (such as CDs and bonds) is most often calculated using **simple interest:** Interest is paid only on the initial deposit for the amount of time it is held. For example, if you held a $100 initial deposit in an account paying 6% interest for 1½ years, you would earn $9 in interest ($1\frac{1}{2} \times 0.06 \times \$100$) over this period. Had you withdrawn $50 at the end of half a year, the total interest earned over the 1½ years would be $6. You would earn $3 interest on $100 for the first half-year ($\frac{1}{2} \times 0.06 \times \$100$) and $3 interest on $50 for the next full year ($1 \times 0.06 \times \$50$).

true rate of interest (return)
the actual rate of interest earned.

When an investment earns simple interest, the stated rate of interest is the **true rate of interest** (or **return**). This is the actual rate of interest earned. In the foregoing example, the true rate of interest is 6%. Because the interest rate reflects the rate at which current income is earned regardless of the size of the deposit, it is a useful measure of current income.

TABLE 4.4 Savings Account Balance Data (5% interest compounded annually)

Date	(1) Deposit (Withdrawal)	(2) Beginning Account Balance	(3) 0.05 × (2) Interest for Year	(4) (2) + (3) Ending Account Balance
1/1/01	$1,000	$1,000.00	$50.00	$1,050.00
1/1/02	(300)	750.00	37.50	787.50
1/1/03	1,000	1,787.50	89.38	1,876.88

TABLE 4.5 **Savings Account Balance Data (5% interest compounded semiannually)**

Date	(1) Deposit (Withdrawal)	(2) Beginning Account Balance	(3) 0.05 × 1/2 × (2) Interest for 6 Months	(4) (2) + (3) Ending Account Balance
1/1/01	$1,000	$1,000.00	$25.00	$1,025.00
7/1/01		1,025.00	25.63	1,050.63
1/1/02	(300)	750.63	18.77	769.40
7/1/02		769.40	19.24	788.64
1/1/03	1,000	1,788.64	44.72	1,833.36
7/1/03		1,833.36	45.83	1,879.19

compound interest
interest paid not only on the initial deposit but also on any interest accumulated from one period to the next.

Compound Interest **Compound interest** is interest paid not only on the initial deposit but also on any interest accumulated from one period to the next. This is the method usually used by savings institutions. When interest is compounded annually over a single year, compound and simple interest calculations provide similar results. In such a case, the stated interest rate and the true interest rate are equal.

The data in Table 4.4 illustrate compound interest. In this case, the interest earned each year is left on deposit rather than withdrawn. The $50 of interest earned on the $1,000 initial deposit during 2001 becomes part of the beginning (initial) balance on which interest is paid in 2002, and so on. *Note that simple interest is used in the compounding process;* that is, interest is paid only on the initial balance held during the given time period.

When an investment earns compound interest, the stated and true interest rates are equal *only* when interest is compounded annually. In general, *the more frequently interest is compounded at a stated rate, the higher the true rate of interest.* The interest calculations for the deposit data in Table 4.4, assuming that interest is compounded semiannually (twice a year), are shown in Table 4.5. The interest for each 6-month period is found by multiplying the beginning (initial) balance for the 6 months by half of the stated 5% interest rate (see column 3 of Table 4.5). You can see that larger returns are associated with more frequent compounding: Compare the end-of-2003 account balance at 5% compounded annually with the end-of-2003 account balance at 5% compounded semiannually. The semiannual compounding results in a higher balance ($1,879.19 versus $1,876.88). Clearly, with semiannual compounding, the true rate of interest is greater than the 5% annually compounded rate. The true rates of interest associated with a 5% stated rate and various compounding frequencies are shown in Table 4.6.

TABLE 4.6 **True Rate of Interest for Various Compounding Frequencies (5% stated rate of interest)**

Compounding Frequency	True Rate of Interest	Compounding Frequency	True Rate of Interest
Annually	5.000%	Monthly	5.120%
Semiannually	5.063	Weekly	5.125
Quarterly	5.094	Continuously	5.127

continuous compounding interest calculation in which interest is compounded over the smallest possible interval of time.

Continuous compounding calculates interest by compounding over the smallest possible interval of time. It results in the maximum true rate of interest that can be achieved with a given stated rate of interest. Table 4.6 shows that the more frequently interest is compounded, the higher the true rate of interest. Because of the impact that differences in compounding frequencies have on return, you should evaluate the true rate of interest associated with various alternatives before making a deposit.

Computational Aids for Use in Time Value Calculations

Time-consuming calculations are often involved in adjusting for the time value of money. Although you should understand the concepts and mathematics underlying these calculations, the application of time value techniques can be streamlined. We will demonstrate the use of financial tables and hand-held financial calculators as computational aids. Personal computers can also be used to simplify time value calculations, using spreadsheets.

Financial Tables Financial tables include various interest factors that simplify time value calculations. The values in these tables are easily developed from formulas, with various degrees of rounding. The tables are typically indexed by the interest rate (in columns) and the number of periods (in rows). Figure 4.1 shows this general layout. The interest factor at a 20% interest rate for 10 years would be found at the intersection of the 20% column and the 10-period row, as shown by the dark blue box. A full set of the four basic financial tables is included in Appendix A at the end of the book. These tables are described more fully later in this chapter.

HOTLINKS

The Time Value software Web site contains several financial calculators—home financing, investment, lease, personal finance, and retirement. To calculate time values on investments, go to Time Value software and then to Investment Calculators. As with any tool, we recommend that you exercise good judgment before relying on the results.

www.timevalue.com/toolinfo.htm

Financial Calculators Financial calculators also can be used for time value computations. Generally, *financial calculators* include numerous preprogrammed financial routines.

Of the keys pictured and defined in Figure 4.2, we typically use four of the five keys in the left column, plus the compute (CPT) key. One of the four keys represents the unknown value being calculated. (Occasionally, all five of the keys are

FIGURE 4.1

Financial Tables

Layout and use of a financial table

	Interest Rate					↓		
Period	1%	2%	···	10%	···	**20%**	···	50%
1			···		···	⋮	···	
2			···		···	⋮	···	
3			···		···	⋮	···	
⋮	⋮	⋮	···	⋮	···	⋮	···	⋮
→ 10	···	···	···	···	···	**X.XXX**	···	···
⋮	⋮	⋮	···	⋮	···	⋮	···	⋮
20			···		···		···	
⋮	⋮	⋮	···	⋮	···	⋮	···	⋮
50			···		···		···	

FIGURE 4.2

Calculator Keys

Important financial keys on the typical calculator

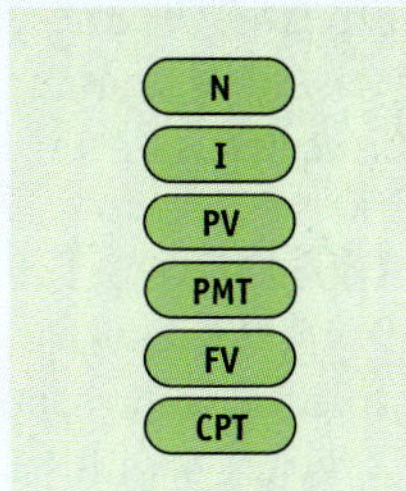

N — Number of periods
I — Interest rate per period
PV — Present value
PMT — Amount of payment (used only for annuities)
FV — Future value
CPT — Compute key used to initiate financial calculation once all values are input

used, with one representing the unknown value.) The keystrokes on some of the more sophisticated calculators are menu-driven: After you select the appropriate routine, the calculator prompts you to input each value; on these calculators, a compute key is not needed to obtain a solution. Regardless, any calculator with the basic time value functions can be used instead of financial tables.

Once you understand the basic underlying concepts, you probably will want to use a calculator to streamline routine financial calculations. With a little practice, you can increase both the speed and accuracy of your financial computations. Note that because of a calculator's greater precision, slight differences are likely to exist between values calculated using financial tables and those found with a financial calculator. Remember that *conceptual understanding of the material is the objective.* An ability to solve problems with a calculator does not necessarily reflect such an understanding, so don't just settle for answers. Work with the material until you are sure you also understand the concepts.

Future Value: An Extension of Compounding

future value
the amount to which a current deposit will grow over a period of time when it is placed in an account paying compound interest.

Future value is the amount to which a current deposit will grow over a period of time when it is placed in an account paying compound interest. Consider a deposit of \$1,000 that is earning 8% (0.08 in decimal form) compounded annually. The following calculation yields the future value of this deposit at the end of 1 year.

Equation 4.1

$$\text{Future value at end of year 1} = \$1{,}000 \times (1 + 0.08) = \underline{\underline{\$1{,}080}}$$

If the money were left on deposit for another year, 8% interest would be paid on the account balance of \$1,080. Thus, at the end of the second year, there would be \$1,166.40 in the account. This amount would represent the beginning-of-year balance of \$1,080 plus 8% of the \$1,080 (\$86.40) in interest. The future value at the end of the second year would be calculated as follows.

Equation 4.2

$$\text{Future value at end of year 2} = \$1{,}080 \times (1 + 0.08) = \underline{\underline{\$1{,}166.40}}$$

To find the future value of the $1,000 at the end of year *n,* the procedure illustrated above would be repeated *n* times. Future values can be determined either mathematically or by using a financial table, financial calculator, or a computer. Here we demonstrate use of a table of future-value interest factors.

INVESTOR FACTS

TIME IS ON YOUR SIDE—It's never too early to begin saving for retirement, even if it seems a long way off. The power of compounding will multiply your funds considerably. If you begin today and sock away $2,000 at the end of each year for just the next 8 years and earn 10% per year on those funds, at the end of 40 years the $16,000 you deposited will have grown to more than $480,000. You can wait, but it will cost you. Time is your biggest investment ally.

TABLE USE The factors in Appendix A, Table A.1 represent the amount to which an initial $1 deposit would grow for various periods (typically years) and interest rates. For example, a dollar deposited in an account paying 8% interest and left there for 2 years would accumulate to $1.166. Using the future-value interest factor for 8% and 2 years (1.166), we can find the future value of an investment that can earn 8% over 2 years: We would *multiply* the amount invested by the appropriate interest factor. In the case of $1,000 left on deposit for 2 years at 8%, the resulting future value is $1,166 (1.166 × $1,000). This agrees (except for a slight rounding difference) with the value calculated in Equation 4.2.

A few points with respect to Appendix A, Table A.1, Future-Value Interest Factors for One Dollar, should be emphasized.

1. The values in the table represent factors for determining the future value of one dollar at the *end* of the given year.
2. As the interest rate increases for any given year, the future-value interest factor also increases. The higher the interest rate, the greater the future value.
3. For a given interest rate, the future value of a dollar increases with the passage of time.
4. The future-value interest factor is always greater than 1. Only if the interest rate were zero would this factor equal 1, and the future value would therefore equal the initial deposit.

Future Value of an Annuity

annuity
a stream of equal cash flows that occur at equal intervals over time.

An **annuity** is a stream of equal cash flows that occur at equal intervals over time. Receiving $1,000 per year at the end of each of the next 8 years is an example of an annuity. The cash flows can be *inflows* of returns earned from an investment or *outflows* of funds invested (deposited) to earn future returns.

ordinary annuity
an annuity for which the cash flows occur at the *end* of each period.

Investors are sometimes interested in finding the future value of an annuity. Their concern is typically with what's called an **ordinary annuity**—one for which the cash flows occur at the *end* of each period. Here we can simplify our calculations by using either tables of these factors for an annuity or a financial calculator. (A complete set of these tables is included in Appendix A, Table A.2.)

TABLE USE The factors in Appendix A, Table A.2 represent the amount to which annual end-of-year deposits of $1 would grow for various periods (years) and interest rates. For example, a dollar deposited at the end of each year for 8 years into an account paying 6% interest would accumulate to $9.897. Using the future-value interest factor for an 8-year annuity earning 6% (9.897), we can find the future value of this cash flow: We would *multiply* the annual investment by the appropriate interest factor. In the case of $1,000 deposited at the end of each year for 8 years at 6%, the resulting future value is $9,897 (9.897 × $1,000).

Present Value: An Extension of Future Value

present value
the *value today* of a sum to be received at some future date; the inverse of future value.

discount rate
the annual rate of return that could be earned currently on a similar investment; used when finding present value; also called *opportunity cost.*

Present value is the inverse of future value. That is, rather than measuring the value of a present amount at some future date, **present value** expresses the *current value of a future sum.* By applying present-value techniques, we can calculate the *value today* of a sum to be received at some future date.

When determining the present value of a future sum, we are answering the basic question "How much would have to be deposited today into an account paying i% interest in order to equal a specified sum to be received so many years in the future?" The applicable interest rate when we are finding present value is commonly called the **discount rate** (or *opportunity cost*). It represents the annual rate of return that could be earned currently on a similar investment.

The basic present-value calculation is best illustrated using a simple example. Imagine that you are offered an opportunity that will provide you, 1 year from today, with exactly $1,000. If you could earn 8% on similar types of investments, how much is the most you would pay for this opportunity? In other words, what is the present value of $1,000 to be received 1 year from now, discounted at 8%? Letting x equal the present value, we can use Equation 4.3 to describe this situation.

Equation 4.3

$$x \times (1 + 0.08) = \$1{,}000$$

Solving Equation 4.3 for x, we get:

Equation 4.4

$$x = \frac{\$1{,}000}{(1 + 0.08)} = \underline{\underline{\$925.93}}$$

Thus the present value of $1,000 to be received 1 year from now, discounted at 8%, is $925.93. In other words, $925.93 deposited today into an account paying 8% interest will accumulate to $1,000 in 1 year. To check this conclusion, *multiply* the future-value interest factor for 8% and 1 year, or 1.080 (from Appendix A, Table A.1), by $925.93. The result is a future value of $1,000 (1.080 × $925.93).

The calculations involved in finding the present value of sums to be received in the distant future are more complex than for a 1-year investment. Here we use tables of present-value interest factors to simplify these calculations. (A complete set of these tables is included in Appendix A, Table A.3.)

TABLE USE The factors in Appendix A, Table A.3 represent the present value of $1 associated with various combinations of periods (years) and discount (interest) rates. For example, the present value of $1 to be received 1 year from now discounted at 8% is $0.926. Using this factor (0.926), we can find the present value of $1,000 to be received 1 year from now at an 8% discount rate by *multiplying* it by $1,000. The resulting present value of $926 (0.926 × $1,000) agrees (except for a slight rounding difference) with the value calculated in Equation 4.4.

Another example may help clarify the use of present-value tables. The present value of $500 to be received 7 years from now, discounted at 6%, is calculated as follows:

$$\text{Present value} = 0.665 \times \$500 = \underline{\underline{\$332.50}}$$

The 0.665 represents the present-value interest factor from Appendix A, Table A.3 for 7 years discounted at 6%.

A few points with respect to Appendix A, Table A.3, Present-Value Interest Factors for One Dollar, should be emphasized.

1. The present-value interest factor for a single sum is always less than 1. Only if the discount rate were zero would this factor equal 1.
2. The higher the discount rate for a given year, the smaller the present-value interest factor. In other words, the greater your opportunity cost, the less you have to invest today in order to have a given amount in the future.
3. The further in the future a sum is to be received, the less it is worth at present.
4. At a discount rate of 0%, the present-value interest factor always equals 1. Therefore, in such a case the future value of a sum equals its present value.

The Present Value of a Stream of Returns

mixed stream
a stream of returns that, unlike an annuity, exhibits no special pattern.

In the preceding paragraphs we illustrated the technique for finding the present value of a single sum to be received at some future date. Because the returns from a given investment are likely to be received at various future dates rather than as a single lump sum, we also need to be able to find the present value of a *stream of returns*. A stream of returns can be viewed as a package of single-sum returns; it may be classified as a mixed stream or an annuity. A **mixed stream** of returns is one that exhibits no special pattern. As noted earlier, an *annuity* is a stream of equal periodic returns. Table 4.7 shows the end-of-year returns illustrating each of these types of patterns. To find the present value of each of these streams (measured at the *beginning* of 2002), we must calculate the total of the present values of the individual annual returns. Because shortcuts can be used for an annuity, calculation of the present value of each type of return stream is illustrated separately.

Present Value of a Mixed Stream To find the present value of the mixed stream of returns given in Table 4.7, we must find and then total the present values of the individual returns. Assuming a 9% discount rate, we can streamline the calculation of the present value of the mixed stream using financial tables.

TABLE 4.7 Mixed and Annuity Return Streams

End of Year	Returns: Mixed Stream	Returns: Annuity
2002	$30	$50
2003	40	50
2004	50	50
2005	60	50
2006	70	50

TABLE 4.8 Mixed-Stream Present-Value Calculation

End of Year	(1) Return	(2) 9% Present-Value Interest Factor	(3) (1) × (2) Present Value
2002	$30	.917	$ 27.51
2003	40	.842	33.68
2004	50	.772	38.60
2005	60	.708	42.48
2006	70	.650	45.50
		Present value of stream	$187.77

Note: Column 1 values are from Table 4.7. Column 2 values are from Appendix A, Table A.3, for a 9% discount rate and 1 through 5 periods (years).

TABLE USE Table A.3 in Appendix A can be used to find the appropriate present-value interest factors for each of the 5 years of the mixed stream's life at the 9% discount rate. Table 4.8 demonstrates the use of these factors, shown in column 2, with the corresponding year's return, shown in column 1, to calculate the present value of each year's return, shown in column 3. The total of the present values of the returns for each of the 5 years is found by summing column 3. The resulting present value of $187.77 represents the amount today (*beginning* of 2002) that, invested at 9%, would provide the same returns as those shown in column 1 of Table 4.8.

Present Value of an Annuity The present value of an annuity can be found in the same way as the present value of a mixed stream. Fortunately, however, there are simpler approaches. Here we simplify our calculations by using tables of these factors for an annuity. (A complete set of these tables is included in Appendix A, Table A.4.)

TABLE USE The factors in Appendix A, Table A.4 represent the present value of a $1 annuity for various periods (years) and discount (interest) rates. For example, the present value of $1 to be received at the end of each year for the next 5 years discounted at 9% is $3.890. Using the present-value interest factor for a 5-year annuity discounted at 9% (3.890), we can find the present value of the $50, 5-year annuity (given in Table 4.7) at a 9% discount rate: We *multiply* the annual return by the appropriate interest factor. The resulting present value is $194.50 (3.890 × $50).

Determining a Satisfactory Investment

satisfactory investment
an investment whose present value of benefits (discounted at the appropriate rate) *equals* or *exceeds* the present value of its costs.

Time value of money techniques can be used to determine an acceptable investment. Ignoring risk at this point, a **satisfactory investment** would be one for which the present value of benefits (discounted at the appropriate rate) *equals* or *exceeds* the present value of its costs. Because the cost of the investment would be incurred initially (at time zero), the cost and its present value are viewed as one and the same. The three possible benefit–cost relationships and their interpretations follow:

1. If the present value of the benefits *just equals the cost,* you would earn a rate of return equal to the discount rate.
2. If the present value of benefits *exceeds the cost,* you would earn a rate of return greater than the discount rate.
3. If the present value of benefits is *less than the cost,* you would earn a rate of return less than the discount rate.

You would prefer only those investments for which the present value of benefits equals or exceeds its cost—situations 1 and 2. In these cases, the rate of return would be equal to or greater than the discount rate.

The information in Table 4.9 demonstrates the application of present value to investment decision making using a financial table. (*Note:* A financial calculator could have been used, as described earlier, to find the present value of this mixed-stream investment.) Assuming an 8% discount rate, we can see that the present value (at the beginning of 2002) of the income (returns) to be received over the assumed 7-year period (year-end 2002 through year-end 2008) is $1,175.28. If the cost of the investment (beginning of 2002) were any amount less than or equal to the $1,175.28 present value, it would be acceptable. At that cost, a rate of return equal to at least 8% would be earned. At a cost above the $1,175.28 present value, the investment would not be acceptable. At that cost, the rate of return would be less than 8%. Clearly, in that case it would be preferable to find an alternative investment with a present value of benefits that equals or exceeds its cost.

TABLE 4.9 Present Value Applied to an Investment

End of Year	(1) Return	(2) 8% Present-Value Interest Factor*	(3) (1) × (2) Present Value
2002	$ 90	.926	$ 83.34
2003	100	.857	85.70
2004	110	.794	87.34
2005	120	.735	88.20
2006	100	.681	68.10
2007	100	.630	63.00
2008	1,200	.583	699.60
		Present value of income	$1, 175.28

* Column 2 values are from Appendix A, Table A.3, for an 8% discount rate and 1 through 7 periods (years).

Measuring Return

LG 4

Thus far, we have discussed the concept of return in terms of its two components (current income and capital gains) and the key factors that affect the level of return (internal characteristics and external forces). These discussions intentionally oversimplified the computations involved in determining the historical or expected return. To compare returns from different investment vehicles, we need to incorporate time value of money concepts that explicitly consider differences in the timing of investment income and capital gains. We must also be able to place a current value on future benefits. Here we will look at several measures that enable us to compare alternative investment vehicles. First, we must define and consider the relationships among various rates of return.

Real, Risk-Free, and Required Returns

Rational investors will choose investments that fully compensate them for the risk involved. The greater the risk, the greater the return required by investors. The return that fully compensates for an investment's risk is called the **required return.** To better understand required returns, it is helpful to consider their makeup. The required return on any investment *j* consists of three basic components: the real rate of return, an expected inflation premium, and a risk premium, as noted in Equation 4.5.

required return
the rate of return an investor must earn on an investment to be fully compensated for its risk.

Equation 4.5

$$\text{Required return on investment } j = \text{Real rate of return} + \text{Expected inflation premium} + \text{Risk premium for investment } j$$

Equation 4.5a

$$r_j = r^* + IP + RP_j$$

real rate of return
the rate of return that could be earned in a perfect world where all outcomes are known and certain—where there was no risk.

expected inflation premium
the average rate of inflation expected in the future.

risk-free rate
the rate of return that can be earned on a risk-free investment; the sum of the real rate of return and the expected inflation premium.

The **real rate of return** is the rate of return that could be earned in a perfect world where all outcomes were known and certain—where there was no risk. In such a world, the real rate of return would create an equilibrium between the supply of savings and the demand for funds. The real rate of return changes with changing economic conditions, tastes, and preferences. Historically, it has been relatively stable and in the range of 1% to 2%. For convenience, we'll assume a real rate of return of 2%.

The **expected inflation premium** represents the average rate of inflation expected in the future. By adding the expected inflation premium to the real rate of return, we get the **risk-free rate.** This is the rate of return that can be earned on a risk-free investment, most commonly a 3-month U.S. Treasury bill. The formula for this rate is shown in Equation 4.6.

Equation 4.6

$$\text{Risk-free rate} = \text{Real rate of return} + \text{Expected inflation premium}$$

Equation 4.6a

$$R_F = r^* + IP$$

risk premium
a return premium that reflects the issue and issuer characteristics associated with a given investment vehicle.

To demonstrate, a real rate of return of 2% and an expected inflation premium of 4% would result in a risk-free rate of return of 6%.

The required return can be found by adding to the risk-free rate a **risk premium,** which varies depending on specific issue and issuer characteristics. *Issue characteristics* are the type of vehicle (stock, bond, etc.), its maturity (2 years, 5 years, infinity, etc.), and its features (voting/nonvoting, callable/noncallable, etc.). *Issuer characteristics* are industry and company factors such as the line of business and financial condition of the issuer. Together, the issue and issuer factors cause investors to require a risk premium above the risk-free rate.

Substituting the risk-free rate, R_F, from Equation 4.6a, into Equation 4.5a for the first two terms to the right of the equal sign ($r^* + IP$), we get Equation 4.7.

Equation 4.7

$$\text{Required return on investment } j = \text{Risk-free rate} + \text{Risk premium for investment } j$$

Equation 4.7a

$$r_j = R_F + RP_j$$

For example, if the required return on IBM common stock is 11% when the risk-free rate is 6%, investors require a 5% risk premium (11% − 6%) as compensation for the risk associated with common stock (the issue) and IBM (the issuer). Later in Chapter 5, we will explore further the relationship between the risk premium and required returns.

Next, we consider the specifics of return measurement.

Holding Period Return

The return to a *saver* is the amount of interest earned on a given deposit. Of course, the amount "invested" in a savings account is not subject to change in value, as is the amount invested in stocks, bonds, and mutual funds. Because we are concerned with a broad range of investment vehicles, we need a measure of return that captures both periodic benefits and changes in value. One such measure is *holding period return.*

The **holding period** is the period of time over which one wishes to measure the return on an investment vehicle. When comparing returns, be sure to use holding periods of the same length. For example, comparing the return on a stock over the 6-month period ended December 31, 2001, with the return on a bond over the 1-year period ended June 30, 2001, could result in a poor investment decision. To avoid this problem, be sure you define the holding period. It is often best to annualize the holding period and use that as a standard. And when comparing the returns from alternative investment vehicles, you should use similar periods in time.

holding period
the period of time over which one wishes to measure the return on an investment vehicle.

Understanding Return Components Earlier in this chapter we identified the two components of investment return: current income and capital gains (or losses). The portion of current income received by the investor during the period is a **realized return.** Most but not all current income is realized. (Accrued interest on taxable zero-coupon bonds is treated as current income for tax purposes but is not a realized return until the bond is sold or matures.) Capital gains returns, on the other hand, are realized only when the investment vehicle is actually sold at the end of the holding period. Until the vehicle is sold, the capital gain is merely a **paper return.**

realized return
current income actually received by an investor during a given period.

paper return
a return that has been achieved but not yet realized by an investor during a given period.

For example, the capital gain return on an investment that increases in market value from $50 to $70 during a year is $20. For that capital gain to be realized, you would have to have sold the investment for $70 at the end of that year.

An investor who purchased the same investment but plans to hold it for another 3 years would also have experienced the $20 capital gain return during the year specified, but he or she *would not have realized the gain in terms of cash flow.* However, *even if the capital gains return is not realized during the period over which the total return is measured, it must be included in the return calculation.*

A second point to recognize about returns is that both the current income and the capital gains component can have a negative value. Occasionally, an investment may have negative current income. That is, you may be required to pay out cash to meet certain obligations. This situation is most likely to occur in various types of property investments. For example, assume you have purchased an apartment complex and the rental income is inadequate to meet the payments associated with its operation. In such a case, you would have to pay the deficit in operating costs, and that payment would represent negative current income. A capital loss can occur on *any* investment vehicle: Stocks, bonds, mutual funds, options, futures, real estate, and gold can all decline in market value over a given holding period.

holding period return (HPR) the total return earned from holding an investment for a specified holding period (*usually 1 year or less*).

Computing the Holding Period Return (HPR) The **holding period return (HPR)** is the total return earned from holding an investment for a specified period of time (the holding period). The HPR is customarily used with holding periods of *1 year or less.* (We'll explain why later.) It represents the sum of current income and capital gains (or losses) achieved over the holding period, divided by the beginning investment value. The equation for HPR is

Equation 4.8

$$\text{Holding period return} = \frac{\begin{matrix}\text{Current income} \\ \text{during period}\end{matrix} + \begin{matrix}\text{Capital gain (or loss)} \\ \text{during period}\end{matrix}}{\text{Beginning investment value}}$$

Equation 4.8a

$$\text{HPR} = \frac{C + CG}{V_0}$$

where

Equation 4.9

$$\begin{matrix}\text{Capital gain (or loss)} \\ \text{during period}\end{matrix} = \begin{matrix}\text{Ending} \\ \text{investment value}\end{matrix} - \begin{matrix}\text{Beginning} \\ \text{investment value}\end{matrix}$$

Equation 4.9a

$$CG = V_n - V_0$$

The HPR equation provides a convenient method for either measuring the total return realized or estimating the total return expected. For example, Table 4.10 summarizes the key financial variables for four investment vehicles over the past year. The total current income and capital gain or loss during the holding period are given in the lines labeled (1) and (3), respectively. The total return over the year is calculated, as shown in line (4), by adding these two sources of return. Dividing the total return value [line (4)] by the beginning-of-year investment value [line (2)], we find the holding period return, given in line (5). Over the 1-year holding period the common stock had the highest HPR (12.25%). The savings account had the lowest (6%).

As these calculations show, all we need to find the HPR is beginning- and end-of-period investment values, along with the value of current income received by the investor during the period. Note that if the current income and

TABLE 4.10 Key Financial Variables for Four Investment Vehicles

	Investment Vehicle			
	Savings Account	Common Stock	Bond	Futures Contract
Cash received				
1st quarter	$15	$10	$ 0	$0
2nd quarter	15	10	70	0
3rd quarter	15	10	0	0
4th quarter	15	15	70	0
(1) Total current income	$60	$45	$140	$0
Investment value				
End-of-year	$1,000	$2,200	$ 970	$3,300
(2) Beginning-of-year	1,000	2,000	1,000	3,000
(3) Capital gain (loss)	$ 0	$ 200	($ 30)	$ 300
(4) Total return [(1) + (3)]	$ 60	$ 245	$ 110	$ 300
(5) Holding period return [(4) ÷ (2)]	6.00%	12.25%	11.00%	10.00%

capital gain (or loss) values in lines (1) and (3) of Table 4.10 had been drawn from a 6-month rather than a 1-year period, the HPR values calculated in line (5) would have been *the same.*

Holding period return can be negative or positive. HPRs can be calculated with Equation 4.8 using either historical data (as in the preceding example) or forecast data.

Using the HPR in Investment Decisions The holding period return is easy to use in making investment decisions. Because it considers both current income and capital gains relative to the beginning investment value, it tends to overcome any problems that might be associated with comparing investments of different size. If we look only at the total returns calculated for each of the four investments in Table 4.10 [line (4)], the futures contract investment appears best, because it has the highest total return. However, the futures contract investment would require the largest dollar outlay ($3,000). The holding period return offers a *relative comparison,* by dividing the total return by the amount of the investment. Comparing HPRs, we find the investment alternative with the *highest return per invested dollar* to be the common stock's HPR of 12.25%. Because the return per invested dollar reflects the efficiency of the investment, the HPR provides a logical method for evaluating and comparing investment returns, particularly for holding periods of 1 year or less.

Yield: The Internal Rate of Return

An alternative way to define a satisfactory investment is in terms of the compound annual rate of return it earns. Why do we need an alternative to the HPR? Because *HPR fails to consider the time value of money.* Although the holding period return is useful with investments held for 1 year or less, it is generally inappropriate for longer holding periods. Sophisticated investors typically do not use HPR when the time period is greater than 1 year. Instead, they use a present-value-based measure, called **yield** (or **internal rate of**

yield (internal rate of return) the compound annual rate of return earned by a long-term investment; the discount rate that produces a present value of the investment's benefits that just equals its cost.

return), to determine the compound annual rate of return earned on investments held for longer than one year. Yield can also be defined as the discount rate that produces a present value of benefits just equal to its cost.

Once you know the yield you can decide whether an investment is acceptable. If the yield on an investment *is equal to or greater than the required return,* then the investment is acceptable. An investment with a yield *below the required return* is unacceptable; it will not compensate you adequately for the risk involved.

The yield on an investment providing a single future cash flow is relatively easy to calculate. The yield on an investment providing a stream of future cash flows generally involves more time-consuming calculations. Many hand-held financial calculators as well as computer software programs are available for simplifying these calculations.

Yield for a Single Cash Flow Some investments, such as U.S. savings bonds, stocks paying no dividends, zero-coupon bonds, and futures contracts are purchased by paying a fixed amount up front. The investor expects them to provide *no periodic income,* but to provide a single—and, the investor hopes, a large—future cash flow at maturity or when the investment is sold. The yield on investments expected to provide a single future cash flow can be estimated using either financial tables or a financial calculator.

TABLE USE Assume you wish to find the yield on an investment costing $1,000 today that you expect will be worth $1,400 at the end of a 5-year holding period. We can find the yield on this investment by solving for the discount rate that causes the present value of the $1,400 to be received 5 years from now to equal the initial investment of $1,000.

The first step involves dividing the present value ($1,000) by the future value ($1,400), which results in a value of 0.714. The second step is to find in the table of present-value interest factors the 5-year factor that is closest to 0.714. Referring to the present-value table (Appendix A, Table A.3), we find that for 5 years the factor closest to 0.714 is 0.713, which occurs at a 7% discount rate. Therefore, the yield on this investment is about 7%. If you require a 6% return, this investment is acceptable (7% expected return ≥ 6% required return).

Yield for a Stream of Income Investment vehicles such as income-oriented stock and bonds typically provide the investor with a *stream of income.* The yield (or internal rate of return) for a stream of income (returns) is generally more difficult to estimate. The most accurate approach is based on searching for the discount rate that produces a present value of income just equal to the cost of the investment. It can be applied using either financial tables or a financial calculator.

TABLE USE If we use the investment in Table 4.9 and assume that its cost is $1,100, we find that the yield must be greater than 8%. At an 8% discount rate, the present value of income (calculated in column 3 of Table 4.9) is greater than the cost ($1,175.28 vs. $1,100). The present values at 9% and 10% discount rates are calculated in Table 4.11. If we look at the present values of income calculated at the 9% and 10% rates, we see that the yield on

TABLE 4.11 Yield Calculation for a $1,100 Investment

Year	(1) Income	(2) 9% Present-Value Interest Factor	(3) (1) × (2) Present Value at 9%	(4) 10% Present-Value Interest Factor	(5) (1) × (4) Present Value at 10%
2002	$ 90	.917	$ 82.53	.909	$ 81.81
2003	100	.842	84.20	.826	82.60
2004	110	.772	84.92	.751	82.61
2005	120	.708	84.96	.683	81.96
2006	100	.650	65.00	.621	62.10
2007	100	.596	59.60	.564	56.40
2008	1,200	.547	656.40	.513	615.60
	Present value of income		$1,117.61		$1,063.08

INVESTOR FACTS

STAY THE COURSE—It's tempting to buy and sell as market returns fluctuate, but consider the results: According to Ibbotson Associates' research, a dollar invested in stocks at the end of 1979 grew to $26.82 by year-end 1999. However, if during those 20 years, the investor for some reason took the dollar out of the market during just the best 15 months for stocks, it would have grown to only $6.81.

Source: Harriet Johnson Brackey, "Study: Female Investors Better: Women Don't Seem to Buy, Sell as Often as Men Do," *Dallas Morning News*, July 31, 2000, p. 4D.

the investment must be somewhere between 9% and 10%. At 9% the present value ($1,117.61) is too high. At 10% the present value ($1,063.08) is too low. The discount rate that causes the present value of income to be closer to the $1,100 cost is 9%, because it is only $17.61 away from $1,100. Thus, if you require an 8% return, the investment is clearly acceptable.

Interest on Interest: The Critical Assumption The critical assumption underlying the use of yield as a return measure is an ability to earn a return equal to the yield on *all income* received during the holding period. This concept can best be illustrated with a simple example. Suppose you buy a $1,000 U.S. Treasury bond that pays 8% annual interest ($80) over its 20-year maturity. Each year you receive $80, and at maturity the $1,000 in principal is repaid. There is no loss in capital, no default; all payments are made right on time. But you must be able to *reinvest* the $80 annual interest receipts in order to earn 8% on this investment.

Figure 4.3 shows the elements of return on this investment to demonstrate the point. If you don't *reinvest* the interest income of $80 per year, you'll end up on the 5% line. You'll have $2,600—the $1,000 principal plus $1,600 interest income ($80/year × 20 years)—at the end of 20 years. (The yield on a single cash flow of $1,000 today that will be worth $2,600 in 20 years is about 5%.) To move to the 8% line, you have to earn 8% on the annual interest receipts. If you do, you'll have $4,661—the $1,000 principal plus the $3,661 future value of the 20-year $80 annuity of interest receipts invested at 8% [$80/year × 45.762 (the 8%, 20-year factor from Appendix A, Table A.2)]—at the end of 20 years. (The yield on a single cash flow of $1,000 today that will be worth $4,661 in 20 years is 8%.) The future value of the investment would be $2,061 greater ($4,661 − $2,600) with interest on interest than without reinvestment of the interest receipts.

It should be clear to you that if you start out with an 8% investment, *you have to earn that same rate of return when reinvesting your income.* The rate of return you start with is the required, or minimum, **reinvestment rate**—the rate of return earned on interest or other income received over the relevant investment horizon. By putting your current income to work at this rate, you'll earn the rate of return you set out to. If you fail to do so, your return will

reinvestment rate
the rate of return earned on interest or other income received from an investment over its investment horizon.

FIGURE 4.3

Earning Interest on Interest

If you invested in a $1,000, 20-year bond with an 8% coupon, you would have only $2,600 at the end of 20 years if you did not reinvest the $80 annual interest receipts—only about a 5% rate of return. If you reinvested the interest at the 8% interest rate, you would have $4,661 at the end of 20 years—an 8% rate of return. To achieve the calculated yield of 8%, you must therefore be able to earn interest on interest at that rate.

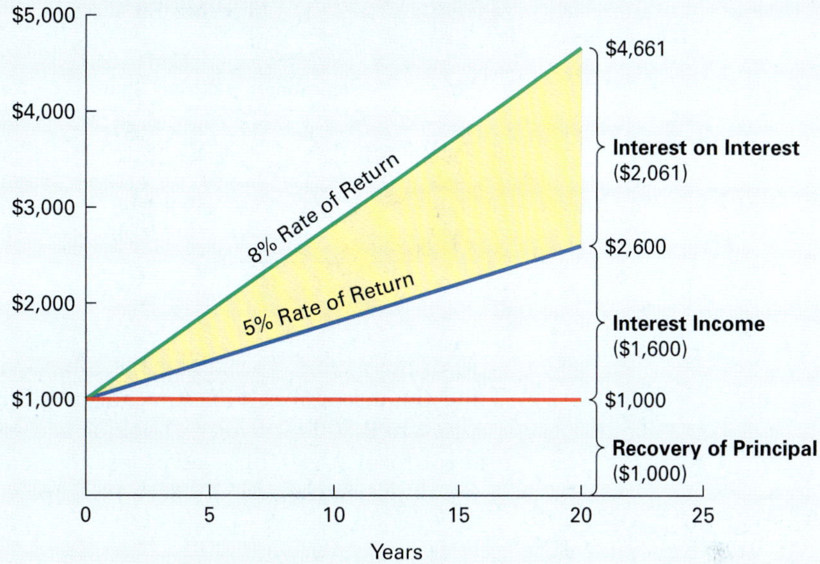

decline accordingly. Even though a bond was used in this illustration, the same principle applies to any other type of investment vehicle.

fully compounded rate of return
the rate of return that includes interest earned on interest.

The earning of interest on interest is what the market refers to as a **fully compounded rate of return.** It's an important concept: You can't start reaping the full potential from your investments until you start earning a fully compounded rate of return on them.

Interest on interest is a particularly important element of return for investment programs that involve a lot of current income. You have to reinvest current income. (With capital gains, the investment vehicle itself is automatically doing the reinvesting.) It follows, therefore, that for investment programs that lean toward income-oriented securities, the continued reinvestment of income plays an important role in investment success.

Finding Growth Rates

rate of growth
the compound annual rate of change in the value of a stream of income.

In addition to finding compound annual rates of return, we frequently need to find the **rate of growth.** This is the compound annual rate of change in the value of a stream of income, particularly dividends or earnings. Here we use an example to demonstrate a simple technique for estimating growth rates using either a financial table or a financial calculator.

Table Use Imagine that you wish to find the rate of growth for the dividends given in Table 4.12. The year numbers in the table show that 1993 is viewed as the base year (year 0); the subsequent years, 1994–2002, are considered years 1 through 9, respectively. Although 10 years of data are presented in Table 4.12, they represent only 9 years of growth, because the value for the earliest year must be viewed as the initial value at time zero.

To find the growth rate, we first divide the dividend for the earliest year (1993) by the dividend for the latest year (2002). The resulting quotient is 0.700 ($2.45 ÷ $3.50). It represents the value of the present-value interest

TABLE 4.12 Dividends Per Share

Year	Year Number	Dividends per Share	Year	Year Number	Dividends per Share
1993	0	$2.45	1998	5	$3.15
1994	1	2.60	1999	6	3.20
1995	2	2.80	2000	7	3.20
1996	3	3.00	2001	8	3.40
1997	4	3.20	2002	9	3.50

factor for 9 years. To estimate the compound annual dividend growth rate, we find the discount rate in Appendix A, Table A.3 associated with the factor closest to 0.700 for 9 years. Looking across year 9 in Table A.3 shows that the factor for 4% is 0.703—very close to the 0.700 value. Therefore, the growth rate of the dividends in Table 4.12 is approximately 4%.

The use of growth rates, which are often an important input to the common stock valuation process, is explored in greater detail in Chapter 8.

Risk: The Other Side of the Coin

LG 5 LG 6

risk
the chance that the actual return from an investment may differ from what is expected.

risk-return tradeoff
the relationship between risk and return, in which investments with more risk should provide higher returns, and vice versa.

Thus far, our primary concern in this chapter has been return. However, we cannot consider return without also looking at risk. Expanding a bit on its definition in Chapter 1, risk is the chance that the actual return from an investment may differ from what is expected.

The risk associated with a given investment is directly related to its expected return. In general, the broader the range of possible returns, the greater the investment's risk, and vice versa. Put another way, riskier investments should provide higher levels of return. Otherwise, what incentive is there for an investor to risk his or her capital? In general, investors attempt to minimize risk for a given level of return or to maximize return for a given level of risk. This relationship between risk and return is called the **risk-return tradeoff.** It is introduced here and will be discussed in greater detail in Chapter 5. Here we begin by examining the key sources of risk. We then consider the measurement and assessment of risk: the risk of a single asset, the assessment of risk associated with a potential investment, and the steps by which return and risk can be combined in the decision process.

Sources of Risk

The risk associated with a given investment vehicle may result from a combination of possible sources. A prudent investor considers how the major sources of risk, discussed below, might affect potential investment vehicles. Of course, as discussed in Chapter 2, *currency exchange risk* should also be considered when investing internationally.

business risk
the degree of uncertainty associated with an investment's earnings and the investment's ability to pay the returns owed investors.

Business Risk In general, **business risk** is the degree of uncertainty associated with an investment's earnings and the investment's ability to pay the returns (interest, principal, dividends) owed investors. For example, business owners may receive no return if the firm's earnings are not adequate to meet obligations. Debtholders, on the other hand, are likely to receive some (but not necessarily all) of the amount owed them, because of the preferential treatment legally accorded to debt.

Much of the business risk associated with a given investment vehicle is related to its kind of business. For example, the business risk of a public utility common stock differs from a high-fashion clothing manufacturer's or an Internet start-up's common stock. Generally, investments in similar kinds of firms have similar business risk, although differences in management, costs, and location can cause varying levels of risk.

financial risk
the degree of uncertainty of payment attributable to the mix of debt and equity used to finance a business; the larger the proportion of debt financing, the greater this risk.

Financial Risk The degree of uncertainty of payment attributable to the mix of debt and equity used to finance a business is **financial risk.** The larger the proportion of debt used to finance a firm, the greater its financial risk. Debt financing obligates the firm to make interest payments as well as to repay the debt, thus increasing risk. Inability to meet obligations associated with the use of debt could result in business failure and in losses for bondholders as well as stockholders and owners.

purchasing power risk
the chance that changing price levels (inflation or deflation) will adversely affect investment returns.

Purchasing Power Risk The chance that changing price levels (inflation or deflation) will adversely affect investment returns is **purchasing power risk.** Specifically, this risk is the chance that generally rising prices (inflation) will reduce *purchasing power* (the amount of a given commodity that can be purchased with a dollar). For example, if last year a dollar would buy three candy bars and today it can buy only two because candy bars now cost 50 cents each, the purchasing power of your dollar has decreased. In periods of declining price levels (deflation), the purchasing power of the dollar increases.

In general, investments whose values move with general price levels have low purchasing power risk and are most profitable during periods of rising prices. Those that provide fixed returns have high purchasing power risk, and they are most profitable during periods of low inflation or declining price levels. The returns on stocks of durable-goods manufacturers, for example, tend to move with the general price level, whereas returns from deposit accounts and bonds do not.

interest rate risk
the chance that changes in interest rates will adversely affect a security's value.

Interest Rate Risk Securities are especially affected by interest rate risk. This is particularly true for those securities that offer purchasers a fixed periodic return. **Interest rate risk** is the chance that changes in interest rates will adversely affect a security's value. The interest rate changes themselves result from changes in the general relationship between the supply of and the demand for money.

As interest rates change, the prices of many securities fluctuate: They typically decrease with increasing interest rates, and they increase with decreasing interest rates. As we will see in greater detail in Chapters 9 and 10, the prices of fixed-income securities such as bonds drop when interest rates rise. They thus provide purchasers with the same rate of return that would be available at prevailing rates. The opposite occurs when interest rates fall: The return on a fixed-income security is adjusted downward to a competitive level by an upward adjustment in its market price.

A second, more subtle aspect of interest rate risk is associated with reinvestment of income. As noted in our earlier discussion of interest on interest, only if you can earn the initial rate of return on income received from an investment can you achieve a *fully compounded rate of return* equal to the initial rate of return. In other words, if a bond pays 8% annual interest, you must be able to earn 8% on the interest received during the bond's holding period in order to earn a fully compounded 8% rate of return over that period. This same aspect of interest rate risk applies to reinvestment of the proceeds received from an investment at its maturity or sale.

A final aspect of interest rate risk is related to investing in short-term securities such as T-bills and certificates of deposit (discussed in Chapter 1). Investors face the risk that when short-term securities mature, their proceeds may have to be invested in lower-yielding, new short-term securities. By initially making a long-term investment, you can lock in a return for a period of years, rather than face the risk of declines in short-term interest rates. Clearly, when interest rates are declining, the returns from a strategy of investing in short-term securities are adversely affected. On the other hand, interest rate increases have a positive impact on such a strategy. The chance that interest rates will decline is therefore the interest rate risk of a short-term security investment strategy.

Most investment vehicles are subject to interest rate risk. Although fixed-income securities are most directly affected by interest rate movements, they also affect other long-term vehicles such as common stock and mutual funds. *Generally, the higher the interest rate, the lower the value of an investment vehicle, and vice versa.*

Liquidity Risk The risk of not being able to liquidate an investment conveniently and at a reasonable price is called **liquidity risk.** The liquidity of a given investment vehicle is an important consideration. In general, investment vehicles traded in *thin markets,* where demand and supply are small, tend to be less liquid than those traded in *broad markets.*

liquidity risk
the risk of not being able to liquidate an investment conveniently and at a reasonable price.

One can generally sell an investment vehicle merely by significantly cutting its price. However, to be liquid, an investment must be easily sold *at a reasonable price.* For example, a security recently purchased for $1,000 would not be viewed as highly liquid if it could be quickly sold only at a greatly reduced price, such as $500. Vehicles such as stocks and bonds of major companies listed on the New York Stock Exchange are generally highly liquid; others, such as the stock of a small company in a declining industry, are not.

Tax Risk The chance that Congress will make unfavorable changes in tax laws is known as **tax risk.** The greater the chance that such changes will drive down the after-tax returns and market values of certain investments, the greater the tax risk. Undesirable changes in tax laws include elimination of tax exemptions, limitation of deductions, and increases in tax rates.

tax risk
the chance that Congress will make unfavorable changes in tax laws, driving down the after-tax returns and market values of certain investments.

In recent years, Congress has passed numerous changes in tax laws. One of the most significant was the Tax Reform Act of 1986, which contained provisions that reduced the attractiveness of many investment vehicles, particularly real estate and other tax shelters. More recently, the maximum rate applicable to capital gains realized on assets held more than 12 months was reduced. Clearly, this change benefits investors and does not represent the unfavorable consequences of tax risk.

Though virtually all investments are vulnerable to increases in tax rates, certain tax-advantaged investments, such as municipal and other bonds, real estate, and natural resources, generally have greater tax risk.

market risk
risk of decline in investment returns because of market factors independent of the given investment.

Market Risk **Market risk** is the risk that investment returns will decline because of market factors independent of the given investment. Examples include political, economic, and social events, as well as changes in investor tastes and preferences. Market risk actually embodies a number of different risks: purchasing power risk, interest rate risk, and tax risk.

The impact of market factors on investment returns is not uniform. Both the degree and the direction of change in return differ among investment vehicles. For example, legislation placing restrictive import quotas on Japanese goods may result in a significant increase in the value (and therefore the return) of domestic automobile and electronics stocks. Essentially, market risk is reflected in the *price volatility* of a security—the more volatile the price of a security, the greater its perceived market risk.

event risk
risk that comes from an unexpected event that has a significant and usually immediate effect on the underlying value of an investment.

Event Risk **Event risk** occurs when something happens to a company that has a sudden and substantial impact on its financial condition. Event risk goes beyond business and financial risk. It does not necessarily mean the company or market is doing poorly. Instead, it involves an unexpected event that has a significant and usually immediate effect on the underlying value of an investment. An example of event risk is the August 2000 offer by Bridgestone/Firestone to replace 6.5 million tires, mainly on Ford light trucks and SUVs, based on 46 deaths and more than 300 incidents involving Firestone tires that were alleged to have shredded on the highway. The stock of Bridgestone Corp.—the Japanese parent company of Bridgestone/Firestone—was quickly and negatively affected. It dropped by about 20% on the Tokyo Exchange during the two days immediately following the announcement.

Event risk can take many forms and can affect all types of investment vehicles. Fortunately, its impact tends to be isolated in most cases. For instance, the stocks of only a small number of companies were directly affected by Bridgestone/Firestone's offer to replace tires.

Risk of a Single Asset

Most people have at some time in their lives asked themselves how risky some anticipated course of action is. In such cases, the answer is usually a subjective judgment, such as "not very" or "quite." Such a judgment may or may not help in decision making. In finance, we are able to quantify the measurement of risk, which improves comparisons between investments and enhances decision making.

The risk or variability of both single assets and portfolios of assets can be measured statistically. Here we focus solely on the risk of single assets. We first consider standard deviation, which is an absolute measure of risk. Then we consider the coefficient of variation, a relative measure of risk.

standard deviation, *s*
a statistic used to measure the dispersion (variation) of returns around an asset's average or expected return.

Standard Deviation: An Absolute Measure of Risk The most common single indicator of an asset's risk is the **standard deviation, *s*.** It measures the dispersion (variation) of returns around an asset's average or expected return. The formula is

Equation 4.10

$$\text{Standard deviation} = \sqrt{\frac{\sum_{j=1}^{n}\left(\begin{array}{c}\text{Return for}\\ \text{outcome } j\end{array} - \begin{array}{c}\text{Average or}\\ \text{expected return}\end{array}\right)^2}{\begin{array}{c}\text{Total number}\\ \text{of outcomes}\end{array} - 1}}$$

Equation 4.10a

$$s = \sqrt{\frac{\sum_{j=1}^{n}(r_j - \bar{r})^2}{n-1}}$$

Consider two competing investments—A and B—described in Table 4.13. Note that both investments earned an average return of 15% over the 6-year period shown. Reviewing the returns shown for each investment in light of their 15% averages, we can see that the returns for investment B vary more from this average than do the returns for investment A.

The standard deviation provides a quantitative tool for comparing investment risk. Table 4.14 demonstrates the calculation of the standard deviations, s_A and s_B, for investments A and B, respectively. Evaluating the calculations, we can see that the standard deviation of 1.49% for the returns on investment A is, as expected, considerably below the standard deviation of 5.24% for investment B. The greater absolute dispersion of investment B's return, reflected in its larger standard deviation, indicates that B is the more risky investment. Of course, these values are absolute measures based on *historical* data. There is no assurance that the risks of these two investments will remain the same in the future.

coefficient of variation, *CV*
a statistic used to measure the *relative* dispersion of an asset's returns; it is useful in comparing the risk of assets with differing average or expected returns.

Coefficient of Variation: A Relative Measure of Risk The **coefficient of variation, *CV*,** is a measure of the *relative* dispersion of an asset's returns. It is useful in comparing the risk of assets with differing average or expected returns. Equation 4.11 gives the formula for the coefficient of variation.

TABLE 4.13 Returns on Investments A and B

	Rate of Return	
Year	Investment A	Investment B
1997	15.6%	8.4%
1998	12.7	12.9
1999	15.3	19.6
2000	16.2	17.5
2001	16.5	10.3
2002	13.7	21.3
Average	15.0%	15.0%

TABLE 4.14 Calculation of Standard Deviations of Returns for Investments A and B

Investment A

Year (j)	(1) Return, r_j	(2) Average Return, $\bar{r}$	(3) (1) − (2) $r_j - \bar{r}$	(4) $(3)^2$ $(r_j - \bar{r})^2$
1997	15.6%	15.0%	.6%	0.36%
1998	12.7	15.0	−2.3	5.29
1999	15.3	15.0	.3	0.09
2000	16.2	15.0	1.2	1.44
2001	16.5	15.0	1.5	2.25
2002	13.7	15.0	−1.3	1.69
				$\sum_{j=1}^{6}(r_j - \bar{r})^2 = 11.12$

$$s_A = \sqrt{\frac{\sum_{j=1}^{6}(r_j - \bar{r})^2}{n-1}} = \sqrt{\frac{11.12}{6-1}} = \sqrt{2.224} = \underline{\underline{1.49\%}}$$

Investment B

Year (j)	(1) Return, r_j	(2) Average Return, $\bar{r}$	(3) (1) − (2) $r_j - \bar{r}$	(4) $(3)^2$ $(r_j - \bar{r})^2$
1997	8.4%	15.0%	−6.6%	43.56%
1998	12.9	15.0	−2.1	4.41
1999	19.6	15.0	4.6	21.16
2000	17.5	15.0	2.5	6.25
2001	10.3	15.0	−4.7	22.09
2002	21.3	15.0	6.3	39.69
				$\sum_{j=1}^{6}(r_j - \bar{r})^2 = 137.16$

$$s_B = \sqrt{\frac{\sum_{j=1}^{6}(r_j - \bar{r})^2}{n-1}} = \sqrt{\frac{137.16}{6-1}} = \sqrt{27.432} = \underline{\underline{5.24\%}}$$

INVESTOR FACTS

VOLATILE STOCKS—from 1926 to 2000, the annual standard deviation for large-company stocks was 20.1%. Therefore, the annual return for about 68% of these stocks fell between 20.1% above and 20.1% below the 13.3% average, or between 33.4% and −6.8%. Bonds were less volatile, with a 5.8% standard deviation during the same period.

Source: Walter Updegrave, "The Skeptical Investor," *Money,* June 2000, p. 134.

Equation 4.11

$$\text{Coefficient of variation} = \frac{\text{Standard deviation}}{\text{Average or expected return}}$$

Equation 4.11a

$$CV = \frac{s}{\bar{r}}$$

As was the case for the standard deviation, the higher the coefficient of variation, the greater the risk.

We can substitute into Equation 4.11a the standard deviation values (from Table 4.14) and the average returns (from Table 4.13) for investments A and B. We get a coefficient of variation for A of 0.099 (1.49% ÷ 15%) and for B of 0.349 (5.24% ÷ 15%). Investment B has the higher coefficient of variation and, as expected, has more relative risk than investment A. Because both investments have the same average return, the coefficient of variation in this case has not provided any more information than the standard deviation.

The real utility of the coefficient of variation is in comparing investments that have *different* expected returns. For example, assume you want to select the less risky of two alternative investments—X and Y. The average return, the standard deviation, and the coefficient of variation for each of these investments are as follows.

Statistics	Investment X	Investment Y
(1) Average return	12%	20%
(2) Standard deviation	9%*	10%
(3) Coefficient of variation [(2) ÷ (1)]	0.75	0.50*

* Preferred investment using the given risk measure.

If you compared the investments solely on the basis of their standard deviations, you would prefer investment X. It has a lower standard deviation than investment Y (9% vs. 10%). But by comparing the coefficients of variation, you can see that you would be making a mistake in choosing X over Y. The *relative* dispersion, or risk, of the investments, as reflected in the coefficient of variation, is lower for Y than for X (0.50 vs. 0.75). Clearly, the coefficient of variation considers the relative size, or average return, of each investment.

HOTLINKS

Access Vanguard site's Education, Planning, and Advice section. Then click on [Investing Primer]. Read the sections on [No Reward Without Risk] and [Defining Investment Risks]. Test your knowledge on the Investing Primer.

personal.vanguard.com/educ/inveduc.html

Assessing Risk

Techniques for quantifying the risk of a given investment vehicle are quite useful. However, they will be of little use if you are unaware of your feelings toward risk. The individual investor typically tends to seek answers to these questions: "Is the amount of perceived risk worth taking to get the expected return?" "Can I get a higher return for the same level of risk or a lower risk for the same level of return?" A look at the general risk-return characteristics of alternative investment vehicles and at the question of an acceptable level of risk will help shed light on how to evaluate risk.

Risk-Return Characteristics of Alternative Investment Vehicles A wide variety of risk-return behaviors are associated with each type of investment vehicle. Some common stocks offer low returns and low risk. Others offer high returns and high risk. In general, though, the risk-return characteristics of the major investment vehicles are as shown in Figure 4.4. Of course, a broad range of risk-return behaviors exists for specific investments of each type. In other words, once you have selected the appropriate type of vehicle, you must still decide which specific security to acquire.

An Acceptable Level of Risk The three basic risk preferences (risk-indifferent, risk-averse, and risk-seeking) are depicted graphically in Figure 4.5.

risk-indifferent
describes an investor who does not require a change in return as compensation for greater risk.

risk-averse
describes an investor who requires greater return in exchange for greater risk.

- For the **risk-indifferent** investor, the required return does not change as risk goes from x_1 to x_2. In essence, no change in return would be required for the increase in risk.
- For the **risk-averse** investor, the required return increases for an increase in risk. Because they shy away from risk, these investors require higher expected returns to compensate them for taking greater risk.

FIGURE 4.4

Risk-Return Tradeoffs for Various Investment Vehicles

A risk-return tradeoff exists such that for a higher risk one expects a higher return, and vice versa. Low-risk-low-return investment vehicles include U.S. government securities and deposit accounts. High-risk-high-return vehicles include real estate and other tangible investments, options, and futures.

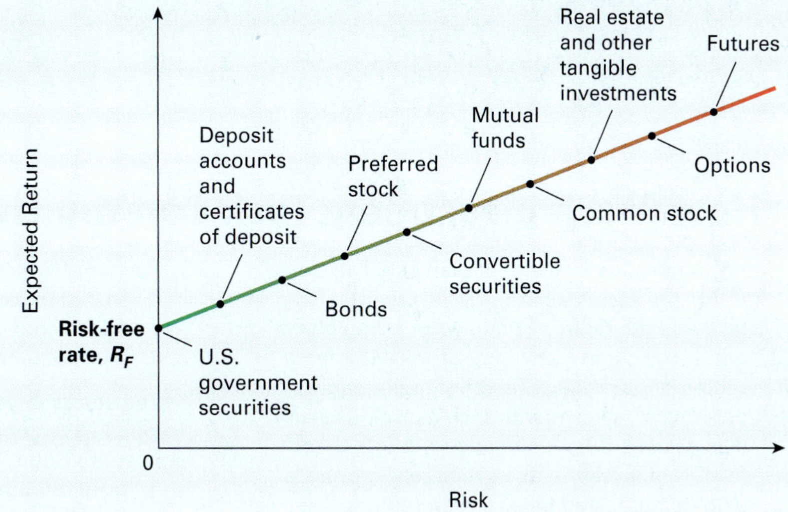

risk-seeking
describes an investor who will accept a lower return in exchange for greater risk.

- For the **risk-seeking** investor, the required return decreases for an increase in risk. Theoretically, because they enjoy risk, these investors are willing to give up some return to take more risk.

Most investors are risk-averse: For a given increase in risk, they require an increase in return. This risk-averse behavior is also depicted in Figure 4.5.

Of course, the amount of return required by each investor for a given increase in risk differs depending on the investor's degree of risk aversion (reflected in the slope of the line). Investors generally tend to be conservative when accepting risk. The more aggressive an investor you are (the farther to the right you operate on the risk-averse line), the greater your tolerance for risk, and the greater your required return. To get a feel for your own risk-taking orientation, read the *Investing in Action* box on page 130.

FIGURE 4.5

Risk Preferences

The risk-indifferent investor requires no change in return for a given increase in risk. The risk-averse investor requires an increase in return for a given risk increase. The risk-seeking investor gives up some return for more risk. The majority of investors are risk-averse.

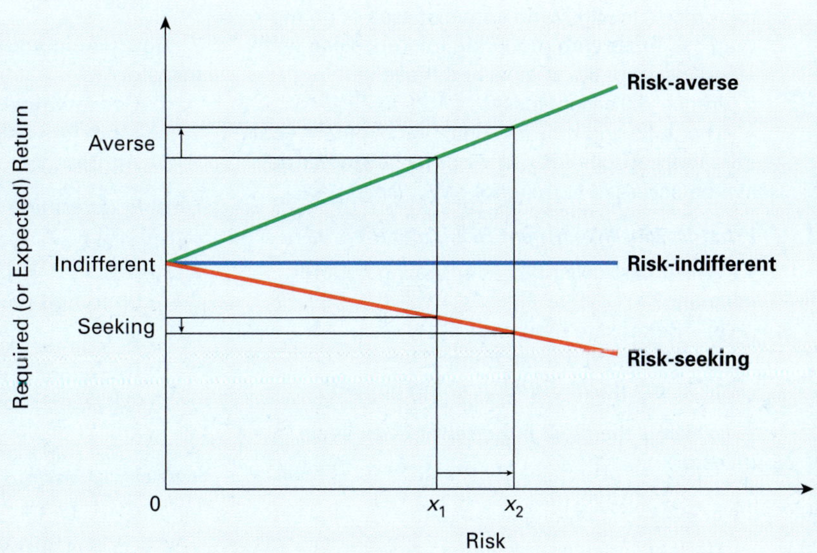

INVESTING in action

How Much Investment Risk Can You Handle?

An effective investment plan is based on a balance between the risks you are willing to take and the returns you need to achieve your goals. The conservative investor saving for retirement or college funding might want to buy only "safe" investments such as U.S. Treasury bills or bank CDs. Historically, though, these fixed-rate investments have barely kept pace with inflation, and taxes lessen returns even further. On the other hand, the stock market—a riskier choice—has far outperformed other investments over the long run. Many financial experts advise having at least 30% to 40% of your portfolio in equities (some suggest even 50% to 75%) if you want to accumulate assets over the long term (more than five to ten years).

The key to risk taking is to determine your personal level of risk tolerance—how comfortable you feel with the volatility of your investments. Understanding your risk tolerance will prevent you from taking more risk than you can handle and will reduce the likelihood that you will panic and abandon your plan midstream.

One way to assess your risk tolerance is to ask yourself how much you could lose on your investments over a 1-year period and still stick to your plan. In general, investors with low risk tolerance can withstand annual losses of no more than 5%, those with moderate tolerance can withstand losses of 6% to 15%, and those with high tolerance will accept losses of 16% to 25%.

The following quiz can help you evaluate your personal capacity for risk. Another, lengthier quiz can be accessed at the book's Web site.

What Is Your Investment Risk Tolerance?

1. Which best describes your feelings about investing?
   a. "Better safe than sorry."
   b. "Moderation in all things."
   c. "Nothing ventured, nothing gained."

2. Which is the most important to you as an investor?
   a. Steady income
   b. Steady income and growth
   c. Rapid price appreciation

3. You won! Which prize would you select?
   a. $4,000 in cash
   b. A 50% chance to win $10,000
   c. A 20% chance to win $100,000

4. The stocks in your retirement account have dropped 20% since last quarter. The market experts are optimistic. What would you do?
   a. Transfer out of stocks to avoid losing more.
   b. Stay in stocks and wait for them to come back.
   c. Shift more money into stocks. If they made sense before, they're a bargain now.

5. The stocks in your retirement account have suddenly gone up 20%. You have no more information. What would you do?
   a. Transfer out of stocks and lock in my gains.
   b. Stay in stocks, hoping for more gains.
   c. Transfer more money into stocks. They might go higher.

6. Would you borrow money to take advantage of a good investment opportunity?
   a. Never
   b. Maybe
   c. Yes

7. How would you characterize yourself as an investor?
   a. Conservative
   b. Moderate risk taker
   c. Aggressive

How to determine your score:

Each (a) answer is worth 1 point. Each (b) is worth 2 points. Each (c) is worth 3 points. Add them up to find your total score.

7–11 points: a conservative investor
12–16 points: a moderate risk taker
17–21 points: an aggressive investor

Sources: Maria Crawford Scott, "Life-Cycle Investing: Investment Decisions and Your Personal Investment Profile," *AAII Journal,* March 1993, pp. 16–19; and Ann Perry, "Putting Stock in the Market," *San Diego Union-Tribune,* July 18, 1993, pp. 11–12.

Steps in the Decision Process: Combining Return and Risk

When you are deciding among alternative investments, you should take the following steps to combine return and risk.

1. Using historical or projected return data, estimate the expected return over a given holding period. Use yield (or present-value) techniques to make sure you give the time value of money adequate consideration.
2. Using historical or projected return data, assess the risk associated with the investment. Subjective risk assessment, use of the standard deviation or coefficient of variation of returns, and use of more sophisticated measures, such as beta (developed in Chapter 5), are the primary approaches available to individual investors.
3. Evaluate the risk-return behavior of each alternative investment to make sure that the return expected is reasonable given the level of risk. If other vehicles with lower levels of risk provide equal or greater returns, the investment is not acceptable.
4. Select the investment vehicles that offer the highest returns associated with the level of risk you are willing to take. As long as you get the highest return for your acceptable level of risk, you have made a "good investment."

Probably the most difficult step in this process is assessing risk. Aside from return and risk considerations, other factors, such as portfolio considerations, taxes, and liquidity, affect the investment decision. We will develop portfolio concepts in Chapter 5 and, in later chapters, will look at all of these factors as they are related to specific investment vehicles.

Summary

LG 1 **Review the concept of return, its components, and the forces that affect the investor's level of return.** Return is the reward for investing. The total return provided by an investment includes current income and capital gains (or losses). Return is commonly calculated on a historical basis and then used to project expected returns. The level of return depends on internal characteristics and external forces, which include the general level of price changes.

LG 2 **Discuss the time value of money and the calculations involved in finding the future value of various types of cash flows.** Because investors have opportunities to earn interest on their funds, money has a time value. Interest can be applied using either simple interest or compound interest. The more frequently interest is compounded at a stated rate, the higher the true rate of interest. Financial tables and financial calculators can be used to streamline time-value calculations. The future value of a present sum or an annuity can be found using compound interest concepts.

LG 3 **Explain the concept of present value, the procedures for calculating present values, and the use of present value in determining whether an investment is satisfactory.** The present value of a future sum is the amount that would have to be deposited today, into an account earning interest at a given rate, to accumulate the specified future sum. The present value of streams of future returns can be found by adding the present values of the individual returns. When the stream is an annuity, its present value can be more simply calculated. A satisfactory investment is one for which the present value of its benefits equals or exceeds the present value of its costs.

LG 4 **Describe real, risk-free, and required returns and the computation and application of holding period return, yield (internal rate of return), and growth rates.** The required return on an investment is the rate of return an investor must earn to be fully compensated for the investment's risk. It represents the sum of the real rate of return and the expected inflation premium (which together represent the risk-free rate), plus the risk premium for the investment. The risk premium varies depending on issue and issuer characteristics. The holding period return (HPR) is the return earned over a specified period of time. It is frequently used to compare returns earned in periods of 1 year or less.

Yield or internal rate of return is the compound annual rate of return earned on investments held for more than 1 year. If the yield is greater than or equal to the required return, the investment is acceptable. Implicit in the use of yield is an ability to earn a return equal to the calculated yield on all income received from the investment during the holding period. Present-value techniques can be used to find a rate of growth, which is the compound annual rate of change in the value of a stream of income, particularly dividends or earnings.

LG 5 **Discuss the key sources of risk and how they might affect potential investment vehicles.** Risk is the chance that the actual return from an investment will differ from what is expected. The total risk associated with a given investment vehicle may result from a combination of sources: business, financial, purchasing power, interest rate, liquidity, tax, market, and event risk. These risks typically have varying effects on different types of investment vehicles.

LG 6 **Understand the risk of a single asset, risk assessment, and the steps that combine return and risk.** The risk of both single assets and portfolios of assets can be measured statistically on an absolute basis by the standard deviation and on a relative basis by the coefficient of variation. There is a tradeoff between risk and return. Generally, each type of investment vehicle displays certain risk-return characteristics. Most investors are risk-averse: In exchange for a given increase in risk, they require an increase in return. The investment decision involves estimating the return and risk of each alternative and then selecting those investments that offer the highest returns for the level of risk the investor is willing to take.

CHAPTER 5

MODERN PORTFOLIO CONCEPTS

Learning Goals

After studying this chapter, you should be able to:

LG 1 Understand portfolio management objectives and the procedures to calculate the return and standard deviation of a portfolio.

LG 2 Discuss the concepts of correlation and diversification, and the effectiveness, methods, and benefits of international diversification.

LG 3 Describe the two components of risk, beta, and the capital asset pricing model (CAPM).

LG 4 Review traditional and modern approaches to portfolio management and reconcile them.

LG 5 Describe the role of investor characteristics and objectives and of portfolio objectives and policies in constructing an investment portfolio.

LG 6 Summarize why and how investors use an asset allocation scheme to construct an investment portfolio.

If you think it's hard to manage a $50,000 investment portfolio, imagine being James Grefenstette. He co-manages $3.4 billion in three mutual funds at Federated Investors. Each fund has different investment strategies.

The first fund, Growth Strategies, invests in companies with total market value over $100 million and above-average growth prospects. In addition to equities, Grefenstette and co-manager Salvatore Esposito may also hold convertible bonds, corporate debt, and ADRs. They diversify by trying to approximate the S&P 500's industry sector weightings. The two also manage the Large Cap Growth Fund, which invests in about 100 large-cap (total market value) companies. Grefenstette and three co-managers also run the specialized Federated Communications Technology Fund, in which at least 65% of the assets are communications technology and service companies.

Federated takes a team approach to fund portfolio management. "If you're ultra-reliant on one person and that person controls the vision and management of the fund, well, if he moves on, the fund may be left without continuity," explains Grefenstette. Federated's team approach protects both the management company and the shareholders. Its managers don't look for star status but focus on providing investors with a fund that follows its stated objectives. "Our goal is to hit a lot of singles, doubles, and the occasional triple, because over time that's what's going to get your customers to enjoy an above-average rate of return with less risk. The people who swing for the fences and hit that occasional home run or grand slam probably strike out a lot."

Federated's strategy provides good lessons for individual investors as well. As we'll see in Chapter 5, understanding your investment objectives and developing appropriate asset allocation strategies are the way to build your own portfolio.

Sources: Jim Grefenstette, "Trimming Technology Close to Market Weight," *Federated Focus*, November 8, 2000, downloaded from www.federatedinvestors.com; Gary Gentile, "This Fund Manager Is a 'Most Valuable Player,'" *Fox Market Wire*, November 1, 1999, downloaded from www.foxmarketwire.com

Principles of Portfolio Planning

LG 1 LG 2

growth-oriented portfolio
a portfolio whose primary objective is long-term price appreciation.

income-oriented portfolio
a portfolio that stresses current dividend and interest returns.

efficient portfolio
a portfolio that provides the highest return for a given level of risk or that has the lowest risk for a given level of return.

Investors benefit from holding portfolios of investments rather than single investment vehicles. Without sacrificing returns, investors who hold portfolios can reduce risk, often to a level below that of any of the investments held in isolation. In other words, when it comes to risk, $1 + 1 < 1$.

As defined in Chapter 1, a portfolio is a collection of investment vehicles assembled to meet one or more investment goals. Of course, different investors have different objectives for their portfolios. The primary goal of a **growth-oriented portfolio** is long-term price appreciation. An **income-oriented portfolio** stresses current dividend and interest returns.

Portfolio Objectives

Setting portfolio objectives involves definite tradeoffs: tradeoffs between risk and return, between potential price appreciation and current income, and between varying risk levels in the portfolio. These will depend on your tax bracket, current income needs, and ability to bear risk. The key point is that the portfolio objectives must be established *before* beginning to invest.

The ultimate goal of an investor is an **efficient portfolio,** one that provides the highest return for a given level of risk or that has the lowest risk for a given level of return. Thus, given the choice between two equally risky investments offering different returns, the investor would be expected to choose the one with the higher return. Likewise, given two vehicles offering the same returns but differing in risk, the *risk-averse* investor would prefer the one with the lower risk. Efficient portfolios aren't necessarily obvious: Investors usually must search out investment alternatives to get the best combinations of risk and return.

Portfolio Return and Standard Deviation

The return on a portfolio is calculated as a weighted average of returns on the assets (investment vehicles) from which it is formed. The portfolio return, r_p, can be found by using Equation 5.1:

Equation 5.1

$$\text{Return on portfolio} = \left(\begin{array}{c}\text{Proportion of}\\ \text{portfolio's total}\\ \text{dollar value}\\ \text{represented by}\\ \text{asset 1}\end{array} \times \begin{array}{c}\text{Return}\\ \text{on asset}\\ 1\end{array}\right) + \left(\begin{array}{c}\text{Proportion of}\\ \text{portfolio's total}\\ \text{dollar value}\\ \text{represented by}\\ \text{asset 2}\end{array} \times \begin{array}{c}\text{Return}\\ \text{on asset}\\ 2\end{array}\right) + \cdots + \left(\begin{array}{c}\text{Proportion of}\\ \text{portfolio's total}\\ \text{dollar value}\\ \text{represented by}\\ \text{asset } n\end{array} \times \begin{array}{c}\text{Return}\\ \text{on asset}\\ n\end{array}\right) = \sum_{j=1}^{n}\left(\begin{array}{c}\text{Proportion of}\\ \text{portfolio's total}\\ \text{dollar value}\\ \text{represented by}\\ \text{asset } j\end{array} \times \begin{array}{c}\text{Return}\\ \text{on asset}\\ j\end{array}\right)$$

Equation 5.1a

$$r_p = (w_1 \times r_1) + (w_2 \times r_2) + \cdots + (w_n \times r_n) = \sum_{j=1}^{n}(w_j \times r_j)$$

TABLE 5.1 Expected Return, Average Return, and Standard Deviation of Returns for Portfolio XY

A. Expected Portfolio Returns

	(1)	(2)	(3)	(4)
	Expected Return			Expected Portfolio
Year	Asset X	Asset Y	Portfolio Return Calculation*	Return, r_p
2003	8%	16%	$(.50 \times 8\%) + (.50 \times 16\%) =$	12%
2004	10	14	$(.50 \times 10\ ) + (.50 \times 14\ ) =$	12
2005	12	12	$(.50 \times 12\ ) + (.50 \times 12\ ) =$	12
2006	14	10	$(.50 \times 14\ ) + (.50 \times 10\ ) =$	12
2007	16	8	$(.50 \times 16\ ) + (.50 \times 8\ ) =$	12

B. Average Expected Portfolio Return, 2003–2007

$$\bar{r}_p = \frac{12\% + 12\% + 12\% + 12\% + 12\%}{5} = \frac{60\%}{5} = \underline{\underline{12\%}}$$

C. Standard Deviation of Expected Portfolio Returns**

$$s_p = \sqrt{\frac{(12\% - 12\%)^2 + (12\% - 12\%)^2 + (12\% - 12\%)^2 + (12\% - 12\%)^2 + (12\% - 12\%)^2}{5 - 1}}$$

$$= \sqrt{\frac{0\% + 0\% + 0\% + 0\% + 0\%}{4}} = \sqrt{\frac{0\%}{4}} = \underline{\underline{0\%}}$$

*Using Equation 5.1.
**Using Equation 4.10 presented in Chapter 4.

Of course, $\sum_{j=1}^{n} w_j = 1$, which means that 100% of the portfolio's assets must be included in this computation.

The *standard deviation of a portfolio's returns* is found by applying Equation 4.10, the formula we used to find the standard deviation of a single asset. Assume that we wish to determine the return and standard deviation of returns for Portfolio XY, created by combining equal portions (50%) of assets X and Y. The expected returns of assets X and Y for each of the next 5 years (2003–2007) are given in columns 1 and 2, in part A of Table 5.1. In columns 3 and 4, the weights of 50% for both assets X and Y, along with their respective returns from columns 1 and 2, are substituted into Equation 5.1 to get an expected portfolio return of 12% for each year, 2003 to 2007. As shown in part B of Table 5.1, the average expected portfolio return, $\bar{r}_p$, over the 5-year period is also 12%. Substituting into Equation 4.10, we calculate Portfolio XY's standard deviation, s_p, of 0% in part C of Table 5.1. This value should not be surprising. Because the expected return each year is the same (12%), no variability is exhibited in the expected returns from year to year shown in column 4 of part A of the table.

HOTLINKS

Several interactive tutorials are available on this NJIT site. Click on [Portfolio return, variance, standard deviation, etc.] link for a two-asset portfolio.

www-ec.njit.edu/~mathis/interactive/index.html

FIGURE 5.1

The Correlation Between Series M, N, and P

The perfectly positively correlated series M and P in the graph on the left move exactly together. The perfectly negatively correlated series M and N in the graph on the right move in exactly opposite directions.

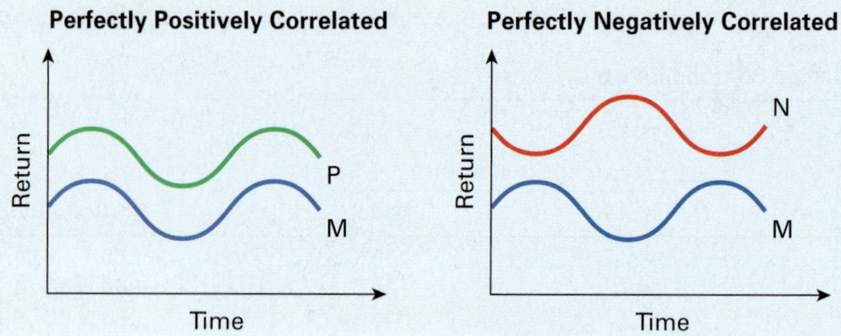

Correlation and Diversification

As noted in Chapter 2, *diversification* involves the inclusion of a number of different investment vehicles in a portfolio. It is an important aspect of creating an efficient portfolio. Underlying the intuitive appeal of diversification is the statistical concept of *correlation.* For effective portfolio planning, you need to understand the concepts of correlation and diversification and their relationship to a portfolio's total risk and return.

correlation
a statistical measure of the relationship, if any, between series of numbers representing data of any kind.

positively correlated
describes two series that move in the same direction.

negatively correlated
describes two series that move in opposite directions.

correlation coefficient
a measure of the degree of correlation between two series.

perfectly positively correlated
describes two positively correlated series that have a correlation coefficient of +1.

perfectly negatively correlated
describes two negatively correlated series that have a correlation coefficient of −1.

uncorrelated
describes two series that lack any relationship or interaction and therefore have a correlation coefficient close to zero.

Correlation **Correlation** is a statistical measure of the relationship, if any, between series of numbers representing data of any kind. If two series move in the same direction, they are **positively correlated.** If the series move in opposite directions, they are **negatively correlated.**

The degree of correlation—whether positive or negative—is measured by the **correlation coefficient.** The coefficient ranges from +1 for **perfectly positively correlated** series to −1 for **perfectly negatively correlated** series. These two extremes are depicted in Figure 5.1 for Series M, N, and P. The perfectly positively correlated series (M and P) move exactly together. The perfectly negatively correlated series (M and N) move in exactly opposite directions.

Diversification To reduce overall risk in a portfolio, it is best to combine assets that have a negative (or a low-positive) correlation. Combining negatively correlated assets can reduce the overall variability of returns, *s,* or risk. Figure 5.2 shows negatively correlated assets F and G, both having the same average expected return, $\bar{r}$. The portfolio that contains those negatively correlated assets also has the same return, $\bar{r}$, but has less risk (variability) than either of the individual assets. Even if assets are not negatively correlated, the lower the positive correlation between them, the lower the resulting risk.

Some assets are **uncorrelated:** They are completely unrelated, with no interaction between their returns. Combining uncorrelated assets can reduce risk—not as effectively as combining negatively correlated assets, but more effectively than combining positively correlated assets. The correlation coefficient for uncorrelated assets is close to zero and acts as the midpoint between perfect positive and perfect negative correlation.

Correlation is important to reducing risk, but it can do only so much. A portfolio of two assets that have perfectly positively correlated returns *cannot* reduce the portfolio's overall risk below the risk of the least risky asset.

FIGURE 5.2

Combining Negatively Correlated Assets to Diversify Risk

The risk or variability of returns, resulting from combining negatively correlated assets F and G, both having the same expected return, $\bar{r}$, results in a portfolio (shown in the rightmost graph) with the same level of expected return but less risk.

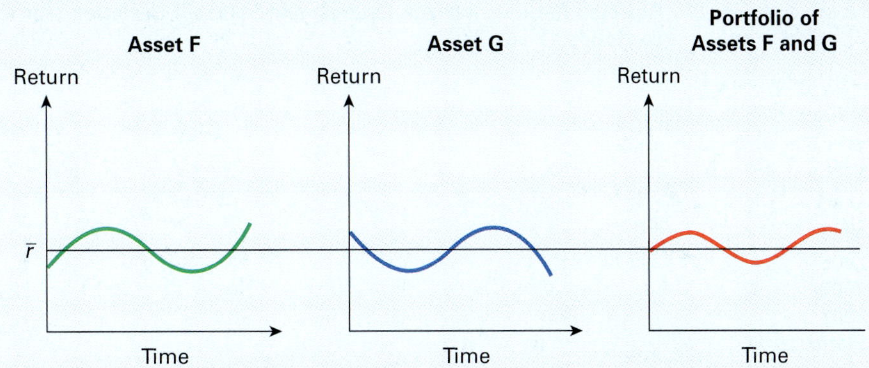

However, a portfolio combining two assets with less than perfectly positive correlation *can* reduce total risk to a level below that of either of the components, which in certain situations may be zero.

For example, assume you own the stock of a machine tool manufacturer that is very *cyclical.* This company has high earnings when the economy is expanding and low earnings during a recession. If you bought stock in another machine tool company, which would have earnings positively correlated with those of the stock you already own, the combined earnings would continue to be cyclical. The risk would remain the same.

As an alternative, however, you could buy stock in a sewing machine manufacturer, which is *countercyclical.* It typically has low earnings during economic expansion and high earnings during recession. Combining the machine tool stock and the sewing machine stock should reduce risk: The low machine tool earnings during a recession would be balanced out by high sewing machine earnings, and vice versa.

A numeric example will provide an even better understanding. Table 5.2 presents the expected returns from three different assets—X, Y, and Z—over the next 5 years (2003–2007), along with their average returns and standard deviations. Each of the assets has an expected value of return of 12% and a standard deviation of 3.16%. The assets therefore have equal return and equal risk, although their return patterns are not identical. The returns of assets X and Y are perfectly negatively correlated, because they move in exactly opposite directions over time. The returns of assets X and Z are perfectly positively correlated: They move in precisely the same direction. (The returns for X and Z are identical, although it is not necessary for return streams to be identical in order for them to be perfectly positively correlated.)

Portfolio XY (shown in Table 5.2) combines equal portions of assets X and Y—the perfectly negatively correlated assets. Calculation of portfolio XY's annual expected returns, average expected return, and the standard deviation of expected portfolio returns was demonstrated in Table 5.1. The risk of the portfolio created by this combination, as reflected in the standard deviation, is reduced to 0%, while its average return remains at 12%. Because both assets have the same average return, are combined in the optimum proportions (a 50–50 mix in this case), and are perfectly negatively correlated, the combination results in the complete elimination of risk. Whenever assets are perfectly negatively correlated, an optimum combination (similar to this 50–50

INVESTOR FACTS

"CORRELATIONSHIP" ADVICE—Most assets that individual investors own are positively correlated, although the extent of that correlation varies. Between 1989 and 1999, the S&P 500 index had a correlation of 0.79 with domestic small-caps (total market values). This high correlation would be expected, because both move in step with the U.S. economy. The S&P 500's correlation with foreign stocks is only 0.53 and is even lower (0.36) with intermediate-term government bonds.

Source: Walter Updegrave, "Investing 101: Why Diversification Pays," *Money*, December 1999, p. 100.

TABLE 5.2 **Expected Returns, Average Returns, and Standard Deviations for Assets X, Y, and Z and Portfolios XY and XZ**

	Assets			Portfolios	
				XY*	XZ**
Year	X	Y	Z	(50%X + 50%Y)	(50%X + 50%Z)
2003	8%	16%	8%	12%	8%
2004	10	14	10	12	10
2005	12	12	12	12	12
2006	14	10	14	12	14
2007	16	8	16	12	16
Statistics:					
Average return†	12%	12%	12%	12%	12%
Standard deviation‡	3.16%	3.16%	3.16%	0%	3.16%

*Portfolio XY illustrates *perfect negative correlation,* because these two return streams behave in completely opposite fashion over the 5-year period. The return values shown here were calculated in part A of Table 5.1.

**Portfolio XZ illustrates *perfect positive correlation,* because these two return streams behave identically over the 5-year period. These return values were calculated using the same method demonstrated for Portfolio XY in part A of Table 5.1.

†The average return for each asset is calculated as the arithmetic average found by dividing the sum of the returns for the years 2003–2007 by 5, the number of years considered.

‡Equation 4.10 was used to calculate the standard deviation. Calculation of the average return and standard deviation for portfolio XY is demonstrated in parts B and C, respectively, of Table 5.1. The portfolio standard deviation can be directly calculated from the standard deviation of the component assets using the following formula:

$$s_p = \sqrt{w_1^2 s_1^2 + w_2^2 s_2^2 + 2w_1 w_2 p_{1,2} s_1 s_2}$$

where w_1 and w_2 are the proportions of the component assets 1 and 2; s_1 and s_2 are the standard deviations of the component assets 1 and 2; and $p_{1,2}$ is the correlation coefficient between the returns of component assets 1 and 2.

mix in assets X and Y) exists for which the resulting standard deviation will equal 0.

Portfolio XZ (shown in Table 5.2) is created by combining equal portions of Assets X and Z—the perfectly positively correlated assets. The risk of this portfolio, reflected by its standard deviation, which remains at 3.16%, is unaffected by this combination. Its average return remains at 12%. Whenever perfectly positively correlated assets such as X and Z are combined, the standard deviation of the resulting portfolio cannot be reduced below that of the least risky asset; the maximum portfolio standard deviation will be that of the riskiest asset. Because assets X and Z have the same standard deviation (3.16%), the minimum and maximum standard deviations are both 3.16%, which is the only value that could be taken on by a combination of these assets.

Impact on Risk and Return In general, the lower (less positive and more negative) the correlation between asset returns, the greater the potential diversification of risk. For each pair of assets, there is a combination that will result in the lowest risk (standard deviation) possible. *The amount of potential risk reduction for this combination depends on the degree of correlation of the two assets.* Many potential combinations could be made, given the expected return of the two assets, the standard deviation for each, and the correlation coefficient. However, *only one combination* of the infinite number of possibilities will minimize risk.

Three possible correlations—perfect positive, uncorrelated, and perfect negative—illustrate the effect of correlation on the diversification of risk and return. Table 5.3 summarizes the impact of correlation on the range of return and risk. The table shows that as you move from perfect positive correlation to perfect negative correlation, you reduce risk. Note that in no case will a portfolio of assets have risk greater than that of the riskiest asset included in the portfolio.

To demonstrate, assume that a firm has carefully calculated the average return, $\bar{r}$, and risk, s, for each of two assets, A and B, as summarized below.

Asset	Average Return, $\bar{r}$	Risk (Standard Deviation), s
A	6%	3%
B	8%	8%

From these data, we can see that asset A is clearly a lower-risk, lower-return asset than asset B.

To evaluate possible combinations, let's consider three possible correlations: perfect positive, uncorrelated, and perfect negative. The results are shown in Figure 5.3. The ranges of return and risk exhibited are consistent with those in Table 5.3. In all cases, the return will range between the 6% return of A and the 8% return of B. The risk, on the other hand, has a wider variability. That variability depends on the degree of correlation: In the case of perfect positive correlation, the risk ranges between the individual risks of A and B (from 3% to 8%). In the uncorrelated case, the risk ranges from below 3% (the risk of A) but greater than 0%, to 8% (the risk of B). In the case of perfect negative correlation, the risk ranges between 0% and 8%.

Note that *only in the case of perfect negative correlation can the risk be reduced to 0%*. As the correlation becomes less positive and more negative (moving from the top of Figure 5.3 down), the ability to reduce risk improves. Keep in mind that the amount of risk reduction achieved also depends on the proportions in which the assets are combined. Although determining the risk-minimizing combination is beyond the scope of this discussion, you should know that it is an important issue in developing portfolios of assets.

TABLE 5.3 Correlation, Return, and Risk for Various Two-Asset Portfolio Combinations

Correlation Coefficient	Range of Return	Range of Risk
+1 (perfect positive)	Between returns of two assets held in isolation	Between risk of two assets held in isolation
0 (uncorrelated)	Between returns of two assets held in isolation	Between risk of most risky asset and less than risk of least risky asset, but greater than 0
−1 (perfect negative)	Between returns of two assets held in isolation	Between risk of most risky asset and 0

FIGURE 5.3

Range of Portfolio Return and Risk for Combinations of Assets A and B for Various Correlation Coefficients

The range of a portfolio's return (r_p) is between that of the lowest and highest component asset returns and is unaffected by the degree of asset correlation. Portfolio risk (s_p), on the other hand, can be reduced below the risk of the least risky asset as the asset correlation moves from perfectly positive to uncorrelated to perfectly negative, where it can be reduced to zero by combining assets in the proper proportion.

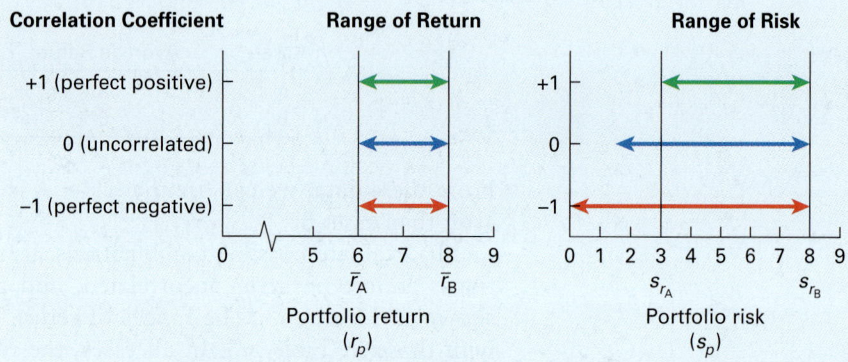

International Diversification

Diversification is clearly a primary consideration when constructing an investment portfolio. Thus far, our focus and examples have been basically domestic. However, as noted earlier, many opportunities for international diversification are now available. Here we consider three aspects of international diversification: effectiveness, methods, and benefits.

Effectiveness of International Diversification Investing internationally obviously offers greater diversification than investing only domestically. That is true for U.S. investors. It is even truer for investors from countries with capital markets that offer much more limited diversification opportunities than are available in the United States.

However, does international diversification actually reduce risk, particularly the variability of rates of return? Two earlier studies overwhelmingly support the argument that well-structured international diversification does indeed reduce the risk of a portfolio and increase the return on portfolios of comparable risk. One study looked at diversification across 12 European countries in 7 different industries between 1978 and 1992. It demonstrated that an investor could actually reduce the risk of a portfolio much more by diversifying internationally *in the same industry* than by diversifying across industries within one country. If the investor diversified both across countries and across industries, the opportunities for risk reduction would be even greater.

Another study examined the risk-return performance between January 1984 and November 1994 of diversified stock portfolios: the S&P 500 in the United States and Morgan Stanley's Europe/Australia/Far East (EAFE) Index. It found that a 100% EAFE portfolio offered a much greater return than a

100% S&P 500 portfolio did—but at much greater risk. However, a portfolio composed of various combinations of the two indexes would have been better: It would have realized both lower risk and a higher return than for the 100% S&P 500 portfolio, and less risk and a moderately lower return than for the 100% EAFE portfolio. For the U.S. investor, a portfolio consisting of 70% S&P 500 coupled with 30% EAFE would have reduced risk by about 5% and increased return by about 7% (from around 14% to more than 15%). Or, for the same degree of risk, an investor could have increased return by about 18% (from around 14% to more than 16.5%).

Methods of International Diversification In later chapters we will examine a wide range of alternatives for international portfolio diversification. We will see that investments in bonds and other debt instruments can be made abroad in U.S. dollars or in foreign currencies—either directly or via foreign mutual funds. Foreign currency investment, however, brings currency exchange risk. This risk can be hedged using various contracts, most commonly currency forwards, futures, and options.

Investing abroad, even if there is little or no currency exchange risk, is generally less convenient, more expensive, and riskier than investing domestically. When making direct investments abroad, you must know what you're doing: You should have a clear idea of the benefits being sought and should have the time to monitor foreign markets.

International diversification can also be achieved by U.S. domestic investments. Several hundred foreign companies list their stocks on U.S. exchanges or over the counter; most of them are Canadian companies. Also, many foreign issuers, both corporate and government, sell their bonds (called *Yankee bonds*) in the United States. The stocks of about 1,200 foreign companies, from about 40 countries, trade in the United States in the form of American Depositary Receipts. Finally, international mutual funds (such as the Fidelity Japan Fund and the Prudential Global Fund) provide investors with a broad range of foreign investment opportunities. These domestic alternatives offer the advantages of convenience and low cost, often with less risk than investments made directly abroad.

It is important to realize that international diversification typically cannot be achieved by investing in U.S. multinationals. In spite of the fact that U.S.-based firms with major foreign operations may generate sizable revenues and profits abroad, most of their costs and expenses—particularly labor costs—are incurred in the United States. The net result is that the firm's behavior tends to be more U.S.-driven than foreign-driven. The multinational firm's results tend to be positively correlated with those in the domestic market, thereby resulting in low diversification. The strategy of investing in domestic companies that have major foreign operations therefore is generally not as effective as investing directly in foreign companies in the given country.

Benefits of International Diversification Can greater returns be found overseas than in the United States? Yes! Can a portfolio's risk be reduced by including foreign investments? Yes! Is international diversification desirable for you? We don't know! A successful global investment strategy depends on many things, just as a purely domestic strategy does. Included are factors such as your resources, goals, sophistication, and psychology. What percentage of your portfolio you allocate to foreign investments depends on your overall

INVESTING in action

Why Venture Abroad?

Why venture abroad, say many U.S. investors, when stock returns on domestic companies have been so high recently? Overseas investments are risky, involving currency fluctuations and political risk.

Yet returns in U.S. markets may not always be the highest. From 1979 to 1989, for example, average annual returns for the Morgan Stanley Capital International Europe Asia and Far East (EAFE) index were 23%, compared with 17.6% for the (domestic) S&P 500. Despite lackluster gains on international investments in the 1990s, the global economy appears poised for significant growth as foreign economies recover from recessions.

"We [Americans] are the most myopic investors in the world, arguably for a good reason," said John J. Brennan, chairman and chief executive of the Vanguard Group. "We have this huge capital market. You can diversify all sorts of ways. . . . But to think that American companies have a lock on success in the future [and that] the American economy will have a lock on growth in the future is naive."

In fact, investing abroad may be a better long-term strategy now than in past years. In 1970, U.S. stock markets represented about two-thirds of the global $1 trillion stock market. Today the worldwide stock market is about $32 trillion, but the U.S. share is down to about half. In the new, tightly linked, technology-dominated world economy, national borders mean less than ever before.

Investment professionals recommend a different approach to international investing today, however. Diversification used to be the primary reason for making foreign investments: If U.S. markets slipped, foreign markets would provide balance and higher returns. Because the major world stock markets tend to move together now, owning non-U.S. stocks doesn't provide the protection it once did.

There are other compelling reasons to include international stocks in your portfolio, however. You may have to look outside the United States to buy stock in worldwide industry leaders. This is particularly true in heavily global sectors like telecommunications, technology, pharmaceuticals, and energy. For example, Finland's Nokia has a 37% share of the U.S. cellular market.

Rather than diversifying by country or region, investors should diversify across industries. "The best way to make money is to pick the best companies and the best businesses, rather than putting 4% of the portfolio in Europe or 5% in Japan," said William Wilby, a portfolio manager with Oppenheimer Funds Inc.

Some investors believe that they can minimize risk by investing in U.S. multinationals to achieve global diversification. This strategy can be restrictive and eliminates solid foreign companies like BMW, Nokia, Nestle, and Sony. "If you choose to buy those products in your daily life," says David Antonelli, international research director for MFS Investment Management in Boston, "why would you limit your ability to invest in those companies?"

If you are not comfortable buying individual company shares, you can use mutual funds to create a global portfolio. Many mutual fund managers follow a global industry sector strategy, and you will find that foreign companies are well represented in sector funds specializing in technology, health care, and other major industry categories.

Sources: Fred Barbash, "Foreign Funds an Answer to Slide in U.S.," *Washington Post*, October 8, 2000, p. H1; Mara der Hovanesian, "So Who Needs Foreign Investing?" *Business Week*, September 11, 2000, p. 166, E12–14; Christopher Farrell, "The New Global Investor," *Business Week*, September 11, 2000, pp. 160–162; and Erika Gonzalez, "International Investors Optimistic," *Denver Rocky Mountain News*, September 19, 2000, downloaded from Electric Library, Business Edition, business.elibrary.com

investment goals and risk preferences. Commonly cited allocations to foreign investments are around 30%, with about two-thirds of this allocation in established foreign markets and the other one-third in emerging markets.

In general, you should avoid investing directly in foreign-currency-denominated instruments. Unless the magnitude of each foreign investment is in hundreds of thousands of dollars, the transactions costs will tend to be high, not just when you are buying and selling but especially when dividends or interest are paid. Therefore, for most investors looking for international diversification, the optimal vehicles are available in the United States. International mutual funds offer diversified foreign investments, coupled with the professional investment expertise of fund managers. ADRs can be used by those who want to make foreign investments in individual stocks. With either mutual funds or ADRs, you can obtain international diversification along with low cost, convenience, transactions in U.S. dollars, protection under U.S. security laws, and (usually) attractive markets (although some ADRs have thin markets).

We shouldn't leave this topic without saying that some of the benefits of international diversification are diminishing over time. Technological advances in communication have greatly improved the quality of information on foreign companies. In addition, new markets and expanded trading hours have improved access to foreign investments. Participation by a growing number of better-informed investors in the foreign markets continues to reduce the opportunities to earn "excess" returns on the additional risk embodied in foreign investments, thereby leveling the playing field for global investors. Although the opportunities to earn excess returns on foreign investments are shrinking, the relatively low correlation of returns in Asian and emerging markets with U.S. returns continues to make international investments appealing as a way to diversify your portfolio. Foreign investments continue to provide greater risk reduction than domestic investments. Clearly, today an important motive for international investment is portfolio diversification rather than realizing sizable excess returns. The *Investing in Action* box on page 142 presents some strategies for international investing in the new millennium.

The Capital Asset Pricing Model (CAPM)

LG 3

From an investor's perspective, the most important aspect of risk is the *overall risk* of the firm. This overall risk significantly affects the returns earned and the value of the firm in the financial marketplace. Clearly, as we'll learn in Chapter 8, the firm's value is directly determined by its risk and the associated return. The basic theory that links return and risk for all assets is the *capital asset pricing model (CAPM)*.

diversifiable (unsystematic) risk
the portion of an investment's risk that results from uncontrollable or random events that are firm-specific; can be eliminated through diversification.

Components of Risk

The risk of an investment consists of two components: diversifiable and nondiversifiable risk. **Diversifiable risk,** sometimes called **unsystematic risk,** results from uncontrollable or random events that are firm-specific, such as labor strikes, lawsuits, and regulatory actions. It is the portion of an investment's

nondiversifiable (systematic) risk
the inescapable portion of an investment's risk attributable to forces that affect all investments and therefore are not unique to a given vehicle.

risk that can be eliminated through diversification. **Nondiversifiable risk,** also called **systematic risk,** is attributed to more general forces such as war, inflation, and political events that affect all investments and therefore are not unique to a given vehicle. The sum of nondiversifiable risk and diversifiable risk is called **total risk.**

Equation 5.2

Total risk = Nondiversifiable risk + Diversifiable risk

total risk
the sum of an investment's nondiversifiable risk and diversifiable risk.

Any careful investor can reduce or virtually eliminate diversifiable risk by holding a diversified portfolio of securities. Studies have shown that investors can eliminate most diversifiable risk by carefully selecting a portfolio of 8 to 15 securities. Therefore, *the only relevant risk is nondiversifiable risk,* which is inescapable. Each security has its own unique level of nondiversifiable risk, which we can measure, as we'll show in the following section.

Beta: A Popular Measure of Risk

During the past 35 years much theory has been developed on the measurement of risk and its use in assessing returns. The two key components of this theory are *beta,* which is a measure of risk, and the *capital asset pricing model (CAPM),* which uses beta to estimate return.

beta
a measure of *nondiversifiable,* or *market, risk* that indicates how the price of a security responds to market forces.

First we will look at **beta,** a number that measures *nondiversifiable,* or *market, risk.* Beta indicates how the price of a security responds to market forces. The more responsive the price of a security is to changes in the market, the higher that security's beta. Beta is found by relating the historical returns for a security to the market return. **Market return** is the average return for all (or a large sample of) stocks. The average return on all stocks in the *Standard & Poor's 500 Stock Composite Index* or some other broad stock index is commonly used to measure market return. You don't have to calculate betas yourself; you can easily obtain them for actively traded securities from a variety of published and online sources. But you should understand how betas are derived, how to interpret them, and how to apply them to portfolios.

market return
the average return on all (or a large sample of) stocks, such as those in the *Standard & Poor's 500 Stock Composite Index.*

Deriving Beta The relationship between a security's return and the market return, and its use in deriving beta, can be demonstrated graphically. Figure 5.4 plots the relationship between the returns of two securities, C and D, and the market return. Note that the horizontal (x) axis measures the market return, and the vertical (y) axis measures the individual security's returns.

The first step in deriving beta is plotting the coordinates for the market return and the security return at various points in time. Such annual market-return and security-return coordinates are shown in Figure 5.4 for security D for the years 1995 through 2002 (the years are noted in parentheses). For example, in 2002 security D's return was 20% when the market return was 10%.

By use of statistical techniques, the "characteristic line" that best explains the relationship between security-return and market-return coordinates is fit to the data points. *The slope of this line is beta.* The beta for security C is about 0.80; for security D it is about 1.30. Security D's higher beta (steeper

FIGURE 5.4

Graphical Derivation of Beta for Securities C and D*

Betas can be derived graphically by plotting the coordinates for the market return and security return at various points in time and using statistical techniques to fit the "characteristic line" to the data points. The slope of the characteristic line is beta. For securities C and D, beta is found to be 0.80 and 1.30, respectively.

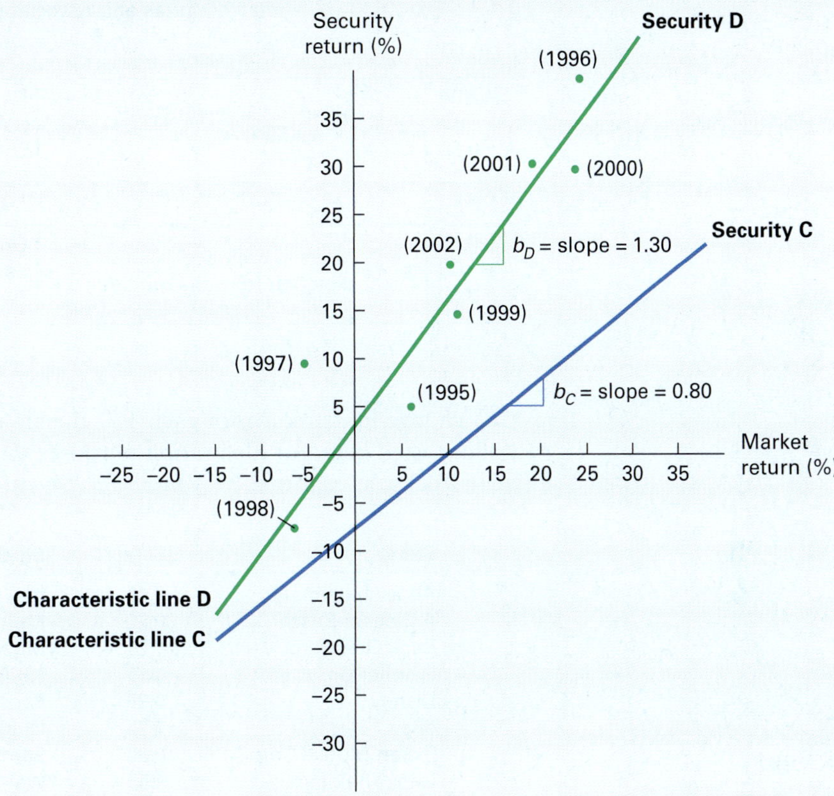

* All data points shown are associated with security D. No data points are shown for security C.

characteristic line slope) indicates that its return is more responsive to changing market returns. *Therefore security D is more risky than security C.*

Interpreting Beta The beta for the overall market is considered to be 1.00. All other betas are viewed in relation to this value. Table 5.4 shows some selected beta values and their associated interpretations. As you can see, betas can be positive or negative, though nearly all betas are positive. The positive or negative sign preceding the beta number merely indicates whether the stock's return changes in the *same direction as the general market* (positive beta) or in the *opposite direction* (negative beta).

Most stocks have betas that fall between 0.50 and 1.75. The return of a stock that is half as responsive as the market (b = 0.50) is expected to change by ½ of 1% for each 1% change in the return of the market portfolio. A stock that is twice as responsive as the market (b = 2.0) is expected to experience a

TABLE 5.4 Selected Betas and Associated Interpretations

Beta	Comment	Interpretation
2.00	Move in same direction as the market	Twice as responsive as the market
1.00		Same response as the market
0.50		Only half as responsive as the market
0		Unaffected by market movement
−0.50	Move in opposite direction from the market	Only half as responsive as the market
−1.00		Same response as the market
−2.00		Twice as responsive as the market

2% change in its return for each 1% change in the return of the market portfolio. Listed here, for illustration purposes, are the actual betas for some popular stocks, as reported by *Value Line Investment Survey* on May 11, 2001:

Stock	Beta	Stock	Beta
Amazon.com	1.80	Int'l Business Machines	1.00
Anheuser-Busch	0.70	Merrill Lynch & Co.	1.85
Bank One Corp.	1.25	Microsoft	1.10
Daimler Chrysler AG	1.15	NIKE, Inc.	0.90
Disney	0.95	PepsiCo, Inc.	0.80
eBay	2.25	Quaker Oats	0.60
Exxon Mobile Corp.	0.80	Sempra Energy	0.55
Gap (The), Inc.	1.55	Wal-Mart Stores	1.15
General Electric	1.25	Xerox	1.05
Intel	1.10	Yahoo! Inc.	1.80

Many large brokerage firms, as well as subscription services like *Value Line,* publish betas for a broad range of securities. They also can be obtained online through sites such as yahoo.com. The ready availability of security betas has enhanced their use in assessing investment risks. The importance of beta in planning and building portfolios of securities will be discussed later in this chapter.

INVESTOR FACTS

MUTUAL FUNDS HAVE BETAS, TOO—For mutual funds, beta can be an important factor in an investor's decision to buy. If you had checked Morningstar.com on November 15, 2000, you would have found that the Dreyfus Premier Technology Growth Fund A, for example, had a beta of 1.54, as you might expect from a fund investing in technology companies. Its beta of 1.54 means that it is about 50% more volatile than the market—in this case, the S&P 500—which is always assigned a beta of 1.00. Another fund from the same family, Dreyfus Appreciation, is less risky than the market, with a beta of 0.87.

Applying Beta Individual investors will find beta useful. It can help in assessing market risk and in understanding the impact the market can have on the return expected from a share of stock. In short, beta reveals how a security responds to market forces. For example, if the market is expected to experience a 10% *increase* in its rate of return over the next period, we would expect a stock with a beta of 1.50 to experience an *increase* in return of about 15% (1.50 × 10%). Because its beta is greater than 1.00, this stock is more volatile than the market as a whole.

For stocks with positive betas, increases in market returns result in increases in security returns. Unfortunately, decreases in market returns are translated into decreasing security returns. In the preceding example, if the market is expected to experience a 10% *decrease,* then a stock with a beta of 1.50 should experience a 15% *decrease* in its return. Because the stock has a beta greater than 1.00, it is more responsive than the market, either up or down.

Stocks that have betas less than 1.00 are, of course, less responsive to changing returns in the market. They are therefore considered less risky. For example, a stock with a beta of 0.50 will increase or decrease its return by about half that of the market as a whole. Thus, if the market went down by 8%, such a stock would probably experience only about a 4% (0.50 × 8%) decline.

Here are some important points to remember about beta:

- Beta measures the nondiversifiable (or market) risk of a security.
- The beta for the market is 1.00.
- Stocks may have positive or negative betas. Nearly all are positive.
- Stocks with betas greater than 1.00 are more responsive to changes in the market return and therefore are more risky than the market. Stocks with betas less than 1.00 are less risky than the market.
- Because of its greater risk, the higher a stock's beta, the greater should be its level of expected return.

The CAPM: Using Beta to Estimate Return

About 35 years ago, finance professors William F. Sharpe and John Lintner developed a model that uses beta to formally link the notions of risk and return. Called the **capital asset pricing model (CAPM),** it explains the behavior of security prices. It also provides a mechanism whereby investors can assess the impact of a proposed security investment on their portfolio's risk and return.

capital asset pricing model (CAPM)
model that formally links the notions of risk and return; it uses beta, the risk-free rate, and the market return to help investors define the required return on an investment.

The CAPM can be viewed both as an equation and as a graph.

The Equation With beta, b, as the measure of nondiversifiable risk, the capital asset pricing model defines the required return on an investment as follows.

Equation 5.3

$$\text{Required return on investment } j = \text{Risk-free rate} + \left[\text{Beta for investment } j \times \left(\text{Market return} - \text{Risk-free rate}\right)\right]$$

Equation 5.3a

$$r_j = R_F + [b_j \times (r_m - R_F)]$$

where

r_j = the required return on investment j, given its risk as measured by beta

R_F = the risk-free rate of return; the return that can be earned on a risk-free investment

b_j = beta coefficient, or index of nondiversifiable risk, for investment j

r_m = the market return; the average return on all securities (typically measured by the average return on all securities in the Standard & Poor's 500 Stock Composite Index or some other broad stock market index)

The equation shows that *as beta increases, the required return for a given investment increases.*

Application of the CAPM can be demonstrated with the following example. Assume you are considering security Z with a beta (b_Z) of 1.25. The risk-free rate (R_F) is 6% and the market return (r_m) is 10%. Substituting these data into the CAPM equation, Equation 5.3a, we get:

$$r_z = 6\% + [1.25 \times (10\% - 6\%)] = 6\% + [1.25 \times 4\%]$$
$$= 6\% + 5\% = \underline{\underline{11\%}}$$

You should therefore expect—indeed, require—an 11% return on this investment as compensation for the risk you have to assume, given the security's beta of 1.25.

If the beta were lower, say 1.00, the required return would be lower:

$$r_z = 6\% + [1.00 \times (10\% - 6\%)] = 6\% + 4\% = \underline{\underline{10\%}}$$

If the beta were higher, say 1.50, the required return would be higher:

$$r_z = 6\% + [1.50 \times (10\% - 6\%)] = 6\% + 6\% = \underline{\underline{12\%}}$$

Clearly, the CAPM reflects the positive mathematical relationship between risk and return, because the higher the risk (beta), the higher the required return.

security market line (SML) the graphical depiction of the capital asset pricing model; reflects the investor's required return for each level of nondiversifiable risk, measured by beta.

The Graph: The Security Market Line (SML) When the capital asset pricing model is depicted graphically, it is called the **security market line (SML).** Plotting the CAPM, we would find that the SML is, in fact, a straight line. For each level of nondiversifiable risk (beta), the SML reflects the required return the investor should earn in the marketplace.

The CAPM at a given point in time can be plotted by simply calculating the required return for a variety of betas. For example, as we saw earlier, using a 6% risk-free rate and a 10% market return, the required return is 11% when the beta is 1.25. Increase the beta to 2.00, and the required return equals 14% (6% + [2.00 × (10% − 6%)]). Similarly, we can find the required return for a number of betas and end up with the following combinations of risk (beta) and required return.

HOTLINKS

You can find the betas for various companies at the Marketguide site. Under [Search for], click on [Symb] and, in the empty box, type in the stock symbol for a company. You can also calculate the beta of a portfolio of stocks at this site.

www.marketguide.com

Risk (beta)	Required Return
0.0	6%
0.5	8
1.0	10
1.5	12
2.0	14
2.5	16

Plotting these values on a graph (with beta on the horizontal axis and required returns on the vertical axis) would yield a straight line like the one in Figure 5.5. It is clear from the SML that as risk (beta) increases, so does the required return, and vice versa.

FIGURE 5.5

The Security Market Line (SML)

The security market line clearly depicts the tradeoff between risk and return. At a beta of 0, the required return is the risk-free rate of 6%. At a beta of 1.0, the required return is the market return of 10%. Given these data, the required return on an investment with a beta of 1.25 is 11%.

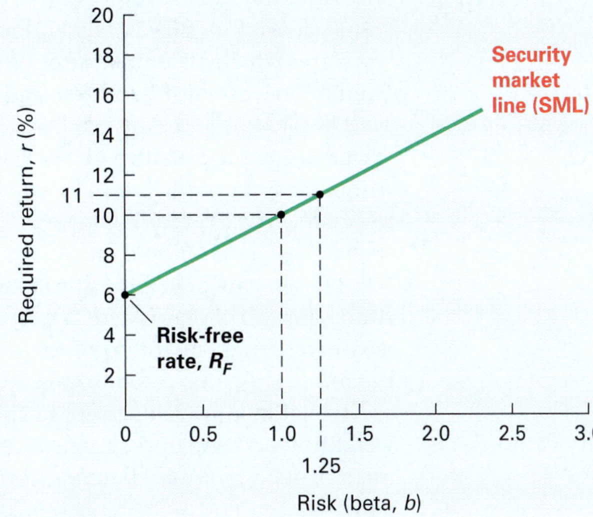

Traditional versus Modern Portfolio

LG 4

Two approaches are currently used by individual and institutional investors to plan and construct their portfolios. The *traditional approach* refers to the less quantitative methods that investors have been using since the evolution of the public securities markets. *Modern portfolio theory (MPT)* is a more recent, more mathematical development that continues to grow in popularity and acceptance. Some MPT concepts are indirectly used by practitioners of the traditional approach, yet there are major differences between the two.

The Traditional Approach

traditional portfolio management
an approach to portfolio management that emphasizes "balancing" the portfolio by assembling a wide variety of stocks and/or bonds of companies from a broad range of industries.

Traditional portfolio management emphasizes "balancing" the portfolio by assembling a wide variety of stocks and/or bonds. The typical emphasis is *interindustry diversification*. This produces a portfolio with securities of companies from a broad range of industries. Traditional portfolios are constructed using the security analysis techniques discussed in Chapters 7 and 8.

Table 5.5 presents the industry groupings and the percentages invested in them by a typical mutual fund that is managed by professionals using the traditional approach. This fund, the Pilgrim Growth Opportunities Fund, is an open-end mutual fund. The portfolio's value at December 31, 2000, was approximately $728 million. Its objective is to seek long-term growth of capital by investing in the common stock of U.S. companies with above average prospects for growth. The Pilgrim Growth Opportunities Fund holds shares of 97 different stocks from 27 industries, as well as some short-term investments.

Analyzing the stock position of the Pilgrim Growth Opportunities Fund, which accounts for 98% of the fund's total assets, we observe the traditional approach to portfolio management at work. This fund holds numerous stocks from a broad cross section of the total universe of available stocks. The stocks are a mix of large and small companies. By far the largest industry group is telecommunications, with 11.93% of the total portfolio. The fund's largest individual holding is BEA Systems, Inc., a provider of e-commerce infrastructure software, which accounts for only 1.94% of the total portfolio. Bristol-Myers Squibb Co., a major producer and distributor of medicines, ranks second, at 1.90%. The third largest holding—1.83%—is Brocade Communication Systems, Inc., a provider of storage area networking infrastructure solutions. Although most of the fund's 97 stocks are those of small companies, in addition to Bristol-Myers Squibb Co., it does include stocks of some major companies, such as America Online, Inc., Gap, Inc., Genentech Inc., and Starbucks Corp.

Those who manage traditional portfolios want to invest in well-known companies for three reasons. First, because these are known as successful business enterprises, investing in them is perceived as less risky than investing in lesser-known firms. Second, the securities of large firms are more liquid and are available in large quantities. Third, institutional investors prefer successful well-known companies because it is easier to convince clients to invest in them. Called *window dressing,* this practice of loading up a portfolio, particularly at the end of a reporting period, with successful well-known stocks makes it easier for institutional investors to sell their services.

Modern Portfolio Theory

During the 1950s, Harry Markowitz, a trained mathematician, first developed the theories that form the basis of modern portfolio theory. Many other

TABLE 5.5 Portfolio of Pilgrim Growth Opportunities Fund, December 31, 2000

The Pilgrim Growth Opportunities Funds appears to adhere to the traditional approach to portfolio management. Its total portfolio value is about $728 million, of which 98% ($713 million) is common stock, including 97 different stocks in 27 industry groupings, plus about 3% ($24 million) in short-term investments, and about −1% (−$9 million) in net liabilities.

Pilgrim Growth Opportunities Fund
Investments by Industry Group
as of December 31, 2000

Industry Group	Percentage	Industry Group	Percentage
Common Stocks	**98.00%**	Internet	0.80%
Apparel	0.94	Leisure time	1.55
Banks	4.72	Machinery—diversified	1.32
Biotechnology	5.61	Media	3.78
Chemicals	0.46	Miscellaneous manufacturing	0.85
Commercial services	0.77	Oil & gas producers	6.48
Computers	5.18	Oil & gas services	1.30
Cosmetics/Personal Care	0.47	Pharmaceuticals	8.53
Diversified financial services	1.41	Pipelines	2.76
Electric	5.24	Retail	4.56
Electronics	1.92	Semiconductors	4.23
Forest products & paper	1.04	Software	8.07
Healthcare—products	1.20	Telecommunications	11.93
Healthcare—services	7.45	**Short-Term Investments**	**3.24**
Insurance	5.43	**Net Liabilities**	**−1.24**

Source: ING Pilgrim U.S. Equity Funds, *2000 Annual Report,* December 31, 2000, pp. 23–24.

modern portfolio theory (MPT) an approach to portfolio management that uses several basic statistical measures to develop a portfolio plan.

scholars and investment experts have contributed to the theory in the intervening years. **Modern portfolio theory (MPT)** utilizes several basic statistical measures to develop a portfolio plan. Included are *expected returns* and *standard deviations* of returns for both securities and portfolios, and the *correlation* between returns. According to MPT, diversification is achieved by combining securities in a portfolio *in such a way that individual securities have negative (or low-positive) correlations between each other's rates of return.* Thus the statistical diversification is the deciding factor in choosing securities for an MPT portfolio.

Two important aspects of MPT are the *efficient frontier* and *beta.*

The Efficient Frontier At any point in time, you are faced with virtually hundreds of investment vehicles from which to choose. You can form any number of possible portfolios. In fact, using only, say, 10 of the vehicles, you could create hundreds of portfolios by changing the proportion of each asset in the portfolio.

If we were to create all possible portfolios, calculate the return and risk of each, and plot each risk-return combination on a set of risk-return axes, we would have the *feasible* or *attainable set* of all possible portfolios. This set is represented by the shaded area in Figure 5.6. It is the area bounded by ABYOZCDEF. As defined earlier, an *efficient portfolio* is a portfolio that provides the highest return for a given level of risk or provides minimum risk for a given level of return. For example, let's compare portfolio T to portfolios B and Y shown in Figure 5.6. Portfolio Y appears preferable to portfolio

FIGURE 5.6

The Feasible or Attainable Set and the Efficient Frontier

The *feasible* or *attainable set* (shaded area) represents the risk-return combinations attainable with all possible portfolios; the *efficient frontier* is the locus of all efficient portfolios. The point O where the investor's highest possible indifference curve is tangent to the efficient frontier is the optimal portfolio. It represents the highest level of satisfaction the investor can achieve given the available set of portfolios.

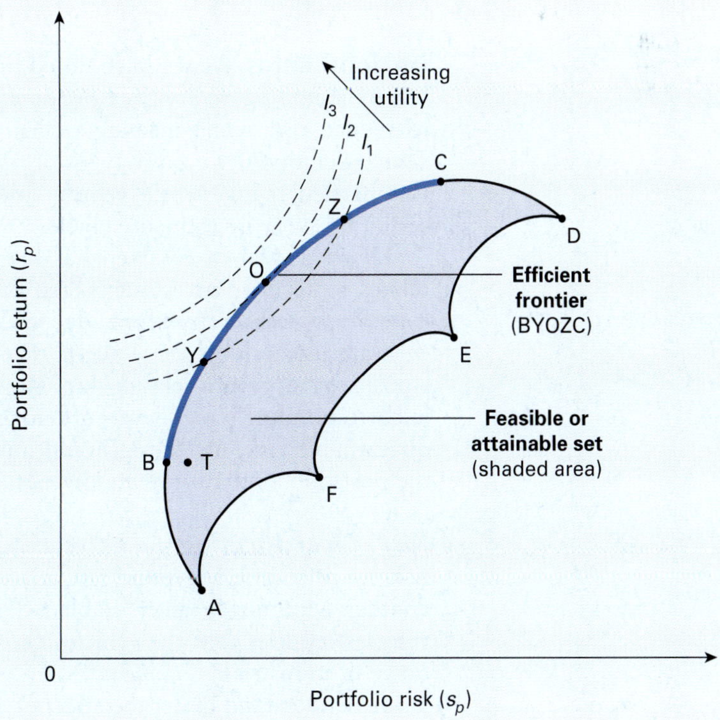

T because it has a higher return for the same level of risk. Portfolio B also "dominates" portfolio T because it has lower risk for the same level of return.

The boundary BYOZC of the feasible set of portfolios represents *all efficient portfolios*—those portfolios that provide the best tradeoff between risk and return. This boundary is called the **efficient frontier.** *All portfolios on the efficient frontier are preferable to all other portfolios in the attainable set.* Any portfolios that would fall to the left of the efficient frontier are not available for investment, because they fall outside of the attainable set. Portfolios that fall to the right of the efficient frontier are *not desirable,* because their risk-return tradeoffs are inferior to those of portfolios on the efficient frontier.

efficient frontier
the leftmost boundary of the *feasible (attainable) set* of portfolios that includes all *efficient portfolios*—those providing the best attainable tradeoff between risk (measured by the standard deviation) and return.

The efficient frontier can, in theory, be used to find the highest level of satisfaction the investor can achieve given the available set of portfolios. To do this, we would plot on the risk-return axes an *investor's utility function* or *risk-indifference curves.* These curves indicate, for a given level of utility (satisfaction), the set of risk-return combinations among which an investor would be indifferent. These curves, labeled I_1, I_2, and I_3 in Figure 5.6, reflect increasing satisfaction as we move from I_1 to I_2 to I_3. The optimal portfolio, O, is the point at which indifference curve I_2 meets the efficient frontier. The higher utility provided by I_3 cannot be achieved given the best available portfolios represented by the efficient frontier.

When coupled with a risk-free asset, the efficient frontier can be used to develop the *capital asset pricing model* (introduced earlier) in terms of portfolio risk (measured by the standard deviation, s_p) and return (r_p). Rather than focus further on theory, let's shift our attention to the more practical aspects of the efficient frontier and its extensions. To do so, we consider the use of *beta* in a portfolio.

Portfolio Betas As we have noted, investors strive to diversify their portfolios by including a variety of noncomplementary investment vehicles in order to reduce risk while meeting return objectives. Remember that investment vehicles embody two basic types of risk: (1) *diversifiable risk,* the risk unique to a particular investment vehicle, and (2) *nondiversifiable risk,* the risk possessed by every investment vehicle.

A great deal of research has been conducted on the topic of risk as it relates to security investments. As we noted earlier, the results show that in general, *to earn more return, one must bear more risk*. More startling, however, are research results showing that only with nondiversifiable risk is there a positive risk-return relationship. High levels of *diversifiable risk* do not result in correspondingly high levels of return. Because there is no reward for bearing diversifiable risk, investors should minimize this form of risk by diversifying the portfolio so that only nondiversifiable risk remains.

Risk Diversification As we've seen, diversification minimizes diversifiable risk by offsetting the poor return on one vehicle with the good return on another. Minimizing diversifiable risk through careful selection of investment vehicles requires that the vehicles chosen for the portfolio come from a wide range of industries.

To understand better the effect of diversification on the basic types of risk, let's consider what happens when we begin with a single asset (security) in a portfolio and then expand the portfolio by randomly selecting additional securities. Using the standard deviation, s_p, to measure the portfolio's *total risk,* we can depict the behavior of the total portfolio risk as more securities are added, as done in Figure 5.7. As securities are added (x-axis) the total portfolio risk (y-axis) declines because of the effects of diversification (explained earlier), and it tends to approach a limit.

Research has shown that, on average, most of the benefits of diversification, in terms of risk reduction, can be gained by forming portfolios containing 8 to 15 randomly selected securities. Unfortunately, because an investor holds but one of a large number of possible x-security portfolios, it is unlikely that he or she will experience the average outcome. As a consequence, some researchers suggest that the individual investor needs to hold about 40 different stocks to achieve efficient diversification. This suggestion tends to support the popularity of investment in mutual funds.

relevant risk
risk that is nondiversifiable.

Because any investor can create a portfolio of assets that will eliminate virtually all diversifiable risk, the only **relevant risk** is that which is nondiversifiable. You must therefore be concerned solely with nondiversifiable risk. The measurement of nondiversifiable risk is thus of primary importance.

Calculating Portfolio Betas As we saw earlier, the *nondiversifiable* or *relevant risk* of a security can be measured using *beta.* The beta for the market is equal to 1.00. Securities with betas greater than 1.00 are more risky than the market, and those with betas below 1.00 are less risky than the market. The beta for the risk-free asset is 0.

portfolio beta, b_p
the beta of a portfolio; calculated as the weighted average of the betas of the individual assets the portfolio includes.

The **portfolio beta, b_p,** is merely the weighted average of the betas of the individual assets it includes. It can be easily estimated using the betas of the component assets. To find the portfolio beta, b_p, we can use Equation 5.4

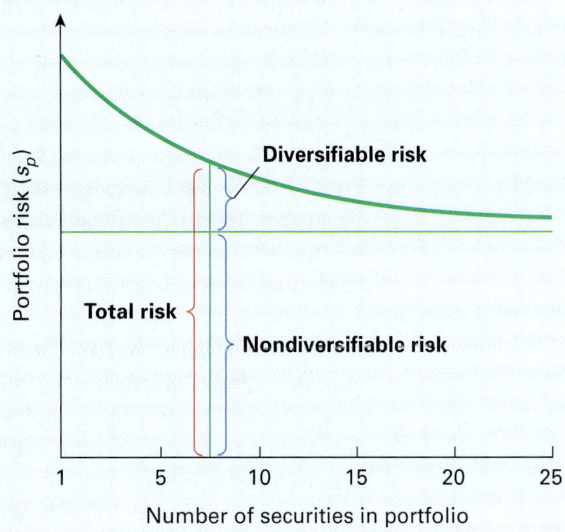

FIGURE 5.7

Portfolio Risk and Diversification

As randomly selected securities are combined to create a portfolio, the total risk of the portfolio (measured by its standard deviation, s_p) declines. The portion of the risk eliminated is the *diversifiable risk;* the remaining portion is the *nondiversifiable* or *relevant risk.* On average, most of the benefits of diversification result from forming portfolios that contain 8 to 15 randomly selected securities.

Equation 5.4

$$\text{Portfolio beta} = \begin{pmatrix} \text{Proportion of portfolio's total dollar value represented by asset 1} \times \text{Beta for asset 1} \end{pmatrix} + \begin{pmatrix} \text{Proportion of portfolio's total dollar value represented by asset 2} \times \text{Beta for asset 2} \end{pmatrix} + \cdots + \begin{pmatrix} \text{Proportion of portfolio's total dollar value represented by asset } n \times \text{Beta for asset } n \end{pmatrix} = \sum_{j=1}^{n} \begin{pmatrix} \text{Proportion of portfolio's total dollar value represented by asset } j \times \text{Beta for asset } j \end{pmatrix}$$

Equation 5.4a

$$b_p = (w_1 \times b_1) + (w_2 \times b_2) + \cdots + (w_n \times b_n) = \sum_{j=1}^{n} (w_j \times b_j)$$

Of course, $\sum_{j=1}^{n} w_j = 1$, which means that 100% of the portfolio's assets must be included in this computation.

Portfolio betas are interpreted in exactly the same way as individual asset betas. They indicate the degree of responsiveness of the *portfolio's* return to changes in the market return. For example, when the market return increases by 10%, a portfolio with a beta of 0.75 will experience a 7.5% increase in its return (0.75 × 10%). A portfolio with a beta of 1.25 will experience a 12.5% increase in its return (1.25 × 10%). Low-beta portfolios are less responsive, and therefore less risky, than high-beta portfolios. Clearly, a portfolio containing mostly low-beta assets will have a low beta, and vice versa.

To demonstrate, consider the Austin Fund, a large investment company that wishes to assess the risk of two portfolios, V and W. Both portfolios contain five assets, with the proportions and betas shown in Table 5.6. The betas for portfolios V and W, b_v and b_w, can be calculated by substituting the appropriate data from the table into Equation 5.4, as follows.

$$\begin{aligned} b_v &= (0.10 \times 1.65) + (0.30 \times 1.00) + (0.20 \times 1.30) + (0.20 \times 1.10) + (0.20 \times 1.25) \\ &= 0.165 + 0.300 + 0.260 + 0.220 + 0.250 = 1.195 \approx \underline{\underline{1.20}} \\ b_w &= (0.10 \times 0.80) + (0.10 \times 1.00) + (0.20 \times 0.65) + (0.10 \times 0.75) + (0.50 \times 1.05) \\ &= 0.080 + 0.100 + 0.130 + 0.075 + 0.525 = \underline{\underline{0.91}} \end{aligned}$$

Portfolio V's beta is 1.20, and portfolio W's is 0.91. These values make sense because portfolio V contains relatively high-beta assets and portfolio W contains relatively low-beta assets. Clearly, portfolio V's returns are more responsive to changes in market returns—and therefore more risky—than portfolio W's.

Using Portfolio Betas The usefulness of beta depends on how well it explains return fluctuations. We can use *the coefficient of determination* (R^2) to evaluate a beta coefficient statistically. This coefficient indicates the percentage of the change in an individual security's return that is explained by its relationship with the market return. R^2 can range from 0 to 1.0. If a regression equation has an R^2 of 0, then none (0%) of the variation in the security's return is explained by its relationship with the market. An R^2 of 1.0 indicates

TABLE 5.6 Austin Fund's Portfolios V and W

	Portfolio V		Portfolio W	
Asset	Proportion	Beta	Proportion	Beta
1	0.10	1.65	0.10	0.80
2	0.30	1.00	0.10	1.00
3	0.20	1.30	0.20	0.65
4	0.20	1.10	0.10	0.75
5	0.20	1.25	0.50	1.05
Total	1.00		1.00	

the existence of perfect correlation (100%) between a security and the market.

Beta is much more useful in explaining a portfolio's return fluctuations than a security's return fluctuations. A well-diversified stock portfolio will have a beta equation R^2 of around 0.90. This means that 90% of the stock portfolio's fluctuations are related to changes in the stock market as a whole. Individual security betas have a wide range of R^2s but tend to be in the 0.20 to 0.50 range. Other factors (diversifiable risk, in particular) also cause individual security prices to fluctuate. When securities are combined in a well-diversified portfolio, most of the fluctuation in that portfolio's return is caused by the movement of the entire stock market.

Interpreting Portfolio Betas If a portfolio has a beta of +1.00, the portfolio experiences changes in its rate of return equal to changes in the market's rate of return. The +1.00 beta portfolio would tend to experience a 10% increase in return if the stock market as a whole experienced a 10% increase in return. Conversely, if the market return fell by 6%, the return on the +1.00 beta portfolio would also fall by 6%.

Table 5.7 lists the expected returns for three portfolio betas in two situations: an increase in market return of 10% and a decrease in market return of 10%. The 2.00 beta portfolio is twice as volatile as the market. When the market return increases by 10%, the portfolio return increases by 20%. When the market return declines 10%, the portfolio's return will fall by 20%. This portfolio would be considered a high-risk, high-return portfolio.

The middle, 0.50 beta portfolio is considered a low-risk, low-return portfolio. This would be a conservative portfolio for investors who wish to maintain a low-risk investment posture. The 0.50 beta portfolio is half as volatile as the market.

A portfolio with a beta of −1.00 moves in the opposite direction from the market. A bearish investor would probably want to own a negative-beta portfolio, because this type of investment tends to rise in value when the stock market declines, and vice versa. Finding securities with negative betas is difficult, however. Most securities have positive betas, because they tend to experience return movements in the same direction as changes in the stock market.

The Risk-Return Tradeoff: Some Closing Comments Another valuable outgrowth of modern portfolio theory is the specific link between nondiversifiable risk and investment return. The basic premise is that an investor must have a

risk-return tradeoff
the positive relationship between the risk associated with a given investment and its expected return.

risk-free rate, R_F
the return an investor can earn on a risk-free investment such as a U.S. Treasury bill or an insured money market account.

portfolio of relatively risky investments to earn a relatively high rate of return. That relationship is illustrated in Figure 5.8. The upward-sloping line shows the **risk-return tradeoff.** The point where the risk-return line crosses the return axis is called the **risk-free rate, R_F.** This is the return an investor can earn on a risk-free investment such as a U.S. Treasury bill or an insured money market deposit account.

As we proceed upward along the risk-return tradeoff line, portfolios of risky investments appear. For example, four investment portfolios, A through D, are depicted. Portfolios A and B are investment opportunities that provide a level of return commensurate with their respective risk levels. Portfolio C provides a high return at a relatively low risk level—and therefore would be an excellent investment. Portfolio D, in contrast, offers high risk but low return—an investment to avoid.

Reconciling the Traditional Approach and MPT

We have reviewed two fairly different approaches to portfolio management: the traditional approach and MPT. The question that naturally arises is which technique you should use. There is no definite answer; the question must be resolved by the judgment of each investor. However, we can offer a few useful ideas.

HOTLINKS

Managing risk and the importance of diversification are emphasized at:

ameritrade.com/educationv2/fhtml/learning/diversification.fhtml

The average individual investor does not have the resources, computers, and mathematical acumen to implement a total MPT portfolio strategy. But most individual investors can extract and use ideas from *both* the traditional and MPT approaches. The traditional approach stresses security selection, which is discussed in Chapters 7 and 8. It also emphasizes diversification of the portfolio across industry lines. MPT stresses negative correlations between rates of return for the securities within the portfolio. This approach calls for diversification, to minimize diversifiable risk. Thus diversification must be accomplished to ensure satisfactory performance with either strategy. Also, beta is a useful tool for determining the level of a portfolio's nondiversifiable risk and should be part of the decision-making process.

We recommend the following portfolio management policy, which uses aspects of both approaches:

TABLE 5.7 Portfolio Betas and Associated Changes in Returns

Portfolio Beta	Change in Market Return	Change in Expected Portfolio Return
+2.00	+10.0%	+20.0%
	−10.0	−20.0
+0.50	+10.0	+ 5.0
	−10.0	− 5.0
−1.00	+10.0	−10.0
	−10.0	+10.0

FIGURE 5.8

The Portfolio risk-Return Tradeoff

As the risk of an investment portfolio increases from zero, the return provided should increase above the risk-free rate, R_F. Portfolios A and B offer returns commensurate with their risk, portfolio C provides a high return at a low-risk level, and portfolio D provides a low return for high risk. Portfolio C is highly desirable; Portfolio D should be avoided.

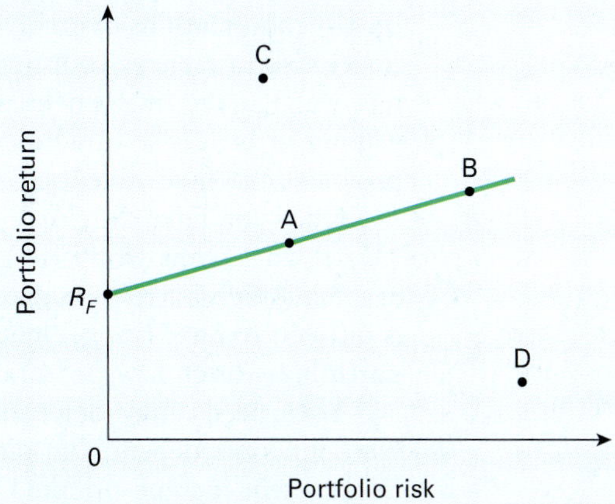

- Determine how much risk you are willing to bear.
- Seek diversification among different types of securities and across industry lines, and pay attention to how the return from one security is related to that from another.
- Consider how a security responds to the market, and use beta in diversifying your portfolio as a way to keep the portfolio in line with your acceptable level of risk.
- Evaluate alternative portfolios to make sure that the portfolio selected provides the highest return for the given level of acceptable risk.

Constructing a Portfolio Using an Asset Allocation Scheme

LG 5 LG 6

In this section we will examine the criteria for constructing a portfolio and then will use these factors to develop a plan for allocating assets in various investment categories. This plan provides a basic, useful framework for selecting individual investment vehicles for the portfolio. In attempting to weave the concepts of risk and diversification into a solid portfolio policy, we will rely on both traditional and modern approaches.

Investor Characteristics and Objectives

Your financial and family situations are important inputs in determining portfolio policy. Vital determinants include: level and stability of income, family factors, net worth, investor experience and age, and disposition toward risk. The types of investments in your portfolio depend on relative income needs and ability to bear risk.

The size of your income and the certainty of your employment also bear on portfolio strategy. An investor with a secure job can handle more risk than one with a less secure position. And, the higher your income, the more important the tax ramifications of an investment program become. Your investment experience also influences your investment strategy. It normally is best to "get one's feet wet" in the investment market by slipping into it gradually rather than leaping in headfirst. A cautiously developed investment program is likely to provide more favorable long-run results than an impulsive one.

Once you have developed a personal financial profile, the next question is "What do I want from my portfolio?" You must generally choose between earning a high current income or obtaining significant capital appreciation. It is difficult to have both. The price of having high appreciation potential in the portfolio is often low potential for current income.

Your needs may determine which avenue is chosen. A retired investor whose income depends on his or her portfolio will probably choose a lower-risk, current-income-oriented approach. In contrast, a high-income, financially secure investor (such as a physician) may be much more willing to take on risky investments in the hope of improving net worth. Thus it should be clear that a portfolio must be built around the individual's needs, which depend on income, responsibilities, financial resources, age, retirement plans, and ability to bear risk.

Portfolio Objectives and Policies

Constructing a portfolio is a logical activity that is best done after you have analyzed your needs and the available investment vehicles. You should consider these objectives when planning and constructing a portfolio: current income needs, capital preservation, capital growth, tax considerations, and risk.

Any one or more of these factors will play an influential role in defining the desirable type of portfolio. For convenience, these factors can be tied together as follows: The first two items, current income and capital preservation, are portfolio objectives consistent with a low-risk, conservative investment strategy. Normally, a portfolio with this orientation contains low-beta (low-risk) securities. The third item, a capital growth objective, implies increased risk and a reduced level of current income. Higher-risk growth stocks, options, futures, and other more speculative investments may be suitable for this investor. The fourth item, an investor's tax bracket, will influence investment strategy. A high-income investor probably wishes to defer taxes and earn investment returns in the form of capital gains. This implies a strategy of higher-risk investments and a longer holding period. Lower-bracket investors are less concerned with how they earn the income, and they may wish to invest in higher-current-income vehicles. The most important item, finally, is risk. The risk-return tradeoff should be considered *in all investment decisions.*

Developing an Asset Allocation Scheme

asset allocation
a scheme that involves dividing one's portfolio into various asset classes to *preserve capital* by protecting against negative developments while taking advantage of positive ones.

Once you have translated your needs into specific portfolio objectives, you can construct a portfolio designed to achieve these goals. Before buying any investment vehicles, however, you must develop an *asset allocation scheme.* **Asset allocation** involves dividing one's portfolio into various asset classes, such as U.S. stocks, U.S. bonds, foreign securities, short-term securities, and other vehicles like tangibles (especially gold) and real estate. The emphasis of asset allocation is on *preservation of capital*—protecting against negative developments while taking advantage of positive developments. Asset allocation, although similar to diversification in its objective, is a bit different: Its focus is on *investment in various asset classes.* Diversification, in contrast, tends to focus more on **security selection**—selecting the *specific* securities to be held *within* an asset class.

security selection
the procedures used to select the *specific* securities to be held *within* an asset class.

Asset allocation is based on the belief that the total return of a portfolio is influenced more by the division of investments into asset classes than by the actual investments. In fact, studies have shown that as much as 90% or more of a portfolio's *return* comes from asset allocation. Therefore, less than 10% can be attributed to the actual security selection. Furthermore, researchers have found that asset allocation has a much greater impact on reducing *total risk* than does selecting the best investment vehicle in any single asset category. Clearly, asset allocation is a very important aspect of portfolio management.

Approaches to Asset Allocation There are three basic approaches to asset allocation: (1) fixed weightings, (2) flexible weightings, and (3) tactical asset allocation. The first two differ with respect to the proportions of each asset category maintained in the portfolio. The third is a more exotic technique used by institutional portfolio managers.

Fixed Weightings The **fixed-weightings approach** allocates a fixed percentage of the portfolio to each of the asset categories, of which there typically are three to five. Assuming four categories—common stocks, bonds, foreign securities, and short-term securities—a fixed allocation might be as follows.

fixed-weightings approach
asset allocation plan in which a fixed percentage of the portfolio is allocated to each asset category.

Category	Allocation
Common stock	30%
Bonds	50
Foreign securities	15
Short-term securities	5
Total portfolio	100%

Generally, the fixed weightings do not change over time. When market values shift, the portfolio may have to be adjusted annually or after major market moves to maintain the desired fixed-percentage allocations.

HOTLINKS
The *Investing in Action* box at the book's Web site offers some basic portfolio-building tips for the novice investor.
www.awl.com/gitman_joehnk

Fixed weights may or may not represent equal percentage allocations to each category. One could, for example, allocate 25% to each of the four categories above. Research has shown that over a long period (1967–1988) equal (20%) allocations to U.S. stocks, foreign stocks, long-term bonds, cash, and real estate resulted in a portfolio that outperformed the S&P 500 in terms of both return and risk. These findings add further support to the importance of even a somewhat naive "buy and hold" asset allocation strategy.

Flexible Weightings The **flexible-weightings approach** involves periodic adjustment of the weights for each asset category on the basis of market analysis. The use of a flexible weighting scheme is often called *strategic asset allocation.* For example, the initial and new allocation based on a flexible weighting scheme may be as follows.

flexible-weightings approach
asset allocation plan in which weights for each asset category are adjusted periodically based on market analysis.

INVESTOR FACTS

STOCKS, BONDS, OR CASH?— Confused about which asset allocation blend to choose? Don't worry—even the pros disagree. The *Wall Street Journal* tracks the asset allocation suggestions of 13 large brokerage firms on a quarterly basis. In the second quarter of 2000, for example, strategists at Morgan Stanley Dean Witter remained bullish, recommending 80% in stocks, 20% in bonds, and nothing in cash. Strategists at Salomon Smith Barney took a more balanced approach, recommending 60% stocks, 35% bonds, and 5% cash.

Source: Terzah Ewing, "Bonds, Cash Beat Stocks in Second Quarter," *Wall Street Journal*, August 24, 2000, p. C1.

Category	Initial Allocation	New Allocation
Common stock	30%	45%
Bonds	40	40
Foreign securities	15	10
Short-term securities	15	5
Total portfolio	100%	100%

A change from the initial to the new allocation would be triggered by shifts in market conditions or expectations. For example, the new allocation shown above may have resulted from an anticipated decline in inflation. That decline would be expected to result in increased domestic stock and bond prices and a decline in foreign and short-term security returns. The weightings were therefore changed to capture greater returns in a changing market.

tactical asset allocation
asset allocation plan that uses stock-index futures and bond futures to change a portfolio's asset allocation based on market behavior.

Tactical Asset Allocation The third approach, **tactical asset allocation,** is a form of market timing that uses stock-index futures and bond futures to change a portfolio's asset allocation. When stocks are forecast to be less attractive than bonds, this strategy involves selling stock-index futures and buying bond futures. Conversely, when bonds are forecast to be less attractive than stocks, the strategy results in buying stock-index futures and selling bond futures. Because this sophisticated technique relies on a large portfolio and the use of quantitative models for market timing, it is generally appropriate only for large institutional investors.

Asset Allocation Alternatives Assuming the use of a fixed-weight asset allocation plan and using, say, four asset categories, we can demonstrate three asset allocations. Table 5.8 shows allocations in each of four categories for conservative (low-return–low-risk), moderate (average-return–average-risk), and aggressive (high-return–high-risk) portfolios. The conservative allocation relies heavily on bonds and short-term securities to provide predictable returns. The moderate allocation consists largely of common stock and bonds and includes more foreign securities and fewer short-term securities than the conservative allocation. Its moderate risk-return behavior reflects a move away from safe, short-term securities to a larger dose of common stock and foreign

TABLE 5.8 Alternative Asset Allocations

	Allocation Alternative		
Category	Conservative (low-return–low-risk)	Moderate (average-return–average-risk)	Aggressive (high-return–high-risk)
Common stock	15%	30%	40%
Bonds	45	40	30
Foreign securities	5	15	25
Short-term securities	35	15	5
Total portfolio	100%	100%	100%

INVESTING in action

University Portfolio Managers Earn an A+

For many portfolio managers, piloting a $6.2-billion portfolio through the ups and down of the current stock market would mean sleepless nights. Laurence Hoagland, chief executive officer for Stanford University's endowment fund, is not worried, however. Although recent market losses may affect the university' s financial standing, Stanford's portfolio is diversified to a point where the university will witness little overall effect from any market slide. "The asset allocation that we have is much more diversified than the typical model for the very reason of dampening the impact of fluctuations," said Hoagland. "Around 25% of our assets are allocated towards investments in the U.S. market, while the typical institution will allocate close to 50% of its assets towards the U.S. market."

Stanford resists the temptation to invest heavily in high-technology companies, many of which were founded by Stanford alumni or faculty. The Stanford Management Company, the group that allocates endowment assets, resolves potential conflicts of interest by using outside money managers with little or no connection to the university. "The money managers that we hire have full discretion over which stocks they buy and sell," said Hoagland. "We deliberately select outside money managers who are likely not to invest as heavily in Silicon Valley stocks, so as to achieve a balance in terms of the assets we hold."

Stanford's domestic-market investments are generally conservative and geared toward the long term. However, 18% of the endowment is in alternative investments, usually partnerships with venture-capital firms. "These have been extremely rewarding in recent years [232% in fiscal 1998–1999], and we have witnessed substantial gains from them," said Hoagland. "However, they are very volatile."

Like Hoagland, investment officers at other universities have been enjoying the high returns from the stock market's run up. The *Chronicle of Higher Education* reports that for the fiscal year ended June 30, 2000, returns at the top 10 schools ranged from Northwestern University's 33.7% to the University of Notre Dame's 62%. However, Notre Dame chief investment officer Scott Malpass warns university trustees that returns are likely to be 13% to 14% for 2001. Jack Meyer, head of Harvard Management Co., agrees. "It is important that we not delude ourselves into thinking that double-digit returns will persist indefinitely."

Not all university portfolio managers follow Stanford's diversification policy. Atlanta's Emory University holds about 40% of its $4.5 billion endowment in Coca-Cola stock, the result of a $105 million gift in 1979. Ten years ago, Emory had the fastest-growing endowment, thanks to this stock. Last year it wasn't so lucky, losing over 12% of its endowment's value as Coke's stock price fell. Yet Wayne Coon, Emory's chief investment officer, does not plan to diversify. "I would worry if I didn't know what caused this," he says.

Sources: Scott Dorfman, "Diversified Portfolio Helps Ensure Against Market," *University Wire*, April 18, 2000; David Marcus, "The New College All-Stars," *U.S. News & World Report*, November 13, 2000, p. 49; Bill Scanlon, "Rising Stock Market Benefits Colleges," *Denver Rocky Mountain News*, February 20, 2000, p. 20A.

securities. Finally, in the aggressive allocation, more dollars are invested in common stock, fewer in bonds, and more in foreign securities, thereby generally increasing the expected portfolio return and risk. The *Investing in Action* box on page 161 describes the success that Stanford University has had using asset allocation for its endowment fund.

Applying Asset Allocation An asset allocation plan should consider the economic outlook and your investments, savings and spending patterns, tax situation, return expectations, and risk tolerance. Such plans must be formulated for the long run, must stress capital preservation, and must provide for periodic revision to maintain consistency with changing investment goals. Generally, to decide on the appropriate asset mix, you must evaluate each asset category in terms of current return, growth potential, safety, liquidity, transaction costs (brokerage fees), and potential tax savings.

HOTLINKS

Learn the basics of asset allocation—how to choose the mix of stocks, bonds, and cash investments that best match your goals, risk tolerance, time horizon, and financial resources—at Vanguard University.

personal.vanguard.com/educ/inveduc.html

Many investors use mutual funds (see Chapter 11) as part of their asset allocation activities, to diversify within each asset category. Or, as an alternative to constructing your own portfolio, you can buy shares in an **asset allocation fund**—a mutual fund that seeks to reduce variability of returns by investing in the right assets at the right time. These funds, like all asset allocation schemes, emphasize diversification. They perform at a relatively consistent level by passing up the potential for spectacular gains in favor of predictability. Some asset allocation funds use fixed weightings, whereas others have flexible weights that change within prescribed limits. As a rule, investors with more than about $100,000 to invest and adequate time can justify do-it-yourself asset allocation. Those with between $25,000 and $100,000 and adequate time can use mutual funds to create a workable asset allocation. Those with less than $25,000 or with limited time may find asset allocation funds most attractive.

asset allocation fund
a mutual fund that seeks to reduce the variability of returns by investing in the right assets at the right time; emphasizes diversification and relatively consistent performance rather than the potential for spectacular gains.

Most important, you should recognize that to be effective an asset allocation scheme *must be designed for the long haul.* Develop an asset allocation scheme you can live with for at least 7 to 10 years, and perhaps longer. Once you have it set, stick with it. The key to success is remaining faithful to your asset allocation; that means fighting the temptation to wander.

Summary

LG 1 **Understand portfolio management objectives and the procedures to calculate the return and standard deviation of a portfolio.** A portfolio is a collection of investment vehicles assembled to achieve one or more investment goals. It involves a tradeoff between risk and return, potential price appreciation and current income, and varying risk levels. The return on a portfolio is calculated as a weighted average of the returns of the assets from which it is formed. The standard deviation of a portfolio's returns is found by applying the same formula that is used to find the standard deviation of a single asset.

LG 2 **Discuss the concepts of correlation and diversification, and the effectiveness, methods, and benefits of international diversification.** Correlation is a statistic used to measure the relationship, if any, between the returns on assets. To diversify, it is best to add assets with negatively correlated returns. In general, the less positive and more negative the correlation between asset returns, the more effectively a portfolio can be diversified to reduce its risk. Through diversification, the risk (standard deviation) of a portfolio can be reduced below the risk of the least risky asset (sometimes to zero); however, the return of the resulting portfolio will be no lower than the smallest return of its component assets. International diversification may allow an investor to reduce portfolio risk without a corresponding reduction in return. It can be achieved by investing abroad or through domestic investment in foreign companies or funds, but it typically cannot be achieved by investing in U.S. multinationals. The preferred method of international diversification for individual investors is the use of ADRs or international mutual funds available in the United States. Although opportunities to earn "excess returns" in international investments are diminishing over time, they continue to be effective diversification vehicles.

LG 3 **Describe the two components of risk, beta, and the capital asset pricing model (CAPM).** The two basic components of total risk are diversifiable (unsystematic) and nondiversifiable (systematic) risk; nondiversifiable risk is the relevant risk. Beta can be used to measure the nondiversible, or market, risk associated with a security investment. It is derived from the historical relationship between a security's return and the market return. The capital asset pricing model (CAPM) relates risk (as measured by beta) to return. It can be depicted graphically as the security market line (SML). The CAPM reflects increasing required returns for increasing risk.

LG 4 **Review traditional and modern approaches to portfolio management and reconcile them.** The traditional approach constructs portfolios by combining a large number of securities issued by companies from a broad cross section of industries. Modern portfolio theory (MPT) uses statistical diversification to develop efficient portfolios. To determine the optimal portfolio, MPT finds the efficient frontier and couples it with an investor's risk-indifference curves. In practice, portfolio betas can be used to develop efficient portfolios consistent with the investor's risk-return preferences. Generally, investors use elements of both the traditional approach and MPT to create portfolios.

LG 5 **Describe the role of investor characteristics and objectives and of portfolio objectives and policies in constructing an investment portfolio.** To construct a portfolio, the investor should consider characteristics such as level and stability of income, family factors, net worth, experience and age, and disposition toward risk. He or she should specify objectives and should plan and construct a portfolio consistent with them. Commonly considered portfolio objectives include current income, capital preservation, capital growth, tax considerations, and level of risk.

LG 6 **Summarize why and how investors use an asset allocation scheme to construct an investment portfolio.** Asset allocation is the key influence on the total return of a portfolio. It involves dividing one's portfolio into various asset classes, whereas diversification tends to focus more on security selection within an asset class. Like diversification, asset allocation aims to protect against negative developments while taking advantage of positive ones. The basic approaches to asset allocation involve the use of fixed weightings, flexible weightings, or tactical asset allocation. Asset allocation can be achieved on a do-it-yourself basis, with the use of mutual funds, or by merely buying shares in an asset allocation fund.

PART THREE

INVESTING IN COMMON STOCK

CHAPTER 6

COMMON STOCK INVESTMENTS

Learning Goals

After studying this chapter, you should be able to:

LG 1 Explain the investment appeal of common stocks and why individuals like to invest in them.

LG 2 Describe stock returns from a historical perspective and understand how current returns measure up to historical standards of performance.

LG 3 Discuss the basic features of common stocks, including issue characteristics, stock quotations, and transaction costs.

LG 4 Understand the different kinds of common stock values.

LG 5 Discuss common stock dividends, types of dividends, and dividend reinvestment plans.

LG 6 Describe various types of common stocks, including foreign stocks, and note how stocks can be used as investment vehicles.

Investing in common stocks is about taking educated risks. It is also about receiving returns—sometimes spectacular ones. In 1971, a company named Intel sold its stock to the public at $23.50 per share. The company was unprofitable and virtually unknown. That year, though, the company made technological history by introducing the world's first microprocessor, the "brains" that control a computer's central processing of data. Today, of course, Intel is a major supplier to the computing industry of chips, boards, systems, and software. And its original investors have been handsomely rewarded: A purchase of 100 shares at $23.50 per share in 1971 grew to over 100,000 shares, worth more than $8.2 million, by mid-year 2000—a return of more than 3,500 times the initial investment.

In hindsight, it looks so easy. But in fact, investors who put their money at risk need to learn as much as possible about each company they consider and the industry in which it operates. They also need to know how to analyze and interpret the information they gather. This chapter looks at common stocks and introduces some of the key concepts and principles of investing in these complex but potentially rewarding securities.

What Stocks Have to Offer

LG 1 LG 2

The basic investment attribute of common stocks is that they enable investors to participate in the profits of the firm. Every shareholder is a part owner of the firm and, as such, is entitled to a piece of the firm's profits. This claim on income is not without limitations, however, because common stockholders are really the **residual owners** of the company. That is, they are entitled to dividend income and a share of the company's earnings only after all other corporate obligations have been met. Equally important, as residual owners, holders of common stock have no guarantee that they will ever receive any return on their investment. The challenge, of course, is to find stocks that will provide the kind of return you're looking for. That's no easy task, for there are literally thousands of actively traded stocks to choose from.

residual owners
owners/stockholders of a firm, who are entitled to dividend income and a prorated share of the firm's earnings only after all the firm's other obligations have been met.

The Appeal of Common Stocks

Common stocks are a popular form of investing, used by millions of individual investors. They are popular, in part, because they offer investors the opportunity to tailor their investment programs to meet individual needs and preferences. Given the size and diversity of the stock market, it's safe to say that no matter what the investment objective, there are common stocks to fit the bill. For people living off their investment holdings, stocks provide a way of earning a steady stream of current income (from the dividends they produce). For investors less concerned about current income, common stocks can serve as the basis for long-run accumulation of wealth. With this strategy, stocks are used very much like a savings account: Investors buy stock for the long haul as a way to earn not only dividends but also a steady flow of capital gains. These investors recognize that stocks have a tendency to go up in price over time, and they simply position themselves to take advantage of that fact. Indeed, it is this potential for capital gains that is the real draw for most investors. Whereas dividends can provide a steady stream of income, the big returns come from capital gains. And few securities can match common stocks when it comes to capital gains.

INVESTOR FACTS

THE SLUMBERING BEAR— Bear markets occur when stock prices are falling. But not all falling markets end up as bears. A drop of *5% or more* in one of the major market indexes, like the Dow Jones Industrial Average (DJIA), is called a **routine decline.** As the name indicates, a routine decline typically occurs several times a year—such as April 14, 2000, when the average dropped 5.6%. A **correction** is a drop of *10% or more* in an index. A correction occurred in mid-summer of 1998, when the DJIA plunged 19.3%. The term **bear market** is reserved for severe market declines of *20% or more*. Bear markets usually occur every 3 to 4 years, but the 1990s were bear-free, although increased market volatility has everyone wondering whether the next bear market isn't just around the corner. (Note: 2000–2001 saw a big-time bear take over the Nasdaq market, as it fell more than 65%, though the Dow, through mid-2001, remained bear-free.)

Putting Stock Price Behavior in Perspective

Given the underlying nature of common stocks, when the market is strong, investors can generally expect to benefit from steady price appreciation. A good example is the performance that took place in 1999, when the market, as measured by the Dow Jones Industrial Average (DJIA), went up by more than 25%. But 1999 was even better for tech stocks and the Nasdaq market, which went up a whopping 85%.

Unfortunately, when the markets falter, so do investor returns. A recent example of such behavior is the 40% drop that occurred in the Nasdaq market in 2000, making it the worst year on record for the Nasdaq. Ironic, isn't it: A year after its best year on record, the Nasdaq recorded its worst year ever! But perhaps, an even more dramatic example of a market gone bad is the hair-raising experience of 1987. In that year, stock prices had shot up almost 30% in the first 6 months, only to experience a terrible crash on October 19. That day was not just another bad day in the market—it was the worst day in the market's history. Stock prices, as measured by the DJIA, fell 508 points on

FIGURE 6.1

The Great Bull Market of 1982–2000

One of the greatest bull markets in history began on August 12, 1982, with the Dow at 777, and has continued for more than 18 years. It was strong enough to survive two market crashes (one in 1987 and another in 1997) and one mild recession (in 1990). Indeed, this bull has had only one down year (1990), as it has charged to a high of over 11,000 on the Dow (so far).

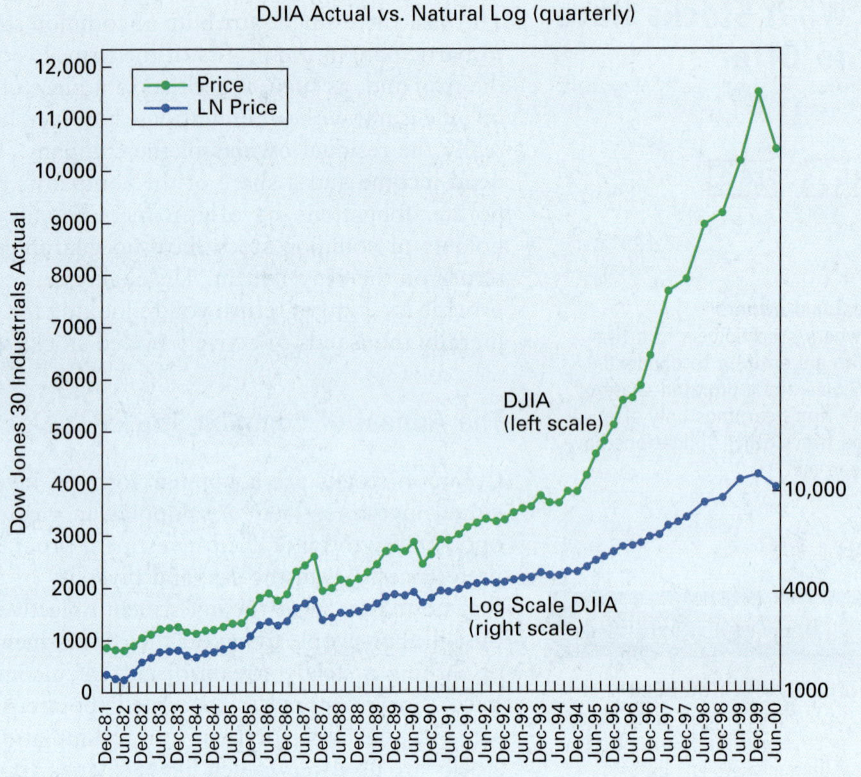

volume of over 600 million shares. The day set a number of records: the largest point drop, the largest 1-day volume of shares traded, and the largest percentage decline (23%), almost twice the previous single-day record.

Ten years later, almost to the day, it happened again. On October 27, 1997, the DJIA set two new records by dropping 554 points on a volume of 685 million shares. In percentage terms, however, the market ended the day down just over 7%, which wasn't even close to the record. (The 7% decline was the 12th largest in percentage terms.) Unlike the 1987 crash, this one didn't last long. The market recovered all of its losses *within 2 weeks*. In stark contrast, it took over 2½ years for the market to recover from the 1987 crash. Then, as the market entered a new century, *an even bigger drop* occurred; on April 14, 2000, the DJIA plunged an eye-popping 617 points. That decline, however, amounted to a fall of "only" 5.5%. It barely compared to the crash of 1987, which in percentage terms was about four times as bad.

Fortunately, days such as these are the exception rather than the rule. More often than not, the stock market offers attractive returns, rather than just risk and wild price volatility. Take a look at Figure 6.1, which shows the behavior of the market over the 19-year period from 1982 through mid-year 2000. This market run, which began in August 1982, when the Dow stood at 777, has seen the DJIA climb to over 11,000 (more than 14 times higher than where it started), making it the biggest market advance of all time! One thing that makes this market stand out is how far it has moved in a relatively short period of time. That is, the Dow has gone from less than 1,000 points to over 11,000 (through mid-2000)—and about 75% of that advance has occurred in the last 6 to 8 years. Movements of the magnitude seen on October 27, 1997, are hard to comprehend calmly. But 100- or 200-point swings are not the same when the DJIA is at 9,000 or 10,000 as when the market was trading at the 2,000 or 3,000 level—which was happening not all that many years ago.

Look again at Figure 6.1. Note the two lines on the graph. The top one tracks the actual behavior of the Dow; the lower one follows the same performance, on a logarithmic ("log") scale that shows the *rate of change* in the market instead of absolute values. Clearly, rather than showing a market that's going through the roof, the second line shows a strong market that's moving up at a far more stable pace. How long the market can continue to do so remains to be seen. The one thing we know for sure is that the market has been very good to investors for the past 18 years. And so long as earnings remain strong and interest rates remain low, there's no reason the market can't continue to climb.

From Stock Prices to Stock Returns

Our discussion so far has centered on *stock prices,* but what's even more important to investors is *stock returns,* which take into account not only price behavior but also dividend income. Table 6.1 uses the DJIA to show annual market returns over the 50-year period from 1950–2000. In addition to total returns, the table breaks market performance down into the two basic sources of return: dividends and capital gains. These figures, of course, reflect the *general behavior of the*

TABLE 6.1 Annual Returns in the Stock Market, 1950–2000 (returns based on performance of the DJIA)

Year	Rate of Return from Dividends	Rate of Return from Capital Gains	Total Rate of Return	Year	Rate of Return from Dividends	Rate of Return from Capital Gains	Total Rate of Return
2000	1.57%	−9.96%	−7.99%	1974	6.12%	−27.57%	−21.45%
1999	1.47	25.22	26.69	1973	4.15	−16.58	−12.43
1998	1.65	16.10	17.75	1972	3.16	14.58	17.74
1997	1.72	22.64	24.36	1971	3.47	6.11	9.58
1996	2.03	26.01	28.04	1970	3.76	4.82	8.58
1995	2.27	33.45	35.72	1969	4.24	−15.19	−10.95
1994	2.75	2.14	4.89	1968	3.32	4.27	7.59
1993	2.65	13.72	16.37	1967	3.33	15.20	18.53
1992	3.05	4.17	7.22	1966	4.06	−18.94	−14.88
1991	3.00	20.32	23.32	1965	2.95	10.88	13.83
1990	3.90	−4.34	−0.44	1964	3.57	14.57	18.14
1989	3.74	26.96	30.70	1963	3.07	17.00	20.07
1988	3.67	11.85	15.52	1962	3.57	−10.81	−7.24
1987	3.67	2.26	5.93	1961	3.11	18.71	21.82
1986	3.54	22.58	26.12	1960	3.47	−9.34	−5.87
1985	4.01	27.66	31.67	1959	3.05	16.40	19.45
1984	5.00	−3.74	1.26	1958	3.43	33.96	37.39
1983	4.47	20.27	24.74	1957	4.96	−12.77	−7.81
1982	5.17	19.60	24.77	1956	4.60	2.27	6.87
1981	6.42	−9.23	−2.81	1955	4.42	20.77	25.19
1980	5.64	14.93	20.57	1954	4.32	43.96	48.28
1979	6.08	4.19	10.27	1953	5.73	−3.77	1.96
1978	6.03	−3.15	2.88	1952	5.29	8.42	13.71
1977	5.51	−17.27	−11.76	1951	6.07	14.37	20.44
1976	4.12	17.86	21.98	1950	6.85	17.63	24.48
1975	4.39	38.32	42.71				

Note: Total return figures are based on both dividend income *and* capital gains (or losses); all figures are compiled from DJIA performance information, as obtained from *Barron's* and the *Wall Street Journal;* 2000 figures are through the second quarter (June 30) of the year.

HOTLINKS

Stockcharts.com gives you the Nasdaq New Highs-New Lows Line ($NAHL). You can scroll down to the bottom of the chart to interpret the chart by clicking on Chart School, at:

www.stockcharts.com/charts/$NAHL.html

market as a whole, not necessarily that of *individual stocks*. Think of them as the return behavior on a well-balanced portfolio of common stocks.

The numbers show a market that, over the past 50 years, has provided annual returns ranging from a low of −21.45% (in 1974) to a high of +48.28% (in 1954). Breaking down the returns into dividends and capital gains reveals that the big returns (or losses) come from capital gains. Overall, as Table 6.2 shows, *stocks provided average annual returns of around 12% over the full 50-year period.* And if you look at just the last 5 to 10 years, you'll find that average returns have been more like 18% to 20%. In fact, over the last 15 years (1985–2000), stocks have produced an average annual return of nearly 18%. Clearly, this market for most of the past 15 years has been anything *but* average.

Keep in mind that the numbers represent market performance; *individual* stocks can and often do perform quite differently. But at least, the averages give us a benchmark against which we can assess current stock returns and our own expectations. For example, if a return of 10% to 12% can be considered a good long-term estimate for stocks, then *sustained* returns of 18% to 20% should definitely be viewed as extraordinary. (These higher returns are possible, of course, but to get them, investors must either take on more risk or hope for a continuation of this incredible market.) Likewise, long-run stock returns of only 6% to 8% should be viewed as substandard performance. If that's the best you think you can do, then you probably should stick with bonds or CDs, where you'll earn almost as much with much less risk.

The Dow, the S&P, and the Nasdaq Most of our discussion in this chapter has been in terms of the DJIA, in large part because the Dow is such a widely followed measure of market performance. However, the DJIA is just one measure of market behavior, and it doesn't always tell the whole story. Two other closely followed market indexes are the S&P (Standard & Poor's) 500 and the Nasdaq Composite.

TABLE 6.2 Holding Period Returns in the Stock Market 1950–2000

Holding Periods	Average Annual Returns	Cumulative Returns	Amount to Which $10,000 Will Grow
5(+) yrs: 1995–2000	21.8%	196.6%	$ 29,662
5 yrs: 1990–94	10.3	63.0	16,296
10(+) yrs: 1990–00	16.0	376.7	47,663
15 yrs: 1985–99	19.1	1,275.8	137,583
25 yrs: 1975–99	16.3	4,327.7	442,769
50 yrs: 1950–99	12.6	36,855.3	3,695,534
The 1990s: 1990–99	18.3	438.9	53,897
The 1980s: 1980–89	17.2	390.5	49,049
The 1970s: 1970–79	5.3	67.9	16,792
The 1960s: 1960–69	5.2	66.0	16,602
The 1950s: 1950–59	18.0	421.7	52,171

Note: Average annual return figures are fully compounded returns and assume that all dividend income *and* capital gains are automatically reinvested. All figures compiled from DJIA performance information, as obtained from *Barron's* and the *Wall Street Journal;* 2000 data through the second quarter.

The problem with the Dow is that it captures the performance of a small, very select group of (just 30) large-cap stocks. Thus, it does not always reflect what's happening in the broad market. In contrast, the *S&P 500* tracks the performance of 500 of the very biggest and most important firms in the market and as such, is felt to be far more representative of market behavior. The *Nasdaq Composite,* on the other hand, tracks the behavior of many of this country's *tech stocks,* from the very largest, like Microsoft and Intel, to most of the newest (and much smaller) dot-com firms.

To see how these three market measures performed in the 1990s, take a look at Figure 6.2. The upper panel shows the DJIA relative to the S&P 500, and the lower panel shows the Dow relative to the Nasdaq Composite. Starting with the upper panel, we can see very similar performances for the DJIA and S&P 500. Indeed, except for a few minor divergences, the two measures moved in very close unison. So much so, in fact, that if you look in Table 6.3, which shows total returns over various holding periods, you'll see that over the decade of the 1990s (from 1/1/90 to 12/31/99), the two had almost identical returns, 18.35% versus 18.20%. Such uniformity isn't surprising because both the Dow and the S&P track the performance of the same segment of the market: large-cap stocks.

You wouldn't expect the same performance, however, when you match the Dow with the Nasdaq, and you don't get it. But look at the lower panel of Figure 6.2: There's probably more similarity between the two measures than you'd expect—especially in the first 5 or 6 years. Indeed, note in Table 6.3 that in the first half of the decade, the DJIA and the Nasdaq Composite had almost the same average annual returns (10.26% for the Dow vs. 10.58% for the Nasdaq). In fact, these two measures tracked one another fairly closely through 1997. Then, in 1998, they went their separate ways. High-tech stocks and the Nasdaq moved up sharply, while large-cap "old economy" stocks continued up at a far more modest pace. Thus, by the end of the decade, whereas the Dow had a very respectable 10-year return of 18.35%, the Nasdaq registered an incredible 24.50% rate of return (see Table 6.3). In dollar terms, this means that a $10,000 investment in the DJIA at the beginning of the decade

TABLE 6.3 Comparative Returns on the Dow, the S&P, and the Nasdaq

Holding Periods and Return Measures`	DJIA	S&P 500	Nasdaq Composite
The Decade of the '90s: 1990–1999			
• Average annual returns	18.35%	18.20%	24.50%
• Cumulative returns	438.97%	432.33%	794.75%
• Amount to which $10,000 will grow	$53,897	$53,233	$89,475
First Half of the Decade: 1990–1994			
• Average annual returns	10.26%	8.69%	10.58%
• Cumulative returns	62.96%	51.70%	65.34%
• Amount to which $10,000 will grow	$16,296	$15,170	$16,534
Last Half of the Decade: 1995–1999			
• Average annual returns	27.03%	28.54%	40.71%
• Cumulative returns	230.75%	250.91%	441.16%
• Amount to which $10,000 will grow	$33,075	$35,091	$54,116

Note: Average annual return figures are fully compounded and assume that all dividends and capital gains are reinvested.

Source: Morningstar Principia Pro, June 2000.

FIGURE 6.2 A Decade of the Dow, the S&P, and the Nasdaq (1990 to 1999, *plus the first half of 2000*)

Here's how the DJIA performed relative to the S&P 500 (top) and the Nasdaq Composite (bottom) in the 1990s. Clearly, the Dow held its own against the S&P but was no match for the tech-heavy Nasdaq.

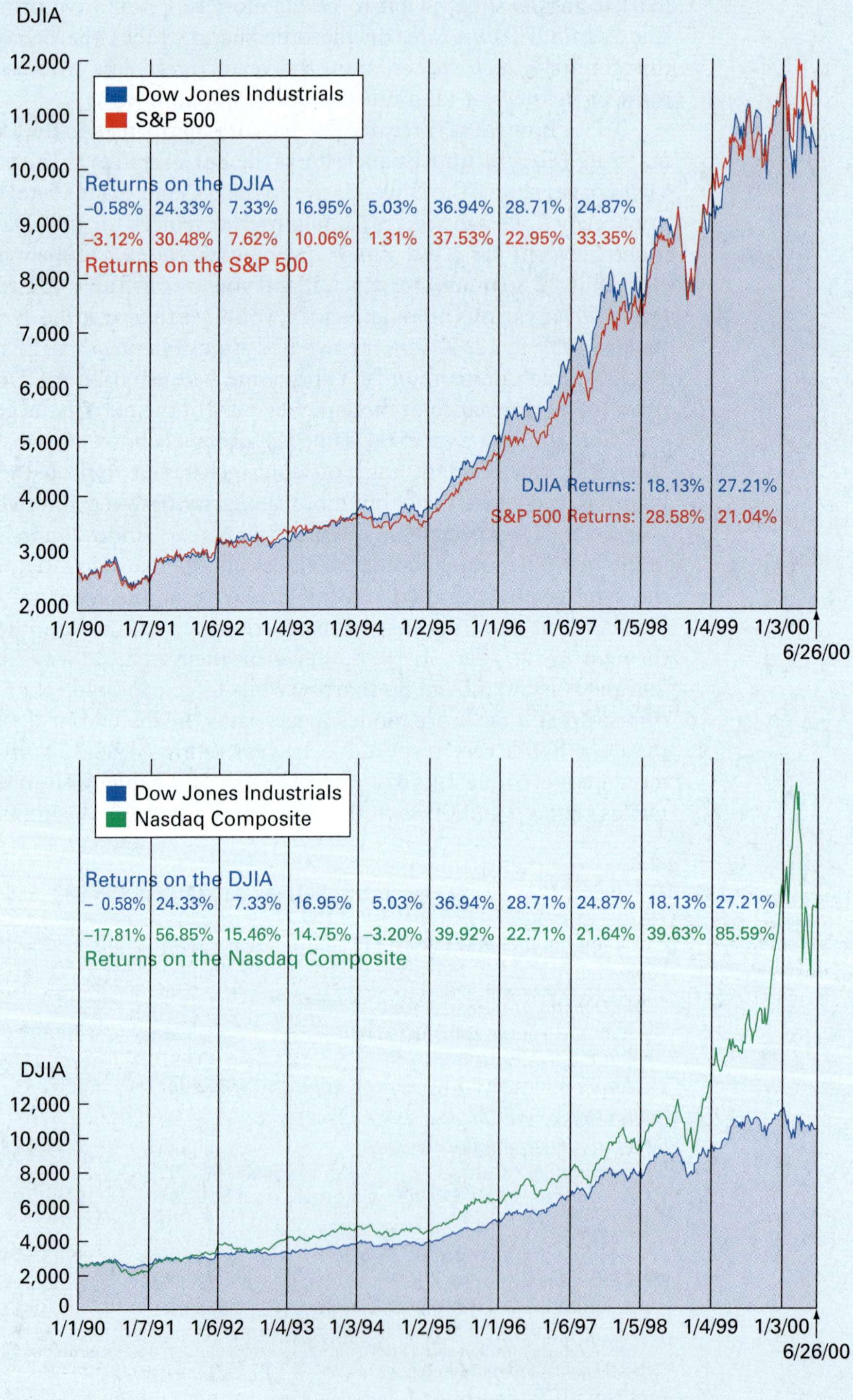

would have been worth more than $50,000 at decade's end, whereas the same amount invested in the Nasdaq would have been worth nearly $90,000.

No matter how you measure it—the Dow, the S&P, or the Nasdaq Composite—the stock market certainly turned in a stellar performance, especially in the last 2 or 3 years of the decade! At least it would appear that way. But what you see isn't always what you get. For as the *Investing in Action* box on page 174 reveals, not all stocks participated equally in this market of the nineties.

The types of (overall) market performance turned in, especially in the last half of the decade, has not come without a price: Since 1997, the level of *market volatility* has increased dramatically. There are some important market statistics to back up this claim. For example, in 1997, 1998, and 1999, the market as measured by the DJIA closed at least 1% higher or lower than the preceding day about one-third of the time. That means that with the the Dow at 9,000 or 10,000, moves of 90 to 100 (or more) points a day have been occurring almost every 3 days over the past 3½ years. The S&P 500 has turned in a similar performance, and even more volatility has occurred in the Nasdaq Composite. Although professional stock traders and day traders may love such price volatility, most investors don't. But when you stop to think about it, it's hard to have one result (outsized returns) without the other (outsized risk/price volatility). After all, the big returns are usually produced when there are big swings in the market.

The Pros and Cons of Stock Ownership

One reason why stocks are so appealing to investors is the substantial return opportunities they offer. As we just saw, stocks generally provide attractive, highly competitive returns over the long haul. Indeed, common stock returns compare very favorably to other investment outlets such as long-term corporate bonds and U.S. Treasury securities. For example, over the 50-year period from 1950 through 2000, high-grade corporate bonds averaged annual returns of around 6%—*about half that of common stocks.* Although long-term bonds sometimes outperform stocks on a year-by-year basis (as they did in the mid-1980s, when interest rates were in a free fall), the opposite is true far more often than not; that is, stocks outperform bonds, and usually by a wide margin. Because stocks can be counted on over most periods to provide returns that exceed annual inflation rates, they make ideal inflation hedges. Indeed, since 1982, stocks have done quite well against inflation. As long as inflation rates remain at reasonably low levels of 3% to 4%, stocks are likely to continue to produce attractive inflation-adjusted returns.

HOTLINKS

Based on broad stock market indexes such as the S&P 500, over long periods of time common stocks have outpaced inflation. Read about outpacing inflation at:

www.putnaminv.com/frames/e101.htm

Stocks offer other benefits as well: They are easy to buy and sell, and the transaction costs are modest. Moreover, price and market information is widely disseminated in the news and financial media. A final advantage is that the unit cost of a share of common stock is usually within the reach of most individual investors. Unlike bonds, which carry minimum denominations of at least $1,000, and some mutual funds that have fairly hefty minimum investments, common stocks don't have such minimums. Instead, most stocks today are priced at less than $75 a share—and any number of shares, no matter how few, can be bought or sold.

INVESTING in action

If the Markets Are Doing So Well, Why Don't I Feel Rich?

During the market's boom times from 1997 to 1999, market indexes soared. Nasdaq was the star performer, rising more than 85% in 1999, compared to the very respectable increases of 25% for DJIA and about 20% for the S&P 500. Investors should have been happy with returns like these. To their dismay, however, most investors discovered that their portfolio returns had not tracked any of these market performance measures.

The reason? Since about 1997, the split between a small group of large-cap stocks and the rest of the market widened, creating a very unbalanced two-tier market. A shrinking number of stocks pushed market averages higher, while other companies languished. The technical term for this is *market breadth*, or how broadly the market is moving. If on a particular day, 80% of the issues on the Nasdaq fell in price, you would hear about a "broad decline."

Many money managers label the current (1997–2000) market a "haves versus have-nots" environment, in which a privileged few drive the rest of the market. In such an environment, even though the market might experience a broad decline, the market index continues to rise. Let's look at some statistics that make this point clear.

- In 1999, the prices of 51% of Nasdaq's companies gained. Technology stocks accounted for almost half of the gainers, with 20% at least doubling in price and some reporting 1,000% increases. However, 48% of Nasdaq companies—especially pharmaceuticals, health care, manufacturing, and financial services—fell in price, with an average decline of 32%. The top performers drove the Nasdaq's performance; without them, the Nasdaq composite index was essentially flat. Seldom has a strong market had so many losers.
- The gap between haves and have-nots is even more apparent in the market capitalization of companies on the Wilshire 5000 Total Market Index,. The market value of the 10 largest companies, led by General Electric (GE), Cisco, and Microsoft, represents 20% of the market's total value of $15.3 trillion. The top 10%, about 700 companies, account for 87% of total value; the bottom 700 account for only 0.02 %. GE alone is as big as the smallest 4,940 companies.

With relatively few power-hitters driving the market, an index can keep rising even though more stock prices post declines than advances. This is exactly what happened from about 1997 through mid-2000. Market watchers keep their eyes on the *advance decline (A/D) line*, which represents a cumulative summary of daily price advances, less price declines, for a particular exchange. You can find graphs of the A/D line, the most widely used measure of market breadth for the major exchanges, at **www.stockcharts.com** These graphs clearly show whether the majority of stocks are following the trend of the market index. If both the market index line and the A/D line are rising, then the market index is fairly representing market performance. When the two move in opposition, it signals that the index is not a good predictor of stock performance.

Another indicator is the *high-low line*, which shows the number of stocks recording their highest or lowest price level in 52 weeks. These are usually shown as moving averages and graphed together to make comparison easy. You'll also find lists of stocks reporting new highs or lows on the stock quotation pages.

Sources: Eric Bjorgen, "A Bull Market? Baloney," *Mututal Funds*, May 2000, p. 28; E. S. Browning, "Nasdaq's Gains Mask a House Divided; Stocks Show Equal Split of Rich ands Poor," *Wall Street Journal*, December 20, 1999, pp. C1, C4; E. S. Browning, "Stocks Approach the Stratosphere," *Wall Street Journal*, January 4, 2000, p. R1; Stockcharts.com, **www.stockcharts.com**; Russ Wiles, "Handful of Companies Dominate Stock Market's Valuation," *Arizona Republic*, April 25, 2000, p. D1.

FIGURE 6.3

The Current Income of Stocks and Bonds

Clearly, the level of current income (dividends) paid to stockholders falls far short of the amount of interest income paid to bondholders.

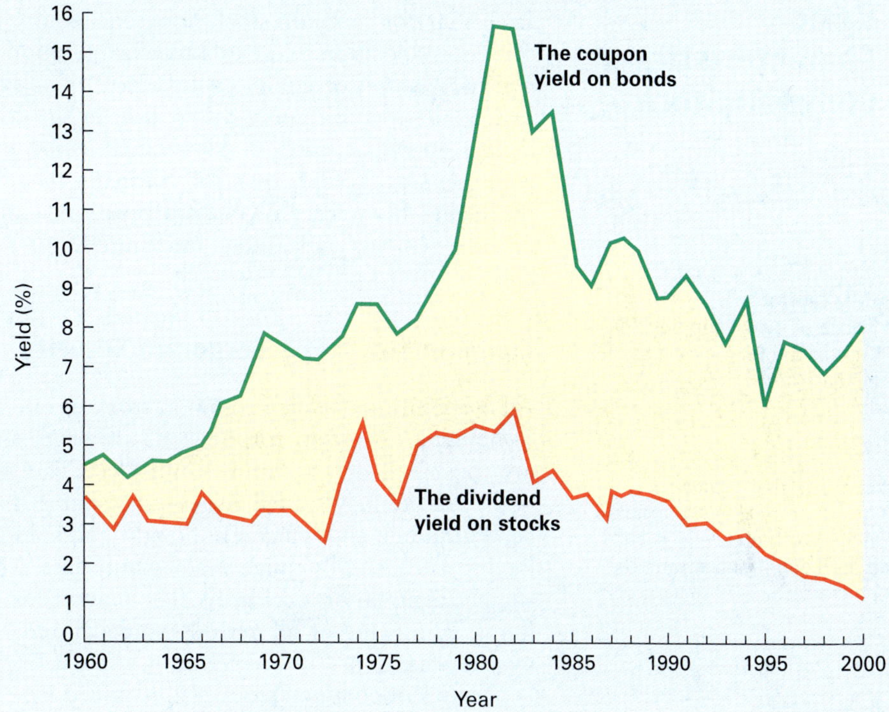

There are also some *disadvantages* to common stock. Risk is perhaps the most significant. Stocks are subject to various types of risk, including business and financial risk, purchasing power risk, market risk, and event risk. All of these can adversely affect a stock's earnings and dividends, its price appreciation, and, of course, the rate of return earned by an investor. Even the best of stocks possess elements of risk that are difficult to overcome, because company earnings are subject to many factors, including government control and regulation, foreign competition, and the state of the economy. Because such factors affect sales and profits, they also affect the price behavior of the stock and possibly even dividends. All of this leads to another disadvantage: The earnings and general performance of stocks are subject to wide swings, so it is difficult to value common stocks and consistently select top performers. The selection process is complex because so many elements go into formulating expectations of stock performance. In other words, not only is the future outcome of the company and its stock uncertain, but the evaluation and selection process itself is far from perfect.

A final disadvantage of stocks is the sacrifice of current income. Several types of investments—bonds, for instance—pay higher levels of current income and do so with much greater certainty. Figure 6.3 compares the dividend yield of common stocks with the coupon yield of bonds. It shows the degree of sacrifice common stock investors make in terms of current income. Clearly, common stocks have a long way to go before they catch up with the *current income levels* available from bonds and most other fixed-income securities.

Basic Characteristics of Common Stock

LG 3 LG 4

Each share of common stock represents equity (ownership) in a company. It's this equity position that explains why common stocks are often referred to as *equity securities* or **equity capital.** Every share entitles the holder to an equal ownership position and participation in the corporation's earnings and dividends, an equal vote, and an equal voice in management. Together, the common stockholders own the company. The more shares an investor owns, the bigger his or her ownership position. Common stock has no maturity date—it remains outstanding indefinitely.

equity capital
evidence of ownership position in a firm, in the form of shares of common stock.

Common Stock as a Corporate Security

All corporations "issue" common stock of one type or another. But the shares of many, if not most, corporations are never traded, because the firms either are too small or are family controlled. The stocks of interest to us in this book are **publicly traded issues**—the shares that are readily available to the general public and which are bought and sold in the open market. The firms issuing such shares range from giants like AT&T and Microsoft to much smaller regional or local firms. The market for publicly traded stocks is enormous: The value of all actively traded listed and OTC stocks in 2000 was over $14 trillion.

publicly traded issues
shares of stock that are readily available to the general public and are bought and sold in the open market.

Shares of common stock can be issued in several different ways. The most widely used procedure today is the **public offering.** In using this procedure, the corporation offers the investing public a certain number of shares of its stock at a certain price. Figure 6.4 shows an announcement for such an offering. In this case, Arena Pharmaceuticals, a small highly-specialized biopharmaceutical company, sold 6.9 million shares of stock at a price of $18 a share.

public offering
an offering to sell to the investing public a set number of shares of a firm's stock at a specified price.

New shares of stock can also be issued using a rights offering. In a rights offering, existing stockholders are given the first opportunity to buy the new issue. They can purchase new shares in proportion to their current ownership position. For instance, if a stockholder currently owns 1% of a firm's stock and the firm issues 10,000 additional shares, the rights offering will give that stockholder the opportunity to purchase 1% (100 shares) of the new issue. The net result of a rights offering is the same as that of a public offering: The firm ends up with more equity in its capital structure, and the number of shares outstanding increases.

Perhaps one of the most creative ways of bringing a new issue to the market is through a **stock spin-off.** Basically, a spin-off occurs when a company gets rid of one of its subsidiaries or divisions. For example, Quaker Oats did this when it spun off its Fisher-Price subsidiary. The company doesn't just sell the subsidiary to some other firm. Rather, it creates a new stand-alone company and then distributes stock in that company to its existing stockholders. Thus every Quaker Oats shareholder received a certain (prorated) number of shares in the newly created, and now publicly traded, Fisher-Price company. There have been hundreds of stock spin-offs in the last 10 years or so. Some of the more notable ones were the spin-off of Agilent by Hewlett-Packard, the partial (15%) spin-off of the online travel service Expedia by Microsoft, and the Eckerd Drugstore spin-off by J.C. Penney. Normally, companies execute stock spin-offs if they believe the subsidiary is no longer a good fit, or if they feel they've become too diversified and want to focus on their

stock spin-off
conversion of one of a firm's subsidiaries to a stand-alone company by distribution of stock in that new company to existing shareholders.

FIGURE 6.4 **An Announcement of a New Stock Issue**

This announcement indicates that Arena Pharmaceuticals (Nasdaq: **ARNA**) is issuing 6.9 million shares of stock at a price of $18 per share. For the company, that will mean nearly $125 million in new capital. Note that even this issue has a global twist to it as the lead banker of this U.S. security offering, ING Barings, is a major multinational investment banking firm headquartered in Amsterdam and London. (*Source: Wall Street Journal,* August 15, 2000.)

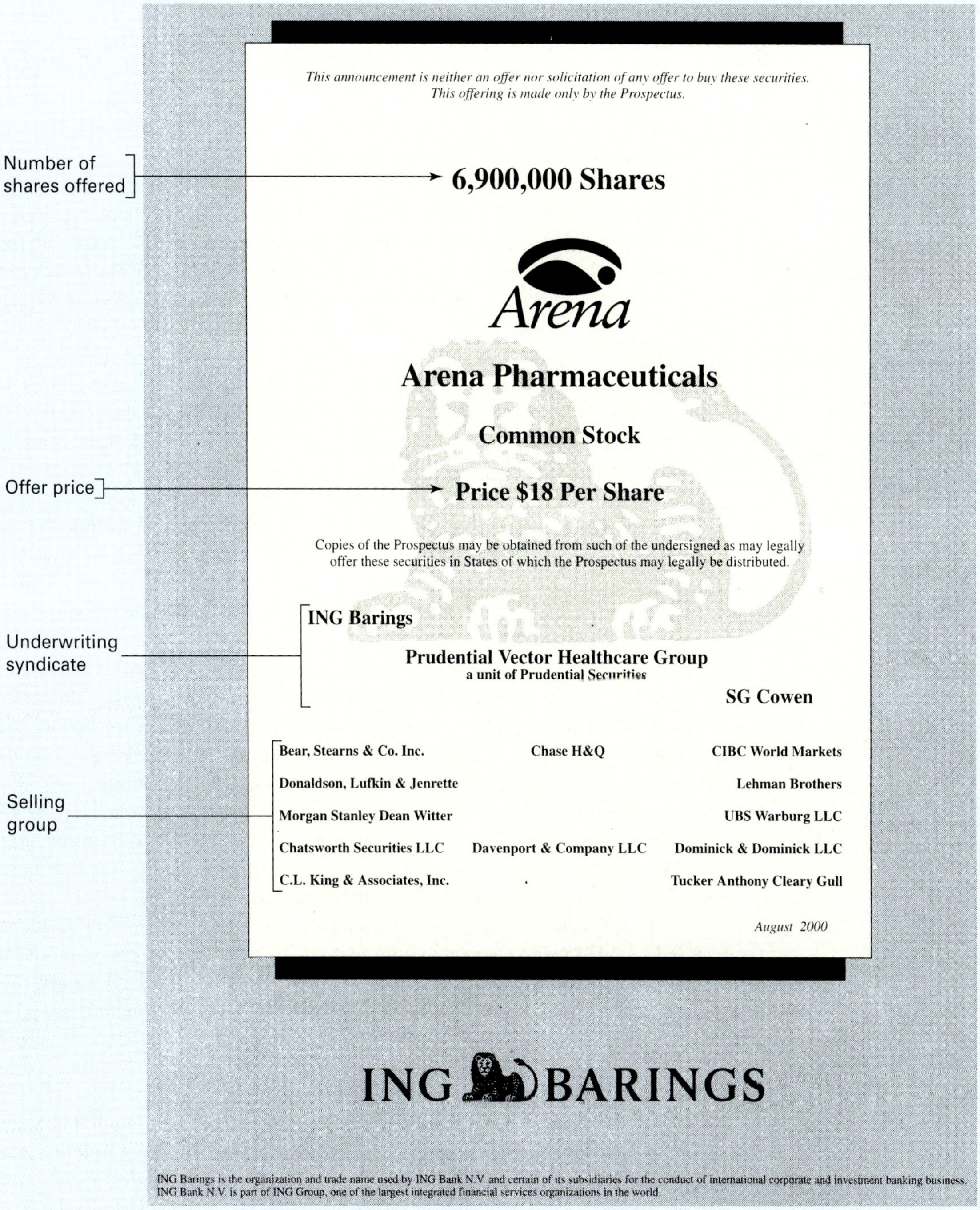

core products. Not surprisingly, such spin-offs often work very well for investors, too.

stock split
a maneuver in which a company increases the number of shares outstanding by exchanging a specified number of new shares of stock for each outstanding share.

Stock Splits Companies can also increase the number of shares outstanding by executing a **stock split.** In declaring a split, a firm merely announces that it will increase the number of shares outstanding by exchanging a specified number of new shares for each outstanding share of stock. For example, in a 2-for-1 stock split, two new shares of stock are exchanged for each old share. In a 3-for-2 split, three new shares are exchanged for every two old shares outstanding. A stockholder who owned 200 shares of stock before a 2-for-1 split becomes the owner of 400 shares; the same investor would hold 300 shares if there had been a 3-for-2 split.

Stock splits are used when a firm wants to enhance its stock's trading appeal by lowering its market price. Normally, the firm gets the desired result: The price of the stock tends to fall in close relation to the terms of the split (unless the stock split is accompanied by a big increase in the level of dividends). For example, using the ratio of the number of old shares to new, we can expect a $100 stock to trade at or close to $50 a share after a 2-for-1 split. Specifically, we divide the original price per share by the ratio of new shares to old. That same $100 stock would trade at about $67 after a 3-for-2 split—that is, $\$100 \div 3/2 = \$100 \div 1.5 = \$67$. (A variation of the stock split, known as a stock dividend, will be discussed later in this chapter.)

HOTLINKS
Get the latest information on stock splits at:
biz.yahoo.com/c/s.html

Treasury Stock Instead of increasing the number of outstanding shares, corporations sometimes find it desirable to *reduce* the number of shares in the hands of the investing public by buying back their own stock. Generally speaking, firms repurchase their own stock when they view it as undervalued in the marketplace. When that happens, the company's own stock becomes an attractive investment candidate. Those firms that can afford to do so will purchase their stock in the open market by becoming investors, like any other individual or institution. When these shares are acquired, they become known as **treasury stock.** Technically, treasury stocks are simply shares of stock that have been issued and subsequently repurchased by the issuing firm. Treasury stocks are kept by the corporation and can be used at a later date for various purposes. Such purposes include mergers and acquisitions, to meet employee stock option plans, or as a means of paying stock dividends. Or the shares can simply be held in treasury for an indefinite time.

treasury stock
shares of stock that have been sold and subsequently repurchased by the issuing firm.

The impact of these share repurchases—or *buybacks,* as they're sometimes called—is not clear. Generally, the feeling is that if the buyback is substantial (involving a significant number of shares), the stockholder's equity position and claim on income will increase. This result is likely to benefit stockholders to the extent that such action has a positive effect on the market price of the stock. However, it has also been suggested that buybacks are often used merely as a way to prop up the price of an overvalued stock.

classified common stock
common stock issued by a company in different classes, each of which offers different privileges and benefits to its holders.

Classified Common Stock For the most part, all the stockholders in a corporation enjoy the same benefits of ownership. Occasionally, a company will issue different classes of common stock, each of which entitles holders to different privileges and benefits. These issues are known as **classified common stock.** Hundreds of publicly traded firms have created such stock classes.

Though issued by the same company, each class of common stock is different and has its own value.

Classified common stock is customarily used to denote either different voting rights or different dividend obligations. For instance, class A could designate nonvoting shares, and class B would carry normal voting rights. Or the class A stock would receive no dividends, and class B would receive regular cash dividends. Notable for its use of classified stock is Ford Motor Company, which has two classes of stock outstanding. Ford's class A stock is owned by the investing public, and class B stock is owned by the Ford family and their trusts or corporations. The two classes of stock share equally in the dividends. But class A stock has one vote per share, whereas the voting rights of the class B stock are structured to give the Ford family a 40% absolute control of the company. Similar types of classified stock are used at the Washington Post, Dillards Department Stores, Dow Jones & Co., Nike, and Berkshire Hathaway. Regardless of the specifics, whenever there is more than one class of common stock outstanding, investors should take the time to determine the privileges, benefits, and limitations of each class.

Buying and Selling Stocks

Whether buying or selling stocks, you should become familiar with how stocks are quoted and with the costs of executing common stock transactions. Certainly, keeping track of *current prices* is an essential element in the buy-and-sell decisions of investors. They are the link in the decision process that lets investors decide when to buy or sell a stock; they also help investors monitor the market performance of their security holdings. Similarly, *transaction costs* are important because of the impact they can have on investment returns. Indeed, the costs of executing stock transactions can sometimes consume most (or all) of the profits from an investment. These costs should not be taken lightly.

Reading the Quotes Investors in the stock market have come to rely on a highly efficient information system that quickly disseminates market prices to the public. The stock quotes that appear daily in the financial press are a vital part of that information system. To see how price quotations work and what they mean, consider the quotes that appear daily (Monday through Friday) in the *Wall Street Journal.* As we'll see, these quotes give not only the most recent price of each stock but also a great deal of additional information.

Some NYSE stock quotes are presented in Figure 6.5—let's use the Disney quotations for purposes of illustration. These quotes were published in the *Wall Street Journal* on Thursday, May 24, 2001. They describe the trading activity that occurred the day before, which in this case was Wednesday, May 23. A glance at the quotations shows that stocks, like most other securities, are now quoted in dollars and cents. That may not sound like a big deal, but it is. Until the year 2000, stocks had been quoted in fractions, mostly in eighths of a dollar, where each ⅛ of a point was worth 12½ cents. That system, which prevailed for well over 100 years, produced stock quotes like 27¼ and 85⅞, which then had to be translated into dollars prices of $27.25 and $85.875. That all changed in 2000, when stock quotes were switched over to "decimals" (dollars and cents).

FIGURE 6.5 Stock Quotations

This figure shows the quotations for a small sample of stocks traded on the NYSE, providing a summary of the transactions that occurred on one day. (*Source: Wall Street Journal,* May 24, 2001.)

YTD % CHG	52 WEEKS HI	LO	STOCK (SYM)	DIV	YLD %	PE	VOL 100S	LAST	NET CHG
+ 14.1	29	19.44	Delta&Pine **DLP**	.16	.7	20	1488	23.88	− 0.27
− 11.1	1.88	0.93	DeltaWdsde **DLW** s		...	1	111	1	...
▲+ 5.8	24.71	16.56	DelticTimber **DEL**	.25	1.0	17	341	25.25	+ 0.55
+ 34.2	28.25	15.99	DeluxeCp **DLX** s	1.48	5.4	...	3196	27.62	− 0.22
− 1.7	**12.30**	**4.31**	♣**DnbryRes DNR**		**...**	**3**	**2216**	**10.81**	**− 0.71**
− 23.6	15.88	7.95	Dept56 **DFS**		...	5	106	8.79	...
+ 24.7	14.38	6.19	DescSA ADR **DES**	e	...	...	308	7.95	+ 0.15
− 22.4	69	20.76	♣DtscheTel ADR **DT**	.56e	2.5	...	31872	22.69	− 0.65
▲+ 30.7	17.30	11.63	DevDivRlty **DDR**	1.48	8.5	16	2256	17.40	+ 0.25
− 9.6	41.50	25.94	DeVry **DV**		...	43	937	34.13	− 0.64
− 3.8	45.49	32.13	Diageo ADS **DEO**	1.38e	3.2	...	2233	42.70	+ 0.34
+ 38.3	78.55	29.69	DiagnstPdt **DP**	.48	.6	35	354	75.52	− 0.80
+ 25.9	15.75	9.88	DialCp **DL**	.16	1.2	dd	1194	13.85	− 0.15
+ 2.6	47.94	29.56	DmndOffshr **DO**	.50	1.2	71	11071	41.03	− 1.72
− 5.0	36.38	22.94	Diebold **DBD**	.64	2.0	20	1644	31.71	− 0.50
+ 52.4	21.50	11.50	DillrdCapTr **DDT**	1.88	9.4	...	142	20	+ 0.04
+ 43.7	**22.50**	**9.44**	**Dillards DDS**	**.16**	**.9**	**15**	**15661**	**16.98**	**− 2.54**
+ 22.8	36.30	14.87	DimeBcp **DME**	.48f	1.3	24	4467	35.99	− 0.19
▲+ 100.0	11.09	2	♣Dimon **DMN**	.20	1.8	18	2660	11	− 0.05
+ 134.7	12.98	4.88	DiscntAuto **DAP**		...	14	135	12.91	− 0.04
+ 14.4	43	26	Disney **DIS**	.21	.6	cc	59521	33.11	− 1.39
− 18.1	19.75	11.90	Dist&Srv ADR **DYS**	.25e	1.8	...	510	14.29	− 0.66
− 7.1	18.80	11.75	DoleFood **DOL**	.40	2.6	13	1429	15.22	− 0.06
− 1.7	24.05	12.80	DlrGenl **DG**	.13	.7	30	21797	18.55	+ 0.05
+ 27.5	24.80	13.63	♣DlrThrfty **DTG**		...	8	416	23.90	− 0.15
▲+ 57.8	25	12.31	DominResVA **DOM**	3.02e	12.4	...	874	24.38	− 0.61
+ 0.6	69.99	42.44	♣DominRes **D**	2.58	3.8	28	8229	67.38	+ 0.79
+ 0.3	66.56	53	♣DominRes PIES n	2.81e	4.5	...	744	62.70	+ 0.40
+ 9.1	11.38	6.63	♣Domtar g **DTC**	.14g	...	...	114	10.02	+ 0.01
+ 11.5	31.80	18.81	♣Donaldson **DCI**	.30	1.0	20	1383	31.02	− 0.61

- Year-to-date changes in price, in percentages
- High and low prices for previous 52 weeks
- Company name and stock symbol
- Annual dividends per share for past 12 months
- Dividend yield (dividends as percent of share price)
- Price/earnings ratio: $\left(\frac{\text{market price}}{\text{earnings per share}}\right)$
- Share volume, in hundreds
- Closing (final) price for the day—this is also the price used to compute dividend yield and the P/E ratio
- Net change in price from previous day

In addition to stock prices, a typical stock quote conveys an array of other information, including

- The first column ("YTD % Chg") gives the stock's year-to-date change in price; note that Disney stock has gone up 14.4% since the first of the year. The next two columns, labeled "Hi" and "Lo," show the highest and lowest prices at which the stock sold during the past 52 weeks—you can see that Disney has traded between \$43 and \$26 a share during the preceding 52-week period.
- Listed to the right of the company's name is its *stock symbol;* Disney goes by the three-letter abbreviation DIS. These symbols are the abbreviations used to identify specific companies; every common stock (and mutual fund) has a unique three- to five-letter symbol that distinguishes it from any other security and is used to execute market trades.

- The figure listed after the stock symbol is the annual cash dividend paid on each share of stock, which for Disney was 21 cents. This is followed by the stock's dividend yield (0.6% for Disney) and its price/earnings (P/E) ratio. Note that the *cc* in the PE column indicates that Disney was trading at more than 100 times its earnings.
- The daily share volume follows the P/E ratio. The sales numbers are listed in lots of 100 shares, so the figure 59521 means that 5,952,100 shares of Disney stock were traded on May 23.
- The next entry, the "Last" column, contains the closing (final) price, $33.11, at which the stock sold on the day in question.
- Finally, as the last ("Net Change") column shows, Disney closed down $1.39. This means the stock closed $1.39 lower than the day before (May 22), when it closed at $34.50.

The same basic quotation system is used for *some* OTC stocks. Actually, for quotation purposes, OTC stocks are divided into two groups: Nasdaq National Market issues and other OTC stocks. The National Market stocks are those of major, actively traded companies; *they are quoted just like NYSE issues.* Other OTC stocks (i.e., Nasdaq Small Cap issues) and AMEX stocks are quoted in a highly abbreviated form that includes only stock name, symbol, volume, closing price, and price change.

Transaction Costs As explained in Chapter 3, common stock can be bought and sold in round or odd lots. A *round lot* is 100 shares of stock or multiples thereof. An *odd lot* is a transaction involving less than 100 shares. The sale of 400 shares of stock would be a round-lot transaction; the sale of 75 shares would be an odd-lot transaction. Trading 250 shares of stock would involve a combination of two round lots and an odd lot.

An investor incurs certain transaction costs when buying or selling stock. In addition to some modest transfer fees and taxes paid by the *seller,* the major cost is the brokerage fee paid—by both *buyer and seller*—at the time of the transaction. As a rule, brokerage fees amount to 1% to 5% of most transactions. But they can go much higher, particularly for very small trades. Higher fees are connected with the purchase or sale of odd lots, which requires a specialist known as an *odd-lot dealer.* This usually results in an *odd-lot differential* of 10 to 25 cents per share, which is tacked on to the normal commission charge, driving up the costs of these small trades. Indeed, the relatively high cost of an odd-lot trade makes it better to deal in round lots whenever possible.

INVESTOR FACTS

MARKET MUSCLE—The total *market value* of a company, defined as the stock price multiplied by the number of shares outstanding, is a measure of what investors think a company is worth. In 2000, General Electric topped the list with a market value of $547 billion, considerably more than the value of the entire Singapore stock market. Some other big-cap companies are Cisco Systems ($369 billion), ExxonMobil ($308 billion), Microsoft ($290 billion), and Pfizer ($274 billion).

Source: Data from "Corporate Snapshots" from www.fortune.com, December 8, 2000.

Common Stock Values

The worth of a share of common stock can be described in a number of ways. Terms such as *par value, book value, market value,* and *investment value* are all found in the financial media. Each designates some accounting, investment, or monetary attribute of a stock.

par value
the stated, or face, value of a stock.

Par Value The term **par value** refers to the stated, or face, value of a stock. Except for accounting purposes, it is relatively useless. In many ways, par value is a throwback to the early days of corporate law, when it was used as a basis for assessing the extent of a stockholder's legal liability. Because the term has little or no significance for investors, many stocks today are issued as no-par or low-par stocks. That is, they may have par values of only a penny or two.

book value
the amount of stockholders' equity in a firm; equals the amount of the firm's assets minus the firm's liabilities and preferred stock.

Book Value **Book value,** another accounting measure, represents the amount of stockholders' equity in the firm. As we will see in the next chapter, it is commonly used in stock valuation. Book value indicates the amount of stockholder funds used to finance the firm. It is calculated by subtracting the firm's liabilities and preferred stock from its assets. Let's assume that a corporation has $10 million in assets, owes $5 million in various forms of short- and long-term debt, and has $1 million worth of preferred stock outstanding. The book value of this firm would be $4 million.

Book value can be converted to a per-share basis—*book value per share*—by dividing it by the number of common shares outstanding. For example, if the firm just described has 100,000 shares of common stock outstanding, then its book value per share is $40. As a rule, most stocks have market prices that are well above their book values.

market value
the prevailing market price of a security.

Market Value **Market value** is one of the easiest stock values to determine. It is simply the prevailing market price of an issue. In essence, market value indicates how the market participants as a whole have assessed the worth of a share of stock. By multiplying the market price of the stock by the number of shares outstanding, we can also find the market value of the firm itself—or what is known as the firm's *market capitalization.* For example, if a firm has 1 million shares outstanding and its stock trades at $50 per share, the company has a market value (or "market cap") of $50 million. Because investors are always interested in an issue's market price, the market value of a share of stock is generally of considerable importance to stockholders.

investment value
the amount that investors believe a security should be trading for, or what they think it's worth.

Investment Value **Investment value** is probably the most important measure for a stockholder. It indicates the worth investors place on the stock—in effect, what they think the stock *should* be trading for. Determining a security's investment value is a complex process based on expectations of the return and risk behavior of a stock. Any stock has two potential sources of return: annual dividend payments and the capital gains that arise from appreciation in market price. In establishing investment value, investors try to determine how much money they will make from these two sources. They then use that estimate as the basis for formulating the return potential of the stock. At the same time, they try to assess the amount of risk to which they will be exposed by holding the stock. Such return and risk information helps them place an investment value on the stock. This value represents the *maximum* price an investor should be willing to pay for the issue. Investment value is the major topic in Chapter 8.

Common Stock Dividends

LG 5

In 1999, U.S. corporations paid out some $365 billion in dividends. Yet, in spite of these numbers, dividends still don't get much respect. Many investors, particularly younger ones, often put very little value on dividends. That's unfortunate, because dividend income is one of the two basic sources of return to investors. And although dividends are subject to higher taxes than long-term capital gains, they're also far less risky. The stream of annual dividends is far more predictable than the capital gains that may or may not occur. Let's now take a closer look at this important source of income.

The Dividend Decision

By paying out dividends, typically on a quarterly basis, companies share with their stockholders some of the profits they've earned. Actually, the question of how much to pay in dividends is decided by a firm's board of directors. The directors evaluate the firm's operating results and financial condition to determine whether dividends should be paid and, if so, in what amount. If the directors decide to pay dividends, they also establish several important payment dates. In this section we'll look at the corporate and market factors that go into the dividend decision. Then we'll briefly examine some of the key payment dates.

earnings per share (EPS)
the amount of annual earnings available to common stockholders, as stated on a per-share basis.

Corporate Versus Market Factors When the board of directors assembles for its regular dividend meeting, it weighs a variety of factors in making a decision to pay out dividends. First, the board looks at the firm's earnings. Even though a company does not have to show a profit to pay dividends, profits still are considered a vital link in the dividend decision. With common stocks, the annual earnings of a firm are usually measured and reported in terms of **earnings per share (EPS)**. Basically, EPS translates total corporate profits into profits on a per-share basis. It provides a convenient measure of the amount of earnings available to stockholders. Earnings per share is found by using the following formula:

Equation 6.1

$$\text{EPS} = \frac{\begin{matrix}\text{Net profit} \\ \text{after taxes}\end{matrix} - \text{Preferred dividends}}{\begin{matrix}\text{Number of shares of} \\ \text{common stock outstanding}\end{matrix}}$$

For example, if a firm reports a net profit of $1.25 million, pays $250,000 in dividends to preferred stockholders, and has 500,000 shares of common outstanding, it has an EPS of $2—that is, ($1,250,000 − $250,000)/500,000. Note in Equation 6.1 that preferred dividends are subtracted from profits, since they must be paid before any funds can be made available to common stockholders.

While assessing profits, the board also looks at the firm's growth prospects. It is very likely some of the firm's present earnings will be needed for investment purposes and to help finance expected growth. The board also considers how much cash the firm has. Finally, the board will want to make sure that it is meeting all legal and contractual constraints. For example, the firm may be subject to a loan agreement that legally limits the amount of dividends it can pay.

After looking at internal matters, the board will consider certain market effects and responses. Most investors feel that if a company is going to retain earnings rather than pay them out in dividends, it should exhibit proportionately higher growth and profit levels. The market's message is clear: If the firm is investing the money wisely and at a high rate of return, fine; otherwise, pay a larger portion of earnings out in the form of dividends. Moreover, to the extent that different types of investors tend to be attracted to different types of firms, the board must make every effort to meet the dividend expectations of its shareholders. For example, income-oriented investors are attracted to firms that generally pay high dividends. Failure to meet those expectations can lead to disastrous results—a sell-off of the firm's stock—in the marketplace.

date of record
the date on which an investor must be a registered shareholder of a firm to be entitled to receive a dividend.

payment date
the actual date on which the company will mail dividend checks to shareholders (also known as the *payable date*).

Some Important Dates Let's assume the directors decide to declare a dividend. They then must indicate the date of payment and other important dates associated with the dividend. Normally, the directors issue a statement to the press indicating their dividend decision, along with the pertinent dividend payment dates. These statements are widely quoted in the financial media. Typical of such releases are the dividend news captions depicted in Figure 6.6.

Three dates are particularly important to the stockholder: date of record, ex-dividend date, and payment date. The **date of record** is the date on which the investor must be a registered shareholder of the firm to be entitled to a dividend. All investors who are official stockholders as of the close of business on that date will receive the dividends that have just been declared. These stockholders are often referred to as *holders of record.* The **payment date,** also set by the board of directors, generally follows the date of record by a week or two. It is the actual date on which the company will mail dividend checks to

FIGURE 6.6

Important Dates and Data About Dividends

The dividend actions of corporations are big news in the financial community. This news release, taken from the *Wall Street Journal,* provides timely information about cash and stock dividends, as well as stocks that have gone ex-dividend. Note that there's even information about recent stock splits. (*Source: Wall Street Journal,* August 15, 2000.)

CORPORATE DIVIDEND NEWS

DIVIDENDS REPORTED AUG. 14

COMPANY	PERIOD	AMT.	PAYABLE DATE	RECORD DATE
Regular				
Advest Group	Q	.06	10-16-00	9-29
Auto Data Proc	Q	.0875	10-01-00	9-15
Avista Corp	Q	.12	9-15-00	8-22
Bergn Brnswg ClA	Q	.01	9-05-00	8-21
Crane Co.	Q	.10	9-12-00	9-01
Cubic Corp	S	.19	9-19-00	8-22
Equality Bancorp	Q	.06	9-22-00	9-08
Jefferson-Pilot	Q	.37	12-05-00	11-10
Kelly Svc clA	Q	.25	9-08-00	8-28
Kelly Svc clB	Q	.25	9-08-00	8-28
Redwood Trust pfB	Q	.755	10-23-00	9-29
Santander BanCorp	Q	.11	10-02-00	9-08
Sears Roebuck	Q	.23	10-02-00	c8-30
Sunsource Cap pf	M	.241667	8-31-00	8-24
Symbol Tchnlgs	S	.01	9-18-00	8-24
White MountainsIns	Q	.40	9-27-00	9-18
Irregular				
Medallion Finl	Q	.36	9-05-00	8-25
Ultrapar ParticADS	–	.1845	10-10-00	8-15
Util Holdrs Tr	–	.054	10-02-00	9-08
Util Holdrs Tr	–	.051	10-16-00	9-15
Util Holdrs Tr	–	.0206	10-03-00	9-01
Funds, REITs, Investment Companies, LPs				
EatonVan Balance A	Q	.035	8-31-00	8-14
EatonVan Balance B	Q	.035	8-17-00	8-14
1st Aust PrimeInco	M	.045	9-15-00	8-31
1st Commonwlth Fd	M	.07	9-15-00	8-31
HancockPatPrDivII	M	.065	9-15-00	8-23
Hyperion 2002 Term	M	.02708	8-31-00	8-22
Hyperion 2005 Inv	M	.03542	8-31-00	8-22
Hyperion Total Ret	M	.0725	8-31-00	8-22
NewPlanRlty	Q	.4125	10-17-00	10-04
NewPlanRlty pfA	Q	.53125	10-16-00	10-04
NewPlanRlty pfB	Q	.539062	10-16-00	10-04
Sizeler Property	Q	.23	9-01-00	8-25
USLife Income Fd	Q	.18	9-01-00	c8-18
VK ConvSecsInc	Q	m4.5691	8-17-00	8-14
m-Reflects $0.16 income and $4.4091 capital gains.				
Stocks				
ACLN Ltd		ss	9-18-00	9-01
s-5-for-4 stock split.				
ABIOMED Inc		ss	10-01-00	8-14
s-2-for-1 stock split.				
Modern Times Grp		ss	8-21-00	8-18
s-s-3.5 shrs of Metro Intl SA Cl B and 1.5 shrs of Metro Intl SA Cl A for each shr held.				
Park Electro		ss	–	10-20
s-3-for-2 stock split subj to shrhldr approval 10/10/00.				
Pericom Semicond		ss	9-08-00	8-24
s-2-for-1 stock split.				
Foreign				
Barclays PLC ADR	–	t1.3155	10-03-00	c8-18
RioTinto PLC ADS	S	t.8444	9-18-00	c8-18

Increased

		AMOUNTS NEW	AMOUNTS OLD		
1st Merchants Corp	Q	.23	.22	9-20-00	9-06
Southwest Water Co	Q	.07	.06	10-20-00	9-30

A-Annual. M-Monthly. Q-Quarterly. S-Semi-annual.

b-Payable in Canadian funds. c-Corrected. h-From Income. k-From capital gains. r-Revised. t-Approximate U.S. dollar amount per American Depository Receipt/Share before adjustment for foreign taxes.

STOCKS EX-DIVIDEND AUG. 16

COMPANY	AMOUNT
AGL Resources Inc	.27
Adams Express Co	.12
All Amer Term Tr	.06
Amerco pfd A	.53125
AmerWaterWks5%pref	.3125
AmerWaterWrks 5%pf	.3125
Apex Municipal Fd	.048893
BP Amoco PLC ADS	t.333
Barclays PLC ADR	t1.3155
Beckman Coulter	.16
Black Hills Corp	.27
Brit Telecomm ADR	t2.1559
CarrAmer Rlty pfB	.5356
CarrAmer Rlty pfC	.5344
CarrAmer Rlty pfD	.5281
CarrAmerica Realty	.4625
Chemed Corp	.10
Chevron Corp	.65
Circor Int'l Inc	.0375
Corp HiYldII	.104887
Corp HiYldIII	.123509
Corp HiYld	.113917
Debt Strat	.066872
Debt StratII	.07878
Debt StratIII	.082246
Diebold Inc	.155
Dun & Bradstreet	.185
Elect Data System	.15
Fedders Corp	.03
Fedders Corp clA	.03
Fleming Cos	.02
Gerber Scientific	.08
Great Lakes Reit A	.609375
HSBC Holdings ADS	t.833
Hanson PLC ADR	t.404629
Harland(John H)Co	.075
Honeywell Intl	.1875
Hudson United Bncp	.25
Imperial Chem Ind	t.8333
Inco OppFd2000	.041666
Insured MuniInco	.064
Intl Paper Co	.25
Invest GrdMuniInco	.075
Liz Claiborne Inc	.1125
Louisiana-Pacific	.14
Macerich Co	.51
Managed HiYldPlus	.11
MidcoastEnergyRes	.07
Milacron Inc	.12
MuniAssets Fund	.068277
Muni Advantage Fd	.06
MuniEnhanced Fd	.0531
MuniHldgsCAInsII	.064945
MuniHldgsInsFL	.061808
MuniHldgsFLInsdV	.06761
MuniHldgs Fd	.068937
MuniHldgsII	.06321
MuniHldgsInsdFd	.060795
MuniHldgsMIInsdII	.072841
r-Revised to include amount.	
MuniHldgsNJInsdIV	.06145

COMPANY	AMOUNT
MuniHldgs NJInsd	.059895
MuniHldgsNYInsdIV	.068786
MuniHldgs NY Ins	.067863
MuniHldgsCAInsdV	.06875
MuniInsd Fd	.039545
MuniVest FdII	.065
MuniVest Fd	.0444
MuniYld AZ Fd	.057
MuniYld CA Fd	.0659
MuniYld CA Insd	.063672
MuniYld CA InsII	.0673
MuniYld FL Insd	.0626
MuniYld FL Fd	.060975
MuniYld Fd	.0714
MuniYld Insd	.07
MuniYld MI Insd	.064625
MuniYld MI Fd	.062299
MuniYld NJ Fund	.065691
MuniYld NJ Insd	.0671
MuniYld NY Insd	.064727
MuniYld PAInsdFd	.065922
MuniYld Qlty	.0678
MuniYld QltyII	.0665
NiSource Inc PIES	.96875
OM Group Inc	.11
Oregon Steel Mills	.02
ParkerHannifin	.17
Petroleum & Res	.20
Pfizer Inc	.09
PharmaHoldrsTr	t.0522
Phelps Dodge Corp	.50
Placer Dome Inc	.05
Protective Life	.13
Questar Corp	.17
RioTinto PLC ADS	t.8444
Russ Berrie & Co	.22
ScottishPwrPLC ADS	t.4364
Sr High Inco Port	.071033
ShellTransp ADR	t.5738
Sherwn-Williams	.135
Smucker (JM) clA	.16
Smucker (JM) clB	.16
Sonoco Products	.20
StanCorp Finl Grp	.07
Target Corp	.055
v-Increased amount payable on post split shrs.	
Timken Co	.18
Tomkins PLC ADR	t.8623
Town & Country Tr	.42
2002 Target Term	.065
2002 Target Term	.10
USLife Income Fd	.18
Ultrapar ParticADS	.1845
Walgreen Co	.03375
Worldwd Dollarvest	.052489

t-Approximate U.S. dollar amount per American Depository Receipt/Share before adjustment for foreign taxes.

holders of record. (Note that in the dividend news reported in Figure 6.6, this date is called the *payable date.*)

Because of the time needed to make bookkeeping entries after a stock is traded, the stock will sell without the dividend (ex-dividend) for three business days prior to the date of record. The **ex-dividend date** will dictate whether you were an official shareholder and therefore eligible to receive the declared dividend. If you sell a stock *on or after* the ex-dividend date, you receive the dividend. If you sell before this date, the new shareholder will receive the recently declared dividend.

ex-dividend date
three business days before the date of record; determines whether one is an official shareholder of a firm and thus eligible to receive a declared dividend.

To see how this all works, consider the following sequence of events. On June 3, the board of directors of Cash Cow, Inc. declares a quarterly dividend of 50 cents a share to holders of record on June 18. Checks will be mailed on the payment date, June 30. The calendar below shows these various dividend dates. If you owned 200 shares of the stock on June 12, you'd receive a check in the mail sometime after June 30 in the amount of $100.

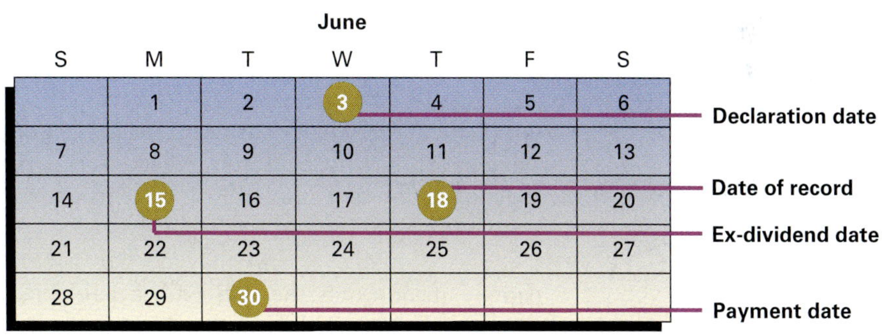

Unlike long-term capital gains, which are subject to a maximum tax rate of 15%, the IRS views cash dividends as *ordinary income* and therefore subject to normal tax rates (of anywhere from 10% to 35%). Thus, unless you hold the stock in some type of tax-sheltered account (such as an IRA or Keogh account), you incur a tax liability with each dividend check you receive.

Types of Dividends

Normally, companies pay dividends in the form of cash, though sometimes they do so by issuing additional shares of stock. The first type of distribution is known as a **cash dividend**; the second is called a **stock dividend.** Occasionally, dividends are paid in still other forms, such as a *stock spin-off* (discussed earlier in this chapter) or perhaps even samples of the company's products. But dividends in the form of either cash or stock remain by far the most popular, so let's take a closer look at them.

cash dividend
payment of a dividend in the form of cash.

stock dividend
payment of a dividend in the form of additional shares of stock.

Cash or Stock More firms use *cash dividends* than any other type of dividend. A nice by-product of cash dividends is that *they tend to increase over time, as companies' earnings grow.* The average annual increase in dividends is around 3% to 5%. Such a tendency appeals to investors because a steady stream of dividends—even better, a *steadily increasing* stream of dividends—shores up stock returns in soft markets.

dividend yield
a measure that relates dividends to share price and puts common stock dividends on a relative (percentage) rather than absolute (dollar) basis.

A convenient way of assessing the amount of dividends received is to measure the stock's **dividend yield.** Basically, this is a measure of dividends on a relative (percentage) basis, rather than on an absolute (dollar) basis. Dividend yield, in effect, indicates the rate of current income earned on the investment dollar. It is computed as follows:

Equation 6.2

$$\text{Dividend yield} = \frac{\text{Annual dividends received per share}}{\text{Current market price of the stock}}$$

Thus a company that annually pays $2 per share in dividends to its stockholders, and whose stock is trading at $40, has a dividend yield of 5%.

dividend payout ratio
the portion of earnings per share (EPS) that a firm pays out as dividends.

To put dividend yield into perspective, it is helpful to look at a company's **dividend payout ratio.** The payout ratio describes that portion of earnings per share (EPS) that is paid out as dividends. It is computed as follows:

Equation 6.3

$$\text{Dividend payout ratio} = \frac{\text{Dividends per share}}{\text{Earnings per share}}$$

A company would have a payout ratio of 50% if it had earnings of $4 a share and paid annual dividends of $2 a share. Although stockholders like to receive dividends, they normally do not like to see payout ratios over 60% to 70%. Payout ratios that high are difficult to maintain and may lead the company into trouble.

Occasionally, a firm may declare a *stock dividend.* A stock dividend simply means that the dividend is paid in additional shares of stock. For instance, if the board declares a 10% stock dividend, each shareholder receives 1 new share of stock for each 10 shares currently owned.

Although they seem to satisfy some investors, *stock dividends really have no value,* because they represent the receipt of something already owned. The market responds to such dividends by adjusting share prices according to the terms of the stock dividend. Thus, in the example above, a 10% stock dividend normally leads to a decline of around 10% in the stock's share price. The market value of your shareholdings after a stock dividend is likely to be the same as it was before the stock dividend. There is, however, one bright spot in all this: Unlike cash dividends, stock dividends are not taxed until the stocks are actually sold.

Dividend Reinvestment Plans

dividend reinvestment plans (DRIPs)
plans in which shareholders have cash dividends automatically reinvested into additional shares of the firm's common stock.

Want to have your cake and eat it too? When it comes to dividends, there is a way to do just that. You can participate in a **dividend reinvestment plan (DRIP).** These are corporate-sponsored programs in which shareholders can have their cash dividends automatically reinvested into additional shares of the company's common stock. (Similar reinvestment programs are offered by mutual funds, which we'll discuss in Chapter 11, and by some brokerage houses, such as Merrill Lynch and Fidelity.) The basic investment philosophy is that *if the company is good enough to invest in, it's good enough to reinvest in.* As Table 6.4 demonstrates, such an approach can have a tremendous impact on your investment position over time.

HOTLINKS

Use the directory of online resources about dividend reinvestment plans (DRIPs) and direct purchase of stocks at

www.stock1.com

TABLE 6.4 Cash or Reinvested Dividends?

Situation: You buy 100 shares of stock at $25 a share (total investment $2,500); the stock currently pays $1 a share in annual dividends. The price of the stock increases at 8% per year; dividends grow at 5% per year.

Investment Period	Number of Shares Held	Market Value of Stock Holdings	Total Cash Dividends Received
	Take Dividends in Cash		
5 years	100	$ 3,672	$ 552
10 years	100	5,397	1,258
15 years	100	7,930	2,158
20 years	100	11,652	3,307
	Full Participation in Dividend Reinvestment Plan (100% of cash dividends reinvested)		
5 years	115.59	$ 4,245	$ 0
10 years	135.66	7,322	0
15 years	155.92	12,364	0
20 years	176.00	20,508	0

Today more than 1,000 companies (including most major corporations) offer dividend reinvestment plans. Each one provides investors with a convenient and inexpensive way to accumulate capital. Stocks in most DRIPs are acquired free of any brokerage commissions, and most plans allow *partial participation.* That is, participants may specify a portion of their shares for dividend reinvestment and receive cash dividends on the rest. Some plans even sell stocks to their DRIP investors at below-market prices—often at discounts of 3% to 5%. In addition, most plans will credit fractional shares to the investor's account, and many will even allow investors to buy additional shares of the company's stock. For example, once enrolled in the General Mills plan, investors can purchase up to $3,000 worth of the company's stock each quarter, free of commissions.

Shareholders can join dividend reinvestment plans simply by sending a completed authorization form to the company. (Generally, it takes about 30 to 45 days for all the paperwork to be processed.) Once you're in, the number of shares you hold will begin to accumulate with each dividend date. There is a catch, however: Even though these dividends take the form of additional shares of stock, you must pay taxes on them *as though they were cash dividends.* Don't confuse these dividends with stock dividends—*reinvested dividends are taxable as ordinary income in the year they're received,* just as though they had been received in cash.

Types and Uses of Common Stock

LG 6

Common stocks appeal to investors because they offer the potential for everything from current income and stability of capital to attractive capital gains. The market contains a wide range of stock, from the most conservative to the highly speculative. Generally, the kinds of stocks that investors seek will depend on their investment objectives and investment programs. We will examine several of the more popular types of common stocks here, as well as the various ways such securities can be used in different types of investment programs.

Types of Stocks

As an investor, one of the things you'll want to understand is the market system used to classify common stock. That's because a stock's general classification reflects not only its fundamental source of return but also the quality of the company's earnings, the issue's susceptibility to market risks, the nature and stability of its earnings and dividends, and even its susceptibility to adverse economic conditions. Such insight is useful in selecting stocks that will best fit your overall investment objectives. Among the many different types of stocks, the following are the most common: blue chips, income stocks, growth stocks, tech stocks, speculative stocks, cyclical stocks, defensive stocks, mid-cap stocks, and small-cap stocks. We will now look at each of these to see what they are and how they might be used.

HOTLINKS

At this site, you can choose stocks by company size and type, and access growth and return rates. Lists show stock prices, quotes, ratios, and charts. For the Stockscreener, go to:

www.stockscreener.com

blue-chip stocks
financially strong, high-quality stocks with long and stable records of earnings and dividends.

Blue-Chip Stocks Blue chips are the cream of the common stock crop. They are stocks that are unsurpassed in quality and have a long and stable record of earnings and dividends. **Blue-chip stocks** are issued by large, well-established firms that have impeccable financial credentials. These companies hold important, often leading positions in their industries and frequently set the standards by which other firms are measured.

Not all blue chips are alike, however. Some provide consistently high dividend yields; others are more growth oriented. Good examples of blue-chip growth stocks are General Electric, Merck, Wal-Mart, SBC Communications, Citigroup, and Home Depot. (Some basic operating and market information about Home Depot's stock, as obtained from the introductory part of a typical *S&P Stock Report,* is shown in Figure 6.7.) Examples of high-yielding

FIGURE 6.7

A Blue-Chip Stock

(*Source:* Standard & Poor's *Stock Reports,* January 8, 2000.)

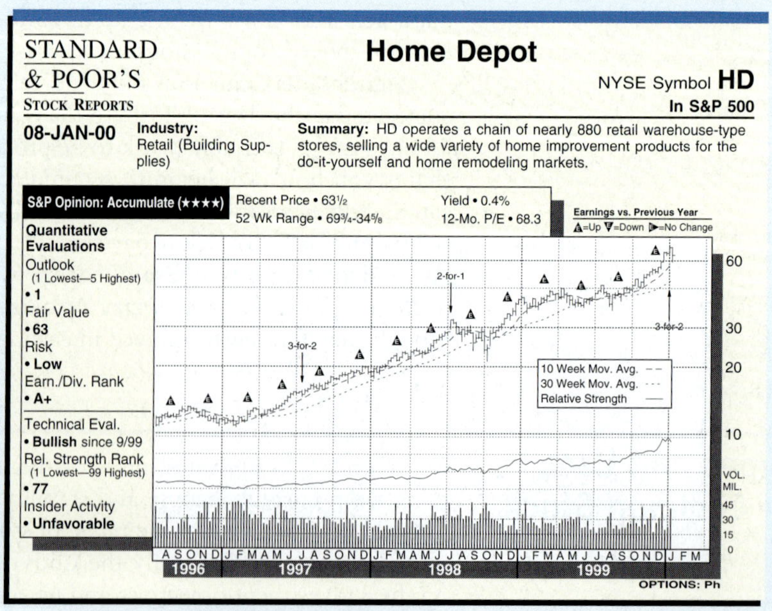

blue chips include such companies as DuPont, Eastman Kodak, International Paper, General Motors, and Philip Morris.

Blue chips are particularly attractive to investors who are looking for quality investment outlets that offer decent dividend yields and respectable growth potential. They're often used for long-term investment purposes and, because of their relatively low risk, as a way of obtaining modest but dependable rates of return. Blue chips are popular with a large segment of the investing public. As a result, they are often relatively high in price, especially when the market is unsettled and investors become more quality-conscious.

income stocks
stocks with long and sustained records of paying higher-than-average dividends.

Income Stocks Some stocks are appealing simply because of the dividends they pay. This is the case with **income stocks.** These are issues that have a long and sustained record of regularly paying higher-than-average dividends. Income stocks are ideal for those who seek a relatively safe and high level of current income from their investment capital. But there's more: Holders of income stocks (unlike bonds and preferred stocks) can expect the dividends they receive to increase regularly over time. Look at Duke Energy, for example. It paid dividends of $1.52 a share in 1989; 10 years later, in 1999, it was paying almost 50% more: $2.20 a share. Percentage-wise, that's a big jump in dividends, and it's something that can have a definite impact on total return.

The major disadvantage of income stocks is that some of them may be paying high dividends because of limited growth potential. Indeed, it's not unusual for income securities to exhibit only low or modest rates of growth in earnings. This does not mean that such firms are unprofitable or lack future prospects. Quite the contrary: Most firms whose shares qualify as income stocks are highly profitable organizations with excellent future prospects. A number of income stocks are among the giants of U.S. industry, and many are also classified as quality blue chips. Many public utilities, such as American Electric Power, Consolidated Edison, DTE Energy, Dominion Resources, and Southern Company, are in this group. Also in this group are phone stocks, such as AT&T and Bell Atlantic, and selected industrial and financial issues, such as Ford, H.J. Heinz, Weyerhaeuser, Bank One, and AmSouth Bancorp. By their very nature, income stocks are not exposed to a great deal of business and market risk. They are, however, subject to a fair amount of interest rate risk.

growth stocks
stocks that experience high rates of growth in operations and earnings.

Growth Stocks Shares that have experienced, and are expected to continue experiencing, consistently high rates of growth in operations and earnings are known as **growth stocks.** A good growth stock might exhibit a *sustained* rate of growth in earnings of 15% to 18% a year over a period when common stocks, on average, are experiencing growth rates of only 6% to 8%. Generally speaking, established growth companies combine steady earnings growth with high returns on equity. They also have high operating margins and plenty of cash flow to service their debt. AIG, Enron Corp., General Dynamics, Starbucks, Lowe's, Reliant Energy, and Staples (shown in Figure 6.8) are all prime examples of growth stocks. As this list suggests, some growth stocks also rate as blue chips and provide quality growth, whereas others represent higher levels of speculation.

HOTLINKS
To read about characteristics of growth and value companies and their performance in recent years, go to:
www.putnaminv.com/frames/e105.htm

Growth stocks normally pay little or nothing in the way of dividends, so their payout ratios seldom exceed 10% to 15% of

FIGURE 6.8

A Growth Stock

(*Source:* Standard & Poor's *Stock Reports,* January 8, 2000.)

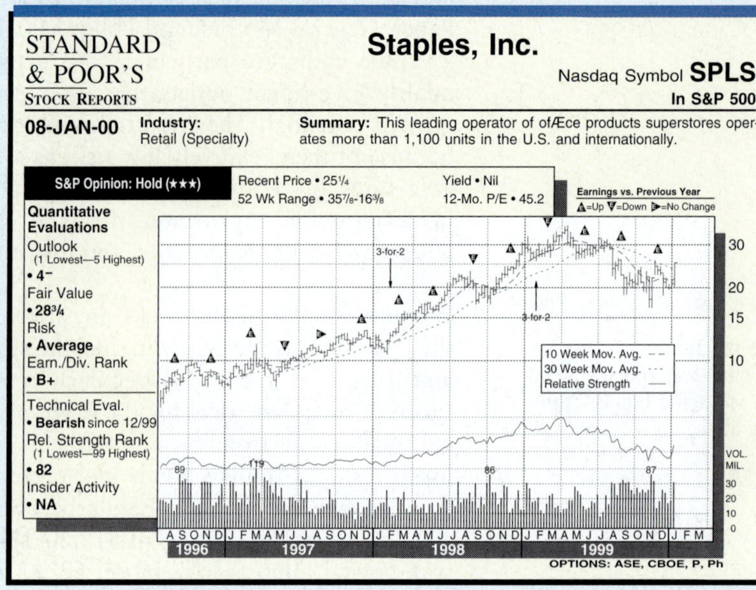

earnings. Instead, all or most of the profits are reinvested in the company and used to help finance rapid growth. Thus the major source of return to investors is price appreciation. Growth shares generally appeal to investors who are looking for attractive capital gains rather than dividends and who are therefore willing to assume a higher element of risk.

tech stocks
stocks that represent the technology, "new-economy" sector of the market.

Tech Stocks Over the past 10 to 15 years, *tech stocks* have become such a dominant force in the market that they deserve to be put in a class all their own. **Tech stocks** basically represent the technology sector of the market and include companies that produce or provide everything from computers, semiconductors, data storage, computer software, and computer hardware to peripherals, Internet services, content providers, networking, and wireless communications. These are the so-called *new-economy* stocks, issued by the companies that are changing the way things are being done in the world. They provide the high-tech equipment, networking systems, and online services to all lines of businesses, education, health care, communications, governmental agencies, and the home. Some of these stocks are listed on the NYSE and AMEX. The vast majority, though, are traded on the Nasdaq, which explains why the Nasdaq Composite index (discussed earlier) did so well.

There are literally thousands of companies that fall into the tech-stock category. They include everything from very small firms that provide some service on the Internet to huge multinational companies. In many cases, these stocks have richly rewarded their investors, even though the companies themselves may have never earned a penny in profits. Certainly, this is a category where it's safe to say that not all stocks are equal. Here you find companies that generate lots of revenues and profits, companies that have lots of revenues but little or no profits, and companies that have little in the way of sales or profits (but supposedly lots of potential).

FIGURE 6.9

A Tech Stock

(*Source:* Standard & Poor's *Stock Reports,* January 8, 2000.)

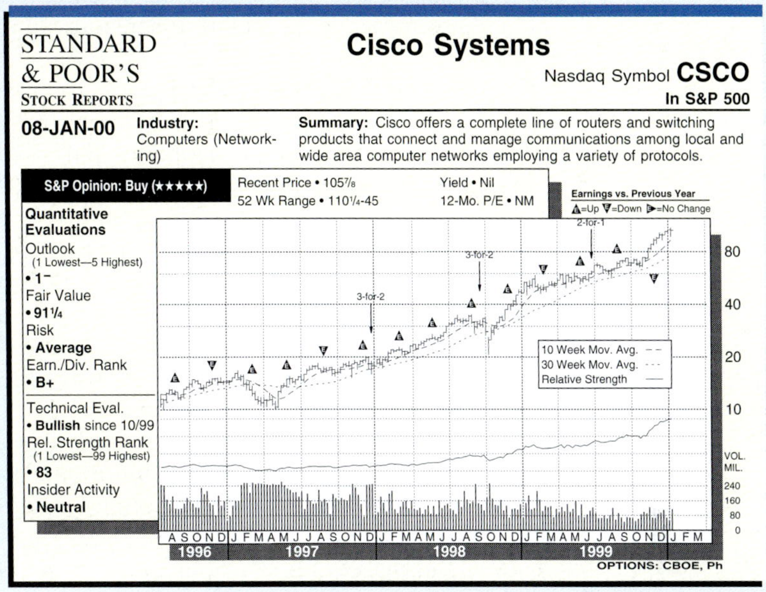

These stocks would probably fall into either the *growth stock* category (see above) or the *speculative stock* class (see below), although some of them are legitimate *blue chips.* Tech stocks may offer the potential for attractive (and, in some cases, phenomenal) returns. But they also involve considerable risk, and are probably most suitable for the more risk-tolerant investor. Included in the tech-stock category you'll find some big names, like Yahoo, Microsoft, Cisco Systems (see Figure 6.9), Adobe Systems, and Amazon.com. You'll also find many not-so-big names, like Intergraph Corp., Synopsys, Abgenix, Exodus, Immuney, and Avid Technology. We'll take another, more detailed look at tech stocks in Chapter 8, including the very difficult job of putting a value on these securities.

speculative stocks
stocks that offer the potential for substantial price appreciation, usually because of some special situation, such as new management or the introduction of a promising new product.

Speculative Stocks Shares that lack sustained records of success but still offer the potential for substantial price appreciation are known as **speculative stocks.** Perhaps investors' hopes are spurred by a new management team that has taken over a troubled company or by the introduction of a promising new product. Other times, it's the hint that some new information, discovery, or production technique will favorably affect the growth prospects of the firm. Speculative stocks are a special breed of securities, and they enjoy a wide following, particularly when the market is bullish.

Generally speaking, the earnings of speculative stocks are uncertain and highly unstable. These stocks are subject to wide swings in price, and they usually pay little or nothing in dividends. On the plus side, speculative stocks such as Cytyc Corp., Krispy Kreme, JAKKS Pacific, Siebel Systems, and Zomax, Inc. offer attractive growth prospects and the chance to "hit it big" in the market. To be successful, however, an investor has to identify the big-money winners before the rest of the market does and the price of the stock is driven up. Speculative stocks are highly risky; they require not only a strong stomach but also a considerable amount of investor know-how. They are used to seek capital gains, and investors will often aggressively trade in and out of these securities as the situation demands.

cyclical stocks
stocks whose earnings and overall market performance are closely linked to the general state of the economy.

Cyclical Stocks **Cyclical stocks** are issued by companies whose earnings are closely linked to the general level of business activity. They tend to reflect the general state of the economy and to move up and down with the business cycle. Companies that serve markets tied to capital equipment spending by business, or to consumer spending for big-ticket, durable items like houses and cars, typically head the list of cyclical stocks. Examples include Caterpillar, Genuine Parts, Maytag Corp., Rohm & Haas, Harnischfeger, and Timken.

Cyclical stocks generally do well when the economy is moving ahead, but they tend to do *especially well* when the country is in the early stages of economic recovery. They are, however, perhaps best avoided when the economy begins to weaken. Cyclical stocks are probably most suitable for investors who are willing to trade in and out of these issues as the economic outlook dictates and who can tolerate the accompanying exposure to risk.

defensive stocks
stocks that tend to hold their own, and even do well, when the economy starts to falter.

Defensive Stocks Sometimes it is possible to find stocks whose prices remain stable or even increase when general economic activity is tapering off. These securities are known as **defensive stocks.** They tend to be less affected than the average issue by downswings in the business cycle. Defensive stocks include the shares of many public utilities, as well as industrial and consumer goods companies that produce or market such staples as beverages, foods, and drugs. An excellent example of a defensive stock is Bandag. This recession-resistant company is the world's leading manufacturer of rubber used to retread tires. Other examples are Checkpoint Systems, a manufacturer of antitheft clothing security clips, and WD-40, the maker of that famous all-purpose lubricant. Perhaps the best known of all defensive stocks, particularly in inflationary periods, are gold mining shares. These stocks blossom when inflation becomes a serious problem. Defensive shares are commonly used by more aggressive investors. Such investors tend to "park" their funds temporarily in defensive stocks while the economy remains soft, or until the investment atmosphere improves.

Mid-Cap Stocks As explained earlier, a stock's size is based on its market value—or, more commonly, on what is known as its *market capitalization* (the market price of the stock times the number of shares outstanding). Generally speaking, the U.S. stock market can be broken into three segments, as measured by a stock's market "cap":

Small-cap	under $1 billion
Mid-cap	$1 billion to $4 or $5 billion
Large-cap	more than $4 or $5 billion

The large-cap stocks are the real biggies—the AT&Ts, GMs, and Microsofts of the investment world. Although there are far fewer large-cap stocks than any other size, these companies account for about 80% to 90% of the total market value of all U.S. equities. But as the saying goes, bigger isn't necessarily better. Nowhere is that statement more accurate than in the stock market. Indeed, both the small-cap and mid-cap segments of the market tend to hold their own, or even to outperform the large stocks over time.

FIGURE 6.10

A Mid-Cap Stock

(*Source:* Standard & Poor's *Stock Reports,* January 8, 2000.)

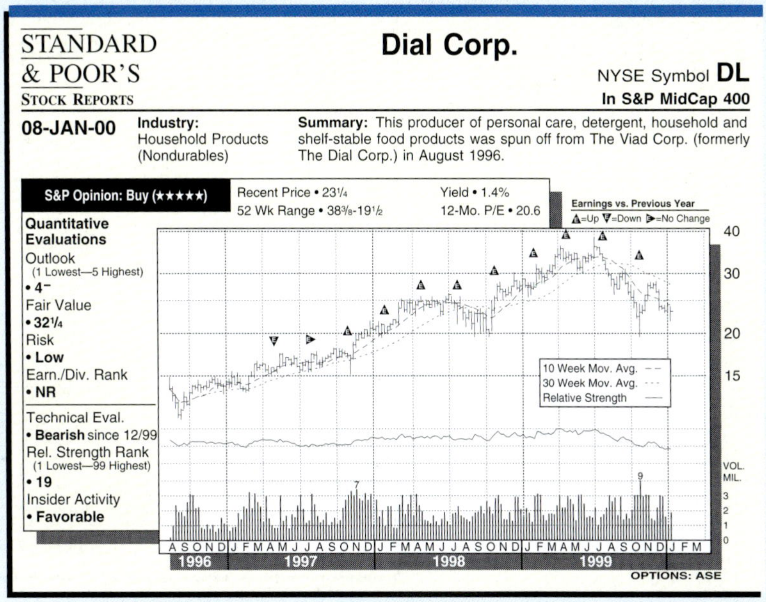

mid-cap stocks
medium-sized stocks, generally with market values of less than \$4 or \$5 billion but more than \$1 billion.

Mid-cap stocks are a special breed, and offer investors some attractive return opportunities. They provide much of the sizzle of small-stock returns, without as much price volatility. (We'll look at small-cap stocks soon.) At the same time, because mid-caps are fairly good-sized companies and many of them have been around for a long time, they offer some of the safety of the big, established stocks. Among the ranks of the mid-caps are such well-known companies as Wendy's International, Barnes & Noble, Dial Corp. (see Figure 6.10), Hertz, Liz Claiborne, Outback Steakhouse, and Keebler Foods. Although these securities offer a nice alternative to large stocks without the uncertainties of small-caps, they probably are most appropriate for investors who are willing to tolerate a bit more risk and price volatility.

One type of mid-cap stock of particular interest is the so-called *baby blue chip*. Also known as "baby blues," these companies have all the characteristics of a regular blue chip *except size*. Like their larger counterparts, baby blues have rock-solid balance sheets, only modest levels of debt, and long histories of steady profit growth. For the most part, they've been able to secure niches in fast-growing specialty markets. Some of these companies, in fact, have been posting gains in annual earnings for 30 to 40 years in a row. Baby blues normally pay a modest level of dividends, but like most mid-caps, they tend to emphasize growth. Thus they're considered ideal for investors seeking quality long-term growth. Some well-known baby blues are Tootsie Roll, Reynolds & Reynolds, Hormel, Keane, Inc., and Herman Miller.

small-cap stocks
stocks that generally have market values of less than \$1 billion but can offer above-average returns.

Small-Cap Stocks Some investors consider small companies to be in a class by themselves in terms of attractive return opportunities. In many cases, this has turned out to be true. Known as **small-cap stocks,** these companies generally have annual revenues of less than \$250 million. Because of their size, spurts of growth can have dramatic effects on their earnings and stock prices. Anchor Financial, Sonic Corp., Papa John's, Sky West, Churchill Downs

FIGURE 6.11

A Small-Cap Stock

(*Source:* Standard & Poor's *Stock Reports,* January 8, 2000.)

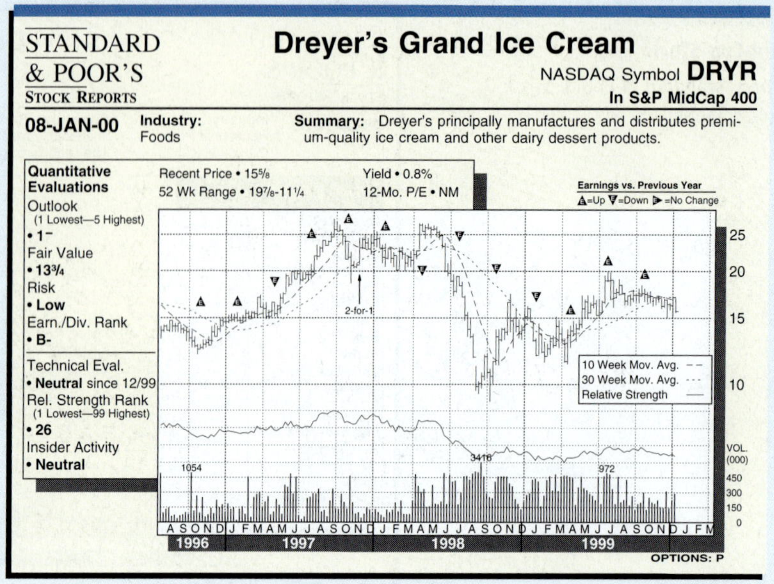

(where the Kentucky Derby is run), and Dreyer's Ice Cream (see Figure 6.11) are some better-known small-cap stocks.

Although some small-caps (like Dreyer's Ice Cream) are solid companies with equally solid financials, that's not the case with most of them. Indeed, because many of these companies are so small, they don't have a lot of stock outstanding, and their shares are not widely traded. In addition, small-company stocks have a tendency to be "here today and gone tomorrow." Although some of these stocks may hold the potential for high returns, investors should also be aware of the very high risk exposure that comes with many of them.

A special category of small-company stock is the so-called *initial public offering (IPO)*. Most IPOs are small, relatively new companies that are going public for the first time. (Prior to their public offering, these stocks were privately held and not publicly traded.) Like other small-cap stocks, IPOs are attractive because of the substantial—sometimes phenomenal—capital gains that investors can earn. Of course, there's a catch: In order to stand a chance of buying some of the better, more attractive IPOs, you need to be either a big-time trader or a preferred client of the broker. Otherwise, the only IPOs you're likely to hear of will be the ones the big guys don't want—which should tell you something about that IPO. More often than not, the small individual investor gets a chance to buy a new issue only after it's been driven way up in price and the initial investors start bailing out, taking their profits with them. Surprisingly, this may take only a few hours or days to occur. If you're not in on the first day, the odds are that your returns will be mediocre, at best. It's an open secret on Wall Street that when it comes to hot IPOs, most individual investors stand little chance of even playing the game, much less winning.

Without a doubt, IPOs are extremely high-risk investments, with the odds stacked against the investor. Because there's no market record to rely on, these stocks should be used only by investors who know what to look for in the company and who can tolerate substantial exposure to risk. IPOs tend to flourish when the market heats up. They very definitely are faddish, their ranks often dominated by trendy retail outlets, food chains, and high-tech firms.

Investing in Foreign Stocks

One of the most dramatic changes to occur in our financial markets in the '80s and '90s was the trend toward globalization. Indeed, globalization became the buzzword of the 1990s, and nowhere was that more evident than in the world equity markets. Consider, for example, that in 1970 the U.S. stock market accounted for fully *two-thirds of the world market.* In essence, our stock market was twice as big as all the rest of the world's stock markets *combined.* That's no longer true: By 1999, the U.S. share of the world equity market had dropped to just over 48%.

Today the world equity markets are dominated by six countries, which together account for about 80% of the total market:

	Market Value (May 2000)
United States	$17.0 trillion
Japan	4.4 trillion
United Kingdom	2.8 trillion
Germany	1.5 trillion
France	1.4 trillion
Canada	820 billion

The United States, still the biggest player, is one of only five countries with trillion-dollar stock markets. In addition to these six, another dozen or so markets are also regarded as major world players. Among the markets in this second tier are Switzerland, Australia, Italy, the Netherlands, Hong Kong, Spain, and Singapore. Finally, some relatively small, emerging markets—South Korea, Mexico, Malaysia, Portugal, Thailand, and Russia—are beginning to make their presence felt. Clearly, the landscape has changed a lot in the last 20 years, and there's every reason to believe that even greater changes lie ahead.

It is clear that the U.S. market dominates in terms of sheer size, as well as in the number of listed companies (over 10,000 of them). But that still leaves unanswered a very important question: How has the U.S. equity market performed in comparison to the rest of the world's major stock markets? The answer: not too well, unfortunately. Table 6.5 summarizes total annual returns (in U.S. dollars) for the 20-year period from 1980 through 1999, for eight of the world's largest equity markets. Note that the United States finished first only once (in 1982). Even so, in the '90s, because the U.S. market consistently finished near the top (every year but 1993), it turned in the best overall performance. Now keep in mind that the returns shown in Table 6.5 *are in U.S. dollars.* As the accompanying *Investing in Action* box reveals, a good deal of the performance of non-U.S. markets is due to the behavior of *currency exchange rates* and not the markets themselves. Indeed, the U.S. stock market is one of the strongest and best performing in the world! Still, the fact remains that when both markets and currencies are combined, some very rewarding opportunities are available to U.S. investors willing to invest in foreign securities.

TABLE 6.5 Comparative Annual Returns in the World's Major Equity Markets, 1980–1999

	Annual Total Returns (in U.S. dollars)								
	Australia	Canada	France	Germany	Japan	Switzerland	United Kingdom	United States	Rank*
1999	18.7%	54.4%	29.7%	20.5%	61.8%	−6.6%	12.4%	26.7%	4th
1998	7.1	−5.7	42.1	29.9	5.2	24.0	17.8	17.8	4th
1997	−9.5	13.3	12.4	25.0	−23.6	44.8	22.6	24.4	3rd
1996	17.7	29.0	21.6	14.0	−15.3	2.8	27.2	28.0	2nd
1995	12.5	19.1	14.8	17.0	0.9	45.0	21.3	35.7	2nd
1994	1.4	−5.1	−7.3	3.1	21.4	30.0	−4.4	4.9	3rd
1993	33.4	17.4	19.6	34.8	23.9	41.7	19.0	16.4	8th
1992	−6.1	−4.6	5.2	−2.1	−26.0	26.0	14.0	7.2	3rd
1991	35.8	12.1	18.6	8.7	9.0	16.8	16.0	23.3	2nd
1990	−16.2	−12.2	−13.3	−8.8	−35.9	−5.1	10.4	−0.4	2nd
1989	10.8	25.2	37.6	48.2	2.3	28.0	23.1	30.7	3rd
1988	38.2	17.9	37.1	19.8	35.4	5.8	4.1	15.5	6th
1987	9.5	14.8	−13.9	−24.6	41.0	−9.2	35.2	5.9	5th
1986	45.0	10.8	79.9	36.4	101.2	34.7	27.7	26.1	7th
1985	21.1	16.2	84.2	138.1	44.0	109.2	53.4	31.7	6th
1984	−12.4	−7.1	4.8	−5.2	17.2	−11.1	5.3	1.2	4th
1983	55.2	32.4	33.2	23.9	24.8	19.9	17.3	24.7	5th
1982	−22.2	2.6	−4.2	10.5	−0.6	2.9	9.0	24.8	1st
1981	−23.8	−10.1	−28.5	−10.3	15.7	−9.5	−10.2	−2.8	2nd
1980	54.7	21.6	−2.0	−10.7	30.4	−7.8	42.0	20.6	5th
	Average Annual Returns Over Extended Holding Periods								
5 years									
1995–99	8.8%	20.5%	23.7%	21.2%	2.1%	20.1%	20.2%	26.4%	
1990–94	7.6	0.9	3.7	6.2	−4.9	20.8	10.7	9.9	
Decades									
1990s	8.6	9.8	13.5	12.8	−0.7	17.4	14.2	17.9	
1980s	13.9	11.6	17.6	16.3	28.6	12.2	19.3	17.2	
20 years									
1980–99	11.2	10.7	15.5	14.5	12.6	14.8	17.3	17.5	

Note: Total return = coupon income + capital gain (or loss) + profit (or loss) from changes in currency exchange rates.

*"Rank" shows how U.S. returns ranked among the listed major markets (e.g., in 1994, the United States ranked third out of the eight markets listed in the table).

Source: International returns obtained from Morgan Stanley Capital International; U.S. returns based on DJIA.

Going Global: Direct Investments or ADRs Basically, there are two ways to invest in foreign stocks: through direct investments or through ADRs. (We'll discuss a third way—international mutual funds—in Chapter 11.) Without a doubt, the most adventuresome way is to *buy shares directly in foreign markets*.

Investing directly is *not* for the uninitiated, however. You have to know what you're doing and be prepared to tolerate a good deal of market risk. Although most major U.S. brokerage houses are set up to accommodate investors interested in buying foreign securities, there are still many logistical problems to be faced. To begin with, you have to cope with currency fluctuations and changing foreign exchange rates. These can have a dramatic impact on your returns. But that's just the start: You also have to deal with different regulatory and accounting standards. The fact is that most foreign markets, even the bigger ones, are not so closely regulated as U.S. exchanges. Investors in foreign markets thus have to put up with insider trading and other practices that can cause wild swings in market prices. Furthermore, accounting standards are often much looser, making detailed information about a company's financial condition and operating results a lot harder to come by. Finally, there are the obvious language barriers, tax problems, and general "red tape" that all too often plague international transactions. There's no doubt that the returns from direct foreign investments can be substantial, but so can the obstacles placed in your way.

HOTLINKS

Visit the CNN financial network to find out which country's stock market has registered the highest percentage change and which registered the lowest percentage change from the previous trading day. Can you cite the reasons why?

cnnfn.cnn.com/markets/world_markets.html

Fortunately, there is an easier way to invest in foreign stocks, and that is to buy *American Depositary Receipts (ADRs)*, or *American Depositary Shares (ADSs)* as they're sometimes called. As we saw in Chapter 2, ADRs are negotiable instruments. Each ADR represents a specific number of shares in a specific foreign company. (The number of shares can range from a fraction of a share to 20 shares or more.) ADRs are great for investors who want foreign stocks but don't want the hassles that often come with them. That's because American Depositary Receipts are bought and sold on U.S. markets just like stocks in U.S. companies. Their prices are quoted in U.S. dollars, not British pounds, Japanese yen, or German marks. Furthermore, dividends are paid in dollars. Although there are about 400 foreign companies *whose shares are directly listed on U.S. exchanges* (over 200 of which are Canadian), most foreign companies are traded in this country as ADRs. Indeed, shares of about 1,000 companies, from more than 40 countries, are traded as ADRs on the NYSE, AMEX, and Nasdaq/OTC markets.

INVESTOR FACTS

FROM RUSSIA WITH LOVE— Want to buy Russian stocks? Head for the New York Stock Exchange, where you can buy ADRs like LUKoil (ticker symbol LKOH), Russia's largest oil company; Rostelecom (ROS), a major telecommunications provider; and Unified Energy Systems (EESR), the primary national electric utility. If you'd prefer to own a diversified portfolio of Russian shares, mutual funds such as the Templeton Russia Fund (TRF) and the Morgan Stanley Dean Witter Eastern Europe Fund (RNE) might be for you. But be prepared for volatility: In 1998, for example, the net asset value (NAV) of RNE dropped 75%; in 1999 it rose 135%!

To see how ADRs are structured, we'll look at Cadbury Schweppes, the British food and household products firm. Each Cadbury ADR represents ownership of four shares of Cadbury stock. These shares are held in a custodial account by a U.S. bank (or its foreign correspondent), which receives dividends, pays any foreign withholding taxes, and then converts the net proceeds to U.S. dollars, which it passes on to investors. Other foreign stocks that can be purchased as ADRs include Sony (a Japanese stock), Ericsson Telephone (from Sweden), Nokia (Finland), Vodafone Airtouch (U.K.), Royal Dutch Petroleum (Netherlands), Nestle's (Switzerland), Shanghai Petro-chemicals (China), Elan Corp. (Ireland), and Grupo Televisa (Mexico). You can even buy ADRs on Russian companies, such as Vimpel-Communications, a Moscow-based cellular phone company whose shares trade (as ADRs) on the NYSE.

Putting Returns in a Global Perspective Whether you buy foreign stocks directly or through ADRs, the whole process of global investing is a bit more complex and more risky than domestic investing. When investing globally, *you have to pick both the right stock and the right market.* Basically, foreign stocks are valued much the same way as U.S. stocks. Indeed, the same variables that drive U.S. share prices (earnings, dividends, etc.) also drive stock values in foreign markets. On top of this, each market reacts to its own set of economic forces (inflation, interest rates, level of economic activity), which set the tone of the market. At any given time, therefore, some markets are performing better than others. The challenge facing global investors is to be in the right market at the right time. As with U.S. stocks, foreign shares produce the same two basic sources of returns: dividends and capital gains (or losses).

INVESTING in action

In International Investing, Currencies Can Make or Break You

Investing overseas can pay off in many ways. Capitalism is spreading around the world like wildfire, and economic development in many developing areas outpaces U.S. growth. Accounting practices have improved, because many foreign companies realize that they must make extensive financial disclosure—beyond their normal comfort level—if they want to attract U.S. investors. Finally, investing overseas can help to diversify and strengthen a portfolio. You may have to look overseas to find industry leaders, and foreign markets may rise if the U.S. market stalls.

Even with these global opportunities, it's difficult to believe that an investor in international stocks can consistently outperform one who invests only in U.S. stocks. Take a look at the accompanying graph: Foreign stocks, represented by the EAFE (Europe/Australia/Far East) index, measured in *U.S. dollars*, appear to have outperformed U.S. equities between 1985 and 1995. What the numbers don't show is the impact of a weakening U.S. dollar. To see that, look at the line for the EAFE in *local currency*. From 1990 to 1995, the compound growth is *below* the U.S. stock market line, because the dollar weakened against the local currencies. For the total period 1985 through mid-2000, *if you exclude the currency factor, then U.S. stocks dwarfed the performance of their overseas counterparts.* The average annual return for U.S. equities was 18.45%, compared to 15.43% for the EAFE in U.S. dollars. When you compare U.S. returns to the EAFE in local currencies, the gap widens even further. The average annual return drops to 11.87%—a significant difference.

A favorable currency movement for a U.S. investor in a foreign market is a *weakening* dollar. Money that is invested overseas is typically converted to a local currencies and later converted back to dollars. If the dollar weakens between the time the investor buys and the time she or he sells the stock, the local currency buys more dollars at the time of the sale.

In contrast, a *strengthening* dollar is bad news for U.S. investors buying overseas securities, because the local currency later buys fewer dollars. In the mid-1990s and again at the turn of the century, the U.S. dollar strengthened against most currencies. Over the 3-year period ending November 30, 2000, for example, the U.S. stock market produced average returns of about 12.4%. The German stock market produced an average annual return of about 17.5% in local currency terms. However, in terms of U.S. dollars, the average annual return in Germany was a very poor 8.4%, because the dollar strengthened against the deutsche mark.

continued on next page

But with global investing, there is a third variable—*currency exchange rates*—that plays an important role in defining returns to U.S. investors. As the U.S. dollar weakens or strengthens relative to a foreign currency, the returns to U.S. investors from foreign stocks increase or decrease accordingly. In a global context, total return to U.S. investors in foreign securities is defined as follows:

Equation 6.4

$$\text{Total return (in U.S. dollars)} = \text{Current income (dividends)} + \text{Capital gains (or losses)} \pm \text{Changes in currency exchange rates}$$

Because current income and capital gains are in the "local currency" (the currency in which the foreign stock is denominated, such as the German mark or the Japanese yen), we can shorten the total return formula to:

INVESTING in action

continued from previous page

Indeed, not too many stock markets outperformed the U.S. in dollar terms. The ones that did—among them Bulgaria, Russia, Turkey, and Zimbabwe—were coming from very low base values. And many of these also carried significant risks beyond currency risk, such as concerns about the stability of their governments, that don't worry investors in U.S. stocks.

Sources: Mara der Hovanesian, "So Who Needs Foreign Investing? *Business Week*, September 11, 2000, p. 12-14; Christopher Farrell, "The New Global Investor," *Business Week*, September 11, 2000, pp. 160–162; Craig Karmin, "Comeback Kids Give the World a Jolt," *Wall Street Journal*, January 3, 2000, p. R21.

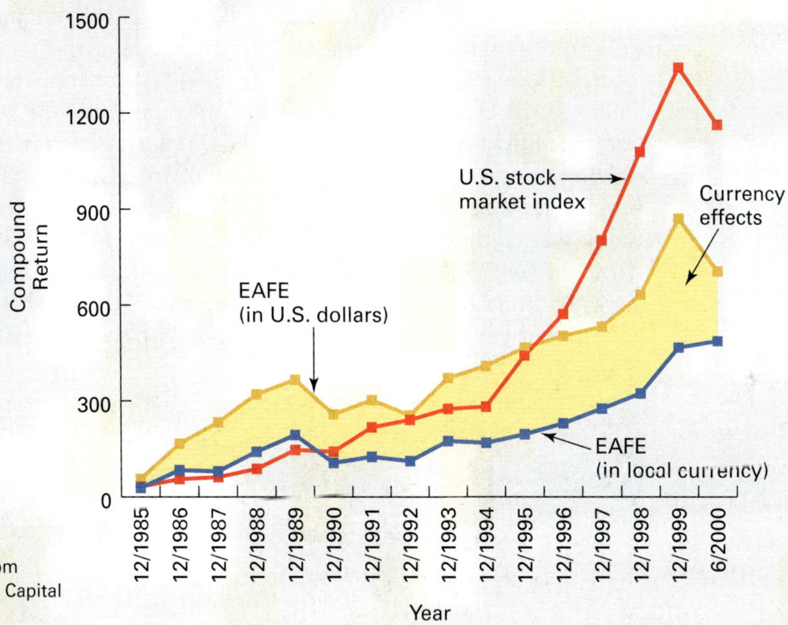

Source: Data from Morgan Stanley Capital International.

Equation 6.5

$$\text{Total return (in U.S. dollars)} = \text{Returns from current income and capital gains (in local currency)} \pm \text{Returns from changes in currency exchange rates}$$

Thus, the two basic components of total return are *those generated by the stocks themselves* (dividends plus change in share prices) and *those derived from movements in currency exchange rates.*

Employing the same two basic components noted above in Equation 6.5, we can compute total return in U.S. dollars by using the following holding period return (HPR) formula, as modified for changes in currency exchange rates.

In Equation 6.6, the "exchange rate" represents the *value of the foreign currency in U.S. dollars*—that is, how much one unit of the foreign currency is worth in U.S. money.

This modified HPR formula is best used over investment periods of one year or less. Also, because it is assumed that dividends are received at the same exchange rate as the ending price of the stock, this equation provides only an approximate (though fairly close) measure of return. Essentially, the first component of Equation 6.6 provides returns on the stock in local currency, and the second element accounts for the impact of changes in currency exchange rates.

Equation 6.6

$$\text{Total return (in U.S. dollars)} = \left[\frac{\text{Ending value of stock in foreign currency} + \text{Amount of dividends received in foreign currency}}{\text{Beginning value of stock in foreign currency}} \times \frac{\text{Exchange rate at } \textit{end} \text{ of holding period}}{\text{Exchange rate at } \textit{beginning} \text{ of holding period}}\right] - 1.00$$

To see how this formula works, consider a U.S. investor who buys several hundred shares of Petrofina, a large Belgian petroleum and chemical company that trades on the Brussels stock exchange. The investor paid a price *per share* of 9,140 Belgian francs (Bf) for the stock, at a time when the exchange rate between the U.S. dollar and the Belgian franc (U.S.\$/Bf) was \$0.0307. At that rate, the Bf was worth a little more than 3 cents. Put another way, this exchange rate amounts to 32.55 Bf per U.S. dollar, so 1 U.S.\$/32.55 B = \$0.0307. The stock paid *annual* dividends of 275 Bf per share. At the end of the year the stock was trading at 9,500 Bf per share, when the U.S.\$/Bf exchange rate was \$0.0336 (29.75 Bf per U.S. dollar). Clearly, the stock went up in price, so the investor must have done all right. To find out just what kind of return this investment generated (in U.S. dollars), we'll have to use Equation 6.6.

$$\begin{aligned}\text{Total return (in U.S. dollars)} &= \left[\frac{9{,}500 + 275}{9{,}140} \times \frac{\$0.0336}{\$0.0307}\right] - 1.00\\ &= [1.0695 \times 1.0945] - 1.00\\ &= [1.1705] - 1.00\\ &= \underline{\underline{17.05\%}}\end{aligned}$$

With a return of 17.05%, the investor seems to have done quite well. However, *most of this return was due to currency movements, not to the behavior of the stock*. Look at just the first part of the equation, which shows the return (in local currency) *earned on the stock* from dividends and capital gains: 1.0695 − 1.00 = 6.95%. Thus the stock itself produced a return of less than 7%. All the rest of the return—more than 10% (i.e., 17.05 − 6.95)—came from the change in currency values. In this case, the value of the U.S. dollar went down relative to the Belgian franc and thus added to the return.

As we've just seen, exchange rates can have a dramatic impact on investor returns. They can convert mediocre returns or even losses into very attractive returns—and vice versa. Only one thing determines whether the so-called *currency effect* is going to be positive or negative: the behavior of the U.S. dollar relative to the currency in which the security is denominated. In essence, *a stronger dollar has a negative impact on total returns to U.S. investors, and a weaker dollar has a positive impact.* Thus, other things being equal, the best time to be in foreign securities is when the dollar is *falling*.

Of course, the greater the amount of fluctuation in the currency exchange rate, the greater the impact on total returns. The challenge facing global investors is to find not only the best-performing foreign stock(s) but also the best-performing foreign currencies. You want the *value of both the foreign stock and the foreign currency to go up over your investment horizon.* And note that this rule applies *both* to direct investment in foreign stocks and to the purchase of ADRs. (Even though ADRs are denominated in dollars, their quoted prices vary with ongoing changes in currency exchange rates.)

Alternative Investment Strategies

Basically, common stocks can be used (1) as a "storehouse" of value, (2) as a way to accumulate capital, and (3) as a source of income. Storage of value is important to all investors; nobody likes to lose money. However, some investors are more concerned about it than others, and therefore, rank safety of principal as their most important stock selection criteria. These investors are more quality-conscious and tend to gravitate toward blue chips and other nonspeculative shares. Accumulation of capital, in contrast, is generally an important goal to those with long-term investment horizons. These investors use the capital gains and/or dividends that stocks provide to build up their wealth. Some use growth stocks for this purpose, others do it with income shares, and still others use a little of both. Finally, some investors use stocks as a source of income. To them, a dependable flow of dividends is essential. High-yielding, good-quality income shares are usually the preferred investment vehicle for these people.

Individual investors can use various *investment strategies* to reach their investment goals. These include buy-and-hold, high income, quality long-term growth, aggressive stock management, and speculation and short-term trading. The first three strategies appeal to investors who consider storage of value important. Depending on the temperament of the investor and the time he or she has to devote to an investment program, any of the strategies might be used to accumulate capital. In contrast, the high-income strategy is the logical choice for those using stocks as a source of income.

Buy-and-Hold Buy-and-hold is the most basic of all investment strategies, and is certainly one of the most conservative. The objective is to place money in a secure investment outlet (safety of principal is vital) and watch it grow over time. In this strategy, investors select high-quality stocks that offer attractive current income and/or capital gains and hold them for extended periods—perhaps as long as 10 to 15 years. This strategy is often used to finance future retirement plans, to meet the educational needs of children, or simply to accumulate capital over the long haul. Generally, investors pick out a few good stocks and then invest in them on a regular basis for long periods of time—until either the investment climate or corporate conditions change dramatically.

Buy-and-hold investors regularly add fresh capital to their portfolios (many treat them like savings plans). Most also plow the income from annual dividends back into the portfolio and reinvest in additional shares (often through dividend reinvestment plans). Long popular with so-called *value-oriented investors,* this approach is used by quality-conscious individuals who are looking for competitive returns over the long haul.

High Income Individual investors often use common stocks to seek high levels of current income. Common stocks are desirable for this purpose not so much for their high dividend yields but also because their *dividend levels tend to increase over time.* In this strategy, safety of principal and stability of income are vital, while capital gains are of secondary importance. Quality income shares are the popular medium for this strategy. Some investors adopt it simply as a way of earning high (and relatively safe) returns on their investment capital. More often, however, a high-income strategy is used by those who are trying to supplement their income. Often, they plan to use the added income for consumption purposes, such as a retired couple supplementing their retirement benefits with income from stocks.

Quality Long-Term Growth This strategy is *less conservative* than either of the first two in that it seeks capital gains as the primary source of return. A fair amount of trading takes place with this approach. Most of the trading is confined to quality growth stocks (including tech stocks, as well as baby blues and other mid-caps) that offer attractive growth prospects and the chance for considerable price appreciation. A number of growth stocks also pay dividends, which many growth-oriented investors consider *an added source of return.* But even so, this strategy still emphasizes capital gains as the principal way to earn big returns. The approach involves a greater element of risk, because of its heavy reliance on capital gains. Therefore, a good deal of diversification is often used. Long-term accumulation of capital is the most common reason for using this approach, but compared to the buy-and-hold tactic, the investor aggressively seeks a bigger payoff by doing considerably more trading and assuming more market risk.

A variation of this investment strategy combines quality long-term growth with high income. This is the so-called *total-return approach* to investing. Though solidly anchored in long-term growth, this approach also considers dividend income as a source of return that should be sought after, rather than relegated to an after-thought or treated as merely a pleasant by-product. In essence, with the total return approach, investors seek attractive long-term returns from *both* dividend income *and* capital gains. These investors hold both income stocks and growth stocks in their portfolios. Or they may hold stocks that provide both dividends and capital gains. In the latter case, the investor doesn't necessarily look for high-yielding stocks, but rather for stocks that offer the potential for *high rates of growth in their dividend streams.* Like their counterparts who employ high-income or quality long-term growth strategies, total-return investors are very concerned about quality. Indeed, about the only thing that separates these investors from high-income and quality long-term growth investors is that to them, what matters is not so much the *source of return* as *the amount of return.* For this reason, total-return investors seek the most attractive returns wherever they can find them—be it from a growing stream of dividends or from appreciation in the price of a stock.

Aggressive Stock Management Aggressive stock management also uses quality issues but seeks attractive rates of return through a fully managed portfolio. Such a portfolio would be one in which the investor aggressively trades in and out of stocks in order to achieve eye-catching returns, primarily from capital gains. Blue chips, growth stocks, big-name tech stocks, mid-caps, and cyclical issues are the primary investment vehicles. More aggressive investors might even consider small-cap stocks, including some of the more speculative tech stocks, foreign shares, and ADRs.

This approach is similar to the quality long-term growth strategy. However, it involves considerably more trading, and the investment horizon is generally much shorter. For example, rather than waiting 2 or 3 years for a stock to move, an aggressive stock trader would go after the same investment payoff in 6 months to a year. Timing security transactions and turning investment capital over fairly rapidly are both key elements of this strategy. These investors try to stay fully invested in stocks when the market is bullish. When it weakens, they shift to a more defensive posture by putting a big chunk of their money into defensive stocks or even into cash and other short-term debt instruments. This strategy has substantial risks. It also places real demands on the individual's time and investment skills. But the rewards can be equally substantial.

Speculation and Short-Term Trading Speculation and short-term trading characterize the least conservative of all investment strategies. The sole objective of this strategy is capital gains. The shorter the time in which the objective can be achieved, the better. Although such investors confine most of their attention to speculative or small-cap stocks and tech stocks, they are not averse to using foreign shares (especially those in so-called *emerging markets*) or other forms of common stock if they offer attractive short-term opportunities. Many speculators find that information about the industry or company is much less important than market psychology or the general tone of the market. It is a process of constantly switching from one position to another as new opportunities unfold. Because the strategy involves so much risk, many transactions yield little or no profit, or even substantial losses. The hope is, of course, that when one does hit, it will be in a big way, and returns will be more than sufficient to offset losses. This strategy obviously requires considerable knowledge and time. Perhaps most important, it also requires the psychological and financial fortitude to withstand the shock of financial losses.

Some Popular Investment Styles

We've just seen that investors can choose from a variety of investment *strategies*—buy-and-hold, speculation, and others. They can also employ different investment *styles* when implementing their investment programs. The selection of an investment style depends in large part on one's investment objectives and risk tolerance. Investment style, in effect, defines the *types of securities* you will want to hold in your equity portfolio. It sets the tone for your investment program by determining how aggressive or conservative you'll be in your security selection. Five types of investment styles dominate the market today: income, growth, value, sector rotation, and momentum investing.

Growth investing and *value investing* are based primarily on fundamental analysis. *Sector rotation* and *momentum investing*, in contrast, are based more on perceived market conditions. The premise behind *income investing* is simple: Buy securities that offer a steady stream of income along with some growth. For equity investors, this means common stocks with a history of regular dividend payments. Utility stocks, some blue chips, and preferred stocks are favorites with income investors who, not surprisingly, tend to follow *high income* as well as *buy-and-hold* investment strategies.

growth investing
investing in stocks with above-average forecasts of earnings growth and high price/earnings ratios in expectation of higher returns.

Growth Investing Investors who prefer **growth investing** are willing to pay premium prices for stocks of companies with above-average expectations of earnings growth. They believe that stock prices of companies with high earnings-growth rates—say, over 15% to 20% a year—should ultimately yield higher returns. These companies have high prices, high price-to-book ratios, and high price/earnings ratios. Most growth stocks pay little or nothing in dividends because management reinvests earnings to "grow" the business. Some growth stocks are large companies, but more often they tend to be "glamour" stocks such as high-tech companies and emerging companies in high-growth industries (the Internet, networking, and biotechnology, for example). Microsoft, Intel, and Cisco are classic examples of growth stocks. Growth investing is riskier than some other styles, as growth stocks tend to rise faster, and fall faster, than the S&P 500. Investors who choose growth stocks need to monitor both company performance and industry trends closely, because these stocks are sensitive to change. Waiting too long to buy or sell can wipe out the rewards of the increased risk. Growth investors tend to use investment strategies that focus on capital appreciation: *quality long-term growth, aggressive stock management,* and possibly even *speculation.*

value investing
investing in stocks of companies that are out of favor with the market for some reason, as reflected by low price/earnings ratios and low prices compared to their fundamentals.

Value Investing In contrast to growth investing, **value investing** focuses on companies that are out of favor with the market. Value investors are "contrarians": They buy stocks whose prices are low compared to their fundamentals (strong balance sheets, earnings, book value per share, cash flow, asset values, or similar quantitative measures). These stocks have lower price/earnings ratios, lower price-to-book ratios, and higher dividend yields than the rest of the market. Value investors analyze *why* the company's valuation is low, and they buy if they expect some particular action—new management, corporate takeover, regulatory change, etc.—to drive up the price. Companies whose prices fall on bad news, such as not meeting earnings targets, may be underpriced bargains. Because the market has undervalued these stocks, value investors believe that the stock price will eventually return to a more "correct" price level, which will produce solid returns over time.

Value companies are often in staid, cyclical industries such as automobiles, chemicals, steel, and financial services. They do best when interest rates are low and the economy is recovering. They peak when economic activity slows. Value investing fell from favor during the strong bull market of the 1990s, when value stocks were harder to find. Patience is definitely a virtue with this style, because it's hard to know just when a company's fortunes will turn. Thus, value investors typically use a *buy-and-hold* strategy.

sector rotation
investing style based on the premise that certain industry sectors perform better during specific stages of the economic cycle.

Sector Rotation With **sector rotation,** investors choose stocks in specific industry sectors that will do best depending on the current and projected stages of the business cycle. The underlying premise is that industries react differently during different stages of the economic cycle—recovery, economic boom, decline, or economic recession. Unlike value and growth investors, who focus on the fundamentals of individual companies, sector rotation investors use a "top-down" approach: They start with the economy as a whole and the forecast for the future. After investors identify industries that should do well in given economic conditions, they select strong companies in those industry sectors. Then, as they anticipate changes in the level of economic activity, they rotate into a different sector.

There are several different ways to define the sectors. One common group divides stocks into four broad sectors: interest-sensitive, consumer durables, capital goods, and defensive. *Interest-sensitive* stocks, like banks, finance companies, and utilities, do well when the economy starts to firm up and interest rates are low. *Consumer durables* are very sensitive to changes in the economy. They tend to do well when the economy is strong, unemployment is low, and consumer disposable income is high. *Capital good manufacturers,* also driven by consumer demand, perform better at a later point in the economic cycle, when economic activity builds greater demand for their products. Finally, *defensive stocks* do well in recessionary periods. Demand for the products that these companies produce remains fairly stable throughout the economic cycle. This sector includes companies that produce staples like food, beverages, and pharmaceuticals, as well as health care providers and utilities.

In sector rotation, investors rotate (move) from one type of stock to the next as the economy moves from one stage of the business cycle to the next. There is obviously a good deal of market timing involved with this approach. Sector rotation investors tend to use investment strategies that focus on *aggressive stock management* and even a bit of *short-term trading.*

momentum investing
investing style that focuses on using relative stock price movement to determine when to buy and sell.

Momentum Investing **Momentum investing** relies heavily on *technical analysis*—an analytical approach that looks at how market forces affect stock prices. (We discuss technical analysis in greater depth in Chapter 8.) Momentum investors focus on relative price movements in the market, rather than on the fundamentals of the underlying companies. They look at stock price, earnings, and other indicators to identify signs that a stock's price is about to soar or fall relative to the market. If the momentum is positive, buying early will produce good returns as more investors jump on the bandwagon and drive the price up even higher.

To select stocks, momentum investors look for stocks in high-growth industries. Momentum stocks tend to have high trading volume and price movements that can be triggered by positive news reports or rumors of high future earnings growth. Basically, momentum investors look for stocks whose prices are rising faster than the S&P 500 (or some other market index or average). They tend to follow either *aggressive stock management* or *speculation and short-term trading* strategies. They typically adopt a relatively short-term approach to investing. Their philosophy is to get in and out fairly quickly—often over no more than a 6- to 12-month period. Some momentum investors are, in fact, very short-term traders, as they will aggressively *day trade* their favorite stock(s), moving in and out on relatively small price changes. Momentum investors have to closely monitor their stocks and watch the direction of the market. This style can be risky if you don't catch the upward movement in time or don't sell before the stock starts to slide.

Summary

LG 1 **Explain the investment appeal of common stocks and why individuals like to invest in them.** Common stocks have long been a popular investment vehicle, largely because of the attractive return opportunities they provide. From current income to capital gains, there are common stocks available to fit just about any investment need.

LG 2 **Describe stock returns from a historical perspective and understand how current returns measure up to historical standards of performance.** Over the long haul, stocks have provided investors with annual returns of around 10% to 15%. Over the past decade or so, stocks have been especially rewarding, generating returns of anywhere from around 20% (on the Dow and the S&P 500) to nearly 30% in the tech-heavy Nasdaq market. Although these returns consist of both dividends and capital gains, it's clear that capital appreciation has been dominant. Whether such returns will continue remains to be seen, but we can probably expect to see highly attractive returns over relatively short periods of time for those willing to assume a greater amount of risk.

LG 3 **Discuss the basic features of common stocks, including issue characteristics, stock quotations, and transaction costs.** Common stocks are a form of equity capital. Each share represents partial ownership of a company. Publicly traded stock can be issued via public offering or through a rights offering to existing stockholders. Companies can also increase the number of shares outstanding through a stock split. To reduce the number of shares of stock in circulation, companies can buy back shares, which are then held as treasury stock. Occasionally, a company issues different classes of common stock, known as classified common stock.

LG 4 **Understand of the different kinds of common stock values.** There are several ways to calculate the value of a share of stock. Book value represents accounting value. Market and investment values, which are most important to investors, represent what the stock is or should be worth.

LG 5 **Discuss common stock dividends, types of dividends, and dividend reinvestment plans.** Companies often share their profits by paying out cash dividends to stockholders. Such actions are normally taken only after carefully considering a variety of corporate and market factors. Sometimes companies declare stock dividends rather than, or in addition to, cash dividends. Many firms that pay cash dividends have dividend reinvestment plans, through which shareholders can have cash dividends automatically reinvested in the company's stock.

LG 6 **Describe various types of common stocks, including foreign stocks, and note how stocks can be used as investment vehicles.** The type of stock selected depends on an investor's needs and preferences. In today's market, investors can choose blue chips, income stocks, growth stocks, tech stocks, speculative issues, cyclicals, defensive shares, mid-cap stocks, small-cap stocks, and initial public offerings. In addition, U.S. investors can buy the common stocks of foreign companies either directly on foreign exchanges or on U.S. markets as American Depositary Receipts (ADRs). Generally speaking, common stocks can be used as a storehouse of value, as a way to accumulate capital, and as a source of income. Different investment strategies (buy-and-hold, high income, quality long-term growth, aggressive stock management, and speculation and short-term trading) as well as different investment styles (income, growth, value, sector rotation, and momentum investing) can be followed to achieve these objectives.

CHAPTER 7

ANALYTICAL DIMENSIONS OF STOCK SELECTION

LEARNING GOALS

After studying this chapter, you should be able to:

LG 1 Discuss the security analysis process, including its goals and functions.

LG 2 Appreciate the purpose and contributions of economic analysis.

LG 3 Describe industry analysis and note how it is used.

LG 4 Demonstrate a basic understanding of fundamental analysis and why it is used.

LG 5 Calculate a variety of financial ratios and describe how financial statement analysis is used to gauge the financial vitality of a company.

LG 6 Use various financial measures to assess a company's performance, and explain how the insights derived form the basic input for the valuation process.

With over 7,000 companies listed on the NYSE and the Nasdaq National Market, how do you decide which ones are good investment candidates? You could start with companies whose goods and services you know. Dell Computer, Disney, Ford, General Electric, McDonald's, and Wal-Mart are just a few companies that come to mind. Familiarity with a company's products is certainly helpful. But it shouldn't be the only criterion for buying securities. You would eliminate many attractive investment opportunities that way.

Take, for example, Medtronic, Inc., a leading medical instrumentation company. Founded in 1949 in a garage in Minneapolis, the company developed the first implantable pacemaker for cardiac-rhythm disorders. In addition to devices that control irregular heartbeats, Medtronic's product line now includes a wide array of implantable and intervention devices for cardiac, neurological, and other disorders.

In addition to the product lineup, you'd also want to know more about its market share, patents on its products, and new products under development. Evaluating this company's products tells you only part of the story, however. After researching the company's stock price history, you'd learn that in the 10 years from January 1, 1991, to December 31, 2000, Medtronic's stock price grew at a compound annual rate of about 33%, compared to the 15.2% annual growth rate of the S&P 500 index over the same period. To put it another way, if you had invested $1,000 in Medtronic stock a decade ago, you have over $17,700; in comparison, $1,000 invested in the stock market as a whole would only be worth about $3,250.

Why did Medtronic's stock perform so much better than the market in general? The answers may lie in analyses of the economy, the medical-device industry, or the company's fundamentals (its financial and operating statistics). This chapter, the first of two on security analysis, introduces some of the techniques and procedures you can use to evaluate the future of the economy, of industries, and of specific companies, such as Medtronics.

Security Analysis

LG 1

The obvious motivation for investing in stocks is to watch your money grow. Consider, for example, the case of the computer software company Oracle Corp. If you had purchased $5,000 worth of Oracle stock in January 1990, that investment would have grown to over $235,000 by the end of the decade (December 1999). That works out to an average annual rate of return of nearly 47%, compared to the 18% or 19% return generated over the same period by the average large-cap stock, as measured by the S&P 500. Unfortunately, for every story of great success in the market, there are dozens more that don't end so well. Most of the disasters can be traced to bad timing, greed, poor planning, or failure to use common sense in making investment decisions. Although these chapters on stock investments cannot offer the keys to sudden wealth, they do provide sound principles for formulating a successful long-range investment program. The techniques described are quite traditional; they are the same proven methods that have been used by millions of investors to achieve attractive rates of return on their capital.

Principles of Security Analysis

security analysis
the process of gathering and organizing information and then using it to determine the intrinsic value of a share of common stock.

intrinsic value
the underlying or inherent value of a stock, as determined through fundamental analysis.

Security analysis consists of gathering information, organizing it into a logical framework, and then using the information to determine the intrinsic value of a common stock. That is, given a rate of return that's compatible to the amount of risk involved in a proposed transaction, **intrinsic value** provides a measure of the underlying worth of a share of stock. It provides a standard for helping you judge whether a particular stock is undervalued, fairly priced, or overvalued. The entire concept of stock valuation is based on the belief that all securities possess an intrinsic value that their market value must approach over time.

In investments, the question of value centers on return. In particular, a satisfactory investment candidate is one *that offers a level of expected return commensurate with the amount of risk involved.* That is, the *minimum rate of return* that you should be able to earn on an investment varies with the amount of risk you have to assume. As a result, not only must an investment candidate be profitable, it must be *sufficiently* profitable—in the sense that you'd expect it to generate a return that's high enough to offset the perceived exposure to risk.

If you could have your way, you'd probably like to invest in something that offers complete preservation of capital, along with sizable helpings of current income and capital gains. The problem, of course, is finding such a security. One approach is to buy whatever strikes your fancy. A more rational approach is to use security analysis to look for promising investment candidates. Security analysis addresses the question of *what to buy* by determining what a stock *ought to be worth*. Presumably, an investor will buy a stock *only if its prevailing market price does not exceed its worth*—its intrinsic value. Ultimately, intrinsic value depends on several factors:

1. Estimates of the stock's future cash flows (the amount of dividends you expect to receive over the holding period and the estimated price of the stock at time of sale).
2. The discount rate used to translate these future cash flows into a present value.
3. The amount of risk embedded in achieving the forecasted level of performance.

Traditional security analysis usually takes a "top-down" approach: It begins with economic analysis and then moves to industry analysis and finally to fundamental analysis. *Economic analysis* assesses the general state of the economy and its potential effects on security returns. *Industry analysis* deals with the industry within which a particular company operates. It looks at how the company stacks up against the major competitors in the industry, and the general outlook for that industry. *Fundamental analysis* looks in depth at the financial condition and operating results of a specific company and the underlying behavior of its common stock. In essence, it looks at the "fundamentals of the company." These fundamentals include the company's investment decisions, the liquidity of its assets, its use of debt, its profit margins and earnings growth, and ultimately the future prospects of the company and its stock.

Fundamental analysis is closely linked to the notion of intrinsic value, because it *provides the basis for projecting a stock's future cash flows.* A key part of this analytical process is *company analysis,* which takes a close look at the actual financial performance of the company. Such analysis is not meant simply to provide interesting tidbits of information about how the company has performed in the past. Rather, company analysis is done to *help investors formulate expectations about the future performance of the company and its stock.* Make no mistake about it: In investments, it's the future that matters. But in order to understand the future prospects of the firm, an investor should have a good handle on the company's current condition and its ability to produce earnings. That's just what company analysis does: It helps investors predict the future by looking at the past and determining how well the company is situated to meet the challenges that lie ahead.

Who Needs Security Analysis in an Efficient Market?

The concept of security analysis in general and fundamental analysis in particular is based on the assumption that investors are capable of formulating reliable estimates of a stock's future behavior. Fundamental analysis operates on the broad premise that some securities may be mispriced in the marketplace at any given point in time. Further, fundamental analysis assumes that, by undertaking a careful analysis of the inherent characteristics of each of the firms in question, it is possible to distinguish those securities that are correctly priced from those that are not.

To many, those two assumptions of fundamental analysis seem reasonable. However, there are others who just don't accept the assumptions of fundamental analysis. These are the so-called *efficient market* advocates. They believe that the market is so efficient in processing new information that securities trade very close to or at their correct values at all times. Thus, they argue, it is virtually impossible to outperform the market on a consistent basis. In its strongest form, the *efficient market hypothesis* asserts the following: (1) Securities are rarely, if ever, substantially mispriced in the marketplace. (2) No security analysis, however detailed, is capable of identifying mispriced securities with a frequency greater than that which might be expected by random chance alone. Is the efficient market hypothesis correct? Is there a place for fundamental analysis in modern investment theory? Interestingly, most financial theorists and practitioners would answer yes to both questions.

The solution to this apparent paradox is quite simple. Basically, fundamental analysis is of value in the selection of alternative investment vehicles for two important reasons. First, financial markets are as efficient as they are because a large number of people and powerful financial institutions invest a great deal of time and money in analyzing the fundamentals of most widely held investments. In other words, markets tend to be efficient, and securities tend to trade at or near their intrinsic values, simply because a great many people have done the research to determine just what their intrinsic values should be. Second, although the financial markets are generally quite efficient, they are by no means perfectly efficient. Pricing errors are inevitable. Those individuals who have conducted the most thorough studies of the fundamentals of a given security are the most likely to profit when errors do occur. We will study the ideas and implications of efficient markets in some detail in Chapter 8. For now, however, we will assume that traditional security analysis is useful in identifying attractive equity investments.

Economic Analysis

LG 2

If we lived in a world where economic activity had absolutely no effect on the stock market or on security prices, we would not need to study the economy. The fact is, of course, that we do not live in such a world. Rather, stock prices are heavily influenced by the state of the economy and by economic events. As a rule, stock prices tend to move up when the economy is strong, and they retreat when the economy starts to soften. It's not a perfect relationship, but it is a powerful one.

The reason why the economy is so important to the market is simple: The overall performance of the economy has a significant bearing on the performance and profitability of the companies that issue common stock. As the fortunes of the issuing firms change with economic conditions, so do the prices of their stocks. Of course, not all stocks are affected in the same way or to the same extent. Some sectors of the economy, like food retailing, may be only mildly affected by the economy. Others, like the construction and auto industries, are often hard hit when times get rough. The *Investing in Action* box on page 211 looks at some of the key factors that drive our economy and at the effects those factors have had on the economic environment.

HOTLINKS

An *Investing in Action* box at the book's homepage details the effects of just one economic condition—unemployment—on the markets.

www.awl.com/gitman_joehnk

economic analysis
a study of general economic conditions that is used in the valuation of common stock.

Economic analysis—a general study of the economy—should not only give an investor a grasp of the *underlying nature of the economic environment* but also enable him or her to assess the *current state of the economy* and formulate expectations about its *future course.* Economic analysis can go so far as to include a detailed examination of each sector of the economy, or it may be done on a very informal basis. However, from a security analysis perspective, its purpose is always the same: to establish a sound foundation for the valuation of common stock.

HOTLINKS

Check out Economics Network, U.S. business cycle dates, at

www.yardeni.com

Economic Analysis and the Business Cycle

Economic analysis sets the tone for security analysis. If the economic future looks bleak, you can probably expect most stock returns to be equally dismal.

INVESTING in action

Seven Engines That Drive the Economy

As the bull market roared through the 1990s, market watchers sought explanations for its continued growth. Jay Mueller, economist at Strong Investments, identified the following seven positive forces as the primary drivers of the strong U.S. economy.

1. **Positive demographics.** The largest age group in the United States today are those who are 40 to 44 years old (those born at the end of postwar baby boom); it is followed by the 35 to 39 age group. These seasoned, experienced workers account for about 17% of the U.S. population. They are major contributors to the increase in U.S. labor productivity, a trend that is expected to continue for 5 to 10 more years.
2. **Deregulation.** As deregulation hit various industries (airlines, oil, trucking, telecommunications, financial services, and competition increased. Consumers enjoyed the benefits of lower prices and more choices, which in turn encouraged higher spending.
3. **Strategic tax rate cuts.** Reductions in the marginal tax rates in the 1980s played a major role in initiating the economic expansion that continued through at least early 2001. Long-term capital gains taxes also fell, the top rate dropping to 20% in 2000. Lower capital gains taxes promote investment. In addition, the elimination of some deductions and tax loopholes shifted the focus to business and investment decisions based on economic fundamentals rather than tax avoidance.
4. **Trade liberalization.** Goods and services flow more freely across national borders since the 1993 passage of the North American Free Trade Agreement (NAFTA) and recent decisions under the General Agreement on Tariffs and Trade (GATT). Other developments in this area include the move toward market-oriented economies in Eastern Europe and Asia. Like deregulation, trade liberalization encourages competition in markets that were formerly closed to new players. The result is higher-quality products and more efficient production, leading to lower prices and economic growth.
5. **The technology revolution.** Technological advances have changed the way we work, play, communicate, and invest. The Internet is a prime mover in this trend, offering not just faster communication and data transfer but even new ways to shop. Computer hardware prices have fallen drastically, making technology affordable to more people than ever. Corporate investments in information technology equipment are now paying off in terms of increased output per worker. Annual U.S. productivity growth, which averaged about 1.8% from 1991 to 1995, jumped to 2.6% between 1996 and 1999.
6. **Welfare reform.** More states now have welfare-to-work programs to help welfare recipients become self-sufficient, productive members of the work force. The percentage of the U.S. population now on welfare is about 2.4%—half of the 1989 figure. The technology revolution has also helped workers with low or no skills enter the labor pool by making it easier to perform certain tasks (such as working at supermarket and other checkout counters) and then upgrade their skills to move up into better paying jobs.
7. **Monetary policy.** The Federal Reserve now takes a more proactive role in using monetary policy to control inflation. Strategic interest rate increases and cuts have stabilized the business cycle and allowed growth to continue.

Keeping an eye on these seven trends will provide you with a sense of what's to come. A weakening of several trends could signal a downshift that will negatively affect the stock market.

Sources: Gene Koretz, "A Test for the New Economy," *Business Week*, December 11, 2000, p. 36; Rich Miller et al., "How Prosperity Is Reshaping the American Economy," *Business Week*, February 14, 2000, pp. 100–110; and Jay N. Mueller, "Seven Engines of the Economy," *Mutual Funds*, August 2000, pp. 38–39.

business cycle
an indication of the current state of the economy, reflecting changes in total economic activity over time.

If the economy looks strong, stocks should do well. As we saw in Chapter 2, the behavior of the economy is captured in the **business cycle,** which reflects changes in total economic activity over time. Two widely followed measures of the business cycle are gross domestic product and industrial production. *Gross domestic product* (GDP) represents the market value of all goods and services produced in a country over the period of a year. *Industrial production* is a measure (it's really an index) of the activity/output in the industrial or productive segment of the economy. Normally, GDP and the index of industrial production move up and down with the business cycle.

Key Economic Factors

Financial and market decisions are made by economic units at all levels, from individual consumers and households to business firms and governments. These various decisions together have an impact on the direction of economic activity. Particularly important in this regard are the following:

Government fiscal policy
Taxes
Government spending
Debt management

Monetary policy
Money supply
Interest rates

Other factors
Inflation
Consumer spending
Business investments
Foreign trade and foreign exchange rates

Government fiscal policy tends to be expansive when it encourages spending—when the government reduces taxes and/or increases the size of the budget. Similarly, monetary policy is said to be expansive when money is readily available and interest rates are relatively low. An expansive economy also depends on a generous level of spending by consumers and business concerns. These same variables moving in a reverse direction can have a contractionary (recessionary) impact on the economy, as for example, when taxes and interest rates increase or when spending by consumers and businesses falls off.

The impact of these major forces filters through the system and affects several key dimensions of the economy. The most important of these are industrial production, corporate profits, retail sales, personal income, the unemployment rate, and inflation. For example, a strong economy exists when industrial production, corporate profits, retail sales, and personal income are moving up and unemployment is down. Thus, when conducting an economic analysis, an investor should keep an eye on fiscal and monetary policies, consumer and business spending, and foreign trade *for the potential impact they have on the economy.* At the same time, he or she must stay abreast of the level of industrial production, corporate profits, retail sales, personal income, unemployment, and inflation *in order to assess the state of the business cycle.*

HOTLINKS

To keep up with the status of the economy, you can view the monthly leading index of economic indicators computed by the Conference Board in New York.

At the White House site, you can visit the economic statistics briefing room. *The Economist* also provides data useful for keeping track of the economy. See the following sites:

www.conference-board.org/
www.whitehouse.gov/fsbr/esbr.html
www.economist.com

To help you keep track of the economy, Table 7.1 provides a brief description of some key economic measures. These economic statistics are compiled by various government agencies and are widely reported in the financial media. (Most of the reports are released monthly.) Take the time to carefully read about the various economic measures and reports cited in Table 7.1. When you understand the behavior of these statistics, you can make your own educated guess as to the current state of the economy and where it's headed.

Developing an Economic Outlook

Conducting an economic analysis involves studying fiscal and monetary policies, inflationary expectations, consumer and business spending, and the state of the business cycle. Often investors do this on a fairly informal basis. As they form their economic judgments, many rely on one or more of the popular published sources (e.g., the *Wall Street Journal, Barron's, Fortune,* and *Business Week*) as well as on periodic reports from major brokerage houses. These sources provide a convenient summary of economic activity and give investors a general feel for the condition of the economy.

HOTLINKS

At this site, choose from the left side of the box Today's Economy, and from the categories, select [Especially for Students]. Read an article that interests you.

www.dismal.com

Once you have developed a general economic outlook, you can use the information in one of two ways. One approach is to construct an economic outlook and then consider where it leads in terms of possible areas for further analysis. For example, suppose you uncover information that strongly suggests the outlook for business spending is very positive. On the basis of such an analysis, you might want to look more closely at capital goods producers, such as office equipment manufacturers. Similarly, if you feel that because of sweeping changes in world politics, U.S. government defense spending is likely to drop off, you might want to avoid the stocks of major defense contractors.

INVESTOR FACTS

THE AMERICAN ADVANTAGE— Driven by the information technology sector, the booming U.S. economy is once again the world leader and has become a model for other countries. In 1999, the most recent year for which comparative statistics were available, the U.S. GDP growth rate was 3.6%, compared to 0.2% for Japan, 1.6% for Germany, 2.2% for the United Kingdom, and 2.9 % for France. The average for the 29 members of the Organization for Economic Cooperation and Development was just 2.5%. Unemployment at year-end 2000 was 4%, compared to 8% in Germany, over 9% in France, and 10% in Italy.

Source: Organization for Economic Cooperation and Development, www.oecd.org/std/gdp.htm; and U.S. Department of Labor, Bureau of Labor Statistics, January 5, 2001, stats.bls.gov

A second way to use information about the economy is to consider specific industries or companies and ask, "How will they be affected by expected developments in the economy?" Take an investor with an interest in *business equipment stocks.* This industry category includes companies involved in the production of everything from business machines and electronic systems to work lockers and high-fashion office furnishings. In this industry you'll find companies like Bell & Howell, Diebold, Herman Miller, Smith Corona, and Steelcase. These stocks are highly susceptible to changing economic conditions. When the economy starts slowing down, companies can put off purchases of durable equipment and fixtures. Especially important to this industry is the outlook for corporate profits and business investments. So long as these economic factors look good, the prospects for business equipment stocks should be positive.

In this instance, our imaginary investor would first want to assess the current state of the business cycle. Using that insight, he would then formulate some expectations about the future of the economy and the potential impact it holds for the stock market in general and business equipment stocks in particular. (Table 7.2 shows how some of the more important economic variables can affect the behavior of the stock market.) To see how this might be done, let's assume that the economy has just gone through a brief (9-month) recession and is now in the recovery stage of the business cycle: Employment is starting to pick up. Inflation and interest rates have come back down. Both

TABLE 7.1 Keeping Track of the Economy

To help you sort out the confusing array of figures that flow almost daily from Washington, D.C., and keep track of what's happening in the economy, here are some of the most important economic measures and reports to watch.

- **Gross domestic product (GDP).** This is the broadest measure of the economy's performance. Issued every 3 months by the Commerce Department, it is an estimate of the total dollar value of all the goods and services produced in this country. Movements in many areas of the economy are closely related to changes in GDP, so it is a good analytic tool. In particular, watch the annual rate of growth or decline in "real" or "constant" dollars. This number eliminates the effects of inflation and thus measures the actual volume of production. Remember, though, that frequent revisions of GDP figures sometimes change the picture of the economy.

- **Industrial production.** Issued monthly by the Federal Reserve Board, this index shows changes in the physical output of U.S. factories, mines, and electric and gas utilities. The index tends to move in the same direction as the economy; it is thus a good guide to business conditions between reports on GDP. Detailed breakdowns of the index give a reading on how individual industries are faring.

- **The index of leading indicators.** This boils down to one number, which summarizes the movement of a dozen statistics that tend to predict—or "lead"—changes in the GDP. This monthly index, issued by the Commerce Department, includes such things as layoffs of workers, new orders placed by manufacturers, changes in the money supply, and the prices of raw materials. If the index moves in the same direction for several months, it's a fairly good sign that total output will move the same way in the near future.

- **Personal income.** A monthly report from the Commerce Department, this shows the before-tax income received in the form of wages and salaries, interest and dividends, rents, and other payments, such as Social Security, unemployment compensation, and pensions. As a measure of individuals' spending power, the report helps explain trends in consumer buying habits, a major part of total GDP. When personal income rises, people often increase their buying. But note a big loophole: Excluded are the billions of dollars that change hands in the so-called underground economy—cash transactions that are never reported to tax or other officials.

- **Retail sales.** The Commerce Department's monthly estimate of total sales at the retail level includes everything from cars to groceries. Based on a sample of retail establishments, the figure gives a rough clue to consumer attitudes. It can also indicate future conditions: A long slowdown in sales can lead to cuts in production.

- **Money supply.** The Federal Reserve reports weekly this measure of the amount of money in circulation. Actually, there are three measures of the money supply: *M1* is basically currency, demand deposits, and NOW accounts. *M2*, the most widely followed measure, equals M1 plus savings deposits, money market deposit accounts, and money market mutual funds. *M3* is M2 plus large CDs and a few other less significant types of deposits/transactions. Reasonable growth in the money supply, as measured by M2, is thought to be necessary for an expanding economy. However, too rapid a rate of growth in money is considered inflationary; in contrast, a sharp slowdown in the growth rate is viewed as recessionary.

- **Consumer prices.** Issued monthly by the Labor Department, this index shows changes in prices for a fixed market basket of goods and services. The most widely publicized figure is for all urban consumers. A second, used in labor contracts and some government programs, covers urban wage earners and clerical workers. Both are watched as a measure of inflation, but many economists believe that flaws cause them to be inaccurate.

- **Producer prices.** This monthly indicator from the Labor Department shows price changes of goods at various stages of production, from crude materials such as raw cotton to finished goods like clothing and furniture. An upward surge may mean higher consumer prices later. However, the index can miss discounts and may exaggerate rising price trends. Watch particularly changes in the prices of finished goods. These do not fluctuate as widely as the prices of crude materials and thus are a better measure of inflationary pressures.

- **Employment.** The percentage of the work force that is involuntarily out of work is a broad indicator of economic health. But another monthly figure issued by the Labor Department—the number of payroll jobs—may be better for spotting changes in business. A decreasing number of jobs is a sign that firms are cutting production.

- **Housing starts.** A pickup in the pace of housing starts usually follows an easing in the availability and cost of money and is an indicator of improving economic health. This monthly report from the Commerce Department also includes the number of new building permits issued across the country, an even earlier indicator of the pace of future construction.

TABLE 7.2 Economic Variables and the Stock Market

Economic Variable	Potential Effect on the Stock Market
Real growth in GDP	Positive impact—it's good for the market.
Industrial production	Continued increases are a sign of strength, which is good for the market.
Inflation	Detrimental to stock prices. Higher inflation leads to higher interest rates and lower price/earnings multiples, and generally makes equity securities less attractive.
Corporate profits	Strong corporate earnings are good for the market.
Unemployment	A downer—an increase in unemployment means business is starting to slow down.
Federal budget surplus or deficit	Budget surpluses have replaced budget deficits (at least for now), which is great news for interest rates and stock prices. Budget deficits, in contrast, may be positive for a depressed economy but can lead to inflation in a stronger economic environment and therefore have a negative impact.
Weak dollar	Often the result of big trade imbalances, a weak dollar has a negative effect on the market. It makes our markets less attractive to foreign investors. However, it also makes our products more affordable in overseas markets and therefore can have a positive impact on our economy.
Interest rates	Another downer—rising rates tend to have a negative effect on the market for stocks.
Money supply	Moderate growth can have a positive impact on the economy and the market. Rapid growth, however, is inflationary and therefore detrimental to the stock market.

GDP and industrial production have experienced sharp increases in the past two quarters. And Congress is putting the finishing touches on a major piece of legislation that would lead to reduced taxes. More important, although the economy is now in the early stages of a recovery, things are expected to get even better in the future. The economy is definitely starting to build steam, and all indications are that both corporate profits and business spending should undergo a sharp increase. All of these predictions should be good news for the producers of business equipment and office furnishings, as a good deal of their sales and an even larger portion of their profits depend on the level of corporate profits and business spending. In short, our investor sees an economy in good shape and set to become even stronger, the consequences of which are favorable not only for the market but for business equipment stocks as well.

Note that these conclusions could have been reached by relying on sources no more sophisticated than *Barron's* or *Business Week*. In fact, about the only "special thing" this investor would have to do is pay careful attention to those economic forces that are particularly important to the business equipment industry (e.g., corporate profits). The economic portion of the analysis, in effect, has set the stage for further evaluation by indicating what type of economic environment to expect in the near future. The next step is to narrow the focus a bit and conduct the industry phase of the analysis.

However, before we continue our analysis, it is vital to clarify a bit the relationship that normally exists between the stock market and the economy. In particular, as we just saw, the economic outlook is used to get a handle on the market and to direct investors to developing industry sectors. Yet it is important to note that changes in stock prices normally occur *before* the actual forecasted changes become apparent in the economy. Indeed, the current trend of stock prices is frequently used to help *predict* the course of the economy itself. The apparent conflict here can be resolved somewhat by noting that because of this relationship, it is even more important to derive a reliable economic outlook and to be sensitive to underlying economic changes that may mean the current outlook is becoming dated. Investors in the stock market tend to look into the future to justify the purchase or sale of stock. If their perception of the future is changing, stock prices are also likely to be changing. Therefore, watching the course of stock prices as well as the course of the general economy can make for more accurate investment forecasting.

Industry Analysis

LG 3

Have you ever thought about buying oil stocks, or autos, or chemicals? How about computer stocks or electric utility stocks? Looking at securities in terms of industry groupings is widely used by both individual and institutional investors. This is a sensible approach because stock prices are influenced by industry conditions. The level of demand in an industry and other industry forces set the tone for individual companies. Clearly, if the outlook is good for an industry, then the prospects are likely to be strong for many of the companies that make up that industry.

Key Issues

industry analysis
study of industry groupings that looks at the competitive position of a particular industry in relation to others and identifies companies that show particular promise within an industry.

The first step in **industry analysis** is to establish the competitive position of a particular industry *in relation to others,* for, as Table 7.3 indicates, not all industries perform alike. The next step is to identify companies *within the industry* that hold particular promise. This sets the stage for a more thorough analysis of individual companies and securities. Analyzing an industry means looking at such things as its makeup and basic characteristics, the key economic and operating variables that drive industry performance, and the outlook for the industry. The investor will also want to keep an eye out for specific companies that appear well situated to take advantage of industry conditions. Companies with strong market positions should be favored over those with less secure positions. Such dominance is indicative of an ability to maintain pricing leadership and suggests that the firm will be in a position to enjoy economies of scale and low-cost production. Market dominance also enables a company to support a strong research and development effort, thereby helping it secure its leadership position for the future.

HOTLINKS

Go to the following site and click [ProSearch], [Industry Groups], [Best and Worst Industries]. Select [1, 6, 18, or 26 week], and 1-, 3-, or 5-year periods to see how the industries fared on returns.

www.wallstreetcity.com

Normally, an investor can gain valuable insight about an industry by seeking answers to the following questions:

TABLE 7.3 A Look at the Stock Performance of Key Industry Groups

In searching for value, an early step is to look at the big picture: *industry-group trends.* One source for such information is Standard & Poor's, which tracks the performance of 115 industries that it breaks into 11 major industrial groups. Shown here is the performance of all 11 of those major industrial groups, plus a wide-ranging sample of 30 separate industries. Each of these groups or industries, in effect, has its own market index (much like, say, the S&P 500) that measures the performance of stocks within that group or industry. As is apparent in the numbers below, some industries simply do much better than others, at least over certain time periods. (*Source: S&P Index Services*, as reported on its Web site, www.spglobal.com, release date, September 29, 2001.)

	Industry Performance (% Price Change)		
	Year to date (through 3rd Qtr. 2000)	1999	5 years
Major Industry Groups			
Basic Material (1)	−28.7%	18.2%	−1.7%
Capital Goods (2)	7.8	25.5	20.1
Communication Services (3)	−24.7	18.2	13.7
Consumer Cyclicals (4)	−19.7	15.0	13.1
Consumer Staples (5)	−3.4	−7.7	12.0
Energy (6)	15.0	17.8	16.3
Financial (7)	20.6	0.8	22.2
Health Care (8)	25.0	−7.8	23.5
Technology (9)	−9.4	75.9	36.6
Transportation (10)	−2.3	−8.3	5.8
Utilities (11)	47.7	−12.9	12.7
Individual Industries			
Aluminum (1)	−36.4%	90.4%	6.9%
Paper Containers & Packaging (1)	−20.1	−6.6	−3.3
Iron & Steel (1)	−42.0	2.7	−13.6
Metal & Glass Containers (2)	−52.6	−21.0	−18.5
Electrical Equipment (2)	11.4	47.8	33.7
Manufacturing (Diversified) (2)	1.0	18.6	17.8
Telecommunications—Wireless (3)	−19.6	208.4	37.9
Telephone (3)	−10.9	5.5	14.3
Building Materials (4)	−36.1	−18.6	−4.8
Publishing (4)	7.3	6.3	16.2
Retail—Speciality Apparel (4)	−36.0	13.5	24.7
Textiles—Speciality (4)	−28.4	−33.6	−19.2
Broadcasting—Radio/TV (5)	−25.6	79.5	23.2
Entertainment (5)	15.3	16.3	21.3
Housewares (5)	−20.9	−16.6	−5.6
Retail Drug Stores (5)	19.2	−25.1	27.8
Oil & Gas Drilling & Equipment (6)	49.7	48.7	23.0
International Oil (6)	5.4	14.6	16.7
Diversified Financial (7)	23.1	29.1	33.6
Multiline Insurance (7)	33.6	26.8	30.4
Investment Banking & Brokerage (7)	45.5	33.1	38.1
Biotechnology (8)	33.5	104.6	36.7
Long-term Health Care (8)	7.2	−56.5	−20.3
Communication Equipment (9)	−28.8	128.9	27.6
Computers—Networking (9)	11.1	129.9	51.5
Electronics—Semiconductors (9)	14.6	66.0	33.0
Railroads (10)	−11.7	−15.6	−1.0
Trucking (10)	−19.4	−6.6	−1.4
Electric Utility Companies (11)	34.5	−22.1	7.0
Independent Power Producers (11)	111.8	50.6	62.0

Note: The parenthetical number behind the industry name represents the industry group to which it belongs. For example, the first three industries are identified with a (1), meaning they belong to the "Basic Materials" industry group, which is also identified with a (1).

1. *What is the nature of the industry?* Is it monopolistic, or are there many competitors? Do a few set the trend for the rest, and if so, who are those few?
2. *To what extent is the industry regulated?* Is it regulated (e.g., public utilities)? If so, how "friendly" are the regulatory bodies?
3. *What role, if any, does labor play in the industry?* How important are labor unions? Are there good labor relations within the industry? When is the next round of contract talks?
4. *How important are technological developments?* Are any new developments taking place? What impact are potential breakthroughs likely to have?
5. *Which economic forces are especially important to the industry?* Is demand for the industry's goods and services related to key economic variables? If so, what is the outlook for those variables? How important is foreign competition to the health of the industry?
6. *What are the important financial and operating considerations?* Is there an adequate supply of labor, material, and capital? What are the capital spending plans and needs of the industry?

growth cycle
a reflection of the amount of business vitality that occurs within an industry (or company) over time.

These questions can sometimes be answered in terms of an industry's **growth cycle**, which reflects the vitality of the industry over time. In the first phase—*initial development*—investment opportunities are usually not available to most investors. The industry is new and untried, and the risks are very high. The second stage is *rapid expansion,* during which product acceptance is spreading and investors can foresee the industry's future more clearly. At this stage, economic and financial variables have little to do with the industry's overall performance (sound a bit like some Internet stocks?). Investors will be interested in investing almost regardless of the economic climate. This is the phase that is of substantial interest to investors, and a good deal of work is done to find such opportunities.

Unfortunately, most industries do not experience rapid growth for long. Instead, they eventually slip into the next category in the growth cycle, *mature growth,* which is the third stage and the one most influenced by economic developments. In this stage, expansion comes from growth of the economy. It is a slower source of overall growth than that experienced in stage 2. In stage 3, the long-term nature of the industry becomes apparent. Industries in this category include defensive ones, like food and apparel, and cyclical industries, like autos and heavy equipment.

The last phase is either *stability* or *decline.* In the decline phase, demand for the industry's products is diminishing, and companies are leaving the industry. Investment opportunities at this stage are almost nonexistent, unless you are seeking only dividend income. Investors want to avoid this stage. However, few really good companies ever reach this final stage because they continually bring new products to the market and, in so doing, remain at least in the mature growth phase.

Developing an Industry Outlook

Industry analysis can be conducted by individual investors themselves. Or, as is more often the case, it can be done with the help of published industry reports such as the popular *S&P Industry Surveys*. These surveys cover all the important economic, market, and financial aspects of an industry, providing commentary as well as vital statistics. Other widely used sources of industry information include brokerage house reports and articles in the popular financial media.

Let's resume our example of the imaginary investor who is thinking about buying business equipment stocks. Recall from our prior discussion that the economic phase of the analysis suggested a strong economy for the foreseeable future—one in which corporate profits and business spending will be expanding. Now the investor is ready to focus on the industry. A logical starting point is to assess the expected industry response to forecasted economic developments. Demand for the product and industry sales would be especially important. The industry is made up of many large and small competitors, and although it is labor-intensive, labor unions are not an important force. Thus, our investor may want to look closely at the potential effect of these factors on the industry's cost structure. Also worth a look is the work being done in research and development (R&D), and in industrial design within the industry. You would want to know which firms are coming out with the new products and fresh ideas, because these firms are likely to be the industry leaders (or potential industry leaders).

Industry analysis yields an understanding of the nature and operating characteristics of an industry, which can then be used to form judgments about the prospects for industry growth. Let's assume that our investor, by using various types of published reports, has examined the key elements of the office equipment industry and has concluded that the industry, *particularly the office furnishings segment,* is well positioned to take advantage of the rapidly improving economy. Many new and exciting products have come out in the last couple of years, and more are on the drawing board or in the R&D stage. Even more compelling is the current emphasis on new products that will contribute to the long-term productivity of businesses and other institutions. Thus the demand for office furniture and fixtures should increase, and although profit margins may tighten a bit, the level of profits should move up smartly, providing a healthy outlook for growth.

In the course of researching the industry, our investor has noticed several companies that stand out, but one looks particularly attractive: Universal Office Furnishings. Long regarded as one of the top design firms in the industry, Universal designs, manufactures, and sells to commercial and institutional users a full line of high-end office furniture and fixtures (desks, chairs, credenzas, modular work stations, filing systems, etc.). In addition, the company produces and distributes state-of-the-art computer furniture and a specialized line of institutional furniture for the hospitality, health care, and educational markets. The company was founded over 50 years ago, and its stock (which trades under the symbol UVRS) has been listed on the NYSE since the late 1960s. Universal would be considered a *mid-cap stock,* with total market capitalization of around $2 or $3 billion. The company experienced rapid growth in the '90s, as it expanded its product line, and is expected to benefit from the strong economic environment now under way. Everything about the economy and the industry looks good for the stock, so our investor decides to take a close look at Universal Office Furnishings.

HOTLINKS

From the main page of the MSN site, go to [Investor], [Markets], [Top 10 Lists], [Industries] to find the 10 best-performing and 10 worst-performing industries.
Go to:

moneycentral.msn.com

Fundamental Analysis

LG 4 LG 5 LG 6

fundamental analysis
the in-depth study of the financial condition and operating results of a firm.

Fundamental analysis is the study of the financial affairs of a business for the purpose of better understanding the nature and operating characteristics of the company that issued the common stock. In this part of the chapter, we will deal with several aspects of fundamental analysis. We will examine the general concept of fundamental analysis, and introduce several types of financial statements that provide the raw material for this analysis. We will then describe the key financial ratios widely used in company analysis, and will conclude with an interpretation of those financial ratios. It's important to understand that this represents the more traditional approach to security analysis. It's commonly used to evaluate both growth and value oriented stocks, as well as income shares, turn-arounds, and other situations where investors can rely on financial statements and other data bases to at least partially form a decision. This approach really has very little, if any, place in the valuation of highly speculative stocks, including many tech stocks, and most IPO's. For now, however, our attention will center on the traditional approach to security analysis; in the latter part of the next chapter (Chapter 8), we'll look at some popular valuation concepts that are being used to evaluate tech stocks.

The Concept

Fundamental analysis rests on the belief that *the value of a stock is influenced by the performance of the company that issued the stock*. If a company's prospects look strong, the market price of its stock is likely to reflect that and be bid up.

HOTLINKS

Get basic fundamental data about a stock at

411stocks.stockselector.com

However, the value of a security depends not only on the return it promises but also on the amount of its risk exposure. Fundamental analysis captures these dimensions (risk and return) and conveniently incorporates them into the valuation process. It begins with a historical analysis of the financial strength of a firm: the so-called *company analysis* phase. Using the insights obtained, along with economic and industry analyses, an investor can then formulate expectations about the future growth and profitability of a company.

In the historical (or company analysis) phase, the investor studies the financial statements of the firm to learn its strengths and weaknesses, identify any underlying trends and developments, evaluate operating efficiencies, and gain a general understanding of the nature and operating characteristics of the firm. The following points are of particular interest:

1. The competitive position of the company.
2. Its composition and growth in sales.
3. Profit margins and the dynamics of company earnings.
4. The composition and liquidity of corporate resources (the company's asset mix).
5. The company's capital structure (its financing mix).

The historical phase is in many respects the most demanding and the most time-consuming. Most investors, however, have neither the time nor the inclination to conduct such an extensive study, so they rely on published reports for the background material. Fortunately, individual investors have a variety of sources to choose from. These include the reports and recommendations of major brokerage houses, the popular financial media, and financial subscription services like S&P and *Value Line,* not to mention a whole

HOTLINKS

To read about company analysis with Marketguide, go to the site below and click on [Learn to Analyze Stocks Using Marketguide].

www.marketguide.com

array of computer-based software and online financial sources, such as CNBC.com, Morningstar Net, MSN Money Central, Quicken.com, Smart Money Interactive, Wall Street City, and Stock Selector.com. These are all valuable sources of information, and the paragraphs that follow are not intended to replace them. Yet to be an intelligent investor, you should understand fully the content and implications of such financial reports. Ultimately, you will be making your own judgment about the company and its stock.

Financial Statements

Financial statements are a vital part of company analysis, because they enable investors to develop an opinion about the operating results and financial condition of a firm. Three types of financial statements are used in company analysis: the balance sheet, the income statement, and the statement of cash flows. The first two statements are essential to carrying out basic financial analysis. (In particular, they contain data needed to compute many of the financial ratios.) The third statement—the cash flow statement—is used primarily to assess the cash/liquidity position of the firm. Company statements are prepared on a quarterly basis (these are *abbreviated* statements, compiled for each 3-month period of operation) and again at the end of each calendar year or *fiscal year* (a 12-month period the company has defined as its operating year, which may or may not end on December 31). Annual financial statements must be fully verified by independent certified public accountants (CPAs). They then must be filed with the U.S. Securities and Exchange Commission, and distributed on a timely basis to all stockholders in the form of annual reports. By themselves, corporate financial statements are a most important source of information to the investor. When used with financial ratios and in conjunction with fundamental analysis, they become even more powerful.

INVESTOR FACTS

NO THANKS, WE'LL PASS— Many companies today use long-term debt as a major source of financing. This is not true in all cases, however. Some big, well-known companies in a variety of industries get along fine with little or no debt. For example, Best Buy, Genentech, Fuji Photo, Intel, Starbucks, and Teradyne have debt-to-equity ratios of just 1% to 3%. And 3COM, Cisco, Microsoft, Paychex, Schering-Plough, Walgreen, and Wrigley have no long-term debt at all in their capital structures.

balance sheet
a financial summary of a firm's assets, liabilities, and shareholders' equity at a single point in time.

The Balance Sheet

The **balance sheet** is a statement of the company's assets, liabilities, and stockholders' equity. The *assets* represent the resources of the company (the things the company owns). The *liabilities* are its debts. *Equity* is the amount of capital the stockholders have invested in the firm. A balance sheet may be thought of as a summary of the firm's assets balanced against its debt and ownership positions *at a single point in time* (on the last day of the calendar or fiscal year, or at the end of the quarter). To balance, the total assets must equal the total amount of liabilities and equity.

A typical balance sheet is illustrated in Table 7.4. It shows the comparative 2000–2001 figures for Universal Office Furnishings, the firm our investor is analyzing. Note that although the Universal name is fictitious, the financial statements are not. *They are the actual financial statements of a real company.* Some of the entries have been slightly modified for pedagogical purposes, but these tables accurately depict what real financial statements look like and how they're used in financial statement analysis.

income statement
a financial summary of the operating results of a firm covering a specified period of time, usually 1 year.

The Income Statement

The **income statement** provides a financial summary of the operating results of the firm. It shows the amount of revenues generated over a period of time, the cost and expenses incurred over the same period, and the company's profits. (Profits are calculated by subtracting all costs and

TABLE 7.4 Corporate Balance Sheet

Universal Office Furnishings, Inc.
Comparative Balance Sheet
December 31
($ in millions)

	2001	2000
Assets		
Current assets		
Cash and equivalents	$ 95.8	$ 80.0
Receivables	227.2	192.4
Inventories	103.7	107.5
Other current assets	73.6	45.2
Total current assets	500.3	425.1
Noncurrent Assets		
Property, plant, & equipment, gross	771.2	646.6
Accumulated depreciation & depletion	(372.5)	(379.9)
Property, plant, & equipment, net	398.7	316.7
Other noncurrent assets	42.2	19.7
Total current liabilities	440.9	336.4
Total assets	**$941.2**	**$761.5**
Liabilities and Stockholders' Equity		
Current liabilities		
Accounts payable	$ 114.2	$ 82.4
Short-term debt	174.3	79.3
Other current liabilities	85.5	89.6
Total current liabilities	374.0	251.3
Noncurrent liabilities		
Long-term debt	177.8	190.9
Other noncurrent liabilities	94.9	110.2
Total noncurrent liabilities	272.7	301.1
Total Liabilities	**$646.7**	**$552.4**
Stockholders' Equity		
Common shares	92.6	137.6
Retained earnings	201.9	71.5
Total equity	294.5	209.1
Total Liabilities and Stockholders' Equity	**$941.2**	**$761.5**

expenses, including taxes, from revenues.) Unlike the balance sheet, the income statement covers activities that have occurred over the course of time, or for a given operating period. Typically, this period extends no longer than a fiscal or calendar year. Table 7.5 shows the income statements for Universal Office Furnishings for 2000 and 2001. Note that these annual statements cover operations for the 12-month period ending on December 31, which corresponds to the date of the balance sheet. The income statement indicates how successful the firm has been in using the assets listed on the balance sheet. That is, management's success in operating the firm is reflected in the profit or loss the company generates during the year.

TABLE 7.5 Corporate Income Statement

Universal Office Furnishings, Inc.
Income Statements
Fiscal Year Ended December 31
($ in millions)

	2001	2000
Net sales	$1,938.0	$1,766.2
Cost of goods sold	1,128.5	1,034.5
Gross operating profit	$ 809.5	$ 731.7
Selling, administrative, and other operating expenses	497.7	445.3
Depreciation & authorization	77.1	62.1
Other income, net	0.5	12.9
Earnings before interest & taxes	$235.2	$237.2
Interest expense	13.4	7.3
Earnings before taxes	$221.8	$229.9
Income taxes	82.1	88.1
Net profit after taxes	**$139.7**	**$141.8**
Dividends paid per share	$0.15	$0.13
Earnings per share (EPS)	$2.26	$2.17
Number of common shares outstanding (in millions)	61.8	65.3

statement of cash flows
a financial summary of a firm's cash flow and other events that caused changes in the company's cash position.

The Statement of Cash Flows The **statement of cash flows** provides a summary of the firm's cash flow and other events that caused changes in its cash position. A relatively new report, first required in 1988, it is also one of the most useful, because it shows how the company is doing in generating cash. The fact is, a company's reported earnings may bear little resemblance to its cash flow. Whereas profits are simply the difference between revenues and the accounting costs that have been charged against them, *cash flow is the amount of money a company actually takes in as a result of doing business.*

Table 7.6 presents the 2000–2001 statement of cash flows for Universal Office Furnishings. This report brings together items from *both* the balance sheet and the income statement to show how the company obtained its cash and how it used this valuable liquid resource. The statement is broken into three parts. The most important part is the first one, labeled "Cash from Operations." It captures the *net cash flow from operations*—the line highlighted on the statement. This is what is often meant by the term *cash flow,* as it represents the amount of cash generated by the company and available for investment and financing activities.

Note that Universal's 2001 cash flow from operations was over $200 million, down a bit from the year before. As it turned out, this gave the company more than enough for its investing activities ($150.9 million) and its financing activities ($35.4 million), so it's actual cash position (see the line near the bottom of the statement, labeled "Net increase (decrease) in cash") increased by some $15.8 million. That result was a big improvement over the year before, when the firm's cash position fell by more than $35 million. A high (and preferably increasing) cash flow means the company has enough money to pay dividends, service debt, and finance growth. In addition, you'd like to see the firm's cash position increase

TABLE 7.6 Statement of Cash Flows

Universal Office Furnishings, Inc.
Statements of Cash Flows
Fiscal Year Ended December 31
($ in millions)

	2001	2000
Cash from Operations		
Net earnings	$139.7	$141.8
Depreciation and amortization	77.1	62.1
Other noncash charges	5.2	16.7
Increase (decrease) in current assets	(41.7)	14.1
Increase (decrease) in current liabilities	21.8	(29.1)
Net cash flow from operations	$202.1	$205.6
Cash from Investing Activities		
Acquisitions of property, plant, and equipment—net	(150.9)	(90.6)
Net cash flow from investing activities	($150.9)	($90.6)
Cash from Financing Activities		
Proceeds from long-term borrowing	749.8	79.1
Reduction in long-term debt, including current maturities and early retirements	(728.7)	(211.1)
Net repurchase of capital stock	(47.2)	(9.8)
Payment of dividends on common stock	(9.3)	(8.5)
Net cash flow from financing activities	($35.4)	($150.3)
Net increase (decrease) in cash	**$15.8**	**($35.3)**
Cash and equivalents at beginning of period	$80.0	$115.3
Cash and equivalents at end of period	$95.8	$80.0

over time because of the positive impact that has on the company's liquidity and its ability to meet operating needs in a prompt and timely fashion.

Key Financial Ratios

To see what accounting statements really have to say about the financial condition and operating results of a firm, it is necessary to turn to *financial ratios*. Such ratios are useful because they provide a different perspective on the financial affairs of the firm—particularly with regard to the balance sheet and income statement—and thus *expand the information content of the company's financial statements*. Ratios lie at the very heart of company analysis. Indeed, company analysis as a system of information would be incomplete without this key ingredient.

ratio analysis
the study of the relationships between financial statement accounts.

Ratio analysis is the study of the relationships between various financial statement accounts. Each measure relates one item on the balance sheet (or income statement) to another, or, as is more often the case, a balance sheet account to an operating (income statement) element. In this way, the investor looks not so much at the absolute size of the financial statement accounts as at what it indicates about the liquidity, activity, or profitability of the firm.

INVESTING in action

The Ten Commandments of Financial Statement Analysis

Individuals must pass a test before obtaining a driver's license, but investors don't need to pass any type of test before trying to use financial statements as part of their investment analyses. Yet analyzing financial statements requires at least as much knowledge and skill as driving an automobile. Perhaps each financial statement should contain a warning to potential users, similar to those found on many products. As a starter, the warning might include these ten commandments:

1. **Thou shalt not use financial statements in isolation.** Instead, use them with other available information, such as data on economy-wide conditions and industry-wide conditions.
2. **Thou shalt not use financial statements as the only source of firm-specific information.** There are many other sources of information about the company. Consider, for example, financial periodicals, analysts' reports, and of course the Internet.
3. **Thou shalt not avoid reading footnotes, which are an integral part of financial statements.** Financial statements cannot be reasonably analyzed without reading and understanding the footnotes.
4. **Thou shalt not focus on a single number. Financial statements are not designed to be reduced to a single number.** Net income is not intended to be the number that summarizes all the information relevant to an investment decision. A user must analyze growth and leverage, among other factors, as well as profitability.
5. **Thou shalt not overlook the implications of what is read.** It is not sufficient simply to know that a company is a high-growth or highly leveraged firm; one must also know that such characteristics typically imply higher risk as well.
6. **Thou shalt not ignore events subsequent to the financial statements.** Financial statements are not forecasts of the future; rather, they report the financial condition of the company as of year-end. They do not capture the effects of events that occur after year-end. They thus become increasingly out of date as the year progresses.
7. **Thou shalt not overlook the limitations of financial statements.** Financial statements report only a specified set of events, not all events or all possible financial effects of a single event. Financial statements do not generally represent estimates of the market values of the reported assets and liabilities, nor do they reflect changes in the market values of those assets and liabilities.
8. **Thou shalt not use financial statements without adequate knowledge.** Investors should be sufficiently competent to read, understand, and analyze financial statements.
9. **Thou shalt not shun professional help.** If unwilling or unable to attain adequate knowledge, the investor should defer to someone who does have this ability, such as a financial analyst or a professional money manager.
10. **Thou shalt not take unnecessary risks.** If unwilling or unable to obtain professional help, the investor should undertake investments where investment risk is minimal or where analysis of financial statements is not an issue.

However, as the accompanying *Investing in Action* box suggests, to get the most from ratio analysis, you must have a good understanding of the uses and limitations of the financial statements themselves.

The most significant contribution of financial ratios is that they enable an investor to assess the firm's past and present financial condition and operating results. The mechanics of ratio analysis are actually quite simple: Selected information is obtained from annual financial statements and used to compute a set of ratios, which are then compared to historical and/or industry standards to evaluate the financial condition and operating results of the company. When historical standards are used, the company's ratios are compared and studied from one year to the next. Industry standards, in contrast, involve comparison of a particular company's ratios to those of other companies in the same line of business.

Remember, the reason we're doing all this is *to develop information about the past that can be used to get a handle on the future.* It's only from an understanding of a company's past performance that you can forecast its future with some degree of accuracy. For example, even if sales have been expanding rapidly over the past few years, you must carefully assess the reasons for the growth before naively assuming that past growth-rate trends will continue into the future. Such insights are obtained from financial ratios and financial statement analysis.

Financial ratios can be divided into five groups: (1) liquidity, (2) activity, (3) leverage, (4) profitability, and (5) common stock, or market, measures. Using the 2001 figures from the Universal financial statements (Tables 7.4 and 7.5), we will now identify and briefly discuss some of the widely used measures in each of these five categories.

liquidity measures
financial ratios concerned with a firm's ability to meet its day-to-day operating expenses and satisfy its short-term obligations as they come due.

Measuring Liquidity **Liquidity** is concerned with the firm's ability to meet its day-to-day operating expenses and satisfy its short-term obligations as they come due. Of major concern is whether a company has adequate cash and other liquid assets on hand to service its debt and operating needs in a prompt and timely fashion. A general overview of a company's liquidity can often be obtained from two simple measures: current ratio and net working capital.

Current Ratio One of the most commonly cited of all financial ratios, the current ratio is computed as follows:

Equation 7.1

$$\text{Current ratio} = \frac{\text{Current assets}}{\text{Current liabilities}}$$

In 2001, Universal Office Furnishings (UVRS) had a current ratio of

$$\text{Current ratio for Universal} = \frac{\$500.3}{\$374.0} = \underline{\underline{1.34}}$$

This figure indicates that UVRS had $1.34 in short-term resources to service every dollar of current debt. That's a fairly good number and, by most standards today, would suggest that the company has more than enough current liquidity.

Net Working Capital Though technically not a ratio, net working capital is often viewed as such. Actually, net working capital is an absolute measure of liquidity and indicates the dollar amount of equity in the working capital position of the firm. It is the difference between current assets and current liabilities. For 2001, the net working capital position for UVRS amounted to

Equation 7.2

$$\text{Net working capital} = \text{current assets} - \text{current liabilities}$$

$$\text{For Universal} = \$500.3 - \$374.0 = \underline{\underline{\$126.3 \text{ million}}}$$

A net working capital figure that exceeds $125,000,000 is indeed substantial (especially for a firm this size) and serves to reinforce our contention that the liquidity position of this firm is very solid—so long as it is not made up of slow-moving, obsolete inventories and/or past-due accounts receivable.

activity ratios
financial ratios that are used to measure how well a firm is managing its assets.

Activity Ratios Measuring general liquidity is only the beginning of the analysis. We must also assess the composition and underlying liquidity of key current assets, and evaluate how effectively the company is managing these assets. **Activity ratios** compare company sales to various asset categories in order to measure how well the company is utilizing its assets. Three of the most widely used activity ratios deal with accounts receivable, inventory, and total assets.

Accounts Receivable Turnover A glance at most financial statements will reveal that the asset side of the balance sheet is dominated by just a few accounts that make up 80% to 90%, or even more, of total resources. Certainly, this is the case with Universal Office Furnishings, where, as you can see in Table 7.4, three entries (accounts receivable, inventory, and net long-term assets) accounted for nearly 80% of total assets in 2001. Like Universal, most firms invest a significant amount of capital in accounts receivable, and for this reason they are viewed as a crucial corporate resource. Accounts receivable turnover is a measure of how these resources are being managed. It is computed as follows:

Equation 7.3

$$\text{Accounts receivable turnover} = \frac{\text{Annual sales}}{\text{Accounts receivable}}$$

$$\text{For Universal} = \frac{\$1{,}938.0}{\$227.2} = \underline{\underline{8.53}}$$

In essence, this turnover figure indicates the kind of return the company is getting from its investment in accounts receivable. Other things being equal, the higher the turnover figure, the more favorable it is. In 2001, UVRS was turning its receivables about 8½ times a year. That excellent turnover rate suggests a very strong credit and collection policy. It also means that each dollar invested in receivables was supporting, or generating, $8.53 in sales.

Inventory Turnover Another important corporate resource—and one that requires a considerable amount of management attention—is inventory. Control of inventory is important to the well-being of a company and is commonly assessed with the inventory turnover measure:

Equation 7.4

$$\text{Inventory turnover} = \frac{\text{Annual sales}}{\text{Inventory}}$$

$$\text{For Universal} = \frac{\$1{,}938.0}{\$103.7} = \underline{\underline{18.69}}$$

Again, the more sales the company can get out of its inventory, the better the return on this vital resource. In 2001, Universal was doing an outstanding job of getting the most from its inventory. A turnover of almost 19 times a year means that the firm is holding inventory for less than a month—actually, for about 20 days (365/18.69 = 19.5). That's the kind of performance you like to see. The higher the turnover figure, the less time an item spends in inventory and the better the return the company is able to earn from funds tied up in inventory.

Total Asset Turnover Total asset turnover indicates how efficiently assets are being used to support sales. It is calculated as follows:

Equation 7.5

$$\text{Total asset turnover} = \frac{\text{Annual sales}}{\text{Total assets}}$$

$$\text{For Universal} = \frac{\$1{,}938.0}{\$941.2} = \underline{\underline{2.06}}$$

Note in this case that UVRS is generating more than $2.00 in revenues from every dollar invested in assets. This is a fairly high number and is important because it has a direct bearing on corporate profitability. The principle at work here is much like the return to an individual investor: Earning $100 from a $1,000 investment is far more desirable than earning the same amount from a $2,000 investment. A high total asset turnover figure suggests that corporate resources are being well managed and that the firm is able to realize a high level of sales (and, ultimately, profits) from its asset investments.

leverage measures
financial ratios that measure the amount of debt being used to support operations and the ability of the firm to service its debt.

Leverage Measures **Leverage** looks at the firm's different types of financing, and indicates the amount of debt being used to support the resources and operations of the company. The amount of indebtedness within the financial structure and the ability of the firm to service its debt are major concerns in leverage analysis. There are two widely used leverage ratios. The first, the debt-equity ratio, measures the *amount of debt* being used by the company. The second, times interest earned, assesses how well the company can *service its debt.*

Debt-Equity Ratio The *debt-equity ratio* measures leverage, or the relative amount of funds provided by lenders and owners. It is computed as follows:

Equation 7.6

$$\text{Debt-equity ratio} = \frac{\text{Long-term debt}}{\text{Stockholders' equity}}$$

$$\text{For Universal} = \frac{\$177.8}{\$294.5} = \underline{\underline{0.60}}$$

Because highly leveraged firms (those that use large amounts of debt) run an increased risk of defaulting on their loans, this ratio is particularly helpful in assessing a stock's risk exposure. The 2001 debt-equity ratio for UVRS is reasonably low (at 60%) and shows that most of the company's capital comes from its owners. Stated another way, there was only 60 cents worth of debt in the capital structure for every dollar of equity.

Times Interest Earned *Times interest earned* is a so-called coverage ratio. It measures the ability of the firm to meet its fixed interest payments and is calculated as follows:

Equation 7.7

$$\text{Times interest earned} = \frac{\text{Earnings before interest and taxes}}{\text{Interest expense}}$$

$$\text{For Universal} = \frac{\$235.2}{\$13.4} = \underline{\underline{17.55}}$$

The ability of the company to meet its interest payments (which, with bonds, are fixed contractual obligations) in a timely and orderly fashion is an important consideration in evaluating risk exposure. Universal's times interest earned ratio indicates that the firm has about $17.50 available to cover every dollar of interest expense. That's an outstanding coverage ratio—way above average! As a rule, a ratio 8 to 9 times earnings is considered very strong, so a ratio that exceeds 17 is definitely up there. To put this number in perspective, there's usually little concern until times interest earned drops to something less than 2 or 3 times earnings.

profitability measures
financial ratios that measure a firm's returns by relating profits to sales, assets, or equity.

Measuring Profitability **Profitability** is a relative measure of success. Each of the various profitability measures relates the returns (profits) of a company to its sales, assets, or equity. There are three widely used profitability measures: net profit margin, return on assets, and return on equity.

Net Profit Margin This is the "bottom line" of operations. Net profit margin indicates the rate of profit being earned from sales and other revenues. It is computed as follows:

Equation 7.8

$$\text{Net profit margin} = \frac{\text{Net profit after taxes}}{\text{Total revenues}}$$

$$\text{For Universal} = \frac{\$139.7}{\$1{,}938.0} = \underline{\underline{7.2\%}}$$

The net profit margin looks at profits as a percent of sales (and other revenues). Because it moves with costs, it also reveals the type of control management has over the cost structure of the firm. Note that UVRS had a net profit margin of 7.2% in 2001. That is, the company's return on sales was better than 7 cents on the dollar. That may be about average for the large U.S. companies, but as we shall see, that's well above average for firms in the business equipment industry.

Return on Assets As a profitability measure, *return on assets (ROA)* looks at the amount of resources needed to support operations. Return on assets reveals management's effectiveness in generating profits from the assets it has available, and is perhaps *the single most important measure of return.* ROA is computed as follows:

Equation 7.9

$$\text{ROA} = \frac{\text{Net profit after taxes}}{\text{Total assets}}$$

$$\text{For Universal} = \frac{\$139.7}{\$941.2} = \underline{\underline{14.8\%}}$$

In the case of Universal Office Furnishings, the company earned almost 15% on its asset investments in 2001. That is a very healthy return, and, indeed, is well above average. As a rule, you'd like to see a company maintain as high an ROA as possible. The higher the ROA, the more profitable the company.

Return on Equity A measure of the overall profitability of the firm, *return on equity (ROE)* is closely followed by investors because of its direct link to the profits, growth, and dividends of the company. Return on equity—or return on investment (ROI), as it's sometimes called—measures the return to the firm's stockholders by relating profits to shareholder equity:

Equation 7.10

$$\text{ROE} = \frac{\text{Net profit after taxes}}{\text{Stockholders' equity}}$$

$$\text{For Universal} = \frac{\$139.7}{\$294.5} = \underline{\underline{47.4\%}}$$

ROE shows the annual payoff to investors, which in the case of UVRS amounts to nearly 48 cents for every dollar of equity. That, too, is an outstanding measure of performance and suggests that the company is doing what it has to do to keep its shareholders happy. Generally speaking, look for a high or increasing ROE. In contrast, watch out for a falling ROE, which could mean trouble later on.

Breaking Down ROA and ROE Both ROA and ROE are important measures of corporate profitability. But to get the most from these two measures, we have to break them down into their component parts. ROA, for example, is made up of two key components: the firm's net profit margin and its total asset turnover. Thus, rather than using Equation 7.9 to find ROA, we can use the following expanded format:

Equation 7.11

$$\text{ROA} = \text{Net profit margin} \times \text{Total asset turnover}$$

Using the net profit margin and total asset turnover figures that we computed (Equations 7.8 and 7.5, respectively), we can find Universal's 2001 ROA.

$$\text{ROA} = 7.2\% \times 2.06 = \underline{\underline{14.0\%}}$$

Note that we end up with the same figure as that found with equation 7.9. So why would you want to use the expanded version of ROA? *The major reason is that it shows you what's driving company profits.* As an investor, you want to know if ROA is moving up (or down) because of improvement (or deterioration) in the company's profit margin and/or its total asset turnover. Ideally, you'd like to see ROA moving up (or staying high) because the company does a good job of managing *both* its profits and its assets.

Just as ROA can be broken into its component parts, so too can the return on equity (ROE) measure. Actually, ROE is nothing more than an extension of ROA. It introduces the company's financing decisions into the assessment of profitability. That is, the expanded ROE measure indicates the extent to which financial leverage (or "trading on the equity") can increase return to stockholders. The use of debt in the capital structure, in effect, means that *ROE will always be greater than ROA.* The question is how much greater. Rather than using the abbreviated version of ROE in Equation 7.10, we can compute ROE as follows:

Equation 7.12

$$\text{ROE} = \text{ROA} \times \text{Equity multiplier}$$

where

$$\text{Equity multiplier} = \frac{\text{Total assets}}{\text{Total stockholders' equity}}$$

To find ROE according to Equation 7.12, we first have to find the equity multiplier.

$$\text{Equity multiplier for Universal} = \frac{\$941.2}{\$294.5} = 3.20$$

Now we can find the 2001 ROE for Universal as follows:

$$\text{ROE} = 14.8 \times 3.20 = \underline{\underline{47.3\%}}$$

Here we can see that the use of debt (the equity multiplier) has magnified—in this case, tripled—returns to stockholders. (Note that small rounding errors account for the difference between the number computed here, 47.3%, and the one computed earlier, 47.4%, when we used Equation 7.10.)

Alternatively, we can expand Equation 7.12 still further by breaking ROA in the equation *into its component parts.* In this case, we could compute ROE as

Equation 7.13

$$\begin{aligned}\text{ROE} &= \text{ROA} \times \text{Equity multiplier}\\ &= (\text{Net profit margin} \times \text{Total asset turnover}) \times \text{Equity multiplier}\end{aligned}$$

$$\text{For Universal} = 7.2\% \times 2.06 \times 3.20 = \underline{\underline{47.4\%}}$$

This expanded version of ROE is especially helpful, because it enables investors to assess the company's profitability in terms of three key components: net profit margin, total asset turnover, and financial leverage. In this way, you can determine whether ROE is moving up simply because the firm is employing more debt, which isn't necessarily beneficial, or because of the way the firm is managing its assets and operations, which certainly does have positive long-term implications. To stockholders, ROE is a critical measure of performance (and thus merits careful attention) because of the impact it has on growth and earnings—both of which, as we'll see in Chapter 8, play vital roles in the stock valuation process.

common stock (market) ratios financial ratios that convert key information about a firm to a per-share basis.

Common Stock Ratios Finally, there are a number of **common stock,** or so-called **market ratios,** that convert key bits of information about the company to a per-share basis. They tell the investor exactly what portion of total profits, dividends, and equity is allocated to each share of stock. Popular common stock ratios include earnings per share, price/earnings ratio, dividends per share, dividend yield, payout ratio, and book value per share. We examined two of these measures (earnings per share and dividend yield) in Chapter 6. Let's look now at the other four.

Price/Earnings Ratio This measure, an extension of the earnings per share ratio, is used to determine how the market is pricing the company's common stock. The price/earnings (P/E) ratio relates the company's earnings per share (EPS) to the market price of its stock.

Equation 7.14

$$P/E = \frac{\text{Market price of common stock}}{\text{EPS}}$$

To compute the P/E ratio, it is necessary first to know the stock's EPS. Using the earnings per share equation from the previous chapter, we see that the EPS for UVRS in 2001 was

$$EPS = \frac{\text{Net profit after taxes} - \text{Preferred dividends}}{\text{Number of common shares outstanding}}$$

$$\text{For Universal} = \frac{\$139.7 - \$0}{61.8} = \underline{\underline{\$2.26}}$$

In this case, the company's profits of \$139.7 million translate into earnings of \$2.26 for *each share* of outstanding common stock. Given this EPS figure and the stock's current market price (assume it is currently trading at \$41.50), we can use Equation 7.14 to determine the P/E ratio for Universal.

$$P/E = \frac{\$41.50}{\$2.26} = \underline{\underline{18.4}}$$

In effect, the stock is currently selling at a multiple of about 18 times its 2001 earnings.

Price/earnings multiples are widely quoted in the financial press and are an essential part of many stock valuation models. Other things being equal, you'd like to find stocks with *rising P/E ratios,* because higher P/E multiples usually translate into higher future stock prices and better returns to stockholders. But even though you'd like to see them going up, you also want to *watch out for P/E ratios that become too high* (relative either to the market or to what the stock has done in the past). When this multiple gets too high, it may be a signal that the stock is becoming overvalued (and may be due for a fall).

One way to assess the P/E ratio is to compare it to the company's rate of growth in earnings. The market has developed a measure of this comparison

INVESTOR FACTS

RATIOS ON THE RISE—Should you buy a stock priced at \$30 a share or one in the same industry selling for \$75 a share? Knowing price alone isn't enough. You'd also want information on P/E ratios, which can provide an indication of how the marketplace values the firm's shares. Recently the average P/E rose to about 23 times based on 2000 earnings, compared to the historical large-company U.S. stock average of about 15. The reason? Many high-tech firms are making little or no profits, and this gives them high P/Es. For example, in early January 2001, Compaq Computer, Nokia, Qualcomm, and Sun Microsystems all had P/E ratios above 80. Even nontechnology companies had high P/Es: Disney was at 67, Coca-Cola, 59, Home Depot 56, and Wal-Mart 44.

Source: Amy Baldwin, "Price-Earnings Ratio a Tricky Stock Gauge," *The Washington Times,* October 13, 2000, p. B10; Eric Tyson, "Stock Price Alone Doesn't Reflect Value," *The Washington Times,* November 3, 2000, p. B11; and Quicken.com Stock Search, **www.quicken.com/investments/stocks/search,** January 11, 2001.

PEG ratio
a financial ratio that relates a stock's price/earnings multiple to the company's rate of growth in earnings.

called the **PEG ratio.** Basically, it looks at the latest P/E relative to the 3- to 5-year rate of growth in earnings. (The earnings growth rate can be all historical—the last 3 to 5 years—or perhaps part historical and part forecasted.) The PEG ratio is computed as

Equation 7.15

$$\text{PEG ratio} = \frac{\text{Stock's P/E ratio}}{\text{3- to 5-year growth rate in earnings}}$$

Universal Office Furnishings had a P/E ratio of 18.4 times earnings in 2001. If corporate earnings for the past 5 years had been growing at an average annual rate of, say, 15%, then its PEG ratio would be

$$\text{For Universal} = \frac{18.4}{15.0} = \underline{\underline{1.21}}$$

A PEG ratio this close to 1.0 is certainly reasonable. It suggests that the company's P/E is not out of line with the earnings growth of the firm. In fact, the idea is to *look for stocks that have PEG ratios that are equal to or less than one.* In contrast, a high PEG means the stock's P/E has outpaced its growth in earnings and, if anything, the stock is probably "fully valued." Some investors, in fact, won't even look at stocks if their PEGs are too high—say, more than 1.5 or 2.0. At the minimum, PEG is probably something you would want to look at, because it is certainly not unreasonable to expect some correlation between a stock's P/E and its rate of growth in earnings.

Dividends per Share The principle here is the same as for EPS: to translate total common dividends paid by the company into a per-share figure. (*Note:* If it is not on the income statement, the amount of dividends paid to common stockholders can usually be found on the statement of cash flows—Table 7.6.) Dividends per share is measured as follows:

Equation 7.16

$$\text{Dividends per share} = \frac{\text{Annual dividends paid to common stock}}{\text{Number of common shares outstanding}}$$

$$\text{For Universal} = \frac{\$9.3}{61.8} = \underline{\underline{\$0.15}}$$

For fiscal 2001, Universal paid out dividends of $0.15 per share—at a quarterly rate of about 3¾ cents per share.

As we saw in the preceding chapter, we can also relate dividends per share to the market price of the stock to determine its dividend yield: i.e., $0.15 ÷ $41.50 = 0.4%. Clearly, you won't find Universal Office Furnishings within the income sector of the market. It pays very little in annual dividends, and thus, has a dividend yield of less than ½ of 1%.

Payout Ratio Another important dividend measure is the dividend payout ratio. It indicates how much of its earnings a company pays out to stockholders in the form of dividends. Well-managed companies try to maintain target payout ratios. If earnings are going up over time, so will its dividends. The payout ratio is calculated as follows:

Equation 7.17

$$\text{Payout ratio} = \frac{\text{Dividends per share}}{\text{Earnings per share}}$$

$$\text{For Universal} = \frac{\$0.15}{\$2.26} = \underline{\underline{0.07}}$$

For Universal in 2001, dividends accounted for about 7% of earnings. Traditionally, most companies that paid dividends tended to pay out somewhere between 40% and 60% of earnings. By that standard, Universal's payout, like its dividend yield, is quite low. However, it is becoming increasingly common for companies, particularly growth-oriented firms, to have low payouts and dividend yields. The fact is that payout ratios have been on the decline in recent years, as companies have become more tax-efficient by retaining more of their earnings or using them for other purposes. (One such purpose is buying back shares of their stock—which UVRS has been doing.) Viewed in this light, Universal's relatively low payout seems perfectly acceptable.

Although low dividend payout ratios are certainly not a cause for concern, high payout ratios may be. In particular, once the payout ratio reaches 70% to 80% of earnings, extra care should be taken. A payout ratio that high is often an indication that the company may not be able to maintain its current level of dividends. That generally means that dividends will have to be cut back to more reasonable levels. And if there's one thing the market doesn't like, it's cuts in dividends.

Book Value per Share The last common stock ratio is book value per share, a measure that deals with stockholders' equity. Actually, book value is simply another term for equity (or net worth). It represents the difference between total assets and total liabilities. And note that in this case we're defining equity as *common stockholders' equity,* which would *exclude* preferred stock. That is, *common stockholders' equity* = *total equity less preferred stocks.* (Universal has no preferred outstanding, so its total equity equals its common stockholders' equity.) Book value per share is computed as follows:

Equation 7.18

$$\text{Book value per share} = \frac{\text{Common stockholders' equity}}{\text{Number of common shares outstanding}}$$

$$\text{For Universal} = \frac{\$294.5}{61.8} = \underline{\underline{\$4.76}}$$

Presumably, a stock should sell for *more* than its book value (as Universal does). If not, it could be an indication that something is seriously wrong with the company's outlook and profitability.

A convenient way to relate the book value of a company to the market price of its stock is to compute the price-to-book-value ratio.

Equation 7.19

$$\text{Price-to-book-value} = \frac{\text{Market price of common stock}}{\text{Book value per share}}$$

$$\text{For Universal} = \frac{\$41.50}{\$4.76} = \underline{\underline{8.72}}$$

Widely used by investors, this ratio shows how aggressively the stock is being priced. Most stocks have a price-to-book-value ratio of more than 1.0—which simply indicates that the stock is selling for more than its book value. In fact, in strong bull markets, it's not uncommon to find stocks trading at four or five times their book values, or even more. Universal's price-to-book ratio of 8.7 times is definitely on the high side. That is something that you'll want to closely evaluate. It may indicate that the stock is already fully priced, or perhaps even overpriced. Or it could result from nothing more than a relatively low owners' equity ratio.

Interpreting the Numbers

Rather than compute all the financial ratios themselves, most investors rely on published reports for such information. Many large brokerage houses and a variety of financial services firms publish such reports. An example is given in Figure 7.1. These reports provide a good deal of vital information in a convenient and easy-to-read format. Best of all, they relieve investors of the chore of computing the financial ratios themselves. (Similar information is also available from a number of online services, as well as from various software providers.) Even so, you, as an investor, must be able to evaluate this published information. To do that, you need not only a basic understanding of financial ratios but also some standard of performance, or benchmark, against which you can assess trends in company performance.

Basically, two types of performance standards are used in financial statement analysis: historical and industry. With *historical standards,* various financial ratios and measures are run on the company for a period of 3 to 5 years (or longer).You would use these to assess developing trends in the company's operations and financial condition. That is, are they improving or deteriorating, and where do the company's strengths and weaknesses lie? In contrast, *industry standards* enable you to compare the financial ratios of the company with comparable firms or with the average results for the industry as a whole. Here, we focus on determining the relative strength of the firm with respect to its competitors. Using Universal Office Furnishings, we'll see how to use both of these standards of performance to evaluate and interpret financial ratios.

Using Historical and Industry Standards Look at Table 7.7. It provides a summary of historical data and average industry figures (for the latest year) for most of the ratios we have discussed. By carefully evaluating these ratios, we should be able to draw some basic conclusions about the financial condition, operating results, and general financial health of the company. By comparing the financial ratios contained in Table 7.7, we can make the following observations about UVRS:

1. Universal's *liquidity position* is a bit below average. But this doesn't seem to be a source of major concern, especially when you consider its receivables and inventory positions. That is, based on its respective turnover ratios (see item 2 below), both of these current assets seem to be very well controlled, which could explain the relatively low current ratio of this company. The current ratio is a bit below average, not because the firm has a lot of current liabilities, but because it is doing such a good job in controlling current assets.

FIGURE 7.1 **An Example of a Published Report with Financial Statistics**

This and similar reports are widely available to investors and play an important part in the security analysis process. (*Source:* Standard & Poor's *Stock Reports,* January 8, 2000.)

STANDARD & POOR'S STOCK REPORTS

Medtronic, Inc.

NYSE Symbol **MDT**

In S&P 500

08-JAN-00

Industry: Health Care (Medical Products & Supplies)

Summary: This global medical device manufacturer has leadership positions in the pacemaker, defibrillator, cardiac stent, orthopedic and other medical markets.

S&P Opinion: Hold (★★★)

Recent Price • 42¼

52 Wk Range • 44⅝-29⅞

Yield • 0.4%

12-Mo. P/E • 82.8

Quantitative Evaluations

Outlook (1 Lowest—5 Highest)
• **3−**

Fair Value
• **42¼**

Risk
• **Low**

Earn./Div. Rank
• **A**

Technical Eval.
• **Neutral** since 12/99

Rel. Strength Rank (1 Lowest—99 Highest)
• **81**

Insider Activity
• **Neutral**

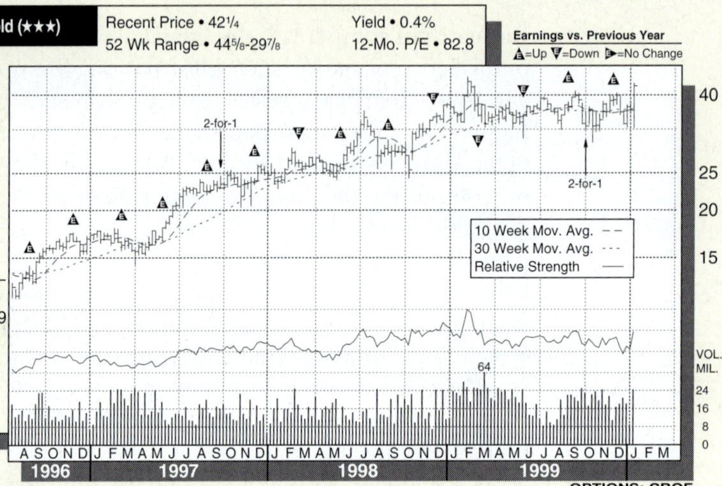

OPTIONS: CBOE

Overview - 23-DEC-99

Revenue growth of 16% is projected for FY 00 (Apr.), reØecting strong growth across the cardiac rhythm management, surgical and spinal/neurological areas. Although the vascular business suffered from difficult comparisons during the first half of the year, we expect strong growth in coming quarters, following the launch of the S670 cardiac stent both in the U.S. and in Japan. Industrywide stent pricing in the U.S. remains generally firm. Revenues in the second half of FY 00 and into FY 01 should also benefit from new product launches in the miniaturized defibrillator and abdominal aortic aneurysm markets. A favorable sales mix should push gross margins toward 74%, although SG&A line improvements could be hindered by the cost of product launches. With R&D costs equal to about 10% of sales, and assuming taxes at 33.0%, we see FY 00 operating EPS growth of about 20%, to $0.92, and look for FY 01 EPS of $1.10.

Valuation - 23-DEC-99

The shares have significantly underperformed the S&P 500 thus far in 1999, falling about 6%, versus a gain of nearly 17% for the S&P 500. Although MDT is one of the more compelling names in the medical technology sector, the health care sector is likely to remain under pressure until signs of a slowdown in earnings growth within the S&P 500, a development that could improve relative valuation measures and result in some sector rotation by investors. In addition, MDT carries an extreme valuation of 38X our FY 00 EPS estimate, nearly 7X projected sales, and 26X operating profits, all of which are far in excess of the company's projected growth rates, medical device group averages, and the P/E for the S&P 500. At recent levels, we would not add to existing positions.

Key Stock Statistics

S&P EPS Est. 2000	0.92	Tang. Bk. Value/Share	1.99
P/E on S&P Est. 2000	45.9	Beta	1.14
S&P EPS Est. 2001	1.10	Shareholders	38,000
Dividend Rate/Share	0.16	Market cap. (B)	$ 50.5
Shs. outstg. (M)	1194.4	Inst. holdings	63%
Avg. daily vol. (M)	3.804		

Value of $10,000 invested 5 years ago: $ 62,064

Fiscal Year Ending Apr. 30

	2000	1999	1998	1997	1996	1995
Revenues (Million $)						
1Q	1,105	991.7	646.3	600.9	523.8	403.8
2Q	1,161	984.5	642.1	598.1	518.5	408.1
3Q	–	1,039	631.4	598.8	529.2	413.7
4Q	–	1,119	685.0	640.5	596.1	516.7
Yr.	–	4,134	2,605	2,438	2,169	1,742
Earnings Per Share ($)						
1Q	**0.21**	**0.20**	**0.15**	**0.13**	0.11	0.07
2Q	**0.22**	**0.10**	**0.15**	**0.13**	0.11	0.08
3Q	**E0.24**	**-0.03**	**0.01**	**0.13**	0.12	0.08
4Q	**E0.25**	**0.13**	**0.17**	**0.15**	0.14	0.10
Yr.	**E0.92**	**0.40**	**0.48**	**0.55**	**0.45**	0.32

Next earnings report expected: late February

Dividend Data (Dividends have been paid since 1977.)

Amount ($)	Date Decl.	Ex-Div. Date	Stock of Record	Payment Date
0.065	Mar. 04	Apr. 07	Apr. 09	Apr. 30 '99
0.080	Jun. 24	Jun. 30	Jul. 02	Jul. 30 '99
2-for-1	Aug. 25	Sep. 27	Sep. 10	Sep. 24 '99
0.040	Oct. 28	Jan. 05	Jan. 07	Jan. 28 '00

TABLE 7.7 Comparative Historical and Industry Ratios

	Historical Figures for Universal Office Furnishings				Industry Averages for the Office Equipment Industry in 2001
	1998	1999	2000	2001	
Liquidity measures					
Current ratio	1.55	1.29	1.69	1.34	1.45
Activity measures					
Receivables turnover	9.22	8.87	9.18	8.53	5.70
Inventory turnover	15.25	17.17	16.43	18.69	7.80
Total asset turnover	1.96	2.12	2.32	2.06	0.85
Leverage measures					
Debt-equity ratio	0.70	0.79	0.91	0.60	1.58
Times interest earned	15.37	26.22	32.49	17.55	5.60
Profitability measures					
Net profit margin	6.6%	7.5%	8.0%	7.2%	4.6%
Return on assets	9.8%	16.4%	18.6%	14.8%	3.9%
Return on equity	25.9%	55.5%	67.8%	47.4%	17.3%
Common stock measures					
Earnings per share	$1.92	$2.00	$2.17	$2.26	N/A
Price/earnings ratio	16.2	13.9	15.8	18.4	16.2
Dividend yield	0.3%	0.4%	0.4%	0.4%	1.1%
Payout ratio	5.2%	5.5%	6.0%	6.6%	24.8%
Price-to-book-value ratio	7.73	10.73	9.34	8.72	3.54

2. Universal's *activity measures* are all way above average. This company consistently has very high turnover measures, which in turn make significant contributions not only to the firm's liquidity position but also to its profitability! Clearly, the company has been able to get a lot more from its assets than the industry as a whole.
3. The *leverage position* of Universal Office Furnishings seems well controlled. The company tends to use a lot less debt in its financial structure than the average firm in the office equipment industry. The payoff for this judicious use of debt comes in the form of a coverage ratio that's well above average.
4. The *profitability picture* for Universal is equally attractive. The profit margin, return on assets, and ROE all remain well above the industry norm. Clearly, the company is doing an outstanding job in managing its profits and is getting as much as it can from its sales, assets, and equity.

In summary, our analysis above shows that this firm is very well managed and highly profitable. The results of this are reflected in *common stock ratios* that are consistently equal or superior to industry averages. Universal does not pay out a lot in dividends, but that's only because it's using those valuable resources to finance its growth and to reward its investors with consistently high ROEs.

Looking at the Competition In addition to analyzing a company historically and relative to the average performance of the industry, it's also useful to evaluate the firm relative to two or three of its major competitors. A lot can be

TABLE 7.8 Comparative Financial Statistics: Universal Office Furnishings and Its Major Competitors
(All Figures are for year-end 2001 or for the 5-year period ended in 2001; $ in millions)

Financial Measure	Universal Office Industries	Cascade Industries	Colwyn Furniture	High Design, Inc.
Total assets	$ 941.2	$ 906.7	$342.7	$3,037.6
Long-term debt	$ 177.8	$ 124.2	$ 73.9	$ 257.8
Stockholders' equity	$ 294.5	$ 501.3	$183.9	$1,562.2
Stockholders' equity as a % of total assets	31.3%	55.3%	53.7%	51.4%
Total revenues	$1,938.0	$1,789.3	$642.2	$3,316.1
Net earnings	$ 139.7	$ 87.4	$ 38.5	$ 184.2
Net profit margin	7.2%	4.9%	6.0%	5.5%
5-year growth rates in:				
Total assets	14.36%	19.44%	17.25%	17.73%
Total revenues	18.84%	17.76%	15.91%	15.84%
EPS	56.75%	38.90%	21.10%	24.66%
Dividends	1.48%	11.12%	N/A	12.02%
Total asset turnover	2.06×	1.97×	1.88×	1.09×
Debt-equity ratio	0.60	0.43	1.46	0.17
Times interest earned	17.55×	13.38×	8.35×	14.36×
ROA	14.8%	9.5%	6.7%	6.7%
ROE	47.4%	18.8%	21.8%	13.0%
P/E ratio	18.4×	14.4×	13.3×	12.4×
PEG ratio	1.21	2.42	1.98	1.09
Payout ratio	6.6%	26.2%	N/A	32.4%
Dividend yield	0.4%	1.8%	N/A	2.6%
Price-to-book-value ratio	8.72	2.71	2.93	1.59

gained from seeing how a company stacks up against its competitors and by determining whether it is, in fact, well positioned to take advantage of unfolding developments. Table 7.8 offers an array of comparative financial statistics for Universal and three of its major competitors. One is about the same size (Cascade Industries), one is much smaller (Colwyn Furniture), and one is much larger (High Design, Inc.). (This type of firm-specific data can generally be obtained from industry surveys similar to those put out by S&P and others—or, again, from the Internet or from various software providers.)

As the data in Table 7.8 show, Universal can hold its own against other leading producers in the industry. Indeed, in virtually every category, Universal's numbers are about equal or superior to those of its three major competitors. It may not be the biggest (or the smallest), but it outperforms them all in profit margins and growth rates (in revenues and earnings). Equally important, it has the highest asset turnover, ROE, and price/earnings ratio. Tables 7.7 and 7.8 clearly show that Universal Office Furnishings is a solid, up-and-coming business that's been able to make a name for itself in a highly competitive industry. The company has done well in the past and appears to be well managed today. Our major concern at this point (and the topic of the first part of Chapter 8) is whether Universal can continue to produce above-average returns to investors.

Summary

LG 1 **Discuss the security analysis process, including its goals and functions.** Success in buying common stocks is largely a matter of careful security selection and investment timing. Security analysis helps the investor make the selection decision by gauging the intrinsic value (underlying worth) of a stock.

LG 2 **Appreciate the purpose and contributions of economic analysis.** Economic analysis evaluates the general state of the economy and its potential effects on security returns. Its purpose is to characterize the future economic environment the investor is likely to face, and is used to set the tone for the security analysis process.

LG 3 **Describe industry analysis and note how it is used.** In industry analysis, the investor focuses on the activities of one or more industries. Especially important are how the competitive position of a particular industry stacks up against others and which companies within an industry hold special promise.

LG 4 **Demonstrate a basic understanding of fundamental analysis and why it is used.** Fundamental analysis looks closely at the financial and operating characteristics of the company—at its competitive position, its sales and profit margins, its asset mix, its capital structure, and, eventually, its future prospects. A key aspect of this analytical process is company analysis, which involves an in-depth study of the financial conditions and operating results of the company.

LG 5 **Calculate a variety of financial ratios and describe how financial statement analysis is used to gauge the financial vitality of a company.** The company's balance sheet, income statement, and statement of cash flows are all used in company analysis. An essential part of this analysis is financial ratios, which expand the perspective and information content of financial statements. There are five broad categories of financial ratios—liquidity, activity, leverage, profitability, and market (common stock) ratios. All involve the study of relationships between financial statement accounts.

LG 6 **Use various financial measures to assess a company's performance, and explain how the insights derived form the basic input for the valuation process.** In order to evaluate financial ratios properly, it is necessary to base the analysis on historical and industry standards of performance. Historical standards are used to assess developing trends in the company. Industry benchmarks enable the investor to see how the firm stacks up against competitors.

CHAPTER 8

STOCK VALUATION AND INVESTMENT DECISIONS

Learning Goals

After studying this chapter, you should be able to:

LG 1 Explain the role that a company's future plays in the stock valuation process and develop a forecast of a stock's expected cash flow.

LG 2 Discuss the concepts of intrinsic value and required rates of return, and note how they are used.

LG 3 Determine the underlying value of a stock using the dividend valuation model, as well as other present value– and price/earnings–based stock valuation models.

LG 4 Gain a basic appreciation of the procedures used to value different types of stocks, from traditional dividend-paying shares to new-economy stocks with their extreme price/earnings ratios.

LG 5 Describe the key attributes of technical analysis, including some popular measures and procedures used to assess the market.

LG 6 Discuss the idea of random walks and efficient markets and note the challenges these theories hold for the stock valuation process.

Tech stocks have been at the forefront of stock market news the past few years. Often this sector, rather than blue-chip industrials, drives the market—both up and down. Take Qualcomm, for example; a company that is a leading developer and supplier of digital wireless communications products and services. It pioneered Code Division Multiple Access (CDMA) technology, a standard for the wireless communications industry. Investors in Qualcomm stock have experienced a roller coaster ride recently. The firm's 1999 stock price started at $6.48 and soared steadily upward to end the year when it hits $176.13—*after* splitting 2-for-1 in May and 4-for-1 in December. This represents an annual return of over 2,600%, the year's best. The following year was another matter, however. Fears of slowing growth sent the stock price into free-fall: It plummeted from $163.25 to $51.50, before rebounding to $82.19 at year end, for a −53% return. Even after the decline, the stock was still trading at a price/earnings ratio of about 85 in early January 2001, a substantial premium over the average P/E of 29 for the S&P 500.

Despite Qualcomm's fluctuating stock price, investors looked with favor on the company's earnings growth—94% from 1997 through 2000, which far outstripped the S&P 500's 14%. The company consistently met or exceeded quarterly earnings estimates, and analysts project continued earnings growth to $1.26 per share in 2001, an increase of 48% over 2000.

What do all these numbers mean in terms of the value of Qualcomm's stock? This chapter explains how to determine a stock's intrinsic value by using dividend valuation, dividend-and-earnings, price/earnings, and other models. We also look at how to value technology stocks. Finally, we'll review the use of technical analysis as a way to assess the state of the market in general.

Sources: Adrienne Carter, "The Big Score," *Money Technology 2000*, October 15, 2000, p.60; "Morningstar Quicktake Report—Qualcomm" *Morningstar.com*, downloaded from www.morningstar.com, January 15, 2001; and Qualcomm Web site, www.qualcomm.com

Valuation: Obtaining a Standard of Performance

LG 1 LG 2

stock valuation
the process by which the underlying value of a stock is established on the basis of its forecasted risk and return performance.

Obtaining a standard of performance that can be used to judge the investment merits of a share of stock is the underlying purpose of **stock valuation.** A stock's intrinsic value provides such a standard because it indicates the future risk and return performance of a security. The question of whether and to what extent a stock is under- or overvalued is resolved by comparing its current market price to its intrinsic value. At any given point in time, the price of a share of common stock depends on investor expectations about the future behavior of the security. If the outlook for the company and its stock is good, the price will probably be bid up. If conditions deteriorate, the price of the stock will probably go down. Let's look now at the single most important issue in the stock valuation process: *the future.*

Valuing a Company and Its Future

Thus far, we have examined several aspects of security analysis: economic and industry analysis, and the historical (company) phase of fundamental analysis. It should be clear, however, that it's *not the past* that's important but *the future.* The primary reason for looking at past performance is to gain insight about the future direction of the firm and its profitability. Granted, past performance provides no guarantees about future returns, but it can give us a good idea of a company's strengths and weaknesses. For example, it can tell us how well the company's products have done in the marketplace, how the company's fiscal health shapes up, and how management tends to respond to difficult situations. In short, the past can reveal how well the company is positioned to take advantage of the things that may occur in the future.

Because *the value of a stock is a function of its future returns,* the investor's task is to use available historical data to project key financial variables into the future. In this way, you can assess the future prospects of the company and the expected returns from its stock. We are especially interested in dividends and price behavior.

Forecasted Sales and Profits The key to our forecast is, of course, the future behavior of the *company* and the most important aspects to consider in this regard are the outlook for sales and the trend in the net profit margin. One way to develop a sales forecast is to assume that the company will continue to perform as it has in the past and simply extend the historical trend. For example, if a firm's sales have been growing at the rate of 10% per year, then assume they will continue at that rate. Of course, if there is some evidence about the economy, industry, or company that suggests a faster or slower rate of growth, the forecast should be adjusted accordingly. More often than not, this "naive" approach will be about as effective as more complex techniques.

Once the sales forecast has been generated, we can shift our attention to the net profit margin. We want to know what kind of return on sales to expect. A naive estimate can be obtained by simply using the average profit margin that has prevailed for the past few years. Again, it should be adjusted to account for any unusual industry or company developments. For most individual investors, valuable insight about future revenues and earnings can be obtained from industry or company reports put out by brokerage houses, advisory services (e.g., *Value Line*), the financial media (e.g., *Forbes*), and from

INVESTOR FACTS

BLIND SPOT—As optical networking companies caught investors' attention, their market value soared. In September 2000, this hype drove the value of JDS Uniphase to $96 billion, which made it the 36th most highly valued company in the world. Investors apparently turned a blind eye to the company's financial results for the fiscal year ended June 30, 2000: Its revenues were $1.4 billion and its losses $905 million. For about the same total market capitalization, you could theoretically buy all 11 of the following major companies—the New York Times, Saks Fifth Avenue, Georgia Pacific, T. Rowe Price, Delta Airlines, Tiffany & Co., Bear Stearns, FedEx, CVS, Gap, and John Hancock—with aggregate revenues of $115 billion and $6.4 billion in profits!

Source: Jon Birger, Pablo Galarza, Laura Lallos, and Jeanne Lee, "Best Stocks & Funds: Invest the Smart Way to Buy Tech," *Money/Tech 2000,* October 15, 2000, pp. 65–66.

HOTLINKS

For help researching a company, see the following sites. At the ClearStation site, enter a stock symbol and click on [Get Graphs].

www.askresearch.com
www.clearstation.com

various investor Web sites. Or, as the accompanying *Investing in Action* box explains, you might even want to take a look at so-called "whisper forecasts" as a way to get a handle on earnings estimates.

Given a satisfactory sales forecast and estimate of the future net profit margin, we can combine these two pieces of information to arrive at future earnings.

Equation 8.1

$$\text{Future after-tax earnings in year } t = \text{Estimated sales for year } t \times \text{Net profit margin expected in year } t$$

The "year *t*" notation in this equation simply denotes a given calendar or fiscal year in the future. It can be next year, the year after that, or any other year in which we are interested. Let's say that in the year just completed, a company reported sales of \$100 million, we estimate that revenues will grow at an 8% annual rate, and the net profit margin should be about 6%. Thus estimated sales next year will equal \$108 million (\$100 million × 1.08). And, with a 6% profit margin, we should expect to see earnings next year of

$$\text{Future after-tax earnings next year} = \$108 \text{ million} \times 0.06 = \underline{\underline{\$6.5 \text{ million}}}$$

Using this same process, we would then estimate sales and earnings *for all other years* in our forecast period.

Forecasted Dividends and Prices At this point we have an idea of the future earnings performance of the company. We are now ready to evaluate the effects of this performance on returns to common stock investors. Given a corporate earnings forecast, we need three additional pieces of information:

- An estimate of future dividend payout ratios.
- The number of common shares that will be outstanding over the forecast period.
- A future price/earnings (P/E) ratio.

For the first two, unless we have evidence to the contrary, we can simply project the firm's recent experience into the future. Payout ratios are usually fairly stable, so there is little risk in using a recent average figure. (Or, if a company follows a fixed-dividend policy, we could use the latest dividend rate in our forecast.) It is also generally safe to assume that the number of common shares outstanding will hold at the latest level or perhaps change at some moderate rate of increase (or decrease) that's reflective of the past.

Getting a Handle on the P/E Ratio The only really thorny issue in this whole process is coming up with an estimate of the future P/E ratio—a figure that has considerable bearing on the stock's future price behavior. Generally speaking, the P/E ratio is a function of several variables, including:

1. The growth rate in earnings.
2. The general state of the market.
3. The amount of debt in a company's capital structure.

INVESTING in action

I've Got a Secret: Whisper Forecasts

As a fiscal quarter ends, investors rush to compare companies' actual reported earnings with consensus (average) security analysts' estimates published by firms such as First Call, Zacks, and I/B/E/S. If a company falls below the analysts' figure by even a penny or two, its stock price can tumble 30% or more in one day. In fact, *Kiplinger's* magazine considers this comparison perhaps the most important factor driving share price performance over the short term, and it affects longer-term performance as well.

Now investors have another set of earnings forecasts to follow. "Whisper forecasts" are unofficial earnings estimates that circulate among traders and investors. They are rumors rather than "official" (analysts') estimates. Whisper numbers tend to be higher than analysts' forecasts, and some market watchers believe they are the analysts' *real* earnings estimates.

Until recently, only the wealthiest individual and institutional investors had access to the super-secret analysts' forecasts. Now whisper numbers are widely available on the Internet. Data come from varied sources: from discussions with stockbrokers, from financial analysts, from investor relations departments, and from investors themselves. For example, Whisper Number (www.whispernumber.com), founded in 1998, combines information from investor forums with polling and daily computer searches of hundreds of thousands of sources, including message boards on Yahoo!, Silicon Investor, Motley Fool, Raging Bull, and America Online. Other Web sites dedicated to these unofficial earnings reports include Earnings Whispers (www.earningswhispers.com), Just Whispers (www.justwhispers.com), and The Whisper Numbers (www.thewhispernumbers.com). Each site claims to have the "real" whisper numbers. (The "Frequently Asked Questions" pages at these sites describe how each compiles its whisper earnings.)

How valid are whisper earnings? Whisper Numbers claims that about 74% of the time, a company that beats the whisper number will see its stock rise within 5 days of its earnings announcement, and those that fail to reach their whisper numbers will see their stock values decline.

A formal study by professors at Purdue and Indiana Universities compared average whisper forecasts and consensus analysts' estimates (from First Call) for 127 mostly high-tech firms from January 1995 to May 1997. The study treated all whispers equally, making no judgments of the poster's credibility. In addition, they used whisper forecasts in several trading strategies. The results showed that whisper forecasts tended to be more accurate than analysts' estimates and also provided information not included in analysts' forecasts. Because whisper forecasts are distributed widely, part of this information is reflected in stock prices before the actual earnings reports. Proponents of whisper forecasts claim that these forecasts also counteract the pessimistic bias of analysts, which derives from corporate pressure to keep estimates low so that positive earnings surprises will be more common than disappointments.

Not everyone believes in whisper forecasts. Some in the industry criticize whisper numbers as rumors, unsubstantiated speculation, or idle gossip from unknown sources that lack accountability. Many observers question the ethics of the practice. Company insiders or short sellers, for example, could plant high numbers to manipulate prices. For this reason, you should use whisper forecasts only in combination with other securities analysis techniques and tools.

Sources: Mark Bagnoli, Messod Daniel Beneish, and Susan G. Watts, "Earnings Expectations: How Important Are the Whispers?" *AAII Journal*, June 2000, pp. 11–14; Just Whispers Web site, www.justwhispers.com; Lynnette Khalfani, "Psst! Get the Scoop on Whisper Numbers," *Wall Street Journal*, January 12, 2001, p. C1; Manual Schiffros, "The Earnings Game," *Kiplinger's*, April 2000, pp. 60–62; and Whisper Numbers Web site, www.whispernumbers.com

4. The current and projected rate of inflation.
5. The level of dividends.

As a rule, higher P/E ratios can be expected with higher rates of growth in earnings, an optimistic market outlook, and lower debt levels (less debt means less financial risk).

The link between the inflation rate and P/E multiples is a bit more complex. Generally speaking, as inflation rates rise, so do bond interest rates. This, in turn, causes required returns on stocks to rise (in order for stock returns to remain competitive with bond returns) and higher required returns on stocks mean lower stock prices and lower P/E multiples. On the other hand, declining inflation (and interest) rates normally translate into higher P/E ratios and stock prices. We can also argue that a high P/E ratio should be expected with high dividend payouts. In practice, however, most companies with high P/E ratios have *low dividend payouts*. The reason: Earnings growth tends to be more valuable than dividends, especially in companies with high rates of return on equity.

A useful starting point for evaluating the P/E ratio is the *average market multiple,* which is simply the average P/E ratio of stocks in the marketplace. The average market multiple indicates the general state of the market. It gives us an idea of how aggressively the market, in general, is pricing stocks. Other things being equal, the higher the P/E ratio, the more optimistic the market. Table 8.1 lists S&P price/earnings multiples for the past 30 years. It shows that market multiples tend to move over a fairly wide range.

relative P/E multiple
a measure of how a stock's P/E behaves relative to the average market multiple.

With the market multiple as a benchmark, you can evaluate a stock's P/E performance relative to the market. That is, you can calculate a **relative P/E multiple** by dividing a stock's P/E by the market multiple. For example, if a stock currently has a P/E of 35 and the market multiple is 25, the stock's relative P/E is 35/25 = 1.40. Looking at the relative P/E, you can quickly get a feel for how aggressively the stock has been priced in the market and what kind of relative P/E is normal for the stock. Other things being equal, a high relative P/E is desirable. The higher this measure, the higher the stock will be priced in the market. But watch out for the downside: High relative P/E multiples can also mean lots of price volatility. (Similarly, we can use average *industry* multiples to get a feel for the kind of P/E multiples that are standard for a given industry. We can then use that information, along with market multiples, to assess or project the P/E for a particular stock.)

Now we can generate a forecast of what the stock's *future* P/E will be over the anticipated *investment horizon* (the period of time over which we expect to hold the stock). For example, with the existing P/E multiple as a base, an *increase* might be justified if you believe the *market multiple* will increase (as the market tone becomes more bullish), and the *relative P/E* is likely to increase also.

Estimating Earnings per Share So far we've been able to come up with an estimate for the dividend payout ratio, the number of shares outstanding, and the price/earnings multiple. We're now ready to forecast the stock's future earnings per share (EPS), which can be done as follows:

Equation 8.2

$$\text{Estimated EPS in year } t = \frac{\text{Future after-tax earnings in year } t}{\text{Number of shares of common stock outstanding in year } t}$$

TABLE 8.1 Average Market P/E Multiples 1971–2000

Year	Market Multiples (Average S&P P/E Ratio)	Year	Market Multiples (Average S&P P/E Ratio)
1971	18.3	1986	16.3
1972	19.1	1987	15.1
1973	12.2	1988	12.2
1974	7.3	1989	15.1
1975	11.7	1990	15.5
1976	11.0	1991	26.2
1977	8.8	1992	22.8
1978	8.3	1993	21.3
1979	7.4	1994	17.0
1980	9.1	1995	17.4
1981	8.1	1996	20.7
1982	10.2	1997	23.9
1983	12.4	1998	32.3
1984	10.0	1999	33.4
1985	13.7	2000	28.5*

**Note:* By May 2001, the average P/E ratio on the S&P 500 was down to about 23 times earnings.

Source: Average year-end multiples derived from various sources, including Standard & Poor's *Index of 500 Stocks* and its *Statistical Service—Security Price Index Record.* Listed P/Es are all year-end (December) figures, except 2000, which is as of end of the third quarter.

Equation 8.2 simply converts aggregate or total corporate earnings to a per-share basis, by relating company (forecasted) profits to the expected number of shares outstanding. Though this approach works quite effectively, some investors would rather bypass the projection of aggregate sales and earnings and instead, *concentrate on earnings from a per-share basis right from the start.* That can be done by looking at the major forces that drive earnings per share: ROE and book value. Quite simply, by employing these two variables, we can define earnings per share as follows:

Equation 8.3

$$\text{EPS} = \text{ROE} \times \text{Book value per share}$$

This formula will produce the same results as the standard EPS equation shown first in Chapter 6 (Equation 6.1) and then again in Chapter 7. The major advantage of this form of the equation is that it allows you to assess the extent to which EPS is influenced by the company's book value and (especially) its ROE. As we saw in the previous chapter, ROE is a key financial measure, because it captures the amount of success the firm is having in managing its assets, operations, and capital structure. And as we see here, ROE not only is important in defining overall corporate profitability but it also plays a crucial role in defining a stock's EPS.

To produce an estimated EPS using Equation 8.3, you would go directly to the two basic components of the formula and try to get a handle on their future behavior. In particular, what kind of growth is expected in the firm's book value per share, *and* what's likely to happen to the company's ROE? In the vast majority of cases, ROE is really the driving force, so it's important to produce a good estimate of that variable. Investors often do that by breaking ROE into its component parts—margin, turnover, and the equity multiplier (see Equation 7.13 in Chapter 7).

Once you have projected ROE and book value per share, you can plug these figures into Equation 8.3 to produce estimated EPS. The bottom line is that, one way or another (using the approach reflected in Equation 8.2 or that in Equation 8.3), you have to arrive at a forecasted EPS number that you are comfortable with. When that's been done, it's a pretty simple matter to use the forecasted payout ratio to estimate dividends per share:

Equation 8.4

$$\begin{matrix}\text{Estimated dividends}\\ \text{per share in year } t\end{matrix} = \begin{matrix}\text{Estimated EPS}\\ \text{in year } t\end{matrix} \times \begin{matrix}\text{Estimated}\\ \text{payout ratio}\end{matrix}$$

The last item is the future price of the stock, which can be determined as

Equation 8.5

$$\begin{matrix}\text{Estimated share price}\\ \text{at end of year } t\end{matrix} = \begin{matrix}\text{Estimated EPS}\\ \text{in year } t\end{matrix} \times \begin{matrix}\text{Estimated P/E}\\ \text{ratio}\end{matrix}$$

Pulling It All Together We've seen the various components that go into our estimates of future dividends and share prices. Now, to see how they all fit together, let's continue with the example we started above. Using the aggregate sales and earnings approach, if the company had 2 million shares of common stock outstanding and that number was expected to hold in the future, then given the estimated earnings of \$6.5 million that we computed earlier, the firm should generate earnings per share (EPS) next year of

$$\begin{matrix}\text{Estimated EPS}\\ \text{next year}\end{matrix} = \frac{\$6.5 \text{ million}}{2 \text{ million}} = \underline{\underline{\$3.25}}$$

This result, of course, would be equivalent to the firm having a projected ROE of, say, 15% and an estimated book value per share of \$21.67. According to Equation 8.3, those conditions would also produce an estimated EPS of \$3.25 (i.e., 0.15 × \$21.67). Using this EPS figure, along with an estimated payout ratio of 40%, we see that dividends per share next year should equal

$$\begin{matrix}\text{Estimated dividends}\\ \text{per share next year}\end{matrix} = \$3.25 \times .40 = \underline{\underline{\$1.30}}$$

If the firm adheres to a *fixed-dividend policy,* this estimate may have to be adjusted to reflect the level of dividends being paid. For example, if the company has been paying annual dividends at the rate of \$1.25 per share *and is expected to continue doing so for the near future,* then you would adjust estimated dividends accordingly (i.e., use \$1.25/share). Finally, if it has been estimated that the stock should sell at 17.5 times earnings, then a share of stock in this company should be trading at a price of about \$56.90 by the *end* of next year.

$$\begin{matrix}\text{Estimated share price}\\ \text{at the end of next year}\end{matrix} = \$3.25 \times 17.5 = \underline{\underline{\$56.88}}$$

Actually, we are interested in the price of the stock at the end of our anticipated investment horizon. Thus the \$56.90 figure would be appropriate if we had a 1-year horizon. However, if we had a 3-year holding period, we would have to extend the EPS figure for 2 more years and repeat our calculations with the new data. As we shall see, *the estimated share price is important because it has embedded in it the capital gains portion of the stock's total return.*

Developing an Estimate of Future Behavior

Using information obtained from Universal Office Furnishings (**UVRS**), we can illustrate the forecasting procedures we discussed above. Recall from Chapter 7 that an assessment of the economy and the office equipment industry was positive and that the company's operating results and financial condition looked strong, both historically and relative to industry standards. Because everything looks favorable for Universal, we decide to take a look at the future prospects of the company and its stock. Assume we have chosen a 3-year investment horizon, because we believe (from earlier studies of economic and industry factors) that the economy and the market for office equipment stocks will start running out of steam near the end of 2004 or early 2005.

Table 8.2 provides selected historical financial data for the company. They cover a 5-year period (ending with the latest fiscal year) and will provide the basis for much of our forecast. The data reveal that, with one or two exceptions, the company has performed at a fairly steady pace and has been able to maintain a very attractive rate of growth. Our economic analysis suggests that the economy is about to pick up, and our research (from Chapter 7) indicates that the industry and company are well situated to take advantage of the upswing. Therefore, we conclude that the rate of growth in sales should pick up dramatically from the abnormally low level of 2001, attaining a growth rate of over 20% in 2002—more in line with the firm's 5-year average. After a modest amount of pent-up demand is worked off, the rate of growth in sales should drop to about 19% in 2003 and to 15% in 2004.

The essential elements of the financial forecast for 2002–2004 are provided in Table 8.3. Highlights of the key assumptions and the reasoning behind them follow.

- *Net profit margin.* Various published industry and company reports suggest a comfortable improvement in earnings, so we decide to use a profit margin of 8.0% in 2002 (up a bit from the latest margin of 7.2% recorded in 2001). We're projecting even better profit margins (8.5%) in 2003 and 2004, as some cost improvements start to take hold.

TABLE 8.2 Selected Historical Financial Data, Universal Office Furnishings

	1997	1998	1999	2000	2001
Total assets (millions)	$554.2	$694.9	$755.6	$761.5	$941.2
Total asset turnover	1.72×	1.85×	1.98×	2.32×	2.06×
Net sales (millions)	$953.2	$1,283.9	$1,495.9	$1,766.2	$1,938.0
Annual rate of growth in sales*	11.5%	34.7%	16.5%	18.1%	9.7%
Net profit margin	4.2%	3.6%	5.0%	8.0%	7.2%
Payout ratio	6.8%	5.6%	5.8%	6.0%	6.6%
Price/earnings ratio	13.5×	21.7×	14.9×	15.7×	18.4×
Number of common shares outstanding (millions)	77.7	78.0	72.8	65.3	61.8

*Annual rate of growth in sales = Change in sales from one year to the next ÷ Level of sales in the base (or earliest) years. For 1998, the annual rate of growth in sales equaled 34.7% = (1998 sales − 1997 sales)/1997 sales = ($1,283.9 − $953.2)/$953.2 = 0.3467.

TABLE 8.3 Summary Forecast Statistics, Universal Office Furnishings

	Latest Actual Figures (Fiscal 2001)	Average for the Past 5 Years (1997–2001)	Forecasted Figures 2002	2003	2004
Annual rate of growth in sales	9.7%	18.1%	22%	19%	15%
Net sales (millions)	$1,938.0	N/A*	$2,364.4**	$2,813.6**	$3,235.6**
× Net profit margin	7.2%	5.6%	8.0%	8.5%	8.5%
= Net after-tax earnings (millions)	$139.7	N/A	$189.2	$239.2	$275.0
÷ Common shares outstanding (millions)	61.8	71.1	61.5	60.5	59.0
= Earnings per share	$ 2.26	N/A	$ 3.08	$ 3.95	$ 4.66
× Payout ratio	6.6%	6.2%	6.0%	6.0%	6.0%
= Dividends per share	$ 0.15	$0.08	$ 0.18	$ 0.24	$ 0.28
Earnings per share	$ 2.26	N/A	$ 3.08	$ 3.95	$ 4.66
× P/E ratio	18.4	16.8	20	19	20
= Share price at year end	$ 41.58	N/A	$ 61.60	$ 75.00	$ 93.20

*N/A: Not applicable.
**Forecasted sales figures: Sales from *preceding* year × Growth rate in sales = Growth in sales; then Growth in sales + Sales from preceding year = Forecast sales for the year. For example, for 2002: $1,938.0 × 0.22 = $426.4 + $1938.0 = $2,364.4.

- *Common shares outstanding.* We believe the company will continue to pursue its share buyback program, but at a substantially lower pace than in the 1998–2001 period. From a current level of 61.8 million shares, we project that the number of shares outstanding will drop to 61.5 million in 2002, to 60.5 million in 2003, and to 59.5 million in 2004.
- *Payout ratio.* We assume that the dividend payout ratio will hold at a steady 6% of earnings, as it has for most of the recent past.
- *P/E ratio.* Primarily on the basis of expectations for improved growth in revenues and earnings, we are projecting a P/E multiple that will rise from its present level of 18½ times earnings to roughly 20 times earnings in 2002. Although this is a fairly conservative increase in the P/E, when it is coupled with the hefty growth in EPS, the net effect will be a big jump in the projected price of Universal stock.

Table 8.3 also shows the sequence involved in arriving at forecasted dividends and price behavior:

1. The company dimensions of the forecast are handled first. These include sales and revenue estimates, net profit margins, net earnings, and the number of shares of common stock outstanding. Note that after-tax earnings are derived according to the procedure described earlier in this chapter.
2. Next we estimate earnings per share, following the procedures established earlier.
3. The bottom line of the forecast is, of course, the returns in the form of dividends and capital gains expected from a share of Universal stock, given that the assumptions about net sales, profit margins, earnings per

share, and so forth hold up. We see in Table 8.3 that dividends should go up to 28 cents a share, which is a big jump. Even so, with annual dividends of a little over a quarter a share, it's clear that dividends still won't account for much of the stock's return. In fact, the dividend yield in 2004 is projected to *fall* to just 3/10 of 1%. The returns from this stock are going to come from capital gains, not dividends. That's clear when you look at year-end share prices, which are expected to more than double over the next 3 years. That is, if our projections are valid, the price of a share of stock should rise from around $41.50 to over $93.00 by year-end 2004.

We now have an idea of what the future cash flows of the investment are likely to be. We now can establish an intrinsic value for Universal Office Furnishings stock.

The Valuation Process

valuation
process by which an investor uses risk and return concepts to determine the worth of a security.

Valuation is a process by which an investor determines the worth of a security using the risk and return concepts introduced in Chapter 5. This process can be applied to any asset that produces a stream of cash flow—a share of stock, a bond, a piece of real estate, or an oil well. To establish the value of an asset, the investor must determine certain key inputs, including the amount of future cash flows, the timing of these cash flows, and the rate of return required on the investment.

In terms of common stock, the essence of valuation is to determine what the stock *ought to be worth*, given estimated returns to stockholders (future dividends and price behavior) and the amount of potential risk exposure. Toward this end, we employ various types of stock valuation models, the end product of which represents the elusive intrinsic value we have been seeking. That is, the stock valuation models determine either an *expected rate of return* or the *intrinsic worth of a share of stock*, which in effect represents the stock's "justified price." In this way, we obtain a standard of performance, based on future stock behavior, that can be used to judge the investment merits of a particular security.

Either of two conditions would make us consider a stock a worthwhile investment candidate: (1) if the computed rate of return equals or exceeds the yield we feel is warranted, or (2) if the justified price (intrinsic worth) is equal to or greater than the current market price. Note especially that a security is considered acceptable even if its yield simply *equals* the required rate of return or if its intrinsic value simply *equals* the current market price of the stock. There is nothing irrational about such behavior. In either case, the security meets your minimum standards to the extent that it is giving you the rate of return you wanted.

HOTLINKS
For a valuation example, see
www.stocksense.com/valuation.html

However, remember this about the valuation process: Even though valuation plays an important part in the investment process, there is *absolutely no assurance* that the actual outcome will be even remotely similar to the forecasted behavior. The stock is still subject to economic, industry, company, and market risks, any one of which could negate *all* your assumptions about the future. Security analysis and stock valuation models are used not to guarantee success but to help you better understand the return and risk dimensions of a proposed transaction.

required rate of return
the return necessary to compensate an investor for the risk involved in an investment.

Required Rate of Return One of the key elements in the stock valuation process is the **required rate of return.** Generally speaking, the amount of return required by an investor should be related to the level of risk that must be assumed in order to generate that return. In essence, the required return establishes a level of compensation compatible with the amount of risk involved. Such a standard helps you determine whether the expected return on a stock (or any other security) is satisfactory. Because you don't know for sure what the cash flow of an investment will be, you should expect to earn a rate of return that reflects this uncertainty. Thus the greater the perceived risk, the more you should expect to earn. As we saw in Chapter 5, this is basically the notion behind the *capital asset pricing model* (CAPM).

Recall that using the CAPM, we define a stock's required return as

Equation 8.6

$$\text{Required rate of return} = \text{Risk-free rate} + \left[\text{Stock's beta} \times \left(\text{Market return} - \text{Risk-free rate}\right)\right]$$

The required inputs for this equation are readily available: You can obtain a stock's beta from *Value Line* or S&P's *Stock Reports* (or from just about any of the many Internet sites, such **as Quicken.com, MSN MoneyCentral,** or **Morningstar.com**). The risk-free rate is basically the average return on Treasury bills for the past year or so. And a good proxy for the market return is the average stock returns over the past 10 to 15 years (like the data reported in Table 6.1).

In the CAPM, the risk of a stock is captured by its beta. For that reason, the required return on a stock increases (or decreases) with increases (or decreases) in its beta. As an illustration of the CAPM at work, consider Universal's stock, which has a beta of 1.30. Given that the risk-free rate is 5.5% and the expected market return is, say, 15%, this stock would have a required return of

$$\text{Required return} = 5.5\% + [1.30 \times (15.0\% - 5.5\%)] = \underline{\underline{17.85\%}}$$

This return—let's round it to 18%—can now be used in a stock valuation model to assess the investment merits of a share of stock.

As an alternative, or perhaps even in conjunction with the CAPM, you could take a more subjective approach to finding required return. For example, if your assessment of the historical performance of the company had uncovered some volatility in sales and earnings, you could conclude that the stock is subject to a good deal of business risk. Also important is market risk, as measured by a stock's beta. A valuable reference point in arriving at a measure of risk is the rate of return available on less risky but competitive investment vehicles. For example, you could use the rate of return on long-term Treasury bonds or high-grade corporate issues as a starting point in defining your desired rate of return. That is, starting with yields on long-term bonds, you could adjust such returns for the levels of business and market risk to which you believe the common stock is exposed.

To see how these elements make up the desired rate of return, let's go back to Universal Office Furnishings. Assume that it is now early 2002 and rates on high-grade corporate bonds are hovering around 9%. Given that our analysis thus far has indicated that the office equipment industry in general and Universal in particular are subject to a "fair" amount of business risk, we would want to adjust that figure upward—probably by around 2 or 3 points. In addition, with its beta of 1.30, we can conclude that the stock carries a good deal of market risk. Thus we should increase our base rate of return even more—say, by another 4 or 5 points. That is, starting from a base (high-grade corporate bond) rate of 9%, we tack on, say, 3% for the company's added business risk and another 4½ or 5% for the stock's market risk. Adding these up, we find that an appropriate required rate of return for Universal's common stock is around 17% or 17½%. This figure is reasonably close to what we would obtain with CAPM using a beta of 1.30, a risk-free rate of 5.5%, and an expected market return of 15% (as in Equation 8.6). The fact that the two numbers are close shouldn't be surprising. If they're carefully (and honestly) done, the CAPM and the subjective approach should yield similar results. Whichever procedure you use, the required rate of return stipulates the minimum return you should expect to receive from an investment. To accept anything less means you'll fail to be fully compensated for the risk you must assume.

Stock Valuation Models

LG 3 LG 4

Take a look at the market and you'll discover that investors employ a number of different types of stock valuation models. Though they all may be aimed at a security's future cash benefits, their approaches to valuation are nonetheless considerably different. Take, for example, those investors who search for value in a company's financials—by keying in on such factors as book value, debt load, return on equity, and cash flow. These are the so-called *value investors*, who rely as much on historical performance as on earnings projections to identify undervalued stock. Then there are the *growth investors*, who concentrate solely on growth in earnings. To them, though past growth is important, the real key lies in projected earnings—that is, in finding companies that are going to produce big earnings, along with big price/earnings multiples, in the future.

HOTLINKS

More often than not, investors tend to be either value investors *or* growth investors. An *Investing in Action* box at the book's homepage discusses the differences.

www.awl.com/gitman_joehnk

There are still other stock valuation models being used in this market—models that employ variables such as dividend yield, price-to-sales ratios, abnormally low P/E multiples, relative price performance over time, and even company size or market caps as key elements in the decision-making process. For purposes of our discussion here, we'll focus on several stock valuation models that are both theoretically sound and widely used. In one form or another, these models use the required rate of return, along with expected cash flows from dividends and/or the future price of the stock, to derive the intrinsic value of an investment. We'll look first at stocks that pay dividends and at a procedure known as the dividend valuation model. From there, we'll look at several valuation procedures that can be used with companies that pay little or nothing in dividends (the more growth-oriented companies). Then we'll move on to tech stocks, many of which not only don't pay dividends but may not even generate earnings (at least for now), or if they do produce earnings, they trade at astronomical P/E multiples.

The Dividend Valuation Model

In the valuation process, the intrinsic value of any investment equals the *present value of the expected cash benefits*. For common stock, this amounts to the cash dividends received each year plus the future sale price of the stock. One way to view the cash flow benefits from common stock is to assume that the dividends will be received over an infinite time horizon—an assumption that is appropriate so long as the firm is considered a "going concern." Seen from this perspective, *the value of a share of stock is equal to the present value of all the future dividends it is expected to provide over an infinite time horizon.*

Although a stockholder can earn capital gains in addition to dividends by selling a stock for more than he or she paid for it, from a strictly theoretical point of view, what is really being sold is the right to all remaining future dividends. Thus, just as the *current* value of a share of stock is a function of future dividends, the *future* price of the stock is also a function of future dividends. In this framework, the *future* price of the stock will rise or fall as the outlook for dividends (and the required rate of return) changes. This approach, which holds that the value of a share of stock is a function of its future dividends, is known as the **dividend valuation model (DVM).**

dividend valuation model (DVM) a model that values a share of stock on the basis of the future dividend stream it is expected to produce; its three versions are zero-growth, constant-growth, and variable-growth.

There are three versions of the dividend valuation model, each based on different assumptions about the future rate of growth in dividends: (1) *The zero-growth model,* which assumes that dividends will not grow over time. (2) *The constant-growth model,* which is the basic version of the dividend valuation model, and assumes that dividends will grow by a fixed/constant rate over time. (3) *The variable-growth model,* which assumes that the rate of growth in dividends varies over time.

Zero Growth The simplest way to picture the dividend valuation model is to assume the stock has a fixed stream of dividends. In other words, dividends stay the same year in and year out, and they're expected to do so in the future. Under such conditions, the value of a zero-growth stock is simply *the capitalized value of its annual dividends.* To find the capitalized value, just divide annual dividends by the required rate of return, which in effect acts as the capitalization rate. That is,

HOTLINKS

See the dividend valuation model at

www.stocksense.com/valuation.html

Equation 8.7

$$\text{Value of a share of stock} = \frac{\text{Annual dividends}}{\text{required rate of return}}$$

For example, if a stock paid a (constant) dividend of $3 a share and you wanted to earn 10% on your investment, the value of the stock would be $30 a share ($3/0.10 = $30).

As you can see, the only cash flow variable that's used in this model is the fixed annual dividend. Given that the annual dividend on this stock never changes, does that mean the price of the stock never changes? Absolutely not! For as the capitalization rate—that is, the required rate of return—changes, so will the price of the stock. Thus, if the capitalization rate goes up to, say, 15%, the price of the stock will fall to $20 ($3/0.15). Although this may be a very simplified view of the valuation model, it's actually not as far-fetched as it may appear. This is basically the procedure used to price preferred stocks in the marketplace.

Constant Growth The zero-growth model is a good beginning, but it does not take into account a growing stream of dividends, which is more likely to be the case in the real world. The standard and more widely recognized version of the dividend valuation model assumes that dividends will grow over time at a specified rate. In this version, the value of a share of stock is still considered to be a function of its future dividends, but such dividends are expected to grow forever (to infinity) at a constant rate of growth, g. Accordingly, the value of a share of stock can be found as follows:

Equation 8.8

$$\text{Value of a share of stock} = \frac{\text{Next year's dividends}}{\text{Required rate of return} - \text{Constant rate of growth in dividends}}$$

Equation 8.8a

$$V = \frac{D_1}{k - g}$$

where

D_1 = annual dividends expected to be paid *next* year (the first year in the forecast period)

k = the capitalization rate, or discount rate (which defines the required rate of return on the investment)

g = the annual rate of growth in dividends, which is expected to hold constant to infinity

This model succinctly captures the essence of stock valuation: *Increase* the cash flow (through D or g) and/or *decrease* the required rate of return (k), and the value of the stock will *increase.* Also note that in the DVM, k defines the total return to the stockholder and g represents the expected capital gains on the investments. We know that, in practice, there are potentially two components that make up the total return to a stockholder: dividends and capital gains. As it turns out, the returns from both dividends and capital gains are captured in the DVM. That is, because k represents total returns and g defines the amount of capital gains embedded in k, it follows that if you subtract g from k ($k - g$), you'll have the expected dividend yield on the stock. Thus the expected total return on a stock (k) equals the returns from capital gains (g) plus the returns from dividends ($k - g$).

The constant-growth DVM should not be used with just any stock. Rather, *it is best suited to the valuation of mature companies* that hold established market positions. These are companies with strong track records that have reached the "mature" stage of growth. This means that you're probably dealing with large-cap (or perhaps even some mature mid-cap) companies that have demonstrated an ability to generate steady—though perhaps not spectacular—rates of growth year in and year out. The growth rates *may not be identical* from year to year, but they tend to move within such a small range that they are seldom far off the average rate. These are companies that have established dividend policies, particularly with regard to the payout ratio, and fairly predictable growth rates in earnings and dividends. Thus, to use the constant-growth DVM on such companies, all that's required is some basic information about the stock's *current* level of dividends and the expected rate of growth in dividends, g.

One popular and fairly simple way to find the dividend growth rate is to look at the *historical* behavior of dividends. If they are growing at a relatively constant rate, you could assume that they'll continue to grow at (or near) that average rate in the future. You can get historical dividend data in a company's annual report, from various online Internet sources, or from publications like *Value Line.* Given this stream of dividends, you can use basic present-value arithmetic to find the average rate of growth. Here's how: Take the level of dividends, say, 10 years ago and the level that's being paid today. Presumably, dividends today will be (much) higher than they were 10 years ago, so, using your calculator, find the present value discount rate that equates the (higher) dividend today to the level paid 10 years earlier. When you find that, you've found the growth rate, because in this case, the *discount rate is the average rate of growth in dividends.* (See Chapter 5 for a detailed discussion of how to use present value to find growth rates.)

Once you've determined the dividend growth rate, g, you can find next year's dividend, D_1, as $D_0 \times (1 + g)$, where D_0 equals the actual (current) level of dividends. Let's say that in the latest year Amalgamated Anything paid \$2.50 a share in dividends. If you expect these dividends to grow at the rate of 6% a year, you can find next year's dividends as follows: $D_1 = D_0\ (1 + g) = \$2.50\ (1 + .06) = \$2.50\ (1.06) = \$2.65$. The only other information you need is the capitalization rate, or required rate of return, k. (Note that k must be greater than g for the constant-growth model to be mathematically operative.)

To see this dividend valuation model at work, consider a stock that currently pays an annual dividend of \$1.75 a share. Let's say that by using the present-value approach described above, you find that dividends are growing at a rate of 8% a year, and you expect they will continue to do so into the future. In addition, you feel that because of the risks involved, the investment should carry a required rate of return of 12%. Given this information, you can use Equation 8.8 to price the stock. That is, given $D_0 = \$1.75$, $g = 0.08$, and $k = 0.12$, it follows that

$$\text{Value of a share of stock} = \frac{D_0\ (1 + g)}{k - g} = \frac{\$1.75\ (1.08)}{0.12 - 0.08} = \frac{\$1.89}{0.04} = \underline{\underline{\$47.25}}$$

Thus, if you want to earn a 12% return on this investment—made up of 8% in capital gains (g), plus 4% in dividend yield (i.e., \$1.89/\$47.25 = 0.04)—then according to the constant-growth dividend valuation model, you should pay no more than \$47.25 a share for this stock.

With this version of the DVM, *the price of the stock will increase over time* so long as k and g don't change. This occurs because the cash flow from the investment will increase as dividends grow. To see how this happens, let's carry our example further. Recall that $D_0 = \$1.75$, $g = 8\%$, and $k = 12\%$. On the basis of this information, we found the current value of the stock to be \$47.25. Now look what happens to the price of this stock if k and g don't change:

Year	Dividend	Stock Price*
(Current year) 0	\$1.75	\$47.25
1	1.89	51.00
2	2.04	
55.00		
3	2.20	59.50
4	2.38	64.25
5	2.57	69.50

*As determined by the dividend valuation model, given $g = 0.08$, $k = 0.12$, and D_0 = dividend level for any given year.

As the table shows, we can also find the expected price of the stock *in the future* by using the standard dividend valuation model. To do this, we simply redefine the appropriate level of dividends. For example, to find the price of the stock in year 3, we use the expected dividend in the third year, \$2.20, and increase it by the factor $(1 + g)$. Thus the stock price in year $3 = D_3 \times (1 + g)/(k - g) = \$2.20 \times (1 + 0.08)/(0.12 - 0.08) = \$2.38/0.04 = \$59.50$. Of course, if future expectations about k or g do change, the *future price* of the stock will change accordingly. Should that occur, an investor could use the new information to decide whether to continue to hold the stock.

Variable Growth Although the constant-growth dividend valuation model is an improvement over the zero-growth model, it still has some shortcomings. The most obvious of these is the fact that it does not allow for changes in expected growth rates. To overcome this problem, we can use a form of the DVM that allows for *variable rates of growth* over time. Essentially, the *variable-growth dividend valuation model* derives, in two stages, a value based on future dividends and the future price of the stock (which price is a function of all future dividends to infinity). The variable-growth version of the model finds the value of a share of stock as follows:

Equation 8.9

$$\text{Value of a share of stock} = \begin{array}{c}\text{Present value of}\\ \text{future dividends}\\ \text{during the initial}\\ \text{variable-growth period}\end{array} + \begin{array}{c}\text{Present value of the price}\\ \text{of the stock at the end of}\\ \text{the variable-growth period}\end{array}$$

Equation 8.9a

$$V = (D_1 \times PVIF_1) + (D_2 \times PVIF_2) + \cdots + (D_v \times PVIF_v) + \left(\frac{D_v(1 + g)}{k - g} \times PVIF_v\right)$$

where

D_1, D_2, etc. = future annual dividends

$PVIF_t$ = present value interest factor, as specified by the required rate of return for a given year t (Table A.3 in the Appendix)

v = number of years in the initial variable-growth period

Note that the last element in this equation is the standard constant-growth dividend valuation model, which is used to find the price of the stock at the end of the initial variable-growth period.

This form of the DVM is appropriate for companies that are expected to experience rapid or variable rates of growth for a period of time—perhaps for the first 3 to 5 years—and then settle down to a constant (average) growth rate thereafter. This, in fact, is the growth pattern of many companies, so the model has considerable application in practice. (It also overcomes one of the operational shortcomings of the constant-growth DVM in that k does not always have to be greater than g. That is, *during the variable-growth period,* the rate of growth, g, can be greater than the required rate of return, k, and the model will still be fully operational.)

Finding the value of a stock using Equation 8.9 is actually a lot easier than it looks. All you need do is follow these steps:

1. Estimate annual dividends during the initial variable-growth period and then specify the constant rate, *g*, at which dividends will grow after the initial period.
2. Find the present value of the dividends expected during the initial variable-growth period.
3. Using the constant-growth DVM, find the price of the stock at the end of the initial growth period.
4. Find the present value of the price of the stock (as determined in step 3). Note that the price of the stock is discounted at the same PVIF as the last dividend payment in the initial growth period, because the stock is being priced (per step 3) at the end of this initial period.
5. Add the two present-value components (from steps 2 and 4) to find the value of a stock.

To see how this works, let's apply the variable-growth model to one of our favorite companies: Sweatmore Industries. Let's assume that dividends will grow at a variable rate for the first 3 years (2001, 2002, and 2003). After that, the annual rate of growth in dividends is expected to settle down to 8% and stay there for the foreseeable future. Starting with the latest (2000) annual dividend of \$2.21 a share, we estimate that Sweatmore's dividends should grow by 20% next year (in 2001), by 16% in 2002, and then by 13% in 2003 before dropping to an 8% rate. Using these (initial) growth rates, we therefore project that dividends in 2001 will amount to \$2.65 a share (\$2.21 × 1.20), and will rise to \$3.08 (\$2.65 × 1.16) in 2002 and to \$3.48 (\$3.08 × 1.13) in 2003. In addition, given Sweatmore's risk profile, we feel that the investment should produce a minimum (required) rate of return (*k*) of at least 14%. We now have all the input we need and are ready to put a value on Sweatmore Industries. Table 8.4 shows the variable-growth DVM in action. The value of Sweatmore stock, according to the variable-growth DVM, is just under \$49.25 a share. In essence, that's the maximum price you should be willing to pay for the stock if you want to earn a 14% rate of return.

Defining the Expected Growth Rate Mechanically, application of the DVM is really quite simple. It relies on just three key pieces of information: future dividends, future growth in dividends, and a required rate of return. But this model is not without its difficulties, and certainly one of the most difficult (and most important) aspects of the DVM is *specifying the appropriate growth rate,* g, *over an extended period of time.* Whether you are using the constant-growth or the variable-growth version of the dividend valuation model, the growth rate, *g*, is a crucial element in the DVM and has an enormous impact on the value derived from the model. Indeed, the DVM is *very sensitive* to the growth rate being used, because that rate affects both the model's numerator and its denominator.

As we saw earlier in this chapter, we can choose the growth rate from a strictly historical perspective (by using present value to find the past rate of growth) and then use it (or something close) in the DVM. That technique might work fine with the constant-growth model, but it has some obvious shortcomings with the variable-growth DVM. One procedure widely used in practice is to define the growth rate, *g*, as follows:

TABLE 8.4 Using the Variable-Growth DVM to Value Sweatmore Stock

Step

1. Projected annual dividends:

2001	\$2.65
2002	\$3.08
2003	\$3.48

Estimated annual rate of growth in dividends, g, for 2004 and beyond: 8%

2. Present value of dividends, using a required rate of return, k, of 14%, during the initial variable-growth period:

Year	Dividends	×	*PVIF* ($k = 14\%$)	=	Present Value
2001	\$2.65		0.877		\$2.32
2002	3.08		0.769		2.37
2003	3.48		0.675		2.35
				Total	\$7.04 (to step 5)

3. Price of the stock at the end of the initial growth period:

$$P_{2003} = \frac{D_{2004}}{k - g} = \frac{D_{2003} \times (1 + g)}{k - g} = \frac{\$3.48 \times (1.08)}{0.14 - 0.08} = \frac{\$3.75}{0.06} = \underline{\underline{\$62.50}}$$

4. Discount the price of the stock (as computed above) back to its present value, at $k = 14\%$:

$PV(P_{2003}) = \$62.50 \times PVIF_{14\%,\,3\text{ yr}} = \$62.50 \times 0.675 = \underline{\underline{\$42.19}}$ (to step 5)

5. Add the present value of the initial dividend stream (step 2) to the present value of the price of the stock at the end of the initial growth period (step 4):

Value of Sweatmore stock = $\$7.04 + \$42.19 = \underline{\underline{\$49.23}}$

Equation 8.10

$$g = \text{ROE} \times \text{The firm's retention rate, } rr$$

where

$$rr = 1 - \text{dividend payout ratio}$$

Both variables in Equation 8.10 (ROE and rr) are *directly related to the firm's rate of growth,* and both play key roles in defining a firm's future growth. The *retention rate* represents the percentage of the firm's profits that are plowed back into the company. Thus, if the firm pays out 35% of its earnings in dividends (i.e., it has a dividend payout ratio of 35%), then it has a retention rate of 65%: $rr = 1 - 0.35 = 0.65$. The retention rate, in effect, indicates the amount of capital that is flowing into the company to finance its growth. Other things being equal, the more money that's being retained in the company, the higher the rate of growth. The other component of Equation 8.10 is the familiar return on equity. Clearly, the more the company can earn on its retained capital, the higher the growth rate.

Let's look at some numbers to see how this actually works. For example, if a company retained, on average, about 80% of its earnings and generated an ROE of around 15%, you'd expect it to have a growth rate of around:

$$g = \text{ROE} \times rr = 0.15 \times 0.80 = \underline{\underline{12\%}}$$

Actually, the growth rate will probably be a bit more than 12%, because Equation 8.10 ignores financial leverage, which in itself will magnify growth. But at least the equation gives you a good idea what to expect. Or it can serve as a starting point in assessing past and future growth. That is, you can use Equation 8.10 to compute expected growth and then assess the two key components of the formula (ROE and *rr*) to see whether they're likely to undergo major changes in the future. If so, then what impact is the change in ROE and/or *rr* likely to have on the growth rate, *g*? The idea is to take the time to study the forces (ROE and *rr*) that drive the growth rate, because the DVM itself is so sensitive to the rate of growth being used. Employ a growth rate that's too high and you'll end up with an intrinsic value that's way too high also. The downside to that, of course, is that you may end up buying a stock that you really shouldn't.

Some Alternatives to the DVM

The variable-growth approach to stock valuation is fairly compatible with the way most people invest. That is, unlike the underlying assumptions in the standard dividend valuation model (which employs an infinite investment horizon), most investors have a holding period that seldom exceeds 5 to 7 years. Under such circumstances, *the relevant cash flows are future dividends and the future selling price of the stock.*

There are some alternatives to the DVM that use such cash flow streams to value stock. One is the so-called *dividends-and-earnings approach,* which in many respects is similar to the variable-growth DVM. Another is the *P/E approach,* which builds the stock valuation process around the stock's price/earnings ratio. One of the major advantages of these procedures is that *they don't rely on dividends as the key input.* Accordingly, they can be used with stocks that are more growth-oriented and pay little or nothing in dividends. It is very difficult, if not impossible, to apply the DVM to stocks that pay little or nothing in dividends. That's not a problem with the dividend-and-earnings approach or the P/E approach. Let's now take a closer look at both of these, as well as a technique that arrives at the expected return on the stock (in percentage terms) rather than a (dollar-based) "justified price."

A Dividends-and-Earnings Approach As we saw earlier the value of a share of stock is a function of the amount and timing of future cash flows and the level of risk that must be taken on to generate that return. A stock valuation model has been developed that conveniently captures the essential elements of expected risk and return and does so in a present-value context. The model is as follows:

Equation 8.11

$$\text{Present value of a share of stock} = \text{Present value of future dividends} + \text{Present value of the price of the stock at date of sale}$$

Equation 8.11a

$$V = (D_1 \times PVIF_1) + (D_2 \times PVIF_2) + \cdots + (D_N \times PVIF_N) + (SP_N \times PVIF_N)$$

where

D_t = future annual dividend in year t

$PVIF_t$ = present-value interest factor, specified at the required rate of return (Table A.3 in the Appendix near the end of the book)

SP_N = estimated share price of the stock at date of sale, year N

N = number of years in the investment horizon

dividends-and-earnings (D&E) approach
stock valuation approach that uses projected dividends, EPS, and P/E multiples to value a share of stock.

This is the so-called **dividends-and-earnings (D&E) approach** to stock valuation. Note its similarities to the variable-growth DVM: It's also present-value-based, and its value is also derived from future dividends and the expected future price of the stock. The big difference between the two procedures revolves around the role that dividends play in determining the future price of the stock. That is, the D&E approach doesn't rely on dividends as the principal player in the valuation process. Therefore, it works just as well with companies that pay little or nothing in dividends as with stocks that pay out a lot in dividends. And along that line, whereas the variable-growth DVM relies on future dividends to price the stock, the D&E approach employs projected earnings per share and estimated P/E multiples. These are the same two variables that drive the price of the stock in the market. Thus, the D&E approach is far more flexible than the DVM and is easier to understand and apply. Using the D&E valuation approach, we focus on projecting future dividends and share price behavior over a defined, finite investment horizon, much as we did for Universal Office Furnishings in Table 8.3.

Especially important in the D&E approach is finding a viable P/E multiple that can be used to project the future price of the stock. This is a critical part of this valuation process, because of the major role that capital gains (and therefore the estimated price of the stock at its date of sale) play in defining the level of security returns. Using market or industry P/Es as benchmarks, you should try to establish a multiple that you feel the stock will trade at in the future. Like the growth rate, g, in the DVM, the P/E multiple is the single most important (and most difficult) variable to project in the D&E approach. Using this input, along with estimated future dividends, this present-value-based model generates a *justified price* based on estimated returns. This intrinsic value represents the price you should be willing to pay for the stock, given its expected dividend and price behavior, and assuming you want to generate a return that is equal to or greater than your required rate of return.

To see how this procedure works, consider once again the case of Universal Office Furnishings. Let's return to our original 3-year investment horizon. Given the forecasted annual dividends and share price from Table 8.3, along with a required rate of return of 18% (as computed earlier using Equation 8.6), we can see that the value of Universal's stock is

$$\begin{aligned}\text{Present value of a share of Universal stock} &= (\$0.18 \times 0.847) + (\$0.24 \times 0.718) + (\$0.28 \times 0.609) \\ &\quad + (\$93.20 \times 0.609) \\ &= \$0.15 + \$0.17 + \$0.17 + \$56.76 \\ &= \underline{\underline{\$57.25}}\end{aligned}$$

According to the D&E approach, Universal's stock should be valued at about \$57 a share. That assumes, of course, that our projections hold up—particularly with regard to our forecasted EPS and P/E multiple in 2004. For example, if the P/E drops from 20 to 17 times earnings, then the value of a share of stock will drop to less than \$50 (to around \$48.75/share). Given that we have confidence in our projections, the present-value figure computed here means that we would realize our (18%) desired rate of return so long as we can buy the stock at no more than \$57 a share. Because UVRS is currently trading at (around) \$41.50, we can conclude that the stock at present is an *attractive investment vehicle*. That is, because we can buy the stock at *less* than its computed intrinsic value, we'll be able to earn our required rate of return, *and then some*. By most standards, Universal would be considered a highly risky investment, if for no other reason than the fact that *nearly all the return is derived from capital gains*. Indeed, dividends alone account for less than 1% of the value of the stock. That is, only 49 cents of the \$57.25 comes from dividends! Clearly, if we're wrong about EPS or the P/E multiple, the future price of the stock (in 2004) could be way off the mark, and so, too, would our projected return.

INVESTOR FACTS

UNEXPECTED RETURNS—No matter how good your estimates of a stock's forecasted dividends or expected return, you can undermine your analytical efforts by trading too frequently. A recent study of returns for over 66,000 investors over the 6 years 1991 to 1997 grouped them according to annual portfolio turnover (how much of the portfolio the investor replaces each year). Buy-and-hold investors, with turnover of 2% a year, earned annual returns of 18.5%. Average traders (76% turnover) fared a little worse at 16.4%. The most active traders, with 258% portfolio turnover, averaged only 11.4% per year, 5 to 7 percentage points less than more patient investors.

Source: Walter Updegrave, "Terms of Trade," *Money*, March 2000, p. 75.

Determining Expected Return

Sometimes investors find it more convenient to deal in terms of expected return rather than a dollar-based justified price. This is no problem, nor is it necessary to sacrifice the present-value dimension of the stock valuation model to achieve such an end. That's because expected return can be found by using the (present-value-based) *internal rate of return (IRR)* procedure first introduced in Chapter 5. This approach to stock valuation uses forecasted dividend and price behavior, along with the *current market price*, to arrive at the fully compounded rate of return you can expect from a given investment.

To see how a stock's expected return is computed, let's look once again at Universal Office Furnishings. Using 2002–2004 data from Table 8.3, along with the stock's current price of \$41.58, we can determine Universal's expected return. To do so, we find the discount rate that equates the future stream of benefits (i.e., the future annual dividends and future price of the stock) to the stock's current market price. In other words, find the discount rate that produces a present value of future benefits equal to the price of the stock, and you have the IRR, or expected return on that stock.

Here's how it works: Using the Universal example, we know that the stock is expected to pay per-share dividends of \$0.18, \$0.24, and \$0.28 over the next 3 years. At the end of that time, we hope to sell the stock for \$93.20. Given that the stock is currently trading at \$41.58, we're looking for the discount rate that will produce a present value (of the future annual dividends and stock price) equal to \$41.58. That is,

$$(\$0.18 \times PVIF_1) + (\$0.24 \times PVIF_2) + (\$0.28 \times PVIF_3) + (\$93.20 \times PVIF_3) = \$41.58$$

We need to solve for the discount rate (the present-value interest factors) in this equation. Through a process of "hit and miss" (and with the help of a personal computer or hand-held calculator), you'll find that with an interest factor of 31.3%, the present value of the future cash benefits from this investment will equal exactly $41.58. That, of course, is our expected return. Thus Universal can be expected to earn a fully compounded annual return of about 31%, assuming that the stock can be bought at $41.58, is held for 3 years (during which time investors receive indicated annual dividends), and then is sold for $93.20 at the end of the 3-year period. When compared to its 18% *required rate of return*, the 31.3% *expected return* makes Universal look like a very attractive investment candidate.

The Price/Earnings (P/E) Approach

price/earnings (P/E) approach
stock valuation approach that tries to find the P/E ratio that's most appropriate for the stock; this ratio along with estimated EPS, is used to determine a reasonable stock price.

One of the problems with the stock valuation procedures we've looked at above is that they are fairly mechanical. They involve a good deal of "number crunching." Although such an approach is fine with some stocks, it doesn't work well with others. Fortunately, there is a more intuitive approach. That alternative is the **price/earnings** (or **P/E**) **approach** to stock valuation.

The P/E approach is a favorite of professional security analysts and is widely used in practice. It's relatively simple to use, because it's based on the standard P/E formula first introduced in Chapter 7 (Equation 7.14). There we showed that a stock's P/E is equal to its market price divided by the stock's EPS. Using this equation and solving for the market price of the stock, we have

Equation 8.12

$$\text{Stock price} = \text{EPS} \times \text{P/E ratio}$$

Equation 8.12 basically captures the P/E approach to stock valuation. That is, given an estimated EPS figure, *you decide on a P/E ratio that you feel is appropriate for the stock. Then you use it in Equation 8.12 to see what kind of price you come up with and how that compares to the stock's current price.*

Actually, this approach is no different from what's used in the market every day. Look at the stock quotes in the *Wall Street Journal.* They include the stock's P/E and show what investors are willing to pay for one dollar of earnings. The higher the multiple, the better investors feel about the company and its future prospects. Essentially, the *Journal* relates the company's earnings per share for the *last* 12 months (known as *trailing earnings*) to the latest price of the stock. In practice, however, investors buy stocks not for their past earnings but for their *expected future earnings.* Thus, in Equation 8.12, it's customary to *use forecasted EPS for next year.*

To implement the P/E approach, the first thing you have to do is come up with forecasted EPS one year out. In the early part of this chapter, we saw how this might be done (see, for instance, Equation 8.3). Given the forecasted EPS, the next task is to evaluate the variables that drive the P/E ratio. Most of that assessment is intuitive. For example, you might want to look at the stock's expected rate of growth in earnings, any potential major changes in the firm's capital structure or dividends, and any other factors such as relative market or industry P/Es that might affect the stock's multiple. You could use such inputs to come up with a base P/E, and then adjust that base, as necessary, to account for the perceived state of the market and/or anticipated changes in the rate of inflation.

Along with estimated EPS, we now have the P/E we need to compute (via Equation 8.12) the price at which the stock should be trading. By comparing that targeted price to the current market price of the stock, we can decide whether the stock is a good buy. For example, we would consider the stock undervalued and therefore a good buy if the computed price of the stock were more than its market price.

Putting a Value on Tech Stocks

Tech stocks have become a major force both in the United States and in equity markets around the world. As a result, they're playing a more important role in a growing number of individual as well as institutional portfolios. As an example of just how important they've become, consider the *Fidelity Blue Chip Growth* fund. According to recent information, 39.4% of the fund was invested in the technology sector, and six of the fund's top ten holdings were tech stocks: Cisco Systems, Intel, EMC Corporation, Microsoft, Sun Microsystems, and IBM. Now, keep in mind, Fidelity Blue Chip Growth is not even considered a tech-stock fund!

Broadly speaking, most investors would define a tech stock as *the stock of a firm whose core business contains a significant technology component.* Admittedly, this definition could include almost any firm, because technology now plays a key role in the development and production of even the most basic products. What separates tech stocks from the rest is that these are the companies that are *providing the technology,* not just using it. Table 8.5 presents an overview of selected tech-stock groups as they are categorized on the Yahoo! Finance Web site (finance.yahoo.com). Some groupings, such as *Computer software,* quickly come to mind—this is, after all, a very large group made up of some 227 firms. We also see some fairly specialized groups, such as *Optical character recognition* (6 firms). Of course, we cannot discuss tech stocks without referring to those firms that specialize in the Internet. Interestingly, Yahoo! has three Internet stock groups: *Internet content, Internet services,* and *Internet software.* In addition, Yahoo! has a closely related group called *Electronic commerce.* Many high-tech firms are fairly young and not exactly household names, while others (like Microsoft and Oracle) are big-name companies with market caps in the hundreds of billions of dollars.

HOTLINKS

See the Internet stock valuation technique at

www.stocksontheweb.com/overview.htm

Tiers of Tech Stocks For valuation purposes, it is often convenient to put tech stocks into three broad categories, or tiers. *Top-tier* tech stocks include firms like Microsoft, Intel, and Cisco Systems. These firms are well-established market leaders with solid track records. There are probably no more than a hundred or so firms that would fall into this category. Most of them have normal financial and market ratios and are valued pretty much like any other growth stock, as described earlier in this chapter.

Next are the *mid-tier* stocks; there are literally hundreds of these firms, such as NVIDIA, Transwitch, and Black Box Corporation. Though many of them may not be household names, they have been around for some time and have demonstrated an ability to not only generate substantial revenues but also to earn solid profits year after year. NVIDIA, for example, had sales of nearly \$650 million in 1999 and profits of over \$80 million. Many of these tech stocks have very high P/E ratios and therefore may not be compatible with standard stock valuation models. A potential problem in valuing some of these mid-tier

TABLE 8.5 Some Tech-Stock Groups

Group Name	Numbers of Firms	Selected Firms
Business information services	22	Gartner Group, Keynote Systems
Computer networks	87	Cisco Systems, Juniper Networks
Computer software	227	Microsoft, Oracle
Defense electronics	27	REMEC, Teledyne
Electrical components-semiconductors	114	Intel, Xilinx
Electronic commerce	59	Amazon.com, eBay
Fiber optics	18	Corning, JDS Uniphase
Industrial automation/robotics	5	Gerber Scientific, Rockwell
Instrumentation—control	10	Datum, Eaton
Internet content	62	CNET, Travelocity.com
Internet services	102	America Online, CMGI
Internet software	94	Ariba, Synquest
Medical—biomedical/gene	145	Amgen, Biogen
Optical character recognition	6	PSC, Scansource
Telecommunications—wireless	57	AT&T Wireless, Vodafone
Telecommunications equipment	139	Lucent, Motorola
Telecommunications services	21	Global Crossing, RCN

Source: Yahoo! finance Web site (finance.yahoo.com).

firms is that they may not have highly diversified product offerings and customer bases. Thus, a shift in industry fundamentals or technology could change their fortunes (i.e., earnings and growth rates) dramatically.

Lower-tier tech stocks include firms like bingo.com and Laser Corporation. Firms at this level typically have yet to generate any earnings. In many cases, they have very little in revenues. Valuation of these firms is extremely difficult and often amounts to little more than hunches. Indeed, these stocks are often bought by investors who pay little attention to fundamentals but instead rely on little more than "stories," such as some media report that's related to the firm's products, an unsubstantiated comment on the Internet, or the advice of a friend who has suddenly become an "expert" at investing.

Tech-Stock Valuation Methods Generally speaking, the methods used to value tech stocks are pretty much the same as those used to value any other type of stock. However, *tech-stock valuation definitely presents some unique challenges.* We'll look at the two primary techniques used to value tech stocks: discounted cash flow analysis and the use of price multiples. After describing each of these methods, we will discuss a concept known as the "burn rate," and then conclude with an example of a tech-stock valuation.

Discounted Cash Flow (DCF) Analysis Earlier in this chapter, we noted that the intrinsic value of any investment is the present value of its expected cash benefits. Actually, that's the principle behind the dividend valuation model (DVM). Recall that in the DVM the value of a share of stock is the present value of its future stream of dividends. The same can be said of the dividends-and-earnings (D&E) approach, except that it relies not only on dividends but also on expected future earnings, P/E multiples, and the future price of the stock. Both the DVM and D&E approaches are examples of discounted cash flow (DCF) models. DCF analysis involves the projection of future cash flows, such as dividends, which are then discounted back to the present at a rate that reflects the investor's required return.

There's an obvious problem in trying to apply the DVM to the valuation of tech stocks: *Very few of them pay dividends.* We could, of course, assume that the companies will *eventually* pay dividends and then discount these dividends back to the present to obtain an estimated value. But far more often than not, such computed values are *highly unreliable!* A viable alternative to the DVM would be to use a variation of the dividends-and-earnings approach. In this version, all of the dividends would be set to zero, so the computed value of the stock would come solely from our future projection of the firm's earnings and P/E ratio—in other words, the future price of the stock. That may work in some cases. But for many tech firms, earnings growth rates are so uncertain that techniques such as the D&E approach are not feasible. In an attempt to get around some of the problems that arise in forecasting earnings, some investors use other measures of cash flow, such as *free cash flow.* But even here, it is difficult to forecast cash flow figures for rapidly growing high-tech firms. In fact, it may be *more difficult* to forecast cash flows for these firms because of all the assumptions that have to be made regarding growth rates, capital expenditures, and working-capital requirements. Thus, although DCF may be useful in valuing some of the larger, more established high-tech companies, most market observers regard it as impractical in the valuation of smaller and newer firms.

Price-Multiple Methods Instead of using DCF, a lot of tech-stock investors base their valuations on *stock price multiples.* To do so, investors identify firms that are comparable to the one being valued, determine the average (or typical) multiples being applied to those comparable firms, and then use it/them to put a value on the firm under consideration. Commonly used multiples include those based on *earnings* (price/earnings), *book value* (price/book value), and *sales* (price/sales). The use of these multiples follows the same steps that we outlined earlier in our discussion of the price/earnings (P/E) approach. That is, given the appropriate P/E multiple, we simply multiply EPS by the P/E ratio, and we have our estimate of the stock price. Similarly, we could *multiply book value per share by the appropriate price/book ratio,* or *sales per share by the appropriate price/sales ratio,* to estimate the value of the stock.

Although price/earnings multiples are widely used in valuation, they can be difficult or even impossible to apply to many tech stocks, because these companies often have earnings that are either highly erratic or even negative. Moreover, the use of price/book ratios may work well when valuing banks or other firms *whose assets are easily measured,* but it can be problematic when valuing tech stocks. The reason is that the book value of the firm as reported on the balance sheet may bear little resemblance to the value of the firm in the marketplace. Much of the marketplace value may stem from *intangible assets* such as the firm's growth potential or technological capabilities. The potential shortcomings of price/earnings and price/book ratios have led many investors to use the price/sales (P/S) ratio as the "multiple of choice" when valuing tech stocks. An advantage of the P/S ratio is that even when earnings are negative, sales are positive.

As is the case with P/E ratios, the P/S multiple can be calculated two ways: on a *trailing* basis or on a *forward* basis. The trailing price/sales ratio is computed simply by dividing share price by the sales per share for the most recent year. Alternatively, the forward price/sales ratio is computed by dividing share price by the *estimated* or *forecasted* sales per share for the *coming year.* This estimate can be obtained from analysts' reports (or, if you are adventurous, you could generate your own forecast). Because it's common for sales to grow over time, the forward price/sales ratio will tend to be lower than the trailing ratio.

Although price/sales ratios are popular in the valuation of tech stocks with little or no earnings, they do have shortcomings. First, although sales will be positive even when earnings are negative, many analysts would argue that our focus should ultimately be on the "bottom line" (earnings and profitability) rather than on the "top line" (sales). A second potential shortcoming of using any price multiple with tech stocks is that the multiple itself is highly volatile because of wide fluctuations in both share price and the characteristic (such as sales) in the denominator. Earlier in this chapter, we showed that there was considerable variation in marketwide P/E multiples over time. For tech stocks, the variation in P/S multiples can be even greater. The problem is this: An investor may determine that a set of comparable firms currently has an average P/S ratio of say, 6½ and then finds that this average has dropped to 3½ only a short time later. Such wide swings introduce into the valuation process the potential for considerable error. In addition, the question arises as to whether the firm being valued should receive the average multiple for the industry, that for a group of comparable firms, or some higher or lower value. Although this is a very difficult question to answer, all else being equal, price multiples do tend to increase with a firm's growth rate and to decrease with higher risk. We noted this earlier for P/E multiples, and the same concept applies to price/sales (P/S) multiples.

burn rate
the rate at which the firm is using up its supply of cash over time.

The "Burn Rate" in Tech Stocks Before proceeding to an example of valuation, we should define one other term that is often used in discussing tech stocks: the **burn rate,** or the **cash burn rate.** The burn rate refers to the *rate at which the firm is using up* ("burning up") *its supply of cash over time.* Because it usually takes a while for many start-up firms to generate cash from operations, their survival depends on their having an adequate supply of cash on hand to meet expenses. The burn rate is determined by examining a firm's statement of cash flows. As we saw in Chapter 7, the statement of cash flows reports the change in the firm's cash position from one period to the next by accounting for the cash flows from operations, investment activities, and financing activities. Other things being equal, a higher burn rate is viewed more negatively, and is likely to result in a lower valuation for the firm.

To illustrate the concept of the "burn rate" refer to Table 8.6, which presents a highly abbreviated statement of cash flows for U.S. Internetworking, Inc. (USIX). This firm implements, operates, and supports packaged software applications over the Internet. The statement of cash flows in Table 8.6 covers the first 9 months of 2000 and the corresponding period for 1999. Let's focus on a few of the key cash flow items relevant to USIX's burn rate. First, the net cash from operations was a *negative* \$93 million for the first 9 months of

2000. This result implies that the core business operations of the firm consumed (burned) cash at the rate of about $10 million per month, largely because of the firm's substantial—and growing—operating loss. Second, USIX made significant capital investment in new assets. As a result, the net cash flow from investing also was *negative,* to the tune of $63 million. That represents another significant use of cash. Indeed, the net cash burned by operations and investing together amounted to over $150 million—or a burn rate of nearly $17 million a month! Some would argue that a more appropriate (and more liberal) way to estimate a firm's burn rate would be to ignore the cash used for investing and simply focus on the cash from operations. But that doesn't seem to be very realistic, because most firms do, in fact, have to make some capital expenditures in order to continue operations. As a compromise, we won't even consider the cash used to meet payments on the firm's long-term debt and lease obligations, as that would just *add* another $2.5 million to the monthly burn rate.

Examination of the firm's financing activities gives us some idea of how USIX met these substantial cashs outflows. In particular, the firm raised nearly $150 million by issuing additional common stock and long-term debt. Because USIX had approximately $81 million in cash at the end of the period, it is likely to run out of cash in about 6 to 8 months, depending on which burn rate you use. USIX can avoid that fate if it (1) significantly decreases its burn rate or perhaps even begins to *generate* cash from operations, or (2) continues to issue significant amounts of debt or equity. Of course, the continued ability to raise additional capital is not guaranteed for any firm and is particularly questionable for risky tech firms.

Tech-Stock Valuation Example As an exercise in tech-stock valuation, let's consider the hypothetical firm Global Applications Software Products (GASP). Actually, although the name is fictitious, the financial statements and values are for a real company operating in roughly the same line of business. GASP is an application software provider, which means that it essentially "hosts" software on its computers and rents this software to other firms. GASP's income statement (see Table 8.7) indicates that revenues for the most recent year were $56.5 million, yet net income was a negative $92.2 million. In other words, the firm had a loss of almost $100 million on sales of some $56 million.

Constructing a set of comparable firms is probably the most challenging part of this valuation process. Investors face a difficult tradeoff: On one hand, the larger the set of comparable firms, the more confident we might be in our estimate of the appropriate multiple. On the other hand, a larger set of comparable firms may include some that are not truly similar to the firm being valued. Let's assume that we have collected data on the price/sales ratios and other financial characteristics for five publicly traded companies in roughly the same line of business as GASP, as shown in Table 8.8.

The sales levels of the comparable firms range from $32.2 million for Corio to $128.8 million for Interliant. *Net losses* range from $164 million for U.S. Internetworking to $44 million for Breakaway Solutions. The levels of sales and net losses for GASP are within those ranges, although GASP had lower sales than average ($56.5 million vs. $79.4 million) and generated less of a loss than the average firm ($92.2 million vs. $110.4 million).

TABLE 8.6 **Statement of Cash Flows**

U.S. Internetworking, Inc.
Statement of Cash Flows
($ in millions)

	For the 9 Months Ended Sept. 30	
	2000	1999
Net loss	($129.4)	($ 69.1)
Other operating activities	36.1	12.6
Net cash flow from operations	**($ 93.3)**	**($ 56.5)**
Net cash flow from investing	**($ 63.0)**	**($ 98.9)**
Payments on long-term debt & capital leases	($ 22.9)	($ 4.5)
Other financing activities	148.0	144.7
Net cash flow from financing	**$125.1**	**$140.2**
Net cash flow	($ 31.2)	($ 15.2)
Cash & equivalents, at beginning of period	$ 112.3	$ 43.8
Cash & equivalents, at end of period	$ 81.1	$ 28.6

Using the price/sales multiple, the simplest approach is to use the average multiple of the comparable firms to find the value of our GASP shares. But first we have to find sales per share for GASP. Using trailing sales, that can be done by taking the firm's total sales for last year and dividing it by the number of shares outstanding. Assuming 30 million shares outstanding, GASP had trailing sales per share of

$56.5 million/30 million = $1.88/share

TABLE 8.7 **Income Statement for a Tech Firm**

Global Applications Software Products
Income Statement
Fiscal Year Ended December 31, 2000
($ in thousands)

Sales	$56,500
Expenses	
Direct cost of services	$64,700
Network and infrastructure costs	35,900
General and administrative	22,400
Sales and marketing	59,300
Depreciation and amortization	31,400
Total costs and expenses	$133,700
Operating loss	($77,200)
Interest expense	15,000
Net loss	**($92,200)**

(No taxes are shown because of the operating loss.)

TABLE 8.8 Financial Data on Five Firms Comparable to GASP

Company Name	Market Cap ($ millions)	Sales ($ millions)	Losses ($ millions)	Price/Sales Ratio
U.S. Internetworking	$532	$ 87	$−164	5.2
Corio	174	32	−161	2.9
Interliant	313	129	−125	2.3
Navisite	311	50	−58	5.7
Breakaway Solutions	76	99	−44	0.6
Averages	$281.2	$79.4	$−110.4	3.34

Now, to find the value of a share of GASP stock, we simply multiply the firm's sales per share by the average price to sales ratio (of 3.34 times):

$$\$1.88 \times 3.34 = \underline{\underline{\$6.28/\text{share}}}$$

Thus we end up with an estimated share price of $6.28.

How does that stack up to our set of comparable firms? To find out, we can convert the GASP share price to a market cap by multiplying price per share by the number of shares outstanding. That results in a market cap of some $188.4 million ($6.28 × 30 million shares). This result is within the range of our five comparable firms, but still below average, so we're probably about where we want to be.

For illustrative purposes, we've greatly simplified the tech-stock valuation process. In practice, you might want to discard one or more of the firms from the comparable analysis, or you might subjectively adjust the average multiple to a higher or lower value on the basis of differences between GASP and the comparables. Or you might want to make some other adjustment based on, say, perceived exposure to risk or perhaps some other variable. The idea is to continue to modify (or "tweak") the P/S ratio until you come up with a multiple that you're comfortable with and that you feel is a proper basis for valuation. Once that's done, the procedure becomes purely mechanical. Simply multiply the ratio you've come up with by the firm's trailing or forward *annual* sales figure. In the case of GASP, if we conclude that a price/sales ratio of around 3.3 to 3.4 is appropriate, then on the basis of trailing annual sales, the stock should be trading for around $6.25 to $6.30 a share. If we can buy it for that price or less, the stock might make a good investment. If not, we'll have to keep looking.

HOTLINKS

To focus on Internet stocks, market news, financials, charts, and analyst reports, see

www.stockset.com

Technical Analysis

How many times have you turned on the TV or radio and in the course of the day's news heard a reporter say, "The market was up 47 points today" or "The market remained sluggish in a day of light trading"? Such comments reflect the importance of the stock market itself in determining the price behavior of common stocks. In fact, some experts believe that studying the

LG 5

market should be the major, if not the only, ingredient in the stock selection process. These experts argue that much of what is done in security analysis is useless because it is the market that matters, not individual companies. Others argue that studying the stock market is only one element in the security analysis process and is useful in helping the investor time decisions.

technical analysis
the study of the various forces at work in the marketplace and their effect on stock prices.

Analyzing the various forces at work in the stock market is known as **technical analysis**. For some investors, it's another piece of information to use when deciding whether to buy, hold, or sell a stock. For others, it's the *only* input they use in their investment decisions. And for still others, technical analysis, like fundamental analysis, is regarded as a big waste of time. Here we will assume that technical analysis does have some role to play in the investment decision process. We will examine the major principles of market analysis, as well as some of the techniques used to assess market behavior.

Principles of Market Analysis

Analyzing market behavior dates back to the 1800s, when there was no such thing as industry or company analysis. Detailed financial information simply was not made available to stockholders, let alone the general public. There were no industry figures, balance sheets, or income statements to study, no sales forecasts to make, and no EPS data or P/E multiples. About the only thing investors could study was the market itself. Some investors used detailed charts in an attempt to monitor what large market operators were doing. These charts were intended to show when major buyers were moving into or out of particular stocks and to provide information that could be used to make profitable buy-and-sell decisions. The charts centered on stock price movements. It was believed that these movements produced certain "formations" that indicated when the time was right to buy or sell a particular stock. The same principle is still applied today: Technical analysts argue that internal market factors, such as trading volume and price movements, often reveal the market's future direction long before it is evident in financial statistics.

If the behavior of stock prices were completely independent of market movements, market studies and technical analysis would be useless. But we have ample evidence that stock prices do, in fact, tend to move with the market. Studies of stock betas have shown that as a rule, anywhere from 20% to 50% of the price behavior of a stock can be traced to market forces. When the market is bullish, stock prices in general can be expected to behave accordingly. When the market turns bearish, you can safely expect most issues to be affected by the "downdraft."

HOTLINKS

It happens to every investor: You've been watching for signs of movement in the market and the prices suddenly fall. For suggestions of what to do in response—other than to panic—see the *Investing in Action* box at our Web site:

www.awl.com/gitman_joehnk

Stock prices, in essence, react to various forces of supply and demand that are at work in the market. After all, it's the *demand* for securities and the *supply* of funds in the market that determine whether we're in a bull or a bear market. So long as a given supply-and-demand relationship holds, the market will remain strong (or weak). When the balance begins to shift, however, future prices can be expected to change as the market itself changes. Thus, more than anything else, technical analysis is intended to monitor the pulse of the supply-and-demand forces in the market and to detect any shifts in this important relationship.

Measuring the Market

If assessing the market is a worthwhile endeavor, then we need some sort of tool or measure to do it. Charts are popular with many investors because they provide a visual summary of the behavior of the market and the price movements of individual stocks. As an alternative or supplement to *charting,* some investors prefer to study various *market statistics.* These statistics include the volume of trading, the amount of short selling, and the buying and selling patterns of small investors (odd-lot transactions). This approach is based on the idea that by assessing some of the key elements of market behavior, investors can gain valuable insights into the general condition of the market and, perhaps, where it's headed over the next few months. Normally, several of these measures are used together, either in an informal way or more formally as a series of complex ratios and measures. Although there are many market measures—or *technical indicators,* as they are called—we will confine our discussion here to several of the more widely followed technical measures: (1) market volume, (2) breadth of the market, (3) short interest, and (4) odd-lot trading. In addition to these, the accompanying *Investing in Action* box describes another popular market measure, the *relative strength index* (RSI for short).

HOTLINKS

At the Bloomberg site shown below, click on charts. At the Equis site, check the Hot Stocks list.

www.bloomberg.com
www.equis.com/java

INVESTOR FACTS

THE JANUARY INDICATOR—Wall Streeters are always on the lookout for new market measures, some of which bear no relationship to the financial world at all. One market adage holds that if the National Football League Conference team wins the Super Bowl, the market will have a good year. Another, more "financial" January-based measure looks at January's market results as a prediction for the year: If the market falls in January, the year will register a decline, and vice versa. From 1900 to 2000, the Dow Jones Industrial Average (DJIA) registered a drop in January 35 times, but this was followed by a full year's decline just 22 times. So this rule of thumb held true only 63% of the time—most recently in 2000, when the January decline was 4.8% and the DJIA ended the year down 6.2%. In 1998, however, the January indicator was wrong: The DJIA fell 2.2% in January but ended the year up 16.1%.

Source: E. S. Browning, "Stocks End Stormy January with Strong Bounce Back," *Wall Street Journal,* February 1, 2000.

Market Volume Market volume is an obvious reflection of the amount of investor interest. Volume is a function of the supply of and demand for stock, and it indicates underlying market strengths and weaknesses. The market is considered *strong* when volume goes up in a rising market or drops off during market declines. It is considered *weak* when volume rises during a decline or drops during rallies. For instance, the market would be considered strong if the Dow Jones Industrial Average went up by, say, 108 points while market volume was heavy. Investor eagerness to buy or sell is felt to be captured by market volume figures. The financial press regularly publishes volume data, and investors can conveniently watch this important technical indicator. An example of this and other vital market information is shown in Figure 8.1.

Breadth of the Market Each trading day, some stocks go up in price and others go down. In market terminology, some stocks *advance* and others *decline.* The breadth-of-the-market indicator deals with these advances and declines. The idea is actually quite simple: So long as the number of stocks that advance in price on a given day exceeds the number that decline, the market is considered strong. The extent of that strength depends on the spread between the number of advances and declines. For example, if the spread narrows so that the number of declines starts to approach the number of advances, market strength is said to be deteriorating. Similarly, the market is considered weak when the number of declines repeatedly exceeds the number of advances. The principle behind this indicator is that the number of advances and declines reflects the underlying sentiment of investors. When the mood is optimistic, for example, look for advances to outnumber declines. Again, data on advances and declines are published daily in the financial press.

Short Interest When investors anticipate a market decline, they sometimes sell a stock short. That is, they sell borrowed stock. The number of stocks sold

INVESTING in action

Relative Strength Weighs In on Buy and Sell Decisions

One of the most widely used technical indicators is the *relative strength index (RSI)*. It is an internal index measuring a security's price relative to itself over time. The RSI indicates a security's momentum, and it gives the best results when used by active investors for short trading periods. It also helps to identify market extremes and points of divergence, signaling that a security is approaching its price top or bottom and may reverse its price trend. (Another type of RSI shows how a security's price movement performs *against a broad market measure* such as the DJIA or S&P 500.)

The RSI is the ratio of the average price change on up days to the average price change on down days during the same period. The index formula is

$$\text{RSI} = 100 - \left[100\Big/\left(1 + \frac{\text{Average price change on up days}}{\text{Average price change on down days}}\right)\right]$$

The RSI can cover various periods of time (days, weeks, or months). The most common RSIs at the popular technical-analysis Web sites are 9-, 14-, and 25-period RSIs.

The RSI ranges between 0 and 100. Most RSIs range between 30 and 70. Generally, RSI values above 70–80 indicate an *overbought* condition (more and stronger buying than the fundamentals justify), which may signal that a reversal of the upward price trend is possible. RSI values below 30 indicate a possible *oversold* condition (more selling than fundamentals might indicate) and a possible reversal of the downward trend. When the RSI crosses these points, it signals a possible trend reversal. The wider 80–20 range is often used with the 9-day RSI, which tends to be more volatile than longer-period RSIs. In bull markets, 80 may be a better upper indicator than 70, whereas in bear markets, 20 is a more accurate lower level. Different sectors and industries have varying RSI threshold levels. By watching the RSI over the long term (one year or more), you can determine the historical RSI trading level and the turning points for a particular stock. Also, the entrance of the RSI into the extreme levels does not mean you should buy or sell, but it does tell you to watch for that possibility.

How can you use the RSI in your own trading? Here are three possible strategies using extremes:

- Buy when the RSI moves above 70 and sell when it falls below 30. However, the trend may have further to run, and you may trade too soon.
- Sell when the RSI crosses below 70 and buy when it moves above 30. This is a popular strategy using 9-day RSIs. However, this strategy has the opposite drawback to the strategy above: You could enter a trade after the trend reversal occurs.
- Sell when an above-70 RSI begins to turn down or buy when a below-30 RSI turns upward. This also has some pitfalls, because the RSI tends to move to extremes during periods of strong price trends and may give false signals.

Another way to use RSIs is to compare price charts and RSIs. Most of the time, both move in the same direction. Hence a divergence between RSI and a price chart can be a strong signal of a changing trend.

Like other technical indicators, the RSI has limitations. It should not be used alone but, rather, works best in combination with other tools such as charting, moving averages, and trendlines. Among the Web sites that offer RSI as a charting option are BigCharts (www.bigcharts.com) and MetaStock Online (www.metastock.com).

Sources: "Using the Relative Strength Index," *Investopedia.com*, www.investopedia.com; Geoffrey N. Smith, "Riding the Wave," *Fidelity Outlook*, Fall 1999, pp. 8–9; and Wayne A. Thorp, "Measuring Internal Strength: Wilder's Indicator," *AAII Journal*, May 2000, pp. 28–32.

FIGURE 8.1

Some Market Statistics

Individual investors can obtain all sorts of technical information at little or no cost from brokerage houses, investment services, the popular financial media, or the Internet. Here, for example, is a sample of information from the *Wall Street Journal.* Note that a variety of information about market volume, new highs and lows, number of advancing and declining stocks, and market averages is available from this one source. (*Source: Wall Street Journal,* October 10, 2000, p. C2.)

STOCK MARKET DATA BANK 10/9/00

MAJOR INDEXES

†12-MO HIGH	†12-MO LOW		DAILY HIGH	DAILY LOW	CLOSE	NET CHG	% CHG	†12-MO CHG	% CHG	FROM 12/31	% CHG
DOW JONES AVERAGES											
11722.98	9796.03	**30 Industrials**	10641.31	10546.23	10568.43	− 28.11	− 0.27	− 79.75	− 0.75	− 928.69	− 8.08
3099.67	2263.59	**20 Transportation**	2543.65	2483.75	2490.63	− 53.02	− 2.08	− 535.39	− 17.69	− 486.57	− 16.34
401.47	269.20	**15 Utilities**	384.72	378.92	381.50	+ 2.52	+ 0.66	+ 85.78	+ 29.01	+ 98.14	+ 34.63
3305.46	2751.55	**65 Composite**	3143.80	3113.62	3120.64	− 11.52	− 0.37	+ 31.57	+ 1.02	− 93.74	− 2.92
364.71	285.95	**DJ US Total Mkt**	330.10	324.80	328.51	− 1.13	− 0.34	+ 22.79	+ 7.46	− 13.06	− 3.82
NEW YORK STOCK EXCHANGE											
677.58	576.17	**Composite**	656.73	651.55	653.55	− 2.57	− 0.39	+ 40.22	+ 6.56	+ 3.25	+ 0.50
851.94	728.87	**Industrials**	815.84	809.44	812.68	− 1.08	− 0.13	+ 37.75	+ 4.87	− 15.53	− 1.88
519.96	443.98	**Utilities**	467.25	462.83	463.74	− 2.90	− 0.62	− 25.86	− 5.28	− 47.41	− 9.28
493.03	353.51	**Transportation**	412.96	405.09	406.04	− 5.82	− 1.41	− 53.23	− 11.59	− 60.66	− 13.00
634.16	442.71	**Finance**	606.34	598.22	599.44	− 6.41	− 1.06	+ 104.11	+ 21.02	+ 82.83	+ 16.03
STANDARD & POOR'S INDEXES											
1527.46	1247.41	**500 Index**	1409.69	1392.48	1402.03	− 6.96	− 0.49	+ 66.82	+ 5.00	− 67.22	− 4.58
1917.64	1544.13	**Industrials**	1687.16	1664.50	1677.99	− 7.04	− 0.42	+ 29.03	+ 1.76	− 163.93	− 8.90
341.15	215.62	**Utilities**	326.33	321.87	325.77	+ 3.90	+ 1.21	+ 87.51	+ 36.73	+ 98.55	+ 43.37
548.60	369.50	**400 MidCap**	513.31	502.85	513.04	+ 0.12	+ 0.02	+ 121.48	+ 31.02	+ 68.37	+ 15.38
225.12	168.96	**600 SmallCap**	206.57	203.02	206.14	− 0.43	− 0.21	+ 29.36	+ 16.61	+ 8.35	+ 4.22
324.40	262.26	**1500 Index**	300.76	296.96	299.32	− 1.36	− 0.45	+ 19.36	+ 6.92	− 9.57	− 3.10
NASDAQ STOCK MARKET											
5048.62	2688.18	**Composite**	3376.92	3233.19	3355.56	− 5.45	− 0.16	+ 439.61	+ 15.08	− 713.75	− 17.54
4704.73	2362.11	**Nasdaq 100**	3359.93	3185.28	3318.90	+ 6.96	+ 0.21	+ 740.02	+ 28.70	− 388.93	− 10.49
2841.00	1549.93	**Industrials**	1886.69	1806.19	1879.09	− 3.45	− 0.18	+ 194.58	+ 11.55	− 359.88	− 16.07
2075.12	1602.08	**Insurance**	1840.73	1818.94	1840.73	− 24.09	− 1.29	− 167.08	− 8.32	− 55.55	− 2.93
1837.10	1340.36	**Banks**	1749.17	1721.52	1735.59	− 13.50	− 0.77	+ 1.98	+ 0.11	+ 44.30	+ 2.62
2964.66	1448.32	**Computer**	1946.91	1855.05	1927.72	− 6.74	− 0.35	+ 346.39	+ 21.90	− 397.68	− 17.10
1230.06	639.02	**Telecommunications**	678.53	645.71	673.67	+ 6.42	+ 0.96	− 33.24	− 4.70	− 341.73	− 33.65
OTHERS											
1036.40	774.49	**Amex Composite**	923.34	914.11	921.90	+ 1.19	+ 0.13	+ 131.88	+ 16.69	+ 44.93	+ 5.12
813.71	646.79	**Russell 1000**	752.37	740.87	748.51	− 3.07	− 0.41	+ 57.05	+ 8.25	− 19.46	− 2.53
606.12	408.90	**Russell 2000**	491.02	481.64	489.53	− 1.49	− 0.30	+ 59.34	+ 13.79	− 15.22	− 3.02
844.78	667.03	**Russell 3000**	776.72	764.94	773.13	− 3.12	− 0.40	+ 61.54	+ 8.65	− 20.18	− 2.54
439.78	394.35	**Value-Line** (geom.)	405.45	401.08	405.16	− 0.15	− 0.04	− 15.49	− 3.68	− 25.88	− 6.00
14751.64	11446.60	**Wilshire 5000**	....	....	13099.79	− 42.37	− 0.32	+ 902.69	+ 7.40	− 712.88	− 5.16

†-Based on comparable trading day in preceding year.

MOST ACTIVE ISSUES

NYSE	VOLUME	CLOSE	CHANGE
Motorola	15,679,200	27.00	− 0.75
Nokia	11,569,900	37.00	− 0.69
NortelNtwks	11,531,400	63.25	+ 0.94
EMC Cp	11,522,500	89.75	+ 0.56
LucentTch	11,443,800	32.31	− 0.94
AT&T	10,183,000	26.56	− 0.69
TX Instr	9,756,500	45.38	− 1.50
GenElec	9,687,200	58.50	− 0.94
SBC Comm	9,384,900	52.44	− 0.88
AmOnline	8,565,400	57.10	− 2.03
AdvMicro	7,879,500	22.38	+ 0.38
MicronTch	7,038,800	39.75	− 1.06
OwenCorn	6,749,100	1.06	+ 0.31
Firstar	6,550,900	17.94	− 1.06
Compaq	6,509,500	25.48	+ 0.47
NASDAQ			
Intel	55,627,000	39.06	− 0.88
CiscoSys	45,487,400	53.69	− 2.50
DellCptr	37,031,700	25.63	+ 0.31
Microsoft	28,166,400	54.19	− 1.38
WorldCom	23,456,400	25.94	+ 0.75
BroadVisn	20,481,800	21.94	+ 3.69
OracleCp	20,037,000	66.75	− 0.88
Connetics	20,027,900	5.31	− 20.19
SunMicrsys	19,674,100	106.81	− 0.69
JDS Uniphs	17,489,000	93.56	+ 2.19
AlteraCp	14,390,100	40.88	− 3.44
AppldMatl	13,702,100	55.75	+ 1.56
Yahoo	12,844,800	85.75	+ 4.50
AMEX			
NASDAQ100	28,825,000	82.63	− 0.38
SPDR	4,499,800	140.00	− 1.06
SPDR Engy	1,375,800	32.75	+ 0.50
Biotch HLDRs	1,028,400	174.50	+ 1.31
S&P Midcap	768,900	94.25	+ 0.25

DIARIES

NYSE	MON	FRI	WK 10/6
Issues traded	3,241	3,284	3,353
Advances	1,194	816	1,265
Declines	1,562	2,009	1,646
Unchanged	485	459	442
New highs	18	47	109
New lows	88	119	75
zAdv vol (000)	302,482	256,079	527,508
zDecl vol (000)	379,166	833,336	438,532
zTotal vol (000)	714,147	1,139,205	1,023,912
Closing tick[1]	−204	−747	−304
Closing Arms[2] (trin)	.96	1.32	.64
zBlock trades	14,794	24,596	21,083
NASDAQ			
Issues traded	4,548	4,596	4,726
Advances	1,497	1,076	1,422
Declines	2,378	2,902	2,731
Unchanged	673	618	573
New highs	16	21	85
New lows	300	313	168
Adv vol (000)	656,400	347,249	445,623
Decl vol (000)	715,415	1,413,816	1,223,868
Total vol (000)	1,401,613	1,801,431	1,721,643
Block trades	n.a.	22,543	20,552
AMEX			
Issues traded	713	742	779
Advances	211	155	225
Declines	346	427	383
Unchanged	156	160	171
New highs	2	3	13
New lows	50	45	32
zAdv vol (000)	8,391	4,400	11,380
zDecl vol (000)	31,759	50,771	30,912
zTotal vol (000)	41,868	57,393	44,746
Comp vol (000)	58,223	78,577	63,237
zBlock trades	n.a.	1,399	954

short interest
the number of stocks sold short in the market at any given time; a technical indicator believed to indicate future market demand.

short in the market at any given point in time is known as the **short interest.** The more stocks that are sold short, the higher the short interest. Because all short sales must eventually be "covered" (the borrowed shares must be returned), a short sale in effect ensures *future demand for the stock.* Thus, the market is viewed optimistically when the level of short interest becomes relatively high by historical standards. The logic is that as shares are bought back to cover outstanding short sales, the additional demand will push stock prices up. The amount of short interest on the NYSE, the AMEX, and Nasdaq's National Market is published monthly in the *Wall Street Journal* and *Barron's.* Figure 8.2 shows the type of information that's available.

Keeping track of the level of short interest can indicate future market demand, but it can also reveal *present* market optimism or pessimism. Short selling is usually done by knowledgeable investors, and a significant buildup or decline in the level of short interest is thought to reveal the sentiment of sophisticated investors about the current state of the market or a company. For example, a significant shift upward in short interest is believed to indicate pessimism concerning the *current* state of the market, even though it may signal optimism with regard to *future* levels of demand.

Odd-Lot Trading A rather cynical saying on Wall Street suggests that the best thing to do is just the opposite of whatever the small investor is doing. The reasoning behind this is that as a group, small investors are notoriously wrong in their timing of investment decisions: The investing public usually does not come into the market in force until after a bull market has pretty much run its course, and it does not get out until late in a bear market. Although its validity is debatable, this is the premise behind a widely followed technical indicator and is the basis for the **theory of contrary opinion.** This theory uses the amount and type of odd-lot trading as an indicator of the current state of the market and pending changes.

theory of contrary opinion
a technical indicator that uses the amount and type of odd-lot trading as an indicator of the current state of the market and pending changes.

Because many individual investors deal in transactions of less than 100 shares, their combined sentiments are supposedly captured in odd-lot figures. The idea is to see what odd-lot investors are doing "on balance." So long as there is little or no difference in the spread between the volume of odd-lot purchases and sales, the theory of contrary opinion holds that the market will probably continue pretty much along its current line (either up or down). When the balance of odd-lot purchases and sales begins to change dramatically, it may be a signal that a bull or bear market is about to end. For example, if the amount of odd-lot purchases starts to exceed odd-lot sales by an ever widening margin, it may suggest that speculation on the part of small investors is starting to get out of control—an ominous signal that the final stages of a bull market may be at hand.

Using Technical Analysis

Investors have a wide range of choices with respect to technical analysis. They can use the charts and complex ratios of the technical analysts. Or they can, more informally, use technical analysis just to get a general sense of the market. In the latter case, market behavior itself is not as important as the implications such behavior can have on the price performance of a particular stock. Thus technical analysis might be used in conjunction with fundamental analysis to determine when to add a particular stock to one's portfolio. Some investors and professional money managers, in fact, look at the technical side of a stock

FIGURE 8.2 Short Interest in the NYSE and the AMEX

The amount of short selling in the market is closely watched by many investment professionals and individual investors. The summary report shown here provides an overview of the extent to which stocks are being shorted in the NYSE and the AMEX. In addition to summary statistics, this monthly report lists all stocks that have been sold short and the number of shares shorted. (*Source: Wall Street Journal*, October 20, 2000.)

NYSE AND AMEX SHORT-SELLING HIGHLIGHTS

LARGEST SHORT POSITIONS

RANK	Oct. 13	Sep. 15	CHANGE
NYSE			
1 Sprint Corp PCS	66,415,612	74,456,483	−8,040,871
2 Citigroup Inc	59,637,216	49,068,672	10,568,544
3 Conseco Inc	59,353,764	66,583,520	−7,229,756
4 Disney (Walt)	58,335,995	56,281,733	2,054,262
5 Nortel Networks	53,909,149	49,342,343	4,566,806
6 VodafoneGroPlcAd	51,661,895	47,106,170	4,555,725
7 America Online Inc	49,938,130	56,219,225	−6,281,095
8 Motorola Inc	43,513,358	37,351,171	6,162,187
9 Rite Aid Corp	41,647,092	37,854,017	3,793,075
10 Lucent Techs	39,733,955	30,721,305	9,012,650
11 AT&T Corp	39,382,017	45,378,252	−5,996,235
12 Deutsche Telkom AG	38,821,574	27,056,296	11,765,278
13 Dow Chemical	35,187,991	33,674,653	1,513,338
14 HCA-Healthcare Co	34,518,092	32,378,947	2,139,145
15 Wal-Mart Stores	33,995,355	35,030,387	−1,035,032
16 Chase Manhattan	30,865,889	7,336,920	23,528,969
17 Adv Micro Dev Inc	30,368,955	25,631,649	4,737,306
18 General Electric	27,419,114	27,622,049	−202,935
19 Telefonos Mex Serl	27,175,400	28,008,846	−833,446
20 Wells Fargo Co	26,907,461	23,438,098	3,469,363
AMEX			
1 Nasdaq-100 Trust	43,061,899	51,574,112	−8,512,213
2 SPDR	15,145,106	14,877,818	267,288
3 Nabor Indus Inc	10,054,415	9,649,077	405,338
4 Trans World Airlin	9,233,693	9,673,034	−439,341
5 Ivax Corp	6,758,079	7,387,020	−628,941

LARGEST CHANGES

RANK	Oct. 13	Sep. 15	CHANGE
NYSE			
POSITIVE			
1 Chase Manhattan	30,865,889	7,336,920	23,528,969
2 Federal-Mogul	18,858,451	4,338,848	14,519,603
3 Deutsche Telkom AG	38,821,574	27,056,296	11,765,278
4 Citigroup Inc	59,637,216	49,068,672	10,568,544
5 Lucent Techs	39,733,955	30,721,305	9,012,650
6 Tyco Intl	25,881,088	17,064,934	8,816,154
7 NiSource Inc	18,143,636	11,517,539	6,626,097
8 Motorola Inc	43,513,358	37,351,171	6,162,187
NEGATIVE			
1 Sprint Corp PCS	66,415,612	74,456,483	−8,040,871
2 Conseco Inc	59,353,764	66,583,520	−7,229,756
3 America Online Inc	49,938,130	56,219,225	−6,281,095
4 AT&T Corp	39,382,017	45,378,252	−5,996,235
5 Compaq Computer	20,483,166	26,301,585	−5,818,419
6 ClearChannelCommun	14,613,705	20,108,201	−5,494,496
7 Micron Technology	12,028,233	16,242,673	−4,214,440
8 Limited Inc	7,468,738	11,520,926	−4,052,188
AMEX			
POSITIVE			
1 SPDR Enrgy Sel XLE	4,328,985	1,511,584	2,817,401
2 SPDR Fin Selct XLF	3,269,081	720,753	2,548,328
3 SPDR Cycl/Trans	1,643,780	232,040	1,411,740
4 Biotech Holdrs Tru	3,194,219	2,195,468	998,751
5 iShares S&P500	1,815,197	1,138,255	676,942
NEGATIVE			
1 Nasdaq-100 Trust	43,061,899	51,574,112	−8,512,213
2 S&P MidCap	2,428,659	3,661,636	−1,232,977
3 U.S. Cellular Corp	3,693,788	4,688,187	−994,399
4 iShares MSCI UK	71,920	793,733	−721,813
5 Ivax Corp	6,758,079	7,387,020	−628,941

NYSE Short Interest

(In millions of shares)

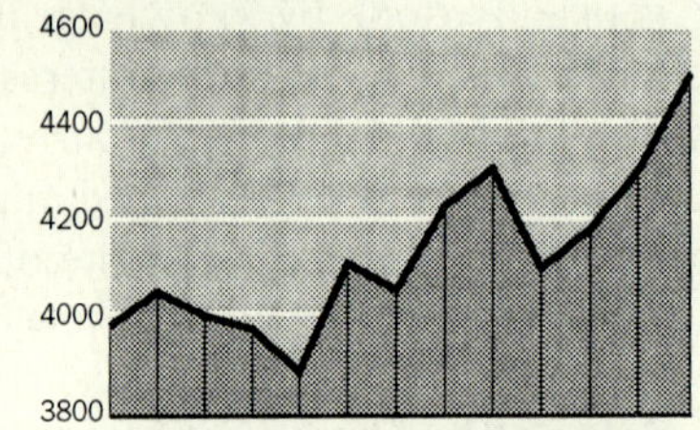

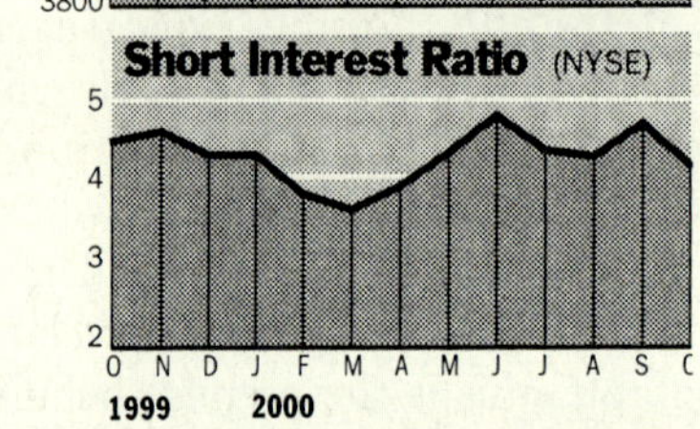

LARGEST SHORT INTEREST RATIOS

The short interest ratio is the number of days it would take to cover the short interest if trading continued at the average daily volume for the month.

RANK	Oct. 13 SHORT INT.	AVG DLY VOL-a	DAYS TO COVER
NYSE			
1 Philippine LdTel-G	1,839,900	1,605	1,146
2 Madeco Adr	4,170,300	15,335	272
3 Quebecor World Inc	1,181,093	5,715	207
4 Comp Cerv Unidas	4,161,100	29,225	142
5 Co Siderurgica ADS	4,034,006	31,815	127
6 Royal Group Techno	3,081,090	26,165	118
7 Compnha Vle DoRioD	14,830,873	151,035	98
8 FltchrChlBlgADS	2,000,900	24,150	83
9 Advocat Inc	1,945,200	29,375	66
10 Vector Group LTD	1,577,345	25,530	62
11 TelecomNZ ADR	4,108,655	65,915	62
12 Revlon Inc. Cl A	3,400,272	58,330	58
13 Total Sys Svcs	1,735,756	29,905	58
14 Nova Chemicals	1,225,518	21,895	56
15 Penn Treaty Americ	954,091	18,175	52
16 Chiquita Brands	3,827,179	78,880	49
17 Aviation Sales	2,563,891	54,405	47
18 Coachmen Indus	1,133,375	24,055	47
AMEX			
1 Blackrock 1999 Ter	1,500,061	6,225	241
2 BioTime Inc	1,441,606	22,630	64
3 iShares MSCI Mexico	2,005,032	33,160	60
4 Hemispherx Biophar	3,584,269	64,320	56
5 Alterra Healthcare	2,493,147	73,055	34

a-Includes securities with average daily volume of 20,000 shares or more. n-New. r-Revised.

Issues that split in the latest month are excluded.

The largest percentage increase and decrease sections are limited to issues with previously established short provisions in both months.

LARGEST % INCREASES

RANK	Oct. 13	Sep. 15	%
NYSE			
1 Conectiv	2,802,595	264,949	957.8
2 Gulf Canada Resour	3,368,086	341,607	886.0
3 GPU Inc	1,808,172	381,978	373.4
4 Federal-Mogul	18,858,451	4,338,848	334.6
5 Chase Manhattan	30,865,889	7,336,920	320.7
6 Alliant Energy	1,306,216	364,477	258.4
7 Gabelli Eqty Tr	964,100	284,662	238.7
8 AmbacFinlGrp	984,589	299,174	229.1
9 Vivendi	4,806,932	1,559,812	208.2
10 JohnsonControls	1,081,475	379,814	184.7
11 Analog Devices Inc	5,289,947	1,893,027	179.4
12 Scana Corp	1,629,705	625,838	160.4
13 Intl Game Tech	2,519,920	1,032,534	144.1
14 Korea Telecom	1,121,799	459,884	143.9
15 Paine Webber Grp	1,957,592	841,000	132.8
16 Rockwell Intl	3,774,401	1,663,914	126.8
17 SunGard Data Systm	3,930,772	1,762,217	123.1
18 Pitney Bowes	4,653,647	2,090,339	122.6
19 United Technolgies	4,558,864	2,051,191	122.3
20 Furniture Brands	1,208,087	545,090	121.6
AMEX			
1 SPDR Cycl/Trans	1,643,780	232,040	608.4
2 SPDR Fin Selct XLF	3,269,081	720,753	353.6
3 SPDR Enrgy Sel XLE	4,328,985	1,511,584	186.4
4 iShares S&P500	1,815,197	1,138,255	59.5
5 Biotech Holdrs Tru	3,194,219	2,195,468	45.5

LARGEST % DECREASES

RANK	Oct. 13	Sep. 15	%
NYSE			
1 Pearson PLC	146,001	1,240,855	−88.2
2 Energy East Cp-Hld	114,351	936,646	−87.8
3 Repsol YPE S.A.Ads	379,705	2,136,419	−82.2
4 Homestake Mining	939,550	4,797,345	−80.4
5 Northeast Util	250,892	1,263,620	−80.1
6 UltramarDiamondShm	353,513	1,408,915	−74.9
7 Unicom Corp	775,030	2,564,199	−69.8
8 Ahold NV ADS	474,805	1,483,099	−68.0
9 Nabisco Grp Hldgs	489,992	1,483,293	−67.0
10 Praxair Inc	700,894	1,877,167	−62.7
11 Scientific-Atlanta	732,349	1,914,601	−61.7
12 TXU Corp	2,328,336	6,079,240	−61.7
13 Lincoln Natl Corp	1,079,785	2,799,976	−61.4
14 Stora Enso Oyj	1,066,432	2,764,438	−61.4
15 OGE Energy Corp	1,180,221	2,946,598	−59.9
16 Taiwan Semi	2,525,063	6,088,230	−58.5
17 Fox Entertainment	1,214,996	2,899,208	−58.1
18 Intrstate Bakeries	537,136	1,263,873	−57.5
19 Sherwn-Williams	729,687	1,694,424	−56.9
20 Hillenbrand Indus	657,187	1,453,999	−54.8
AMEX			
1 iShares MSCI UK	71,920	793,733	−90.9
2 S&P MidCap	2,428,659	3,661,636	−33.7
3 U.S. Cellular Corp	3,693,788	4,688,187	−21.2
4 Diamonds Trust	1,981,893	2,375,294	−16.6
5 Nasdaq-100 Trust	43,061,899	51,574,112	−16.5

before doing any fundamental analysis. If the stock is found to be technically sound, then they'll look at its fundamentals; if not, they'll look for another stock. For these investors, the concerns of technical analysis are still the same: *Do the technical factors indicate that this might be a good stock to buy?*

HOTLINKS

Other technical analysis sites that help with research are the following:

www.dailystocks.com
www.chartpatterns.com
www.stockcharts.com
stockmaster.com
my.zacks.com

Most investors rely on published sources, such as those put out by brokerage firms—or, now, widely available on the Internet—to obtain necessary technical insights. They often find it helpful to use several different approaches. For example, an investor might follow market P/Es and dividend yields and also keep track of market volume and breadth of the market. Such information provides the investor with a convenient and low-cost way of staying abreast of the market. Certainly, trying to determine the right (or best) time to get into the market is a principal objective of technical analysis—and one of the major pastimes of many investors.

Charting

charting
the activity of charting price behavior and other market information and then using the patterns these charts form to make investment decisions.

Charting is perhaps the best-known activity of the technical analyst. Technicians—analysts who believe it is chiefly (or solely) supply and demand that drives stock prices—use various types of charts to plot the behavior of everything from the Dow Jones Industrial Average to the share price movements of individual listed and OTC stocks. Just about every kind of technical indicator is charted in one form or another. Figure 8.3 on page 276 shows a typical stock chart. In this case, the price behavior of Medtronic, Inc. has been plotted, along with a variety of supplementary technical information about the stock.

Charts are popular because they provide a visual summary of activity over time. Perhaps more important (in the eyes of technicians, at least), they contain valuable information about developing trends and the future behavior of the market and/or individual stocks. Chartists believe price patterns evolve into *chart formations* that provide signals about the future course of the market or a stock. We will now briefly review the practice of charting, including popular types of charts, chart formations, and investor uses of charts.

bar chart
the simplest kind of chart, on which share price is plotted on the vertical axis and time on the horizontal axis; stock prices are recorded as vertical bars showing high, low, and closing prices.

Bar Charts The simplest and probably most widely used type of chart is the **bar chart.** Market or share prices are plotted on the vertical axis, and time is plotted on the horizontal axis. This type of chart derives its name from the fact that prices are recorded as vertical bars that depict high, low, and closing prices. A typical bar chart is shown in Figure 8.4 on page 276. Note that on December 31, this particular stock had a high price of 29 a low of 27, and closed at 27.50. Because these charts contain a time element, technicians frequently plot a variety of other pertinent information on them. For example, volume is often put at the base of bar charts (see the Medtronic chart in Figure 8.3).

point-and-figure charts
charts used to keep track of emerging price patterns by plotting significant price changes with *X*s and *O*s but with no time dimension used.

Point-and-Figure Charts **Point-and-figure charts** are used strictly to keep track of emerging price patterns. Because there is no time dimension on them, they are *not* used for plotting technical measures. Point-and-figure charts are unique in two other ways: First, only *significant* price changes are recorded on these charts. That is, prices have to move by a certain minimum amount—usually at least a point or two—before a new price level is recognized. Second, price *reversals* show up only after a predetermined change in direction occurs. Normally, only closing

FIGURE 8.3 **A Stock Chart**

This chart for Medtronics, Inc. contains information about the daily price behavior of the stock, along with the stock's relative strength, its moving average, its trading volume, and several other pieces of supplementary data. (*Source:* Chart courtesy of Stockcharts.com *Note:* Visit this Web site's glossary for expanded definitions.)

FIGURE 8.4

A Bar Chart

Bar charts are widely used to track stock prices, market averages, and numerous other technical measures.

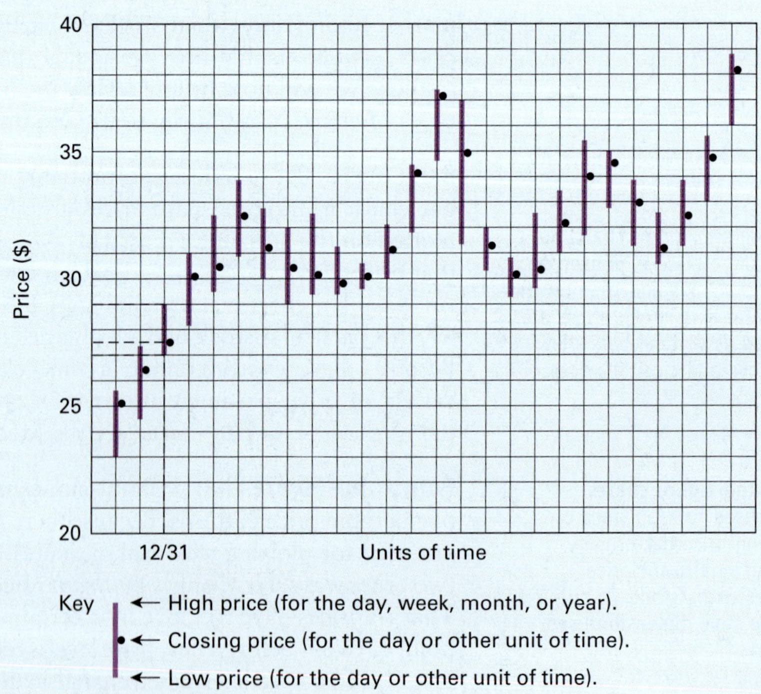

prices are charted, though some point-and-figure charts use all price changes during the day. An X is used to denote an increase in price, an O a decrease.

Figure 8.5 shows a common point-and-figure chart. In this case, the chart employs a 2-point box: The stock must move by a minimum of 2 points before any changes are recorded. The chart can cover a span of one year or less if the stock is highly active. Or it can cover a number of years if the stock is not very active. As a rule, low-priced stocks are charted with 1-point boxes, moderately priced shares with increments of 2 to 3 points, and high-priced securities with 3- to 5-point boxes.

Here is how point-and-figure charts work: Suppose we are at point A on the chart in Figure 8.5. The stock has been hovering around this \$40–\$41 mark for some time. Assume, however, that it just closed at \$42.25. Now, because the minimum 2-point movement has been met, the chartist would place an X in the box immediately *above* point A. The chartist would remain with this new box as long as the price moved (up or down) within the 2-point range of 42 to 44. Although the chartist follows *daily* prices, a new entry is made on the chart only after the price has changed by a certain minimum amount and moved into a new 2-point box. We see that from point A, the price generally moved up over time to nearly \$50 a share. At that point (indicated as point B on the chart), things began to change as a reversal set in. That is, the price of the stock began to drift downward and in time moved out of the \$48–\$50 box. This reversal prompts the chartist to change columns and symbols, by moving one column to the right and recording the new price level with an O in the \$46–\$48 box. The chartist will continue to use Os as long as the stock continues to close on a generally lower note.

Chart Formations The information that charts supposedly contain about the future course of the market (or a stock) is thought by some to be revealed in chart *formations*. That is, chartists believe that in response to certain supply and demand forces, emerging price patterns result in various formations that historically have indicated that certain types of market behavior are imminent. If you

FIGURE 8.5

A Point-and-Figure Chart

Point-and-figure charts are unusual because they have no time dimension. Rather, a column of Xs is used to reflect a general upward drift in prices, and a column of Os is used when prices are drifting downward.

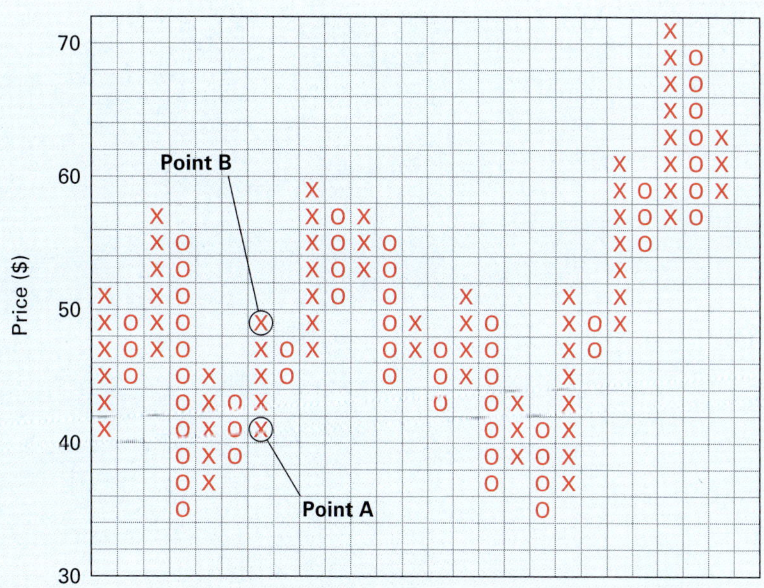

know how to interpret charts (which is no easy task), you can see formations building and recognize buy and sell signals. These chart formations are often given some pretty exotic names, such as *head and shoulders, falling wedge, scallop and saucer, ascending triangle,* and *island reversal,* to name just a few.

Figure 8.6 shows four formations. The patterns form "support levels" and "resistance lines" that, when combined with the basic formations, yield buy and sell signals. Panel A is an example of a *buy* signal that occurs when prices break out above a resistance line in a particular pattern. In contrast, when prices break out below a support level, as they do at the end of the formation in panel B, a *sell* signal is said to occur. Supposedly, a sell signal means everything is in place for a major drop in the market (or in the price of a share of stock). A buy signal indicates that the opposite is about to occur. Unfortunately, one of the major problems with charting is that the formations rarely appear as neatly and cleanly as those in Figure 8.6. Rather, identifying and interpreting them often demands considerable imagination.

Investor Uses Charts are merely tools used by market analysts and technicians to assess conditions in the market and/or the price behavior of individual stocks. Unlike other types of technical measures, charting is seldom done on an informal basis. Either you chart because you believe in its value, or you don't chart at all. A chart by itself tells you little more than where the market

FIGURE 8.6

Some Popular Chart Formations

To chartists, each of these formations has meaning about the future course of events.

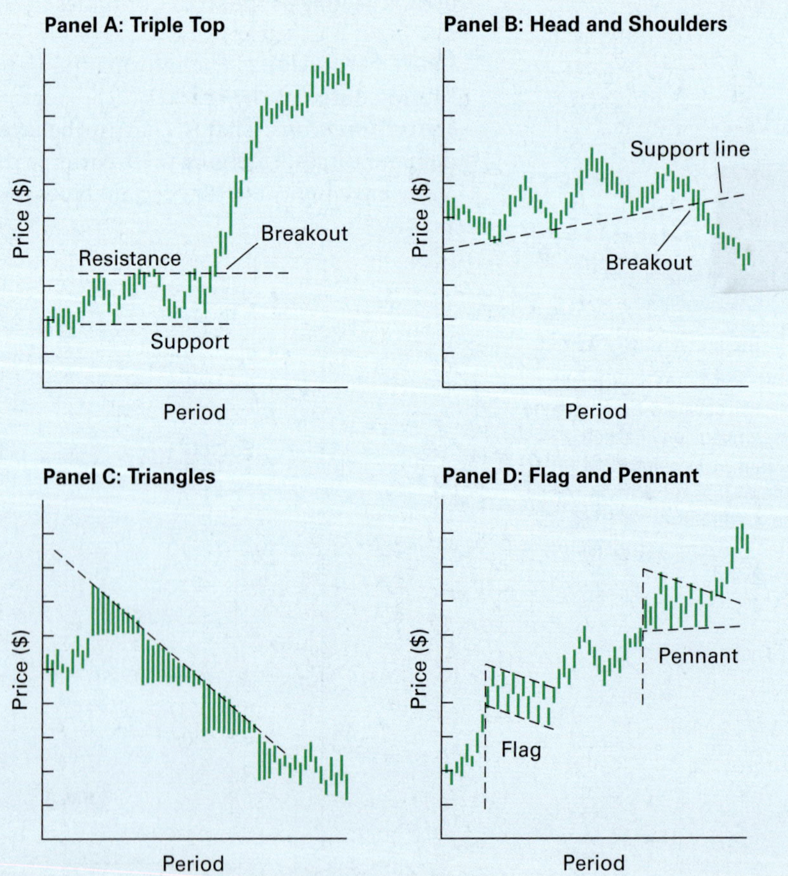

or a stock has been. But to chartists, those price patterns yield formations that, along with things like resistance lines, support levels, and breakouts, tell them what to expect in the future. Chartists believe that history repeats itself, so they study the historical reactions of stocks (or the market) to various formations, and they devise trading rules based on these observations. It makes no difference to chartists whether they are following the market or an individual stock. *It is the formation that matters,* not the issue being plotted. The value of charts lies in knowing how to "read" them and how to respond to the signals they are said to give about the future. A long-standing debate (some would call it a feud) still rages on Wall Street regarding the merits of charting. Although a large segment of investors and investment professionals may scoff at it, to avid chartists, charting is no laughing matter.

Random Walks and Efficient Markets

LG 6

random walk hypothesis
the theory that stock price movements are unpredictable, so there's no way to know where prices are headed.

If a drunk were abandoned in an open field at night, where would you begin to search for him the next morning? The answer, of course, is the spot where the drunk was left the night before, because there's no way to predict where he will go. To some analysts, stock prices seem to wander about in a similar fashion. Observations of such erratic movements have led to a body of evidence called the random walk hypothesis. Its followers believe that price movements are unpredictable and therefore security analysis will not help to predict future market behavior. This hypothesis obviously has serious implications for much of what we have discussed in the last two chapters.

A Brief Historical Overview

To describe stock prices as a random walk suggests that price movements cannot be expected to follow any type of pattern. Or, put another way, price movements are independent of one another. In order to find a theory for such behavior, researchers developed the concept of efficient markets. As we discussed briefly in Chapter 7, the basic idea behind an efficient market is that the market price of securities always fully reflects available information. This means that it would be difficult, if not impossible, to consistently outperform the market by picking "undervalued" stocks.

Random Walks The first evidence of random price movements dates back to the early 1900s. During that period, statisticians noticed that commodity prices seemed to follow a "fair game" pattern. That is, prices seemed to move up and down randomly, giving no advantage to any particular trading strategy. Although a few studies on the subject appeared in the 1930s, thorough examination of the randomness in stock prices did not begin until 1959. From that point on, particularly through the decade of the 1960s, the random walk issue was one of the most keenly debated topics in stock market literature. The development of high-speed computers has helped researchers compile convincing evidence that stock prices do, in fact, come very close to a random walk.

Efficient Markets Given the extensive random walk evidence, market researchers were faced with another question: What sort of market would produce prices that seem to fluctuate randomly? Such behavior could be the result of investors who are irrational and make investment decisions on whim. However, it has been argued much more convincingly that investors are not irrational. Rather, random price movements are evidence of highly efficient markets.

efficient market
a market in which securities reflect all possible information quickly and accurately.

An **efficient market** is one in which securities fully reflect all possible information quickly and accurately. The concept holds that investors incorporate all available information into their decisions about the price at which they are willing to buy or sell. At any point in time, then, the current price of a security incorporates all information. Additionally, the current price reflects not only past information, such as might be found in company reports and financial publications, but also information about events that have been announced but haven't yet occurred, like a forthcoming dividend payment. Furthermore, the current price reflects *predictions* about future information: Investors actively forecast important events and incorporate those forecasts into their estimates. Obviously, because of keen competition among investors, when new information becomes known, the price of the security adjusts quickly. This adjustment is not always perfect. Sometimes it is too large and at other times too small. But on average it balances out and is correct. The new price, in effect, is set after investors have fully assessed the new information.

Why Should Markets Be Efficient?

efficient markets hypothesis (EMH)
basic theory of the behavior of efficient markets, in which there are a large number of knowledgeable investors who react quickly to new information, causing securities prices to adjust quickly and accurately.

Active markets, such as the New York Stock Exchange, are efficient because they are made up of many rational, highly competitive investors who react quickly and objectively to new information. Investors, searching for market profits, compete vigorously for new information and do extremely thorough analyses. The **efficient markets hypothesis (EMH)**, which is the basic theory describing the behavior of such a market, has several tenets:

1. There are many knowledgeable investors actively analyzing, valuing, and trading any particular security. No one of these individual traders alone can affect the price of any security.
2. Information is widely available to all investors at approximately the same time, and this information is practically "free," or nearly so.
3. Information on events, such as labor strikes, industrial accidents, and changes in product demand, tends to occur randomly.
4. Investors react quickly and accurately to new information, causing prices to adjust quickly and, on average, accurately.

For the most part, the securities markets do, in fact, exhibit these characteristics.

Levels of Market Efficiency

The efficient markets hypothesis is concerned with *information*—not only the type and source of information, but also the quality and speed with which it is disseminated among investors. It is convenient to discuss the EMH in three cumulative categories or forms: past prices only; past prices *plus* all other public data, and, finally, past prices and public data *plus* private information. Together, these three ways of looking at information flows in the market represent three forms of the EMH: the weak, semi-strong, and strong forms.

weak form (EMH)
form of the EMH holding that past data on stock prices are of no use in predicting future prices.

Weak Form The **weak form of the EMH** holds that past data on stock prices are of no use in predicting future price changes. If prices follow a random walk, price changes over time are random. Today's price change is unrelated to yesterday's or to that of any other day, just as each step by a drunk is unrelated to previous steps. If new information arrives randomly, then prices will change randomly.

A number of people have asserted that it is possible to profit from "runs" in a stock's price. They contend that when a stock's price starts moving up, it will continue to move up for a period of time, developing momentum. If you can spot a run, then, on the basis of past prices alone, you can develop a trading strategy that will produce a profit. The results from much careful research suggest that momentum in stock prices does exist, and if investors quickly trade at the beginning of the run, large profits can be made. But there's a problem: In addition to spotting a run (no easy task), an investor would have to make numerous trades; when commissions are factored in, the person most likely to make a profit is the broker. Many other trading rules have been tested to determine whether profits can be made by examining past price movements, and there is very little, if any, evidence that a trading rule *based solely on past price data* can outperform a simple buy-and-hold strategy.

semi-strong form (EMH)
form of the EMH holding that abnormally large profits cannot be consistently earned using publicly available information.

Semi-Strong Form The **semi-strong form of the EMH** holds that abnormally large profits cannot be consistently earned using publicly available information. This information includes not only past price and volume data but also data such as corporate earnings, dividends, inflation, and stock splits. The semi-strong information set includes all of the information publicly considered in the weak form*, as well as all other information publicly available.* Tests of the semi-strong form of the EMH are basically concerned with the speed at which information is disseminated to investors. The research conclusions of research tests support the position that stock prices adjust very rapidly to new information and therefore support the semi-strong form of the EMH.

Most tests of semi-strong efficiency have examined how a stock price changes in response to an economic or financial event. A famous study involved stock splits. A stock split does not change the value of a company, so the value of the stock should not be affected by a stock split. The research indicated that there are sharp increases in the price of a stock *before* a stock split, but the changes after the split are random. Investors, therefore, cannot gain by purchasing stocks on or after the announcement of a split. To earn abnormal profits they would have to purchase before the split is announced. By the time of the announcement, the market has already incorporated into the price any favorable information associated with the split.

Other studies have examined the impact of major events on stock prices. The overwhelming evidence indicates that stock prices react within minutes, if not seconds, to any important new information. Certainly, by the time an investor reads about the event in the newspaper, the stock price has almost completely adjusted to the news. Even hearing about the event on the radio or television usually allows too little time to complete the transaction in time to make an abnormal profit.

strong form (EMH)
form of the EMH that holds that there is no information, public or private, that allows investors to earn abnormal profits consistently.

Strong Form The **strong form of the EMH** holds that there is no information, public or private, that allows investors to consistently earn abnormal profits. It states that stock prices immediately adjust to any information, even if it isn't available to every investor. This extreme form of the EMH has not received universal support.

One type of private information is the kind obtained by corporate insiders, such as officers or directors of a corporation. They have access to valuable information about major strategic and tactical decisions the company makes. They also have detailed information about the financial state of the firm that may not be available to other shareholders. Corporate insiders may legally trade shares of stock in their company, if they report the transactions to the Securities and Exchange Commission (SEC) each month. This information is then made public, usually within several weeks. It should not be surprising to learn that most studies of corporate insiders find that they consistently earn abnormally large profits when they sell their company stock. They are able to sell stock holdings before major announcements are made to the public and can thereby profit from the stock price adjustment that comes quickly after important news is released.

Other market participants occasionally have inside—nonpublic—information that they obtained *illegally.* With this information, they can gain an unfair advantage that permits them to earn an excess return. Clearly, those who trade securities on the basis of illegal inside information have an unfair advantage. Empirical research has confirmed that those with such inside information do indeed have an opportunity to earn an excess return—but there might be an awfully high price attached, such as spending time in prison, if they're caught.

Possible Implications

The concept of an efficient market holds serious implications for investors. In particular, it could have considerable bearing on traditional security analysis and stock valuation procedures. Some, in fact, contend that investors should spend less time analyzing securities and more time on such matters as reducing taxes and transaction costs, eliminating unnecessary risk, and constructing a widely diversified portfolio. Make no mistake about it: *Even in an efficient market, all sorts of return opportunities are available.* But to proponents of efficient markets, the only way to increase returns is to invest in a portfolio of higher-risk securities.

Implications for Technical Analysis The most serious challenge the random walk evidence presents is to technical analysis. If price fluctuations are purely random, charts of past prices are unlikely to produce significant trading profits. In a highly efficient market, shifts in supply and demand occur so rapidly that technical indicators simply measure after-the-fact events, with no implications for the future. But if markets are less than perfectly efficient, information may be absorbed slowly, producing gradual shifts in supply and demand conditions—and profit opportunities for those who recognize the shifts early. Although the great bulk of evidence supports a random walk, many investors follow a technical approach because they believe it improves their investment results.

Implications for Fundamental Analysis Many strict fundamental analysts were at first pleased by the random walk attack on technical analysis. Further development of the efficient markets concept, however, was not so well received: In an efficient market, it's argued, prices react so quickly to new information that not even security analysis will enable investors to realize consistently superior returns. Because of the extreme competition among investors, security prices are seldom far above or below their justified levels, and fundamental analysis thus loses much of its value. The problem is not that fundamental analysis is poorly done. On the contrary, it is done all too well! So many investors, competing so vigorously for profit opportunities, simply eliminate the opportunities before other investors can capitalize on them.

So Who Is Right?

Some type of fundamental analysis probably has a role in the stock selection process, for even in an efficient market, there is no question that stock prices reflect a company's profit performance. Some companies are fundamentally strong and others fundamentally weak, and investors must be able to distinguish between the two. Thus some time can profitably be spent in evaluating a company and its stock to determine, not if it is undervalued, but whether it is fundamentally strong.

The level of investor return, however, is more than a function of the fundamental condition of the company; it is also related to risk exposure. Fundamental analysis can help assess risk exposure and identify securities that possess risk commensurate with the return they offer.

The extent to which the markets are efficient is still subject to considerable debate. At present, there seems to be a growing consensus that although the markets may not be *perfectly* efficient, evidence suggests that they are at least *reasonably* efficient.

In the final analysis, the individual investor must decide on the merits of fundamental and technical analysis. Certainly, a large segment of the investing public believes in security analysis, even in a market that may be efficient. What is more, the principles of stock valuation—that promised return should be commensurate with exposure to risk—are valid in any type of market setting.

Summary

LG 1 **Explain the role a company's future plays in the stock valuation process and develop a forecast of a stock's expected cash flow.** The final phase of security analysis involves an assessment of the investment merits of a specific company and its stock. The focus here is on formulating expectations about the company's prospects and the risk and return behavior of the stock. In particular, we would want some idea of the stock's future earnings, dividends, and share prices, because that's ultimately the basis of our return.

LG 2 **Discuss the concepts of intrinsic value and required rates of return, and note how they are used.** Information such as projected sales, forecasted earnings, and estimated dividends are important in establishing intrinsic value. This is a measure, based on expected return and on risk exposure, of what the stock ought to be worth. A key element is the investor's required rate of return, which is used to define the amount of return that should be earned given the stock's perceived exposure to risk. The more risk in the investment, the more return one should require.

LG 3 **Determine the underlying value of a stock using the dividend valuation model, as well as other present value– and price/earnings–based stock valuation models.** The dividend valuation model derives the value of a share of stock from the stock's future growth in dividends. Another popular valuation procedure is the dividends-and-earnings approach, which uses a finite investment horizon to derive a present value–based "justified price." There's also the price/earnings approach to stock valuation, which uses projected EPS and the stock's P/E ratio to determine whether a stock is fairly valued. At times, investors find it more convenient to deal in terms of expected returns than in dollar-based justified prices. To do so, one would find the fully compounded rate of return by solving for the discount rate in the present value–based stock valuation model.

LG 4 **Gain a basic appreciation of the procedures used to value different types of stock, from traditional dividend-paying shares to new-economy stocks with their extreme price/earnings ratios.** Various forms of the dividend valuation model work fine for companies that pay dividends. For those that pay little or nothing in dividends, the dividend-and-earnings and P/E approaches are used. But even these procedures often don't work well with many of the new-economy tech stocks, which may not have dividends, may not even have profits, and may sell at astronomical P/E ratios. To value these stocks, we use the discounted cash flow approach (which is like the D&E approach except that value is based solely on the estimated future price of the stock) or some type of price multiple (usually, the price/sales multiple). Though far from perfect, these procedures at least enable investors to get a rough idea of the value of these high-flying tech stocks.

LG 5 **Describe the key attributes of technical analysis, including some popular measures and procedures used to assess the market.** Technical analysis is another phase of the analytical process. It deals with the behavior of the stock market itself and the various economic forces at work in the marketplace. A number of tools can be used to assess the state of the market, including market measures like volume of trading, breadth of the market, short-interest positions, odd-lot trading, and relative strength. Some investors use charting to assess the condition of everything from the overall market to specific stocks.

LG 6 **Discuss the idea of random walks and efficient markets, and note the challenges these theories hold for the stock valuation process.** In recent years, both technical and fundamental analysis have been seriously challenged by the random walk and efficient market hypotheses. Indeed, considerable evidence indicates that stock prices do move in a random fashion. The efficient market hypothesis is an attempt to explain *why* prices behave randomly. The idea behind an efficient market is that available information is always fully reflected in the price of securities, so investors should *not* expect to outperform the market consistently.

PART FOUR

INVESTING IN FIXED-INCOME SECURITIES

CHAPTER 9
BOND INVESTMENTS

CHAPTER 10
BOND VALUATION AND ANALYSIS

CHAPTER 9

BOND INVESTMENTS

Learning Goals

After studying this chapter, you should be able to:

LG 1 Explain the basic investment attributes of bonds and their use as investment vehicles.

LG 2 Describe the essential features of a bond and distinguish among different types of call, refunding, and sinking-fund provisions.

LG 3 Describe the relationship between bond prices and yields, and explain why some bonds are more volatile than others.

LG 4 Identify the different types of bonds and the kinds of investment objectives these securities can fulfill.

LG 5 Discuss the global nature of the bond market and the difference between dollar-denominated and non-dollar-denominated foreign bonds.

LG 6 Describe the role that bond ratings play in the market and the quotation system used with various types of bonds.

We've all seen ads for telecommunications companies like Sprint, promising to integrate into one neat package all our communications needs: wire-line long-distance and local phone and data services, wireless communications, and Internet services. Sprint is in a good position to deliver on its promises. The company built and operates the first nationwide all-digital, fiber-optic network and is a leader in advanced data communications services. Through its Sprint Integrated ON-Demand Network (Sprint ION), the company delivers simultaneous voice, video, and data services over a single existing connection.

Maintaining Sprint's telecommunications edge is expensive. The company spends from $5 billion to $7 billion a year to upgrade to fiber-optic networks and implement other advanced technologies. Making these and future expenditures for technology and also for acquisitions is essential to the company's survival in today's competitive telecommunications industry. With deregulation, any company that doesn't keep up with cutting-edge technology will lose customers to eager competitors.

Like other companies in capital-intensive businesses, Sprint uses debt as well as equity to finance its growth. Its September 2000 quarterly balance sheet showed $17 billion in long-term debt. Sprint issues bonds through its Sprint Capital Corp. subsidiary. Current debt offerings have maturities ranging from 1 to 20 years. Because its debt obligations are rated Baa1/BBB+ by Moody's and Standard & Poor's, Sprint will have to offer higher interest rates than competitors such as WorldCom (rated A3/A–), AT&T (rated A2/A or better), and Southwestern Bell (rated AA2/AA). As you will see in this chapter, investors in bonds like Sprint's have to consider credit quality, interest rates, maturity, and other factors to decide whether to invest in these securities.

Source: Sprint Web page, **www.sprint.com**; CNNfn Bond Center, **cnnfn.cnn.com/markets/bondcenter**

Why Invest in Bonds

LG 1

bonds
negotiable, publicly traded long-term debt securities, whereby the issuer agrees to pay a fixed amount of interest over a specified period of time and to repay a fixed amount of principal at maturity.

In contrast to stocks, *bonds are liabilities*—they are nothing more than publicly traded IOUs where the bondholders are actually *lending money* to the issuer. Technically, **bonds** can be described as negotiable, publicly traded, long-term debt securities. They are issued in various denominations, by a variety of borrowing organizations, including the U.S. Treasury, agencies of the U.S. government, state and local governments, and corporations. Bonds are often referred to as *fixed-income securities* because the debt-service obligations of the issuers are fixed. That is, the issuing organization agrees to pay a fixed amount of interest periodically and to repay a fixed amount of principal at maturity.

Like any other type of investment vehicle, bonds provide investors with two kinds of income: (1) They provide a generous amount of current income, and (2) given the right market environment, they can also be used to generate substantial amounts of capital gains. The current income, of course, is derived from the interest payments received over the life of the issue. Capital gains, in contrast, are earned whenever market interest rates fall. A basic trading rule in the bond market is that *interest rates and bond prices move in opposite directions*. When interest rates rise, bond prices fall. When rates drop, bond prices move up. Thus, it is possible to buy bonds at one price and to sell them later at a higher price. Of course, it is also possible to incur a capital loss, should market rates move against you. Taken together, the current income and capital gains earned from bonds can lead to attractive returns.

Bonds are also a versatile investment outlet. They can be used conservatively by those who seek high current income, or they can be used aggressively by those who go after capital gains. Although bonds have long been considered attractive investments for those seeking current income, it wasn't until the late-'60s and the advent of volatile interest rates that they also become recognized for their capital gains potential and as trading vehicles. Investors found that, given the relation of bond prices to interest rates, the number of profitable trading opportunities increased substantially as wider and more frequent swings in interest rates began to occur.

In addition, certain types of bonds can be used for tax shelter: Municipal obligations are perhaps the best known in this regard. But as we'll see later in this chapter, Treasury and certain federal agency issues also offer some tax advantages. Finally, because of the general high quality of many bond issues, they can also be used for the preservation and long-term accumulation of capital. For with quality issues, not only do investors have a high degree of assurance that they'll get their money back at maturity, but the stream of interest income is also highly dependable.

Putting Bond Market Performance in Perspective

The bond market is driven by interest rates. In fact, *the behavior of interest rates is the single most important force in the bond market.* Interest rates determine not only the amount of current income investors will receive but also the amount of capital gains (or losses) bondholders will incur. It's not surprising, therefore, that bond market participants follow interest rates closely and that bond market performance is often portrayed in terms of market interest rates.

Figure 9.1 provides a look at bond interest rates over the 40-year period from 1961 through 2000. It shows that from a state of relative stability, interest rates rose steadily in the latter half of the 1960s. Over the course of the next 15 years, the rates paid on high-grade bonds almost tripled. Indeed, interest rates rose from the 4% to 5% range in the early 1960s to over 16% by 1982. But then rates dropped sharply. By 1986 they were back to the single-digit range once again. Thus, after a protracted bear market, bonds abruptly reversed course, and the strongest bull market on record occurred from 1982 to early 1987. (The bond market is considered *bearish* when market interest rates are high or rising, *bullish* when rates are low or falling.) Even though interest rates did move back up for a short time in 1987–1988, they quickly retreated and by 1998–1999, had fallen to levels not seen in over 30 years. Indeed, by early 1999, long-term Treasury bonds were yielding *less than* 5%.

HOTLINKS

For information on the impact of economic news on bonds, go to:

www.briefing.com/FreeServices/fs_bondbrf.htm

Historical Returns As with stocks, *total returns* in the bond market are made up of both current income and capital gains (or losses). Tables 9.1 and 9.2 provide an overview of (total) returns in the bond market—on an annual basis and for various investment horizons—over the 40-year period from 1961 through the second quarter of the year 2000. Take a look at Table 9.1, which lists *year-end market yields* and total *annual returns* for high-grade corporate bonds. Note how bond returns started to slip in 1965, as market yields began to climb. In fact, from 1965 to 1981, there were no fewer than 8 years when average returns were negative. In contrast, look what happened over the 16-year period from 1982 through 1998, when rates were in a general state of decline: There were only 2 years of negative returns (in 1987 and 1994), whereas double-digit returns (of 10.7% to 43.8%) occurred in no fewer than 10 of the 16 years.

FIGURE 9.1

The Behavior of Interest Rates Over Time—1961–2000

From an era of relative stability, bond interest rates rose dramatically and became highly volatile. The net result was that bond yields not only became competitive with the returns offered by other securities but also provided investors with attractive capital gains opportunities. (2000 yields through the second quarter, June 2000.)

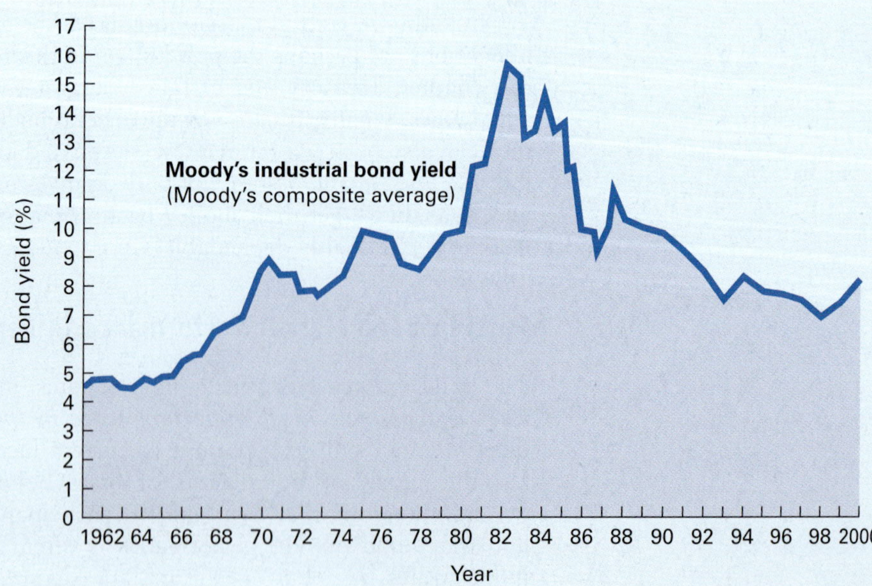

TABLE 9.1 Historical Annual Yields and Returns in the Bond Market, 1961–2000*
(Yields and returns based on performance of high-grade corporate bonds)

Year	Year-End Bond Yields*	Total Rates of Return**	Year	Year-End Bond Yields*	Total Rates of Return**
2000*	7.15%	2.62%	1980	3.15%	−2.62%
1999	7.05	−5.76	1979	10.87	−4.18
1998	6.53	9.16	1978	9.32	−0.07
1997	7.16	13.46	1977	8.50	1.71
1996	7.43	2.20	1976	8.14	18.65
1995	6.86	27.94	1975	8.97	14.64
1994	8.64	−5.76	1974	8.89	−3.06
1993	7.31	13.64	1973	7.79	1.14
1992	8.34	9.34	1972	7.41	7.26
1991	8.58	20.98	1971	6.48	11.01
1990	9.61	6.48	1970	6.85	18.37
1989	9.18	15.29	1969	7.83	−8.09
1988	9.81	10.49	1968	6.62	2.57
1987	10.33	1.47	1967	6.30	−4.95
1986	9.02	18.71	1966	5.55	0.20
1985	10.63	30.90	1965	4.79	−0.46
1984	12.05	16.39	1964	4.46	4.77
1983	12.76	4.70	1963	4.46	2.19
1982	11.55	43.80	1962	4.34	7.95
1981	14.98	−0.96	1961	4.56	4.82

*Year-end bond yields are for (S&P) AA-rated corporate (industrial and utility) bonds; 2000 yields and returns through the second quarter (June) 2000.

**Total return figures are based on interest income as well as capital gains (or losses).

Sources: Annual yields derived from Standard & Poor's *S&P Trade and Security Statistics.* Total return figures (for 1961–1985) from Ibbotson and Sinquefield, *Stocks, Bonds, Bills, and Inflation: Historical Returns.* Total returns for 1986 through the second quarter of 2000 obtained from the *Lehman Bros. Long-Term Corporate Bond* database.

Table 9.2 contains return performance over various holding periods of 5 to 40 years. These figures demonstrate the type of long-term returns possible from bonds and show that *average annual returns of around 8% to 10% on high-grade issues are not out of the question.* Although such performance may lag behind that of stocks (which it should, in light of the reduced exposure to risk), it really isn't that bad, especially from the the perspective of risk-adjusted rate of return. The big question facing bond investors, however, is what kind of returns will they be able to produce over the next 10 to 12 years? The 1980s and early 1990s were very good for bond investors. *But that market was driven by falling interest rates, which in turn produced hefty capital gains and outsize returns.* Whether market interest rates will (or even can) continue on that path is doubtful. Most market observers, in fact, caution against expecting abnormally high rates of return over the next decade or so.

Bonds Versus Stocks Although bonds definitely have their good points (low risk, high levels of current income, and desirable diversification properties), they also have a significant downside: their *comparative* returns. The fact is, *relative to stocks,* the long-run returns on bonds just don't hold up too well. Look at Figure 9.2. It tracks the comparative returns of stocks (via the S&P 500) and bonds (using the Lehman Bros. Long-Term Corporate Bond Index) over the 1990s. As can be seen, for the first half of the period, bonds held up very well,

TABLE 9.2 Holding Period Returns in the Bond Market: 1961–2000*

	Average Annual Returns*	Cumulative Total Returns	Amount to Which a $10,000 Investment Will Grow Over the Holding Period
5(+) years: 1995–2000*	8.50%	56.61%	$ 15,661
5 years: 1990–94	8.57	50.85	15,085
10(+) years: 1990–2000*	8.53	136.24	23,624
15 years: 1985–99	10.58	352.06	45,206
25 years: 1975–99	9.77	929.37	102,937
40 years: 1961–99	7.08	1,440.13	154,013
The 1960s: 1960–69	1.7%	18.1%	$11,809
The 1970s: 1970–79	6.2	83.1	18,305
The 1980s: 1980–89	13.0	240.2	34,022
The 1990s: 1990–99	8.7	130.2	23,020

*Average annual return figures are fully compounded returns and are based on interest income as well as capital gains (or losses). 2000 data through the second quarter (June).

Sources: Annual yields derived from Standard & Poor's *S&P Trade and Security Statistics.* Total return figures (1961–85) from Ibbotson and Sinquefield, *Stocks, Bonds, and Inflation: Historical Returns.* Total return data for 1986 through the second quarter of 2000 from *Lehman Bros. Long-Term Corporate Bond* series.

pretty much matching the returns in the stock market. But things started to change in 1995, as stock returns shot up, while bond returns began to level off. The net result was that for the decade as a whole, bonds produced average annual returns of 8.7%, whereas stocks turned in average returns of 18.2%. That difference meant that a $10,000 investment in bonds would have led to a terminal value of some $23,000, compared to more than $53,000 for stocks.

That's a high opportunity cost to pay for holding bonds, and it prompted some market observers to question whether bonds should have *any place at all* in an investment portfolio. They reason that if interest rates have, in fact, bottomed out, then bonds won't have much to offer, other than relatively low returns. But that view ignores one of the key aspects of bonds: *the element of stability they add to a portfolio.* The fact is, bonds possess excellent portfolio diversification properties and, except for the most aggressive of investors, have a lot to contribute from a portfolio perspective. Indeed, as a general rule, adding bonds to a portfolio will, *up to a point,* have a much greater impact on lowering risk than on return. Face it: you don't buy bonds for their high returns (except when you think interest rates are heading down). Rather, you buy them for their current income and/or for the stability they bring to your portfolio. And that's still true, even today. What's more, it's important to keep in mind that most of the comparative return performance in the '90s was due to a phenomenal 5-year run (from 1995–1999) for stocks. Thus, when stock returns come back down to earth and return to more normal levels (which has to happen, sooner or later), bond returns will once again become more competitive.

HOTLINKS

For information on bond investment considerations, go to the Bond Market Association's site whose address is shown below. Click on [Bond Basics]: Key bond investment considerations.

www.investinginbonds.com

Exposure to Risk

Like any other type of investment vehicle, fixed-income securities should be viewed in terms of their risk and return. Generally speaking, bonds are

FIGURE 9.2 Comparative Performance of Stocks and Bonds in the 1990s—January 1990–December 1999

This graph shows what happened to $10,000 invested in bonds over the decade of the '90s, versus the same amount invested in stocks. Obviously, while the beginning amount was the same, the ending (or "terminal") amounts were not. And, we should point out, the difference would have been even bigger had we used the Nasdaq Composite Index instead of the S&P 500—indeed, a $10,000 investment in the Nasdaq Composite would have grown to nearly $89,500, due in part to the phenomenal year in 1999, when the Nasdaq shot up more than 85%. (*Source: Morningstar Principia Pro for Mutual Funds,* release date March 31, 2000.)

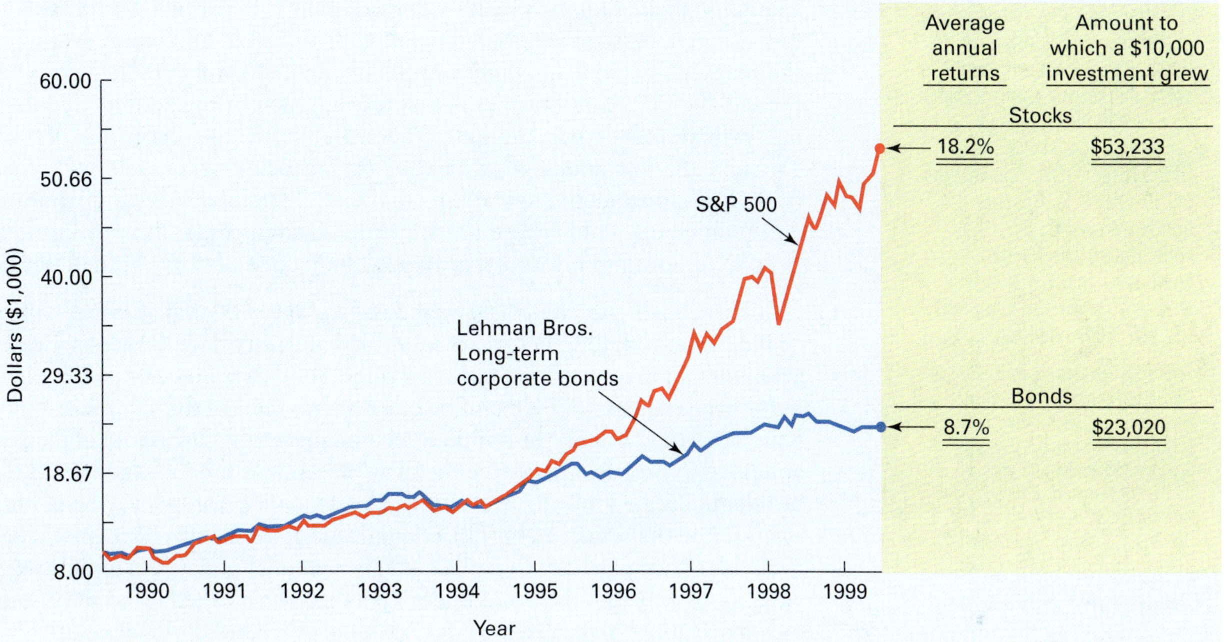

Note: Performance figures and graphs are based on fully compounded rates of return and include reinvested current income (dividends and interest) as well as capital gains (or losses); taxes have been ignored in all calculations.

exposed to five major types of risks: interest rate risk, purchasing power risk, business/financial risk, liquidity risk, and call risk.

- **Interest Rate Risk.** Interest rate risk is the number one source of risk to fixed-income investors, *because it's the major cause of price volatility in the bond market.* For bonds, interest rate risk translates into market risk: The behavior of interest rates, in general, affects *all* bonds and cuts across *all* sectors of the market, even the U.S. Treasury market. When market interest rates rise, bond prices fall, and vice versa. And as interest rates become more volatile, so do bond prices.

- **Purchasing Power Risk.** Purchasing power risk accompanies inflation. During periods of mild inflation, bonds do pretty well, because their returns tend to outstrip inflation rates. Purchasing power risk really heats up when inflation takes off, as it did in the late 1970s; when that happens, bond yields start to lag behind inflation rates. The reason: Even though market yields are rising with inflation, your return is locked in by the fixed coupon rate on your bond.

INVESTOR FACTS

BONDS REWARD THE FAITHFUL—Although the percentage of bond holdings in investor portfolios dropped to an all-time low of 8% in April 2000, those who remained loyal to fixed-income securities were winners in 2000. Bonds outperformed the stock market for the first time since 1993. The Lehman Brothers Aggregate Bond Index rose 11.6%, and returns on 30-year U.S. Treasury bonds were 20%. By comparison, the Nasdaq Composite Index was down almost 40% for the year, and the S&P 500 index fell 10%.

Source: Janet Kidd Stewart, "Bonds Find Few Friends in Fast-Paced Markets," *San Diego Union Tribune,* July 16, 2000, pp. I-3, I-6; and Gregory Zuckerman and Michael Derby, "Government Bonds Provide a Safe Haven as High-Yield Market Delivers a Bruising," *Wall Street Journal,* January 2, 2001, p. R8.

- **Business/Financial Risk.** This is basically the risk that the *issuer will default on interest and/or principal payments.* Also known as *credit risk,* business/financial risk has to do with the quality and financial integrity of the issuer. The stronger the issuer, the less business/financial risk there is to worry about. This risk doesn't even exist for some securities (e.g., U.S. Treasuries). For others, such as corporate and municipal bonds, it's a very important consideration.
- **Liquidity Risk.** Liquidity risk is the risk that a bond will be difficult to unload, at a reasonable price, if you want to sell it. In certain sectors of the market, this is a far bigger problem than investors realize. For even though the U.S. bond market is enormous, much of the activity occurs in the primary/new-issue market. Therefore, with the exception of the Treasury market and a good deal of the agency market, relatively little trading is done in the secondary markets, particularly with corporates and municipals. And where there's little trading, there's lots of liquidity risk. So, if liquidity is important to you, steer clear of thinly traded bonds.
- **Call Risk.** Call risk, or *prepayment risk,* is the risk that a bond will be "called" (retired) long before its scheduled maturity date. Issuers are often given the opportunity to prepay their bonds, and they do so by calling them in for prepayment. (We'll examine call features later in this chapter.) When issuers call their bonds, the bondholders end up getting cashed out of the deal and have to find another place for their investment funds—and there's the problem. Because bonds are nearly always called for prepayment after interest rates have taken a big fall, comparable investment vehicles just aren't available. Thus you have to replace a high-yielding bond with a much lower-yielding issue. From the bondholder's perspective, a called bond means not only a disruption in cash flow but also a sharply reduced rate of return.

Essential Features of a Bond

LG 2 LG 3

A *bond* is a negotiable, long-term debt instrument that carries certain obligations (including the payment of interest and the repayment of principal) on the part of the issuer. Because bondholders are only lending money to the issuer, they are not entitled to any of the rights and privileges that go along with an ownership position. But bondholders, as well as bond issuers, do have a number of well-defined rights and privileges that together help define the essential features of a bond. We'll now take a look at some of these features. As you will see, when it comes to bonds, it's especially important to know what you're getting into, *for many seemingly insignificant features (like a bond's coupon or maturity) can have dramatic effects on its price behavior and investment return.* This is especially true in periods of low interest rates, because knowing what to buy and when to buy can mean the difference between earning a mediocre return and earning a highly competitive one.

Bond Interest and Principal

In the absence of any trading, a bond investor's return is limited to fixed interest and principal payments. That's because bonds involve a fixed claim on the issuer's income (as defined by the size of the periodic interest payments) and a fixed claim on the assets of the issuer (equal to the repayment of principal at maturity). As a rule, bonds pay interest every 6 months. There are exceptions, however; some issues carry interest payment intervals as short as a month, and a few as long as a year. The amount of interest due is a function of the **coupon,** which defines the annual interest income that will be paid by the issuer to the bondholder. For instance, a $1,000 bond with an 8% coupon pays $80 in interest annually—generally in the form of two $40 semiannual payments. The **principal** amount of a bond, also known as an issue's *par value,* specifies the amount of capital that must be repaid at maturity. For example, there is $1,000 of principal in a $1,000 bond.

coupon
feature on a bond that defines the amount of annual interest income.

principal
on a bond, the amount of capital that must be paid at maturity.

Of course, debt securities regularly trade at market prices that differ from their principal (par) values. This occurs whenever an issue's coupon differs from the prevailing market rate of interest. That is, the price of the issue changes inversely with interest rates until its yield is compatible with the prevailing market yield. Such behavior explains why a 7% issue will carry a market price of only $825 in a 9% market. The drop in price from its par value of $1,000 is necessary to raise the yield on this bond from 7% to 9%. In essence, the new, higher yield is produced in part from annual coupons and in part from capital gains, as the price of the issue moves from $825 back to $1,000 at maturity.

Maturity Date

maturity date
the date on which a bond matures and the principal must be repaid.

Unlike common stock, all debt securities have limited lives and will expire on a given date in the future, the issue's **maturity date.** Although a bond carries a series of specific interest payment dates, the principal is repaid only once: on or before maturity. The maturity date is fixed (and never changes). It not only defines the life of a new issue but also denotes the amount of time remaining for older, outstanding bonds. Such a life span is known as an issue's *term to maturity.* For example, a new issue may come out as a 25-year bond, but 5 years later, it will have only 20 years remaining to maturity.

term bond
a bond that has a single, fairly lengthy maturity date.

serial bond
a bond that has a series of different maturity dates.

note
a debt security originally issued with a maturity of from 2 to 10 years.

Two types of bonds can be distinguished on the basis of maturity: term and serial issues. A **term bond** has a single, fairly lengthy maturity date and is the most common type of issue. A **serial bond,** in contrast, has a series of different maturity dates, perhaps as many as 15 or 20, within a single issue. For example, a 20-year term bond issued in 1999 has a single maturity date of 2019, but that same issue as a serial bond might have 20 annual maturity dates that extend from 1999 through 2019. At each of these annual maturity dates, a certain portion of the issue would come due and be paid off. Maturity is also used to distinguish a *note* from a *bond.* That is, a debt security that's originally issued with a maturity of 2 to 10 years is known as a **note,** whereas a *bond* technically has an initial term to maturity of more than 10 years. In practice, notes are often issued with maturities of 5 to 7 years, whereas bonds normally carry maturities of 20 to 30 years or more.

Call Features—Let the Buyer Beware!

Consider the following situation: You've just made an investment in a high-yielding, 25-year bond. Now all you have to do is sit back and let the cash flow in, right? Well, perhaps. Certainly, that will happen for the first several years. But, if market interest rates drop, it's also likely that you'll receive a notice from the issuer that the bond is being *called.* This means that the issue is being retired before its maturity date. There's really nothing you can do but turn in the bond and invest your money elsewhere. It's all perfectly legal because every bond is issued with a **call feature,** which stipulates whether and under what conditions a bond can be called in for retirement prior to maturity.

call feature
feature that specifies whether and under what conditions the issuer can retire a bond prior to maturity.

Basically, there are three types of call features:

1. A bond can be *freely callable,* which means the issuer can prematurely retire the bond at any time.
2. A bond can be *noncallable,* which means the issuer is prohibited from retiring the bond prior to maturity.
3. The issue could carry a *deferred call,* which means the issue cannot be called until after a certain length of time has passed from the date of issue. In essence, the issue is noncallable during the deferment period and then becomes freely callable thereafter.

Obviously, in our illustration above, either the high-yielding bond was issued as freely callable or it became freely callable with the end of its call deferment period.

Call features are placed on bonds *for the benefit of the issuers.* They're used most often to replace an issue with one that carries a lower coupon, and the issuer benefits by the reduction in annual interest cost. Thus, when market interest rates undergo a sharp decline, as they did in 1982–1987 and again in 1991–1993, bond issuers retire their high-yielding bonds (by calling them in) and replace them with lower-yielding obligations. *The net result is that the investor is left with a much lower rate of return than anticipated.*

call premium
the amount added to a bond's par value and paid to investors when a bond is retired prematurely.

call price
the price the issuer must pay to retire a bond prematurely; equal to par value plus the call premium.

In a halfhearted attempt to compensate investors who find their bonds called out from under them, a **call premium** is tacked onto a bond and paid to investors, along with the issue's par value, when the bond is called. The sum of the par value plus call premium represents the issue's **call price.** This is the amount the issuer must pay to retire the bond prematurely. As a general rule, call premiums usually equal about 8 to 12 months' interest at the earliest date of call and then become progressively smaller as the issue nears maturity. Using this rule, the initial call price of a 9% bond could be as high as $1,090, where $90 represents the call premium.

refunding provisions
provisions that prohibit the premature retirement of an issue from the proceeds of a lower-coupon refunding bond.

In addition to call features, some bonds may also carry **refunding provisions.** These are much like call features except that they prohibit just one thing: the premature retirement of an issue from the proceeds of a lower-coupon bond. For example, a bond could come out as freely callable but *nonrefundable* for 5 years. In this case, the bond would probably be sold by brokers as a *deferred refunding issue,* with little or nothing said about its call feature. The distinction is important, however. It means that a nonrefunding or deferred refunding issue *can still be called and prematurely retired for any reason other than refunding.* Thus, an investor could face a call on a high-yielding nonrefundable issue if the issuer has the cash to retire the bond prematurely.

sinking fund
a provision that stipulates the amount of principal that will be retired annually over the life of a bond.

Sinking Funds

Another provision that's important to investors is the **sinking fund,** which stipulates how a bond will be paid off over time. This provision applies only to term bonds, of course, because serial issues already have a predetermined method of repayment. Not all (term) bonds have sinking-fund requirements, but for those that do, a sinking fund specifies the annual repayment schedule that will be used to pay off the issue. It indicates how much principal will be retired each year. Sinking-fund requirements generally begin 1 to 5 years after the date of issue and continue annually thereafter until all or most of the issue is paid off. Any amount not repaid (which might equal 10% to 25% of the issue) would then be retired with a single "balloon" payment at maturity. Unlike a call or refunding provision, the issuer generally does not have to pay a call premium with sinking-fund calls. Instead, the bonds are normally called at par for sinking-fund purposes.

There's another difference between sinking-fund provisions and call or refunding features. That is, whereas a call or refunding provision gives the issuer the *right* to retire a bond prematurely, a sinking-fund provision *obligates* the issuer to pay off the bond systematically over time. The issuer has no choice. It must make sinking-fund payments in a prompt and timely fashion or run the risk of being in default.

senior bonds
secured debt obligations, backed by a legal claim on specific property of the issuer.

mortgage bonds
senior bonds secured by real estate.

collateral trust bonds
senior bonds backed by securities owned by the issuer but held in trust by a third party.

equipment trust certificates
senior bonds secured by specific pieces of equipment; popular with transportation companies such as airlines.

first and refunding bonds
bonds secured in part with both first and second mortgages.

junior bonds
debt obligations backed only by the promise of the issuer to pay interest and principal on a timely basis.

debenture
an unsecured (junior) bond.

subordinated debentures
unsecured bonds whose claim is secondary to other debentures.

income bonds
unsecured bonds requiring that interest be paid only after a specified amount of income is earned.

Secured or Unsecured Debt

A single issuer may have a number of different bonds outstanding at any given point in time. In addition to coupon and maturity, one bond can be differentiated from another by the type of collateral behind the issue. Issues can be either junior or senior. **Senior bonds** are secured obligations, which are backed by a legal claim on some specific property of the issuer. Such issues would include **mortgage bonds,** which are secured by real estate; **collateral trust bonds,** which are backed by financial assets owned by the issuer but held in trust by a third party; **equipment trust certificates,** which are secured by specific pieces of equipment (e.g., boxcars and airplanes) and are popular with railroads and airlines; and **first and refunding bonds,** which are basically a combination of first mortgage and junior lien bonds (i.e., the bonds are secured in part by a first mortgage on some of the issuer's property and in part by second or third mortgages on other properties). (Note that first and refunding bonds are *less secure* than, and should *not* be confused with, straight first-mortgage bonds.)

Junior bonds, on the other hand, are backed only by the promise of the issuer to pay interest and principal on a timely basis. There are several classes of unsecured bonds, the most popular of which is known as a **debenture.** Figure 9.3 shows the announcement for a very large issue that came out in June 2000. This particular issue happens to be a *note,* but just like a debenture, it too is unsecured (essentially, this note is nothing more than a short-term debenture). Even though there was no collateral backing up this obligation, the issuer, Hewlett-Packard, was able to sell $1.5 *billion* worth of these securities at an interest rate of just 7.15%.

Subordinated debentures can also be found in the market. These issues have a claim on income secondary to other debenture bonds. **Income bonds,** the most junior of all bonds, are unsecured debts requiring that interest be paid only after a certain amount of income is earned. With these bonds, there is no legally binding requirement to meet interest payments on a timely or regular basis so long as a specified amount of income has not been earned. These issues are similar in many respects to *revenue bonds* found in the municipal market.

FIGURE 9.3

Announcement of a New Corporate Debt Issue

This $1.5 billion global note was issued by Hewlett-Packard in 2000 and is secured by nothing more than the good name of the company. Raising this kind of money without having to put up any collateral may be hard to imagine, but for big, financially secure companies like HP, it's done all the time. And note that the price was right: The coupon on this unsecured debt is only 7.15%, which at the time was considerably less than what the average homeowner would have had to pay to get a $150,000 mortgage. Even so, over the short, 5-year life of this note, HP will be paying more than $100,000,000 in interest! (*Source: Wall Street Journal*, July 12, 2000.)

This announcement is neither an offer to sell nor a solicitation of offers to buy any of these securities. The offering is made only by the Prospectus and the related Prospectus Supplement, copies of which may be obtained in any State or jurisdiction in which this announcement is circulated only from such of the underwriters as may legally offer these securities in such State or jurisdiction.

NEW ISSUE June 6, 2000

$1,500,000,000

hp®

invent

7.15% Global Notes due June 15, 2005

Price 99.666%

plus accrued interest, if any, from June 9, 2000

Credit Suisse First Boston Salomon Smith Barney

Bear, Stearns & Co. Inc.

Chase Securities Inc.

Goldman, Sachs & Co.

Morgan Stanley Dean Witter

The Williams Capital Group, L.P.

Principles of Bond Price Behavior

The price of a bond is a function of its coupon, its maturity, and the movement of market interest rates. The relationship of bond prices to market interest rates is captured in Figure 9.4. Basically, the graph reinforces the *inverse relationship* that exists between bond prices and market rates: *Lower* rates lead to *higher* bond prices.

premium bond
a bond with a market value in excess of par; occurs when interest rates drop below the coupon rate.

discount bond
a bond with a market value lower than par; occurs when market rates are greater than the coupon rate.

Figure 9.4 also shows the difference between premium and discount bonds. A **premium bond** is one that sells for more than its par value. A premium results whenever market interest rates drop below the bond's coupon rate. A **discount bond,** in contrast, sells for less than par. The discount is the result of market rates being greater than the issue's coupon rate. Thus, the 10% bond in Figure 9.4 trades at a premium when market rates are at 8%, but at a discount when rates are at 12%.

When a bond is first issued, it is usually sold to the public at a price that equals or is very close to its par value. Likewise, when the bond matures—some 15, 20, or 30 years later—it will once again be priced at its par value. What happens to the price of the bond in between is of considerable interest to most bond investors. We know that the extent to which bond prices move depends not only on the *direction* of change in interest rates but also on the *magnitude* of such change: The greater the moves in interest rates, the greater the swings in bond prices.

However, bond price volatility also varies according to an issue's coupon and maturity. That is, bonds with *lower coupons* and/or *longer maturities* respond more vigorously to changes in market rates and therefore undergo sharper price swings. (Note in Figure 9.4 that for a given change in interest rates—e.g., from 10% to 8%—the largest change in price occurs when the bond has the greatest number of years to maturity.) Therefore, if a *decline* in interest rates is anticipated, you should seek lower coupons and longer maturities (to maximize capital gains). When interest rates move *up*, you should do just the opposite: seek high coupons with short maturities. This choice will minimize price variation and act to preserve as much capital as possible.

Actually, of the two variables, the *maturity* of an issue has the greater impact on price volatility. For example, look what happens to the price of an 8% bond when market interest rates rise by 1, 2, or 3 percentage points:

	Change in the Price of an 8% Bond When Interest Rates Rise by:		
Bond Maturity	1 Percentage Point	2 Percentage Points	3 Percentage Points
5 years	−4.0%	−7.7%	−11.2%
25 years	−9.9%	−18.2%	−25.3%

For purposes of this illustration, we assume the changes in interest rate occur "instantaneously," so the maturities remain fixed, at 5 or 25 years. Given the computed price changes, it's clear that the shorter (5-year) bond offers a lot more price stability. Such behavior is universal with all fixed-income securities, and is very important. It means that if you want to reduce your exposure to capital loss or, more to the point, to lower the price volatility in your bond holdings, then just *shorten your maturities.*

FIGURE 9.4 The Price Behavior of a Bond

A bond will sell at its par value so long as the prevailing market interest rate remains the same as the bond's coupon—in this case, 10%. However, when market rates drop, bond prices move up. When rates rise, bond prices move down. As a bond approaches its maturity, the price of the issue moves toward its par value regardless of the level of prevailing interest rates.

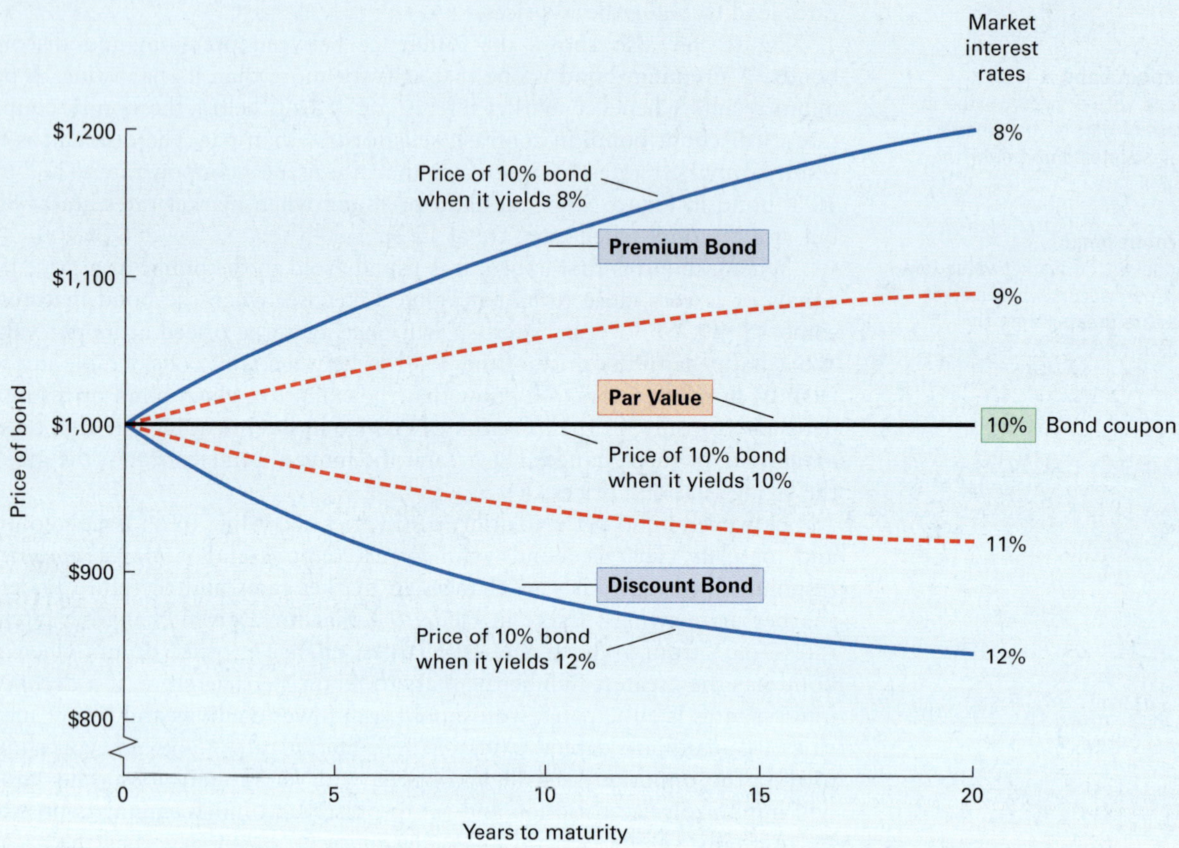

The Market for Debt Securities

LG 4 LG 5

Thus far, our discussion has dealt with basic bond features. We now shift attention to a review of the market in which these securities are traded. To begin with, the bond market is chiefly over-the counter in nature, as listed bonds represent only a small portion of total outstanding obligations. In addition, this market is far more stable than the stock market. Indeed, although interest rates—and therefore bond prices—do move up and down over time, when bond price activity is measured on a daily basis, it is *remarkably stable.* There are two other things that stand out about the bond market: It's big, and it has been growing rapidly. From a $250 billion market in 1950, it has grown to the point where, in early 2000, the amount of bonds outstanding in this country reached nearly *$15 trillion!* That makes the bond market even bigger than the U.S. stock market, although the gap is definitely narrowing.

Here's what the U.S. bond market looked like at the beginning of the new millenium (January 2000):

	Amount Outstanding ($ in trillions)
U.S. Treasury securities	$ 2.46
Agency securities	1.62
Municipal bonds	1.35
Corporate bonds	4.13
Mortgage-backed securities	2.29
Foreign issues and Eurodollar bonds	2.74
Total	$14.59

Source: "Size & Structure of the World Bond Market: 2000," Merrill Lynch, April 2000.

The growth in this market has been remarkable. It has doubled in size since 1992, which translates into a compound rate of growth of more than 10% per year. Domestic issues alone (*excluding* foreign issues and Eurodollar bonds) account for $11.9 trillion, or 81% of the total U.S. market. Let's now take a look at each of these various segments.

Major Market Segments

There are bonds available in today's market to meet almost any investment objective and to suit just about any type of investor. As a matter of convenience, the bond market is normally separated into four major segments, according to type of issuer: Treasury, agency, municipal, and corporate. As we shall see, each sector has developed its own features, as well as its own trading characteristics.

Treasury Bonds "Treasuries" (or "governments," as they are sometimes called) are a dominant force in the fixed-income market. If not the most popular type of bond, they certainly are the best known. In addition to T-bills (a popular short-term debt security), the U.S. Treasury issues notes and bonds. It also issues *inflation-indexed securities,* which are the newest type of Treasury debt, introduced in January 1997. All Treasury obligations are of the highest quality because they are all backed by the "full faith and credit" of the U.S. government. This backing, along with their liquidity, makes them very popular with individual and institutional investors both here and abroad. Indeed, Treasury securities are traded in all the major markets of the world, from New York to London to Sydney and Tokyo.

HOTLINKS

For more information on Treasury bonds, go to Investorama.com and click on [What are the different types of treasury bonds and how can I invest in them?]

www.investorama.com/askinvestorama/bonds

Treasury notes are issued with maturities of 2, 5, and 10 years, whereas **Treasury bonds** carry 30-year maturities. (The Treasury last issued 20-year bonds in 1986.) The Treasury issues its notes and bonds at regularly scheduled auctions, the results of which are widely reported by the financial media (see Figure 9.5). In this auction process, the Treasury establishes the initial yields and coupons on the securities it issues.

Treasury notes
U.S. Treasury debt securities that are issued with maturities of 2 to 10 years or less.

Treasury bonds
U.S. Treasury debt securities that are issued with 30-year maturities.

Actually, because of the ever-widening federal budget *surplus,* the Treasury has announced that it will be sharply reducing the issuance of new

FIGURE 9.5 The Reported Results of a Treasury Note Auction

Treasury auctions are closely followed by the financial media; here, the results of a 10-year Treasury note auction are reported. These auctions are highly competitive. The number of bids submitted generally far exceeds the size of the issue, so the spread between the highest and lowest bids is quite small—sometimes as small as 2 basis points, or 2/100 of 1%. (*Source:* Department of the Treasury—Bureau of Public Debt, and *Wall Street Journal.*)

Here are details of yesterday's 10-year note auction:

All bids are awarded at a single price at the market-clearing yield. Rates are determined by the difference between that price and the face value.

10-YEAR NOTES

Applications	$20,940,987,000	The amount of bids submitted
Accepted bids	$ 8,005,987,000	Size of the issue—the number of bids accepted
Bids at market-clearing yield accepted	38%	
Accepted noncompetitively	$108,592,000	The number of noncompetitive bids submitted (and accepted)
Auction price (rate)	100.153 (6.475%)	The average price and yield (rate) on the issue
Interest rate	6 1/2%	The coupon that the issue will carry, which is set after the auction
CUSIP number	912827521	

The notes are dated February 15, 2000, will be issued May 15, 2000, and mature February 15, 2010.

notes and bonds. Indeed, the supply of these securities is to be reduced across the board as the Treasury eliminates the auctions of some maturities all together and reduces the size or frequency of others. Even so, a full array of Treasury notes and bonds is still available in the aftermarket. But many of those may soon become extinct, as the Treasury uses part of the budget surplus to pay down the national debt by buying back outstanding securities.

All Treasury notes and bonds are sold in $1,000 denominations. Interest income from these securities is subject to normal federal income tax but *is exempt from state and local taxes.* The Treasury today issues only *noncallable* securities. The last time the U.S. Treasury issued callable debt was in 1984. Until then, most Treasury bonds carried long-term call deferments, under which the bonds became freely callable during the last 5 years of the issue's life. There are still some deferred-call Treasuries outstanding; they're easy to identify because the deferred-call features are a specific part of the bond listing system. For example, a 10% issue of 2005–10 signifies that this Treasury bond has a maturity date of 2010 and a deferred-call feature that extends through 2005.

Treasury inflation-indexed obligations (TIPS)
a type of Treasury security that provides protection against inflation by adjusting investor returns for the annual rate of inflation.

As noted above, the newest form of Treasury security is the **Treasury inflation-indexed obligation.** Also known as **TIPS,** which stands for "Treasury inflation-protection securities," they are issued as notes (with 10-year maturities) and bonds (with 30-year maturities). They offer investors the opportunity to stay ahead of inflation by periodically adjusting their returns for any inflation that has occurred. That is, if inflation is running at an annual rate of, say, 3%, then at the end of the year, the par (maturity) value of the bond will increase by 3%. (Actually, the adjustments to par value are done every 6 months.) Thus the $1,000 par value will grow to $1,030 at the end of the first year. If the 3% inflation rate continues for the second year, the par value will once again increase, this time from $1,030 to $1,061 ($1,030 × 1.03). Unfortunately, the coupons on these securities are set very low, because they're meant to provide investors with so-called *real (inflation-adjusted) returns.* Thus one of these bonds might carry a coupon of only 3.5% at a time when regular T-bonds are paying, say, 6.5% or 7%. But there's an advantage even to this: *The actual size of the coupon payment will increase over time as the par value on the bond goes up.* For investors who are concerned about inflation protection, these securities may be just the ticket. But as the *Investing in Action* box on page 302 suggests, TIPS are a lot more complex than the traditional Treasury bond.

agency bonds
debt securities issued by various agencies and organizations of the U.S. government.

Agency Bonds **Agency bonds** are debt securities issued by various agencies and organizations of the U.S. government, such as the Federal Home Loan Bank, the Federal Farm Credit Systems, the Small Business Administration, the Student Loan Marketing Association, and the Federal National Mortgage Association. Though these securities are the closest things to Treasuries, they are not obligations of the U.S. Treasury and technically should not be considered the same as a Treasury bond. Even so, *they are very high-quality securities that have almost no risk of default.* In spite of the similar default risk exposure, these securities usually provide yields that are comfortably above the market rates for Treasuries. Thus they offer investors a way to increase returns with little or no real difference in risk.

There are basically two types of agency issues: government-sponsored and federal agencies. Although there are only six government-sponsored organizations, the number of federal agencies exceeds two dozen. To overcome some of the problems in the marketing of many relatively small federal agency securities, Congress established the Federal Financing Bank to consolidate the financing activities of all federal agencies. (As a rule, the generic term *agency* is used to denote both government-sponsored and federal agency obligations.)

Selected characteristics of some of the more popular agency bonds are presented in Table 9.3. As the list of issuers shows, most of the government agencies that exist today were created to support either agriculture or housing. Although agency issues are not direct liabilities of the U.S. government, a few of them actually do carry government guarantees and therefore represent the full faith and credit of the U.S. Treasury. But even those issues that do not carry such guarantees are highly regarded in the marketplace. They are all viewed as *moral obligations* of the U.S. government, as it's highly unlikely that Congress would ever allow one of them to default. Also, like Treasury securities, agency issues are normally noncallable or carry lengthy call deferment features. One final point: Since 1986 *all new agency (and Treasury) securities* have been issued in *book entry form.* This means that no certificate of ownership is issued to the buyer of the bonds. Rather, the buyer receives a "confirmation" of the transaction, and his or her name is entered in a computerized logbook, where it remains as long as the security is owned.

HOTLINKS

To access a database of corporate, agency, and municipal bond offerings, go to

www.bondtrac.com/info/infoServices.html

INVESTING in action

Some Hints on TIPS

Bondholders look at inflation like Superman looks at kryptonite. Superman weakens when faced with the dreaded substance and would die if exposed to it for long. Bondholders weaken when inflation heats up because it causes bond prices to buckle and fixed payments to lose their purchasing power. Some people have the mistaken impression that they can't lose money investing in Treasury bonds. But they can because bond prices fall in an inflationary environment. So that investors can buy its bonds without fearing inflation, in 1997 Uncle Sam created TIPS, Treasury inflation-protected securities.

Here's how TIPS work: The government issues a 10-year bond with a $1,000 face value that pays, say, 3% interest—and that rate stays fixed for the life of the issue. But if the consumer price index rises, so does the face amount of the bond. For example, because the CPI rose 3.4% in 2000, the new face amount was adjusted up to $1,000 × 1.034 = $1,034. Therefore, in 2001, the annual interest payment would be $31.02 (3% of $1,034). When the TIPS mature in 10 years, the investor gets the inflation-adjusted face value at that time, which could be as much as $2,000 if inflation really takes off. A lot can change over a decade, but inflation looks pretty tame these days. As one professional investor puts it, buying TIPS now is like buying flood insurance during a drought. TIPS also protect you if deflation occurs. The bond's value will not fall below its initial face value (of $1,000).

Are TIPS a good deal or not? They certainly are for the government, which is able to pay 3% interest instead of an inflation-adjusted premium like 6% or 7%. Taxpayers should like that too, because it helps keep government interest payments down. And, unlike the case with conventional fixed-income securities, the investor doesn't have to worry about the Treasury bond's value plummeting if inflation heats up.

Take a look at what happens to a conventional bond if inflation is rekindled beyond the implied inflation premium (in this case, 3%). Investors get 6% per year, or $60, no matter what happens to the level of prices. In 10 years, that $1,000 principal will certainly have less purchasing power than it does today. It might be able to buy just $700 worth of goods. In addition, rising inflation generally means rising interest rates. In the marketplace, conventional bond prices fall when interest rates rise. Therefore, an investor who wishes to sell a conventional bond prior to maturity is likely to take a loss if interest rates are higher than when the bond was purchased.

TIPS protect investors from such erosion in bond prices. TIPS are not so great, however, if inflation stays dormant, because the investors are getting only 3% on their money. You could get that kind of interest at your local bank, and you don't need to lock up your money nearly as long as you do with TIPS.

There's one other downside to TIPS: taxes. Investors have to pay a tax on the increasing face value of their bonds—$34 in the first year in the foregoing example. That may not seem like much, but the government doesn't actually pay out the increase in the bond's face value until maturity. Thus you end up paying taxes on income you've earned but don't have in hand. For that reason, TIPS probably make the most sense for individual retirement accounts (IRAs) and other tax-deferred retirement accounts.

TIPS are also a good idea for investors who want to allocate a portion of their assets to income-generating securities and don't want to worry that inflation will erode their value. But the tradeoff for that protection is significant: loss of about half the income.

Sources: Robert Barker, "A Bond Anybody Can Love," *Business Week,* June 19, 2000, p.260; and James Grant, "An Inflation Tip," *Forbes,* October 30, 2000, p. 402.

municipal bonds
debt securities issued by states, counties, cities, and other political subdivisions; most of these bonds are tax-exempt (free of federal income tax on interest income).

Municipal Bonds **Municipal bonds** are the issues of states, counties, cities, and other political subdivisions (such as school districts and water and sewer districts). This is a trillion-dollar market today, and it's the only segment of the bond market that's dominated by individual investors: About two-thirds of all municipal bonds are held by individuals. (There are few tax incentives for

TABLE 9.3 Characteristics of Some Popular Agency Issues

Type of Issue	Minimum Denomination	Initial Maturity	Tax Status* Federal	State	Local
Federal Farm Credit System	$ 1,000	13 months to 15 years	T	E	E
Federal Home Loan Bank	10,000	1 to 20 years	T	E	E
Federal Land Banks	1,000	1 to 10 years	T	E	E
Farmers Home Administration	25,000	1 to 25 years	T	T	T
Federal Housing Administration	50,000	1 to 40 years	T	T	T
Federal Home Loan Mortgage Corp.** ("Freddie Mac")	25,000	18 to 30 years	T	T	T
Federal National Mortgage Association** ("Fannie Mae")	25,000	1 to 30 years	T	T	T
Government National Mortgage Association** (GNMA—"Ginnie Mae")	25,000	12 to 40 years	T	T	T
Student Loan Marketing Association	10,000	3 to 10 years	T	E	E
Tennessee Valley Authority (TVA)	1,000	5 to 50 years	T	E	E
U.S. Postal Service	10,000	25 years	T	E	E
Federal Financing Corp.	1,000	1 to 20 years	T	E	E

*T = taxable; E = tax-exempt
**Mortgage-backed securities.

institutional investors to hold these securities.) These bonds are often issued as *serial obligations,* which means that the issue is broken into a series of smaller bonds, each with its own maturity date and coupon.

HOTLINKS

For information on municipal bonds, go to the following sites. At Investorama.com click on [When would muni bonds make sense for me?] and at investinginbonds.com click on [Updated: Muni Bonds].

www.Investorama.com/askinvestorama/bonds
www.investinginbonds.com

Municipal bonds ("munis") are brought to the market as either general obligation or revenue bonds. **General obligation bonds** are backed by the full faith, credit, and taxing power of the issuer. **Revenue bonds,** in contrast, are serviced by the income generated from specific income-producing projects (e.g., toll roads). Although general obligations used to dominate the municipal market, the vast majority of munis today come out as revenue bonds (accounting for about 70% to 75% of the new-issue volume).

The distinction between a general obligation bond and a revenue bond is important for a bondholder, because the issuer of a revenue bond is obligated to pay principal and interest *only if a sufficient level of revenue is generated.* If the funds aren't there, the issuer does not have to make payment on the bond. General obligation bonds, however, are required to be serviced in a prompt and timely fashion irrespective of the level of tax income generated by the municipality. Obviously, revenue bonds involve a lot more risk than general obligations, and because of that, they provide higher yields. Regardless of the type, municipal bonds are customarily issued in $5,000 denominations.

general obligation bonds
municipal bonds backed by the full faith, credit, and taxing power of the issuer.

revenue bonds
municipal bonds that require payment of principal and interest only if sufficient revenue is generated by the issuer.

municipal bond guarantees
guarantees from a party other than the issuer that principal and interest payments will be made in a prompt and timely manner.

A somewhat unusual aspect of municipal bonds is the widespread use of **municipal bond guarantees.** With these guarantees, a party other than the issuer assures the bondholder that principal and interest payments will be made in a prompt and timely manner. The third party, in essence, provides an additional source of collateral in the form of insurance, placed on the bond at the date of issue, that is nonrevocable over the life of the obligation. As a result of the guarantee, bond quality is improved. The three principal insurers are the Municipal Bond Investors Assurance Corporation (MBIA), the American Municipal Bond Assurance Corporation (AMBAC), and the Financial

Guaranty Insurance Co. (FGIC). These guarantors will normally insure any general obligation or revenue bond as long as it carries an S&P rating of triple-B or better. (We'll explore bond ratings later in this chapter.) Municipal bond insurance results in higher ratings (usually triple-A) and improved liquidity for these bonds, which are generally more actively traded in the secondary markets. Insured bonds are especially common in the revenue market, and insurance markedly boosts their attractiveness. Whereas an uninsured revenue bond lacks certainty of payment, a guaranteed issue is very much like a general obligation bond because the investor knows that principal and interest payments will be made on time.

Tax Advantages Without a doubt, the thing that makes municipal securities unique is the fact that, in most cases, their interest income is exempt from federal income taxes. That's why these issues are known as *tax-free,* or *tax-exempt,* bonds. Normally, the obligations are also exempt from state and local taxes *in the state in which they were issued.* For example, a California issue is free of California tax if the bondholder lives in California, but its interest income is subject to state tax if the investor resides in Arizona. Note that *capital gains on municipal bonds are not exempt from taxes.*

Individual investors are the biggest buyers of municipal bonds, and tax-free yield is certainly a major draw. Table 9.4 shows what a taxable bond would have to yield to equal the net yield of a tax-free bond. *It demonstrates how the yield attractiveness of municipals varies with an investor's income level.* Clearly, the higher the individual's tax bracket, the more attractive municipal bonds become. Generally speaking, an investor has to be in one of the higher federal tax brackets before municipal bonds offer yields that are competitive with fully taxable issues. This is so because municipal yields are lower than those available from fully taxable issues (such as corporates); and unless the tax effect is sufficient to raise the yield on a municipal to a figure that equals or surpasses taxable rates, it doesn't make much sense to buy municipal bonds.

taxable equivalent yield
the return a fully taxable bond would have to provide to match the after-tax return of a lower-yielding, tax-free municipal bond.

We can determine the level of return a fully taxable bond would have to provide in order to match the after-tax return of a lower-yielding, tax-free issue by computing what is known as a municipal's **taxable equivalent yield**. This measure can be calculated according to the following simple formula:

Equation 9.1

$$\text{Taxable equivalent yield} = \frac{\text{Yield of municipal bond}}{1 - \text{Federal tax rate}}$$

For example, if a municipal offered a yield of 6.5%, then an individual in the 39.6% tax bracket in the year 2000 would have had to find a fully taxable bond with a yield of 10.76% (i.e., 6.5%/0.604 = 10.76%) to reap the same after-tax returns as the municipal.

Note, however, that Equation 9.1 considers *federal taxes only.* As a result, the computed taxable equivalent yield applies only to certain situations: (1) to states that have no state income tax, (2) to situations where the investor is looking at an out-of-state bond (which would be taxable by the investor's state of residence), or (3) where the investor is comparing a municipal bond to a Treasury (or agency) bond—in which case *both* the Treasury and the municipal bonds are free from state income tax. Under any of these conditions, the only tax that's relevant is federal income tax, so using Equation 9.1 is appropriate. But what if the investor is comparing an in-state bond to, say, a corporate

TABLE 9.4 Taxable Equivalent Yields for Various Tax-Exempt Returns

Taxable Income*			Tax-Free Yield							
Joint Returns ($000)	Individual Returns ($000)	Federal Tax Bracket	5%	6%	7%	8%	9%	10%	12%	14%
$0–$43.8	$0–$26.2	15%	5.88	7.06	8.24	9.41	10.59	11.76	14.12	16.47
$43.8–$105.9	$26.2–$63.5	28	6.94	8.33	9.72	11.11	12.50	13.89	16.67	19.44
$105.9–$161.4	$63.5–$132.6	31	7.25	8.70	10.15	11.59	13.04	14.49	17.39	20.29
$161.4–$288.3	$132.6–$288.3	36	7.81	9.38	10.94	12.50	14.06	15.63	18.75	21.88
$288.3 and above	$288.3 and above	39.6	8.28	9.93	11.59	13.25	14.90	16.56	19.87	23.18

*Taxable income and federal tax rates that were in effect in January 1, 2000.

bond? In this case, the in-state bond would be free from both federal and state taxes, but the corporate bond would not. As a result, Equation 9.1 could not be used. Instead, the investor should use a form of the equivalent yield formula that considers *both* federal and state income taxes:

Equation 9.2

$$\text{Taxable equivalent yield for both federal and state taxes} = \frac{\text{Municipal bond yield}}{1 - \left[\text{Federal tax rate} + \text{State tax rate}\left(1 - \text{Federal tax rate}\right)\right]}$$

When both federal and state taxes are included in the calculations, the net effect is to *increase* the taxable equivalent yield. Of course, the size of the increase depends on the level of state income taxes. In a high-tax state like California, for example, the impact can be substantial. Return to the 6.5% municipal bond introduced above: If a California resident in the maximum federal and state tax brackets (39.6% and 11%, respectively) in the year 2000 were considering a corporate issue, she would have had to get a yield of 12.09% on the corporate to match the 6.5% yield on the California bond:

$$\text{Taxable equivalent yield for both federal and state taxes} = \frac{6.5}{1 - [.396 + .11(1 - .3960]}$$

$$= \frac{6.5}{1 - [.396 + .066]}$$

$$= \underline{\underline{12.09\%}}$$

This yield compares to a taxable equivalent yield of 10.76% when only federal taxes were included in the calculation. That's a difference of more than one full percentage point—certainly *not* an insignificant amount.

Corporate Bonds Corporations are the major nongovernmental issuers of bonds. The market for corporate bonds is customarily subdivided into four segments: *industrials* (the most diverse of the groups), *public utilities* (the dominant group in terms of volume of new issues), *rail and transportation bonds,* and *financial issues* (banks, finance companies, etc.). Not only is there a full range of bond quality available in the corporate market, but there is also a wide assortment of different types of bonds. These range from first-mortgage obligations to convertible bonds' debentures, subordinated debentures, senior subordinated issues, capital notes (a type of unsecured debt issued by banks and other financial institutions), and income bonds. Interest on corporate bonds is paid semiannually, and sinking funds are fairly common. The bonds usually come in $1,000 denominations and are issued on a term basis with a single maturity date. Maturities usually range from 25 to 40 years or more. Many corporates, especially the longer ones, carry call deferment provisions that prohibit prepayment for the first 5 to 10 years. Corporate issues are popular with individuals because of their relatively attractive yields.

Most corporates fit the general description above. One that does not is the *equipment trust certificate,* a security issued by railroads, airlines, and other transportation concerns. The proceeds from equipment trust certificates are used to purchase equipment (e.g., jumbo jets and railroad engines) that serves as the collateral for the issue. These bonds are usually issued in serial form and carry uniform annual installments throughout. They normally carry maturities that range from 1 year to a maximum of 15 to 17 years. An attractive feature of equipment trust certificates is that despite a near-perfect payment record that dates back to pre-Depression days, these issues generally offer above-average yields to investors.

Specialty Issues

In addition to the basic bond vehicles described above, investors can also choose from a number of *specialty issues*—bonds that possess unusual issue characteristics. For the most part, these bonds have coupon or repayment provisions that are out of the ordinary. Most are issued by corporations, although they are being used increasingly by other issuers as well. Four of the most actively traded specialty issues today are zero-coupon bonds, mortgage-backed securities, asset-backed securities, and high-yield junk bonds. All four of these rank as some of the more popular bonds on Wall Street. Let's now take a closer look at each of these specialty issues.

zero-coupon bonds
bonds with no coupons that are sold at a deep discount from par value.

Zero-Coupon Bonds As the name implies, **zero-coupon bonds** have no coupons. Rather, these securities are sold at a deep discount from their par values and then increase in value over time at a compound rate of return so that at maturity, they are worth much more than their initial investment. Other things being equal, the cheaper the zero-coupon bond, the greater the return an investor can earn: For example, a 6% might cost $420, but one with a 10% yield might cost only $240.

Because they don't have coupons, these bonds do not pay interest semiannually. In fact, they pay *nothing* to the investor until the issue matures. As strange as it might seem, this feature is the main attraction of zero-coupon bonds. Because there are no interest payments, investors do not have to worry about reinvesting coupon income twice a year. Instead, the fully compounded rate of return on a zero-coupon bond is virtually guaranteed at the rate stated when the issue was purchased. For example, in mid-2000, U.S. Treasury zero-coupon bonds with 20-year maturities were available at yields of around 6.25%. Thus, for less than $300, you could buy a bond that would be worth more than three times that amount, or $1,000, at maturity in 20 years. Best of all, you would be *locking in* a 6.25% compound rate of return on your investment for the full 20-year life of the issue.

The foregoing advantages notwithstanding, zeros do have some serious disadvantages. One is that if rates do move up over time, you won't be able to participate in the higher return (you'll have no coupon income to reinvest). In addition, zero-coupon bonds are subject to tremendous price volatility: If market rates climb, you'll experience a sizable capital loss as the prices of zero-coupons plunge. (Of course, if interest rates *drop,* you'll reap enormous capital gains if you hold long-term zeros. Indeed, such issues are unsurpassed in capital gains potential.) A final disadvantage is that the IRS has ruled that zero-coupon bondholders must report *interest as it is accrued,* even though no interest is actually received. For this reason, most fully taxable zero-coupon bonds should either be used in tax-sheltered investments, such as IRAs, or be held by minor children who are likely to be taxed at the lowest rate, if at all.

HOTLINKS

To read about Treasury strips, go to:

www.bondsonline.com/asp/treas/zeros.asp

Zeros are issued by corporations, municipalities, and federal agencies. You can even buy U.S. Treasury notes and bonds in the form of zero-coupon securities. They're known as **Treasury strips,** or **strip-Ts,** for short. Actually, the Treasury does *not* issue zero-coupon bonds. Instead, it *allows government securities dealers to sell regular coupon-bearing notes and bonds in the form of zero-coupon securities.* Essentially, the coupons are stripped from the bond, repackaged, and then sold separately as zero-coupon bonds. For example, a 20-year Treasury bond has 40 semiannual coupon payments, plus one principal payment. These 41 cash flows can be repackaged and sold as 41 different zero-coupon securities, with maturities that range from 6 months to 20 years. Because they sell at such large discounts, Treasury strips are often sold in minimum denominations (par values) of $10,000. But with their big discounts, that means you probably will pay only $2,800 or $2,900 for $10,000 worth of 20-year strip-Ts. Because there's an active secondary market for Treasury strips, investors can get in and out of these securities with ease just about any time they want. Strip-Ts offer the maximum in issue quality, a full array of different maturities, and an active secondary market—all of which explains why they are so popular.

Treasury strips (Strip-Ts) zero-coupon bonds created from U.S. Treasury securities.

Mortgage-Backed Securities Simply put, a **mortgage-backed bond** is a debt issue that is secured by a pool of residential mortgages. An issuer, such as the Government National Mortgage Association (GNMA), puts together a pool of home mortgages and then issues securities in the amount of the total mortgage pool. These securities, also known as *pass-through securities* or *participation certificates,* are usually sold in minimum denominations of $25,000. Though their maturities can go out as far as 30 years, the average life is generally much shorter (perhaps as short as 8 to 10 years) because many of the mortgages are paid off early.

mortgage-backed bond a debt issue secured by a pool of home mortgages; issued primarily by federal agencies.

As an investor in one of these securities, you hold an undivided interest in the pool of mortgages. When a homeowner makes a monthly mortgage payment, that payment is essentially passed through to you, the bondholder, to pay off the mortgage-backed bond you hold. Although these securities come with normal coupons, *the interest is paid monthly rather than semiannually.* Actually, the monthly payments received by bondholders are, like mortgage payments, made up of both principal and interest. Because the principal portion of the payment represents return of capital, it

HOTLINKS

For an index of agency issues and mortgage-backed bonds, see:

stocks.about.com/money/stocks/cs/bonds_mortgage/index.htm

is considered tax-free. The interest portion, however, is subject to ordinary state and federal income taxes.

Mortgage-backed securities are issued primarily by three federal agencies. Although there are some state and private issuers (mainly big banks and S&Ls), agency issues dominate the market and account for 90% to 95% of the activity. The major agency issuers of mortgage-backed securities (MBSs) are:

- *Government National Mortgage Association (GNMA).* Known as Ginnie Mae, it is the oldest and largest issuer of MBSs.
- *Federal Home Loan Mortgage Corporation (FHLMC).* Known as Freddie Mac, it was the first to issue pools containing conventional mortgages. Stock in FHLMC is publicly owned and traded on the NYSE.
- *Federal National Mortgage Association (FNMA).* Known as Fannie Mae, it's the newest agency player and the leader in marketing seasoned/older mortgages. Its stock is also publicly owned and traded on the NYSE.

Together, these securities represent an important and rapidly growing segment of the U.S. bond market. Indeed, it has been estimated that by 2002 or 2003 *the mortgage-backed market will actually be bigger than the U.S. Treasury market.*

One problem with mortgage-backed securities is that they *are self-liquidating investments;* a portion of the monthly cash flow to the investor is repayment of principal. Thus the investor is always receiving back part of the original investment capital; at maturity there is *no* big principal payment. To counter this problem, a number of *mutual funds* were formed that invest in mortgage-backed securities *but* automatically and continually reinvest the capital/principal portion of the cash flows. Mutual fund investors therefore receive only the interest from their investments and are thus able to preserve their capital.

collateralized mortgage obligation (CMO)
mortgage-backed bond whose holders are divided into classes based on the length of investment desired; principal is channeled to investors in order of maturity, with short-term classes first.

Collateralized Mortgage Obligations Loan prepayments are another problem with mortgage-backed securities. In fact, it was in part an effort to defuse some of the prepayment uncertainty in standard mortgage-backed securities that led to the creation of **collateralized mortgage obligations (CMOs).** Normally, as pooled mortgages are prepaid, all bondholders receive a prorated share of the prepayments. The net effect is to sharply reduce the life of the bond. A CMO, in contrast, divides investors into classes (called "tranches," which is French for "slice"), depending on whether they want a short, intermediate, or long-term investment. Although interest is paid to all bondholders, all principal payments go first to the shortest tranche until it is fully retired. Then the next class in the sequence becomes the sole recipient of principal, and so on until the last tranche is retired.

Basically, CMOs are *derivative securities* created from traditional mortgage-backed bonds, which are placed in a trust. Participation in this trust is then sold to the investing public in the form of CMOs. The net effect of this transformation is that CMOs look and behave very much like any other bond: They offer predictable interest payments and have (relatively) predictable maturities. However, although they carry the same triple-A ratings and implicit U.S. government backing as the mortgage-backed bonds that underlie them, CMOs represent a quantum leap in complexity. Some types of CMOs can be as simple and safe as Treasury bonds. But others can be far more volatile—and risky—than the standard MBSs they're made from. That's because when putting CMOs together, Wall Street performs the financial equivalent of gene splicing: Investment bankers isolate the interest and principal payments from the underlying MBSs and rechannel them to the different tranches. It's not issue quality or risk of default that's the problem here, but rather prepayment, or call, risk. All the bonds will be paid off; it's just a matter of when. Different types of CMO tranches have different levels of prepayment risk. The overall risk in a CMO cannot, of course, exceed that of the underlying mortgage-backed bonds, so in order for there to be some tranches with very little (or no) prepayment risk, others have to endure a lot more. The net effect is that while some CMO tranches are low in risk, others are extremely volatile.

Unfortunately, CMOs became so complex and so exotic that nobody, not even professional money managers, knew exactly what they were getting into. When market interest rates shot way up in 1994, CMO investors took huge losses. In the process, they lost much of their appetite for these securities. Of course, the mortgage market still exists today, but investors are no longer so interested in the "exotics." Instead, their attention has shifted back to "plain vanilla" MBSs or to simpler, less exotic (i.e., less risky) CMOs.

securitization
the process of transforming lending vehicles such as mortgages into marketable securities.

asset-backed securities (ABS)
securities similar to mortgage-backed securities that are backed by a pool of bank loans, leases, and other assets.

Asset-Backed Securities The creation of mortgage-backed securities and CMOs quickly led to the development of a new market technology—the process of **securitization**, whereby various lending vehicles are transformed into marketable securities, much like a mortgage-backed security. Investment bankers are now selling billions of dollars worth of pass-through securities, known as **asset-backed securities (ABS)**, which are backed by pools of auto loans and credit card bills (two of the principal types of collateral), as well as computer leases, hospital receivables, small business loans, truck rentals, and even royalty fees. These securities, first introduced in the mid-1980s, are created when an investment banker bundles together some type of debt linked asset (such as loans or receivables), and then sells investors—via asset-backed securities—the right to receive all or part of the future payments made on that debt. For example, GMAC, the financing arm of General Motors, is a regular issuer of collateralized *auto loan* securities. When it wants to get some of its car loans off its books, GMAC takes the monthly cash flow from a pool of auto loans and pledges them to a new issue of bonds, which are then sold to investors. In similar fashion, *credit card receivables* are regularly used as collateral for these bonds (indeed, they represent the biggest segment of the ABS market), as are *home equity loans,* the second-biggest type of ABS.

Investors are drawn to ABSs for a number of reasons. One is the relatively *high yields* they offer. Another is their *short maturities,* which often extend out no more than 3 to 5 years. A third is the *monthly, rather than semiannual, principal/interest payments* that accompany many of these securities. Also important to investors is their *high credit quality.* That's due to the fact that most of these deals are backed by generous credit protection. For example, the securities are often overcollateralized, which means that the pool of assets backing the bonds may be 25% to 50% larger than the bond issue itself. For whatever reason, the vast majority of ABS receive the highest credit rating possible (triple-A) from the leading agencies.

Most of the ABS market is centered on the three major forms of collateral—credit card receivables, home equity loans, and auto loans. The rest of the

INVESTOR FACTS

THE DREAM FACTORY—Which would you rather own—mundane financial assets like home mortgages and credit card receivables, or a piece of a rock star or best-selling author? Wall Street financier David Pullman made it possible to own part of a rock star in 1997 with "Bowie bonds," asset backed securities based on royalties of David Bowie songs. Since then his firm has offered more than $200 million of bonds secured by works of stars such as James Brown, Marvin Gaye, and the Isley Brothers. What's next for Pullman? He believes any form of intellectual property is a good securitization candidate: authors' earnings, patents, and screenplays.

Source: Daniel Kadlec, "Creative Bonds: Banking on the Stars," *Time*, October 16, 2000, p. 82.

market is anything but traditional, though. Indeed, it seems that just about anything can be securitized, from trade receivables and aircraft loans to taxi medallions and lottery winnings.

Junk Bonds **Junk bonds** or (*high-yield bonds,* as they're also called) are highly speculative securities that have received low, sub-investment-grade ratings (typically Ba or B). These bonds are issued primarily by corporations and, also, by municipalities. Junk bonds generally take the form *of subordinated debentures,* which means the debt is unsecured and has a low claim on assets. These bonds are called "junk" because of their high risk of loss. The companies that issue them generally have excessive amounts of debt in their capital structures, and their ability to service that debt is subject to considerable doubt. Probably the most unusual type of junk bond is something called a **PIK-bond.** PIK stands for *payment in kind* and means that rather than paying the bond's coupon in cash, the issuer can make annual interest payments in the form of additional debt. This "financial printing press" usually goes on for 5 or 6 years, after which time the issuer is supposed to start making interest payments in real money.

junk bonds
high-risk securities that have low ratings but produce high yields.

PIK-bond
a payment-in-kind junk bond that gives the issuer the right to make annual interest payments in new bonds rather than in cash.

Traditionally, the term *junk bond* was applied to the issues of troubled companies, which might have been well rated when first issued but slid to low ratings through corporate mismanagement, heavy competition, or other factors. That all changed during the 1980s, when the vast majority of junk bonds originated not with troubled companies but with a growing number of mature (fairly well-known) firms that used enormous amounts of debt to finance takeovers and buyouts. These companies would change overnight from investment-grade firms to junk as they piled on debt to finance a takeover—or the threat of one. (Wall Street refers to these firms as "fallen angels.")

Why would any rational investor be drawn to junk bonds? The answer is simple: They offer very high yields. Indeed, in a typical market, relative to investment-grade bonds, you can expect to pick up anywhere from 2.5 to 5 percentage points in added yield. In mid-2000, for example, investors were getting 11% or 12% yields on junk bonds, compared to 7% or 8% on investment-grade corporates. Obviously, *such yields are available only because of the correspondingly higher exposure to risk.* However, as we saw earlier in this chapter, there's more to bond returns than yield alone: The *returns* you end up with don't always correspond to the *yields* you went in with. Junk bonds are subject to a good deal of risk, and their prices are unstable. Indeed, unlike investment-grade bonds, whose prices are closely linked to the behavior of market interest rates, junk bonds tend to behave more like stocks. As a result, the returns you actually end up with are highly unpredictable. Accordingly, only investors who are thoroughly familiar with the risks involved, and who are comfortable with such risk exposure, should use these securities.

A Global View of the Bond Market

Globalization has hit the bond market, just as it has the stock market. Foreign bonds have caught on with U.S. investors because of their high yields and attractive returns. There are risks with foreign bonds, of course, but high risk of default is *not* one of them. Instead, the big risk with foreign bonds has to do with the impact that currency fluctuations can have on returns in U.S. dollars.

By year-end 1999, the total value of the world bond market reached some $31 trillion. The United States has the biggest debt market, accounting for about 47% of the total. Far behind the Unites States is Japan, with about 18% of the world market, followed by Germany (at 8%), then Italy, the U.K., France, and Canada. Together, these seven countries account for nearly 85% of the world bond market. Worldwide, various forms of government bonds (e.g., Treasuries, agencies, and munis) dominate the market, accounting for about 55% of the total.

Although the United States today accounts for about half of the available fixed-income securities, that percentage is sure to decline in the future as foreign markets continue to expand. Therefore, by investing solely in U.S. fixed-income securities, an investor is excluding not only half of the investment possibilities worldwide but, more important, the faster growing half. Also, as Table 9.5 reveals, investors in U.S. bonds are missing out on some pretty attractive returns. (The results reported in the table *are total returns in U.S. dollars* and include coupon income, capital gains or losses, and the effects of changes in currency exchange rates.) In fact, over the 20-year period from 1980 through 1999, the U.S. market provided the highest annual return just once (in 1982). A lot of the difference between U.S. and foreign returns in the bond market is due, of course, to the impact of currency exchange rates. Still, the fact remains that from an international perspective, better returns to U.S. investors are usually available to those willing to go offshore.

U.S.-Pay Versus Foreign-Pay Bonds There are several different ways to invest in foreign bonds (*excluding* foreign bond mutual funds, which we'll examine in Chapter 11). From the perspective of a U.S. investor, foreign bonds can be divided into two broad categories on the basis of the currency in which the bond is denominated: *U.S.-pay* (or dollar-denominated) bonds and *foreign-pay* (or non-dollar-denominated) bonds. All the cash flows—including purchase price, maturity value, and coupon income—from dollar denominated foreign bonds are in U.S. dollars, whereas the cash flows from nondollar bonds are designated in a foreign currency or in a basket of foreign currencies, such as the European Currency Unit (ECU).

Dollar-Denominated Bonds Dollar-denominated foreign bonds are of two types: Yankee bonds and Eurodollar bonds. Yankee bonds are issued by foreign governments or corporations or by so-called supernational agencies, like the World Bank and the InterAmerican Bank. These bonds are issued and traded in the United States; they're registered with the SEC, and all transactions are in U.S. dollars. Buying a Yankee bond is really no different from buying any other U.S. bond: These bonds are traded on U.S. exchanges and the OTC market, and *because everything is in dollars, there's no currency exchange risk to deal with.* The bonds are generally very high in quality (which is not surprising, given the quality of the issuers) and offer highly competitive yields to investors.

Eurodollar bonds
foreign bonds denominated in dollars but not registered with the SEC, thus restricting sales of new issues.

Eurodollar bonds, in contrast, are issued and traded outside the United States. They are denominated in U.S. dollars, but they are not registered with the SEC, which means underwriters are legally prohibited from selling new issues to the U.S. public. (Only "seasoned" Eurodollar issues can be sold in this country.) The Eurodollar market today is dominated by foreign-based investors (though that is changing) and is primarily aimed at institutional investors.

TABLE 9.5 Comparative Annual Returns in the World's Major Bond Markets

Annual Total Returns (in U.S. dollars)

	Australia	Canada	France	Germany	Italy	Japan	U.K.	U.S.
1980	−19.0%	−1.6%	−11.0%	−10.3%	−11.8%	24.0%	31.2%	−2.6%
1981	−7.1	−4.7	−18.8	−8.8	−25.0	8.4	−18.8	−0.9
1982	15.0	1.4	5.3	16.5	11.5	3.6	28.8	43.8
1983	0.5	1.9	−0.4	−7.7	15.1	12.3	8.1	4.7
1984	4.9	1.1	6.6	1.4	21.9	2.3	−12.4	16.4
1985	−13.2	34.0	34.4	41.8	37.5	36.8	38.6	30.9
1986	17.1	19.5	27.6	38.4	88.6	36.4	36.4	19.8
1987	29.1	10.4	2.2	28.6	14.2	41.4	41.4	−0.3
1988	29.8	18.9	2.2	−6.6	−1.0	2.6	2.5	6.8
1989	5.1	16.1	8.9	5.6	15.5	−14.5	−3.7	14.0
1990	16.3	7.2	22.4	14.8	28.8	7.2	31.3	8.6
1991	24.3	21.5	13.4	9.8	15.1	23.4	12.8	14.8
1992	−0.1	−0.5	4.6	6.2	−14.4	11.3	−3.9	7.2
1993	16.2	11.4	13.1	7.3	14.0	27.1	19.5	10.1
1994	6.2	−9.9	4.6	9.1	2.1	8.5	−1.7	−2.9
1995	14.9	23.2	27.8	26.5	20.7	10.4	15.8	17.3
1996	19.8	11.3	4.8	−0.3	29.6	−5.9	18.3	2.9
1997	−7.3	4.8	−7.0	−8.9	−1.6	−4.3	10.4	10.0
1998	3.8	2.1	21.2	20.3	20.8	15.9	21.1	10.3
1999	4.1	4.3	−17.2	−16.5	−17.0	15.7	−4.4	−2.9
Average Annual Returns Over Extended Holding Periods								
5 years:								
1995–99	7.1%	9.1%	5.9%	4.2%	10.5%	6.4%	12.2%	7.5%
1990–94	12.6	6.0	11.6	9.4	9.1	15.5	11.6	7.6
10 years:								
1990–99 (the '90s)	9.8%	7.5%	8.8%	6.8%	9.8%	10.9%	11.9%	7.5%
1980–89 (the '80s)	5.0	9.1	4.6	8.3	13.4	14.0	13.1	12.4
15 years:								
1985–99	11.1%	11.6%	10.9%	11.7%	16.9%	14.1%	15.6%	9.8%
20 years:								
1980–99	8.0%	8.6%	7.2%	8.4%	13.2%	13.1%	13.6%	10.4%

Note: Total return = Coupon income + Capital gain (or loss) + Profit (or loss) from changes in currency exchange rates. The returns shown here are *government bond returns* and as such, *the U.S. returns* will differ a bit from those shown in Tables 9.1 and 9.2 (which are yields and returns for *corporate bonds*).

Source: Datastream

Foreign-Pay Bonds From the standpoint of U.S. investors, foreign-pay international bonds encompass all those issues denominated in a currency other than dollars. These bonds are issued and traded overseas and are not registered with the SEC. Examples are German government bonds, which are payable in deutsche marks; Japanese bonds, issued in yen; and so forth. When investors speak of *foreign bonds*, it's this segment of the market that most of them are thinking of.

Foreign-pay bonds are subject to changes in currency exchange rates, which can dramatically affect total returns to U.S. investors. The returns on foreign-pay bonds are a function of three things: (1) the level of coupon (interest) income earned on the bonds; (2) the change in market interest rates, which determine the level of capital gains (or losses); and (3) the behavior of currency exchange rates. The first two variables are the same as those that drive bond returns in this country and are, of course, just as important to foreign bonds as they are to domestic bonds. Thus, if you're investing overseas, you still want to know what the yields are today and where they're headed. *It's really the third variable that separates the return behavior of dollar-denominated from foreign-pay bonds.*

We can assess returns from foreign-pay bonds by employing the same (modified) holding period return formula first introduced in our discussion of foreign stock returns. (See Equation 6.6 in Chapter 6.) For example, assume a U.S. investor purchased a German government bond, in large part because of the attractive 10% coupon it carried. If the bond was bought at par and market rates fell over the course of the year, the security itself would have provided a return in excess of 10% (because the decline in rates would provide some capital gains). However, if the deutsche mark (DM) fell relative to the dollar, the total return (in U.S. dollars) could have actually ended up at a lot less than 10%, depending on what happened to the U.S. $/DM exchange rate. To find out exactly how this investment turned out, you could use Equation 6.6, and make a few (very minor) modifications to it (e.g., use interest income in place of dividends received). Like foreign stocks, *foreign-pay bonds can pay off from both the behavior of the security and the behavior of the currency.* As Table 9.5 shows, that combination, in many cases, means superior returns to U.S. investors. Knowledgeable investors find these bonds attractive not only because of their competitive returns but also because of *the positive diversification effects they have on bond portfolios.*

Trading Bonds

LG 6

In large part as a result of the perceived safety and stability of bonds, many individual investors view bond investing as a relatively simple process. Such thinking, however, can often lead to unsatisfactory results, even losses. The fact is that not all bonds are alike, and picking the right security for the time is just as important for bond investors as it is for stock investors. Indeed, success in the bond market demands a thorough understanding not only of the different types of bonds but also of the many technical factors that drive bond yields, prices, and returns—things like call features, refunding provisions, and the impact that coupon and maturity can have on bond price volatility. Also, because bond ratings are so important to a smooth-running bond market, investors should become thoroughly familiar with them. Let's now take a look at these ratings and at the quotation system used for bonds.

Bond Ratings

bond ratings
letter grades that designate investment quality and are assigned to a bond issue by rating agencies.

Bond ratings are like grades: A letter grade that designates investment quality is assigned to an issue on the basis of extensive, professionally conducted financial analysis. Ratings are widely used and are an important part of the municipal and corporate bond markets, where issues are regularly evaluated and rated by one or more of the rating agencies. Even some agency issues, like the Tennessee Valley Authority (TVA), are rated, though they always receive ratings that confirm the obvious—that the issues are prime grade. The two largest and best-known rating agencies are Moody's and Standard & Poor's; another lesser known but still important bond-rating agency is Fitch Investors Service.

How Ratings Work Every time a large new issue comes to the market, it is analyzed by a staff of professional bond analysts to determine default risk exposure and investment quality. (A fee, usually ranging from $1,000 to $15,000 and paid by the issuer or the underwriter of the securities, is charged for rating each bond.) The rating agency thoroughly studies the financial records of the issuing organization and assesses its future prospects. Although the specifics of the actual credit analysis conducted by the rating agencies change with each issue, several major factors enter into most bond ratings. With a corporate issue, for example, these factors include an analysis of the issue's indenture provisions, an in-depth study of the firm's earning power (including the stability of its earnings), a look at the company's liquidity and how it is managed, a study of the company's relative debt burden, and an in-depth exploration of its coverage ratios to determine how well it can service both existing debt and any new bonds that are being contemplated or proposed. As you might expect, the firm's financial strength and stability are very important in determining the appropriate bond rating. Indeed, although there is far more to setting a rating than cranking out a few financial ratios, a strong relationship exists between the operating results and financial condition of the firm and the rating its bonds receive. Generally, the higher ratings are associated with more profitable companies that rely *less* on debt as a form of financing, are more liquid, have stronger cash flows, and have no trouble servicing their debt in a prompt and timely fashion.

Table 9.6 lists the various ratings assigned to bonds by the two major services. In addition to the standard rating categories noted in the table, Moody's uses numerical modifiers (1, 2, or 3) on bonds rated double-A to B, while S&P uses plus (+) or minus (−) signs on the same rating classes to show relative standing within a major rating category. For example, A+ (or A1) means a strong, high A rating, whereas A− (or A3) indicates that the issue is on the low end of the A rating scale. Except for slight variations in designations (Aaa vs. AAA), the meanings and interpretations are basically the same.

Note that the top four ratings (Aaa through Baa, or AAA through BBB) designate *investment-grade* bonds. Such ratings are highly coveted by issuers, as they indicate financially strong, well-run companies. The next two ratings (Ba/B or BB/B) are reserved for junk bonds. These ratings mean that although *the principal and interest payments on the bonds are still being met in a timely fashion,* the risk of default is relatively high. The issuers of these bonds generally lack the financial strength that backs investment-grade issues. (Sometimes the Caa1/CCC+ category is counted as part of the junk category, although technically the C rating class is meant to designate bonds that are already in default or getting very close to it.) Most of the time, Moody's and S&P assign identical ratings. Sometimes, however, an issue carries two different ratings. These **split ratings** are viewed simply as "shading" the quality of an issue one way or another. For example, an issue might be rated Aa by Moody's but A or A+ by S&P.

split ratings
different ratings given to a bond issue by the two major rating agencies.

TABLE 9.6 Bond Ratings

Moody's	S&P	Definition
Aaa	AAA	*High-grade investment bonds.* The highest rating assigned, denoting extremely strong capacity to pay principal and interest. Often called "gilt-edge" securities.
Aa	AA	*High-grade investment bonds.* High quality by all standards but rated lower primarily because the margins of protection are not quite as strong.
A	A	*Medium-grade investment bonds.* Many favorable investment attributes, but elements may be present that suggest susceptibility to adverse economic changes.
Baa	BBB	*Medium-grade investment bonds.* Adequate capacity to pay principal and interest but possibly lacking certain protective elements against adverse economic conditions.
Ba	BB	*Speculative issues.* Only moderate protection of principal and interest in varied economic times. (This is one of the ratings carried by junk bonds.)
B	B	*Speculative issues.* Generally lacking desirable characteristics of investment bonds. Assurance of principal and interest may be small; this is another junk-bond rating.
Caa	CCC	*Default.* Poor-quality issues that may be in default or in danger of default.
Ca	CC	*Default.* Highly speculative issues, often in default or possessing other market shortcomings.
C		*Default.* These issues may be regarded as extremely poor in investment quality.
	C	*Default.* Rating given to income bonds on which no interest is paid.
	D	*Default.* Issues actually in default, with principal or interest in arrears.

Source: Moody's *Bond Record* and Standard & Poor's *Bond Guide.*

Also, just because a bond is given a certain rating at the time of issue doesn't mean it will keep that rating for the rest of its life. Ratings change as the financial condition of the issuer changes. In fact, all rated issues are reviewed on a regular basis to ensure that the assigned rating is still valid. Many issues do carry a single rating to maturity, but it is not uncommon for ratings to be revised up or down. As you might expect, the market responds to rating revisions by adjusting bond yields accordingly. For example, an upward revision (e.g., from A to AA) causes the market yield on the bond to drop, as a reflection of the bond's improved quality. One final point: Although it may appear that the firm is receiving the rating, it is actually the *issue* that receives it. As a result, a firm's different issues can have different ratings. The senior securities, for example, might carry one rating and the junior issues another, lower rating.

HOTLINKS

For further explanation of Moody's bond ratings, go to:

www.moneypages.com/syndicate/bonds/index.html

What Ratings Mean Most bond investors pay close attention to agency ratings, because ratings can affect not only potential market behavior but comparative market yields as well. Specifically, the higher the rating, the lower the yield, other things being equal. For example, whereas an A-rated bond might offer a 7.5% yield, a comparable triple-A issue would probably yield something like 7%. Furthermore, investment-grade securities are far more interest-sensitive and tend to exhibit more uniform price behavior than junk bonds and other lower-rated issues. Perhaps most important, *bond ratings serve to relieve individual investors of the drudgery of evaluating the investment quality of an issue on their own.* Large institutional investors often have their own staff of credit analysts who independently assess the creditworthiness of various corporate and municipal issuers; individual investors, in contrast, have little if anything to gain from conducting their own credit analysis. After all, credit analysis is time-consuming and costly, and it demands a good deal more expertise than the average individual investor possesses. Most important, the ratings are closely adhered to by a large segment of the bond investment community, in large part because it has been shown that *the rating agencies do a remarkably good job of assessing bond quality.* Thus individual investors can depend on assigned agency ratings as a viable measure of the creditworthiness of the issuer and an issue's risk of default. A word of caution is in order, however: Bear in mind that bond ratings are intended to measure only an issue's *default risk,* which has no bearing whatsoever on an issue's exposure to *market risk.* Thus if interest rates increase, even the highest-quality issues go down in price, subjecting investors to capital loss and market risk.

INVESTOR FACTS

BETTING ON AN UPGRADE—"You say *potayto* and I say *potahto,*" as the old song goes. It turns out that some corporate bonds appear to be of investment-grade quality to one credit rating agency but look like junk to another. Such bonds—which are given a low *investment-grade* rating by one agency and a lower *junk bond* rating by another—are known as *crossover bonds,* and they are proving to be popular with investors. For one thing, they usually pay higher interest rates than a purely investment-grade bond, because one rating agency thinks the credit risk is greater. But they also offer investors the opportunity for capital appreciation. The reason: Often, the rating agency that called the bond junk eventually upgrades its credit rating, making the bond more valuable.

Reading the Quotes

One thing you quickly learn in the bond market is that transactions are not always as easy to conduct as they may seem. In the first place, many bonds have relatively "thin" markets. Indeed, some issues may trade only five or ten bonds a week, and many have no secondary market at all. There are, of course, numerous high-volume issues, but even so, you should pay particularly close attention to an issue's trading volume—especially if you're looking for lots of price action and need prompt order executions. In addition, it's not always easy to obtain current information on bond prices. That's because most bonds trade in over-the-counter markets, which are somewhat specialized, rather than on centralized exchanges; and except for Treasury securities, the financial pages provide little information on general market activity and even less on particular securities. Indeed, daily price quotes are widely available on only a few of the thousands of publicly traded corporate and municipal bonds. Finally, investors often have to look to both brokers and bankers to complete transactions. Most brokerage houses tend to confine their activities to new issues and to secondary market transactions of listed Treasury obligations, agency issues, and corporate bonds. Commercial banks, in contrast, are still the major dealers in municipal bonds and are active in Treasury and agency securities as well.

Except for municipal issues (which are usually quoted in terms of the yield they offer), bonds are quoted on the basis of their dollar prices. Such quotes are always interpreted as a *percent of par.* Thus, a quote of 97½ does not mean $97.50 but, instead, means that the issue is trading at 97.5% of the par value of the obligation. In the bond market, it's assumed that we're dealing with bonds that have par values of $1,000—or some multiple thereof. Accordingly, a quote of 97½ translates into a dollar price of $975. (With bond quotes, 1 point = $10, and ⅛ of a point = $1.25.) As you can see in the bond quotes in Figure 9.6, one quotation system is used for corporate bonds and another for governments. (Treasuries and agencies are quoted the same.)

HOTLINKS

Two great sites for getting bond quotes, as well as a lot of other information about bonds, are:

www.bondsonline.com
www.investinginbonds.com

Corporate Bond Quotes To understand the system used with corporate bonds, look at the Duke Energy issue highlighted in Figure 9.6. The group of numbers immediately following the company name (which is often highly abbreviated) gives the coupon and the year in which the bond matures. Thus,

FIGURE 9.6 **Price Quotations for Corporate and Government Bonds**

Both corporate and Treasury bonds are quoted as a percent of their par value. But note that corporate bonds are quoted in eighths of a point, whereas Treasuries are quoted in thirty-seconds. Also observe that both coupon and maturity play vital roles in the quotation system. (*Source: Wall Street Journal,* July 7, 2000.)

CORPORATES

Bonds	Cur Yld.	Vol	Close	Net Chg
ChespkE $9\frac{1}{8}$06	9.6	20	95	...
ChespkE $8\frac{1}{2}$12	9.9	17	86	+ 2
ChiqBr 10s09	12.7	15	$78\frac{1}{2}$	+ $\frac{3}{8}$
vjClardg $11\frac{3}{4}$02f	...	10	$49\frac{3}{4}$	− $1\frac{1}{4}$
ClrkOil $9\frac{1}{2}$04	10.3	51	$91\frac{7}{8}$	+ $1\frac{7}{8}$
Coastl $9\frac{3}{4}$03	9.4	25	$103\frac{1}{2}$	− $1\frac{7}{8}$
Consec $8\frac{1}{8}$03	9.7	109	$83\frac{1}{2}$	− 1
Conseco $10\frac{1}{2}$04	12.5	22	$83\frac{7}{8}$	− $\frac{1}{8}$
Conseco $10\frac{1}{2}$02	14.1	472	$72\frac{3}{4}$	+ $\frac{1}{4}$
ConPort 11s06	15.6	21	$70\frac{1}{2}$	+ $\frac{1}{2}$
DR Hrtn 10s06	10.2	10	98	− $1\frac{3}{4}$
DevonE 4.9s08	cv	10	$96\frac{1}{4}$	+ $\frac{3}{4}$
Dole 7s03	7.5	10	$93\frac{5}{8}$	+ $\frac{1}{4}$
DukeEn $6\frac{3}{4}$25	7.9	10	85	+ $1\frac{1}{4}$
DukeEn $7\frac{1}{2}$25	7.9	25	$94\frac{1}{2}$	+ $1\frac{3}{4}$
Exxon 6s05	6.2	6	$96\frac{1}{4}$	...
Florsh $12\frac{3}{4}$02	13.7	2	93	+ 1
GEICap $7\frac{7}{8}$06	7.6	25	104	− $\frac{3}{4}$
GMA $5\frac{1}{2}$01	5.6	14	$97\frac{3}{8}$	− $\frac{1}{8}$
GMA $9\frac{5}{8}$01	9.3	35	$103\frac{1}{2}$	+ $1\frac{5}{8}$
GMA $6\frac{7}{8}$01	7.0	5	$98\frac{7}{8}$	...
GMA 7s02	7.0	15	$99\frac{5}{8}$	...
GMA $8\frac{1}{2}$03	8.3	35	$102\frac{5}{8}$	...
GMA $8\frac{3}{4}$05	8.3	16	105	...
GMA zr12	...	12	$37\frac{1}{2}$	− 2
vjGenesH $9\frac{3}{4}$05f	...	105	$12\frac{1}{2}$	+ 1
HRPT $7\frac{1}{2}$03	cv	5	90	+ 1
Hallwd 10s05	11.0	5	91	− $\frac{7}{8}$
HlthcrR 6.55s02	cv	40	86	− 4
Hilton 5s06	cv	589	80	+ $1\frac{1}{8}$
Hollngr $9\frac{1}{4}$06	9.3	10	$99\frac{7}{8}$	+ $1\frac{3}{4}$
Honywll zr2000	...	45	$98\frac{5}{32}$	...
Honywll zr03	...	40	$79\frac{1}{2}$	+ $\frac{3}{4}$
HousF $9\frac{5}{8}$00	9.7	9	$99\frac{5}{8}$	− $\frac{1}{4}$
IBM $7\frac{1}{4}$02	7.2	10	$100\frac{3}{8}$	− $\frac{1}{8}$
IBM 6.45s07	6.7	50	$96\frac{7}{8}$	+ $\frac{5}{8}$
IBM $7\frac{1}{2}$13	7.5	5	$100\frac{3}{8}$	− $1\frac{7}{8}$
IntShip 9s03	9.0	33	$99\frac{1}{2}$	...
JCPL $6\frac{3}{8}$03	6.6	1	$96\frac{1}{2}$	+ $\frac{3}{8}$
KaufB $9\frac{3}{8}$03	9.5	80	99	− $\frac{1}{4}$
KaufB $7\frac{3}{4}$04	8.4	10	$92\frac{1}{4}$	+ $\frac{5}{8}$
KaufB $9\frac{5}{8}$06	9.8	68	98	+ $\frac{5}{8}$
KerrM $7\frac{1}{2}$14	cv	1	97	+ $1\frac{3}{4}$
Leucadia $8\frac{1}{4}$05	8.6	20	96	...
Leucadia $7\frac{3}{4}$13	8.9	29	$87\frac{1}{4}$	...
LibPrp 8s01	cv	19	134	+ 2
Loews $3\frac{1}{8}$07	cv	78	$81\frac{1}{2}$	− $\frac{1}{2}$
Lucent $7\frac{1}{4}$06	7.4	20	$98\frac{1}{8}$	− $1\frac{7}{8}$
MBNA 8.28s26	9.8	101	$84\frac{3}{4}$	− $2\frac{3}{8}$
MSC Sf $7\frac{7}{8}$04	cv	50	87	...
MailWell 5s02	cv	18	83	+ 3

Duke Energy bond

GMAC zero-coupon bond

10¾% Treasury bond (noncallable)

U.S. TREASURY STRIPS

Mat.	Type	Bid	Asked	Chg.	Ask Yld.
Feb 13	ci	45:23	45:29	−7	6.28
May 13	ci	45:01	45:06	−7	6.28
Aug 13	ci	44:10	44:15	−8	6.28
Nov 13	ci	43:20	43:25	−7	6.28
Feb 14	ci	42:29	43:02	−8	6.29
May 14	ci	42:08	42:13	−8	6.29
Aug 14	ci	41:19	41:24	−8	6.29
Nov 14	ci	40:30	41:04	−8	6.29
Feb 15	ci	40:09	40:14	−8	6.30
Feb 15	bp	40:09	40:15	−8	6.30
May 15	ci	39:21	39:26	−7	6.30
Aug 15	ci	39:01	39:07	−7	6.30
Aug 15	bp	39:04	39:10	−8	6.28
Nov 15	ci	38:14	38:19	−7	6.30
Nov 15	bp	38:19	38:24	−8	6.27
Feb 16	ci	37:27	38:01	−7	6.30
Feb 16	bp	38:02	38:07	−8	6.26
May 16	ci	37:09	37:15	−7	6.29
May 16	bp	37:22	37:27	−8	6.23
Aug 16	ci	36:23	36:29	−7	6.29
Nov 16	ci	36:06	36:11	−7	6.29
Nov 16	bp	36:15	36:21	−8	6.24
Feb 17	ci	35:20	35:26	−3	6.28
May 17	ci	35:03	35:09	−4	6.28
May 17	bp	35:07	35:13	−6	6.26
Aug 17	ci	34:19	34:24	−6	6.28
Aug 17	bp	34:23	34:28	−6	6.26
Nov 17	ci	33:30	34:03	−6	6.30
Feb 18	ci	33:16	33:22	−6	6.28
May 18	ci	33:00	33:06	−6	6.28
May 18	bp	33:02	33:08	−6	6.27

Stripped (zero-coupon) Treasuries

TREASURIES

Rate	Maturity Mo/Yr	Bid	Asked	Chg.	Ask Yld.
$11\frac{1}{8}$	Aug 03	113:03	113:07	−7	6.36
$4\frac{1}{4}$	Nov 03n	93:27	93:29	−6	6.29
$11\frac{7}{8}$	Nov 03	116:09	116:13	−7	6.36
$4\frac{3}{4}$	Feb 04n	95:02	95:04	−7	6.28
$5\frac{7}{8}$	Feb 04n	98:22	98:24	−7	6.27
$5\frac{1}{4}$	May 04n	96:16	96:18	−7	6.26
$7\frac{1}{4}$	May 04n	103:06	103:08	−6	6.28
$12\frac{3}{8}$	May 04	120:07	120:13	−8	6.32
6	Aug 04n	99:03	99:05	−7	6.23
$7\frac{1}{4}$	Aug 04n	103:14	103:16	−6	6.27
$13\frac{3}{4}$	Aug 04	126:11	126:17	−8	6.32
$5\frac{7}{8}$	Nov 04n	98:18	98:19	−7	6.25
$7\frac{7}{8}$	Nov 04n	105:30	106:00	−7	6.28
$11\frac{5}{8}$	Nov 04	119:31	120:05	−8	6.26
$7\frac{1}{2}$	Feb 05n	104:27	104:29	−8	6.26
$6\frac{1}{2}$	May 05n	101:05	101:07	−6	6.20
$6\frac{3}{4}$	May 05n	102:14	102:15	−7	6.15
12	May 05	123:17	123:23	−8	6.26
$6\frac{1}{2}$	Aug 05n	101:03	101:05	−7	6.23
$10\frac{3}{4}$	Aug 05	119:08	119:12	−9	6.26
$5\frac{7}{8}$	Nov 05n	98:11	98:13	−8	6.23
$5\frac{5}{8}$	Feb 06n	97:04	97:06	−6	6.22
$9\frac{3}{8}$	Feb 06	114:15	114:19	−8	6.25
$6\frac{7}{8}$	May 06n	103:01	103:03	−7	6.23
7	Jul 06n	103:24	103:26	−7	6.23
$6\frac{1}{2}$	Oct 06n	101:10	101:12	−7	6.23
$3\frac{3}{8}$	Jan 07i	96:03	96:04	....	4.06
$6\frac{1}{4}$	Feb 07n	100:06	100:08	−7	6.20
$7\frac{5}{8}$	Feb 02-07	101:18	101:20	−3	6.54
$6\frac{5}{8}$	May 07n	102:07	102:09	−7	6.21
$6\frac{1}{8}$	Aug 07n	99:15	99:17	−7	6.21
$7\frac{7}{8}$	Nov 02-07	102:25	102:27	−4	6.55
$3\frac{5}{8}$	Jan 08i	97:04	97:05	....	4.07
$5\frac{1}{2}$	Feb 08n	95:26	95:28	−8	6.19
$5\frac{5}{8}$	May 08n	96:18	96:20	−8	6.17
$8\frac{3}{8}$	Aug 03-08	104:31	105:01	−7	6.56
$4\frac{3}{4}$	Nov 08n	90:28	90:30	−9	6.15
$8\frac{3}{4}$	Nov 03-08	106:17	106:19	−6	6.53
$3\frac{7}{8}$	Jan 09i	98:20	98:21	....	4.06
$5\frac{1}{2}$	May 09n	95:21	95:23	−11	6.13
$9\frac{1}{8}$	May 04-09	108:22	108:24	−6	6.52
6	Aug 09n	99:01	99:02	−17	6.13
$10\frac{3}{8}$	Nov 04-09	114:14	114:18	−6	6.48
$4\frac{1}{4}$	Jan 10i	101:22	101:23	....	4.03
$6\frac{1}{2}$	Feb 10n	103:09	103:10	−15	6.04
$11\frac{3}{4}$	Feb 05-10	120:18	120:24	−9	6.47
10	May 05-10	114:11	114:15	−9	6.48
$12\frac{3}{4}$	Nov 05-10	127:29	128:03	−10	6.46
$13\frac{7}{8}$	May 06-11	135:18	135:24	−12	6.44
14	Nov 06-11	138:25	138:31	−12	6.43
$10\frac{3}{8}$	Nov 07-12	122:26	123:00	−13	6.40
12	Aug 08-13	134:26	135:00	−16	6.40
$13\frac{1}{4}$	May 09-14	145:20	145:26	−17	6.39

13⅞% Treasury bond (deferred call)

the 7½ means that this particular bond carries a 7½% annual coupon and will mature in the year 2025.

The next column, labeled "Cur Yld," provides the *current yield*—in this case, 7.9%—being offered by the issue at its *current market price.* **Current yield** is a measure of the amount of annual interest income a bond provides relative to its prevailing market price. It is found by dividing annual coupon income by the closing price of the issue. In many respects, it is equivalent to the dividend yield measure used with stocks. We'll look at this bond valuation measure in more detail in Chapter 10.

current yield
measure of the annual interest income a bond provides relative to its current market price.

The next entry in the Duke Energy quote in Figure 9.6 is the "Vol" column, which shows the actual number of bonds traded. In this case, 25 bonds were traded on the day of the quotes. The last two columns provide the bond's closing price for the day and the net change in the closing price. Thus the bond's closing (or last) price was 94½, up a point and three-quarters (+1¾) from its last close. In dollars, that means the bond traded at $945, which was $17.50 higher than its previous close. Note that corporate bonds are usually quoted in eighths of a point (as are munis) although, as we'll see, that's not the case with Treasury and agency bonds.

Government Bond Quotes In contrast to corporates (and munis), U.S. government bonds (Treasuries as well as agency issues) are listed in thirty-secondths of a point. With government bonds, the figures to the right of the colon (:) indicate the number of thirty-seconds in the fractional bid or ask price. For example, look at the ask price of the highlighted 10¾% Treasury issue in Figure 9.6: It is being quoted at 119:12 (ask). Translated, that means the bond is being quoted at 119$^{12}/_{32}$, or 119.375% of par. Thus if you wanted to buy, say, $15,000 worth of this issue, you would have to pay $17,906.25 ($15,000 × 1.19375). Actually, the amount would be more than that after transaction costs were tacked on. Here's an example of a bond that is trading at a big premium (some 19 percent *above* its par value), in large part because market interest rates have fallen well below the bond's coupon.

Treasury (and agency) bond quotes include not only the coupon (see the "Rate" column) but also the year and *month* of maturity. Note also that when there's more than one date in the maturity column (e.g., see the 13⅞% Treasury bond, which shows a maturity of May 06–11), it's the *second* figure that indicates the issue's maturity date; the first one shows when the bond becomes freely callable. Thus the 13⅞% bond matures in May 2011, and it carries a call deferment provision that extends through May 2006. In contrast, a Treasury note or bond with a single maturity date, such as the 10¾% bond of August 2005, indicates that the issue is *noncallable.*

Unlike corporates, government bonds are quoted in bid/ask terms. The bid price signifies what the bond dealers are willing to pay for the securities (which is how much you can sell them for). The ask price is what the dealers will sell the bonds for (what you have to pay to buy them). Again, keep in mind that these bid/ask prices ignore transaction costs. When transaction costs are factored in, you'll end up getting *less* than the quoted price when you sell and paying *more* than the quoted price when you buy. This is especially true in the Treasury, agency, and municipal markets, where secondary market trades of, say, $25,000 or less can involve transactions costs of as much as *1% to 5%* of the amount traded. Finally, note that the "Yld" column with Treasuries is not the current yield of the issue but rather the bond's *promised yield-to-maturity.*

Promised yield-to-maturity is basically a fully compounded measure of return that captures both current income and capital gains or losses. (We'll examine yield-to-maturity in Chapter 10.)

Quotes on Zero-Coupon Bonds Also highlighted in both the corporate and Treasury quotes are some zero-coupon bonds. Look at the GMAC ("GMA") bonds highlighted in the corporate column; these are zero-coupon bonds. Such bonds are easy to pick out because they're identified by the letters *zr* in place of their coupons. For example, with the highlighted GMAC bonds, the *zr12* tells you the issue is a zero-coupon bond that matures in 2012.

Zeros are even easier to pick out in the Treasury quotes, because they're all listed under the heading "U.S. Treasury Strips." As we discussed earlier in this chapter, these securities are created by "stripping" the coupons from their bond issues and selling them separately from the principal. Thus the principal and interest *cash flows* can be sold on their own. (Look at the Strips quotes: A *ci* behind the maturity date means the issue is made up of coupon/interest cash flow, whereas a *bp* means it is made up of bond principal.) Regardless of whether they're corporates or stripped Treasuries, the prices of most zeros are quite low compared to regular coupon bonds. This is particularly true for longer maturities. Thus the quoted price of 37½ for the highlighted GMAC issue is *not* a misprint. Rather, it means that you could have purchased this bond for $375 (or 37.5% of par) and in the year 2012, receive $1,000 in return. Likewise, you could have purchased the (highlighted) February 15 stripped Treasury for just $400 (and change) and in 2015, receive a payment of $1,000 (which, by the way, would provide you with a fully compounded return of 6.30%).

Summary

LG 1

Explain the basic investment attributes of bonds and their use as investment vehicles. Bonds are publicly traded debt securities that provide investors with two basic sources of return: (1) current income and (2) capital gains. Current income is derived from the coupon (interest) payments received over the life of the issue. Capital gains can be earned whenever market interest rates fall. In addition to their yields and returns, bonds can also be used to shelter income from taxes and for the preservation and long-term accumulation of capital. Just as important, the diversification properties of bonds are such that they can greatly enhance portfolio stability.

LG 2

Describe the essential features of a bond and distinguish among different types of call, refunding, and sinking-fund provisions. All bonds carry some type of coupon, which specifies the annual rate of interest to be paid by the issuer. Bonds also have predetermined maturity dates: Term bonds carry a single maturity date, and serial bonds have a series of maturity dates. Every bond is issued with some type of call feature, be it freely callable, noncallable, or deferred callable. Call features spell out whether an issue can be prematurely retired and, if so, when. Some bonds (temporarily) prohibit the issuer from paying off one bond with the proceeds from another by including a refunding provision. Others are issued with sinking-fund provisions, which specify how a bond is to be paid off over time.

LG 3

Describe the relationship between bond prices and yields, and explain why some bonds are more volatile than others. The price behavior of a bond depends on the issue's coupon and maturity and on the movement in market interest rates. When interest rates go down, bond prices go up, and vice versa. However, the extent to which bond prices move up or down depends on the coupon and maturity of an issue. Bonds with lower coupons and/or longer maturities generate larger price swings.

LG 4 **Identify the different types of bonds and the kinds of investment objectives these securities can fulfill.** The bond market is divided into four major segments: Treasuries, agencies, municipals, and corporates. Treasury bonds are issued by the U.S. Treasury and are virtually default-free. Agency bonds are issued by various political subdivisions of the U.S. government and make up an increasingly important segment of the bond market. Municipal bonds are issued by state and local governments in the form of either general obligation or revenue bonds. Corporate bonds make up the major non-government sector of the market and are backed by the assets and profitability of the issuing companies. Generally speaking, Treasuries are attractive because of their high quality, agencies and corporates because of the added returns they provide, and munis because of the tax shelter they offer.

LG 5 **Discuss the global nature of the bond market and the difference between dollar-denominated and non-dollar-denominated foreign bonds.** There's growing investor interest in foreign bonds, particularly foreign-pay securities, because of their highly competitive yields and returns. Foreign-pay bonds cover all those issues that are denominated in some currency other than U.S. dollars. These bonds have an added source of return: currency exchange rates. In addition, there are dollar-denominated foreign bonds—Yankee bonds and Eurodollar bonds. These have no currency exchange risk because they are issued in U.S. dollars.

LG 6 **Describe the role that bond ratings play in the market and the quotation system used with various types of bonds.** Municipal and corporate issues are regularly rated for bond quality by independent rating agencies. A rating of Aaa indicates an impeccable record. Lower ratings, such as A or Baa, indicate more risk. As with all investments, the returns required of lower-quality instruments generally are higher than those required of high-quality bonds. The bond market also has its own quotation system, wherein bonds are quoted as a percent of par. Thus, 1 point in the bond market represents $10 (not $1 as in the stock market).

CHAPTER 10

BOND VALUATION AND ANALYSIS

Black & Decker Corp. is one of the nation's largest and most diversified manufacturers, ranking 356 on the Fortune 500 and ninth in its industry group. Over the years, Black & Decker has used acquisitions of smaller companies to expand into many different areas beyond its original line of power tools and accessories. Black & Decker's product line today also includes residential security hardware, household appliances, and metal and plastic fasteners/fastening systems for commercial applications.

To finance its growth, Black & Decker often used long-term bonds. In 1991 the company had $2.6 billion of long-term debt on its books, giving it a debt-to-equity ratio of 2.56—well above industry averages. Although the company reduced its debt load steadily, it still had $1.6 billion as of 1997. Its six issues, with maturities from 2000 to 2028, carried interest rates ranging from 6.55% to 7.5%. Because of the relatively large amount of debt on Black & Decker's balance sheet, Standard & Poor's Corporation rated its bonds BBB–, the lowest investment grade rating. As a result, the company had to pay more interest on its debt than a higher-rated company. Had the company's financial position weakened further, S&P might have downgraded the bonds to BB or lower—the high-yield, or "junk," bond category. The market price of Black & Decker bonds would have declined in reaction to such a move. However, in April 1999, S&P upgraded Black & Decker's bonds to BBB as the company continued to make significant strides in reducing its debt. By December 31, 2000, long-term debt was just under $800 million, and the debt-to-equity ratio, though still above industry standards, was 1.15.

As we'll see in this chapter, a bond's price is affected by many factors, including credit quality and the general level of interest rates. Investors must evaluate these factors when deciding whether the market value of a bond will provide the return they need.

LEARNING GOALS

After studying this chapter, you should be able to:

LG 1 Explain the behavior of market interest rates, and identify the forces that cause interest rates to move.

LG 2 Describe the term structure of interest rates, and note how these so-called yield curves can be used by investors.

LG 3 Understand how bonds are valued in the marketplace.

LG 4 Describe the various measures of yield and return, and explain how these standards of performance are used in bond valuation.

LG 5 Understand the basic concept of duration, how it can be measured, and its use in the management of bond portfolios.

LG 6 Discuss various bond investment strategies and the different ways these securities can be used by investors.

The Behavior of Market Interest Rates

LG 1 LG 2

You will recall from Chapter 4 that rational investors try to earn a return that fully compensates them for risk. In the case of bondholders, that required return (r_i) has three components: the real rate of return (r^*), an expected inflation premium (IP), and a risk premium (RP). Thus the required return on a bond can be expressed by the following equation:

Equation 10.1

$$r_i = r^* + IP + RP$$

The real rate of return and inflation premium are external economic factors, and together they equal the risk-free rate (R_F). Now, to find the required return, we need to consider the unique features and properties of the bond issue itself; we can do this by adding the bond's risk premium to the risk-free rate. A bond's risk premium (RP) will take into account key issue and issuer characteristics, including such variables as the type of bond, the issue's term-to-maturity, its call features, and bond rating. Together, the three components in Equation 10.1 (r^*, IP, and RP) determine the level of interest rates at any given point in time.

Because interest rates have a significant bearing on bond prices and yields, both conservative and aggressive investors closely monitor them. Conservative investors watch interest rates because one of their major objectives is to lock in high yields. Aggressive traders also have a stake in interest rates because their investment programs are often built on the capital gains opportunities that accompany major swings in rates.

Keeping Tabs on Market Interest Rates

yield spreads
differences in interest rates that exist among various sectors of the market.

Just as there is no single bond market but a series of different market sectors, so too there is no single interest rate that applies to all segments of the market. Rather, each segment has its own, unique level of interest rates. Granted, the various rates tend to drift in the same direction over time and follow the same general pattern of behavior. But it's also common for **yield spreads** (interest rate differentials) to exist among the various market sectors. We can summarize the more important market yields and yield spreads as follows:

- Municipal bonds usually carry the lowest market rates because of their tax-exempt feature. As a rule, their market yields are about 20% to 30% lower than corporates. In the taxable sector, Treasuries have the lowest yields (because they have the least risk), followed by agencies and then corporates, which provide the highest returns.
- Issues that normally carry bond ratings (e.g., municipals or corporates) generally display the same behavior: the lower the rating, the higher the yield.
- There is generally a direct relationship between the coupon an issue carries and its yield. Discount (low-coupon) bonds yield the least, and premium (high-coupon) bonds yield the most.
- In the municipal sector, revenue bonds yield more than general obligation bonds.
- Bonds that are freely callable generally provide the highest returns, at least at date of issue. These are followed by deferred call obligations and then by noncallable bonds, which yield the least.

- As a rule, bonds with long maturities tend to yield more than short issues. However, this rule does not hold; sometimes, as in mid-2000, short-term yields equal or exceed the yields on long-term bonds.

The preceding list can be used as a general guide to the higher-yielding segments of the market. For example, income-oriented municipal bond investors might do well to consider certain high-quality revenue bonds as a way to increase yields; and investors who like to stick to high-quality issues might select agency bonds, rather than Treasuries, for the same reason.

As an investor, you should pay close attention to interest rates and yield spreads, and try to stay abreast not only of the current state of the market but also of the *future direction in market rates.* For example, if you are a conservative (income-oriented) investor and think that rates have just about peaked, that should be a clue to try to lock in the prevailing high yields with some form of call protection. (For example, buy bonds, like Treasuries or double-A-rated utilities, that are noncallable or still have lengthy call deferments.) In contrast, if you're an aggressive bond trader who thinks rates have peaked (and are about to drop), that should be a signal to buy bonds that offer maximum price appreciation potential (low-coupon bonds that still have a long time before they mature.) Clearly, in either case, *the future direction of interest rates is important!*

But how do you formulate such expectations? Unless you have considerable training in economics, you will probably have to rely on various published sources. Fortunately, a wealth of such information is available. Your broker is an excellent source for such reports, as are investor services like Moody's and Standard & Poor's; and, of course, there are numerous online sources. Finally, there are widely circulated business and financial publications (the *Wall Street Journal, Forbes, Business Week,* and *Fortune,* to name a few) that regularly address the current state and future direction of market interest rates. One of the best sources is illustrated in Figure 10.1. Predicting the direction of interest rates is not easy. However, by taking the time to read some of these publications and reports regularly and carefully, you, too, can keep track of the behavior of interest rates and at least get a handle on what experts predict is likely to occur in the near future—say, over the next 6 to 12 months, perhaps even longer.

What Causes Rates to Move?

Although interest rates are a complex economic issue, we do know that certain forces are especially important in influencing their general behavior. Serious bond investors should make it a point to become familiar with the major determinants of interest rates and try to monitor those variables, at least informally.

And in that regard, perhaps no variable is more important than *inflation.* Changes in the inflation rate (or even expectations about its future course) have a direct and pronounced effect on market interest rates. Clearly, if inflation is expected to slow down, then market interest rates should fall as well. To gain an appreciation of the extent to which interest rates are linked to inflation, take a look at Figure 10.2. Note that as inflation drifts up, so do interest rates. On the other hand, a drop in inflation is matched by a similar decline in interest rates.

FIGURE 10.1 A Popular Source of Information About Interest Rates and the Credit Markets

The "Credit Markets" column, which appears every day in the *Wall Street Journal,* provides a capsule view of the current conditions and future prospects in the bond market. Note that on this particular day, a good deal of the article was devoted to the heavy calendar of upcoming new issues, inflation expectations, and Alan Greenspan. (*Source: Wall Street Journal,* July 11, 2000.)

CREDIT MARKETS

Bond Prices Finish Lower After a Thin Session, Depressed by Expected Heavy New-Issue Slate

By Michael S. Derby
And Gregory Zuckerman
Staff Reporters of The Wall Street Journal

NEW YORK—The afterglow of Friday's noninflationary employment report died out quickly yesterday, as bonds slipped in weak trading, weighed down by what is expected to be a heavy calendar of corporate-bond sales this week.

At 4 p.m., the price of the 10-year Treasury note was down 5/32, or $1.5625 per $1,000 face amount, at 103 14/32. Its yield rose to 6.022% from 6.001% Friday, as yields move inversely to prices.

Meanwhile, the price of the 30-year Treasury bond was down 9/32 at 105 5/32, as its yield rose to 5.881% from 5.861%.

Treasury prices spent most of the day losing ground. But Treasurys were able to stage a small rally late in the day, aided by a little bit of bargain-hunting buying that came amid thin overall levels of trade, traders said.

"We've done quite a bit better toward the close, but we're sort of in a hangover mode from Friday" and its overly optimistic price increases, said Richard Hollocher, vice president with broker-dealer A.G. Edwards in St. Louis.

Traders said that while Friday's employment figures were reassuring, they weren't good enough to help the bond market break out of its recent range. But if inflation data in coming weeks prove benign, a rally could begin. "We're laying the building blocks now to a rally," said one long-bond trader.

On Friday, Treasurys posted robust gains after the June jobs report showed a nonfarm payroll gain of 11,000 jobs, far below expectations and the smallest monthly increase in the past four years. The report comforted some bond traders worried that the Federal Reserve in August will feel a need to raise interest rates, to ward off inflation.

Treasury Yield Curve

Yields as of 4:30 p.m. Eastern time

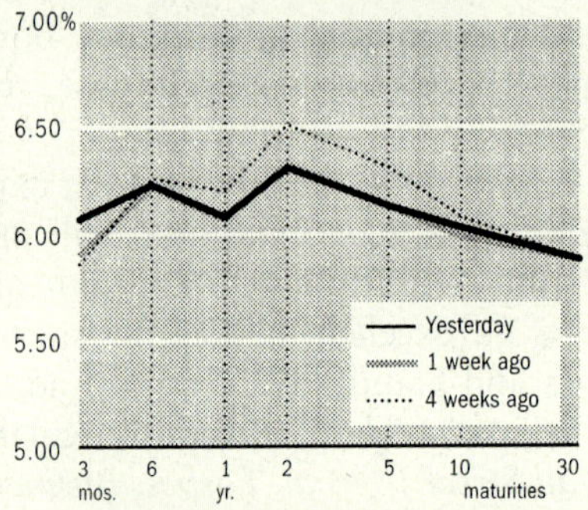

Source: Reuters

YIELD COMPARISONS

Based on Merrill Lynch Bond Indexes, priced as of midafternoon Eastern time.

	7/10	7/7	–52 Week– High	Low
Corp.-Govt. Master	6.91%	6.89%	7.43%	6.16%
Treasury 1-10yr	6.32	6.29	6.90	5.52
10+ yr	6.21	6.20	6.93	6.02
Agencies 1-10yr	7.06	7.02	7.65	6.17
10+ yr	6.91	6.89	7.35	6.50
Corporate				
1-10 yr High Qlty	7.33	7.32	7.89	6.30
Med Qlty	7.91	7.88	8.43	6.79
10+yr High Qlty	7.84	7.83	8.24	7.05
Med Qlty	8.33	8.32	8.76	7.50
Yankee bonds(1)	7.60	7.58	8.10	7.01
Current-coupon mortgages (2)				
GNMA 7.50%	7.66	7.64	8.15	7.22
FNMA 8.00%	7.91	7.89	8.39	7.16
FHLMC8.00%	7.92	7.91	8.41	7.19
High-yield corporates	12.11	12.12	12.50	10.18
Tax-Exempt Bonds				
7-12-yr G.O. (AA)	4.98	4.98	5.50	4.71
12-22-yr G.O. (AA)	5.61	5.62	6.14	5.14
22+yr revenue (A)	5.86	5.87	6.35	5.38

Note: High quality rated AAA-AA; medium quality A-BBB/Baa; high yield, BB/Ba-C.

(1) Dollar-denominated, SEC-registered bonds of foreign issuers sold in the U.S. (2) Reflects the 52-week high and low of mortgage-backed securities indexes rather than the individual securities shown.

"failed to stage a breakout" from their recent trading range, and may head lower as a result.

A number of market participants also tied some of the market's weakness to nervousness ahead of two scheduled speeches by Federal Reserve Chairman Alan Greenspan, and key wholesale and inflation data to be released on Friday. Mr. Greenspan will speak on the "New Economy" today and global economic challenges tomorrow.

Mark Sauvigne, a government-bond trader at Chase Securities in New York, said that "everyone's going to wait for the news this week" before they'll be willing to shift into bonds.

Richard Hinderlie, who manages fixed-income funds for Invesco in Denver, said: "We think the economy is going to slow down a little bit. But is that enough to get the Fed off of our backs?"

Treasurys showed little reaction to a Fed coupon-pass action, in which it purchased securities maturing between August 2003 and May 2005.

Corporate & Junk Bonds

Electric utility **Dominion Resources** sold $1.1 billion of notes in two parts, the first of several jumbo corporate-bond offerings expected this week.

The Richmond, Va., utility's $400 million of three-year notes were priced at a yield margin of 1.30 percentage points over Treasurys, while the $700 million five-year notes came at 1.55 points over Treasurys.

Both issues came at yield margins that were narrower than early indications, a sign of strong demand for the credit as well as an improved market tone following the recent benign economic data, said Jim Probert, managing director and head of U.S. syndicate at Banc of America Securities, which was a joint lead manager on the deal with Chase Securities and Lehman Brothers.

FIGURE 10.2

The Impact of Inflation on the Behavior of Interest Rates

The behavior of interest rates has always been closely tied to the movements in the rate of inflation. What changed in the early 1980s, however, was the spread between inflation and interest rates. Whereas a spread of roughly 3 points was common in the past, it has held at about 5 to 6 percentage points since 1982.

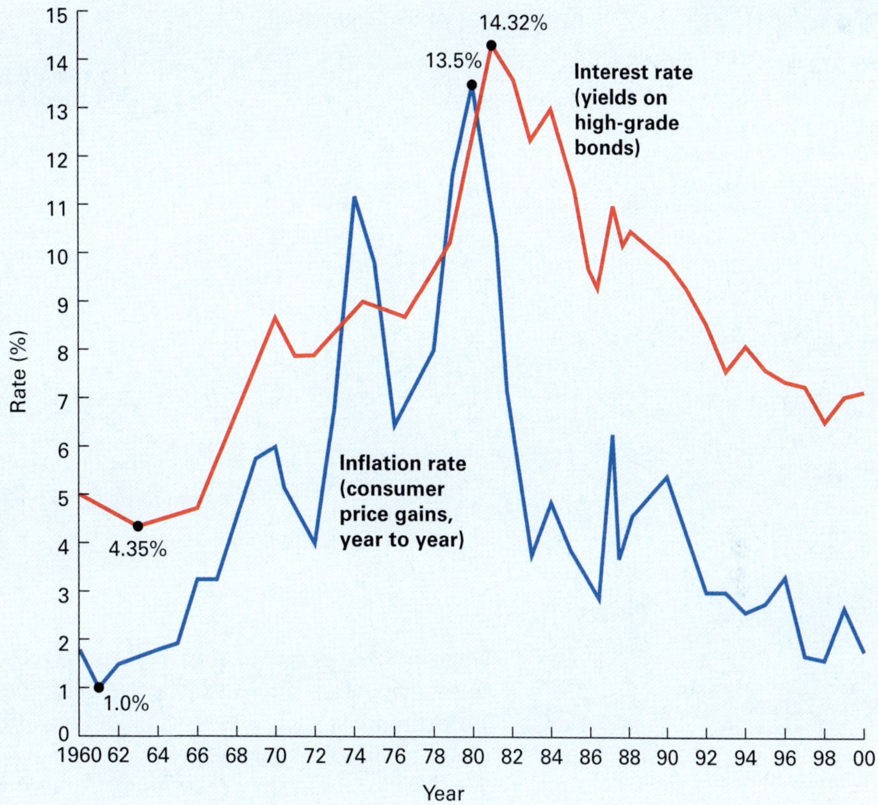

In addition to inflation, there are at least five other important economic variables that can significantly affect the level of interest rates:

- *Changes in the money supply.* An increase in the money supply pushes rates down (as it makes more funds available for loans), and vice versa. This is true only up to a point, however. If the growth in the money supply becomes excessive, it can lead to inflation, which, of course, means higher interest rates.
- *The size of the federal budget surplus.* What arguably was one of the biggest problems facing the U.S. economy at the beginning of the '90s had completely reversed course by the end of the decade, as 30 years of growing budget deficits gave way to a new era of *budget surpluses.* Because the U.S Treasury no longer needed to borrow money to cover deficits, the decreased demand for funds reduced pressure on interest rates which, in turn, promoted lower rates. That's why bond market participants viewed a budget surplus so favorably.
- *The level of economic activity.* Businesses need more capital when the economy expands. This need increases the demand for funds, and rates tend to rise. During a recession, economic activity contracts, and rates typically fall.
- *Policies of the Federal Reserve.* Actions of the Federal Reserve to control inflation also have a major effect on market interest rates. For example,

FIGURE 10.3

Two Types of Yield Curves

A yield curve relates term-to-maturity to yield-to-maturity at a given point in time. Although yield curves come in many shapes and forms, the most common is the *upward-sloping curve.* It shows that investor returns (yields) increase with longer maturities.

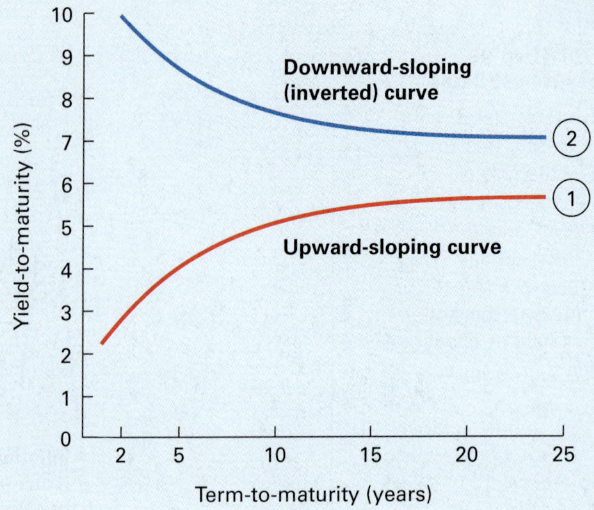

when the Fed wants to slow real (or perceived) inflation, it usually does so by driving up interest rates, as it did several times in 1999–2000. Unfortunately, such actions can also have the nasty side effect of slowing down business activity as well.

- *The level of interest rates in major foreign markets.* Today, investors look beyond national borders for investment opportunities. If rates in major foreign markets rise, that puts pressure on rates in the United States to rise as well; if they don't rise, foreign investors may be tempted to dump their dollars to buy higher-yielding foreign securities.

The Term Structure of Interest Rates and Yield Curves

term structure of interest rates the relationship between the interest rate or rate of return (yield) on a bond and its time to maturity.

yield curve a graph that represents the relationship between a bond's term to maturity and its yield at a given point in time.

Although many factors affect the behavior of market interest rates, one of the most popular and widely studied is *bond maturity.* The relationship between interest rates (yield) and time to maturity for any class of similar-risk securities is called the **term structure of interest rates.** This relationship can be depicted graphically by a **yield curve,** which relates a bond's *term* to maturity to its *yield* to maturity at a given point in time. A particular yield curve exists for only a short period of time. As market conditions change, so do the yield curve's shape and location.

Types of Yield Curves Two different types of yield curves are illustrated in Figure 10.3. By far, the most common type is curve 1, the *upward-sloping* curve. It indicates that yields tend to increase with longer maturities. The longer a bond has to go until maturity, the greater the potential for price volatility and the risk of loss. Investors, therefore, require higher risk premiums to induce them to buy the longer, riskier bonds. Occasionally, the yield curve becomes *inverted,* or downward-sloping, as shown in curve 2, which occurs when short-term rates are higher than long-term rates. This curve generally results from actions by the Federal Reserve to curtail inflation by driving short-term interest rates way up. In addition to these, there are two other types of yield curves that appear from time to time: the *flat* yield curve, when rates for short- and long-term debt are essentially the same, and the *humped* yield curve, when intermediate-term rates are the highest.

Plotting Your Own Curves Yield curves are constructed by plotting the yields for a group of bonds that are similar in all respects but maturity. Treasury securities (bills, notes, and bonds) are typically used to construct yield curves. There are several reasons for this: Their yields are easily found in financial publications, they have no risk of default, and they are homogeneous with regard to quality and other issue characteristics. Investors can also construct yield curves for other classes of debt securities, such as A-rated municipal bonds, Aa-rated corporate bonds, or even certificates of deposit.

HOTLINKS

For the latest information on the U.S. economy and bonds, go to the SmartMoney Web site at:

www.smartmoney.com/bonds

Figure 10.4 shows the yield curves for Treasury securities on two dates, November 18, 1997, and July 10, 2000. To draw these curves, you need Treasury quotes from the *Wall Street Journal*. (Note that actual quoted yields for curve 2 are provided in the boxed information right below the graph.) Given the required quotes, select the yields for the Treasury bills, notes, and bonds maturing in approximately 3 months, 6 months, and 1, 2, 5, 10, 20, and 30 years. The yields used for this curve are highlighted. (You could include more points, but they would not have much effect on the general shape of the curve.) Next, plot the points on a graph whose horizontal (x) axis represents time to maturity in years and whose vertical (y) axis represents yield to maturity. Connect the points to create the curves shown in Figure 10.4. You'll notice that because curve 2 is downward-sloping (i.e., the 30-year yield is less than T-bills rates), it ended with a lower yield than curve 1, even though it started at a substantially higher level.

Explanations of the Term Structure of Interest Rates As we noted earlier, the shape of the yield curve can change over time. Three commonly cited theories—the expectations hypothesis, the liquidity preference theory, and the market segmentation theory—explain more fully the reasons for the general shape of the yield curve.

expectations hypothesis
theory that the shape of the yield curve reflects investor expectations of future interest rates.

Expectations Hypothesis The **expectations hypothesis** suggests that the yield curve reflects investor expectations about the future behavior of interest rates. This theory argues that the relationship between rates today and rates expected in the future is due primarily to investor expectations about inflation. If investors anticipate higher rates of inflation in the future, they will require higher long-term interest rates today, and vice versa. To see how this explanation can be applied in practice, consider the behavior of U.S. Treasury securities.

Because Treasury securities are considered essentially risk-free, only two components determine their yield: the real rate of interest and inflation expectations. Because the real interest rate is the same for all maturities, variations in yields are caused by differing inflation expectations associated with different maturities. This hypothesis can be illustrated using the July 10, 2000, yields for four of the Treasury maturities in Figure 10.4. If we assume that the real rate of interest is 3%, then the inflation expectation during the period to maturity is as shown in column 3 of the following table.

FIGURE 10.4

Yield Curves on U.S. Treasury Issues

Here we see two yield curves constructed from actual market data (quotes). Note the different shapes of the two curves: Curve 1 has a normal upward slope, and Curve 2 is actually downward sloping. As a result, Curve 2 started well above Curve 1, but ended well below it. (*Source: Wall Street Journal,* July 11, 2000.)

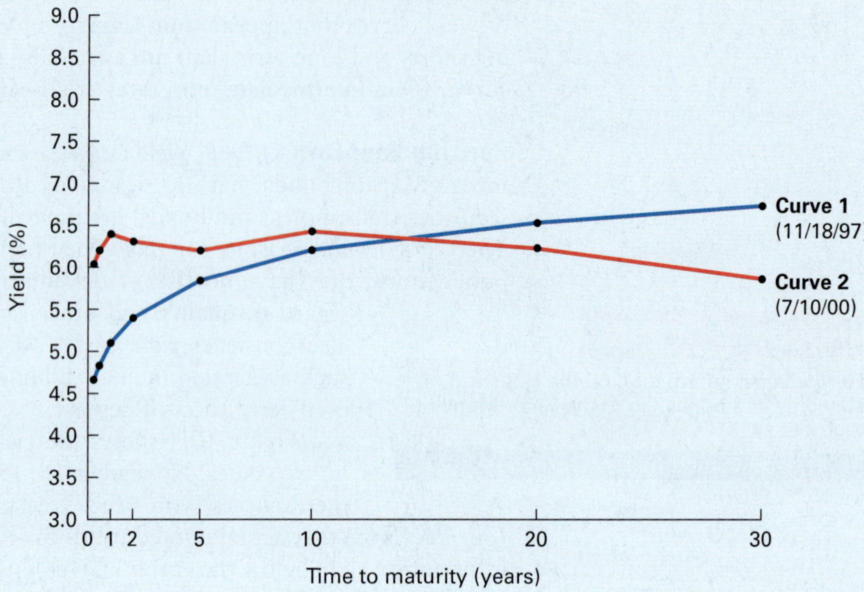

Yield Data for Curve 2
Treasury Issues—Bills, Notes, and Bonds
Monday, July 10, 2000

TREASURY BILLS

	Maturity	Days to Mat.	Bid	Asked	Chg.	Ask Yld.
	Jul 13 '00	2	5.92	5.84	+0.35	5.92
	Jul 20 '00	9	5.77	5.69	−0.05	5.78
	Jul 27 '00	16	5.50	5.42	+0.02	5.51
	Aug 03 '00	23	5.65	5.57	−0.02	5.67
	Aug 10 '00	30	5.73	5.69	−0.01	5.80
	Aug 17 '00	37	5.78	5.74	−0.04	5.85
	Aug 24 '00	44	5.70	5.66	−0.04	5.78
	Aug 31 '00	51	5.81	5.77	+0.02	5.90
	Sep 07 '00	58	5.83	5.79	+0.03	5.93
	Sep 14 '00	65	5.82	5.80	+0.03	5.94
	Sep 21 '00	72	5.82	5.80	+0.04	5.95
	Sep 28 '00	79	5.84	5.82	+0.05	5.98
3 Month →	**Oct 05 '00**	**86**	**5.88**	**5.87**	**+0.02**	**6.04**
	Oct 12 '00	93	5.91	5.89	+0.02	6.06
	Oct 12 '00	93	5.88	5.87	+0.02	6.04
	Oct 19 '00	100	5.88	5.86	+0.02	6.04
	Oct 26 '00	107	5.86	5.84	+0.06	6.03
	Nov 02 '00	114	5.92	5.90	+0.01	6.10
	Nov 09 '00	121	5.92	5.90	....	6.10
	Nov 16 '00	128	5.92	5.90	+0.02	6.11
	Nov 24 '00	136	5.91	5.89	+0.01	6.11
	Nov 30 '00	142	5.91	5.89	+0.01	6.11
	Dec 07 '00	149	5.94	5.92	+0.02	6.15
	Dec 14 '00	156	5.95	5.93	+0.01	6.17
	Dec 21 '00	163	5.94	5.92	+0.01	6.17
	Dec 28 '00	170	5.96	5.94	+0.02	6.20
6 Month →	**Jan 04 '01**	**177**	**5.95**	**5.94**	**+0.02**	**6.20**
	Jan 11 '01	184	5.94	5.93	−0.01	6.20
	Feb 01 '01	205	5.91	5.89	+0.01	6.16
	Mar 01 '01	233	5.56	5.54	+0.01	5.79
	May 31 '01	324	5.75	5.74	+0.01	6.06

GOVT. BONDS & NOTES

	Rate	Maturity Mo/Yr	Bid	Asked	Chg.	Ask Yld.
	5	Feb 01n	99:03	99:05	....	6.36
	$5\frac{5}{8}$	Feb 01n	99:16	99:18	+ 1	6.32
	$4\frac{7}{8}$	Mar 01n	98:27	98:29	+ 1	6.44
	$6\frac{3}{8}$	Mar 01n	99:28	99:30	....	6.45
	5	Apr 01n	98:27	98:29	....	6.40
	$6\frac{1}{4}$	Apr 01n	99:26	99:28	....	6.40
	$5\frac{5}{8}$	May 01n	99:10	99:12	+ 1	6.38
	8	May 01n	101:07	101:09	....	6.40
	$13\frac{1}{8}$	May 01	105:13	105:15	-1	6.35
	$5\frac{1}{4}$	May 01n	98:31	99:01	+ 1	6.38
	$6\frac{1}{2}$	May 01n	100:00	100:02	....	6.42
	$5\frac{3}{4}$	Jun 01n	99:10	99:12	+ 1	6.42
	$6\frac{5}{8}$	Jun 01n	100:04	100:06	+ 1	6.42
1 Year →	$5\frac{1}{2}$	Jul 01n	99:01	99:03	+ 1	6.40
	$6\frac{5}{8}$	Jul 01n	100:05	100:07	....	6.40
	$7\frac{7}{8}$	Aug 01n	101:15	101:17	....	6.40
	$13\frac{3}{8}$	Aug 01	107:07	107:09	-1	6.38
	$6\frac{1}{2}$	May 02n	100:06	100:08	-1	6.35
	$6\frac{5}{8}$	May 02n	100:14	100:15	-2	6.35
	$6\frac{1}{4}$	Jun 02n	99:26	99:28	....	6.32
2 Year →	**$6\frac{3}{8}$**	**Jun 02n**	**100:04**	**100:05**	**-1**	**6.29**
	$3\frac{5}{8}$	Jul 02i	99:12	99:13	....	3.93
	6	Jul 02n	99:11	99:13	....	6.31
	$11\frac{5}{8}$	Nov 04	120:01	120:07	-6	6.24
	$7\frac{1}{2}$	Feb 05n	104:30	105:00	-4	6.23
	$6\frac{1}{2}$	May 05n	101:07	101:09	-4	6.19
	$6\frac{3}{4}$	**May 05n**	**102:18**	**102:19**	**-4**	**6.12**
	12	May 05	123:19	123:25	-5	6.23
5 Year →	$6\frac{1}{2}$	Aug 05n	101:07	101:09	-3	6.20
	$10\frac{3}{4}$	Aug 05	119:10	119:14	-6	6.24
	$5\frac{7}{8}$	Nov 05n	98:15	98:17	-3	6.20
	$5\frac{5}{8}$	Feb 06n	97:07	97:09	-4	6.21
	$9\frac{3}{8}$	Feb 06	114:19	114:23	-4	6.22
	$6\frac{7}{8}$	May 06n	103:05	103:07	-4	6.21
	7	Jul 06n	103:28	103:30	-3	6.20

GOVT. BONDS & NOTES (CONT.)

	Rate	Maturity Mo/Yr	Bid	Asked	Chg.	Ask Yld.
	$6\frac{1}{2}$	**Feb 10n**	**103:11**	**103:12**	**-7**	**6.03**
	$11\frac{3}{4}$	Feb 05-10	120:23	120:29	-2	6.42
10 Year →	10	May 05-10	114:17	114:21	....	6.43
	$12\frac{3}{4}$	Nov 05-10	128:02	128:08	-1	6.42
	$13\frac{7}{8}$	May 06-11	135:25	135:31	-1	6.40
	14	Nov 06-11	139:00	139:06	-2	6.39
	$10\frac{3}{8}$	Nov 07-12	122:31	123:05	-4	6.37
	9	Nov 18	129:25	129:31	-5	6.23
	$8\frac{7}{8}$	Feb 19	128:20	128:26	-6	6.24
	$8\frac{1}{8}$	Aug 19	120:26	121:00	-4	6.23
	$8\frac{1}{2}$	Feb 20	125:10	125:16	-5	6.23
20 Year →	$8\frac{3}{4}$	May 20	128:10	128:16	-5	6.23
	$8\frac{3}{4}$	Aug 20	128:17	128:23	-4	6.23
	$7\frac{7}{8}$	Feb 21	118:31	119:03	-4	6.22
	$8\frac{1}{8}$	May 21	121:31	122:05	-3	6.21
	$8\frac{1}{8}$	Aug 21	122:04	122:10	-4	6.21
	8	Nov 21	120:27	121:01	-4	6.21
	$7\frac{1}{4}$	Aug 22	112:16	112:20	-3	6.19
	$7\frac{5}{8}$	Nov 22	117:00	117:04	-3	6.20
	$7\frac{1}{8}$	Feb 23	111:05	111:09	-3	6.19
	$6\frac{1}{4}$	Aug 23	100:28	100:30	-2	6.17
	$7\frac{1}{2}$	Nov 24	116:18	116:22	-1	6.17
	$7\frac{5}{8}$	Feb 25	118:09	118:13	....	6.16
	$6\frac{7}{8}$	Aug 25	109:01	109:03	-1	6.16
	6	Feb 26	98:01	98:03	....	6.15
	$6\frac{3}{4}$	Aug 26	107:24	107:26	+ 1	6.14
	$6\frac{1}{2}$	Nov 26	104:19	104:21	....	6.14
	$6\frac{5}{8}$	Feb 27	106:10	106:12	+ 1	6.14
	$6\frac{3}{8}$	Aug 27	103:06	103:08	+ 2	6.13
	$6\frac{1}{8}$	Nov 27	100:01	100:03	+ 2	6.12
	$3\frac{5}{8}$	Apr 28i	95:17	95:18	....	3.89
	$5\frac{1}{2}$	Aug 28	92:00	92:02	+ 1	6.09
	$5\frac{1}{4}$	Nov 28	88:27	88:29	+ 2	6.07
	$5\frac{1}{4}$	Feb 29	89:02	89:04	+ 2	6.05
	$3\frac{7}{8}$	Apr 29i	100:16	100:17	....	3.84
	$6\frac{1}{8}$	Aug 29	101:06	101:07	-9	6.03
30 Year →	**$6\frac{1}{4}$**	**May 30**	**105:13**	**105:16**	**+ 3**	**5.86**

Maturity	(1) November 18, 1997 Yield	(2) Real Rate of Interest	(3) Inflation Expectation [(1) − (2)]
3 months	6.04%	3.00%	3.04%
1 year	6.40	3.00	3.40
5 years	6.20	3.00	3.20
10 years	6.43	3.00	3.43

According to the expectations hypothesis, the numbers in column 3 would suggest that in early July 2000, investors didn't foresee much of a problem with inflation. As a result, the yield curve (in Figure 10.4) was a lot flatter in 2000 than it was in 1997.

Generally, under the expectations hypothesis, an increasing inflation expectation results in an upward-sloping yield curve, a decreasing inflation expectation results in a downward-sloping yield curve, and a stable inflation expectation results in a relatively flat yield curve. Although, as we'll see below, other theories do exist, the observed strong relationship between inflation and interest rates lends considerable credence to this widely accepted theory.

liquidity preference theory
theory that investors tend to prefer the greater liquidity of short-term securities and therefore require a premium to invest in long-term securities.

Liquidity Preference Theory More often than not, yield curves have at least a mild upward slope, as in 1997. One explanation for the frequency of upward-sloping yield curves is the **liquidity preference theory.** This theory states that, intuitively, long-term bond rates should be higher than short-term rates because of the added risks involved with the longer maturities. In other words, because of the risk differential (real or perceived) between long- and short-term debt securities, rational investors will prefer the less risky, short-term obligations *unless they can be motivated, via higher interest rates, to invest in the longer bonds.*

Actually, there are a number of reasons why rational investors should prefer short-term securities. To begin with, they are more liquid (more easily converted to cash) and less sensitive to changing market rates, which means there is less risk of loss of principal. For a given change in market rates, the prices of longer-term bonds will show considerably more movement than the prices of short-term bonds. Simply put, uncertainty increases over time, and investors therefore require a premium to invest in long maturities. In addition, just as investors tend to require a premium for tying up funds for longer periods, borrowers will also pay a premium in order to obtain long-term funds. Borrowers thus assure themselves that funds will be available, and they avoid having to roll over short-term debt at unknown and possibly unfavorable rates. All of these preferences and market forces explain why higher rates of interest should be associated with longer maturities and why it's perfectly rational to expect upward-sloping yield curves.

market segmentation theory
theory that the market for debt is segmented on the basis of maturity, that supply and demand within each segment determines the prevailing interest rate, and that the slope of the yield curve depends on the relationship between the prevailing rates in each segment.

Market Segmentation Theory Another often-cited theory, the **market segmentation theory,** suggests that the market for debt is segmented on the basis of maturity preferences of different types of financial institutions and investors. According to this theory, the yield curve changes as the supply and demand for funds within each maturity segment determines its prevailing interest rate. The equilibrium between the financial institutions that supply the funds for short-term maturities (e.g., banks) and the borrowers of those short-term funds (e.g., businesses with seasonal loan requirements) establishes interest rates in the short-term markets. Similarly, the equilibrium between suppliers and demanders in such long-term markets as life insurance and real estate determines the prevailing long-term interest rates.

The shape of the yield curve can be either upward- or downward-sloping, as determined by the general relationship between rates in each market segment. When supply outstrips demand for short-term loans, short-term rates are relatively low. If, at the same time, the demand for long-term loans is higher than the available supply of funds, then long-term rates will move up. Thus, low rates in the short-term segment and high rates in the long-term segment cause an upward-sloping yield curve, and vice versa.

Which Theory Is Right? It is clear *that all three theories* of the term structure have merit in explaining the shape of the yield curve. From them, we can conclude that at any time, the slope of the yield curve is affected by (1) inflationary expectations, (2) liquidity preferences, and (3) the supply and demand conditions in the short- and long-term market segments. Upward-sloping yield curves result from higher inflation expectations, lender preferences for shorter-maturity loans, and greater supply of short- rather than of long-term loans relative to the respective demand in each market segment. The opposite behavior, of course, results in a flat or downward-sloping yield curve. At any point in time, the interaction of these forces determines the prevailing slope of the yield curve.

Using the Yield Curve in Investment Decisions Bond investors often use yield curves in making investment decisions. As noted earlier, yield curves change in accordance with market conditions. Analyzing the changes in yield curves over time provides investors with information about future interest rate movements and how they can affect price behavior and comparative returns. For example, if the yield curve begins to rise sharply, it usually means that inflation is starting to heat up or is expected to do so in the near future. In that case, investors can expect that interest rates, too, will rise. Under these conditions, most seasoned bond investors turn to short or intermediate (3 to 5 years) maturities, which provide reasonable returns and at the same time minimize exposure to capital loss when interest rates go up (and bond prices fall). A downward-sloping yield curve, though unusual, generally results from actions of the Federal Reserve to reduce inflation. As suggested by the expectations hypothesis, this would signal that rates have peaked and are about to fall.

Another factor to consider is the difference in yields on different maturities—the "steepness" of the curve. For example, a steep yield curve is one where long rates are *much higher* than short rates. This shape is often seen as an indication that long-term rates may be near their peak and are about to fall, thereby narrowing the spread between long and short rates. Steep yield curves are generally viewed as a bullish sign. For aggressive bond investors, they could be the signal to start moving into long-term securities. Flatter yield curves, on the other hand, sharply reduce the incentive for going long-term. For example, look at yield curve 2 in Figure 10.4. Note that the difference in yield between the 5- and 20-year maturities is quite small. (In fact, it's almost nonexistent. It amount to *only 3 basis points,* or 3/100 of 1%.) As a result, there's not much incentive to

HOTLINKS

For an informative guide to bonds, go to:

www.bondsonline.com

go long-term. Under these conditions, investors would be well advised to just stick with the 5- to 10-year maturities, which will generate about the same yield as long bonds but without the risks. You'll also notice that in July 2000, the 30-year bonds had even lower yields. A lot of this was due to a "scarcity effect" as the Treasury began to sharply curtail the supply of long bonds. In other words, because there was more demand than supply, rates fell.

The Pricing of Bonds

LG 3

If there's one common denominator in the bond market, it's the way bonds are priced. No matter who the issuer is, what kind of bond it is, or whether it's fully taxable or tax-free, all bonds are priced pretty much the same. In particular, all bonds (including *notes* with maturities of more than a year) are priced according to the *present value of their future cash flow* streams. Indeed, once the prevailing or expected market yield is known, the whole process becomes rather mechanical.

Bond prices are driven by market yields. That's because in the marketplace, the *appropriate yield at which the bond should sell is determined first,* and then that yield is used to find the price (or market value) of the bond. The appropriate yield on a bond is a function of certain market and economic forces (e.g., the risk-free rate of return and inflation), as well as key issue and issuer characteristics (e.g., years to maturity and the bond rating). Together, these forces combine to form the *required rate of return,* which is the rate of return the investor would like to earn in order to justify an investment in a given fixed-income security. In the bond market, required return is market driven and is generally considered to be the issue's market yield. That is, the required return defines the yield at which the bond should be trading and serves as the *discount rate* in the bond valuation process.

Basically, bond investors are entitled to two distinct types of cash flows: (1) the periodic receipt of coupon income over the life of the bond, and (2) the recovery of principal (or par value) at the end of the bond's life. Thus, in valuing a bond, you're dealing with an *annuity* of coupon payments plus a large *single cash flow,* as represented by the recovery of principal at maturity. These cash flows, along with the required rate of return on the investment, are then used in a present-value-based bond valuation model to find the dollar price of a bond. We'll demonstrate the bond valuation process in two ways. First, we'll use *annual compounding*—that is, because of its computational simplicity, we'll assume we're dealing with coupons that are paid once a year. Second, we'll examine bond valuation under conditions of *semiannual compounding,* which is more like the way most bonds actually pay their coupons.

We'll use present-value interest factors to define and illustrate the various bond price and yield measures. But all these calculations can be done just as easily (in fact, more easily) on a good hand-held calculator. Even so, before you revert to the regular use of one of these calculators we strongly encourage you to work through the bond valuation model at least once or twice, using the procedures outlined below. Doing so will help you gain a thorough understanding of what's embedded in a bond price or yield measure.

Annual Compounding

Along with a table of present-value interest factors (see Appendix A, Tables A.3 and A.4), the following information is needed to value a bond: (1) the size of the annual coupon payment, (2) the bond's par value, and (3) the number of years remaining to maturity. The prevailing market yield (or an estimate of future market rates) is then used as the discount rate to compute the price of a bond, as follows:

Equation 10.2

$$\text{Bond price} = \frac{\text{Present value of the annuity}}{\text{of annual interest income}} + \frac{\text{Present value of the}}{\text{bond's par value}}$$

Equation 10.2a

$$\text{BP} = (I \times PVIFA) + (PV \times PVIF)$$

where

I = amount of annual interest income

$PVIFA$ = present-value interest factor for an *annuity* (Appendix A, Table A.4)

PV = par value of the bond, which is assumed to be $1,000

$PVIF$ = present-value interest factor for a *single cash flow* (Appendix A, Table A.3)

To illustrate the bond price formula in action, consider a 20-year, 9½% bond that is being priced to yield 10%. From this we know the bond pays an annual coupon of 9½% (or $95), has 20 years left to maturity, and should be priced to provide a market yield of 10%. As we saw in Chapter 4, the maturity and market yield information is used to find the appropriate present-value interest factors (in Appendix A, Tables A.3 and A.4). Given these interest factors, we can now use Equation 10.2 to find the price of our bond.

$$\begin{aligned}\text{Bond price} &= (\$95 \times PVIFA \text{ for } 10\% \text{ and } 20 \text{ years}) + \\ &\quad (\$1{,}000 \times PVIF \text{ for } 10\% \text{ and } 20 \text{ years}) \\ &= (\$95 \times 8.514) + (\$1{,}000 \times .149) = \underline{\underline{\$957.83}}\end{aligned}$$

Note that because this is a coupon-bearing bond, we have an annuity of coupon payments of $95 a year for 20 years, plus a single cash flow of $1,000 that occurs at the end of year 20. Thus, in bond valuation, we find the present value of the coupon annuity and then add that amount to the present value of the recovery of principal at maturity. In this particular case, you should be willing to pay about $958 for this bond, so long as you're satisfied with earning 10% on your money.

Semiannual Compounding

Although using annual compounding, as we did above, simplifies the valuation process a bit, it's not the way bonds are actually valued in the marketplace. In practice, most (domestic) bonds pay interest every 6 months, so semiannual compounding is used in the valuation of bonds. Fortunately, it's relatively easy to go from annual to semiannual compounding: All you need do is cut the annual coupon payment in half, and make two minor modifications to the present-value interest factors. Given these changes, finding the price of a bond under conditions of semiannual compounding is much like pricing a bond using annual compounding. That is,

Equation 10.3

$$\text{Bond price (with semiannual compounding)} = \text{Present value of an annuity of } \textit{semiannual} \text{ coupon payments} + \text{Present value of the bond's par value}$$

Equation 10.3a

$$\text{BP} = (I/2 \times PVIFA^*) + (PV \times PVIF^*)$$

where

$PVIFA^*$ = present-value interest factor for an annuity, with required return and years-to-maturity adjusted for *semiannual compounding* (Appendix A, Table A.4)

$PVIF^*$ = present-value interest factor for a single cash flow, with required return and years-to-maturity adjusted for *semiannual compounding* (Appendix A, Table A.3)

I, PV = as described above

Note that in Equation 10.3, we adjusted the present-value interest factors (both $PVIFA$ and $PVIF$) to accommodate semiannual compounding. By simply cutting the required return in half and doubling the number of years to maturity, we are, in effect, dealing with a semiannual measure of return and using the number of 6-month periods to maturity (rather than *years*). For example, in our bond illustration above, we wanted to price a 20-year bond to yield 10%. With semiannual compounding, we would be dealing with a semiannual return of 10%/2 = 5%, and with 20 × 2 = 40 semiannual periods to maturity. Thus we'd find the present-value interest factors for 5% and 40 periods from Table A.4 (for $PVIFA^*$) and from Table A.3 (for $PVIF^*$). Note that we adjust the present-value interest factor for the $1,000 par value, because that too will be subject to semiannual compounding, even though the cash flow will still be received in one lump sum.

To see how this all fits together, consider once again the 20-year, 9½% bond. This time assume it's being priced to yield 10%, *compounded semiannually*. Using Equation 10.3, you'd have:

$$\begin{aligned}\text{Bond price (with semiannual compounding)} &= (\$95/2 \times PVIFA^* \text{ for } 5\% \text{ and } 40 \text{ periods}) \\ &\quad + (\$1{,}000 \times PVIF^* \text{ for } 5\% \text{ and } 40 \text{ periods}) \\ &= (\$47.50 \times 17.159) + (\$1{,}000 \times .142) = \underline{\underline{\$957.02}}\end{aligned}$$

The price of the bond in this case ($957.02) is slightly less than the price we obtained with annual compounding ($957.83). Clearly, it doesn't make much difference whether we use annual or semiannual compounding, though the differences do tend to increase a bit with lower coupons and shorter maturities.

INVESTOR FACTS

PRICES GO UP, PRICES GO DOWN—We all know that when market rates go up, bond prices go down (and vice versa). But bond prices don't move up and down at the same speed, because they don't move in a straight line. Rather, the relationship between market yields and bond prices is "convex," meaning bond prices will rise at an increasing rate when yields fall and decline at a decreasing rate when yields rise. That is, *bond prices go up faster than they go down*. This is known as *positive convexity*, and it's a property of all noncallable bonds. Thus, for a given change in yield, you stand to make more money when prices go up than you'll lose when prices move down!

Measures of Yield and Return

LG 4

As surprising as it may seem, in the bond market, investment decisions are made more on the basis of a bond's yield than its dollar price. Not only does yield affect the price at which a bond trades, it also serves as an important measure of return. To use yield as a measure of return, we *simply reverse the bond valuation process* described above and solve for yield rather than price. Actually, there are three widely used measures of yield: current yield, yield-to-maturity, and yield-to-call. We'll look at all three of them here, along with a concept known as *expected return,* which measures the expected (or actual) rate of return earned over a specific holding period.

Current Yield

Current yield is the simplest of all return measures, but it also has the most limited application. This measure looks at just one source of return: *a bond's interest income.* In particular, it indicates the amount of current income a bond provides relative to its prevailing market price. It is calculated as follows:

Equation 10.4

$$\text{Current yield} = \frac{\text{Annual interest}}{\text{Current market price of the bond}}$$

For example, an 8% bond would pay \$80 per year in interest for every \$1,000 of principal. However, if the bond were currently priced at \$800, it would have a current yield of 10% (\$80/\$800 = 0.10). Current yield is a measure of a bond's annual coupon income, so it would be of interest primarily to investors seeking high levels of current income.

Yield-to-Maturity

yield-to-maturity (YTM) the fully compounded rate of return earned by an investor over the life of a bond, including interest income and price appreciation.

promised yield same as yield-to-maturity.

Yield-to-maturity (YTM) is the most important and widely used bond valuation measure. It evaluates both interest income and price appreciation and considers total cash flow received over the life of an issue. Also known as **promised yield,** YTM shows the fully compounded rate of return earned by an investor, *given that the bond is held to maturity and all principal and interest payments are made in a prompt and timely fashion.* This measure of yield is used not only to gauge the return on a single issue but also to track the behavior of the market in general. In other words, market interest rates are basically a reflection of the average promised yields that exist in a given segment of the market. Promised yield provides valuable insight about an issue's investment merits and is used to assess the attractiveness of alternative investment vehicles. Other things being equal, the higher the promised yield of an issue, the more attractive it is.

Although there are a couple of ways to compute promised yield, the best and most accurate procedure is one that is derived directly from the bond valuation model described above. That is, assuming annual compounding, you can use Equation 10.2 to measure the YTM on a bond. The difference is that now, rather than trying to determine the price of the bond, *we know its price and are trying to find the discount rate that will equate the present value of the bond's cash flow (coupon and principal payments) to its current market price.* This procedure may sound familiar: It's just like the *internal rate of return* measure described in Chapter 4. Indeed, we're basically looking for the internal rate of return on a bond. When we find that, we have the bond's yield-to-maturity.

Unfortunately, unless you have a hand-held calculator or computer software that will do the calculations for you, finding yield-to-maturity is a matter of trial and error. Let's say we want to find the yield-to-maturity on a 7½% ($1,000 par value) bond that has 15 years remaining to maturity and is currently trading in the market at $809.50. From Equation 10.2, we know that

$$\text{Bond price} = (I \times PVIFA) + (PV \times PVIF)$$

As it now stands, we know the current market price of the bond ($809.50), the amount of annual interest/coupon income (7½% = $75), the par value of the bond ($1,000), and the number of years to maturity (15). To compute yield-to-maturity, we need to find the discount rate (in the present-value interest factors) that produces a bond price of $809.50.

Here's what we have so far:

$$\text{Bond price} = (I \times PVIFA) + (PV \times PVIF)$$

$$\$809.50 = (\$75 \times PVIFA \text{ for 15 years and a discount rate of ?\%}) + (\$1{,}000 \times PVIF \text{ for 15 years and a discount rate of ?\%})$$

Right now we know only one thing about the yield on this bond—it has to be more than 7½%. (Why? Because this is a discount bond, so the yield-to-maturity must exceed the coupon rate.) Through trial and error, we might start with a discount rate of, say, 8% or 9% (or any number above the bond's coupon). Sooner or later, we'll move to a discount rate of 10%. And look what happens at that point: Using Equation 10.2 to price this bond at a discount rate of 10%, we see that

$$\begin{aligned}\text{Bond price} &= (\$75 \times PVIFA \text{ for 15 years and 10\%}) + (\$1{,}000 \times PVIFA \text{ for 15 years and 10\%}) \\ &= (\$75 \times 7.606) + (\$1{,}000 \times 0.239) \\ &= \underline{\underline{\$809.45}}\end{aligned}$$

The computed price of $809.45 is reasonably close to the bond's current market price of $809.50. As a result, the 10% rate represents the yield-to-maturity on this bond. That is, 10% is the discount rate that leads to a *computed bond price* equal (or very close) to the bond's *current market price*. In this case, if you were to pay $809.50 for the bond and hold it to maturity, you would expect to earn a yield of 10.0%. Now there's no doubt that promised yield is an important measure of performance. However, as discussed in the *Investing in Action* box on page 337, this measure tells only part of the story.

Using Semiannual Compounding Given some fairly simple modifications, it's also possible to find yield-to-maturity using semiannual compounding. To do so, we cut the annual coupon in half, double the number of years (periods) to maturity, and use the bond valuation model in Equation 10.3. Returning to our 7½%, 15-year bond, let's see what happens when we try a discount rate of 10%. In this case, with semiannual compounding, we'd use a discount rate of 5% (10% ÷ 2); using this discount rate and 30 six-month periods to maturity (15 × 2) to specify the present-value interest factor, we have

$$\text{Bond price} = (\$75/2 \times PVIFA^{*} \text{ for } 5\% \text{ and } 30 \text{ periods}) + (\$1{,}000 \times PVIFA \text{ for } 5\% \text{ and } 30 \text{ periods})$$
$$= (\$37.50 \times 15.373) + (\$1{,}000 \times 0.231) = \underline{\underline{\$807.49}}$$

As you can see, a semiannual discount rate of 5% results in a computed bond value that's a bit short of our target price of \$809.50. Given the inverse relationship between price and yield, it follows that if we need a higher price, we'll have to try a lower yield (discount rate). Therefore, we know the semiannual yield on this bond has to be something less than 5%. Through interpolation, we find that a semiannual discount rate of (around) 4.97% gives us a computed bond value that's very close to \$809.50.

At this point, because we're dealing with semiannual cash flows, to be technically accurate we should find the bond's "effective" annual yield. However, that's not the way it's done in practice. Rather, *market convention is to simply state the annual yield as twice the semiannual yield.* This practice produces what the market refers to as the **bond-equivalent yield.** Returning to the bond-yield problem we started above, we know that the issue has a semiannual yield of 4.97%. According to the bond-equivalent yield convention, all we have to do now is *double the solving rate in order to obtain the annual rate of return on this bond.* Doing this gives us a yield-to-maturity (or promised yield) of 4.97% × 2 = 9.94%. This is the annual rate of return we'll earn on the bond if we hold it to maturity.

bond-equivalent yield
the annual yield on a bond, calculated as twice the semiannual yield.

Yield Properties Actually, in addition to holding the bond to maturity, there are a couple of other critical assumptions embedded in any yield-to-maturity figure. The promised yield measure—whether computed with annual or semiannual compounding—is based on present-value concepts and therefore contains important reinvestment assumptions. That is, the yield-to-maturity figure itself is the *minimum required reinvestment rate the investor must subsequently earn on each of the interim coupon receipts* in order to generate a return equal to or greater than the promised yield. In essence, the calculated yield-to-maturity figure is the return "promised" only so long as the issuer meets all interest and principal obligations on a timely basis and the investor reinvests all coupon income (from the date of receipt to maturity) at an average rate equal to or greater than the computed promised yield. In our example above, the investor would have to reinvest (to maturity) each of the coupons received over the next 15 years at a rate of about 10%. *Failure to do so would result in a realized yield of less than the 10% promised.* In fact, if the worst did occur and the investor made no attempt to reinvest any of the coupons, he or she would earn a realized yield over the 15-year investment horizon of just over 6½%—far short of the 10% promised return. Clearly, unless it's a zero-coupon bond, a significant portion of a bond's total return over time is derived from the *reinvestment of coupons.*

INVESTING in action

There's More to Bond Returns Than Yield Alone

When individuals choose bond investments, they usually focus on yields, in the belief that higher yields generate better returns. But yields and returns are two different things, and investors who blindly chase higher yields can end up regretting it.

The fact is that yield is only part of the story: It tells you what you can expect going into an investment, not what you'll actually end up earning on the deal. Indeed, yield is often a poor proxy for return, and confusing the two can be damaging to your wealth!

Total return for fixed-income investments is made up of not only the initial yield but also (1) interest on reinvested interest and (2) price change. Only in the case of short-term investments, such as 1-year CDs or Treasury bills, is yield a good gauge of return. For long-term bonds and bonds purchased at prices far above or below face value, other factors often dwarf yield in determining returns. That's true even when the bonds are of triple-A quality.

For instance, interest on interest easily becomes the biggest factor in returns for buy-and-hold investors in long-term bonds, especially if interest rates rise during the life of the bond. If you bought a 30-year Treasury bond yielding 6.0% today and interest rates subsequently rose so that your average reinvestment rate was 8.0% over the life of the bond, more than 75% of your total return at maturity would come from income on reinvested interest. On the other hand, although interest on interest dominates bond returns for long holding periods, price change dominates return for short-term investors. In either case, *future interest rate changes are the major concern for investors who want to safeguard their total returns.*

The starting yield on a bond becomes a bigger boon or burden to investors the longer the bond's maturity—which makes total returns on longer-term bonds much more sensitive to interest rate swings. For instance, from 1950 to 1980, long-term Treasury bonds actually had lower total returns than money market funds, despite their persistently higher yields. Unfortunately, steadily rising interest rates erased an average of 2.5% a year from the value of long-term bond portfolios during that period, more than wiping out the bonds' yield advantage over T-bills. In the 1980s and 1990s, by contrast, a steady decline in interest rates meant long-term bonds put on a much better showing than yields would have indicated. Rising bond prices, caused by falling market rates, pushed total returns on Treasury bonds up to an average of 12.6% a year, beating T-bill returns by 3.7 percentage points.

In the year 2000, rising prices were again the biggest component of bond returns. Yields on all types of high-grade long-term bonds dropped as the economy slowed. By year-end, yields on 10-year Treasury notes fell to 5.11% and on 30-year Treasury bonds to 5.46%. Thus principal values (prices) rose so that total returns for the 10- and 30-year securities were 14.8% and 21.0%, respectively.

Of course, no one really knows where interest rates will go—and trying to predict them can prove to be a fruitless exercise. But investors can get a handle on the risks they face in the short run by considering how total returns on different investments might react to interest rate changes over, say, the next 12 months. For example, if interest rates were to fall 1 percentage point over the next 12 months, a typical portfolio of long-term bonds (with lives of more than 10 years) would generate an estimated total return of about 13%. But if interest rates were to rise by 1 percentage point, the total return would shrink to about 1%, making a money fund return look good by comparison. Looking at the problem this way tells the investor how much rates would have to rise before the returns on long-term bonds were reduced to the level of, say, bank CDs or some other short-term benchmark. Clearly, the farther rates have to rise, the more cushion you have and the more secure your investments.

The old adage "You can't judge a book by its cover" certainly does apply to the bond market: Just because a bond promises a yield of *x* percent doesn't mean that's the return you'll actually end up with.

Sources: Tom Petruno, "Quality Bond Funds Had a Good Year," *Newsday,* December 16, 2000, p. F4; Gregory Zuckerman and Michael Derby, "Government Bonds Provide a Safe Haven as High-Yield Market Delivers a Bruising," *Wall Street Journal,* January 2, 2001, p. R8.

Finding the Yield on a Zero The same promised-yield procedures described above (Equation 10.2 with annual compounding or Equation 10.3 with semiannual compounding) can also be used to find the yield-to-maturity on a zero-coupon bond. The only difference is that the coupon portion of the equation can be ignored because it will, of course, equal zero. All you have to do to find the promised yield on a zero is to divide the current market price of the bond by $1,000 (the bond's par value) and then look for the computed interest factor in the present-value Table A.3 (in Appendix A).

To illustrate, consider a 15-year zero-coupon issue that can be purchased today for $315. Dividing this amount by the bond's par value of $1,000, we obtain an interest factor of $315/$1,000 = 0.315. Now, using annual compounding, look in Table A.3 (the table of present-value interest factors for single cash flows). Go down the first column to year 15 and then look across that row until you find an interest factor that equals (or is very close to) 0.315. Once you've found the factor, look up the column to the "Interest Rate" heading and you've got the promised yield of the issue. Using this approach, we see that the bond in our example has a promised yield of 8%. Had we been using semiannual compounding, we'd do exactly the same thing, except we'd go down to "year 30" and start the process there.

Yield-to-Call

Bonds can be either noncallable or callable. Recall from Chapter 9 that a *noncallable bond* prohibits the issuer from calling the bond in for retirement prior to maturity. Because such issues will remain outstanding to maturity, they can all be valued by using the standard *yield-to-maturity* measure. In contrast, a *callable bond* gives the issuer the right to retire the bond prematurely, so the issue may or may not remain outstanding to maturity. As a result, YTM may not always be the appropriate measure of value. Instead, we must consider the impact of the bond being called. A common way to do that is to use a measure known as **yield-to-call (YTC)**, which shows the yield on a bond if the issue remains outstanding *not* to maturity but, rather, until its first (or some other specified) call date.

yield-to-call (YTC)
the yield on a bond if it remains outstanding only until a specified call date.

Yield-to-call is commonly used with bonds that carry *deferred-call provisions*. Remember that such issues start out as noncallable bonds and then, after a call deferment period (of 5 to 10 years), become freely callable. Under these conditions, *YTC would measure the expected yield on a deferred-call bond assuming that the issue is retired at the end of the call deferment period* (that is, when the bond first becomes freely callable). We can find YTC by making two simple modifications to the standard YTM equation (Equation 10.2 or 10.3). First, we define the length of the investment horizon (N) as *the number of years to the first call date,* not the number of years to maturity. Second, instead of using the bond's par value ($1,000), we *use the bond's call price* (which is stipulated in the indenture and is nearly always greater than the bond's par value).

For example, assume you want to find yield-to-call on a 20-year, 10½% deferred-call bond that is currently trading in the market at $1,204, but has 5 years to go to first call (that is, before it becomes freely callable), at which time it can be called in at a price of $1,085. Thus, rather than using the bond's maturity of 20 years in the valuation equation (Equation 10.2 or 10.3), we use the number of years to first call (5 years), and rather than the bond's par value,

\$1,000, we use the issue's call price, \$1,085. Note, however, we still use the bond's coupon (10½%) and its current market price (\$1,204). Thus, for annual compounding, here's what we'd have:

Equation 10.5

$$\text{Bond price} = (I \times PVIFA) + (CP \times PVIF)$$

$$\$1{,}204.00 = (\$105 \times PVIFA \text{ for 5 years and a discount rate of ?\%}) + (\$1{,}085 \times PVIF \text{ for 5 years and a discount rate of ?\%})$$

In Equation 10.5, *CP* equals the call price on the issue, and the present-value interest factors (for both *PVIFA* and *PVIF*) are for the number of years to first call date, not the term to maturity.

Through trial and error, we finally hit upon a discount rate of 7%. At that point, the present value of the future cash flows (coupons over the next 5 years, plus call price) will exactly (or very nearly) equal the bond's current market price of \$1,204. That is,

$$\text{Bond price} = (\$105 \times PVIFA_{5\text{ years, }7\%}) + (\$1{,}085 \times PVIF_{5\text{ years, }7\%})$$
$$= (\$105 \times 4.100) + (\$1{,}085 \times 0.713)$$
$$= \$430.50 + \$773.61 = \underline{\$1{,}204.11}$$

Thus *the YTC on this bond is 7%*. In contrast, the bond's YTM is 8.36%. In practice, bond investors normally compute *both* YTM and YTC for deferred-call bonds that are *trading at a premium*. They do this to find which of the two yields is lower; market convention is to *use the lower, more conservative measure of yield (YTM or YTC) as the appropriate indicator of value*. As a result, the premium bond in our example would be valued relative to its yield-to-call. The assumption is that because interest rates have dropped so much (the bond is trading 2 percentage points below its coupon), it will be called in the first chance the issuer gets. However, the situation is totally different when this or any bond trades at a discount. Why? Because YTM on any *discount bond*, whether callable or not, *will always be less* than YTC. Thus YTC is a totally irrelevant measure for discount bonds—it's used only with premium bonds.

Expected Return

Rather than just buying and holding bonds, some investors prefer to actively trade in and out of these securities over fairly short investment horizons. As a result, yield-to-maturity and yield-to-call have relatively little meaning, other than as indicators of the rate of return used to price the bond. These investors obviously need an alternative measure of return that can be used to assess the investment appeal of those bonds they intend to trade in and out of. Such an alternative measure is **expected return.** It indicates the rate of return an investor can expect to earn by holding a bond over a period of time that's less than the life of the issue. (Expected return is also known as **realized yield,** because it shows the return an investor would realize by trading in and out of bonds over short holding periods.)

expected return
the rate of return an investor can expect to earn by holding a bond over a period of time that's less than the life of the issue.

realized yield
same as expected return.

Expected return lacks the precision of yield-to-maturity (and YTC), because the major cash flow variables are largely the product of investor estimates. In particular, going into the investment, both the length of the holding period and the future selling price of the bond are pure estimates and therefore subject to uncertainty. Even so, we can use pretty much the same procedure to find realized yield as we did to find promised yield. That is, with some simple modifications to the standard bond-pricing formula, we can use the following equation to find the expected return on a bond.

Equation 10.6

$$\text{Bond price} = \begin{array}{c}\text{Present value of the bond's}\\ \text{annual interest income}\\ \text{over the holding period}\end{array} + \begin{array}{c}\text{Present value of the bond's}\\ \text{future price at the}\\ \text{end of the holding period}\end{array}$$

Equation 10.6a

$$BP = (I \times PVIFA) + (FV \times PVIF)$$

where the present-value interest factors (for both *PVIFA* and *PVIF*) are for the length of the expected holding period only, not for the term to maturity, and *FV* is the expected future price of the bond.

Note that in this case, the *expected future price* of the bond is used in place of par value ($1,000), and *the length of the holding period* is used in place of term to maturity. As indicated above, we must determine the *future price* of the bond when computing expected realized yield; this is done by using the standard bond price formula, as described earlier. The most difficult part of deriving a reliable future price is, of course, coming up with future market interest rates that you feel will exist when the bond is sold. By evaluating current and expected market interest rate conditions, *the investor estimates a promised yield that the issue is expected to carry at the date of sale and then uses that yield to calculate the bond's future price.*

To illustrate, take one more look at our 7½%, 15-year bond. This time, let's assume that you feel the price of the bond, which is now trading at a discount, will rise sharply as interest rates fall over the next few years. In particular, assume the bond is currently priced at $810 (to yield 10%) and that you anticipate holding the bond for 3 years. Over that time, you expect market rates to drop, so the price of the bond should rise to around $960 by the end of the 3-year holding period. (Actually, we found the future price of the bond—$960—by assuming interest rates would fall to 8% in 3 year. We then used the standard bond price formula—in this case Equation 10.2—to find the value of a 7½%, 12-year obligation, which is how many years to maturity a 15-year bond will have at the end of a 3-year holding period.) Thus, we are assuming that you will buy the bond today at a market price of $810 and sell it 3 years later—after interest rates have declined to 8%—at a price of $960. Given these assumptions, the expected return (realized yield) on this bond is 14.6%, which is the discount rate in the following equation that will produce a current market price of $810.

$$\begin{aligned}\text{Bond price} &= (\$75 \times \textit{PVIFA} \text{ for 3 years and 14.6\%})\\ &\quad + (\$960 \times \textit{PVIF} \text{ for 3 years and 14.6\%})\\ &= (\$75 \times 2.301) + (\$960 \times 0.664) = \underline{\underline{\$810.02}}\end{aligned}$$

The better-than-14½% return on this investment is fairly substantial, but keep in mind that this is only a measure of *expected return*. It is, of course, subject to variation if things do not turn out as anticipated, particularly with regard to the market yield expected at the end of the holding period. (*Note:* This illustration uses annual compounding, but you could just as easily have used *semiannual compounding,* which, everything else being the same, would have resulted in an expected yield of 14.4% rather than the 14.6% found with annual compounding. Also, if the anticipated horizon is 1 year or less, you would want to use the simple *holding-period return (HPR)* measure described in Chapter 4.)

Valuing a Bond

Depending on investor objectives, the value of a bond can be determined by either its promised yield or its expected return. Conservative, income-oriented investors employ *promised yield* (YTM or YTC) to value bonds. Coupon income over extended periods of time is their principal objective, and promised yield provides a viable measure of return—assuming, of course, the reinvestment assumptions embedded in the yield measure are reasonable. More aggressive bond traders, on the other hand, use *expected return* to value bonds. The capital gains that can be earned by buying and selling bonds over relatively short holding periods is their chief concern, and expected return is more important to them than the promised yield at the time the bond is purchased.

In either case, promised or expected yield provides a *measure of return* that can be used to determine the relative attractiveness of fixed-income securities. But to do so, we must evaluate the measure of return in light of the *risk* involved in the investment. Bonds are no different from stocks in that the amount of return (promised or expected) should be sufficient to cover the investor's exposure to risk. Thus, the greater the amount of perceived risk, the greater the amount of return the bond should generate. If the bond meets this hurdle, it could then be compared to other potential investment outlets. If you find it difficult to do better in a risk–return sense, then the bond under evaluation should be given serious consideration as an investment outlet.

HOTLINKS

To answer questions such as "What is my yield to maturity?" "What is my yield to call?" "How will rate changes affect my bond's current value?" you can use the bond calculators at:

www.aaii.com/otherinv/calc/

Duration and Immunization

LG 5

One of the problems with yield-to-maturity (YTM) is that it assumes you can reinvest the bond's periodic coupon payments at the same rate over time. But if you reinvest this interest income at a lower rate (or if you spend it), your real return will be much lower than that indicated by YTM. The assumption that interest rates will remain constant is a key weakness of YTM. Another flaw is that YTM assumes the issuer will make all payments on time and won't call the bonds before maturity, as often happens when interest rates drop. For bonds that are not held to maturity, prices will reflect prevailing interest rates, which are likely to differ from YTM. If rates have moved up since a bond was purchased, the bond will sell at a discount. If interest rates have dropped, it will sell at a premium. The sales price will obviously have a major impact on the total return earned.

The problem with yield-to-maturity, then, is that it fails to take into account the effects of reinvestment risk and price (or market) risk. To see how reinvestment and price risks behave relative to one another, consider a situation in which market interest rates have undergone a sharp decline. Under such conditions, you might be tempted to cash out your holdings and take some gains (i.e., do a little "profit taking"). Indeed, selling before maturity is the only way to take advantage of falling interest rates, because a bond will pay its par value at maturity, regardless of prevailing interest rates. But there's a downside to falling rates: When interest rates fall, so do the opportunities to invest at high rates. Therefore, although you gain on the price side, you lose on the reinvestment side. Even if you don't sell out, you are faced with increased reinvestment risk, because in order to earn the YTM promised on your bonds, you have to be able to reinvest each coupon payment at the same YTM rate. Obviously, as rates fall, you'll find it increasingly difficult to reinvest the stream of coupon payments at or above the YTM rate. When market rates rise, just the opposite happens: The price of the bond falls, but your reinvestment opportunities improve.

What is needed is a measure of performance that overcomes these deficiencies and takes into account both price and reinvestment risks. Such a yardstick is provided by something called **duration.** It captures in a single measure the extent to which the price of a bond will react to different interest rate environments. Because duration gauges the price volatility of a bond, it gives you an idea of how likely you are to earn the YTM you expect. That in turn will help you tailor your holdings to your expectations of interest rate movements.

duration
a measure of bond price volatility, which captures both price and reinvestment risks and which is used to indicate how a bond will react in different interest rate environments.

The Concept of Duration

The concept of duration was first developed in 1938 by actuary Frederick Macaulay to help insurance companies match their cash inflows with payments. When applied to bonds, duration recognizes that the amount and frequency of interest payments, yield-to-maturity, and time to maturity all affect the "time dimension" of a bond. Time to maturity is important because it influences how much a bond's price rises or falls as interest rates change. In general, when rates move, bonds with longer maturities fluctuate more than shorter-term issues. However, maturity alone isn't a sufficient measure of the time dimension of bonds. Maturity tells you only when the last payment will be made; it doesn't say anything about interim payments. The amount of reinvestment risk is also directly related to the size of a bond's coupons: Bonds that pay high coupons have greater reinvestment risk simply because there's more to reinvest.

Any change in interest rates will cause price risk and reinvestment risk to push and pull bonds in opposite directions. An increase in rates will produce a drop in price but will lessen reinvestment risk by making it easier to reinvest coupon payments at or above the YTM rate. Declining rates, in contrast, will boost prices but increase reinvestment risk. At some point in time, these two forces should exactly offset each other. *That point in time is the bond's duration.*

In general, bond duration possesses the following properties:

- Higher coupons result in shorter durations.
- Longer maturities mean longer durations.
- Higher yields (YTMs) lead to shorter durations.

A bond's coupon, maturity, and yield interact to produce the issue's measure of duration. Knowing a bond's duration is helpful because it captures the underlying price *volatility* of a bond. That is, since *a bond's duration and volatility are directly related, it follows that the shorter the duration, the less volatility there is in bond prices—and vice versa, of course.*

Measuring Duration

Duration is a measure of the effective, as opposed to actual, maturity of a fixed-income security. As we will see, only those bonds promising a single payment to be received at maturity (zero-coupon bonds) have durations equal to their actual years to maturity. For all other bonds, *duration measures are always less than their actual maturities.*

Although a bond's term to maturity is a useful concept, it falls short of being a reliable measure of a bond's effective life, because it does not consider all of the bond's cash flows or the time value of money. Duration is a far superior measure of the effective timing of a bond's cash flows, as it explicitly considers both the time value of money and the bond's coupon and principal payments. Duration may be thought of as the *weighted-average life of a bond*, where the weights are the relative future cash flows of the bond, all of which are discounted to their present values. Mathematically, we can find the duration of a bond as follows:

Equation 10.7

$$\text{Duration} = \sum_{t=1}^{T}\left[\frac{PV(C_t)}{P_{\text{bond}}} \times t\right]$$

where

$PV(C_t)$ = present value of a future coupon or principal payment

P_{bond} = current market price of the bond

t = year in which the cash flow (coupon or principal) payment is received

T = remaining life of the bond, in years

The duration measure obtained from Equation 10.7 is commonly referred to as *Macaulay duration*—named after the actuary who developed the concept.

Although duration often is computed using semiannual compounding, Equation 10.7 uses *annual coupons and annual compounding* in order to keep the ensuing discussion and calculations as simple as possible. But even so, the formula looks more formidable than it really is. If you follow the basic steps noted below, you'll find that duration is not tough to calculate. Here are the steps involved:

Step 1. Find the present value of each annual coupon or principal payment [$PV(C_t)$]. *Use the prevailing YTM on the bond as the discount rate.*

Step 2. Divide this present value by the current market price of the bond (P_{bond}).

Step 3. Multiply this relative value by the year in which the cash flow is to be received (t).

Step 4. Repeat steps 1 through 3 for each year in the life of the bond, and then *add up* the values computed in step 3.

Duration for a Single Bond Table 10.1 illustrates the four-step procedure for calculating the duration of a 7½%, 15-year bond priced (at $957) to yield 8%. Note that this particular 15-year bond has a duration of less than 9½ years (9.36 years, to be exact). Here's how we found that value: Along with the current market price of the bond ($957), the first three columns of Table 10.1 provide the basic input data: Column (1) is the year (*t*) of the cash flow. Column (2) is the amount of the annual cash flows (from coupons and principal). And column (3) lists the appropriate present-value interest factors, given an 8% discount rate (which is equal to the prevailing YTM on the bond).

The first thing we do (step 1) is find the present value of each of the annual cash flows (column 4). Then (step 2) we divide each of these present values by the current market price of the bond (column 5). Multiplying the relative cash flows from column (5) by the year (*t*) in which the cash flow occurs (step 3) results in a time-weighted value for each of the annual cash flow streams (column 6). Adding up all the values in column (6) (step 4) yields the duration of the bond. As you can see, the duration of this bond is a lot less than its maturity—a condition that would exist with any coupon-bearing bond. In addition, keep in mind *that the duration on any bond will change over time* as YTM and term to maturity change. For example, the duration on this 7½%, 15-year bond will fall as the bond nears maturity and/or as the market yield (YTM) on the bond increases.

INVESTOR FACTS

DIFFERENT BONDS, SAME DURATIONS—Sometimes, you really can't judge a book—or a bond, for that matter—by its cover. Here are three bonds that, on the surface, appear to be totally different:

- An 8-year, zero-coupon bond priced to yield 6%.
- A 12-year, 8¾% bond that trades at a yield of 8%.
- An 18-year, 10½% bond priced to yield 13%.

Although these three bonds have different coupons and different maturities, they have one thing in common: They all have *identical durations* of 8 years. Thus if interest rates went up or down by 50 to 100 basis points, the market prices of these bonds would all behave pretty much the same!

Duration for a Portfolio of Bonds The concept of duration is not applied merely to single securities. It can also be applied to whole portfolios of fixed-income securities. The duration of an entire portfolio is fairly easy to calculate. All we need are the durations of the individual securities in the portfolio and their weights (i.e., the proportion that each security contributes to the overall value of the portfolio). Given this, *the duration of a portfolio is simply the weighted average of the durations of the individual securities in the portfolio.* For example, consider the following five-bond portfolio:

Bond	Amount Invested*	Weight	×	Bond Duration	=	Portfolio Duration
Government bonds	$ 270,000	0.15		6.25		0.9375
Aaa corporates	180,000	0.10		8.90		0.8900
Aa utilities	450,000	0.25		10.61		2.6525
Agency issues	360,000	0.20		11.03		2.2060
Baa industrials	540,000	0.30		12.55		3.7650
	$1,800,000	1.00				10.4510

*Amount invested = Current market price × Par value of the bonds. That is, if the government bonds are quoted at 90 and the investor holds $300,000 in these bonds, then 0.90 × $300,000 = $270,000.

In this case, the $1.8 million bond *portfolio* has an average duration of approximately 10.5 years. Obviously, if you want to change the duration of the portfolio, you can do so by either (1) changing the asset mix of the portfolio (shift the weight of the portfolio to longer- or shorter-duration bonds, as desired) and/or (2) adding new bonds to the portfolio with the desired duration characteristics. As we will see below, this approach is often used in a bond portfolio strategy known as *bond immunization*.

TABLE 10.1 Duration Calculation for a 7½%, 15-year Bond Priced to Yield 8%

(1)	(2)	(3)	(4)	(5)	(6)
Year *(t)*	Annual Cash Flow (C_t)	*PVIF* (at 8%)	Present Value of Annual Cash Flows $[PV(C_t)]$ (2) × (3)	$PV(C_t)$ Divided by Current Market Price of the Bond* (4) ÷ $957	Time-Weighted Relative Cash Flow (1) × (5)
1	$ 75	.926	$ 69.45	.0726	.0726
2	75	.857	64.27	.0672	.1343
3	75	.794	59.55	.0622	.1867
4	75	.735	55.12	.0576	.2304
5	75	.681	51.08	.0534	.2668
6	75	.630	47.25	.0494	.2962
7	75	.583	43.72	.0457	.3198
8	75	.540	40.50	.0423	.3386
9	75	.500	37.50	.0392	.3527
10	75	.463	34.72	.0363	.3628
11	75	.429	32.18	.0336	.3698
12	75	.397	29.78	.0311	.3734
13	75	.368	27.60	.0288	.3749
14	75	.340	25.50	.0266	.3730
15	1,075	.315	338.62	.3538	5.3076
					Duration: 9.36 yrs.

*If this bond is priced to yield 8%, it will be quoted in the market at $957.

Bond Duration and Price Volatility

A bond's price volatility is, in part, a function of its term to maturity and, in part, a function of its coupon yield. Unfortunately, there is no exact relationship between bond maturities and bond price volatilities with respect to interest rate changes. There is, however, a fairly close relationship between bond duration and price volatility—at least, so long as the market doesn't experience wide swings in yield. Duration can be used as a viable predictor of price volatility *only so long as the yield swings are relatively small* (no more than 50 to 100 basis points, or so). That's because whereas duration is a straight-line relationship, the price-yield relationship of a bond is convex in nature. That is, when bond yields change, bond prices actually move in a curved (convex) manner rather than in a straight line, as depicted by duration. Thus, when the market (or bond) undergoes a *big change* in yield, duration will *understate* the appreciation in price when rates fall and *overstate* the price decline when rates rise. Assuming that's not the case (i.e., that we're dealing with relatively small changes in market yield), then multiplying a bond's duration value by −1 results in its price elasticity with respect to interest rate changes. Thus, by calculating a bond's duration, we can obtain a fairly accurate measure of how much its price will change relative to a given (reasonably small) change in market interest rates.

The mathematical link between bond price and interest rate changes involves the concept of *modified duration*. To find modified duration, we simply take the (Macaulay) duration for a bond (as found from Equation 10.7) and adjust it for the bond's yield to maturity.

Equation 10.8

$$\text{Modified duration} = \frac{\text{(Macaulay) Duration in years}}{1 + \text{Yield to maturity}}$$

Thus the modified duration for the 15-year bond discussed above is

$$\text{Modified duration} = \frac{9.36}{1 + 0.08} = \underline{\underline{8.67}}$$

Note that here we use the bond's computed (Macaulay) duration of 9.36 years and the same YTM we used to compute duration in Equation 10.7; in this case, the bond was priced to yield 8%, so we use a yield-to-maturity of 8%.

To determine, in percentage terms, how much the price of this bond would change as market interest rates increased from, say, 8% to 8½%, we multiply the modified duration value calculated above first by −1 (because of the inverse relationship between bond prices and interest rates) and then by the change in the level of the market interest rates. That is,

Equation 10.9

$$\begin{aligned}\text{Percent change in bond price} &= -1 \times \text{Modified duration} \times \text{Change in interest rates} \\ &= -1 \times 8.67 \times 0.5\% = \underline{\underline{-4.33\%}}\end{aligned}$$

Thus a 50-basis-point (or ½ of 1%) increase in market interest rates will lead to an almost 4½% drop in the price of this 15-year bond. Such information is useful to bond investors seeking—or trying to avoid—price volatility.

Uses of Bond Duration Measures

Bond investors have learned to use duration analysis in many ways. For example, as we saw above, you can use modified duration to measure the potential price volatility of a particular issue. Another, perhaps more important use of duration is in the *structuring of bond portfolios*. That is, if you thought that interest rates were about to increase, you could calculate the expected percentage decrease in the value of the portfolio, given a certain change in market interest rates, and then reduce the overall duration of the portfolio by selling higher-duration bonds and buying those of shorter duration bonds. Such a strategy would prove profitable, because short-duration bonds do not decline in value to the same degree as longer bonds. On the other hand, if you felt that interest rates were about to decline, the opposite strategy would be appropriate.

Although active, short-term investors frequently use duration analysis in their day-to-day operations, longer-term investors also employ it in planning their investment decisions. Indeed, a strategy known as *bond portfolio immunization* represents one of the most important uses of duration.

Bond Immunization Some investors hold portfolios of bonds not for the purpose of "beating the market" but, rather, to *accumulate a specified level of wealth by the end of a given investment horizon*. For these investors, bond portfolio immunization often proves to be of great value. Immunization allows you to derive a specified rate of return from bond investments over a given investment interval *regardless of what happens to market interest rates over the course of the* *holding period*. In essence, you are able to "immunize" your portfolio from the effects of changes in market interest rates over a given investment horizon.

To understand how and why bond portfolio immunization is possible, you need to understand that changes in market interest rates lead to two distinct and opposite changes in bond valuation: The first effect is known as the *price effect*. It results in portfolio valuation changes when interest rates change before the end of the desired investment horizon. This is true because interest rate decreases lead to bond price increases, and vice versa. The second effect is known as the *reinvestment effect*. It arises because the YTM calculation assumes that all coupon payments will be reinvested at the YTM rate that existed when the bond was purchased. If interest rates increase, however, the coupons may be reinvested at a higher rate, leading to increases in investor wealth. Of course, the opposite is true when interest rates decrease. Thus, whereas an increase in rates has a negative effect on a bond's price, it has a positive effect on the reinvestment of coupons. Therefore, when interest rate changes do occur, the price and reinvestment effects work against each other from the standpoint of the investor's wealth.

When do these counteracting effects offset each other and leave the investor's position unchanged? You guessed it: when the average duration of the portfolio just equals the investment horizon. This should not come as much of a surprise, because such a property is already embedded in the duration measure itself. And, if it applies to a single bond, it should also apply to the *weighted-average duration of a bond portfolio*. When such a condition (of offsetting price and reinvestment effects) exists, *a bond portfolio is said to be immunized*. More specifically, your wealth position is immunized from the effects of interest rate changes *when the weighted-average duration of the bond portfolio exactly equals your desired investment horizon*. Table 10.2 provides an example of bond immunization using a 10-year, 8% coupon bond with a duration of 8 years. Here, we assume the investor's desired investment horizon is also 8 years in length.

The example in Table 10.2 assumes that you originally purchased the 8% coupon bond at par. It further assumes that market interest rates for bonds of this quality drop from 8% to 6% at the end of the fifth year. Because you had an investment horizon of exactly 8 years and desire to lock in an interest rate return of exactly 8%, it follows that you expect to have a terminal value of \$1,850.90 [i.e., \$1,000 invested at 8% for 8 years = $\$1,000 \times (1.08)^8 =$ \$1,850.90], regardless of interest rate changes in the interim. As can be seen from the results in Table 10.2, the immunization strategy netted you a total of \$1,850.31—just 59 cents short of your desired goal. Note that in this case, although reinvestment opportunities declined in years 5, 6, and 7 (when market interest rates dropped to 6%), that same lower rate led to a higher market price for the bond. That higher price, in turn, provided enough capital gains to offset the loss in reinvested income. This remarkable result clearly demonstrates the power of bond immunization and the versatility of bond duration. And note that even though the table uses a single bond for purposes of illustration, the same results can be obtained from a bond *portfolio* that is maintained at the *proper weighted-average duration*.

Although bond immunization is a powerful investment tool, it is clearly not a passive investment strategy. Maintaining a fully immunized portfolio (of more than one bond) requires *continual portfolio rebalancing*. Indeed, every time interest rates change, the duration of a portfolio changes. Because effective immunization requires that the portfolio have a duration value equal in

HOTLINKS

Streaming files on bond price dynamics, modified duration, and term structure of interest rates are available from the Duke University site at:

www.duke.edu/~charvey/Classes/ba350_1997/350hyper.htm

length to the *remaining investment horizon*, the composition of the portfolio must be rebalanced each time interest rates change. Further, even in the absence of interest rate changes, a bond's duration declines more slowly than its term to maturity. This, of course, means that the mere passage of time will dictate changes in portfolio composition. Such changes will ensure that the duration of the portfolio continues to match the remaining time in the investment horizon. In summary, portfolio immunization strategies can be extremely effective, but it is important to realize that immunization is not a passive strategy and is not without potential problems, the most notable of which are associated with portfolio rebalancing.

Bond Investment Strategies

LG 6

Generally, bond investors tend to follow one of three kinds of investment programs. First, there are those who live off the income: the conservative, quality-conscious, income-oriented investors who seek to maximize current income. Then there are the speculators (bond traders), who have a considerably different investment objective: to maximize capital gains, often within a short time span. This investment approach requires considerable expertise, because it is based almost entirely on estimates of the future course of interest rates. Finally, there are the serious long-term investors, whose objective is to maximize *total return*—from both current income and capital gains—over fairly long holding periods.

In order to achieve the objectives of any one of these three programs, you need to adopt a strategy that is compatible with your goals. Professional money managers use a variety of techniques to manage the multi-million (or multi-billion) dollar bond portfolios under their direction. These range from passive approaches, to semiactive strategies, to active, fully managed strategies using interest rate forecasting and yield spread analysis. Most of these strategies are fairly complex and require substantial computer support. Even so, we can look briefly at some of the more basic strategies to gain an appreciation of

TABLE 10.2 Bond Immunization

Year	Cash Flow from Bond						Terminal Value of Reinvested Cash Flow
1	$80	×	$(1.08)^4$	×	$(1.06)^3$	=	$ 129.63
2	80	×	$(1.08)^3$	×	$(1.06)^3$	=	120.03
3	80	×	$(1.08)^2$	×	$(1.06)^3$	=	111.14
4	80	×	(1.08)	×	$(1.06)^3$	=	102.90
5	80	×	$(1.06)^3$			=	95.28
6	80	×	$(1.06)^2$			=	89.89
7	80	×	(1.06)			=	84.80
8	80					=	80.00
8	$1,036.64*					=	1,036.64
				Total			$1,850.31
				Investor's required wealth at 8%			$1,850.90
				Difference			$ .59

*The bond could be sold at a market price of $1,036.64, which is the value of an 8% bond with 2 years to maturity that is priced to yield 6%.

Note: Bond interest coupons are assumed to be paid at year-end. Therefore, there are 4 years of reinvestment at 8% and 3 years at 6% for the first year's $80 coupon.

INVESTING in action

Getting Started in Bond Investing

After the stock market's wild ride in the late 1990s and the even wilder ride in 2000 and 2001, you may be beginning to think that perhaps bonds may make a good addition to your portfolio. Perhaps you want to preserve capital or think that bonds would exert a stabilizing influence on your portfolio. You'll need to answer some basic questions before you start. Do you want a taxable or a tax-exempt security? The answer depends on your tax bracket and on whether you are buying the securities for a tax-advantaged account such as your 401(k) retirement account. The next question is a bit harder: *Should you buy individual bonds or a bond mutual fund* (an investment company that invests shareholders' money in bonds)?

Individual bonds offer certain advantages. You know the interest rate you will earn and how much you will get back when the bond matures. Individual bonds may suit your needs if you have a specific goal in mind or a specific date on which you will need funds. In this case, zero-coupon bonds are a good choice, because you buy them at a discount and get the par value at maturity. The returns are modest, but the risk is correspondingly low. Finally, individual bonds are less costly to purchase than bond mutual funds, which have ongoing fees. However, investing in bonds is not always simple. For one thing, it can be hard to find information. Credit research is more difficult on corporate and municipal bonds than on stocks. You also need to understand a bond's features, such as call options. One way around a lot of these problems is to invest in bond funds, rather than individual issues.

With a bond mutual fund, a professional manager deals with these and other problems. Unlike individual bonds, however, you have no guarantee of a fixed interest rate. Bond fund returns are governed by the fund's portfolio and market interest rate trends, so you can't predict the value of your fund shares in the future. They are also more subject to market fluctuations, because the manager is buying and selling securities. Investors in a bond fund could lose their principal, which is not likely with individual bonds of good credit quality held to maturity. And of course you should factor in expenses. (Chapter 11 discusses mutual fund costs.)

Some factors are important whether you choose individual bonds or bond funds. Both react to interest rate changes, and the duration of the bond or the fund tells you just how sensitive it is to interest rates. The duration of a bond mutual fund is the average of the durations of the bonds in its portfolio. The duration of money market funds is close to zero. For short-term funds it is 1–3 years; for medium-term funds, 4–6 years; and for long-term funds, 7–10 years. If interest rates increase 1 point, a long-term fund with a duration of 12 will fall about 12%. As you'd expect, longer-term bonds or bond funds are most sensitive to interest rate fluctuations. At the Morningstar Web site (**www.morningstar.com**), you can find taxable and tax-exempt bond funds categorized by their potential interest rate sensitivity, as measured by average portfolio durations.

Sources: Sarah C. Bush, "Five Tips for Choosing a Bond Fund," *Morningstar.com*, June 8, 2000, and "Why Bond Funds Can Get So Wild," *Morningstar.com*, October 4, 1999, both downloaded from **news.morningstar.com/news**; Chris Kelsch, "How Risky IS Your Bond Fund?" *Morningstar.com*, March 24, 2000, downloaded from **news.morningstar.com/news**; Peter Di Teresa, "Should You Buy Bonds or Bond Funds?" *Morningstar.com*, August 24, 2000, downloaded from **news.morningstar.com/news**; and Tom Petruno, "Quality Bond Funds Had a Good Year," *Newsday*, December 16, 2000, p. F4.

HOTLINKS

Another bond portfolio strategy is called a *barbell*. For information on that approach, see the Investing in Action box at:

www.awl.com/gitman_joehnk

the different ways in which fixed-income securities can be used to reach different investment objectives. Before doing that, however, you might want to take a look at the nearby *Investing in Action* box, which offers some guidelines for getting started in bonds and introduces another way to invest in bonds—via mutual funds (a topic we discuss in detail in Chapter 11).

Passive Strategies

The bond immunization strategies we have discussed are considered to be primarily *passive* in nature, to the extent that investors using these tools typically are *not* attempting to beat the market. Rather, these investors immunize their portfolios in an effort to lock in specified rates of return (or terminal values) that they deem acceptable, given the risks involved. Generally speaking, passive investment strategies are characterized by a lack of input regarding investor expectations of changes in interest rate and/or bond price. Further, these strategies typically do not generate significant transaction costs. A *buy-and-hold* strategy is perhaps the most passive of all investment strategies: All that is required is that the investor replace bonds that have deteriorating credit ratings, have matured, or have been called. Although buy-and-hold investors restrict their ability to earn above-average returns, they also minimize the losses that transaction costs represent.

HOTLINKS

Prudential Securities has an informative article about laddering at:

www.prusec.com/financial_concerns/ladder.htm

One popular approach that is a bit more active than buy-and-hold is the use of so-called **bond ladders.** In this strategy, equal amounts are invested in a *series* of bonds with staggered maturities. Here's how a bond ladder works: Suppose you want to confine your investing to fixed-income securities with maturities of 10 years or less. Given that maturity constraint, you could set up a ladder by investing in (roughly) equal amounts of, say, 3-, 5-, 7-, and 10-year issues. When the 3-year issue matures, the money from it (along with any new capital) would be put into a new 10-year note. The process would continue rolling over like this so that eventually you would hold a full ladder of staggered 10-year notes. By rolling into new 10-year issues every 2 or 3 years, you can do a kind of dollar-cost averaging and thereby lessen the impact of swings in market rates. Actually, the laddered approach is a safe, simple, and almost automatic way of investing for the long haul. Indeed, once the ladder is set up, it should be followed in a fairly routine manner. A key ingredient of this or any other passive strategy is, of course, the use of high-quality investment vehicles that possess attractive features, maturities, and yields.

bond ladders
an investment strategy wherein equal amounts of money are invested in a series of bonds with staggered maturities.

INVESTOR FACTS

KEY QUESTIONS TO ASK ABOUT A BOND INVESTMENT—There are several key variables to consider before investing in bonds. The following factors help to determine the value of the investment and how well it meets your financial goals:

- What is the bond's maturity?
- Can it be redeemed early through call features?
- What is the credit quality? What is the bond rating? Is it insured?
- What is the price?
- What is the yield to maturity? What is the yield to call?
- Is it taxable or tax-exempt?

Source: Investing in Bonds, www.investinginbonds.com/info/checklist.htm

Trading on Forecasted Interest Rate Behavior

In contrast, a highly risky approach to bond investing is the *forecasted interest rate* approach. It seeks attractive capital gains when interest rates are expected to decline and preservation of capital when an increase in interest rates is anticipated. It's risky because it relies on the imperfect forecast of future interest rates. The idea is to increase the return on a bond portfolio by making strategic moves in anticipation of interest rate changes. Such a strategy is essentially *market timing*. An unusual feature of this tactic is that most of the trading is done with *investment-grade securities,* because a high degree of interest rate sensitivity is required to capture the maximum amount of price behavior.

Once interest rate expectations have been specified, this strategy rests largely on technical matters. For example, when a decline in rates is anticipated, aggressive bond investors often seek to lengthen the maturity (or duration) of their bonds (or bond portfolios). The reason: Longer-term bonds rise more in price than shorter-term issues. At the same time, investors look for low-coupon and/or moderately discounted bonds, which will add to duration and increase the amount of potential price volatility. These interest swings are usually short-lived, so bond traders try to earn as much as possible in as short a time as possible. (Margin trading—the use of borrowed money to buy bonds—is also used as a way of magnifying returns when rate declines are expected.) When rates start to level off and move up, these investors begin to shift their money out of long, discounted bonds and into high-yielding issues with short maturities. In other words, they do a complete reversal. During those periods when bond prices are dropping, investors are more concerned about preservation of capital, so they take steps to protect their money from capital losses. Thus, they tend to use such short-term obligations as Treasury bills, money funds, short-term (2–5 year) notes, or even variable-rate notes.

Bond Swaps

bond swap
an investment strategy wherein an investor liquidates one bond holding and simultaneously buys a different issue in its place.

In a **bond swap,** an investor simply liquidates one position and at the same time buys a different issue in its place. Swaps can be executed to increase current yield or yield-to-maturity, to take advantage of shifts in interest rates, to improve the quality of a portfolio, or for tax purposes. Although some swaps are highly sophisticated, most are fairly simple transactions. They go by a variety of colorful names, such as "profit takeout," "substitution swap," and "tax swap," but they are all used for one basic reason: *to seek portfolio improvement.* We will briefly review two types of bond swaps that are fairly simple and hold considerable appeal: the yield pickup swap and the tax swap.

yield pickup swap
replacement of a low-coupon bond for a comparable higher-coupon bond in order to realize an increase in current yield and yield-to-maturity.

In a **yield pickup swap,** an investor switches out of a low-coupon bond into a comparable higher-coupon issue in order to realize an instantaneous pickup of current yield and yield-to-maturity. For example, you would be executing a yield pickup swap if you sold 20-year, A-rated, 6½% bonds (which were yielding 8% at the time) and replaced them with an equal amount of 20-year, A-rated, 7% bonds that were priced to yield 8½%. By executing the swap, you would improve your current yield (your coupon income would increase from $65 a year to $70 a year) as well as your yield-to-maturity (from 8 to 8½%). Basically, such swap opportunities arise because of the *yield spreads* that normally exist between, say, industrial and public utility bonds. The mechanics are fairly simple, and you can execute such swaps simply by watching for swap candidates and/or asking your broker to do so. In fact, the only thing you have to be careful of is that transaction costs do not eat up all the profits.

tax swap
replacement of a bond that has a capital loss for a similar security; used to offset a gain generated in another part of an investor's portfolio.

The other type of swap that's popular with many investors is the **tax swap,** which is also relatively simple and involves few risks. The technique can be used whenever an investor has a substantial tax liability that has come about as a result of selling some security holdings at a profit. The objective is to execute a swap so that the tax liability accompanying the capital gains can be *eliminated or substantially reduced.* This is done by selling an issue that has undergone capital *loss* and replacing it with a comparable obligation. For example, assume that you had $10,000 worth of corporate bonds that you sold (in the current year) for $15,000, resulting in a capital gain of $5,000. You can eliminate the tax liability accompanying the capital gain by selling securities that have *capital losses of $5,000.* Let's assume you find you hold a 20-year, 4¾% municipal bond that (strictly by coincidence, of course) has undergone a $5,000 drop in value. Thus you have the required tax shield in your portfolio. All you have to do is find a viable swap candidate. Suppose you find a comparable 20-year, 5% municipal issue currently trading at about the same price as the issue being sold. By selling the 4¾s and simultaneously buying a comparable amount of the 5s, you will not only increase your tax-free yields (from 4¾% to 5%) but also eliminate the capital gains tax liability. The only precaution is that *identical issues cannot be used* in such swap transactions. The IRS would consider that a "wash sale" and disallow the loss. Moreover, the capital loss must occur in the same taxable year as the capital gain. This limitation explains why the technique is so popular with knowledgeable investors, particularly at year-end, when tax loss sales and tax swaps multiply as investors hurry to establish capital losses.

HOTLINKS

For details on IRS regulations regarding wash sales, go to the book's Web site and click on Chapter 17. Go to the section on Strategies that Trade Current Income for Capital Gains and then on Tax Swaps.

www.awl.com/gitman_joehnk

Summary

LG 1 **Explain the behavior of market interest rates, and identify the forces that cause interest rates to move.** The behavior of interest rates is the single most important force in the bond market. It determines not only the amount of current income an investor will receive but also the investor's capital gains (or losses). Changes in market interest rates can have a dramatic impact on the total returns obtained from bonds over time.

LG 2 **Describe the term structure of interest rates, and note how these yield curves can be used by investors.** Many forces drive the behavior of interest rates over time, including inflation, the cost and availability of funds, and the level of interest rates in major foreign markets. One particularly important force is the term structure of interest rates, which relates yield-to-maturity to term-to-maturity.

LG 3 **Understand how bonds are valued in the marketplace.** Bonds are valued (priced) in the marketplace on the basis of their required rates of return (or market yields). The whole process of pricing a bond begins with the yield it should provide. Once that piece of information is known (or estimated), a standard, present-value-based model is used to find the dollar price of a bond.

LG 4 **Describe the various measures of yield and return, and explain how these standards of performance are used in bond valuation.** Four types of yields are important to investors: current yield, promised yield, yield-to-call, and expected yield (or return). Promised yield (yield-to-maturity) is the most widely used bond valuation measure. It captures both the current income and the price appreciation of an issue. The same can be said of yield-to-call, which assumes the bond will be outstanding only until its first call date. Expected return, in contrast, is a valuation measure that's used by aggressive bond traders to show the total return that can be earned from trading in and out of a bond long before it matures.

LG 5 **Understand the basic concept of duration, how it can be measured, and its use in the management of bond portfolios.** Bond duration is an important concept in bond valuation. Duration takes into account the effects of both reinvestment and price (or market) risks. It captures, in a single measure, the extent to which the price of a bond will react to different interest rate environments. Equally important, duration can be used to immunize whole bond portfolios from the often devastating forces of changing market interest rates.

LG 6 **Discuss various bond investment strategies and the different ways these securities can be used by investors.** As investment vehicles, bonds can be used as a source of income, as a way to seek capital gains by speculating on the movement in interest rates, or as a way to earn attractive long-term returns. To achieve these objectives, investors often employ one or more of the following strategies: passive strategies such as buy-and-hold, bond ladders, and portfolio immunization; bond trading based on forecasted interest rate behavior; and bond swaps.

Part Five
PORTFOLIO MANAGEMENT

CHAPTER 11

MUTUAL FUNDS: PROFESSIONALLY MANAGED INVESTMENT PORTFOLIOS

LEARNING GOALS

After studying this chapter, you should be able to:

LG 1 Describe the basic features of mutual funds, and note what they have to offer as investment vehicles.

LG 2 Distinguish between open- and closed-end funds, as well as other types of professionally managed investment companies, and discuss the various types of fund loads, fees, and charges.

LG 3 Discuss the types of funds available and the variety of investment objectives these funds seek to fulfill.

LG 4 Discuss the investor services offered by mutual funds and how these services can fit into an investment program.

LG 5 Gain an appreciation of the investor uses of mutual funds, along with the variables to consider when assessing and selecting funds for investment purposes.

LG 6 Identify the sources of return and compute the rate of return earned on a mutual fund investment.

Imagine learning that the Dow Jones Industrial Average had dropped 600 points and the Nasdaq, 300 points, and thinking, "Cool!" That was Blaine Rollins's reaction on April 14, 2000. Rollins, a manager for Janus Funds, had previously moved significant fund assets into cash and was ready to buy heavily for the fund. "I basically bought my 10 worst-performing names of the day, which were all down 15%, 25%, and 30%," Rollins said. "I thought, 'Hey, cheap stock.' "

Not many individual investors would have had the courage to follow Rollins into the market at a time when stocks were tumbling. And that's exactly why mutual funds are so appealing: They offer the expertise of professional money managers who study market trends and invest in a portfolio of securities. Buying shares in one of the nearly 8,000 mutual funds gives an investor shares in a diversified portfolio.

Janus's investment philosophy centers on bottom-up, company-focused fundamental research rather than on more "macro" trends in the economy or markets. Its analysis emphasizes sustainable future earnings growth, cash flow, return on invested capital, dominant franchises, and shareholder-focused management. Unlike funds that diversify broadly, Janus's various funds own about 550 different stocks (compared to almost 2,000 at Putnam Funds and 3,370 at Fidelity). Its concentration strategy—buying relatively few high-priced growth stocks—paid off in the late 1990s when the bull market was at its peak. However, when the market dipped in 2000, the value of Janus Funds' holdings did also.

If Janus's investment strategy doesn't appeal to you, you can find a different approach at another mutual fund. Approaches range from funds that track the movement of a particular market index to emerging-markets funds that invest in stocks in developing economies. As you'll learn in this chapter, mutual funds can help you reach your investment goals.

Sources: Lisa Gibbs, "Glory Days at Janus," Money, June 2000, pp. 122–130; "About Janus," Janus Funds Web site, www.janus.com

The Mutual Fund Phenomenon

LG 1 LG 2

Questions of which stock or bond to select, when to buy, and when to sell have plagued investors for as long as there have been organized securities markets. Such concerns lie at the very heart of the mutual fund concept and in large part explain the growth that mutual funds have experienced. Many investors lack the time, know-how, or commitment to manage their own portfolios, so they turn to professional money managers and simply let them decide which securities to buy and when to sell. More often than not, when investors look for professional help, they look to mutual funds.

Basically, a mutual fund is a type of financial services organization that receives money from its shareholders and then invests those funds on their behalf in a diversified portfolio of securities. Thus, when investors buy shares in a mutual fund, they actually become *part owners of a widely diversified portfolio of securities.* In an abstract sense, a mutual fund can be thought of as the *financial product* sold to the public by an investment company. That is, the investment company builds and manages a portfolio of securities and sells ownership interests—shares of stock—in that portfolio through a vehicle known as a mutual fund.

Recall from Chapter 5 that portfolio management deals with both asset allocation and security selection decisions. By investing in mutual funds, investors delegate some, if not all, of the *security selection decisions* to professional money managers. As a result, they can concentrate on key asset allocation decisions—which, of course, play a vital role in determining long-term portfolio returns. Indeed, it's for this reason that *many investors consider mutual funds to be the ultimate asset allocation vehicle.* For with mutual funds, all investors have to do is decide where they want to invest—in large-cap stocks, for example, or in technology stocks, high-yield bonds, the S&P 500 index, or international securities—and then let the professional money managers at the mutual funds do the rest, that is, decide which securities to buy and sell, and when.

Mutual funds have been a part of the investment landscape for over 75 years. The first one (MFS) was started in Boston in 1924 and is still in business today. By 1940 the number of mutual funds had grown to 68, and by 1980 there were 564 of them. But that was only the beginning: The next 20 years saw unprecedented growth in the mutual fund industry, as assets under management grew from less than $100 billion in 1980 to over $7 trillion in 2000. Indeed, by *2000 there were nearly 8,000 publicly traded mutual funds.* (Actually, counting duplicate and multiple fund offerings from the same portfolio, there are more like *12,000 funds available.*) To put that number in perspective, *there are more mutual funds in existence today than there are stocks listed on the New York and American exchanges combined.* The mutual fund industry has grown so much, in fact, that it is now *the largest financial intermediary* in this country—even ahead of banks. Obviously, the funds must be doing something right!

An Overview of Mutual Funds

Mutual funds are big business in the United States and, indeed, all over the world. As the year 2000 began, an estimated 83 million individuals in 48 million U.S. households owned mutual funds. That's nearly half of all U.S. households! Table 11.1 provides some additional statistics about mutual funds in this country and abroad. Clearly, mutual funds appeal to a lot of investors—

TABLE 11.1 Some Mutual Fund Statistics

I. Total Number of U.S. Shareholder Accounts (in millions)

	1990*	1999*
Stock funds	22.2	149.0
Bond funds	13.6	20.7
Money market funds	23.0	43.6
Other funds	3.2	14.4
Total	62.0	227.7

II. Total Number of Funds

	1990*	1999*
Stock funds	1,100	3,952
Bond funds	1,046	2,261
Money market funds	741	1,045
Other funds	194	533
Total—U.S. funds	3,081	7,791
Number of funds in other countries**	N/A	35,979
Total—worldwide	N/A	43,770

III. Total Net Assets Under Management (in billions of dollars)

	1990*	1999*
Stock funds	$239.5	$4,041.9
Bond funds	291.3	808.1
Money market funds	498.3	1,613.1
Other funds	36.1	383.2
Total—U.S. funds	$1,065.2	$ 6,846.3
Net assets under mgmt. in other countries**	N/A	$ 3,687.5
Total—worldwide	N/A	$10,533.8

IV. Composition of Mutual Fund Ownership in U.S. (relative to total mutual fund assets)

Owned by U.S. households	1990*	1999*
in dollars	$790 billion	$5.5 trillion
% of total	74.0%	81.0%
Owned by institutions		
in dollars	$275 billion	$1.3 trillion
% of total	26.0%	19.0%

Notes: *All data are for year-end 1990 and 1999.
**Totals for 30 countries, the major ones being Canada, France, Germany, U.K., Japan, Hong Kong, Italy, Korea, and Spain.

Source: 2000 Mutual Fund Fact Book, Investment Company Institute, 2000; obtained from www.ici.org

investors from all walks of life and all income levels. They range from inexperienced to highly experienced investors who all share a common view: Each has decided, for one reason or another, to turn over at least a part of his or her investment management activities to professionals.

Pooled Diversification As noted above, an investment in a mutual fund really represents *an ownership position in a professionally managed portfolio*

FIGURE 11.1 A Partial List of Portfolio Holdings

This exhibit represents just *two pages* of security holdings for this particular fund. The total list of holdings goes on for 28 pages and includes stocks in hundreds of different companies. Certainly, this is far more diversification than most individual investors could ever hope to achieve. (*Source: Fidelity Low-Priced Stock Fund,* January 2000.)

Common Stocks – continued	Shares	Value (Note 1) (000s)
SERVICES – continued		
Services – continued		
The Go-Ahead Group PLC	225,000	$ 2,170
Thomas Group (a)	170,900	1,987
Velcro Industries NV	114,500	1,489
Viad Corp.	2,000,000	52,625
Wesco, Inc.	200,000	745
		202,600
TOTAL SERVICES		408,763
TECHNOLOGY – 17.9%		
Communications Equipment – 0.6%		
Champion Technology Holdings Ltd.	100,000	7
KTK Telecommunications Engineering Co. Ltd.	100,000	493
Kyosan Electric Manufacturing Co. Ltd.	500,000	1,173
LoJack Corp. (a)	110,500	856
Perceptron, Inc. (a)	233,500	934
Tollgrade Communications, Inc. (a)(d)	509,000	29,586
Turnstone Systems, Inc.	1,200	35
		33,084
Computer Services & Software – 5.4%		
Affiliated Computer Services, Inc. Class A (a)	1,000,000	39,750
Aladdin Knowledge Systems Ltd. (a)	315,000	5,906
Analysts International Corp.	100,000	1,256
Avant! Corp. (a)	1,227,600	21,867
Black Box Corp. (a)(d)	1,400,000	82,775
Computer Learning Centers, Inc. (a)(d)	1,161,200	2,177
Condor Technology Solutions, Inc. (a)	134,000	184
Cotelligent, Inc. (a)	352,800	1,852
Daitec Co. Ltd.	425,200	6,215
Directrix, Inc. (a)	90,000	529
Fair, Isaac & Co., Inc.	520,000	23,790
GSE Systems, Inc. (a)(d)	353,800	1,548
Infinium Software, Inc. (a)	152,500	867
Informa Group PLC	875,000	8,312
JDA Software Group, Inc. (a)	1,000,000	20,000
Mapics, Inc. (a)	676,000	10,140
Meta Group, Inc. (a)	75,000	1,697
National Data Corp.	5,000	160

Common Stocks – continued	Shares	Value (Note 1) (000s)
TECHNOLOGY – continued		
Computer Services & Software – continued		
Ontrack Data International, Inc. (a)	244,000	$ 1,800
Phoenix Technologies Ltd. (a)	1,000,000	20,625
Project Software & Development, Inc. (a)	700,000	33,075
Prophet 21, Inc. (a)	115,500	1,444
Remedy Corp. (a)	100,000	4,044
RWD Technologies, Inc. (a)	62,000	605
SPSS, Inc. (a)(d)	861,100	22,227
Symantec Corp. (a)	100,000	5,006
Timberline Software Corp.	353,600	4,177
Unigraphics Solutions, Inc. Class A (a)(d)	520,000	12,253
		334,281
Computers & Office Equipment – 4.3%		
Adaptec, Inc. (a)	375,000	19,641
Advanced Digital Information Corp. (a)	1,250,000	61,250
Amplicon, Inc.	523,400	5,757
Caere Corp. (a)	25,000	219
Cybex Corp. (a)(d)	674,000	35,385
Equinox Systems, Inc. (a)(d)	535,000	5,083
Kronos, Inc. (a)(d)	935,000	56,100
Maezawa Kasei Industries Co. Ltd.	200,000	3,203
Nam Tai Electronics, Inc.	431,500	5,825
Nam Tai Electronics, Inc. warrants 11/24/00 (a)	140,000	144
Pomeroy Computer Resources, Inc. (a)(d)	1,179,800	19,172
PSC, Inc. (a)	60,000	480
Quantum Corp. – DLT & Storage Systems (a)	550,010	5,294
SBS Technologies, Inc. (a)(d)	495,000	17,696
SED International Holdings, Inc. (a)(d)	960,000	1,830
Tech Data Corp. (a)	20,000	446
Zebra Technologies Corp.	500,000	29,594
		267,119
Electronic Instruments – 1.0%		
BTU International, Inc. (a)(d)	603,300	4,148
Cohu, Inc.	300,000	12,375
Halma PLC	750,000	1,393
Hurco Companies, Inc. (a)(d)	379,028	1,469
Intest Corp. (a)(d)	650,000	13,366
Mesa Laboratories, Inc. (a)	125,400	494
MOCON, Inc.	119,600	673

of securities. To appreciate the extent of such diversification, look at Figure 11.1. It provides a partial list of the securities held in the portfolio of a major mutual fund. (The exhibit shows just two pages out of a 28-page list of security holdings.) Note that in January 2000, this fund owned anywhere from 1,200 shares of Turnstone Systems to 2 *million* shares of Viad Corporation. Furthermore, note that within each industry segment, the fund diversified its holdings across a number of different stocks. Clearly, this is far more diversification than most investors could ever attain. Yet each investor who owns shares in this fund is, in effect, a part owner of this diversified portfolio.

Of course, not all funds are as big or as widely diversified as the one depicted in Figure 11.1. But whatever the size of the fund, as the securities held by it move up and down in price, the market value of the mutual fund shares moves accordingly. And when dividend and interest payments are received by the fund, they too are passed on to the mutual fund shareholders and distributed on the basis of prorated ownership. For example, if you own 1,000 shares in a mutual fund and that represents 1% of all shares outstanding, you will receive 1% of the dividends paid by the fund. When a security held by the fund is sold for a profit, the capital gain is also passed on to fund shareholders. The whole mutual fund idea, in fact, rests on the concept of **pooled diversification**. This process works very much like health insurance, whereby individuals pool their resources for the collective benefit of all the contributors.

INVESTOR FACTS

WHO OWNS THE FUNDS, AND WHY?—The average mutual fund shareholder is 45 years old, married, college-educated, and employed, with $69,000 of household income, $74,400 of mutual fund assets, and $199,000 of total financial assets. Almost 90% own equity mutual funds, and about half own money market funds. Nearly all mutual fund investors consider their holdings as long-term savings. The top four reasons why they select mutual funds are professional management, investment diversification, potential for high returns, and ease of making investments.

Source: 2000 Mutual Fund Fact Book (Washington, DC: Investment Company Institute, May 2000), downloaded from www.ici.org

pooled diversification
a process whereby investors buy into a diversified portfolio of securities for the collective benefit of the individual investors.

management fee
a fee levied annually for professional mutual fund services provided; paid regardless of the performance of the portfolio.

Attractions and Drawbacks of Mutual Fund Ownership

The attractions of mutual fund ownership are numerous. One of the most important is *diversification.* It benefits fund shareholders by spreading out holdings over a wide variety of industries and companies, thus reducing risk. Another appeal of mutual funds is *full-time professional management,* which relieves investors of many day-to-day management and record-keeping chores. What's more, the fund is probably able to offer better investment expertise than individual investors can provide. Still another advantage is that most mutual fund investments can be started with a *modest capital outlay.* Sometimes no minimum investment is required, and after the initial investment additional shares can usually be purchased in small amounts. The *services that mutual funds offer* also make them appealing to many investors: These include automatic reinvestment of dividends, withdrawal plans, and exchange privileges. Finally, mutual funds offer *convenience.* They are relatively easy to acquire; the funds handle the paperwork and record keeping; their prices are widely quoted; and it is possible to deal in fractional shares.

There are, of course, some major drawbacks to mutual fund ownership. One of the biggest disadvantages is that mutual funds in general can be costly and involve *substantial transaction costs.* Many funds carry sizable commission fees ("load charges"). In addition, a **management fee** is levied annually for the professional services provided. It is deducted right off the top, regardless of whether the fund has had a good or a bad year. And, even in spite of all the professional management and advice, it seems that *mutual fund performance* over the long haul is at best about equal to what you would expect from the market as a whole. There are some notable exceptions, of course, but most funds do little more than keep up with the market. In many cases, they don't even do that.

Figure 11.2 shows the investment performance for 12 different types of equity (or equity-oriented) funds over the 10½-year period from January 1990 through mid-2000. The reported returns are average, fully compounded annual rates of return. They assume that all dividends and capital gains distributions are reinvested into additional shares of stock. Note that when compared to the S&P 500, only three fund categories outperformed the market, whereas several fell far short. The message is clear: *Consistently beating the market is no easy task,* even for professional money managers. Although a handful of funds have given investors above-average and even spectacular rates of return, most mutual funds simply do not meet those levels of performance. This is not to say that the long-term returns from mutual funds are substandard or that they fail to equal what you could achieve by putting your money in, say, a savings account or some other risk-free investment outlet. Quite the contrary: The long-term returns from mutual funds have been substantial (and perhaps even better than what a lot of individual investors could have achieved on their own), but most of these returns can be traced to strong market conditions and/or to the reinvestment of dividends and capital gains.

HOTLINKS

To see the corrosive effect that fees paid have on return (or profit), use the fee analyzer at:

www.smartmoney.com/fundfeeanalyzer/

FIGURE 11.2 **The Comparative Performance of Mutual Funds Versus the Market**

Even with the services of professional money managers, it's tough to outperform the market. In this case, the average performance of 9 out of the 12 fund categories failed to meet the market's standard of return (for the period from January 1990 to mid-2000). (*Source: Morningstar,* June 2000.)

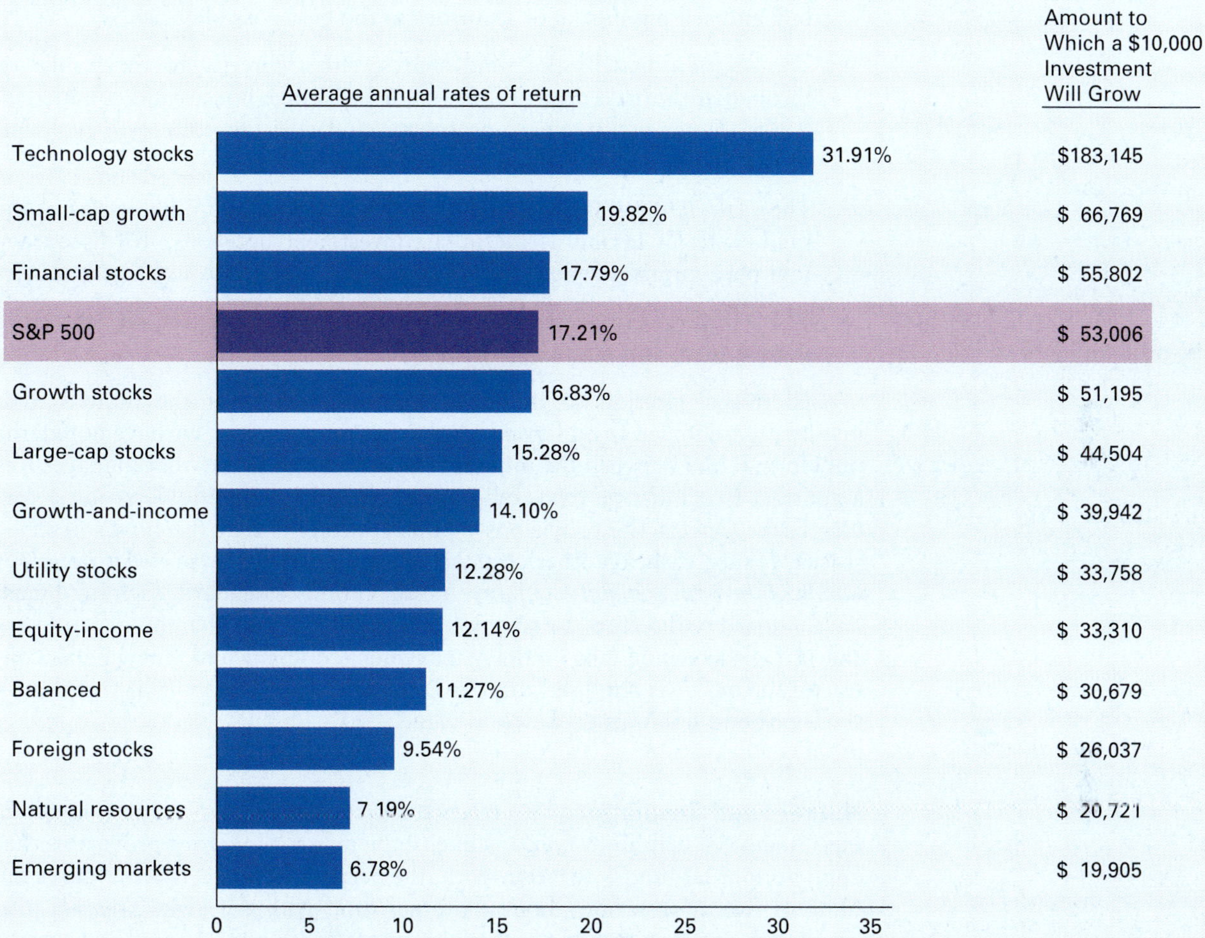

How Mutual Funds Are Organized and Run Although it's tempting to think of a mutual fund as a single large entity, that view is not really accurate. Various functions—investing, record keeping, safekeeping, and others—are split among two or more companies. To begin with, there's the fund itself, which is organized as a separate corporation or trust and is owned by the shareholders, not by the firm that runs it. In addition, there are several other main players:

- The *management company* runs the fund's daily operations. Management companies are the firms we know as Fidelity, Vanguard, T. Rowe Price, American Century, and Dreyfus. They are the ones that create the funds in the first place. Usually, the management firm also serves as investment adviser.

- The *investment adviser* buys and sells stocks or bonds and otherwise oversees the portfolio. Usually, three parties participate in this phase of the operation: (1) *The money manager,* who actually runs the portfolio and makes the buy and sell decisions; (2) *Securities analysts,* who analyze securities and look for viable investment candidates; and (3) *traders,* who buy and sell big blocks of securities at the best possible price.
- The *distributor* sells the fund shares, either directly to the public or through authorized dealers (like major brokerage houses and commercial banks). When you request a prospectus and sales literature, you deal with the distributor.
- The *custodian* physically safeguards the securities and other assets of the fund, without taking a role in the investment decisions. To discourage foul play, an independent party (usually a bank) serves in this capacity.
- The *transfer agent* keeps track of purchase and redemption requests from shareholders and maintains other shareholder records.

All this separation of duties is designed to protect the mutual fund investor/shareholder. In addition to the separation of duties we have noted, the only formal link between the mutual fund and the company that manages it is a contract that must be renewed—and approved by shareholders—on a regular basis. One of the provisions of this contract is that the fund's assets—stocks, bonds, cash, or other securities in the portfolio—can *never be in the hands of the management company.* As still another safeguard, each fund must have a board of directors, or trustees, who are elected by shareholders and are charged with keeping tabs on the management company and renewing its contract. Obviously, as a mutual fund investor, you will lose money if your fund's stock or bond holdings go down in value.

Mutual Fund Regulations We discussed securities regulations in Chapter 2, but it might be helpful to review some of the major regulatory provisions that apply to mutual funds. To begin with, the *Securities Act of 1933* requires the filing of full information about a mutual fund with the SEC. This act also requires the fund to provide potential investors with a fund profile or current prospectus. This document discloses the fund's management, its investment policies and objectives, and other essential data. In addition, the purchase and sale of mutual fund shares are subject to the antifraud provisions of the *Securities Exchange Act of 1934,* while the *Investment Advisers Act of 1940* regulates the activities of the investment advisers that work for mutual funds. Most important, in order to qualify for investment company status, a fund must comply with the provisions of the *Investment Company Act of 1940.* That comprehensive piece of legislation provides the foundation for the regulation of the mutual fund industry and, among other things, establishes standards of income distribution, fee structures, and diversification of assets.

From a tax perspective, a mutual fund can be treated as an essentially tax-exempt organization (and thereby avoid the double taxation of dividends and income) so long as it qualifies under *Subchapter M* of the Internal Revenue Code of 1954. Briefly, to operate as a regulated investment company and enjoy the attendant tax benefits, a fund must annually distribute to its shareholders all of its realized capital gains and at least 90% of its interest and dividend income. That way, the fund will pay *no* taxes on any of its earnings, whether they're derived from current income or capital gains.

Open- or Closed-End Funds

Although investing in mutual funds has been made as simple as possible, investors nevertheless should have a clear understanding of what they're getting into. For starters, it's essential that you be aware of the different organizational structures, particularly with regard to open- and closed-end funds, as well as a type of fund that combines the characteristics of open- and closed-end funds, the so-called "exchange-traded funds."

open-end investment company
a type of investment company in which investors buy shares from, and sell them back to, the mutual fund itself, with no limit on the number of shares the fund can issue.

Open-End Investment Companies The term *mutual fund* is commonly used to describe an open-end investment company. In an **open-end investment company,** investors buy their shares from, and sell them back to, the mutual fund itself. When an investor buys shares in an open-end fund, the fund issues new shares of stock and fills the purchase order with those new shares. There is no limit, other than investor demand, to the number of shares the fund can issue. (Occasionally, funds *temporarily* close themselves to new investors—they won't open any new accounts—in an attempt to keep fund growth in check.) All open-end mutual funds stand behind their shares and buy them back when investors decide to sell. There is never any trading between individuals.

HOTLINKS

Vanguard's mututal fund investor education glossary is at:

www.vanguard.com/educ/glossary/glossintro.html

Open-end mutual funds are the dominant type of investment company and account for well over 95% of the assets under management. All the statistics cited above, including those in Table 11.1, pertain to these types of funds. Many of these funds are very large and hold *billions* of dollars' worth of securities. Indeed, in 2000, the typical stock or bond fund held an average portfolio of some $750 million, and there were more than 800 billion-dollar funds.

Both buy and sell transactions in (open-end) mutual funds are carried out at prices based on the current market value of all the securities held in the fund's portfolio. (Technically, this would also include the book value of any other assets, such as cash and receivables from securities transactions, that the fund might hold at the time, though for all practical purposes, these other assets generally account for only a tiny fraction of the fund's total portfolio.) Known as the fund's **net asset value (NAV)**, this current market value is calculated at least once a day and represents the underlying value of a share of stock in a particular mutual fund. NAV is found by taking the total market value of all assets held by the fund, less any liabilities, and dividing this amount by the number of fund shares outstanding. For example, if the market value of all the assets held by the XYZ mutual fund on a given day equaled $10 million, and if XYZ on that particular day had 500,000 shares outstanding, the fund's net asset value per share would be $20 ($10,000,000 ÷ 500,000). This figure, as we will see, is then used to derive the price at which the fund shares are bought and sold.

net asset value (NAV)
the underlying value of a share of stock in a particular mutual fund.

closed-end investment companies
a type of investment company that operates with a fixed number of shares outstanding.

Closed-End Investment Companies Although the term *mutual fund* is supposed to be used only with open-end funds, it is also commonly used to refer to closed-end investment companies. **Closed-end investment companies** operate with a fixed number of shares outstanding, and do not regularly issue new shares of stock. In effect, they have a capital structure like that of any other corporation, except that the corporation's business happens to be investing in marketable securities. Shares in closed-end investment companies, like those of any other common stock, are actively traded in the secondary market. But unlike open-end funds, *all trading in closed-end funds is done between investors in the open market.* The fund itself plays no role in either buy or sell transactions. Once the shares are issued, the fund is out of the picture. By far, most closed-end investment companies are traded on the New York Stock Exchange, a few are traded on the American Exchange, and occasionally some are traded in the OTC market or on some other exchange. Even so, while these shares are traded (on the NYSE, AMEX, or Nasdaq) like any other stock, their quotes are listed separately—in the *Wall Street Journal* at least. Figure 11.3 shows the quotes for a small sample of closed-end funds listed on the NYSE, including Gabelli Equity Trust (one of the bigger closed-end investment companies). These quotes are grouped by the exchange on which the funds are traded, and are just like any other NYSE or Nasdaq National Market quotes, except they don't show the P/E ratio.

A closed-end fund is, in many respects, both a common stock and an investment company. As the original form of investment company, closed-end funds have enjoyed a long history that dates back to nineteenth-century England and Scotland. In the United States, closed-end funds were actively traded during the 1920s bull market, when they far outnumbered their open-end relatives. During that freewheeling era, however, they were highly leveraged and consequently were hit hard during the Crash of 1929, earning a bad reputation with investors. They remained something of an oddity for decades afterward. It wasn't until the bull market that began in the early 1980s that closed-end funds came back into fashion.

Many of the investment advisers that today run closed-end funds (like Putnam, Kemper, Nuveen, MFS, and Franklin-Templeton) also manage open-end funds, often with similar investment objectives. They offer both closed- and open-end funds because they are really *two different investment products.* For although it may not appear so at first glance, there are some major differences between these two types of funds. To begin with, closed-end funds have a fixed amount of capital to work with. Therefore, they don't have to be concerned about keeping cash on hand (or readily available) to meet redemptions. Equally important, because there is no pressure on portfolio managers to cash in these securities at inopportune times, they can be more aggressive in their investment styles by investing in obscure yet attractive securities that may not be actively traded. And, of course, because they don't have new money flowing in all the time, portfolio managers don't have to worry about finding new investments. Instead, they can concentrate on a set portfolio of securities.

Of course, this also puts added pressures on the money managers, since their investment styles and fund portfolios are closely monitored and judged by the market. That is, the share prices of closed-end companies are determined not only by their net asset values but also by general supply and

FIGURE 11.3

Stock Quotations for Closed-End Investment Companies

The quotes for closed-end investment companies are listed separately from other common stocks. Nonetheless, except for the lack of a P/E ratio, their quotes are pretty much the same as any other NYSE or Nasdaq National Market stock. (*Source: Wall Street Journal,* May 24, 2001.)

Gabelli Equity Trust →

CLOSED-END FUNDS

YTD %CHG	52 WEEKS HI	LO	STOCK (SYM)	DIV	YLD %	VOL 100S	CLOSE	NET CHG
+ 7.0	8.48	6.88	Fortis Sec **FOR** x	.67	8.5	99	7.89	− 0.02
− 14.8	15.75	8	FraGrthFd **FRF**	3.18e	35.5	98	8.95	− 0.07
+ 6.5	9.05	7.25	FrnklnMulti **FMI**	.67a	7.5	118	8.92	− 0.07
+ 8.1	8.74	6.75	FrnklnUnvlTr **FT**	.80a	10.0	213	8.04	+ 0.01
+ 17.9	11.60	8.63	GabelliConv **GCV**	.80a	7.4	72	10.76	− 0.13
+ 3.1	12.69	10	GabelliTr **GAB**	1.08a	9.2	1173	11.79	− 0.06
+ 10.3	15.69	9.32	GabelliMlti **GGT**	1.56e	13.7	115	11.37	− 0.47
+ 1.7	9.38	7.63	GabelliUt **GUT**	.60a	6.7	102	8.90	− 0.02
+ 6.6	39.70	31.49♣	GenAmInv **GAM**	4.05e	10.6	371	38.37	− 0.15
− 9.5	12.98	7.75♣	GermanyFd **GER**	2.39	27.8	604	8.60	+ 0.01
− 13.7	13.02	6.75♣	NewGrmnyFd **GF**	.08	1.0	565	7.66	− 0.14
+ 6.4	14.20	11.69	GlblHiInco **GHI**	1.61	11.7	439	13.76	− 0.09
+ 13.0	12.30	9.88	GlblIncFd **GDF**	1.42	12.2	223	11.65	+ 0.14
+ 31.9	11.10	7.44♣	GtChina **GCH**	.03	.3	115	10.80	− 0.02
+ 6.2	37.81	18.08♣	H&Q Hlth **HQH**	4.97e	19.1	258	26.03	− 0.42
+ 4.9	32.56	15 ♣	H&Q LifeSci **HQL**	4.08e	17.9	131	22.75	− 0.35
− 0.6	9.31	6.63♣	HnckJ BkOpp **BTO**	.77	8.7	1387	8.82	− 0.12
+ 1.8	15.25	12.63♣	HnckJ IncSec **JHS**	1.03m	7.0	65	14.70	...
+ 1.6	20.10	16.56♣	HnckJ Invst **JHI**	1.37m	7.0	134	19.56	− 0.08
+ 4.2	12.65	10.25♣	HnckJ PtGlb **PGD**	.97	7.8	37	12.50	+ 0.10
+ 6.4	12.20	10	HnckJ PtPfd	.86	7.4	25	11.70	+ 0.10
+ 2.9	9.90	7.88♣	HnckJ PtPrem **PDF**	.65	7.2	87	9	+ 0.09
+ 2.3	11	9.06♣	HnckJ PtPremII **PDT**	.78	7.2	121	10.81	+ 0.05
+ 12.1	14.80	11.81♣	HnckJ PtSel **DIV**	1.08	7.4	70	14.64	+ 0.16
+ 2.6	14.19	11.88	HatterasSec **HAT**	1.02	7.5	5	13.66	− 0.05
+ 5.2	9.75	7.63♣	HiIncoFd **HIO**	.97	10.7	770	9.07	+ 0.07
+ 5.4	6.34	4.44	HiYldFd **HYI**	.60	10.5	76	5.73	− 0.02
− 0.5	7	4.76	HiYldPlsFd **HYP**	.87	14.9	1174	5.85	− 0.26
+ 4.4	9.22	7.94	Hyperion02 **HTB**	.10	1.1	151	9.20	...
+ 5.8	9.20	7.63	Hyperion05 **HTO**	.55f	6.0	276	9.19	+ 0.08
+ 2.1	9.50	7.38	HyperionFd **HTR**	.87	9.9	625	8.81	+ 0.01
− 12.0	15.13	9.29	IndiaFd **IFN**	j	...	2180	10.61	+ 0.16

demand conditions in the stock market. As a result, depending on the market outlook and investor expectations, closed-end companies generally trade at a discount or premium to NAV. (They almost never trade at net asset value.) Share price discounts and premiums can at times become quite large. In fact, it's not unusual for such spreads to amount to as much as 25% to 30% of net asset value (occasionally more) depending on market judgments and expectations. And while these funds can trade at either premiums or discounts, price discounts are, in fact, far more common.

Exchange-Traded Funds

Combine some of the operating characteristics of an open-end fund with some of the trading characteristics of a closed-end fund, and what you'll end up with is something called an *exchange-traded fund.* These securities are being promoted as the newest product to hit the fund world, but they're really a recreation of a product that's been around since the early 1990s. Technically, an **exchange-traded fund (ETF)** is a type of open-end mutual fund that trades as a listed security on one of the stock exchanges (mostly the AMEX). Actually, all EFTs thus far (mid-year 2000) have been structured as *index funds* set up to match the performance of a certain segment of the market. They do this by owning all, or a representative sample, of the stocks in a targeted market segment or index. (We'll examine traditional index funds in more detail later in this chapter.) Thus, ETFs offer the professional money management of traditional mutual funds *and* the liquidity of an exchange-traded stock.

exchange-traded fund (ETF) an open-end mutual fund that trades as a listed security on a stock exchange.

Even though these securities are like closed-end funds in that ETFs are traded on listed exchanges, *they are in reality open-end mutual funds,* where the number of shares outstanding can be increased or decreased in response to market demand. That is, although ETFs can be bought or sold like any stock on a listed exchange, *the ETF distributor can also create new shares or redeem old shares.* This is done through a special type of security known as a *payment-in-kind creation unit.* This is done to prevent the fund from trading at (much of) a premium or discount and thereby avoid one of the pitfalls of closed-end funds. For the most part, individual investors are *not* involved in the creation or redemption of shares (that's done with the big institutional investors). Instead, individual investors will buy and sell ETFs in the secondary market by placing orders with their brokers, as they would normally do with any stock.

HOTLINKS

Which are the most active index shares—Nasdaq 100 index shares, SPDRs, Midcap SPDRs, or Diamonds? To find out, visit:

amex.com

By mid-2000, there were more than 60 ETFs listed on the American Stock Exchange, and every one of them was based on some domestic or international stock market index. The biggest and oldest (started in 1993) are based on the S&P 500 and are known as *spiders*. In addition to spiders, there are *diamonds* (which are based on the DJIA) and *qubes* (based on the Nasdaq 100 and so-named because of their QQQ ticker symbol). There also are ETFs based on 19 international markets (from Australia and Canada to Germany, Japan, and the U.K.). Just about every major U.S. index, in fact, has its own ETF. So do a lot of minor indexes (some of which were created by the distributors) that cover very specialized (and sometimes fairly small) segments of the market. The net asset values of ETFs are set at a fraction of the underlying index value at any given time. For example, if the S&P 500 index stands at, say, 1464.46, the ETF on that index will trade at around 146.50 (that is, at about 1/10 of the index). Likewise, the ETF on the Dow is set at 1/100 of the DJIA. (Thus, when the DJIA is at say, 10449.30, the ETF will trade at around 104.50).

ETFs combine many of the advantages of closed-end funds with those of traditional (open-end) index funds. As with closed-end funds, you can buy and sell ETFs at *any time of the day* by placing an order through your broker (and paying a standard commission, just as you would with any other stock). In contrast, you *cannot* trade a traditional open-end fund on an intraday basis; all buy and sell orders for those funds are filled at the end of the trading day, at closing prices. What's more, because ETFs are passively managed, they offer all the advantages of any index fund: low cost, low portfolio turnover, and low taxes. In fact, the fund's tax liability is kept very low, because ETFs rarely distribute any capital gains to shareholders. Thus, you could hold one of these things for decades and never pay a dime in capital gains taxes (at least not until you sell the shares). The *Investing in Action* box on page 366 provides some additional information about ETFs—information that might help you decide whether they are right for you.

Some Important Considerations

When you buy or sell shares in a *closed-end* investment company (or in *ETFs*, for that matter), you pay a commission, just as you would with any other listed or OTC stock. This is not the case with open-end mutual funds, however. The cost of investing in an open-end fund depends on the types of fees and load charges that the fund levies on its investors.

load fund
a mutual fund that charges a commission when shares are bought; also known as a *front-end load fund.*

no-load fund
a mutual fund that does not charge a commission when shares are bought.

low-load fund
a mutual fund that charges a small commission (2% to 3%) when shares are bought.

back-end load
a commission charged on the *sale* of shares in a mutual fund.

12(b)-1 fee
a fee levied annually by some mutual funds to cover management and other operating costs; amounts to as much as 1% of the average net assets.

Load and No-Load Funds The *load charge* on an open-end fund is the commission the investor pays when buying shares in a fund. Generally speaking, the term **load fund** is used to describe a mutual fund that charges a commission when shares are bought. (Such charges are also known as *front-end loads.*) In a **no-load fund** no sales charges are levied. Load charges can be fairly substantial and can amount to as much as 8½% of the *purchase price* of the shares. However, very few funds charge the maximum. Instead, many funds charge commissions of only 2% or 3%. Such funds are known as **low-load funds.**

Although there may be little or no difference in the performance of load and no-load funds, *the cost savings with no-load funds tend to give investors a head start in achieving superior rates of return.* Unfortunately, the true no-load fund is becoming harder to find, as more and more no-loads are becoming *12(b)-1 funds.* While these funds do not directly charge commissions at the time of purchase, they *annually* assess what are known as 12(b)-1 charges to make up for any lost commissions. (These charges are more fully described below.) Overall, less than 40% of the funds sold today are pure no-loads; the rest charge some type of load or fee.

Occasionally, a fund will have a **back-end load,** which means commissions are levied when shares are sold. These loads may amount to as much as 7¼% of the value of the shares sold, although back-end loads tend to decline over time and usually disappear altogether after 5 or 6 years from date of purchase. The stated purpose of back-end loads is to enhance fund stability by discouraging investors from trading in and out of the funds over short investment horizons. In addition, a substantial (and growing) number of funds charge something called a **12(b)-1 fee** that's assessed annually for as long as you own the fund. Known appropriately as *hidden loads,* these fees are designed to help funds (particularly the no-loads) cover their distribution and marketing costs. They can amount to as much as 1% per year of assets under management. In good markets and bad, these fees are paid right off the top, and that can take its toll. Consider, for instance, $10,000 invested in a fund that charges a 1% 12(b)-1 fee. That translates into a charge of $100 a year—certainly not an insignificant amount of money.

The latest trend in mutual fund fees is the so-called *multiple-class sales charge.* You'll find such arrangements at firms like American Capital, Dreyfus, Merrill Lynch, MFS, Keystone, Smith Barney, and Prudential. The mutual

INVESTING in action

Adding ETFs to Your Investment Portfolio

Exchange-traded funds (ETFs), which are one of the fastest-growing investment vehicles today, are similar to index mutual funds but trade like stocks. Each share represents a basket of securities that closely tracks one specific index. New types of ETFs are being introduced regularly, such as bond ETFs that track the Lehman Brothers and other bond indexes. Some fund companies are even proposing actively managed ETFs that don't track an index.

Because ETFs trade on the stock market, it's easy to buy and sell them through a brokerage account throughout the day—not just after the markets close, as with mutual funds. ETFs also have extremely low costs because they have no research or management fees and minimal back-office costs. For example, annual expenses for SPDRS (S&P 500 Depositary Receipts) are just 0.12%—$12 per $10,000 investment; Barclays iShares S&P 500 charges just 0.0945%. Another benefit is their tax advantage. Because they are not actively managed, ETFs have little or no taxable income and capital gains distributions.

ETFs do have some drawbacks, though. Although fees are low, investors incur brokerage commissions any time they trade ETFs, as well as a small bid/ask spread. Frequent trades can quickly wipe out any profits. ETFs do not offer dividend reinvestment or monthly purchase programs. Traditional mutual funds can reinvest dividends and capital gains immediately to continuously compound their gains, whereas ETFs can reinvest the cash only monthly or quarterly. And some ETFs have highly concentrated portfolios: for example, 43% of QQQs' holdings are in just 10 stocks, with Cisco and Intel accounting for about 15% of the portfolio.

Despite the downside, ETFs offer investors a quick way to get exposure to a market segment. They provide diversification and precise market tracking, and they appeal to both active traders and long-term investors. It's easy to add a specific equity component on the basis of one of the following:

- **Style:** Choose an ETF that tracks a growth or value index such as the S&P 400 Mid Cap Barra Growth or the S&P 600 Small Cap Value.
- **Size:** Market capitalization is another ETF segmentation strategy. You will find ETFs that track small-, mid-, and large-caps, using the S&P, Dow, Nasdaq, and Russell indexes.
- **Sector**: Many ETFs, including Barclays' iShares and Merrill Lynch HOLDRS, target specific industries or sectors, such as biotechnology, real estate investment trusts, pharmaceuticals, telecommunications, health care, energy, noncyclical companies, and subsectors of the Internet industry. They offer exposure to a small part of an industry that mutual funds may not cover and give broader coverage than one could obtain buying several individual stocks.
- **Region:** ETFs make it easy to achieve geographical diversification—whether to just one country or to an entire region—without the high loads and fees of most foreign stock funds. Barclays' iShares include Webs (World Equity Benchmark shares) that track the Morgan Stanley Capital International (MSCI) indexes for 20 countries as well as regional ETFs that track the S&P Europe 350 and Global 100 and MSCI European Monetary Union. However, international index funds are a less costly way to get broad exposure.

The bottom line on any investment is how well it performs over time. Investors can track ETF total returns and compare them to traditional mutual funds in similar sectors at Morningstar.com (**www.morningstar.com/Cover/ETF.html**) and with the *Wall Street Journal's* monthly Mutual Fund Report.

Sources: "About iShares," Barclays iShares Web site, www.ishares.com; "Better Than Index Funds," *Forbes*, August 21, 2000, p. 268; Diane Forrest, "Weighing the Risks," *Maclean's*, January 29, 2001; Odette Galli, "Not Just for Day Traders," *Smart Money*, September 2000, p. 124; Eric Jacobson, "Barclays to Roll Out Exchange-Traded Bond Funds, *Morningstar.com*, January 8, 2001, downloaded from www.morningstar.com; Mark Mclaughlin, "Xtreme Indexing," *Kiplinger's Personal Finance Magazine*, June, 2000; and Anne Tergesen, "All Abroad for Exchange-Traded Funds," *Business Week*, September 11, 2000, p. 166; and Chet Currier, "Understanding Prospectuses Leads to Informed Investing," *Dallas Morning News*, June 18, 2000, p. 11H.

fund simply issues different classes of stocks on the same portfolio of securities, with each class having a different fee structure. For example, class A shares might have normal (relatively high) front-end loads; class B shares might have no front-end loads but substantial back-end loads along with a modest annual 12(b)-1 fee; and class C shares might carry only maximum 12(b)-1 fees. In other words, you "choose your own poison."

To try to bring some semblance of order to fund charges and fees, in 1992 the SEC instituted a series of caps on mutual fund fees. Under the 1992 rules, a mutual fund cannot charge more than 8½% in *total sales charges and fees*, including front- and back-end loads as well as 12(b)-1 fees. Thus, if a fund charges a 5% front-end load and a 1% 12(b)-1 fee, it can charge a maximum of only 2½% in back-end load charges without violating the 8½% cap. In addition, the SEC set a 1% cap on annual 12(b)-1 fees and, perhaps more significantly, stated that true no-load funds cannot charge more than 0.25% in annual 12(b)-1 fees. If they do, they have to drop the no-load label in their sales and promotional material.

Other Fees and Costs Another cost of owning mutual funds is the *management fee*. This is the compensation paid to the professional managers who administer the fund's portfolio. It must be paid regardless of whether a fund is load or no-load, and whether it is an open- or closed-end fund, or an exchange-traded fund. Unlike load charges, which are one-time costs, management fees and 12(b)-1 charges, if imposed, are levied annually. They are paid regardless of the fund's performance. In addition, there are the administrative costs of operating the fund. These are fairly modest and represent the normal cost of doing business (e.g., the commissions paid when the fund buys and sells securities). The various fees that funds charge generally range from less than 0.5% to as much as 3% or 4% of average assets under management. Total expense ratios bear watching, because high expenses take their toll on performance. As a point of reference, in 2000, domestic stock funds had average expense ratios of around 1.45%, foreign stock funds of around 1.90%, stock index funds of around 0.65%, and domestic bond funds of around 1.10%.

A final cost of mutual funds is the taxes paid on securities transactions. To avoid double taxation, nearly all mutual funds operate as *regulated investment companies*. This means that all (or nearly all) of the dividend and interest income is passed on to the investor, as are any capital gains realized when securities are sold. The mutual fund therefore passes the tax liability on to its shareholders. This holds true whether such distributions are reinvested in the company (in the form of additional mutual fund shares) or paid out in cash. Mutual funds annually provide each stockholder with a summary report on the amount of dividends and capital gains received and the amount of taxable income earned by the fund shareholder.

Keeping Track of Fund Fees and Loads Critics of the mutual fund industry have come down hard on the proliferation of fund fees and charges. Some argue that the different charges and fees are meant to do one thing: confuse the investor. A lot of funds were going to great lengths (lowering a cost here, tacking on a fee there, hiding a charge somewhere else) to make themselves look like something they weren't. The funds were following the letter of the law, and were fully disclosing all their expenses and fees. The trouble was that the funds were able to hide all but the most conspicuous charges in "legalese." Fortunately, steps have been taken to bring fund fees and loads out into the open.

For one thing, fund charges are more widely reported now than they were in past. Most notably, today you can find detailed information about the types and amounts of fees and charges on just about any mutual fund by accessing a variety of Web sites, such as www.quicken.com/investments/mutualfunds, www.kiplinger.com/investing/funds/, or www.morningstar.com/Cover/Funds.html. Figure 11.4 provides excerpts from one of these sites and shows the kind of information that's readily available, at no charge, on the Web.

HOTLINKS

Study the impact of load, expense ratio, 12b-1 fee, and taxes on fund performance at:

www.smartmoney.com/fundfeeanalyzer/

Alternatively, you can use the mutual fund quotes that appear daily in most major, large-city newspapers or in the *Wall Street Journal.* For example, look at the *Wall Street Journal* quotations in Figure 11.5. Note the use of the letters *r, p,* and *t* behind the name of the fund. An *r* behind a fund's name means that the fund charges some type of redemption fee, or back-end load, when you sell your shares. This is the case, for example, with the Dreyfus Aggressive Value Fund. A *p* in the quotes means that the fund levies a 12(b)-1 fee, which you'll have to pay, for example, if you invest in the Dreyfus Global Growth Fund. Finally, a *t* indicates funds that charge both redemption fees and 12(b)-1 fees. Note, for example, that the FBR Financial Services Fund is one such fund.

The quotations, of course, tell you only the *kinds* of fees charged by the funds. They do not tell you *how much* is charged. To get the specifics on the amount charged, you'll have to turn to other sources. Furthermore, these published quotes (which are fairly representative of what you'd find in other major newspapers) *tell you nothing about the front-end loads,* if any, charged by the funds. Refer once again to the quotes in Figure 11.5, and compare the Dodge & Cox Balanced and FPA Paramount Funds. They look alike, don't they? But they're not. For even though neither of them charges redemption or 12(b)-1 fees, only one of them is a no-load fund. Dodge & Cox does not charge a front-end load, and is in fact a no-load fund. The FPA fund, in contrast, comes with a hefty 6½% front-end load. As a point of interest, the other three funds highlighted in Figure 11.5—Dreyfus Aggressive Value, Global Growth, and FBR Financial Services—don't charge front-end loads either, but you'd never know that from the quotes. (It should be noted that the *Wall Street Journal* also publishes a *Monthly Mutual Fund Review* on the first or second Monday of each month. Among other things, it provides some specifics on front-end loads and annual expense charges, including 12(b)-1 fees.

In addition to the public sources noted above, the mutual funds themselves are required by the SEC to disclose all of their fees and expenses fully in a standardized, easy-to-understand format. Every fund profile or prospectus must contain, up front, a fairly detailed *fee table,* much like the one illustrated in Table 11.2. This table has three parts. The first specifies *all shareholder transaction costs.* In effect, this tells you what it's going to cost to buy and sell shares in the mutual fund. The next section lists the *annual operating expenses* of the fund. Showing these expenses as a percentage of average net assets, the fund must break out management fees, 12(b)-1 fees, and any other expenses. The third section provides a rundown of *the total cost over time* of buying,

FIGURE 11.4 Fund Fees and Charges on the Web

The Internet has become the motherlode of information on just about any topic imaginable, including mutual fund fees and charges. Here's an example of information taken from the Kiplinger Web site. These excerpts show, among other things, all the fees and expenses levied by each fund. The two funds in the exhibit provide a stark contrast in fees and expenses. The Smith Barney fund carries both a high front-end load and a 12(b)-1 fee, plus a substantial management fee/expense ratio. The Vanguard fund, on the other hand, provides a vivid example of a truly low-cost fund: no loads or fees and a *very low* management fee/expense ratio. (*Source:* www.kiplinger.com/investing/funds/, August 2, 2000.)

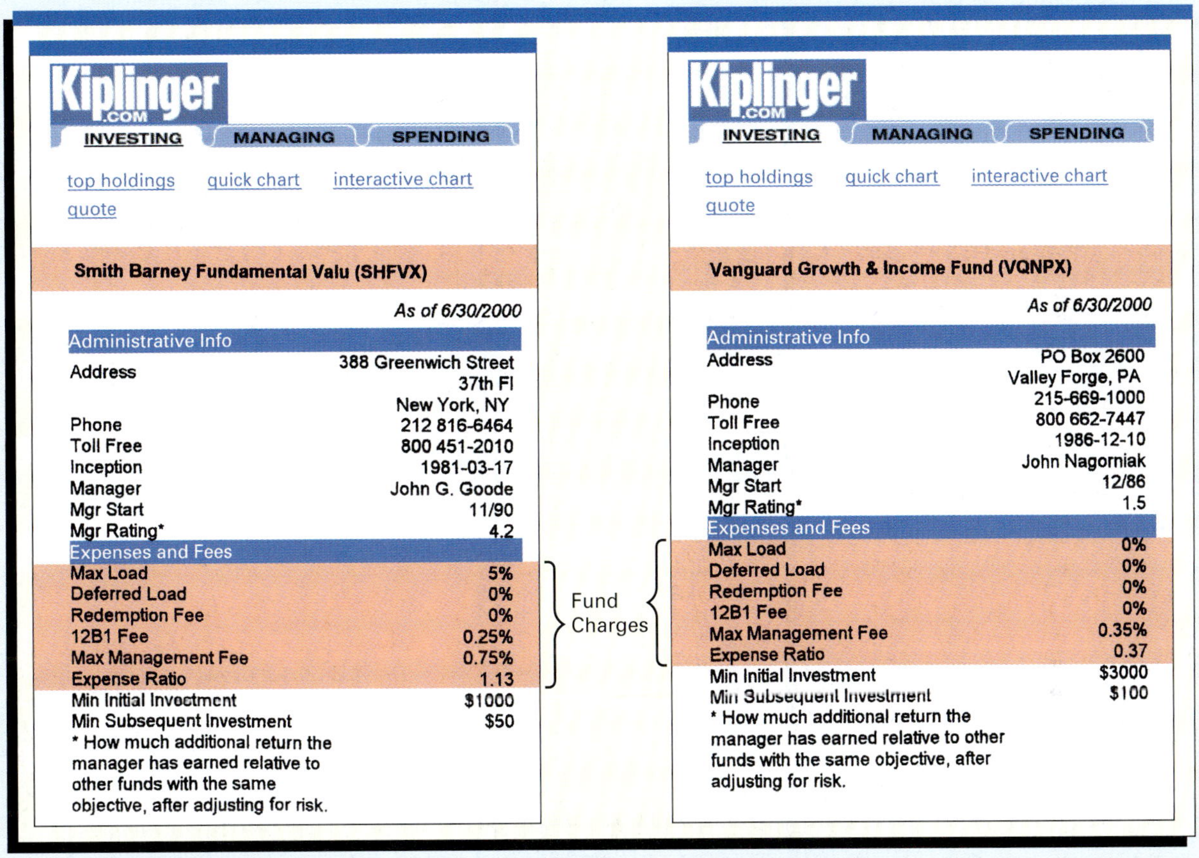

Kiplinger.COM — INVESTING | MANAGING | SPENDING

top holdings quick chart interactive chart quote

Smith Barney Fundamental Valu (SHFVX)

As of 6/30/2000

Administrative Info	
Address	388 Greenwich Street 37th Fl New York, NY
Phone	212 816-6464
Toll Free	800 451-2010
Inception	1981-03-17
Manager	John G. Goode
Mgr Start	11/90
Mgr Rating*	4.2
Expenses and Fees	
Max Load	5%
Deferred Load	0%
Redemption Fee	0%
12B1 Fee	0.25%
Max Management Fee	0.75%
Expense Ratio	1.13
Min Initial Investment	$1000
Min Subsequent Investment	$50

* How much additional return the manager has earned relative to other funds with the same objective, after adjusting for risk.

Fund Charges

Kiplinger.COM — INVESTING | MANAGING | SPENDING

top holdings quick chart interactive chart quote

Vanguard Growth & Income Fund (VQNPX)

As of 6/30/2000

Administrative Info	
Address	PO Box 2600 Valley Forge, PA
Phone	215-669-1000
Toll Free	800 662-7447
Inception	1986-12-10
Manager	John Nagorniak
Mgr Start	12/86
Mgr Rating*	1.5
Expenses and Fees	
Max Load	0%
Deferred Load	0%
Redemption Fee	0%
12B1 Fee	0%
Max Management Fee	0.35%
Expense Ratio	0.37
Min Initial Investment	$3000
Min Subsequent Investment	$100

* How much additional return the manager has earned relative to other funds with the same objective, after adjusting for risk.

selling, and owning the fund. This part of the table contains both transaction and operating expenses and shows what the total costs would be over hypothetical 1-, 3-, 5-, and 10-year holding periods. To ensure consistency and comparability, the funds must follow a rigid set of guidelines when constructing the illustrative costs.

HOTLINKS

For a detailed discussion of two other types of investment companies—real estate investment trusts and annuities—see our Web site, at:

www.awl.com/gitman_joehnk

Other Types of Investment Companies

In addition to open-end, closed-end, and exchange-traded funds, there are three other types of investment companies: (1)

FIGURE 11.5

Mutual Fund Quotes

Open-end mutual funds are listed separately from other securities. They have their own quotation system, an example of which, from the *Wall Street Journal,* is shown here. Note that these securities are quoted in dollars and cents and that the quotes include not only the fund's NAV but year-to-date (YTD) returns as well. Also included is an indication of whether the fund charges redemption and/or 12(b)-1 fees. (*Source: Wall Street Journal,* August 2, 2000.)

Mutual Fund Quotations

Name	NAV	Net Chg	YTD %ret
EqInc p	20.67	+0.30	− 4.0
EqVal p	NA	...	NA
GovCorp p	12.01	+0.02	+ 3.5
Gro&Inc p	28.58	+0.07	− 3.7
HiQual p	11.30	+0.01	+ 3.4
HiYldBd p	9.92	−0.01	− 0.7
InLHorSA	13.26	+0.04	− 1.6
IntGvt p	10.77	+0.01	+ 3.8
IntHorSA	12.39	+0.03	− 0.6
IntlEq p	19.25	+0.12	− 6.5
LgHorSA	11.86	+0.04	− 3.5
SpecEq p	23.87	−0.26	− 2.5
StHorSA	10.55	+0.02	+ 2.2
StkIdx p	11.24	+0.05	NN
Dodge & Cox:			
Balan	64.01	+0.55	+ 2.6
Inco	11.56	+0.03	+ 4.8
Stock	95.63	+1.12	+ 1.0
Dom Social	39.99	+0.01	− 4.5
DomISocial	23.15	...	− 4.3
Dreyfus:			
A Bond	13.53x	−0.05	+ 4.7
AggGr	14.32	−0.05	− 0.3
AggVal r	26.82	+0.43	+11.8
Aprec p	46.51	+0.42	+ 2.7
Balanced	15.74	+0.09	+ 0.9
BdMktInv p	9.53	+0.01	NN
BsicIntMu	12.88	+0.01	+ 5.3
BsicMu	12.93	+0.01	+ 7.2
CalTx r	14.23	+0.02	+ 7.7
Cal Int r	13.54	...	+ 5.0
CT Int r	13.48	...	+ 3.7
DiscIntR	11.77	+0.02	+ 4.3
Discp	42.85	+0.12	+ 0.2
DisSmCp t	18.05	+0.01	− 5.6
Dr500In t	42.14	+0.22	− 1.8
Dreyf	12.68	+0.05	− 3.2
DreyMid r	24.34	+0.14	+10.9
EmgLd	37.24	−0.07	+ 1.4
EmgMkt	14.19	+0.08	− 8.5
FL Int r	12.97	+0.01	+ 3.7
GlbGrth p	37.91	+0.11	−11.2
GnCA r	12.62	+0.01	+ 7.7
GMBd t	13.36	+0.01	+ 5.9
GNY t	19.06	+0.01	+ 6.2
GNM p	13.86x	−0.05	+ 3.9
GrInc	18.78	+0.18	− 2.3
FBR Funds:			
FinSvcA t	14.45	+0.15	+ 5.9
SmCpFinA p	14.38	+0.05	+ 7.0
SmCpVl A p	19.20	−0.54	+ 1.9
FFTW Funds:			
Instl	8.12	+0.01	− 3.9
LtdDur	9.67	...	+ 3.8
US Sht	9.65	−0.01	+ 3.6
WWFxIHg	10.72	+0.01	NN
WWFxdIn	8.75	+0.01	− 1.0
FMI FocusFd	33.85	−0.19	+29.6
FPA Funds:			
Capit	25.47	+0.08	+ 0.7
NwInc	10.32	+0.01	+ 3.9
Parmt	7.22	...	−20.8
Peren	19.70	+0.03	− 0.2
FTI Funds:			
Bond	9.33	+0.01	+ 3.8
IntlEq	16.86	+0.03	−12.4
LCapGr	12.39	+0.02	+ 2.8
LCapGrIn	10.11	+0.01	+ 1.3
Muni	9.60	...	+ 3.6
SmCapEq	23.54	−0.11	+ 4.0
Fairmt	19.85	−0.19	−16.5
Fasciano	32.98	−0.15	+ 0.8

NAV: The price you get when you *sell* shares, or what you pay when you *buy* no-load funds.

Dodge & Cox Balanced: A true no-load fund (no front-end, back-end, or 12b-1 fees).

Dreyfus Aggressive Value: A fund with a redemption fee (r).

Dreyfus Global Growth: A fund with a 12(b)-1 fee (p).

FBR Financial Services: A fund with both a redemption fee and a 12(b)-1 fee (t).

FPA Paramount: A fund with a 6½% front-end load (but no redemption or 12(b)-1 fees).

TABLE 11.2 Mutual Fund Fee Table (Required by Federal Law)

The following table describes the fees and expenses that are incurred when you buy, hold, or sell shares of the fund.

Shareholder Fees (paid by the investor directly)	
Maximum sales charge (load) on purchases (as a % of offering price)	3%
Sales charge (load) on reinvested distributions	None
Deferred sales charge (load) on redemptions	None
Exchange fees	None
Annual account maintenance fee (for accounts under $2,500)	$12.00
Annual fund operating expenses (paid from fund assets}	
Management fee	0.45%
Distribution and Service (12b-1) fee	None
Other expenses	0.20%
Total annual fund operating expenses	0.65%

Example

This example is intended to help an investor compare the cost of investing in different funds. The example assumes a $10,000 investment in the fund for one, three, five, and ten years and then a redemption of all fund shares at the end of those periods. The example also assumes that an investment returns 5 percent each year and that the fund's operating expenses remain the same. Although actual costs may be higher or lower, based on these assumptions an investor's costs would be:

1 year	$364
3 years	$502
5 years	$651
10 years	$1,086

HOTLINKS

For a detailed discussion of two other types of investment companies—real estate investment trusts and annuities—see our Web site, at:

www.awl.com/gitman_joehnk

unit investment trusts, (2) real estate investment trusts, and (3) annuities. Unit investment trusts and annuities are similar to mutual funds to the extent that they, too, invest primarily in marketable securities, such as stocks and bonds. Real estate investment trusts, in contrast, invest primarily in various types of real estate–related investments, like mortgages. We'll look at unit investment trusts in this section. The other two types of investment companies are not discussed in this book.

unit investment trust (UIT)
a type of investment vehicle whereby the trust sponsors put together a fixed/unmanaged portfolio of securities and then sell ownership units in the portfolio to individual investors.

Unit Investment Trusts A **unit investment trust** (UIT) represents little more than an interest in an *unmanaged* pool of investments. UITs are like mutual funds to the extent that they involve a portfolio of securities. But that's where the similarity ends. Once a portfolio of securities is put together, it is simply held in safekeeping for investors under conditions set down in a trust agreement. Traditionally, these portfolios were made up of various types of *fixed-income securities,* with long-term municipal bonds being the most popular type of investment vehicle. There is no trading in the portfolios, so the returns, or yields, are fixed and fairly predictable—at least for the short term. Not surprisingly, these unit investment trusts appeal mainly to income-oriented investors looking for a safe, steady stream of income.

In the early 1990s, brokerage firms began aggressively marketing a new type of investment product, the *stock-oriented UIT.* These new equity trusts caught on quickly with investors seeking capital gains and attractive returns. By year-end 1999, these products accounted for nearly 70% of this $95 billion market. A popular theme among equity trusts is the "dogs of the Dow" strategy (selecting and holding the five or ten companies in the DJIA that pay the highest dividend yields), although growth stock, high dividend yield, and market index trusts also do well. Stock trusts are normally offered with terms that range from 1-year (typical of the Dow-dogs products) to 5 years or more (found on many stock index trusts). Except for the shorter terms (1 to 5 years for equity trusts vs. 15 to 30 years for fixed-income products), these trusts are no different from the traditional bond-oriented UITs: Once the portfolios are put together, they usually remain untouched for the life of the trust.

Various sponsoring brokerage houses put together these pools of securities and then sell units of the pool to investors. (Each unit is like a share in a mutual fund.) For example, a brokerage house might put together a pool of corporate securities that amounts to, say, $100 million. The sponsoring firm would then sell units in this pool to the investing public at anywhere from $250 (for many equity trusts) to $1,000 per unit (common for fixed-income products). The sponsoring organization does little more than routine recordkeeping. It services the investments by collecting coupons or dividends and distributing the income (often on a monthly basis) to the holders of the trust units.

There is a dark side to UITs, however. *They tend to be very costly.* These products can have not only substantial up-front transaction costs but also hefty annual fees. For example, many equity UITs assess load charges of 1% to 3% and then another 1½% to 2½% in annual fees. Both of these amounts are well above what you'd pay for a typical equity mutual fund. Brokers argue that they earn those fat fees by removing fear and greed from the investment process and by enabling investors to build a well-diversified portfolio at a reasonable cost.

Types of Funds and Services

LG 3 LG 4

Some mutual funds specialize in stocks, others in bonds. Some have maximum capital gains as an investment objective, and some high current income. Some funds appeal to speculators, while others are of interest primarily to income-oriented investors. Every fund has a particular investment objective, and each fund is expected to do its best to conform to its stated investment policy and objective. Categorizing funds according to their investment policies and objectives is a common practice in the mutual fund industry. The categories indicate similarities in how the funds manage their money, and also their risk and return characteristics. Some of the more popular types of mutual funds are growth, aggressive growth, value, equity-income, balanced, growth-and-income, bond, money market, index, sector, socially responsible, asset allocation, and international funds. Let's look now at these various types of mutual funds to see what they are and how they operate.

Types of Mutual Funds

growth fund
a mutual fund whose primary goals are capital gains and long-term growth.

Growth Funds The objective of a **growth fund** is simple: capital appreciation. Long-term growth and capital gains are the primary goals. Growth funds invest principally in well-established, large- or mid-cap companies that have above-average growth potential. They may offer little (if anything) in the way of dividends and current income. Because of the uncertain nature of their investment income, growth funds may involve a fair amount of risk exposure. They are usually viewed as long-term investment vehicles most suitable for the more aggressive investor who wants to build up capital and has little interest in current income.

aggressive growth fund
a highly speculative mutual fund that seeks large profits from capital gains.

Aggressive Growth Funds Aggressive growth funds are the so-called performance funds that tend to increase in popularity when markets heat up. **Aggressive growth funds** are highly speculative investment vehicles that seek large profits from capital gains. Also known as *capital appreciation* or *small-cap* funds, many are fairly small, and their portfolios consist mainly of "high-flying" common stocks. These funds often buy stocks of small, unseasoned companies, stocks with relatively high price/earnings multiples, and common stocks whose prices are highly volatile. They seem to be especially fond of turnaround situations and may even use leverage in their portfolios (i.e., buy stocks on margin); they also use options fairly aggressively, various hedging techniques, and perhaps even short selling. These techniques are designed, of course, to yield big returns. But aggressive funds are also highly speculative and are among the most volatile of all mutual funds. When the markets are good, aggressive growth funds do well; but when the markets are bad, these funds often experience substantial losses.

HOTLINKS

For more information on fund objectives, go to the site listed below. Click on [education] and then [mfs], [How to Read a Prospectus]. Read the objectives ("Investment Style") section.

value fund
a mutual fund that seeks stocks that are undervalued in the market by investing in shares that have low P/E multiples, high dividend yields, and promising futures.

Value Funds **Value funds** confine their investing to stocks considered to be *undervalued* by the market. That is, the funds look for stocks that are fundamentally sound but have yet to be discovered. These funds hold stocks as much for their underlying intrinsic value as for their *growth potential.* In stark contrast to growth funds, value funds look for stocks with relatively low price/earnings ratios, high dividend yields, and moderate amounts of financial leverage. They prefer undiscovered companies that offer the potential for growth, rather than those that are already experiencing rapid growth.

Value investing is not easy. It involves extensive evaluation of corporate financial statements and any other documents that will help fund managers uncover value (investment opportunities) *before the rest of the market does* (that's the key to the low P/Es). And the approach seems to work. For even though value investing is generally regarded as *less risky* than growth investing (lower P/Es, higher dividend yields, and fundamentally stronger companies all translate into reduced risk exposure), the long-term return to investors in value funds is competitive with that from growth funds and even aggressive growth funds. Thus, value funds are often viewed as a viable investment alternative for relatively conservative investors who are looking for the attractive returns that common stocks have to offer, yet want to keep share price volatility and investment risk in check.

equity-income fund
a mutual fund that emphasizes current income and capital preservation and invests primarily in high-yielding common stocks.

Equity-Income Funds **Equity-income funds** emphasize current income by investing primarily in high-yielding common stocks. Capital preservation is also important, and so are capital gains, although capital appreciation is not a primary objective of equity-income funds. These funds invest heavily in high-grade common stocks, some convertible securities and preferred stocks, and occasionally even junk bonds or certain types of high-grade foreign bonds. As far as their stock holdings are concerned, they lean heavily toward blue chips (including perhaps even "baby blues"), public utilities, and financial shares. They like securities that generate hefty dividend yields but also consider potential price appreciation over the longer haul. In general, because of their emphasis on dividends and current income, these funds tend to hold higher-quality securities that are subject to less price volatility than the market as a whole. They're generally viewed as a fairly low-risk way of investing in stocks.

balanced fund
a mutual fund whose objective is to generate a balanced return of both current income and long-term capital gains.

Balanced Funds **Balanced funds** tend to hold a balanced portfolio of both stocks and bonds for the purpose of generating a well-balanced return of both current income and long-term capital gains. In many respects, they're much like equity-income funds, but balanced funds usually put more into fixed-income securities; generally, they keep at least 25% to 50% of their portfolios in bonds. The bonds are used principally to provide current income, and stocks are selected mainly for their long-term growth potential.

The funds can, of course, shift the emphasis in their security holdings one way or the other. Clearly, the more the fund leans toward fixed-income securities, the more income-oriented it will be. For the most part, balanced funds tend to confine their investing to high-grade securities, including growth-oriented blue-chip stocks, high-quality income shares, and high-yielding investment-grade bonds. Balanced funds are usually considered a relatively safe form of investing, in which you can earn a competitive rate of return without having to endure a lot of price volatility.

growth-and-income fund
a mutual fund that seeks both long-term growth and current income, with primary emphasis on capital gains.

Growth-and-Income Funds **Growth-and-income funds** also seek a balanced return made up of both current income and long-term capital gains, but they place a greater emphasis on growth of capital. Unlike balanced funds, growth-and-income funds put most of their money into equities. In fact, it's not unusual for these funds to have 80% to 90% of their capital in common stocks. They tend to confine most of their investing to quality issues, so growth-oriented blue-chip stocks appear in their portfolios, along with a fair amount of high-quality income stocks. Part of the appeal of these funds is the fairly substantial returns many have generated over the long haul. Of course, these funds involve a fair amount of risk, if for no other reason than the emphasis they place on stocks and capital gains. Thus growth-and-income funds are most suitable for those investors who can tolerate the risk and price volatility.

bond fund
a mutual fund that invests in various kinds and grades of bonds, with income as the primary objective.

Bond Funds As the name implies, **bond funds** invest exclusively in various types and grades of bonds—from Treasury and agency bonds to corporates and municipals. Income is the primary investment objective, although capital gains are not ignored. There are three important advantages of buying shares in bond funds rather than investing directly in bonds. First, the bond funds are generally more liquid than direct investments in bonds. Second, they offer a cost-effective way of achieving a high degree of diversification in an otherwise expensive investment vehicle. (Most bonds carry minimum denominations of $1,000 to $5,000.) Third, bond funds will automatically reinvest interest and other income, thereby allowing the investor to earn fully compounded rates of return.

Bond funds are generally considered to be a fairly conservative form of investment. But they are not without risk; that's because *the prices of the bonds held in the fund's portfolio fluctuate with changing interest rates.* Many bond funds are managed pretty conservatively, but a growing number are becoming increasingly aggressive. In fact, much of the growth that bond funds have experienced recently can be attributed to a more aggressive investment attitude. In today's market, investors can find everything from high-grade government bond funds to highly speculative funds that invest in nothing but junk bonds or even in highly volatile derivative securities. Indeed, exotic derivative securities became a real problem in 1993–1994, when many of the bond funds that had large positions in derivatives experienced eye-popping losses. These losses taught investors a valuable lesson: Watch out for funds with heavy exposure to exotic derivative securities, or at least recognize that if the fund is heavily invested in such securities, you may be in for a very bumpy ride.

Bond funds today remain a sound investment and continue to be popular with investors who seek a relatively conservative investment outlet. Here's a list of the different types of domestic bond funds available to investors:

- *Government bond funds,* which invest in U.S. Treasury and agency securities.
- *Mortgage-backed bond funds,* which put their money into various types of mortgage-backed securities of the U.S. government (e.g., GNMA issues). These funds appeal to investors for several reasons: (1) They provide diversification. (2) They are an affordable way to get into mortgage-backed securities. (3) They allow investors (if they so choose) to reinvest the principal portion of the monthly cash flow, thereby enabling them to preserve rather than consume their capital.
- *High-grade corporate bond funds,* which invest chiefly in investment-grade securities rated triple-B or better.
- *High-yield corporate bond funds,* which are risky investments that buy junk bonds for the yields they offer.
- *Convertible bond funds,* which invest primarily in securities (domestic and possibly foreign) that can be converted or exchanged into common stocks. These funds offer investors some of the price stability of bonds, along with the capital appreciation potential of stocks.
- *Municipal bond funds,* which invest in tax-exempt securities and are suitable for investors who seek tax-free income. Like their corporate counterparts, municipal funds can be packaged as either high-grade or high-yield funds. A special type of municipal bond fund is the so-called *single-state fund,* which invests in the municipal issues of only one state, thus producing (for residents of that state) interest income that is *fully exempt* from both federal and state taxes (and possibly even local/city taxes as well).

- *Intermediate-term bond funds,* which invest in bonds with maturities of 7 to 10 years or less and offer not only attractive yields but relatively low price volatility as well. Shorter (2- to 5-year) funds are also available; these shorter-term funds are often used as substitutes for money market investments by investors looking for higher returns on their money, especially when short-term rates are way down.

Clearly, no matter what you're looking for in a fixed-income security, you're likely to find a bond fund that fits the bill. The number and variety of such funds have skyrocketed in the past 15 years or so, and by mid-2000, there were nearly 3,000 publicly traded bond funds that together had almost *$1 trillion* worth of bonds under management.

Money Market Funds The first money market mutual fund, or money fund for short, was set up in November 1972 with just $100,000 in total assets. It was a new idea that applied the mutual fund concept to the buying and selling of short-term money market instruments—bank certificates of deposit, U.S. Treasury bills, and the like. For the first time, investors with modest amounts of capital were given access to the high-yielding money market, where many instruments require minimum investments of $100,000 or more. The idea caught on quickly, and the growth in money funds was nothing short of phenomenal. That growth temporarily peaked in 1982, when the introduction of money market deposit accounts by banks and S&Ls caused money fund assets to level off and eventually decline. It didn't take long for the industry to recover, however, and by mid-2000, there were some 1,200 money funds that together held nearly $1.7 *trillion* in assets.

There are several different kinds of money market mutual funds:

- *General-purpose money funds,* which invest in any and all types of money market investment vehicles, from Treasury bills and bank CDs to corporate commercial paper. The vast majority of money funds are of this type. They invest their money wherever they can find attractive short-term yields.

- *Government securities money funds,* which were established as a way to meet investor concerns for safety. They effectively eliminate any risk of default by confining their investments to Treasury bills and other short-term securities of the U.S. government, or its agencies.

- *Tax-exempt money funds,* which limit their investing to very short (30- to 90-day) tax-exempt municipal securities. Because their income is free from federal income taxes, they appeal predominantly to investors in high tax brackets. The yields on these funds are about 30% to 35% below the returns on other types of money funds, so you need to be in a high enough tax bracket to produce a competitive after-tax return. Some tax-exempt funds confine their investing to the securities of a single state so that residents of high-tax states can enjoy income that's free from both federal and state taxes.

Just about every major brokerage firm has at least four or five money funds of its own, and hundreds more are sold by independent fund distributors. Most require minimum investments of $1,000 (although $2,500 to $5,000 minimums are not uncommon). Because the maximum average maturity of their holdings cannot exceed 90 days, money funds are highly liquid investment vehicles. They're also very low in risk and virtually immune to capital loss, because at least 95% of the fund's assets must be invested in top-rated/prime-grade securities. Since the fund's interest income tends to follow general interest rate conditions, the returns to shareholders are subject to the ups and downs of market interest rates. Even so, the yields on money funds are highly competitive with those of other short-term securities. And with the check-writing privileges they offer, money funds are just as liquid as checking or savings accounts. They are viewed by many investors as a convenient, safe, and profitable way to accumulate capital and temporarily store idle funds.

index fund
a mutual fund that buys and holds a portfolio of stocks (or bonds) equivalent to those in a specific market index.

Index Funds "If you can't beat 'em, join 'em." That saying pretty much describes the idea behind index funds. Essentially, an **index fund** is a type of mutual fund that buys and holds a portfolio of stocks (or bonds) equivalent to those in a market index like the S&P 500. An index fund that's trying to match the S&P 500, for example, would hold the same 500 stocks that are held in that index, in exactly (or very nearly) the same proportions. Rather than trying to beat the market, as most actively managed funds do, *index funds simply try to match the market*. That is, they seek to match the performance of the index on which the fund is based. They do this through low-cost investment management. In fact, in most cases, the whole portfolio is run almost entirely by a computer that matches the fund's holdings with those of the targeted index.

The approach of index funds is strictly buy-and-hold. Indeed, about the only time an index-fund portfolio changes is when the targeted market index alters its "market basket" of securities. (Occasionally an index will drop a few securities and replace them with new ones.) A pleasant by-product of this buy-and-hold approach is that the funds have extremely low portfolio turnover rates and, therefore, very little in *realized* capital gains. As a result, aside from a modest amount of dividend income, these funds produce very little taxable income from year to year, which leads many high-income investors to view them as a type of tax-sheltered investment.

In addition to their tax shelter, these funds provide something else: By simply trying to match the market, index funds actually produce *highly competitive returns*. It's very tough to outperform the market, whether you are a professional money manager or a seasoned individual investor. Index funds readily acknowledge this fact and don't even try to outperform the market; instead, all they try to do is match market returns. Surprisingly, the net result of this strategy, combined with *a very low cost structure,* is that most index funds outperform the vast majority of all other types of stock funds. Historical data show that only about 20% to 25% of stock funds outperform the market. Because an index fund pretty much matches the market, these funds tend to produce better returns than 75% to 80% of competing stock funds. Granted, every now and then the fully managed stock funds will have a year when they outperform index funds. But this is the exception rather than the rule, especially when you look at multi-year returns, covering periods of 3 to 5 years or more—indeed, over most multi-year periods, the vast majority of fully managed stock funds just can't keep up with index funds.

Besides the S&P 500, which is the most popular index, a number of other market indexes are used, including the S&P Midcap 400, the Russell 2000 Small Stock, and the Wilshire 5000 indexes, as well as value-stock indexes, growth-stock indexes, international-stock indexes, and even bond indexes. When picking index funds, be sure to avoid high-cost funds, as such fees significantly *reduce* the chance that the fund will be able to match the market. Also, avoid index funds that use gimmicks as a way to "enhance" yields: That is, rather than follow the index, these funds will "tilt" their portfolios in an attempt to outperform the market. Your best bet is to buy a *true* index fund (one that has no added "bells and whistles"), and a low-cost one at that.

sector fund
a mutual fund that restricts its investments to a particular segment of the market.

Sector Funds One of the hottest products on Wall Street is the so-called **sector fund,** a mutual fund that restricts its investments to a particular sector (or segment) of the market. These funds concentrate their investment holdings in one or more industries that make up the sector being aimed at. For example, a health care sector fund would focus on such industries as drug companies, hospital management firms, medical suppliers, and biotech concerns. The portfolio of a sector fund would consist of promising growth stocks from these particular industries. Among the more popular sector funds are those that concentrate their investments in technology, financial services, leisure and entertainment, natural resources, electronics, chemicals, computers, telecommunications, utilities, and, of course, health care—all the "glamour" industries.

The overriding investment objective of a sector fund is *capital gains.* A sector fund is similar to a growth fund in many respects and should be considered speculative. The sector fund concept is based on the belief that the really attractive returns come from small segments of the market. So rather than diversifying your portfolio across the market, put your money where the action is! It's an interesting notion that may warrant consideration by investors willing to take on the added risks that often accompany these funds.

Socially Responsible Funds For some, investing is far more than just cranking out financial ratios and calculating investment results. To these investors, the security selection process doesn't end with bottom lines, P/E ratios, growth rates, and betas. Rather, it also includes the *active, explicit consideration of moral, ethical, and environmental issues.* The idea is that social concerns should play just as big a role in investment decisions as do profits and other financial matters. Not surprisingly, a number of funds cater to such investors: Known as **socially responsible funds,** they actively and directly incorporate ethics and morality into the investment decision. Their investment decisions revolve around *both* morality and profitability.

socially responsible fund
a mutual fund that actively and directly incorporates ethics and morality into the investment decision.

Socially responsible funds consider only certain companies for inclusion in their portfolios. If a company doesn't meet the fund's moral, ethical, or environmental tests, fund managers simply won't consider buying the stock, no matter how good the bottom line looks. Generally speaking, these funds refrain from investing in companies that derive revenues from tobacco, alcohol, gambling, or weapons, or that operate nuclear power plants. In addition, the funds tend to favor firms that produce "responsible" products or services, that have strong employee relations and positive environmental records, and that are socially responsive to the communities in which they operate. Although these screens might seem to eliminate a lot of stocks from consideration, these funds (most of which are fairly small) still find plenty of securities to choose from. As far as performance is concerned, the general perception is that there's a price to pay, in the form of lower average returns, for socially responsible investing. That's not too surprising, however, for whenever you add more investment hurdles, you're likely to reduce return potential. But to those who truly believe in socially responsible investing, the sacrifice apparently is worth it.

Asset Allocation Funds Studies have shown that the most important decision an investor can make is where to allocate his or her investment assets. As we saw in Chapter 5, *asset allocation* involves deciding how you're going to divide up your investments among different types of securities. For example, what portion of your money do you want to devote to money market securities, what portion to stocks, and what portion to bonds? Asset allocation deals in broad terms (types of securities) and does not address individual security selection. Strange as it may seem, asset allocation has been found to be a far more important determinant of total portfolio returns than individual security selection.

Because many individual investors have a tough time making asset allocation decisions, the mutual fund industry has created a product to do the job for them. Whereas most mutual funds concentrate on one type of investment—whether stocks, bonds, or money market securities—asset allocation funds put money into all these markets. Many of them also include foreign securities in the asset allocation scheme. Some even include inflation-resistant investments, such as gold or real estate. By mid-year 2000, there were nearly 300 asset allocation funds in existence. All were designed for people who want to hire fund managers not only to select individual securities but also to allocate money among the various markets.

Here's how a typical asset allocation fund works. The money manager establishes a desired allocation mix, which might look something like this: 50% of the portfolio goes to U.S. stocks, 30% to bonds, 10% to foreign securities, and 10% to money market securities. Securities are then purchased for the fund in these proportions, and the overall portfolio maintains the desired mix. Actually, each segment of the fund is managed almost as a separate portfolio. Thus securities within, say, the stock portion are bought, sold, and held as the market dictates.

What really separates asset allocation funds from the rest of the pack is that *as market conditions change over time, the asset allocation mix changes as well.* For example, if the U.S. stock market starts to soften, funds will be moved out of stocks to some other area. As a result, the stock portion of the portfolio might drop to, say, 35%, and the foreign securities portion might increase to 25%. Of course, there's no assurance that the money manager will make the right moves at the right time, but the expectation is that he or she will. (It's interesting to note that *balanced funds* are really a form of asset allocation fund, except that they tend to follow a *fixed-mix* approach to asset allocation. That is, the fund may put, say, 60% of the portfolio into stocks and 40% into bonds, and then pretty much stick to that mix, no matter what the markets are doing.)

Asset allocation funds are supposed to provide investors with one-stop shopping. That is, you find an asset allocation fund that fits your needs and invest in it, rather than buying a couple of stock funds, a couple of bond funds, and so on. The success of these funds rests not only on how well the money manager picks securities but also on how well he or she times the market and moves capital among different segments of the market.

international fund
a mutual fund that does all or most of its investing in foreign securities.

International Funds In their search for higher yields and better returns, U.S. investors have shown a growing interest in foreign securities. Sensing an opportunity, the mutual fund industry was quick to respond with a proliferation of so-called **international funds**—a type of mutual fund that does all or most of its investing in foreign securities. Just compare the number of international funds that are around today with those in existence a few years ago: In 1985 there were only about 40 of these funds; by 2000, the number had grown to nearly 1,900. The fact is that a lot of people would like to invest in foreign securities but simply don't have the experience or know-how to do so. International funds may be just the vehicle for such investors, *provided they have at least a basic appreciation of international economics.* Because these funds deal with the international economy, balance-of-trade positions, and currency valuations, investors should have a fundamental understanding of what these issues are and how they can affect fund returns.

Technically, the term *international fund* describes a type of fund that invests *exclusively in foreign securities.* Such funds often confine their activities to specific geographic regions (e.g., Mexico, Australia, Europe, or the Pacific Rim). In contrast, *global funds* invest not only in foreign securities but also in U.S. companies—usually multinational firms. As a rule, global funds provide more diversity and, with access to both foreign and domestic markets, can go wherever the action is.

Regardless of whether they're global or international (we'll use the term *international* to apply to both), you'll find just about any type of fund you could possibly want in the international sector. There are international stock funds, international bond funds, even international money market funds. There are aggressive growth funds, balanced funds, long-term growth funds, high-grade bond funds, and so forth. There are funds that confine their investing to large, established markets (like Japan, Germany, and Australia) and others that stick to the more exotic (and risky) emerging markets (such as Thailand, Mexico, Chile, and even former Communist countries like Poland). No matter what your investment philosophy or objective, you're likely to find what you're looking for in the international area.

Basically, these funds attempt to take advantage of international economic developments in two ways: (1) by capitalizing on changing market conditions and (2) by positioning themselves to benefit from devaluation of the dollar. They can make money either from rising share prices in a foreign market or, perhaps just as important, from a falling dollar (which in itself produces capital gains for U.S. investors in international funds). Many of these funds, however, attempt to protect their investors from currency exchange risks by using various types of *hedging strategies.* That is, by using foreign currency options and futures, or some other type of derivative product, the fund tries to eliminate (or reduce) the effects of fluctuating currency exchange rates. Some funds, in fact, do this on a permanent basis: In essence, these funds hedge away exchange risk so that they can concentrate on the higher returns offered by the foreign securities themselves. Others use currency hedges only occasionally, when they feel there's a real chance of a substantial swing in currency values. But even with currency hedging, international funds are still considered fairly high-risk investments and should be used only by investors who understand and are able to tolerate such risks.

Investor Services

Ask most investors why they buy a particular mutual fund and they'll probably tell you that the fund provides the kind of income and return they're looking for. Now, no one would question the importance of return in the investment decision, but there are some other important reasons for investing in mutual funds, not the least of which are the valuable services they provide. Some of the most sought-after *mutual fund services* are automatic investment and reinvestment plans, regular income programs, conversion and phone-switching privileges, and retirement programs.

automatic investment plan
a mutual fund service that allows shareholders to automatically send fixed amounts of money from their paychecks or bank accounts into the fund.

Automatic Investment Plans It takes money to make money. For an investor, that means being able to accumulate the capital to put into the market. Unfortunately, that's not always easy. But mutual funds have come up with a program that makes savings and capital accumulation as painless as possible. The program is the **automatic investment plan.** This service allows fund shareholders to automatically funnel fixed amounts of money *from their paychecks or bank accounts* into a mutual fund. It's much like a payroll deduction plan.

This fund service has become very popular, because it enables shareholders to invest on a regular basis without having to think about it. Just about every fund group offers some kind of automatic investment plan for virtually all of its stock and bond funds. To enroll, you simply fill out a form authorizing the fund to siphon a set amount (usually a minimum of \$25 to \$100 per period) from your bank account or paycheck at regular intervals, such as monthly or quarterly. Once enrolled, you'll be buying more shares every month or quarter (most funds deal in fractional shares). Of course, if it's a load fund, you'll still have to pay normal sales charges on your periodic investments. To remain diversified, you can divide your money among as many funds (within a given fund family) as you like. Finally, you can get out of the program any time, without penalty, by simply calling the fund. Although convenience is perhaps the chief advantage of automatic investment plans, they also make solid investment sense: One of the best ways of building up a sizable amount of capital is to *add funds to your investment program systematically over time.* The importance of making regular contributions to your investment portfolio cannot be overstated; it ranks right up there with compound interest.

automatic reinvestment plan
a mutual fund service that enables shareholders to automatically buy additional shares in the fund through the reinvestment of dividends and capital gains income.

Automatic Reinvestment Plans An automatic reinvestment plan is another of the real draws of mutual funds and is offered by just about every open-ended fund. Whereas automatic investment plans deal with money the shareholder is putting into a fund, automatic *re*investment plans deal with the dividends the funds pay to their shareholders. Much like the dividend reinvestment plans we looked at with stocks (in Chapter 6), the **automatic reinvestment plans** of mutual funds enable you to keep your capital fully employed. Through this service, dividend and/or capital gains income is automatically used to buy additional shares in the fund (most funds deal in fractional shares). Such purchases are often commission-free. Keep in mind, however, that even though you may reinvest all dividends and capital gains distributions, the IRS still treats them as cash receipts and taxes them as investment income in the year in which they were received.

Automatic reinvestment plans are especially attractive because they enable you to earn fully compounded rates of return. That is, by plowing back profits, you can essentially put them to work in generating even more earnings. Indeed, the effects of these plans on total accumulated capital over the long run can be substantial. Figure 11.6 shows the long-term impact of one

FIGURE 11.6 The Effects of Reinvesting Income

Reinvesting dividends or capital gains can have a tremendous impact on one's investment position. This graph shows the results of a hypothetical investor who initially invested $10,000 and, for a period of 15 years, reinvested all dividends and capital gains distributions in additional fund shares. (No adjustment has been made for any income taxes payable by the shareholder, which is appropriate so long as the fund was held in an IRA or Keogh account.) (*Source: Morningstar Principia.*)

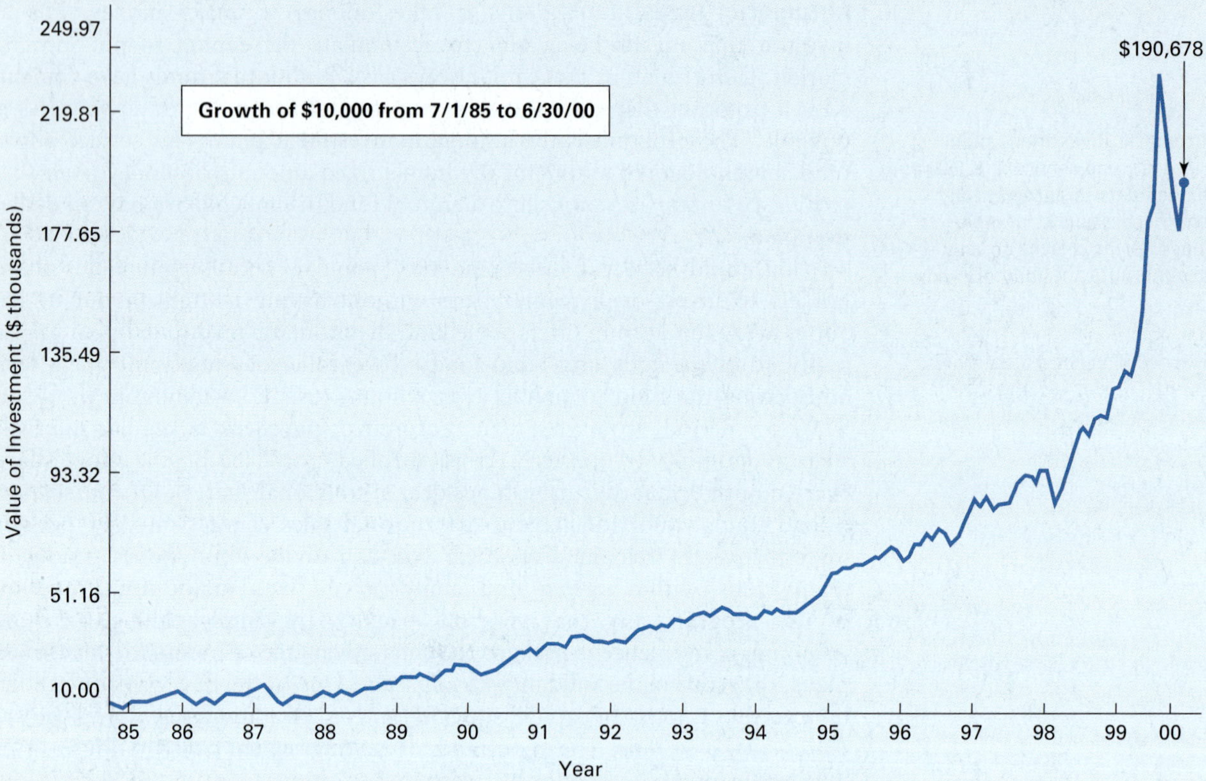

such plan. (These are the actual performance numbers for a *real* mutual fund, Fidelity Growth Company.) In the illustration, we assume the investor starts out with $10,000 and, except for the reinvestment of dividends and capital gains, *adds no new capital over time.* Even so, note that the initial investment of $10,000 grew to nearly $191,000 over a 15-year period (which amounts to a compounded rate of return of almost 21%). Of course, not all periods will match this performance, nor will all mutual funds be able to perform as well, even in strong markets. The point is that as long as care is taken in selecting an appropriate fund, *attractive benefits can be derived from the systematic accumulation of capital offered by automatic reinvestment plans.*

systematic withdrawal plan
a mutual fund service that enables shareholders to automatically receive a predetermined amount of money every month or quarter.

Regular Income Although automatic investment and reinvestment plans are great for the long-term investor, what about the investor who's looking for a steady stream of income? Once again, mutual funds have a service to meet this need. Called a **systematic withdrawal plan,** it's offered by most open-ended funds. Once enrolled in one of these plans, an investor automatically receives a predetermined amount of money every month or quarter. Most funds require a minimum investment of $5,000 or more in order to participate. The size of the minimum payment must normally be $50 or more per period (with no limit on the maximum). The funds will pay out the monthly or quarterly income first from dividends and realized capital gains. If this source proves to be inadequate and the shareholder so authorizes, the fund can then tap the principal or original paid-in capital to meet the required periodic payments.

Conversion Privileges and Phone Switching Sometimes investors find it necessary to switch out of one fund and into another. For example, an investor's objectives or the investment climate itself may have changed. **Conversion** (or **exchange**) **privileges** were devised to meet such needs conveniently and economically. Investment management companies that offer a number of different funds—known as **fund families**—often provide conversion privileges. These enable shareholders to move easily from one fund to another. With *phone switching* you simply pick up the phone to move money among funds. The only constraint is that the switches must be confined to the same *family* of funds. For example, you can switch from a Dreyfus growth fund to a Dreyfus money fund, or any other fund managed by Dreyfus.

conversion (exchange) privilege
feature of a mutual fund that allows shareholders to move money from one fund to another, within the same family of funds.

fund families
different kinds of mutual funds offered by a single investment management company.

With some fund families, the alternatives open to investors seem almost without limit. Indeed, some of the larger families offer literally hundreds of funds. Fidelity has over 300 different funds in its family: from high-performance stock funds to bond funds, tax-exempt funds, a couple of dozen sector funds, and a couple of dozen money funds. More than 400 fund families are in operation today. They all provide low-cost conversion/phone-switching privileges. Some even provide these privileges free, although most have limits on the number of times such switches can occur each year. Twenty of the largest fund families are listed in Table 11.3 on page 384. Together these 20 families have nearly $2.5 *trillion* in assets under management and offer more than 3,400 different mutual funds to the investing public. (Many of these funds are actually duplicates of the same portfolio, because fund distributors often use multiple distribution channels or have multiple load/commission structures. As a result, several "different" mutual funds are sold from the same portfolio of securities.)

HOTLINKS

You can obtain details on the various IRA programs, as well as other tax-sheltered retirement plans at the book's Web site. Click on the Web-chapter titled Tax-Advantaged Investments and then on Tax Deferred Retirement Programs. To access our Web site, go to:

www.awl.com/gitman_joehnk

Conversion privileges are usually considered beneficial for shareholders. They allow investors to meet their ever-changing long-term goals. They also permit investors to manage their mutual fund holdings more aggressively by allowing them to move in and out of funds as the investment environment changes. Unfortunately, there is one major drawback: For tax purposes, the exchange of shares from one fund to another is regarded as a sale transaction followed by a subsequent purchase of a new security. As a result, if any capital gains exist at the time of the exchange, the investor is liable for the taxes on that profit, even though the holdings were not truly liquidated.

Retirement Programs As a result of government legislation, self-employed individuals are permitted to divert a portion of their pretax income into self-directed retirement plans. And all working Americans, whether or not they are self-employed, are allowed to establish individual retirement arrangements (IRAs). Indeed, with legislation passed in 1997, *qualified investors* can now

TABLE 11.3 **Twenty of the Biggest Fund Families**

Fund Families	Total Number of Funds Available	Total Amount of Assets Under Management ($ billions)
Fidelity	326	$628.8
Vanguard	90	508.4
Putnam	201	237.4
Franklin-Templeton	207	156.8
T. Rowe Price	81	154.7
American Century	95	93.2
MFS	168	92.8
American Express	108	91.4
Morgan Stanley Dean Witter	263	83.9
Oppenheimer	151	75.5
Merrill Lynch	284	67.2
Van Kampen	135	59.6
Dreyfus	261	54.4
Evergreen	204	37.6
Prudential	200	36.3
Smith Barney	144	34.5
Kemper	144	34.2
Eaton Vance	142	25.8
Wells Fargo	97	17.8
Goldman Sachs	167	17.5

Note: Number of funds in existence at mid-year 2000; assets under management for stock-and-bond funds only.

Source: Principia Pro for Mutual Funds, Morningstar, Release date, June 30, 2000.

choose between deductible and nondeductible (Roth) IRAs. Even those who make too much to qualify for one of these programs can set up special nondeductible IRAs. Today all mutual funds provide a special service that allows individuals to set up tax-deferred retirement programs as either IRA or Keogh accounts—or, through their place of employment, to participate in a tax-sheltered retirement plan, such as a 401(k). The funds set up the plans and handle all the administrative details so that the shareholder can easily take full advantage of available tax savings.

Investing in Mutual Funds

LG 5 LG 6

Suppose you are confronted with the following situation: You have money to invest and are trying to select the right place to put it. You obviously want to pick a security that meets your idea of acceptable risk and will generate an attractive rate of return. The problem is that you have to make the selection from a list of nearly 8,000 securities. Sound like a "mission impossible"? Well that's basically what you're up against when trying to select a suitable mutual fund. However, if you approach the problem systematically, it may not be so formidable a task. First, it might be helpful to examine more closely the various investor uses of mutual funds. With this background, we can then look at the selection process and at several measures of return that can be used to assess performance. As we will see, it is possible to whittle down the list of alternatives by matching your investment needs with the investment objectives of the funds.

INVESTOR FACTS

FUNDS FOR THE LITTLE GUY—You don't need a large bank account to begin investing in mutual funds. Many mutual funds require minimum investments of $500 or less and additional purchases of $50. Although some may be limited to 401(k) retirement plans, others are open to general investors and cover a variety of investment categories. You don't have to give up performance because the funds court small investors. Those that performed in the top quarter of their peer group from 1995 to 2000 include Excelsior's Value and Restructuring and Blended Equity Funds ($500 minimum initial investment), Strong Asset Allocation Fund, and the socially responsible Pax World Fund ($250 minimum).

Source: Jeff D. Opdyke, "Cheap Funds: Putting Your Pennies to Work," *Wall Street Journal*, July 10, 2000, p. C14.

Investor Uses of Mutual Funds

Mutual funds can be used in a variety of ways. For instance, performance funds can serve as a vehicle for capital appreciation, whereas bond funds can provide current income. Regardless of the kind of income a mutual fund provides, investors tend to use these securities for one of three reasons: (1) as a way to accumulate wealth, (2) as a storehouse of value, or (3) as a speculative vehicle for achieving high rates of return.

Accumulation of Wealth Accumulation of wealth is probably the most common reason for using mutual funds. Basically, the investor uses mutual funds over the long haul to build up investment capital. Depending on investor goals, a modest amount of risk may be acceptable, but usually preservation of capital and capital stability are considered important. The whole idea is to form a "partnership" with the mutual fund in building up as big a capital pool as possible: *You provide the capital by systematically investing and reinvesting in the fund, and the fund provides the return by doing its best to invest your resources wisely.*

Storehouse of Value Investors also use mutual funds as a storehouse of value. The idea is to find a place where investment capital can be fairly secure and relatively free from deterioration yet still generate a relatively attractive rate of return. Short- and intermediate-term bond funds are logical choices for such purposes, and so are money funds. Capital preservation and income over the long term are very important to some investors. Others might seek storage of value only for the short term, using, for example, money funds as a place to "sit it out" until a more attractive opportunity comes along.

Speculation and Short-Term Trading Although speculation is becoming more common, it is still not widely used by mutual fund investors. The reason, of course, is that most mutual funds are long-term in nature and thus not meant to be used as aggressive trading vehicles. However, a growing number of funds (e.g., sector funds) now cater to speculators. Some investors find that mutual funds are, in fact, attractive outlets for speculation and short-term trading.

One way to do this is to trade in and out of funds aggressively as the investment climate changes. Load charges can be avoided (or reduced) by dealing in families of funds offering low-cost conversion privileges and/or by dealing only in no-load funds. Other investors might choose to invest in funds for the long run but still seek high rates of return by investing in aggressive mutual funds. A number of funds follow very aggressive trading strategies, which may appeal to investors willing to accept substantial risk exposure. These are usually the fairly specialized, smaller funds. Examples are sophisticated enhanced-yield funds, leverage funds, option funds, emerging-market funds, small-cap aggressive growth funds, and sector funds. In essence, investors in such funds are simply applying the basic mutual fund concept to their investment needs by letting professional money managers handle their accounts in a way they would like to see them handled: *aggressively.*

The Selection Process

When it comes to mutual funds, there is one question every investor has to answer: Why invest in a mutual fund to begin with—why not just go it alone by buying individual stocks and bonds directly? For beginning investors and investors with little capital, the answer is simple: With mutual funds, investors are able to achieve far more diversification than they could ever get on their own, and they get the help of professional money managers at a very reasonable cost. For more seasoned investors, the answers are probably a bit more involved. Certainly, diversification and professional money management come into play, but there are other reasons as well. The competitive returns offered by mutual funds are a factor with many investors, as are the services they provide. Many seasoned investors simply have decided they can get better returns over the long haul by carefully selecting mutual funds than by investing on their own. As a result, they put all or a big chunk of their money into funds. Some of these investors use part of their capital to buy and sell individual securities on their own and use the rest *to buy mutual funds that invest in areas they don't fully understand or don't feel well informed about.* For example, they'll use mutual funds to get into foreign markets, to buy mortgage-backed securities, to buy junk bonds (where diversification is so very important), or to buy value funds (because that's such a tricky and time-consuming way to invest).

Once you have decided to use mutual funds, you have to decide which fund(s) to buy. In many respects, the selection process is critical in determining how much success you will have with mutual funds. It means putting into action all you know about funds, in order to gain as much return as possible from an acceptable level of risk. The selection process begins with an assessment of your own investment needs, which sets the tone of the investment program. Obviously, what you want to do is select from those 8,000 or so funds the one or two (or three or four) that will best meet your total investment needs.

Objectives and Motives for Using Funds Selecting the right investment means finding those funds that are most suitable to your investment needs. The place to start is with your own investment objectives. In other words, why do you want to invest in a mutual fund, and what are you looking for in a fund? Obviously, an attractive rate of return would be desirable, but there is also the matter of a tolerable amount of risk exposure. Probably, when you look at your own risk temperament in relation to the various types of mutual funds available, you will discover that certain types of funds are more appealing to you than others. For instance, aggressive growth or sector funds are usually *not* attractive to individuals who wish to avoid high exposure to risk.

Another important factor in the selection process is the intended use of the mutual fund. That is, do you want to invest in mutual funds as a means of accumulating wealth, as a storehouse of value, or to speculate for high rates of return? This information puts into clearer focus the question of exactly what you are trying to do with your investment dollars. Finally, there is the matter of the types of services provided by the fund. If you are particularly interested in certain services, you should be sure to look for them in the funds you select. Having assessed what you are looking for in a fund, you are ready to look at what the funds have to offer.

FIGURE 11.7 **Some Relevant Information About Specific Mutual Funds**

Investors who want in-depth information about the operating characteristics, investment holdings, and market behavior of specific mutual funds, such as the Fidelity Growth Company profiled here, can usually find what they're looking for in publications like *Morningstar Mutual Funds* or, as shown here, from computer-based information sources like *Morningstar's Principia*. (*Source:* Morningstar, Inc., *Principia Pro Plus,* release date: March 22, 2000.)

Fidelity Growth Company

Ticker	Load	NAV	Yield	Total Assets	Mstar Category
FDGRX	None	$109.84	0.0%	$37,589.4 mil	Large Growth

Prospectus Objective: Growth

Fidelity Growth Company Fund seeks capital appreciation.

The fund invests primarily in various common stocks including preferreds, convertibles, and warrants issued by companies that the advisor believes have above-average growth potential, measured by earnings or gross sales. To select investments, the advisor focuses mainly on smaller, lesser-known companies in emerging areas of the economy. It may also seek investment opportunities in revitalized or well-positioned larger companies in mature industries.

The fund was formerly named Fidelity Mercury Fund.

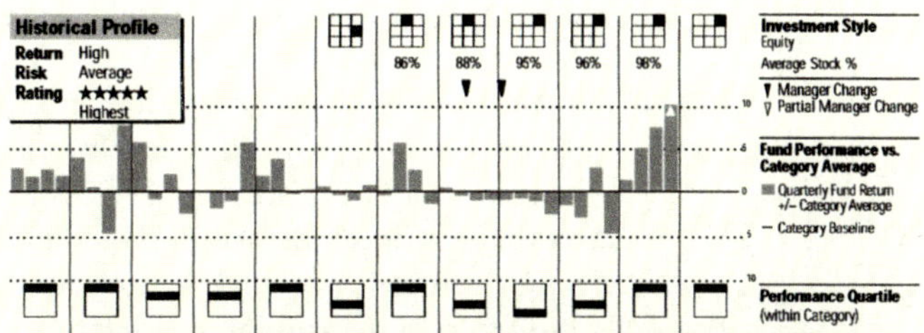

1989	1990	1991	1992	1993	1994	1995	1996	1997	1998	1999	02-00	History
18.92	19.60	27.09	27.64	29.06	27.26	36.29	40.46	43.32	51.02	84.30	109.84	NAV
41.64	3.59	48.33	7.94	16.19	−2.22	39.61	16.81	18.91	27.23	79.48	31.80	Total Return %
9.96	6.71	17.85	0.33	6.13	−3.54	2.08	−6.14	−14.44	−1.35	58.44	38.62	+/– S&P 500
3.96	2.23	8.93	4.05	16.26	−7.08	0.96	−8.71	−14.83	−17.87	49.80	36.28	+/– Russ Top 200 Grt
0.95	0.00	0.41	0.34	0.25	0.76	0.59	0.78	0.54	0.21	0.00	0.00	Income Return %
40.69	3.59	47.92	7.61	15.94	−2.98	39.03	16.03	18.36	27.02	79.48	31.80	Capital Return %
10	13	28	29	23	51	12	65	79	72	6	1	Total Rtn % Rank Cat
0.14	0.00	0.08	0.09	0.07	0.22	0.16	0.28	0.22	0.09	0.00	0.00	Income $
2.00	0.00	1.73	1.48	2.92	0.92	1.57	1.60	4.35	3.73	6.29	0.95	Capital Gains $
0.95	1.14	1.07	1.09	1.07	1.05	0.95	0.85	0.68	0.63	0.72	—	Expense Ratio %
1.42	1.51	0.75	0.52	0.43	0.64	0.76	0.96	0.54	0.24	−0.11	—	Income Ratio %
269	189	174	250	159	135	97	78	93	76	86	—	Turnover Rate %
298.7	601.7	1,376.4	1,810.7	2,542.7	2,993.4	6,278.8	9,272.6	10,509.4	11,440.4	24,337.2	37,589.4	Net Assets $mil

Portfolio Manager(s)

Steven S. Wymer. Since 1-1997. BS 1985 U. of Illinois; MBA 1989 U. of Chicago. Wymer joined Fidelity Investments as an analyst in 1989. He has been a portfolio manager since 1990. From 1985 to 1987, he was an emerging-business consultant for Deloitte Haskins & Sells. Funds previously managed: Fidelity Sel Chemicals (01-1993 - 01-1995), Fidelity Sel Automotive (10-1990 - 02-1993), Fidelity Dividend Growth (05-1995 - 01-1997).

Performance 02-29-00

	1st Qtr	2nd Qtr	3rd Qtr	4th Qtr	Total
1995	7.04	16.04	11.84	0.50	39.61
1996	5.61	4.49	2.64	3.13	16.81
1997	−2.72	15.70	9.57	−3.58	18.91
1998	12.80	1.57	−8.34	21.16	27.23
1999	9.00	9.56	3.99	44.52	79.48

Trailing	Total Return%	+/– S&P 500	+/–Russ Top 200 Grth	% Rank All	% Rank Cat	Growth of $10,000
3 Mo	60.47	61.81	56.33	3	2	16,047
6 Mo	86.86	82.75	72.61	5	4	18,686
1 Yr	130.96	119.23	109.20	4	3	23,096
3 Yr Avg	51.14	29.36	20.55	3	4	34,523
5 Yr Avg	41.47	16.33	9.95	2	5	56,656
10 Yr Avg	27.55	9.52	6.16	2	4	114,007
15 Yr Avg	23.50	5.83	—	1	2	237,223

Tax Analysis	Tax-Adj Ret%	%Rank Cat	%Pretax Ret	%Rank Cat
3 Yr Avg	47.79	5	93.5	31
5 Yr Avg	38.66	3	93.2	23
10 Yr Avg	25.20	4	91.5	16

Potential Capital Gain Exposure: 55% of assets

Risk Analysis

Time Period	Load-Adj Return %	Risk %Rank[1] All	Risk %Rank[1] Cat	Morningstar Return	Morningstar Risk	Morningstar Risk-Adj Rating
1 Yr	130.96					
3 Yr	51.14	55	11	3.78	0.81	★★★★★
5 Yr	41.47	67	16	3.31	0.87	★★★★★
10 Yr	27.55	77	45	3.36	1.02	★★★★★

Average Historical Rating (170 months): 3.9★s

[1]1=low, 100=high

Category Rating (3 Yr)

1 2 3 4 5
Worst Best

Return High
Risk Below Avg

Other Measures	Standard Index S&P 500	Best Fit Index Wil 4500
Alpha	28.1	18.7
Beta	0.93	1.03
R-Squared	37	77
Standard Deviation		30.66
Mean		51.14
Sharpe Ratio		1.29

Portfolio Analysis 11-30-99

Share change since 05-99 Total Stocks: 280	Sector	PE	YTD Ret%	% Assets
⊕ Microsoft	Technology	56.2	−23.40	3.00
⊕ Cisco Sys	Technology	NMF	23.40	2.84
⊕ Natl Semicon	Technology	—	75.47	2.76
⊕ Network Appliance	Technology	NMF	127.20	2.43
⊕ JDS Uniphase	Technology	—	63.42	2.43
⊖ MedImmune	Health	NMF	19.67	1.86
⊕ PE Corp - PE Biosystems Grp	Industrials	95.0	74.58	1.83
⊕ Research in Motion	Technology	NMF	192.80	1.75
General Elec	Industrials	41.1	−14.40	1.66
☼ Genentech	Health	—	43.40	1.48
⊕ QLT Phototherapeutics	Health	—	21.49	1.44
⊕ Wal-Mart Stores	Retail	40.4	−29.20	1.39
⊕ Sepracor	Health	—	104.40	1.37
⊖ Corning	Industrials	96.4	45.81	1.30
⊕ Conexant Sys	Technology	—	48.02	1.30
⊕ CIENA	Technology	—	177.90	1.29
⊕ Fannie Mae	Financials	14.3	−14.70	1.22
⊕ PE Corp - Celera Genomics Gr	Health	—	227.50	1.21
⊕ America Online	Technology	NMF	−22.40	1.15
⊕ Nike	Durables	15.3	−42.60	1.13
⊕ McDonald's	Services	22.6	−21.50	1.11
⊕ Biogen	Health	77.1	27.74	1.10
⊕ Intel	Technology	53.6	37.32	1.06
☼ Vignette	Technology	—	41.41	0.95
⊕ Bristol-Myers Squibb	Health	27.8	−10.40	0.92

Current Investment Style

Style: Value Blnd Growth; Size: Large Med Small

	Stock Port Avg	Relative S&P 500 Current	Relative S&P 500 Hist	Rel Cat
Price/Earnings Ratio	45.1	1.17	1.21	1.04
Price/Book Ratio	16.5	1.54	1.10	1.26
Price/Cash Flow	32.5	1.24	1.20	1.07
3 Yr Earnings Growth	29.0[†]	1.66	1.24	1.10
1 Yr Earnings Est%	28.1	1.51	—	1.12
Med Mkt Cap $mil	22,139	0.3	0.4	0.31

[†]figure is based on 50% or less of stocks

Special Securities % assets 11-30-99	
Restricted/Illiquid Secs	0
Emerging-Markets Secs	0
Options/Futures/Warrants	No

Composition % assets 11-30-99	
Cash	2.7
Stocks*	97.4
Bonds	0.0
Other	0.0
*Foreign (% stocks)	7.7

Market Cap	
Giant	27.6
Large	32.5
Medium	35.4
Small	4.3
Micro	0.2

Sector Weightings	% of Stocks	Rel S&P	5-Year High	5-Year Low
Utilities	0.3	0.2	3	0
Energy	2.8	0.5	7	1
Financials	6.2	0.5	18	6
Industrials	10.3	1.0	18	4
Durables	2.0	1.1	7	0
Staples	3.5	0.8	11	0
Services	8.8	0.7	17	8
Retail	4.0	0.7	17	4
Health	18.6	2.0	27	7
Technology	43.5	1.3	48	16

Analysis by Scott Cooley 03-16-00

With Fidelity Growth Company, it's deja vu all over again.

Fidelity diversified funds tend to go through a typical life cycle. The story goes something like this: Fund notches big returns with small-to-moderate-size asset base. Investors come piling in. Fund gets too large to operate with as much flexibility as it did in the past. Manager spreads the fund across more stocks, cuts turnover, and ultimately invests in larger companies. Fund becomes reliably above average but loses the explosive potential it once had.

After a dazzling 1999 return, manager Steve Wymer may be facing the size issue here. Since the end of 1998, the fund's net assets have tripled, topping $35 billion as of the end of February, the last date Fidelity made that figure available. Wymer has already taken some steps to accommodate the fund's girth. He now holds nearly 300 stocks rather than the 220 or so he says he'd prefer to own. Wymer also acknowledges that he will need more ideas or bigger ones to deploy the fund's incoming cash. And he says he's giving a close look to some giant caps, partly in an effort to soak up the fund's inflows. He also says giant caps' valuations are becoming more attractive, as most haven't run up as much as mid-caps have recently.

That said, the fund is in good hands with Wymer. He has repeatedly beaten his rivals into now-hot areas, ranging from biotechnology and cellular to fiber optics. Moreover, his play on mid-cap stocks, particularly in the technology area, paid huge dividends in 1999 and again in 2000's first two-and-a-half months. Indeed, during Wymer's tenure, the fund has handily outpaced its average large-cap growth rival.

Of course, those sorts of mid-cap plays will become increasingly difficult to execute as the fund's asset base expands. Thus, investors should expect this to become more of a typical large-growth fund, albeit one managed by a very talented stock-picker.

Address:	82 Devonshire Street Boston, MA 02109 800-544-8888
Web Address:	www.fidelity.com
Inception:	01-17-83
Advisor:	Fidelity Management & Research
Subadvisor:	FMR (U.K.)/FMR (Far East)
NTF Plans:	Fidelity, Fidelity Inst., Muriel Siebert, Waterhouse

Minimum Purchase:	$2500	Add: $250	IRA: $500
Min Auto Inv Plan:	$2500	Add: $100	
Sales Fees:	No-load		
Management Fee:	0.30%+0.52% max./0.27% min.(G)+(–)0.20%P		
Actual Fees:	Mgt: 0.51%	Dist: —	
Expense Projections:	3Yr: $237	5Yr: $411	10Yr: $918
Avg Brok Commission:	—	Income Distrib: Annually	
Total Cost (relative to category):		Low	

MORNINGSTAR Mutual Funds

What the Funds Offer Just as each individual has a set of investment needs, each fund has its own *investment objective,* its own *manner of operation,* and its own *range of services.* These three parameters are useful in helping you to assess investment alternatives. But where do you find such information? One obvious place is the fund's *profile,* or its prospectus ("Statement of Additional Information"), which supplies information on investment objectives, portfolio composition, management, and past performance. Publications such as the *Wall Street Journal, Barron's, Money, Fortune,* and *Forbes* also offer useful information about mutual funds. These sources provide a wealth of operating and performance statistics in a convenient and easy-to-read format. For instance, each year *Forbes* rates a couple thousand mutual funds, and every quarter *Barron's* publishes an extensive mutual fund performance report.

A number of reporting services also provide background information and assessments on funds. Among the best in this category are *Morningstar Mutual Funds* (a sample of which is shown in Figure 11.7), Wiesenberger's *Investment Companies* (an annual publication with quarterly updates), Standard & Poor's/Lipper Analytical's *Mutual Fund ProFiles* (a publication that comes out quarterly), and *Value Line Mutual Fund Survey* (which produces a mutual fund report similar to its stock report). In addition, all sorts of performance statistics are available on disks and on the Internet for easy use on home computers. For example, quarterly or annually updated software is available, at very low cost, from Morningstar or from the American Association of Individual Investors (AAII).

Using sources like these, investors can obtain information on such things as investment objectives, load charges and annual expense rates, summary portfolio analyses, services offered, historical statistics, and reviews of past performance. Or, you can look to the publications put out by the funds themselves, as explained in the *Investing in Action* box on page 390.

INVESTOR FACTS

SOME MUTUAL FUND FACTS EVERY INVESTOR SHOULD KNOW . . .

- Even bad funds sometimes rank as top performers.
- Stock funds that get hit hard in market crashes aren't necessarily bad investments.
- Even great funds have bad years now and then.
- Most stock (and bond) funds fail to beat the market.
- You don't need a broker to buy mutual funds.
- A fund that doesn't charge a sales commission isn't necessarily a no-load fund.
- If you own more than a dozen different funds, you probably own too many.

Whittling Down the Alternatives At this point, the fund selection becomes a process of elimination. A large number of funds can be eliminated from consideration simply because they fail to meet stated needs. Some funds may be too risky; others may be unsuitable as a storehouse of value. Thus, rather than trying to evaluate 8,000 different funds, you can narrow down the list to two or three *types* of funds that best match your investment needs. From here, you can whittle down the list a bit more by introducing other constraints. For example, because of cost considerations, you may want to deal only in no-load or low-load funds (more on this topic below). Or you may be seeking certain services that are important to your investment goals.

Now we introduce the final (but certainly not the least important) element in the selection process: the *fund's investment performance.* Useful information includes (1) how the fund has performed over the past 5 to 7 years, (2) the type of return it has generated in good markets as well as bad, (3) the level and stability of dividend and capital gains distributions, and (4) the amount of volatility/risk in the fund's return. Note that the dividend and capital gains distribution is an important indication not only of how much current income the fund distributes annually but also of the fund's *tax efficiency.* As a rule, funds that have low dividends and low asset turnover expose their shareholders to less taxes and therefore have higher tax-efficiency ratings. And while you're looking at performance, it probably wouldn't hurt to check out the fund's *fee structure.* Be on guard for funds that charge abnormally high management fees; they can really hurt returns over time.

Note that in this decision process, considerable weight is given to *past performance.* Now as a rule, the past is given little or no attention in the investment decision. After all, it's the future that matters. Although the *future performance* of a mutual fund is still the variable that holds the key to success, investors should look carefully at past investment results to see how successful the fund's investment managers have been. In essence, the success of a mutual fund rests in large part on the *investment skills of the fund managers.* Therefore, look for consistently good performance, in up as well as down markets, over *extended* periods of time (5 years or more). Most important, check whether the same key people are still running the fund. Although past success is certainly no guarantee of future performance, a strong team of money managers can have a significant bearing on the level of fund returns.

Stick with No-Loads or Low-Loads There's a long-standing "debate" in the mutual fund industry regarding load funds and no-load funds. Do load funds add value? If not, then why pay the load charges? As it turns out, empirical results generally do not support the idea that load funds provide added value. Load fund returns, in general, don't seem to be any better than the returns from no-load funds. In fact, in many cases, the funds with abnormally high loads and 12(b)-1 charges often produce returns that are far less than what you can get from no-load funds. In addition, because of compounding, the differential returns tend to widen with longer holding periods. But that should come as no surprise, because big load charges and/or 12(b)-1 fees reduce your investable capital—and therefore the amount of money you have working for you. In fact, the only way a load fund can overcome this handicap is to produce *superior returns,* which is no easy thing to do, year in and year out. Granted, a handful of load funds have produced very attractive returns over extended periods of time, but they are the exception rather than the rule.

Obviously, it's in your best interest to pay close attention to load charges (and other fees). As a rule, to maximize returns, you should *seriously consider sticking to no-load funds or to low-loads* (funds that have total load charges, including 12(b)-1 fees, of 3% or less). At the very minimum, you should consider a more expensive load fund *only* if it has a much better performance record (and offers more return potential) than a less expensive fund. There may well be times when the higher costs are justified. But far more often than not, you're better off trying to minimize load charges. That shouldn't be difficult to do, however, because there are literally thousands of no-load and low-load funds to choose from. And they come in all types and sizes. What's more, most of the top-performing funds are found in the universe of no-loads or low-loads. So why would you even want to look anywhere else?

Investing in Closed-End Funds

The assets of closed-end funds (CEFs) represent only a fraction of the more than $7 trillion invested in open-end funds. Indeed, in early 2000 there were over 500 CEFs, which together held total assets of "only" $158 billion (about

INVESTING in action

Knowing Where to Look Is Half the Battle

Only a lawyer could love a mutual fund prospectus. So many words, so little meaning. No wonder half of the investing public ignores the admonition to "read the prospectus before you invest." But the prospectus really does contain a wealth of information if you know how to separate the wheat from the chaff. Among the most important data are the mutual fund's *expenses*. The Expenses section explains whether the fund has a sales load and how much it is; it also breaks out management and marketing fees for your approval or disapproval.

The Investment Objective section will tell you about the fund's *investment style*—whether it seeks value, growth, income, or whatever. You might get some real detail here, such as the information that the fund buys small stocks with market values between $100 million and $500 million. Then there's the discussion of *risk*. A good prospectus alerts you to specific risks that pertain to your portfolio. For example, the prospectus could tell you that the fund's bias toward high-dividend stocks could limit its potential for capital appreciation. In contrast, a poorly prepared prospectus provides general risk information that applies to all mutual funds. Such general information can go on for pages, and it probably protects the mutual fund company in the event of a lawsuit. Unfortunately, it doesn't help the investor make a prudent investment decision.

Most funds list long-term *total returns* in the prospectus. You might discover that the fund's returns are very volatile and not to your liking. If the prospectus does not list total returns, it may be because the results aren't very good.

A prospectus also gives you a biography of the *portfolio manager*. Why is this important information? If the manager is brand new, then the total return is irrelevant because the current manager didn't compile it.

Still, reading a prospectus has not always been something that most people like to do. But now, rules adopted by the SEC give investors the choice of buying into a mutual fund on the basis of a brief (2 to 6 pages), concise, readable document called a fund profile, or requesting a more detailed prospectus from the fund company. The *fund profile* is designed to tell you (in plain English and in a standardized format) the most important things you need to know about a fund (e.g., its investment objectives, principle risks, fees and expenses, etc.) without overwhelming you in a bunch of unnecessary legalese. Likewise, the fund prospectuses are now far more user-friendly, as they too must be simplified and downsized (by removing all the irrelevant "boilerplate"); and they must be written in plain English, as well.

Should you want even more information than provided in either the profile or prospectus, you can always ask for a copy of the fund's *Statement of Additional Information,* which provides detailed information on the fund's investment objectives, portfolio composition, management, and past performance. Or, ask to see the fund company's last annual or semiannual report. That document usually has a lot to say about a fund's performance, what the portfolio includes, and the portfolio managers' outlook for the future.

2% of the amount held by open-end funds). Like open-end funds, CEFs come in a variety of different types and styles, including funds that specialize in municipal bonds, taxable bonds, various types of equity securities, and international securities, as well as regional and single-country funds. Both taxable and tax-free bonds dominate the CEF universe. In fact, municipal bonds alone account for about 46% of CEF assets. In addition to bonds and the domestic equity market, many closed-end funds target foreign stock markets. For example, regional funds focus on a group of countries within a broad geographic area, such as Europe or Latin America. In contrast, *single-country funds* target either *emerging markets* (such as Brazil, China, the Czech Republic, India, Indonesia, Mexico, the Philippines, and Turkey) or *developed markets* (such as France, Germany, Japan, and the United Kingdom).

Some Key Differences Between Closed-End and Open-End Funds Because closed-end funds trade like stocks, you must deal with a broker to buy or sell shares, and the usual brokerage commissions apply. Open-end funds, in contrast, are bought from and sold to the fund operators themselves. Another important difference between open- and closed-end funds is their liquidity. You can buy and sell relatively large dollar amounts of an open-end mutual fund at its NAV without worrying about affecting the price. However, a relatively large buy or sell order for a CEF could easily bump its price up or down. Thus, the greater liquidity of open-end funds gives them a distinct advantage. Like open-end funds, most CEFs offer dividend reinvestment plans, but in many cases, that's about it. CEFs simply don't provide the full range of services that mutual fund investors are accustomed to.

All things considered, probably the most important difference is the way these funds are priced in the marketplace. This is important because it *directly affects* investor costs and returns. Whereas open-end funds can be bought and sold at NAV (plus any front-end load or minus any redemption charge), CEFs *have two values*—a market value (or stock price) and net asset value (NAV). The two are rarely the same, because CEFs typically trade at either a premium or a discount. A *premium* occurs when a fund trades for more than its NAV; a *discount* occurs when it trades for less. As a rule, CEFs trade at discounts. Indeed, at mid-year 2000, the typical CEF traded at an average *discount of around 10%*. Premiums and discounts are reported weekly in *Barron's*, the *Wall Street Journal*, and other newspapers.

The premium or discount is calculated as follows:

Equation 11. 1

$$\text{Premium (or discount)} = (\text{Share price} - \text{NAV}) / \text{NAV}$$

Suppose Fund A has a NAV of \$10. If its share price is \$8, it will sell at a 20% discount. That is,

$$\begin{aligned}\text{Premium (or discount)} &= (\$8 - \$10)/\$10 \\ &= -\$2/\$10 = -.20 = \underline{\underline{-20\%}}\end{aligned}$$

Because this value is negative, the fund is trading at a *discount* (or below its NAV). On the other hand, if this same fund were priced at \$12 per share, it would be trading at a *premium* of 20%—that is, (\$12 − \$10)/\$10 = \$2/\$10 = 0.20. Because the value is positive, the fund is trading at a premium (above its NAV).

What to Look for in a Closed-End Fund If you know what to look for and your timing and selection are good, you may find that some *deeply discounted CEFs* provide a great way to earn attractive returns. For example, if a fund trades at a 20% discount, you pay only 80 cents for each dollar's worth of assets. At certain times, the market offers the opportunity to pick up funds at attractive prices. (This could well be the case when double-digit discounts exist.) At other times, discounts may be too narrow to represent any special value. If you can buy a fund at an abnormally wide discount and sell it when the discount narrows or turns to a premium, you can enhance your overall return. In fact, even if the discount does not narrow, your return will be improved, because the yield on your investment is higher than it would be with an otherwise equivalent open-end fund. The reason: You're investing less money. Here's a simple example. Suppose a CEF trades at $8, a 20% discount from its NAV of $10. If the fund distributed $1 in dividends for the year, it would yield 12.5% ($1 divided by its $8 price). However, if it was a no-load, open-end fund, it would be trading at its higher NAV and therefore would yield only 10% ($1 divided by its $10 NAV). Thus, when investing in CEFs, pay close attention to the size of the premium and discount. In particular, keep your eyes open for funds trading at deep discounts, because that feature alone can enhance potential returns.

For the most part, except for the premium or discount, a CEF should be analyzed just like any other mutual fund. That is, pay attention to the expense ratio, portfolio turnover rate, past performance, cash position, and so on. In addition, study the history of the discount. Information on closed-end funds can be found in such publications as *Morningstar Closed-End Funds,* Standard & Poor's *Stock Reports,* and *Value Line Investment Survey.* Also, keep in mind that with CEFs, you probably won't get a prospectus (as you might with an open-end fund), because they do not continuously offer new shares to investors.

One final point to keep in mind when developing a closed-end fund investment program: Stay clear of new issues (IPOs) of closed-end funds and funds that sell at steep *premiums.* Never buy new CEFs when they are brought to the market as IPOs. Why? Because IPOs are always brought to the market at *hefty premiums.* You therefore face the almost inevitable risk of losing money as the shares fall to a discount within a month or two. This drop in price occurs because the IPO funds have to be offered at a premium just to cover the amount of the underwriting spread. You also want to avoid funds that are trading at premiums—especially at steep premiums—such as volatile single-country portfolios. That too can lead to built-in losses when, if sentiment sours, these premiums quickly turn to discounts.

Measuring Performance

As in any investment decision, return performance is a major dimension in the mutual fund selection process. The level of dividends paid by the fund, its capital gains, and its growth in capital are all important aspects of return. Such return information enables you to judge the investment behavior of a fund and to appraise its performance in relation to other funds and investment vehicles. Here, we will look at different measures that mutual fund investors use to assess return. Also, because risk is so important in defining the investment behavior of a fund, we will examine mutual fund risk as well.

Sources of Return An open-end mutual fund has three potential sources of return: (1) dividend income, (2) capital gains distribution, and (3) change in the price (or net asset value) of the fund. Depending on the type of fund, some mutual funds derive more income from one source than another. For example, we would normally expect income-oriented funds to have much higher dividend income than capital gains distributions.

Open-end mutual funds regularly publish reports that recap investment performance. One such report is the *Summary of Income and Capital Changes,* an example of which is provided in Table 11.4. This statement is

TABLE 11.4 A Report of Mutual Fund Income and Capital Changes (For a share outstanding throughout the year)

	2001	2000	1999
1. Net asset value, beginning of period	**$24.47**	**$27.03**	**$24.26**
2. Income from investment operations:			
3. Net investment income	$0.60	$0.66	$0.50
4. Net gains on securities (realized and unrealized)	6.37	(1.74)	3.79
5. Total from investment operations	6.97	(1.08)	4.29
6. Less distributions:			
7. Dividends from net investment income	($0.55)	($0.64)	($0.50)
8. Distributions from realized gains	(1.75)	(.84)	(1.02)
9. Total distributions	(2.30)	(1.48)	(1.52)
10. Net asset value, end of period	$29.14	$24.47	$27.03
11. Total return	28.48%	(4.00%)	17.68%
12. Ratios/supplemental data			
13. Net assets, end of period ($000)	$307,951	$153,378	$108,904
14. Ratio of expenses to average net assets	1.04%	0.85%	0.94%
15. Ratio of net investment income to average net assets	1.47%	2.56%	2.39%
16. Portfolio turnover rate*	85%	144%	74%

**Portfolio turnover rate* relates the number of shares bought and sold by the fund to the total number of shares held in the fund's portfolio. A high turnover rate (in excess of 100%) means the fund has been doing a lot of trading.

found in the fund's profile or prospectus. It gives a brief overview of the fund's investment activity, including expense ratios and portfolio turnover rates. Of interest to us here is the top part of the report (which runs from "net asset value, beginning of period" to "net asset value, end of period"—lines 1 to 10). This part reveals the amount of dividend income and capital gains distributed to the shareholders, along with any change in the fund's net asset value.

dividend income
income derived from the dividend and interest income earned on the security holdings of a mutual fund.

Dividend income (see line 7 of Table 11.4) is derived from the dividend and interest income earned on the security holdings of the mutual fund. It is paid out of the *net investment income* that's left after all operating expenses have been met. When the fund receives dividend or interest payments, it passes these on to shareholders in the form of dividend payments. The fund accumulates all of the current income it has received for the period and then pays it out on a prorated basis. If a fund earned, say, $2 million in dividends and interest in a given year and if that fund had 1 million shares outstanding, each share would receive an annual dividend payment of $2.

capital gains distributions
payments made to mutual fund shareholders that come from the profits that a fund makes from the sale of its securities.

Capital gains distributions (see line 8) work on the same principle, except that these payments are derived from the capital gains earned by the fund. It works like this: Suppose the fund bought some stock a year ago for $50 and sold that stock in the current period for $75 per share. Clearly, the fund has achieved capital gains of $25 per share. If it held 50,000 shares of this stock, it would have realized a total capital gain of $1,250,000 ($25 × 50,000 = $1,250,000). Given that the fund has 1 million shares outstanding, each share is entitled to $1.25 in the form of a capital gains distribution. Note that this capital gains distribution applies only to *realized* capital gains (that is, the security holdings were actually sold and the capital gains actually earned).

unrealized capital gains (paper profits)
a capital gain made only "on paper"-that is, not realized until the fund's holdings are sold.

Unrealized capital gains (or **paper profits**) are what make up the third and final element of a mutual fund's return. When the fund's holdings go up or down in price, the net asset value of the fund moves accordingly. Suppose an investor buys into a fund at $10 per share and sometime later the fund is quoted at $12.50. The difference of $2.50 per share is the unrealized capital gains. It represents the profit that shareholders would receive (and are entitled to) if the fund were to sell its holdings. (Actually, as Table 11.4 shows, some of the change in net asset value can also be made up of undistributed income.)

The return on *closed-end* investment companies is derived from the same three sources as that of open-end funds and from a *fourth source* as well: changes in price discounts or premiums. But because discount or premium is already embedded in the share price of a fund, it follows that, for a closed-end fund, the third element of return—change in share price—is made up not only of change in net asset value but also of change in price discount or premium.

What About Future Performance? There's no doubt that a statement like the one in Table 11.4 provides a convenient recap of a fund's past behavior. Looking at past performance is useful, but it doesn't tell you what the future will be. Ideally, you want an indication of what the same three elements of return—dividend income, capital gains distribution, and change in NAV—*will be.* But it's extremely difficult—if not impossible—to get a firm grip on what the future holds in dividends, capital gains, and NAV. This is because a mutual fund's future performance is directly linked to the *future make-up of the securities in its portfolio,* something that is next to impossible to get a clear reading on. It's not like evaluating the expected performance of a share of stock, in which case you're keying in on one company. With mutual funds, investment performance depends on the behavior of many different stocks and bonds.

HOTLINKS

You can research risk, price history, and managers of mutual funds at the MSN site:

moneycentral.msn.com/investor/research/wizards/FRW.asp?Funds=1

Where, then, do you look for insight on future performance? Most market observers suggest that the first place to look is the market itself. In particular, try to get a fix on the future direction of *the market as a whole.* This is important because the behavior of a well-diversified mutual fund tends to reflect the general tone of the market. Thus, if the feeling is that the market is going to be drifting up, so should the investment performance of mutual funds. Also spend some time evaluating the *track records* of mutual funds in which you are interested. Past performance has a lot to say about the investment skills of the fund's money managers. In essence, look for funds that you think will be able to capture the best of what the future market environment holds.

Measures of Return A simple but effective measure of performance is to describe mutual fund return in terms of the three major sources noted above: dividends earned, capital gains distributions received, and change in price. When dealing with investment horizons of 1 year or less, we can easily convert these fund payoffs into a return figure by using the standard holding period return (HPR) formula. The computations necessary are illustrated below using the 2001 figures from Table 11.4. Referring to the exhibit, we can see that in 2001, this hypothetical no-load, open-end fund paid 55 cents per share in dividends and another $1.75 in capital gains distributions. It had a price at the beginning of the year of $24.47 that rose to $29.14 by the end of the year. Thus, summarizing this investment performance, we have

Price (NAV) at the *beginning* of the year	\$24.47
Price (NAV) at the *end* of the year	29.14
Net increase	\$ 4.67
Return for the year:	
Dividends received	\$ .55
Capital gains distributions	1.75
Net increase in price (NAV)	4.67
Total return	\$ 6.97
Holding period return (HPR)	**28.5%**
(Total return/beginning price)	

This HPR measure (which is shown in Table 11.4 as "Total Return" on line 11) not only captures all the important elements of mutual fund return but also provides a handy indication of yield. Note that the fund had a total dollar return of \$6.97. On the basis of a beginning investment of \$24.47 (the initial share price of the fund), the fund produced an annual return of 28.5%.

HPR with Reinvested Dividends and Capital Gains Many mutual fund investors have their dividends and/or capital gains distributions reinvested in the fund. How, then, do you obtain a measure of return when you receive your (dividend/capital gains) payout in additional shares of stock rather than cash? With slight modifications, you can continue to use holding period return. The only difference is that you have to keep track of the number of shares acquired through reinvestment. To illustrate, let's continue with the example above and assume that you initially bought 200 shares in the mutual fund. Assume also that you were able to acquire shares through the fund's reinvestment program at an average price of \$26.50 a share. Thus, the \$460 in dividends and capital gains distributions [(\$.55 + \$1.75) × 200] provided you with another 17.36 shares in the fund (\$460/\$26.50). Holding period return under these circumstances would relate the market value of the stock holdings at the beginning of the period with holdings at the end:

Equation 11. 2

$$\text{Holding period return} = \frac{\left(\begin{array}{c}\text{Number of}\\ \text{shares at } \textit{end}\\ \text{of period}\end{array} \times \begin{array}{c}\text{ending}\\ \text{price}\end{array}\right) - \left(\begin{array}{c}\text{Number of}\\ \text{shares at } \textit{beginning}\\ \text{of period}\end{array} \times \begin{array}{c}\text{Initial}\\ \text{price}\end{array}\right)}{\begin{array}{c}\text{Number of shares}\\ \text{at } \textit{beginning} \text{ of period}\end{array} \times \begin{array}{c}\text{Initial}\\ \text{price}\end{array}}$$

Thus the holding period would be

$$\text{Holding period return} = \frac{(217.36 \times \$29.14) - (200 \times \$24.47)}{(200 \times \$24.47)}$$

$$= \frac{(\$6,333.87) - (\$4,894.00)}{\$4,894.00} = \underline{\underline{29.4\%}}$$

This holding period return, like the preceding one, provides a rate-of-return measure that can now be used to compare the performance of this fund to those of other funds and investment vehicles.

Measuring Long-Term Returns Rather than using 1-year holding periods, it is sometimes necessary to assess the performance of mutual funds over extended periods of time. In these cases, it would be inappropriate to employ holding period return as a measure of performance. When faced with multiple-year investment horizons, we can use the present-value-based *internal rate of return* (IRR) procedure to determine the fund's average annual compound rate of return. To illustrate, refer once again to Table 11.4. Assume that this time we want to find the annual rate of return over the full 3-year period (1999 through 2001). In this case, we see that the mutual fund had the following annual dividends and capital gains distribution.

	2001	2000	1999
Annual dividends paid	\$ .55	\$ .64	\$ .50
Annual capital gains distributed	\$1.75	\$ .84	
\$1.02			
Total distributions	\$2.30	\$1.48	\$1.52

Now, given that the fund had a price of \$24.26 at the beginning of the period (1/1/99) and was trading at \$29.14 at the end of 2001 (3 years later), we have the following time line of cash flows:

Initial Cash Flow	Subsequent Cash Flows		
	Year 1	Year 2	Year 3
\$24.26 (Beginning Price)	\$1.52 (Distributions)	\$1.48 (Distributions)	\$2.30 + \$29.14 (Distributions + Ending Price)

The idea is to find the discount rate that will equate the annual dividends/capital gains distributions *and* the ending price in year 3 to the beginning (1999) price of the fund (\$24.26).

Using standard present-value calculations, we find that the mutual fund in Table 11.4 provided its investors with an annual rate of return of 13.1% over the 3-year period from 1999 through 2001. That is, at 13.1%, the present values of the cash flows in years 1, 2, and 3 equal the beginning price of the fund (\$24.26). Such information helps us assess fund performance and compare the return performance of one fund to other funds and investment vehicles. According to SEC regulations, if mutual funds report historical return behavior, they must do so in a standardized format that employs fully compounded, total-return figures similar to those obtained from the above present value-based measure of return. The funds are not required to report such information. But, if they do cite performance in their promotional material, they must follow a full-disclosure manner of presentation that takes into account not only dividends and capital gains distributions but also any increases or decreases in the fund's NAV that have occurred over the past 1-, 3-, 5-, and 10-year periods.

Returns on Closed-End Funds The returns of CEFs are customarily reported on the basis of their NAVs. That is, *price premiums and discounts are ignored when computing various return measures.* At the same time, it's becoming increasingly common to see return performance expressed in terms of actual market prices, a practice that captures the impact of changing market premiums or discounts on holding period returns. As you might expect, the greater the premiums or discounts and the greater the changes in these values over time, the greater their impact on reported returns. It's not at all uncommon for CEFs to have different market-based and NAV-based holding period returns. When NAVs are used, you find the returns on CEFs in exactly the same way as you do the returns on open-end funds. In contrast, when market values are used to measure return, all you need do *is substitute the market price of the fund* (with its embedded premium or discount) *for the corresponding NAV in the holding period or internal rate of return* measure. Some CEF investors like to run *both* NAV-based and market-based measures of return to see how changing premiums (or discounts) have added to or hurt the returns on their mutual fund holdings. Even so, as a rule, NAV-based return numbers are generally viewed as the preferred measures of performance. Because fund managers often have little or no control over changes in premium or discounts, NAV-based measures are felt to give a truer picture of the performance of the fund itself.

The Matter of Risk Because most mutual funds are so diversified, their investors are largely immune to the business and financial risks normally present with individual securities. Even with extensive diversification, however, the investment behavior of most funds is still exposed to a considerable amount of *market risk*. In fact, because mutual fund portfolios are so well diversified, they often tend to perform very much like the market—or some segment of the market that's being targeted by the fund. Although a few funds, like gold funds, tend to be defensive (countercyclical), market risk is an important behavioral ingredient in a large number of mutual funds, both open- and closed-end. Investors should be aware of the effect the general market has on the investment performance of a mutual fund. For example, if the market is trending downward and you anticipate that trend to continue, it might be best to place any new investment capital into something like a money fund until the market reverses itself. At that time, you can make a more long-term commitment.

Another important risk consideration revolves around the management practices of the fund itself. If the portfolio is managed conservatively, the risk of a loss in capital is likely to be much less than for aggressively managed funds. Obviously, the more speculative the investment goals of the fund, the greater the risk of instability in the net asset value. But, a conservatively managed portfolio does not necessarily eliminate all price volatility. The securities in the portfolio are still subject to inflation, interest rate, and general market risks. However, these risks are generally reduced or minimized as the investment objectives and portfolio management practices of the funds become more conservative.

Summary

LG 1

Describe the basic features of mutual funds, and note what they have to offer as investment vehicles. Mutual fund shares represent ownership in a diversified, professionally managed portfolio of securities. Many investors who lack the time, know-how, or commitment to manage their own money turn to mutual funds. Mutual funds shareholders benefit from a level of diversification and investment performance they might otherwise find difficult to achieve. In addition, they can establish an investment program with a limited amount of capital and obtain a variety of investor services not available elsewhere.

LG 2 **Distinguish between open- and closed-end mutual funds, as well as other types of professionally managed investment companies, and discuss the various types of fund loads, fees, and charges.** Open-end funds have no limit on the number of shares they may issue. Closed-end funds have a fixed number of shares outstanding and trade in the secondary markets like any other share of common stock. Exchange-traded funds possess characteristics of both open-end and closed-end funds. Other types of investment companies are unit investment trusts, REITs (which invest primarily in various types of real estate products), and variable annuities. Mutual fund investors face an array of loads, fees, and charges, including front-end loads, back-end loads, annual 12(b)-1 charges, and annual management fees. Some of these costs are one-time charges (e.g., front-end loads). Others are paid annually [e.g., 12(b)-1 and management fees]. Investors should understand fund costs, which can be a real drag on fund performance and return.

LG 3 **Discuss the types of funds available and the variety of investment objectives these funds seek to fulfill.** Each fund has an established investment objective that determines its investment policy and identifies it as a certain type of fund. Some of the more popular types of funds are growth funds, aggressive growth funds, value funds, equity-income funds, balanced funds, growth-and-income funds, asset allocation funds, index funds, bond funds, money funds, sector funds, socially responsible funds, and international funds. The different categories of funds have different risk-return characteristics.

LG 4 **Discuss the investor services offered by mutual funds and how these services can fit into an investment program.** Mutual funds also offer special services, such as automatic investment and reinvestment plans, systematic withdrawal programs, low-cost conversion and phone-switching privileges, and retirement programs.

LG 5 **Gain an appreciation of the investor uses of mutual funds, along with the variables to consider when assessing and selecting funds for investment purposes.** Mutual funds can be used to accumulate wealth, as a storehouse of value, or as a vehicle for speculation and short-term trading. The fund selection process generally starts by assessing the investor's needs and wants. The next step is to consider what the funds have to offer, particularly with regard to investment objectives, risk exposure, and investor services. The investor then narrows down the alternatives by aligning his or her needs with the types of funds available and, from this short list of funds, applies the final selection tests: fund performance and cost.

LG 6 **Identify the sources of return and compute the rate of return earned on a mutual fund investment.** The payoff from investing in a mutual fund includes dividend income, distribution of realized capital gains, growth in capital (unrealized capital gains), and—for closed-end funds—the change in premium or discount. Various measures of return recognize these elements and provide simple yet effective ways of gauging the annual rate of return from a mutual fund. Risk is also important to mutual fund investors. A fund's extensive diversification may protect investors from business and financial risks. But considerable market risk still remains because most funds tend to perform much like the market, or like that segment of the market in which they specialize.

Appendix A
Financial Tables

Table A.1
Future-Value Interest Factors for One Dollar, FVIF

Table A.2
Future-Value Interest Factors for a One-Dollar Annuity, FVIFA

Table A.3
Present-Value Interest Factors for One Dollar, PVIF

Table A.4
Present-Value Interest Factors for a One-Dollar Annuity, PVIFA

TABLE A.1 Future-Value Interest Factors for One Dollar, *FVIF*

Period	1%	2%	3%	4%	5%	6%	7%	8%	9%	10%	11%	12%	13%	14%	15%	16%	17%	18%	19%	20%
1	1.010	1.020	1.030	1.040	1.050	1.060	1.070	1.080	1.090	1.100	1.110	1.120	1.130	1.140	1.150	1.160	1.170	1.180	1.190	1.200
2	1.020	1.040	1.061	1.082	1.102	1.124	1.145	1.166	1.188	1.210	1.232	1.254	1.277	1.300	1.322	1.346	1.369	1.392	1.416	1.440
3	1.030	1.061	1.093	1.125	1.158	1.191	1.225	1.260	1.295	1.331	1.368	1.405	1.443	1.482	1.521	1.561	1.602	1.643	1.685	1.728
4	1.041	1.082	1.126	1.170	1.216	1.262	1.311	1.360	1.412	1.464	1.518	1.574	1.630	1.689	1.749	1.811	1.874	1.939	2.005	2.074
5	1.051	1.104	1.159	1.217	1.276	1.338	1.403	1.469	1.539	1.611	1.685	1.762	1.842	1.925	2.011	2.100	2.192	2.288	2.386	2.488
6	1.062	1.126	1.194	1.265	1.340	1.419	1.501	1.587	1.677	1.772	1.870	1.974	2.082	2.195	2.313	2.436	2.565	2.700	2.840	2.986
7	1.072	1.149	1.230	1.316	1.407	1.504	1.606	1.714	1.828	1.949	2.076	2.211	2.353	2.502	2.660	2.826	3.001	3.185	3.379	3.583
8	1.083	1.172	1.267	1.369	1.477	1.594	1.718	1.851	1.993	2.144	2.305	2.476	2.658	2.853	3.059	3.278	3.511	3.759	4.021	4.300
9	1.094	1.195	1.305	1.423	1.551	1.689	1.838	1.999	2.172	2.358	2.558	2.773	3.004	3.252	3.518	3.803	4.108	4.435	4.785	5.160
10	1.105	1.219	1.344	1.480	1.629	1.791	1.967	2.159	2.367	2.594	2.839	3.106	3.395	3.707	4.046	4.411	4.807	5.234	5.695	6.192
11	1.116	1.243	1.384	1.539	1.710	1.898	2.105	2.332	2.580	2.853	3.152	3.479	3.836	4.226	4.652	5.117	5.624	6.176	6.777	7.430
12	1.127	1.268	1.426	1.601	1.796	2.012	2.252	2.518	2.813	3.138	3.498	3.896	4.334	4.818	5.350	5.936	6.580	7.288	8.064	8.916
13	1.138	1.294	1.469	1.665	1.886	2.133	2.410	2.720	3.066	3.452	3.883	4.363	4.898	5.492	6.153	6.886	7.699	8.599	9.596	10.699
14	1.149	1.319	1.513	1.732	1.980	2.261	2.579	2.937	3.342	3.797	4.310	4.887	5.535	6.261	7.076	7.987	9.007	10.147	11.420	12.839
15	1.161	1.346	1.558	1.801	2.079	2.397	2.759	3.172	3.642	4.177	4.785	5.474	6.254	7.138	8.137	9.265	10.539	11.974	13.589	15.407
16	1.173	1.373	1.605	1.873	2.183	2.540	2.952	3.426	3.970	4.595	5.311	6.130	7.067	8.137	9.358	10.748	12.330	14.129	16.171	18.488
17	1.184	1.400	1.653	1.948	2.292	2.693	3.159	3.700	4.328	5.054	5.895	6.866	7.986	9.276	10.761	12.468	14.426	16.672	19.244	22.186
18	1.196	1.428	1.702	2.026	2.407	2.854	3.380	3.996	4.717	5.560	6.543	7.690	9.024	10.575	12.375	14.462	16.879	19.673	22.900	26.623
19	1.208	1.457	1.753	2.107	2.527	3.026	3.616	4.316	5.142	6.116	7.263	8.613	10.197	12.055	14.232	16.776	19.748	23.214	27.251	31.948
20	1.220	1.486	1.806	2.191	2.653	3.207	3.870	4.661	5.604	6.727	8.062	9.646	11.523	13.743	16.366	19.461	23.105	27.393	32.429	38.337
21	1.232	1.516	1.860	2.279	2.786	3.399	4.140	5.034	6.109	7.400	8.949	10.804	13.021	15.667	18.821	22.574	27.033	32.323	38.591	46.005
22	1.245	1.546	1.916	2.370	2.925	3.603	4.430	5.436	6.658	8.140	9.933	12.100	14.713	17.861	21.644	26.186	31.629	38.141	45.923	55.205
23	1.257	1.577	1.974	2.465	3.071	3.820	4.740	5.871	7.258	8.954	11.026	13.552	16.626	20.361	24.891	30.376	37.005	45.007	54.648	66.247
24	1.270	1.608	2.033	2.563	3.225	4.049	5.072	6.341	7.911	9.850	12.239	15.178	18.788	23.212	28.625	35.236	43.296	53.108	65.031	79.496
25	1.282	1.641	2.094	2.666	3.386	4.292	5.427	6.848	8.623	10.834	13.585	17.000	21.230	26.461	32.918	40.874	50.656	62.667	77.387	95.395
30	1.348	1.811	2.427	3.243	4.322	5.743	7.612	10.062	13.267	17.449	22.892	29.960	39.115	50.949	66.210	85.849	111.061	143.367	184.672	237.373
35	1.417	2.000	2.814	3.946	5.516	7.686	10.676	14.785	20.413	28.102	38.574	52.799	72.066	98.097	133.172	180.311	243.495	327.988	440.691	590.657
40	1.489	2.208	3.262	4.801	7.040	10.285	14.974	21.724	31.408	45.258	64.999	93.049	132.776	188.876	267.856	378.715	533.846	750.353	1051.642	1469.740
45	1.565	2.438	3.781	5.841	8.985	13.764	21.002	31.920	48.325	72.888	109.527	163.985	244.629	363.662	538.752	795.429	1170.425	1716.619	2509.583	3657.176
50	1.645	2.691	4.384	7.106	11.467	18.419	29.456	46.900	74.354	117.386	184.559	288.996	450.711	700.197	1083.619	1670.669	2566.080	3927.189	5988.730	9100.191

TABLE A.1 *(Continued)*

Period	21%	22%	23%	24%	25%	26%	27%	28%	29%	30%	31%	32%	33%	34%	35%	40%	45%	50%
1	1.210	1.220	1.230	1.240	1.250	1.260	1.270	1.280	1.290	1.300	1.310	1.320	1.330	1.340	1.350	1.400	1.450	1.500
2	1.464	1.488	1.513	1.538	1.562	1.588	1.613	1.638	1.664	1.690	1.716	1.742	1.769	1.796	1.822	1.960	2.102	2.250
3	1.772	1.816	1.861	1.907	1.953	2.000	2.048	2.097	2.147	2.197	2.248	2.300	2.353	2.406	2.460	2.744	3.049	3.375
4	2.144	2.215	2.289	2.364	2.441	2.520	2.601	2.684	2.769	2.856	2.945	3.036	3.129	3.224	3.321	3.842	4.421	5.063
5	2.594	2.703	2.815	2.932	3.052	3.176	3.304	3.436	3.572	3.713	3.858	4.007	4.162	4.320	4.484	5.378	6.410	7.594
6	3.138	3.297	3.463	3.635	3.815	4.001	4.196	4.398	4.608	4.827	5.054	5.290	5.535	5.789	6.053	7.530	9.294	11.391
7	3.797	4.023	4.259	4.508	4.768	5.042	5.329	5.629	5.945	6.275	6.621	6.983	7.361	7.758	8.172	10.541	13.476	17.086
8	4.595	4.908	5.239	5.589	5.960	6.353	6.767	7.206	7.669	8.157	8.673	9.217	9.791	10.395	11.032	14.758	19.541	25.629
9	5.560	5.987	6.444	6.931	7.451	8.004	8.595	9.223	9.893	10.604	11.362	12.166	13.022	13.930	14.894	20.661	28.334	38.443
10	6.727	7.305	7.926	8.594	9.313	10.086	10.915	11.806	12.761	13.786	14.884	16.060	17.319	18.666	20.106	28.925	41.085	57.665
11	8.140	8.912	9.749	10.657	11.642	12.708	13.862	15.112	16.462	17.921	19.498	21.199	23.034	25.012	27.144	40.495	59.573	86.498
12	9.850	10.872	11.991	13.215	14.552	16.012	17.605	19.343	21.236	23.298	25.542	27.982	30.635	33.516	36.644	56.694	86.380	129.746
13	11.918	13.264	14.749	16.386	18.190	20.175	22.359	24.759	27.395	30.287	33.460	36.937	40.745	44.912	49.469	79.371	125.251	194.620
14	14.421	16.182	18.141	20.319	22.737	25.420	28.395	31.691	35.339	39.373	43.832	48.756	54.190	60.181	66.784	111.119	181.614	291.929
15	17.449	19.742	22.314	25.195	28.422	32.030	36.062	40.565	45.587	51.185	57.420	64.358	72.073	80.643	90.158	155.567	263.341	437.894
16	21.113	24.085	27.446	31.242	35.527	40.357	45.799	51.923	58.808	66.541	75.220	84.953	95.857	108.061	121.713	217.793	381.844	656.841
17	25.547	29.384	33.758	38.740	44.409	50.850	58.165	66.461	75.862	86.503	98.539	112.138	127.490	144.802	164.312	304.911	553.674	985.261
18	30.912	35.848	41.523	48.038	55.511	64.071	73.869	85.070	97.862	112.454	129.086	148.022	169.561	194.035	221.822	426.875	802.826	1477.892
19	37.404	43.735	51.073	59.567	69.389	80.730	93.813	108.890	126.242	146.190	169.102	195.389	225.517	260.006	299.459	597.625	1164.098	2216.838
20	45.258	53.357	62.820	73.863	86.736	101.720	119.143	139.379	162.852	190.047	221.523	257.913	299.937	348.408	404.270	836.674	1687.942	3325.257
21	54.762	65.095	77.268	91.591	108.420	128.167	151.312	178.405	210.079	247.061	290.196	340.446	398.916	466.867	545.764	1171.343	2447.515	4987.883
22	66.262	79.416	95.040	113.572	135.525	161.490	192.165	228.358	271.002	321.178	380.156	449.388	530.558	625.601	736.781	1639.878	3548.896	7481.824
23	80.178	96.887	116.899	140.829	169.407	203.477	244.050	292.298	349.592	417.531	498.004	593.192	705.642	838.305	994.653	2295.829	5145.898	11222.738
24	97.015	118.203	143.786	174.628	211.758	256.381	309.943	374.141	450.974	542.791	652.385	783.013	938.504	1123.328	1342.781	3214.158	7461.547	16834.109
25	117.388	144.207	176.857	216.539	264.698	323.040	393.628	478.901	581.756	705.627	854.623	1033.577	1248.210	1505.258	1812.754	4499.816	10819.242	25251.164
30	304.471	389.748	497.904	634.810	807.793	1025.904	1300.477	1645.488	2078.208	2619.936	3297.081	4142.008	5194.516	6503.285	8128.426	24201.043	69348.375	191751.000
35	789.716	1053.370	1401.749	1861.020	2465.189	3258.053	4296.547	5653.840	7423.988	9727.598	12719.918	16598.906	21617.363	28096.695	36448.051	130158.687	*	*
40	2048.309	2846.941	3946.340	5455.797	7523.156	10346.879	14195.051	19426.418	26520.723	36117.754	49072.621	66519.313	89962.188	121388.437	163433.875	700022.688	*	*
45	5312.758	7694.418	11110.121	15994.316	22958.844	32859.457	46897.973	66748.500	94739.937	134102.187	*	*	*	*	*	*	*	*
50	13779.844	20795.680	31278.301	46889.207	70064.812	104354.562	154942.687	229345.875	338440.000	497910.125	*	*	*	*	*	*	*	*

*Not shown because of space limitations.

TABLE A.2 Future-Value Interest Factors for a One-Dollar Annuity, FVIFA

Period	1%	2%	3%	4%	5%	6%	7%	8%	9%	10%	11%	12%	13%	14%	15%	16%	17%	18%	19%	20%
1	1.000	1.000	1.000	1.000	1.000	1.000	1.000	1.000	1.000	1.000	1.000	1.000	1.000	1.000	1.000	1.000	1.000	1.000	1.000	1.000
2	2.010	2.020	2.030	2.040	2.050	2.060	2.070	2.080	2.090	2.100	2.110	2.120	2.130	2.140	2.150	2.160	2.170	2.180	2.190	2.200
3	3.030	3.060	3.091	3.122	3.152	3.184	3.215	3.246	3.278	3.310	3.342	3.374	3.407	3.440	3.472	3.506	3.539	3.572	3.606	3.640
4	4.060	4.122	4.184	4.246	4.310	4.375	4.440	4.506	4.573	4.641	4.710	4.779	4.850	4.921	4.993	5.066	5.141	5.215	5.291	5.368
5	5.101	5.204	5.309	5.416	5.526	5.637	5.751	5.867	5.985	6.105	6.228	6.353	6.480	6.610	6.742	6.877	7.014	7.154	7.297	7.442
6	6.152	6.308	6.468	6.633	6.802	6.975	7.153	7.336	7.523	7.716	7.913	8.115	8.323	8.535	8.754	8.977	9.207	9.442	9.683	9.930
7	7.214	7.434	7.662	7.898	8.142	8.394	8.654	8.923	9.200	9.487	9.783	10.089	10.405	10.730	11.067	11.414	11.772	12.141	12.523	12.916
8	8.286	8.583	8.892	9.214	9.549	9.897	10.260	10.637	11.028	11.436	11.859	12.300	12.757	13.233	13.727	14.240	14.773	15.327	15.902	16.499
9	9.368	9.755	10.159	10.583	11.027	11.491	11.978	12.488	13.021	13.579	14.164	14.776	15.416	16.085	16.786	17.518	18.285	19.086	19.923	20.799
10	10.462	10.950	11.464	12.006	12.578	13.181	13.816	14.487	15.193	15.937	16.722	17.549	18.420	19.337	20.304	21.321	22.393	23.521	24.709	25.959
11	11.567	12.169	12.808	13.486	14.207	14.972	15.784	16.645	17.560	18.531	19.561	20.655	21.814	23.044	24.349	25.733	27.200	28.755	30.403	32.150
12	12.682	13.412	14.192	15.026	15.917	16.870	17.888	18.977	20.141	21.384	22.713	24.133	25.650	27.271	29.001	30.850	32.824	34.931	37.180	39.580
13	13.809	14.680	15.618	16.627	17.713	18.882	20.141	21.495	22.953	24.523	26.211	28.029	29.984	32.088	34.352	36.786	39.404	42.218	45.244	48.496
14	14.947	15.974	17.086	18.292	19.598	21.015	22.550	24.215	26.019	27.975	30.095	32.392	34.882	37.581	40.504	43.672	47.102	50.818	54.841	59.196
15	16.097	17.293	18.599	20.023	21.578	23.276	25.129	27.152	29.361	31.772	34.405	37.280	40.417	43.842	47.580	51.659	56.109	60.965	66.260	72.035
16	17.258	18.639	20.157	21.824	23.657	25.672	27.888	30.324	33.003	35.949	39.190	42.753	46.671	50.980	55.717	60.925	66.648	72.938	79.850	87.442
17	18.430	20.012	21.761	23.697	25.840	28.213	30.840	33.750	36.973	40.544	44.500	48.883	53.738	59.117	65.075	71.673	78.978	87.067	96.021	105.930
18	19.614	21.412	23.414	25.645	28.132	30.905	33.999	37.450	41.301	45.599	50.396	55.749	61.724	68.393	75.836	84.140	93.404	103.739	115.265	128.116
19	20.811	22.840	25.117	27.671	30.539	33.760	37.379	41.446	46.018	51.158	56.939	63.439	70.748	78.968	88.211	98.603	110.283	123.412	138.165	154.739
20	22.019	24.297	26.870	29.778	33.066	36.785	40.995	45.762	51.159	57.274	64.202	72.052	80.946	91.024	102.443	115.379	130.031	146.626	165.417	186.687
21	23.239	25.783	28.676	31.969	35.719	39.992	44.865	50.422	56.764	64.002	72.264	81.698	92.468	104.767	118.809	134.840	153.136	174.019	197.846	225.024
22	24.471	27.299	30.536	34.248	38.505	43.392	49.005	55.456	62.872	71.402	81.213	92.502	105.489	120.434	137.630	157.414	180.169	206.342	236.436	271.028
23	25.716	28.845	32.452	36.618	41.430	46.995	53.435	60.893	69.531	79.542	91.147	104.602	120.203	138.295	159.274	183.600	211.798	244.483	282.359	326.234
24	26.973	30.421	34.426	39.082	44.501	50.815	58.176	66.764	76.789	88.496	102.173	118.154	136.829	158.656	184.166	213.976	248.803	289.490	337.007	392.480
25	28.243	32.030	36.459	41.645	47.726	54.864	63.248	73.105	84.699	98.346	114.412	133.333	155.616	181.867	212.790	249.212	292.099	342.598	402.038	471.976
30	34.784	40.567	47.575	56.084	66.438	79.057	94.459	113.282	136.305	164.491	199.018	241.330	293.192	356.778	434.738	530.306	647.423	790.932	966.698	1181.865
35	41.659	49.994	60.461	73.651	90.318	111.432	138.234	172.314	215.705	271.018	341.583	431.658	546.663	693.552	881.152	1120.699	1426.448	1816.607	2314.173	2948.294
40	48.885	60.401	75.400	95.024	120.797	154.758	199.630	259.052	337.872	442.580	581.812	767.080	1013.667	1341.979	1779.048	2360.724	3134.412	4163.094	5529.711	7343.715
45	56.479	71.891	92.718	121.027	159.695	212.737	285.741	386.497	525.840	718.881	986.613	1358.208	1874.086	2590.464	3585.031	4965.191	6879.008	9531.258	13203.105	18280.914
50	64.461	84.577	112.794	152.664	209.341	290.325	406.516	573.756	815.051	1163.865	1668.723	2399.975	3459.344	4994.301	7217.488	10435.449	15088.805	21812.273	31514.492	45496.094

TABLE A.2 (Continued)

Period	21%	22%	23%	24%	25%	26%	27%	28%	29%	30%	31%	32%	33%	34%	35%	40%	45%	50%
1	1.000	1.000	1.000	1.000	1.000	1.000	1.000	1.000	1.000	1.000	1.000	1.000	1.000	1.000	1.000	1.000	1.000	1.000
2	2.210	2.220	2.230	2.240	2.250	2.260	2.270	2.280	2.290	2.300	2.310	2.320	2.330	2.340	2.350	2.400	2.450	2.500
3	3.674	3.708	3.743	3.778	3.813	3.848	3.883	3.918	3.954	3.990	4.026	4.062	4.099	4.136	4.172	4.360	4.552	4.750
4	5.446	5.524	5.604	5.684	5.766	5.848	5.931	6.016	6.101	6.187	6.274	6.362	6.452	6.542	6.633	7.104	7.601	8.125
5	7.589	7.740	7.893	8.048	8.207	8.368	8.533	8.700	8.870	9.043	9.219	9.398	9.581	9.766	9.954	10.946	12.022	13.188
6	10.183	10.442	10.708	10.980	11.259	11.544	11.837	12.136	12.442	12.756	13.077	13.406	13.742	14.086	14.438	16.324	18.431	20.781
7	13.321	13.740	14.171	14.615	15.073	15.546	16.032	16.534	17.051	17.583	18.131	18.696	19.277	19.876	20.492	23.853	27.725	32.172
8	17.119	17.762	18.430	19.123	19.842	20.588	21.361	22.163	22.995	23.858	24.752	25.678	26.638	27.633	28.664	34.395	41.202	49.258
9	21.714	22.670	23.669	24.712	25.802	26.940	28.129	29.369	30.664	32.015	33.425	34.895	36.429	38.028	39.696	49.152	60.743	74.887
10	27.274	28.657	30.113	31.643	33.253	34.945	36.723	38.592	40.556	42.619	44.786	47.062	49.451	51.958	54.590	69.813	89.077	113.330
11	34.001	35.962	38.039	40.238	42.566	45.030	47.639	50.398	53.318	56.405	59.670	63.121	66.769	70.624	74.696	98.739	130.161	170.995
12	42.141	44.873	47.787	50.895	54.208	57.738	61.501	65.510	69.780	74.326	79.167	84.320	89.803	95.636	101.840	139.234	189.734	257.493
13	51.991	55.745	59.778	64.109	68.760	73.750	79.106	84.853	91.016	97.624	104.709	112.302	120.438	129.152	138.484	195.928	276.114	387.239
14	63.909	69.009	74.528	80.496	86.949	93.925	101.465	109.611	118.411	127.912	138.169	149.239	161.183	174.063	187.953	275.299	401.365	581.858
15	78.330	85.191	92.669	100.815	109.687	119.346	129.860	141.302	153.750	167.285	182.001	197.996	215.373	234.245	254.737	386.418	582.980	873.788
16	95.779	104.933	114.983	126.010	138.109	151.375	165.922	181.867	199.337	218.470	239.421	262.354	287.446	314.888	344.895	541.985	846.321	1311.681
17	116.892	129.019	142.428	157.252	173.636	191.733	211.721	233.790	258.145	285.011	314.642	347.307	383.303	422.949	466.608	759.778	1228.165	1968.522
18	142.439	158.403	176.187	195.993	218.045	242.583	269.885	300.250	334.006	371.514	413.180	459.445	510.792	567.751	630.920	1064.689	1781.838	2953.783
19	173.351	194.251	217.710	244.031	273.556	306.654	343.754	385.321	431.868	483.968	542.266	607.467	680.354	761.786	852.741	1491.563	2584.665	4431.672
20	210.755	237.986	268.783	303.598	342.945	387.384	437.568	494.210	558.110	630.157	711.368	802.856	905.870	1021.792	1152.200	2089.188	3748.763	6648.508
21	256.013	291.343	331.603	377.461	429.681	489.104	556.710	633.589	720.962	820.204	932.891	1060.769	1205.807	1370.201	1556.470	2925.862	5436.703	9973.762
22	310.775	356.438	408.871	469.052	538.101	617.270	708.022	811.993	931.040	1067.265	1223.087	1401.215	1604.724	1837.068	2102.234	4097.203	7884.215	14961.645
23	377.038	435.854	503.911	582.624	673.626	778.760	900.187	1040.351	1202.042	1388.443	1603.243	1850.603	2135.282	2462.669	2839.014	5737.078	11433.109	22443.469
24	457.215	532.741	620.810	723.453	843.032	982.237	1144.237	1332.649	1551.634	1805.975	2101.247	2443.795	2840.924	3300.974	3833.667	8032.906	16579.008	33666.207
25	554.230	650.944	764.596	898.082	1054.791	1238.617	1454.180	1706.790	2002.608	2348.765	2753.631	3226.808	3779.428	4424.301	5176.445	11247.062	24040.555	50500.316
30	1445.111	1767.044	2160.459	2640.881	3227.172	3941.953	4812.891	5873.172	7162.785	8729.805	10632.543	12940.672	15737.945	19124.434	23221.258	60500.207	154105.313	383500.000
35	3755.814	4783.520	6090.227	7750.094	9856.746	12527.160	15909.480	20188.742	25596.512	32422.090	41028.887	51868.563	65504.199	82634.625	104134.500	325394.688	*	*
40	9749.141	12936.141	17153.691	22728.367	30088.621	39791.957	52570.707	69376.562	91447.375	120389.375	*	*	*	*	*	*	*	*
45	25294.223	34970.230	48300.660	66638.937	91831.312	126378.937	173692.875	238384.312	326686.375	447005.062	*	*	*	*	*	*	*	*

*Not shown because of space limitations.

TABLE A.3 Present-Value Interest Factors for One Dollar, PVIF

Period	1%	2%	3%	4%	5%	6%	7%	8%	9%	10%	11%	12%	13%	14%	15%	16%	17%	18%	19%	20%
1	.990	.980	.971	.962	.952	.943	.935	.926	.917	.909	.901	.893	.885	.877	.870	.862	.855	.847	.840	.833
2	.980	.961	.943	.925	.907	.890	.873	.857	.842	.826	.812	.797	.783	.769	.756	.743	.731	.718	.706	.694
3	.971	.942	.915	.889	.864	.840	.816	.794	.772	.751	.731	.712	.693	.675	.658	.641	.624	.609	.593	.579
4	.961	.924	.888	.855	.823	.792	.763	.735	.708	.683	.659	.636	.613	.592	.572	.552	.534	.516	.499	.482
5	.951	.906	.863	.822	.784	.747	.713	.681	.650	.621	.593	.567	.543	.519	.497	.476	.456	.437	.419	.402
6	.942	.888	.837	.790	.746	.705	.666	.630	.596	.564	.535	.507	.480	.456	.432	.410	.390	.370	.352	.335
7	.933	.871	.813	.760	.711	.665	.623	.583	.547	.513	.482	.452	.425	.400	.376	.354	.333	.314	.296	.279
8	.923	.853	.789	.731	.677	.627	.582	.540	.502	.467	.434	.404	.376	.351	.327	.305	.285	.266	.249	.233
9	.914	.837	.766	.703	.645	.592	.544	.500	.460	.424	.391	.361	.333	.308	.284	.263	.243	.225	.209	.194
10	.905	.820	.744	.676	.614	.558	.508	.463	.422	.386	.352	.322	.295	.270	.247	.227	.208	.191	.176	.162
11	.896	.804	.722	.650	.585	.527	.475	.429	.388	.350	.317	.287	.261	.237	.215	.195	.178	.162	.148	.135
12	.887	.789	.701	.625	.557	.497	.444	.397	.356	.319	.286	.257	.231	.208	.187	.168	.152	.137	.124	.112
13	.879	.773	.681	.601	.530	.469	.415	.368	.326	.290	.258	.229	.204	.182	.163	.145	.130	.116	.104	.093
14	.870	.758	.661	.577	.505	.442	.388	.340	.299	.263	.232	.205	.181	.160	.141	.125	.111	.099	.088	.078
15	.861	.743	.642	.555	.481	.417	.362	.315	.275	.239	.209	.183	.160	.140	.123	.108	.095	.084	.074	.065
16	.853	.728	.623	.534	.458	.394	.339	.292	.252	.218	.188	.163	.141	.123	.107	.093	.081	.071	.062	.054
17	.844	.714	.605	.513	.436	.371	.317	.270	.231	.198	.170	.146	.125	.108	.093	.080	.069	.060	.052	.045
18	.836	.700	.587	.494	.416	.350	.296	.250	.212	.180	.153	.130	.111	.095	.081	.069	.059	.051	.044	.038
19	.828	.686	.570	.475	.396	.331	.277	.232	.194	.164	.138	.116	.098	.083	.070	.060	.051	.043	.037	.031
20	.820	.673	.554	.456	.377	.312	.258	.215	.178	.149	.124	.104	.087	.073	.061	.051	.043	.037	.031	.026
21	.811	.660	.538	.439	.359	.294	.242	.199	.164	.135	.112	.093	.077	.064	.053	.044	.037	.031	.026	.022
22	.803	.647	.522	.422	.342	.278	.226	.184	.150	.123	.101	.083	.068	.056	.046	.038	.032	.026	.022	.018
23	.795	.634	.507	.406	.326	.262	.211	.170	.138	.112	.091	.074	.060	.049	.040	.033	.027	.022	.018	.015
24	.788	.622	.492	.390	.310	.247	.197	.158	.126	.102	.082	.066	.053	.043	.035	.028	.023	.019	.015	.013
25	.780	.610	.478	.375	.295	.233	.184	.146	.116	.092	.074	.059	.047	.038	.030	.024	.020	.016	.013	.010
30	.742	.552	.412	.308	.231	.174	.131	.099	.075	.057	.044	.033	.026	.020	.015	.012	.009	.007	.005	.004
35	.706	.500	.355	.253	.181	.130	.094	.068	.049	.036	.026	.019	.014	.010	.008	.006	.004	.003	.002	.002
40	.672	.453	.307	.208	.142	.097	.067	.046	.032	.022	.015	.011	.008	.005	.004	.003	.002	.001	.001	.001
45	.639	.410	.264	.171	.111	.073	.048	.031	.021	.014	.009	.006	.004	.003	.002	.001	.001	.001	*	*
50	.608	.372	.228	.141	.087	.054	.034	.021	.013	.009	.005	.003	.002	.001	.001	.001	*	*	*	*

**PVIF* is zero to three decimal places.

TABLE A.3 *(Continued)*

Period	21%	22%	23%	24%	25%	26%	27%	28%	29%	30%	31%	32%	33%	34%	35%	40%	45%	50%
1	.826	.820	.813	.806	.800	.794	.787	.781	.775	.769	.763	.758	.752	.746	.741	.714	.690	.667
2	.683	.672	.661	.650	.640	.630	.620	.610	.601	.592	.583	.574	.565	.557	.549	.510	.476	.444
3	.564	.551	.537	.524	.512	.500	.488	.477	.466	.455	.445	.435	.425	.416	.406	.364	.328	.296
4	.467	.451	.437	.423	.410	.397	.384	.373	.361	.350	.340	.329	.320	.310	.301	.260	.226	.198
5	.386	.370	.355	.341	.328	.315	.303	.291	.280	.269	.259	.250	.240	.231	.223	.186	.156	.132
6	.319	.303	.289	.275	.262	.250	.238	.227	.217	.207	.198	.189	.181	.173	.165	.133	.108	.088
7	.263	.249	.235	.222	.210	.198	.188	.178	.168	.159	.151	.143	.136	.129	.122	.095	.074	.059
8	.218	.204	.191	.179	.168	.157	.148	.139	.130	.123	.115	.108	.102	.096	.091	.068	.051	.039
9	.180	.167	.155	.144	.134	.125	.116	.108	.101	.094	.088	.082	.077	.072	.067	.048	.035	.026
10	.149	.137	.126	.116	.107	.099	.092	.085	.078	.073	.067	.062	.058	.054	.050	.035	.024	.017
11	.123	.112	.103	.094	.086	.079	.072	.066	.061	.056	.051	.047	.043	.040	.037	.025	.017	.012
12	.102	.092	.083	.076	.069	.062	.057	.052	.047	.043	.039	.036	.033	.030	.027	.018	.012	.008
13	.084	.075	.068	.061	.055	.050	.045	.040	.037	.033	.030	.027	.025	.022	.020	.013	.008	.005
14	.069	.062	.055	.049	.044	.039	.035	.032	.028	.025	.023	.021	.018	.017	.015	.009	.006	.003
15	.057	.051	.045	.040	.035	.031	.028	.025	.022	.020	.017	.016	.014	.012	.011	.006	.004	.002
16	.047	.042	.036	.032	.028	.025	.022	.019	.017	.015	.013	.012	.010	.009	.008	.005	.003	.002
17	.039	.034	.030	.026	.023	.020	.017	.015	.013	.012	.010	.009	.008	.007	.006	.003	.002	.001
18	.032	.028	.024	.021	.018	.016	.014	.012	.010	.009	.008	.007	.006	.005	.005	.002	.001	.001
19	.027	.023	.020	.017	.014	.012	.011	.009	.008	.007	.006	.005	.004	.004	.003	.002	.001	*
20	.022	.019	.016	.014	.012	.010	.008	.007	.006	.005	.005	.004	.003	.003	.002	.001	.001	*
21	.018	.015	.013	.011	.009	.008	.007	.006	.005	.004	.003	.003	.003	.002	.002	.001	*	*
22	.015	.013	.011	.009	.007	.006	.005	.004	.004	.003	.003	.002	.002	.002	.001	.001	*	*
23	.012	.010	.009	.007	.006	.005	.004	.003	.003	.002	.002	.002	.001	.001	.001	*	*	*
24	.010	.008	.007	.006	.005	.004	.003	.003	.002	.002	.002	.001	.001	.001	.001	*	*	*
25	.009	.007	.006	.005	.004	.003	.003	.002	.002	.001	.001	.001	.001	.001	.001	*	*	*
30	.003	.003	.002	.002	.001	.001	.001	.001	*	*	*	*	*	*	*	*	*	*
35	.001	.001	.001	.001	*	*	*	*	*	*	*	*	*	*	*	*	*	*
40	*	*	*	*	*	*	*	*	*	*	*	*	*	*	*	*	*	*
45	*	*	*	*	*	*	*	*	*	*	*	*	*	*	*	*	*	*
50	*	*	*	*	*	*	*	*	*	*	*	*	*	*	*	*	*	*

**PVIF* is zero to three decimal places.

TABLE A.4 Present-Value Interest Factors for a One-Dollar Annuity, PVIFA

Period	1%	2%	3%	4%	5%	6%	7%	8%	9%	10%	11%	12%	13%	14%	15%	16%	17%	18%	19%	20%
1	.990	.980	.971	.962	.952	.943	.935	.926	.917	.909	.901	.893	.885	.877	.870	.862	.855	.847	.840	.833
2	1.970	1.942	1.913	1.886	1.859	1.833	1.808	1.783	1.759	1.736	1.713	1.690	1.668	1.647	1.626	1.605	1.585	1.566	1.547	1.528
3	2.941	2.884	2.829	2.775	2.723	2.673	2.624	2.577	2.531	2.487	2.444	2.402	2.361	2.322	2.283	2.246	2.210	2.174	2.140	2.106
4	3.902	3.808	3.717	3.630	3.546	3.465	3.387	3.312	3.240	3.170	3.102	3.037	2.974	2.914	2.855	2.798	2.743	2.690	2.639	2.589
5	4.853	4.713	4.580	4.452	4.329	4.212	4.100	3.993	3.890	3.791	3.696	3.605	3.517	3.433	3.352	3.274	3.199	3.127	3.058	2.991
6	5.795	5.601	5.417	5.242	5.076	4.917	4.767	4.623	4.486	4.355	4.231	4.111	3.998	3.889	3.784	3.685	3.589	3.498	3.410	3.326
7	6.728	6.472	6.230	6.002	5.786	5.582	5.389	5.206	5.033	4.868	4.712	4.564	4.423	4.288	4.160	4.039	3.922	3.812	3.706	3.605
8	7.652	7.326	7.020	6.733	6.463	6.210	5.971	5.747	5.535	5.335	5.146	4.968	4.799	4.639	4.487	4.344	4.207	4.078	3.954	3.837
9	8.566	8.162	7.786	7.435	7.108	6.802	6.515	6.247	5.995	5.759	5.537	5.328	5.132	4.946	4.772	4.607	4.451	4.303	4.163	4.031
10	9.471	8.983	8.530	8.111	7.722	7.360	7.024	6.710	6.418	6.145	5.889	5.650	5.426	5.216	5.019	4.833	4.659	4.494	4.339	4.192
11	10.368	9.787	9.253	8.760	8.306	7.887	7.499	7.139	6.805	6.495	6.207	5.938	5.687	5.453	5.234	5.029	4.836	4.656	4.486	4.327
12	11.255	10.575	9.954	9.385	8.863	8.384	7.943	7.536	7.161	6.814	6.492	6.194	5.918	5.660	5.421	5.197	4.988	4.793	4.611	4.439
13	12.134	11.348	10.635	9.986	9.394	8.853	8.358	7.904	7.487	7.013	6.750	6.424	6.122	5.842	5.583	5.342	5.118	4.910	4.715	4.533
14	13.004	12.106	11.296	10.563	9.899	9.295	8.745	8.244	7.786	7.367	6.982	6.628	6.302	6.002	5.724	5.468	5.229	5.008	4.802	4.611
15	13.865	12.849	11.938	11.118	10.380	9.712	9.108	8.560	8.061	7.606	7.191	6.811	6.462	6.142	5.847	5.575	5.324	5.092	4.876	4.675
16	14.718	13.578	12.561	11.652	10.838	10.106	9.447	8.851	8.313	7.824	7.379	6.974	6.604	6.265	5.954	5.668	5.405	5.162	4.938	4.730
17	15.562	14.292	13.166	12.166	11.274	10.477	9.763	9.122	8.544	8.022	7.549	7.120	6.729	6.373	6.047	5.749	5.475	5.222	4.990	4.775
18	16.398	14.992	13.754	12.659	11.690	10.828	10.059	9.372	8.756	8.201	7.702	7.250	6.840	6.467	6.128	5.818	5.534	5.273	5.033	4.812
19	17.226	15.679	14.324	13.134	12.085	11.158	10.336	9.604	8.950	8.365	7.839	7.366	6.938	6.550	6.198	5.877	5.584	5.316	5.070	4.843
20	18.046	16.352	14.878	13.590	12.462	11.470	10.594	9.818	9.129	8.514	7.963	7.469	7.025	6.623	6.259	5.929	5.628	5.353	5.101	4.870
21	18.857	17.011	15.415	14.029	12.821	11.764	10.836	10.017	9.292	8.649	8.075	7.562	7.102	6.687	6.312	5.973	5.665	5.384	5.127	4.891
22	19.661	17.658	15.937	14.451	13.163	12.042	11.061	10.201	9.442	8.772	8.176	7.645	7.170	6.743	6.359	6.011	5.696	5.410	5.149	4.909
23	20.456	18.292	16.444	14.857	13.489	12.303	11.272	10.371	9.580	8.883	8.266	7.718	7.230	6.792	6.399	6.044	5.723	5.432	5.167	4.925
24	21.244	18.914	16.936	15.247	13.799	12.550	11.469	10.529	9.707	8.985	8.348	7.784	7.283	6.835	6.434	6.073	5.746	5.451	5.182	4.937
25	22.023	19.524	17.413	15.622	14.094	12.783	11.654	10.675	9.823	9.077	8.422	7.843	7.330	6.873	6.464	6.097	5.766	5.467	5.195	4.948
30	25.808	22.396	19.601	17.292	15.373	13.765	12.409	11.258	10.274	9.427	8.694	8.055	7.496	7.003	6.566	6.177	5.829	5.517	5.235	4.979
35	29.409	24.999	21.487	18.665	16.374	14.498	12.948	11.655	10.567	9.644	8.855	8.176	7.586	7.070	6.617	6.215	5.858	5.539	5.251	4.992
40	32.835	27.356	23.115	19.793	17.159	15.046	13.332	11.925	10.757	9.779	8.951	8.244	7.634	7.105	6.642	6.233	5.871	5.548	5.258	4.997
45	36.095	29.490	24.519	20.720	17.774	15.456	13.606	12.108	10.881	9.863	9.008	8.283	7.661	7.123	6.654	6.242	5.877	5.552	5.261	4.999
50	39.196	31.424	25.730	21.482	18.256	15.762	13.801	12.233	10.962	9.915	9.042	8.304	7.675	7.133	6.661	6.246	5.880	5.554	5.262	4.999

TABLE A.4 *(Continued)*

Period	21%	22%	23%	24%	25%	26%	27%	28%	29%	30%	31%	32%	33%	34%	35%	40%	45%	50%
1	.826	.820	.813	.806	.800	.794	.787	.781	.775	.769	.763	.758	.752	.746	.741	.714	.690	.667
2	1.509	1.492	1.474	1.457	1.440	1.424	1.407	1.392	1.376	1.361	1.346	1.331	1.317	1.303	1.289	1.224	1.165	1.111
3	2.074	2.042	2.011	1.981	1.952	1.923	1.896	1.868	1.842	1.816	1.791	1.766	1.742	1.719	1.696	1.589	1.493	1.407
4	2.540	2.494	2.448	2.404	2.362	2.320	2.280	2.241	2.203	2.166	2.130	2.096	2.062	2.029	1.997	1.849	1.720	1.605
5	2.926	2.864	2.803	2.745	2.689	2.635	2.583	2.532	2.483	2.436	2.390	2.345	2.302	2.260	2.220	2.035	1.876	1.737
6	3.245	3.167	3.092	3.020	2.951	2.885	2.821	2.759	2.700	2.643	2.588	2.534	2.483	2.433	2.385	2.168	1.983	1.824
7	3.508	3.416	3.327	3.242	3.161	3.083	3.009	2.937	2.868	2.802	2.739	2.677	2.619	2.562	2.508	2.263	2.057	1.883
8	3.726	3.619	3.518	3.421	3.329	3.241	3.156	3.076	2.999	2.925	2.854	2.786	2.721	2.658	2.598	2.331	2.109	1.922
9	3.905	3.786	3.673	3.566	3.463	3.366	3.273	3.184	3.100	3.019	2.942	2.868	2.798	2.730	2.665	2.379	2.144	1.948
10	4.054	3.923	3.799	3.682	3.570	3.465	3.364	3.269	3.178	3.092	3.009	2.930	2.855	2.784	2.715	2.414	2.168	1.965
11	4.177	4.035	3.902	3.776	3.656	3.544	3.437	3.335	3.239	3.147	3.060	2.978	2.899	2.824	2.752	2.438	2.185	1.977
12	4.278	4.127	3.985	3.851	3.725	3.606	3.493	3.387	3.286	3.190	3.100	3.013	2.931	2.853	2.779	2.456	2.196	1.985
13	4.362	4.203	4.053	3.912	3.780	3.656	3.538	3.427	3.322	3.223	3.129	3.040	2.956	2.876	2.799	2.469	2.204	1.990
14	4.432	4.265	4.108	3.962	3.824	3.695	3.573	3.459	3.351	3.249	3.152	3.061	2.974	2.892	2.814	2.478	2.210	1.993
15	4.489	4.315	4.153	4.001	3.859	3.726	3.601	3.483	3.373	3.268	3.170	3.076	2.988	2.905	2.825	2.484	2.214	1.995
16	4.536	4.357	4.189	4.033	3.887	3.751	3.623	3.503	3.390	3.283	3.183	3.088	2.999	2.914	2.834	2.489	2.216	1.997
17	4.576	4.391	4.219	4.059	3.910	3.771	3.640	3.518	3.403	3.295	3.193	3.097	3.007	2.921	2.840	2.492	2.218	1.998
18	4.608	4.419	4.243	4.080	3.928	3.786	3.654	3.529	3.413	3.304	3.201	3.104	3.012	2.926	2.844	2.494	2.219	1.999
19	4.635	4.442	4.263	4.097	3.942	3.799	3.664	3.539	3.421	3.311	3.207	3.109	3.017	2.930	2.848	2.496	2.220	1.999
20	4.657	4.460	4.279	4.110	3.954	3.808	3.673	3.546	3.427	3.316	3.211	3.113	3.020	2.933	2.850	2.497	2.221	1.999
21	4.675	4.476	4.292	4.121	3.963	3.816	3.679	3.551	3.432	3.320	3.215	3.116	3.023	2.935	2.852	2.498	2.221	2.000
22	4.690	4.488	4.302	4.130	3.970	3.822	3.684	3.556	3.436	3.323	3.217	3.118	3.025	2.936	2.853	2.498	2.222	2.000
23	4.703	4.499	4.311	4.137	3.976	3.827	3.689	3.559	3.438	3.325	3.219	3.120	3.026	2.938	2.854	2.499	2.222	2.000
24	4.713	4.507	4.318	4.143	3.981	3.831	3.692	3.562	3.441	3.327	3.221	3.121	3.027	2.939	2.855	2.499	2.222	2.000
25	4.721	4.514	4.323	4.147	3.985	3.834	3.694	3.564	3.442	3.329	3.222	3.122	3.028	2.939	2.856	2.499	2.222	2.000
30	4.746	4.534	4.339	4.160	3.995	3.842	3.701	3.569	3.447	3.332	3.225	3.124	3.030	2.941	2.857	2.500	2.222	2.000
35	4.756	4.541	4.345	4.164	3.998	3.845	3.703	3.571	3.448	3.333	3.226	3.125	3.030	2.941	2.857	2.500	2.222	2.000
40	4.760	4.544	4.347	4.166	3.999	3.846	3.703	3.571	3.448	3.333	3.226	3.125	3.030	2.941	2.857	2.500	2.222	2.000
45	4.761	4.545	4.347	4.166	4.000	3.846	3.704	3.571	3.448	3.333	3.226	3.125	3.030	2.941	2.857	2.500	2.222	2.000
50	4.762	4.545	4.348	4.167	4.000	3.846	3.704	3.571	3.448	3.333	3.226	3.125	3.030	2.941	2.857	2.500	2.222	2.000

CREDITS

8 Reprinted with permission of Money Magazine, "What's Your Investing IQ?" Laura Lallos, *Money,* August 2000, pp. 91–92. © 2000 Time Inc. All rights reserved.

38 Reprinted with permission of Reliant Resources, Inc., public offering of common stock, April 16, 2001, p. 1.

38 Reprinted with permission of The Wall Street Journal via the Copyright Clearance Center, "Initial Public Offerings, Top to Bottom," *The Wall Street Journal,* January 3, 2000, p. R4.

80 Reprinted with permission of The Value Line Investment Survey, Ratings and Reports December 25, 2000 for © PepsiCo, Inc.

85 Reprinted with permission © PepsiCo, Inc. 2000.

91 Reprinted with permission from Yodlee Inc., screen capture from www.yodlee.com/demo/demo.html.

96 Reprinted with permission of The Wall Street Journal via the Copyright Clearance Center, Stock Market Data Bank, *The Wall Street Journal,* September 29, 2000, p. C2.

97 Reprinted with permission of The Wall Street Journal via the Copyright Clearance Center, Graph of the Dow Jones Industrial Average from 3/31/00 through 9/28/00 from *The Wall Street Journal,* September 29, 2000, p. C3.

110 Reprinted with permission of Ameritrade Holding Corporation, all rights in the copyrightable content and trademarks are owned and reserved by Ameritrade Holding Corporation, and that Ameritrade ® is a registered trademark of Ameritrade Holding Corporation.

132 Reprinted with permission of Morningstar, Inc., "Stock Returns," November 9, 2000, www.morningstar.com.

152 Reprinted with permission of Knight Ridder/Tribune Information Services, "Study: Female Investors Better: Women Don't Seem to Buy, Sell As Often As Men Do," by Harriet Johnson Brackey, July 31, 2000, p. 4D.

160 Reprinted with permission of Money, "The Skeptical Investor," by Walter Updegrave, June 2000, p. 134. © Time Inc. All rights reserved.

179 Reprinted with permission of Money, "Investing 101: Why Diversification Pays," by Walter Updegrave, December 1999. © 2000 Time Inc. All rights reserved.

193 Reprinted with permission of ING Pilgrim, Table of Pilgrim Growth Opportunities Fund, Investments by Industry Group, 2000 Annual Report, December 31, 2000.

203 Reprinted with permission of The Wall Street Journal via the Copyright Clearance Center, "Bonds,Cash Beat Stocks in Second Quarter," by Terzah Ewing *The Wall Street Journal,* August 24, 2000.

231 Reprinted with permission of Morningstar, Inc., Table compiled of graphs – Average annual return figures 90s decade, June 2000.

233 Reprinted with permission of Arena Pharmaceuticals. Announcement of new stock issue August 15, 2000.

237 Reprinted with permission of The Wall Street Journal via the Copyright Clearance Center, Stock Quotations, *The Wall Street Journal,* September 7, 2000.

238 Reprinted with permission of Fortune Magazine, "Corporate Snapshots" from www.fortune.com, December 8, 2000.

242 Reprinted with permission of The Wall Street Journal via the Copyright Clearance Center, Corporate Dividend News, *The Wall Street Journal,* August 15, 2000.

246 Reprinted with permission of Standard and Poor's, Stock Reports – Home Depot, *Standard and Poors,* January 8, 2000.

247 Reprinted with permission of Standard and Poor's, Stock Reports – Staples, Inc., *Standard and Poors,* January 8, 2000.

248 Reprinted with permission of Standard and Poor's, Stock Reports – Cisco Systems, *Standard and Poors,* January 8, 2000.

251 Reprinted with permission of Standard and Poor's, Stock Reports – Dial Corp., *Standard and Poors,* January 8, 2000.

251 Reprinted with permission of Standard and Poor's, Stock Reports – Dreyer's Grand Ice Cream, *Standard and Poors,* January 8, 2000.

255 Reprinted with permission of Morgan Stanley, Graph based on data from Morgan Stanley Capital International.

276 Reprinted from December 11, 2000 issue of Business Week by special permission, © 2000 by The McGraw-Hill Companies, Inc. "A Test for the New Economy," by Gene Koretz.

276 Reprinted with permission of Mutual Funds, "Seven Engines of the Economy," by Jay N. Mueller, August 2000, pp. 38–39.

283 Reprinted with permission of Standard and Poor's, S&P Index Services as reported on its website, www.spglobal.com, September 29, 2000.

301 Reprinted with permission of Standard and Poor's, Stock Report—Medtronic, Inc., *Standard and Poor's,* January 8, 2000.

315 Reprinted with permission of Money/Tech 2000, "Best Stocks & Funds: Invest the Smart Way to Buy Tech," by Jon Birger, Pablo Galarza, Laura Lallos, Jeanne Lee, October 15, 2000. © 2000 Time Inc. All rights reserved.

334 Reprinted with permission of Money, "Terms of Trade," by Walter Updegrave, March 2000. © 2000 Time Inc. All rights reserved.

337 Reprinted with permission of The Research Works, Inc., at www.stocksontheweb.com.

346 Reprinted with permission of The Wall Street Journal via the Copyright Clearance Center, Stock Market Data Bank, *The Wall Street Journal,* October 10, 2000, p. C2.

347 Reprinted with permission of The Wall Street Journal via the Copyright Clearance Center, "Stocks End Stormy January with Strong Bounce Back," by E.S. Browning, *The Wall Street Journal,* February 1, 2000.

348 Reprinted with permission of The Wall Street Journal via the Copyright Clearance Center, NYSE and AMEX Short-Selling Highlights, *The Wall Street Journal,* October 20, 2000.

350 Reprinted with permission of StockCharts.com, at www.stockcharts.com.

375 Reprinted with permission of Morningstar, Inc. Graph based on data from Morningstar-Comparative Performance of Stocks and Bonds in the 90s.

380 Reproduced with permission of Hewlett-Packard Company, Announcement of a new bond issue. © June 6, 2000.

397 Reprinted with permission of Datastream, Comparative Annual Returns in the World's Major Bond Markets. © Thomson Financial Datastream. All Rights Reserved.

403 Reprinted with permission of The Wall Street Journal via the Copyright Clearance Center, Quotations for Corporate and Government Bonds, *The Wall Street Journal,* July 7, 2000.

416 Reprinted with permission of The Wall Street Journal via the Copyright Clearance Center, "Bond Prices Finish Lower After a Thin Session, Depressed by Expected Heavy New-Issue Slate," by Michael S. Derby and Gregory Zuckerman, *The Wall Street Journal,* July 11, 2000.

493 Reprinted with permission of Morningstar, Inc., Fidelity Low-Priced Stock Fund, list of common stocks, January 2000.

494 Reprinted with permission of the Investment Company Institute, Who Owns the Funds, and Why?, downloaded from 2000 Mutual Fund Fact Book, www.ici.org.

495 Reprinted with permission of Morningstar, Inc., Comparative Performance of Mutual Funds versus the Market, June 2000.

499 Reprinted with permission of The Wall Street Journal via the Copyright Clearance Center, Stock Quotations, *The Wall Street Journal,* July 19, 2000.

505 Reprinted with permission from the August 2, 2000 Issue of Kiplinger's Personal Finance.com, © 2000, The Kiplinger's Washington Editors, Inc.

506 Reprinted with permission of The Wall Street Journal via the Copyright Clearance Center, Mutual Fund Quotes, *The Wall Street Journal,* August 2, 2000.

519 Reprinted with permission of Morningstar, Inc., Graph of Growth of $10,000, from 7/1/85 to 6/30/00.

520 Reprinted with permission of Morningstar, Inc., Table of 20 of the 50 Biggest Fund Families, adapted from Morningstar Principia Pro for Mutual Funds, June 30, 2000.

522 Reprinted with permission of The Wall Street Journal via the Copyright Clearance Center, "Cheap Funds: Putting Your Pennies to Work," by Jeff D. Opdyke, *The Wall Street Journal,* July 10, 2000, p. C14.

524 Reprinted with permission of Morningstar, Inc., Fidelity Growth Company, Morningstar Mutual Funds Principia Pro released March 22, 2000.

GLOSSARY

A

(ADRs) dollar-denominated negotiable receipts for the stocks of foreign companies that are held in the vaults of banks in the companies' home countries.

12(b)-1 fee a fee levied annually by some mutual funds to cover management and other operating costs; amounts to as much as 1% of the average net assets.

accrual-type securities securities for which interest is paid when the bond is cashed, on or before maturity, rather than periodically over the life of the bond.

activity ratios financial ratios that are used to measure how well a firm is managing its assets.

agency bonds debt securities issued by various agencies and organizations of the U.S. government.

aggressive growth fund a highly speculative mutual fund that seeks large profits from capital gains.

American depositary receipts (ADRs) dollar-denominated negotiable receipts for the stocks of foreign companies that are held in the vaults of banks in the companies' home countries.

AMEX composite index measure of the current price behavior of the stocks listed on the AMEX, relative to a base of 100 set at August 31, 1973.

analytical information available current data in conjunction with projections and recommendations about potential investments.

annuity a stream of equal cash flows that occur at equal intervals over time.

arbitration a formal dispute resolution process in which a customer and a broker present their argument before a panel, which then decides the case.

ask price the lowest price at which a dealer is willing to sell a given security.

asset allocation a scheme that involves dividing one's portfolio into various asset classes to *preserve capital* by protecting against negative developments while taking advantage of positive ones.

asset allocation fund a mutual fund that seeks to reduce the variability of returns by investing in the right assets at the right time; emphasizes diversification and relatively consistent performance rather than the potential for spectacular gains.

asset management account a comprehensive deposit account that combines checking, investing, and borrowing activities; it automatically "sweeps" excess balances into short-term investments and borrows to meet shortages.

asset-backed securities (ABS) securities similar to mortgage-backed securities that are backed by a pool of bank loans, leases, and other assets.

automatic investment plan a mutual fund service that allows shareholders to automatically send fixed amounts of money from their paychecks or bank accounts into the fund.

automatic reinvestment plan a mutual fund service that enables shareholders to automatically buy additional shares in the fund through the reinvestment of dividends and capital gains income.

averages numbers used to measure the general behavior of stock prices by reflecting the arithmetic average price behavior of a representative group of stocks at a given point in time.

B

back-end load a commission charged on the sale of shares in a mutual fund.

back-office research reports a brokerage firm's analyses of and recommendations on investment prospects; available on request at no cost to existing and potential clients or for purchase at some Web sites.

balance sheet a financial summary of a firm's assets, liabilities, and shareholders' equity at a single point in time.

balanced fund a mutual fund whose objective is to generate a balanced return of both current income and long-term capital gains.

banker's acceptances short-term, low-risk investment vehicles arising from bank guarantees of business transactions; are sold at a discount from their face value and generally provide yields slightly below those of CDs and commercial paper.

bar chart the simplest kind of chart, on which share price is plotted on the vertical axis and time on the horizontal axis; stock prices are recorded as vertical bars showing high, low, and closing prices.

Barron's a weekly business newspaper; a popular source of financial news.

bear markets unfavorable markets normally associated with falling prices, investor pessimism, economic slowdown, and government restraint.

beta a measure of *nondiversifiable,* or *market, risk* that indicates how the price of a security responds to market forces.

bid price the highest price offered by a dealer to purchase a given security.

blue-chip stocks financially strong, high-quality stocks with long and stable records of earnings and dividends.

bond fund a mutual fund that invests in various kinds and grades of bonds, with income as the primary objective.

bond ladders an investment strategy wherein equal

amounts of money are invested in a series of bonds with staggered maturities.

bond ratings letter grades that designate investment quality and are assigned to a bond issue by rating agencies.

bond swap an investment strategy wherein an investor liquidates one bond holding and simultaneously buys a different issue in its place.

bond yield summary measure of the total return an investor would receive on a bond if it were purchased at its current price and held to maturity; reported as an annual rate of return.

bond-equivalent yield the annual yield on a bond, calculated as twice the semiannual yield.

bonds long-term debt instruments (IOUs), issued by corporations and governments, that offer a known interest return plus return of the bond's *face value* at maturity.

bonds negotiable, publicly traded long-term debt securities, whereby the issuer agrees to pay a fixed amount of interest over a specified period of time and to repay a fixed amount of principal at maturity.

book value the amount of stockholders' equity in a firm; equals the amount of the firm's assets minus the firm's liabilities and preferred stock.

brokered CDs certificates of deposit sold by stockbrokers; offer slightly higher yields than other CDs and typically can be sold prior to maturity without incurring a penalty.

bull markets favorable markets normally associated with rising prices, investor optimism, economic recovery, and government stimulus.

burn rate the rate at which the firm is using up its supply of cash over time.

business cycle an indication of the current state of the economy, reflecting changes in total economic activity over time.

business risk the degree of uncertainty associated with an investment's earnings and the investment's ability to pay the returns owed investors.

C

call feature feature that specifies whether and under what conditions the issuer can retire a bond prior to maturity.

call premium the amount added to a bond's par value and paid to investors when a bond is retired prematurely.

call price the price the issuer must pay to retire a bond prematurely; equal to par value plus the call premium.

capital asset pricing model (CAPM) model that formally links the notions of risk and return; it uses beta, the risk-free rate, and the market return to help investors define the required return on an investment.

capital gains the amount by which the sale price of an asset *exceeds* its original purchase price.

capital gains distributions payments made to mutual fund shareholders that come from the profits that a fund makes from the sale of its securities.

capital loss the amount by which the proceeds from the sale of a capital asset are *less than* its original purchase price.

capital market market in which *long-term* securities such as stocks and bonds are bought and sold.

cash account a brokerage account in which a customer can make only cash transactions.

cash dividend payment of a dividend in the form of cash.

certificates of deposit (CDs) savings instruments in which funds must remain on deposit for a specified period; withdrawals prior to maturity incur interest penalties.

charting the activity of charting price behavior and other market information and then using the patterns these charts form to make investment decisions.

churning an illegal and unethical practice engaged in by a broker to increase commissions by causing excessive trading of clients' accounts.

classified common stock common stock issued by a company in different classes, each of which offers different privileges and benefits to its holders.

closed-end investment companies a type of investment company that operates with a fixed number of shares outstanding.

coefficient of variation, *CV* a statistic used to measure the *relative* dispersion of an asset's returns; it is useful in comparing the risk of assets with differing average or expected returns.

collateral trust bonds senior bonds backed by securities owned by the issuer but held in trust by a third party.

collateralized mortgage obligation (CMO) mortgage-backed bond whose holders are divided into classes based on the length of investment desired; principal is channeled to investors in order of maturity, with short-term classes first.

commercial paper short-term, unsecured promissory notes (IOUs) issued by corporations with very high credit standings.

common stock equity investment that represents ownership in a corporation; each share represents a fractional ownership interest in the firm.

common stock (market) ratios financial ratios that convert key information about a firm to a per-share basis.

compound interest interest paid not only on the initial deposit but also on any interest accumulated from one period to the next.

continuous compounding interest calculation in which interest is compounded over the smallest possible interval of time.

conversion (exchange) privilege feature of a mutual fund that allows shareholders to move money from one fund to another, within the same family of funds.

convertible security a fixed-income obligation (bond or preferred stock) with a feature permitting conversion into a specified number of shares of common stock.

correlation a statistical measure of the relationship, if any, between series of numbers representing data of any kind.

correlation coefficient a measure of the degree of correlation between two series.

coupon feature on a bond that defines the amount of annual interest income.

currency exchange rate the relationship between two currencies on a specified date.

currency exchange risk the risk caused by the varying exchange rates between the currencies of two countries.

current income usually cash or near-cash that is periodically received as a result of owning an investment.

current yield measure of the annual interest income a bond provides relative to its current market price.

custodial account the brokerage account of a minor; requires a parent or guardian to be part of all transactions.

cyclical stocks stocks whose earnings and overall market performance are closely linked to the general state of the economy.

D

date of record the date on which an investor must be a registered shareholder of a firm to be entitled to receive a dividend.

day trader an investor who buys and sells stocks quickly throughout the day in hopes of making quick profits.

dealers traders who "make markets" by offering to buy or sell certain over-the-counter securities at stated prices.

debenture an unsecured (junior) bond.

debit balance the amount of money being borrowed in a margin loan.

debt funds lent in exchange for interest income and the promised repayment of the loan at a given future date.

defensive stocks stocks that tend to hold their own, and even do well, when the economy starts to falter.

deflation a period of generally declining prices.

derivative securities securities that are structured to exhibit characteristics similar to those of an underlying security or asset and that derive their value from the underlying security or asset.

descriptive information factual data on the past behavior of the economy, the market, the industry, the company, or a given investment vehicle.

direct investment investment in which an investor directly acquires a claim on a security or property.

discount basis a method of earning interest on a security by purchasing it at a price below its redemption value; the difference is the interest earned.

discount bond a bond with a market value lower than par; occurs when market rates are greater than the coupon rate.

discount broker broker who charges low commissions to make transactions for customers but provides little or no free research information or investment advice.

discount rate the annual rate of return that could be earned currently on a similar investment; used when finding present value; also called *opportunity cost.*

diversifiable (unsystematic) risk the portion of an investment's risk that results from uncontrollable or random events that are firm-specific; can be eliminated through diversification.

diversification the inclusion of a number of different investment vehicles in a portfolio to increase returns or reduce risk.

dividend income income derived from the dividend and interest income earned on the security holdings of a mutual fund.

dividend payout ratio the portion of earnings per share (EPS) that a firm pays out as dividends.

dividend reinvestment plans (DRIPs) plans in which shareholders have cash dividends automatically reinvested into additional shares of the firm's common stock.

dividend valuation model (DVM) a model that values a share of stock on the basis of the future dividend stream it is expected to produce; its three versions are zero-growth, constant-growth, and variable-growth.

dividend yield a measure that relates dividends to share price and puts common stock dividends on a relative (percentage) rather than absolute (dollar) basis.

dividends periodic payments made by firms to their shareholders.

dividends-and-earnings (D&E) approach stock valuation approach that uses projected dividends, EPS, and P/E multiples to value a share of stock.

domestic investments debt, equity, and derivative securities of U.S.-based companies.

Dow Jones bond averages mathematical averages of the *closing prices* for groups of utility, industrial, and composite bonds.

Dow Jones Industrial Average (DJIA) a stock market average made up of 30 high-quality stocks selected for total market value and broad public ownership and believed to reflect overall market activity.

dual listing listing of a firm's shares on more than one exchange.

duration a measure of bond price volatility, which captures both price and reinvestment risks and which is used to indicate how a bond will react in different interest rate environments.

E

earnings per share (EPS) the amount of annual earnings available to common stockholders, as stated on a per-share basis.

economic analysis a study of general economic conditions that is used in the valuation of common stock.

efficient frontier the leftmost boundary of the feasible (attainable) set of portfolios that includes all efficient portfolios—those providing the best attainable tradeoff between risk (measured by the standard deviation) and return.

efficient market a market in which securities reflect all possible information quickly and accurately.

efficient markets hypothesis (EMH) basic theory of the behavior of efficient markets, in which there are a large number of knowledgeable investors who react quickly to new information, causing securities prices to adjust quickly and accurately.

efficient portfolio a portfolio that provides the highest return for a given level of risk or that has the lowest risk for a given level of return.

electronic communications networks (ECNs) privately owned electronic trading networks that automatically match buy and sell orders that customers place electronically.

equipment trust certificates senior bonds secured by specific pieces of equipment; popular with transportation companies such as airlines.

equity ongoing ownership in a business or property.

equity capital evidence of ownership position in a firm, in the form of shares of common stock.

equity-income fund a mutual fund that emphasizes current income and capital preservation and invests primarily in high-yielding common stocks.

ethics standards of conduct or moral judgment.

Eurodollar bonds foreign bonds denominated in dollars but not registered with the SEC, thus restricting sales of new issues.

event risk risk that comes from an unexpected event that has a significant and usually immediate effect on the underlying value of an investment.

excess margin more equity than is required in a margin account.

exchange-traded fund (ETF) an open-end mutual fund that trades as a listed security on a stock exchange.

ex-dividend date three business days before the date of record; determines whether one is an official shareholder of a firm and thus eligible to receive a declared dividend.

expectations hypothesis theory that the shape of the yield curve reflects investor expectations of future interest rates.

expected inflation premium the average rate of inflation expected in the future.

expected return the rate of return an investor can expect to earn by holding a bond over a period of time that's less than the life of the issue; the return an investor thinks an investment will earn in the future.

F

fair disclosure rule (Regulation FD) rule requiring senior executives to disclose critical information simultaneously to investment professionals and the public via press releases or SEC filings.

financial institutions organizations that channel the savings of governments, businesses, and individuals into loans or investments.

financial leverage the use of debt financing to magnify investment returns.

financial markets forums in which suppliers and demanders of funds make financial transactions.

financial portals supersites on the Web that bring together many investing features, including real-time quotes, stock and mutual fund screens, portfolio trackers, news, research, and transaction capabilities, along with other personal finance features.

financial risk the degree of uncertainty of payment attributable to the mix of debt and equity used to finance a business; the larger the proportion of debt financing, the greater this risk.

first and refunding bonds bonds secured in part with both first and second mortgages.

fixed-commission schedules fixed brokerage commissions that typically apply to the small transactions usually made by individual investors.

fixed-income securities investment vehicles that offer a fixed periodic return.

fixed-weightings approach asset allocation plan in which a fixed percentage of the portfolio is allocated to each asset category.

flexible-weightings approach asset allocation plan in which weights for each asset category are adjusted periodically based on market analysis.

foreign investments debt, equity, and derivative securities of foreign-based companies.

Form 10-K a statement that must be filed annually with the SEC by all firms having securities listed on an organized exchange or traded in the Nasdaq market.

fourth market transactions made directly between large institutional buyers and sellers of securities.

full-service broker broker who, in addition to executing clients' transactions, provides them with a full array of brokerage services.

fully compounded rate of return the rate of return that includes interest earned on interest.

fund families different kinds of mutual funds offered by a single investment management company.

fundamental analysis the in-depth study of the financial condition and operating results of a firm.

future value the amount to which a current deposit will grow over a period of time when it is placed in an account paying compound interest.

futures legally binding obligations stipulating that the sellers of such contracts will make delivery and the buyers of the contracts will take delivery of a specified commodity or financial instrument at some specific date, at a price agreed on at the time the contract is sold.

G

general obligation bonds municipal bonds backed by the full faith, credit, and taxing power of the issuer.

growth cycle a reflection of the amount of business vitality that occurs within an industry (or company) over time.

growth fund a mutual fund whose primary goals are capital gains and long-term growth.

growth investing investing in stocks with above-average forecasts of earnings growth and high price/earnings ratios in expectation of higher returns.

growth stocks stocks that experience high rates of growth in operations and earnings.

growth-and-income fund a mutual fund that seeks both long-term growth and current income, with primary emphasis on capital gains.

growth-oriented portfolio a portfolio whose primary objective is long-term price appreciation.

H

holding period the period of time over which one wishes to measure the return on an investment vehicle.

holding period return (HPR) the total return earned from holding an investment for a specified holding period (*usually 1 year or less*).

I

income bonds unsecured bonds requiring that interest be paid only after a specified amount of income is earned.

income statement a financial summary of the operating results of a firm covering a specified period of time, usually 1 year.

income stocks stocks with long and sustained records of paying higher-than-average dividends.

income-oriented portfolio a portfolio that stresses current dividend and interest returns.

index fund a mutual fund that buys and holds a portfolio of stocks (or bonds) equivalent to those in a specific market index.

indexes numbers used to measure the general behavior of stock prices by measuring the current price behavior of a representative group of stocks in relation to a base value set at an earlier point in time.

indirect investment investment made in a *portfolio*, or collection of securities or properties.

individual investors investors who manage their own funds.

industry analysis study of industry groupings that looks at the competitive position of a particular industry in relation to others and identifies companies that show particular promise within an industry.

inflation a period of generally rising prices.

initial margin the minimum amount of equity that must be provided by a margin investor *at the time of purchase.*

initial public offering (IPO) the first public sale of a company's stock.

insider trading the illegal use of *nonpublic* information about a company to make profitable securities transactions.

institutional investors investment professionals paid to manage other people's money.

interest the "rent" paid by a borrower for use of the lender's money.

interest rate risk the chance that changes in interest rates will adversely affect a security's value.

international fund a mutual fund that does all or most of its investing in foreign securities.

intrinsic value the underlying or inherent value of a stock, as determined through fundamental analysis.

investment any vehicle into which funds can be placed with the expectation that it will generate positive income and/or preserve or increase its value.

investment banker financial intermediary that specializes in selling new security issues and advising firms with regard to major financial transactions.

investment goals the financial objectives that one wishes to achieve by investing.

investment letters newsletters that provide, on a subscription basis, the analyses, conclusions, and recommendations of experts in securities investment.

investment plan a written document describing how funds will be invested and specifying the target date for achieving each investment goal and the amount of tolerable risk.

investment value the amount that investors believe a security should be trading for, or what they think it's worth.

J

junior bonds debt obligations backed only by the promise of the issuer to pay interest and principal on a timely basis.

junk bonds high-risk securities that have low ratings but produce high yields.

L

leverage measures financial ratios that measure the amount of debt being used to support operations and the ability of the firm to service its debt.

limit order an order to buy at or below a specified price or to sell at or above a specified price.

liquidity the ability of an investment to be converted into cash quickly and with little or no loss in value.

liquidity measures financial ratios concerned with a firm's ability to meet its day-to-day operating expenses and satisfy its short-term obligations as they come due.

liquidity preference theory theory that investors tend to prefer the greater liquidity of short-term securities and therefore require a premium to invest in long-term securities.

liquidity risk the risk of not being able to liquidate an investment conveniently and at a reasonable price.

load fund a mutual fund that charges a commission when shares are bought; also known as a *front-end load fund.*

long purchase a transaction in which investors buy securities in the hope that they will increase in value and can be sold at a later date for profit.

long-term investments investments with maturities of longer than a year or with no maturity at all.

low-load fund a mutual fund that charges a small commission (2% to 3%) when shares are bought.

M

maintenance margin the absolute minimum amount of margin (equity) that an investor must maintain in the margin account at all times.

management fee a fee levied annually for professional mutual fund services provided; paid regardless of the performance of the portfolio.

margin account a brokerage account for which margin trading is authorized; a brokerage account in which the customer has been extended borrowing privileges by the brokerage firm.

margin call notification of the need to bring the equity of an account whose margin is below the maintenance level up to the initial margin level or to have enough margined holdings sold to reach this standard.

margin loan vehicle through which borrowed funds are made available, at a stated interest rate, in a margin transaction.

margin requirement the minimum amount of equity that must be a margin investor's own funds; set by the Federal Reserve Board (the "Fed").

margin trading the use of borrowed funds to purchase securities; magnifies returns by reducing the amount of equity that the investor must put up.

market order an order to buy or sell stock at the best price available when the order is placed.

market return the average return on all (or a large sample of) stocks, such as those in the *Standard & Poor's 500 Stock Composite Index.*

market risk risk of decline in investment returns because of market factorsindependent of the given investment.

market segmentation theory theory that the market for debt is segmented on the basis of maturity, that supply and demand within each segment determines the prevailing interest rate, and that the slope of the yield curve depends on the relationship between the prevailing rates in each segment.

market timing the process of identifying the current state of the economy/market and assessing the likelihood of its continuing on its present course.

market value the prevailing market price of a security.

maturity date the date on which a bond matures and the principal must be repaid.

mediation an informal, voluntary dispute resolution process in which a customer and a broker agree to a mediator, who facilitates negotiations between them to resolve the case.

mid-cap stocks medium-sized stocks, generally with market values of less than $4 or $5 billion but more than $1 billion.

mixed stream a stream of returns that, unlike an annuity, exhibits no special pattern.

modern portfolio theory (MPT) an approach to portfolio management that uses several basic statistical measures to develop a portfolio plan.

momentum investing investing style that focuses on using relative stock price movement to determine when to buy and sell.

money market market in which *short-term* securities are bought and sold.

money market deposit accounts (MMDAs) a bank deposit account with limited check-writing privileges; has no legal minimum balance, but many banks impose their own.

money market mutual fund (MMMF) a mutual fund that pools the capital of a large number of investors and uses it to invest exclusively in high-yielding, short-term securities.

Moody's Investor Services publisher of a variety of financial material, including *Moody's Manuals.*

mortgage bonds senior bonds secured by real estate.

mortgage-backed bond a debt issue secured by a pool of home mortgages; issued primarily by federal agencies.

municipal bond guarantees guarantees from a party other than the issuer that principal and interest payments will be made in a prompt and timely manner.

municipal bonds debt securities issued by states, counties, cities, and other political subdivisions; most of these bonds are tax-exempt (free of federal income tax on interest income).

mutual fund a company that raises money from sale of its shares and invests in and professionally manages a diversified portfolio of securities.

N

Nasdaq (National Association of Securities Dealers Automated Quotation) system an automated system that provides up-to-date bid and ask prices on certain selected, highly active OTC securities.

Nasdaq indexes measures of current price behavior of securities sold OTC, relative to a base of 100 set at February 5, 1971.

Nasdaq National Market a list of national or international Nasdaq stocks that meet certain qualification standards of financial size, performance, and trading activity.

negatively correlated describes two series that move in opposite directions.

negotiated commissions brokerage commissions agreed to by the client and the broker as a result of their negotiations; typically apply on large institutional transactions and to individual investors who maintain large accounts.

net asset value (NAV) the underlying value of a share of stock in a particular mutual fund.

net losses the amount by which capital losses exceed capital gains; up to $3,000 of net losses can be applied against ordinary income in any year.

no-load fund a mutual fund that does not charge a commission when shares are bought.

nondiversifiable (systematic) risk the inescapable portion of an investment's risk attributable to forces that affect all investments and therefore are not unique to a given vehicle.

note a debt security originally issued with a maturity of from 2 to 10 years.

NOW (negotiated order of withdrawal) account a bank checking account that pays interest; has no legal minimum balance, but many banks impose their own.

NYSE composite index measure of the current price behavior of the stocks listed on the NYSE, relative to a base of 50 set at December 31, 1965.

O

odd lot less than 100 shares of stock.

online broker typically a deep-discount broker through which investors can execute trades electronically online via a commercial service or on the Internet.

open-end investment company a type of investment company in which investors buy shares from, and sell them back to, the mutual fund itself, with no limit on the number of shares the fund can issue.

options securities that give the investor an opportunity to sell or buy another security at a specified price over a given period of time.

ordinary annuity an annuity for which the cash flows occur at the *end* of each period.

organized securities exchanges centralized institutions in which transactions are made in already outstanding securities.

over-the-counter (OTC) market widely scattered telecommunications network through which transactions are made in both *initial public offerings* (IPOs) and already outstanding securities.

P

paper return a return that has been achieved but not yet realized by an investor during a given period.

par value the stated, or face, value of a stock.

passbook savings account a savings account, offered by banks, that generally pays a low rate of interest and has no minimum balance.

payment date the actual date on which the company will mail dividend checks to shareholders (also known as the *payable date*).

PEG ratio a financial ratio that relates a stock's price/earnings multiple to the company's rate of growth in earnings.

perfectly negatively correlated describes two negatively correlated series that have a correlation coefficient of −1.

perfectly positively correlated describes two positively correlated series that have a correlation coefficient of +1.

PIK-bond a payment-in-kind junk bond that gives the issuer the right to make annual interest payments in new bonds rather than in cash.

point-and-figure charts charts used to keep track of emerging price patterns by plotting significant price changes with Xs and Os but with no time dimension used.

pooled diversification a process whereby investors buy into a diversified portfolio of securities for the collective benefit of the individual investors.

portfolio collection of securities or properties, typically constructed to meet one or more investment goals.

portfolio beta, *bp* the beta of a portfolio; calculated as the weighted average of the betas of the individual assets the portfolio includes.

positively correlated describes two series that move in the same direction.

preferred stock ownership interest in a corporation; has a stated dividend rate, payment of which is given preference over common stock dividends of the same firm.

premium bond a bond with a market value in excess of par; occurs when interest rates drop below the coupon rate.

present value the *value today* of a sum to be received at some future date; the inverse of future value.

price/earnings (P/E) approach stock valuation approach that tries to find the P/E ratio that's most appropriate for the stock; this ratio along with estimated EPS, is used to determine a reasonable stock price.

primary market the market in which *new issues* of securities are sold to the public.

prime rate the lowest interest rate charged the best business borrowers.

principal on a bond, the amount of capital that must be paid at maturity.

private placement the sale of new securities directly to selected groups of investors, without SEC registration.

profitability measures financial ratios that measure a firm's returns by relating profits to sales, assets, or equity.

promised yield same as yield-to-maturity.

property investments in real property or in tangible personal property.

prospectus a portion of a security registration statement that describes the key aspects of the issue, the issuer, and its management and financial position.

public offering an offering to sell to the investing public a set number of shares of a firm's stock at a specified price; the sale of a firm's securities to the general public.

publicly traded issues shares of stock that are readily available to the general public and are bought and sold in the open market.

purchasing power risk the chance that changing price levels (inflation or deflation) will adversely affect investment returns.

pyramiding the technique of using paper profits in margin accounts to partly or fully finance the acquisition of additional securities.

Q

quotations price information about various types of securities, including current price data and statistics on recent price behavior.

R

random walk hypothesis the theory that stock price movements are unpredictable, so there's no way to know where prices are headed.

rate of growth the compound annual rate of change in the value of a stream of income.

ratio analysis the study of the relationships between financial statement accounts.

real estate entities such as residential homes, raw land, and income property.

real rate of return the rate of return that could be earned in a perfect world where all outcomes are known and certain—where there was no risk.

realized return current income actually received by an investor during a given period.

realized yield same as expected return.

red herring a preliminary prospectus made available to prospective investors during the waiting period between the registration statement's filing with the SEC and its approval.

refunding provisions provisions that prohibit the premature retirement of an issue from the proceeds of a lower-coupon refunding bond.

reinvestment rate the rate of return earned on interest or other income received from an investment over its investment horizon.

relative P/E multiple a measure of how a stock's P/E behaves relative to the average market multiple.

relevant risk risk that is nondiversifiable.

required rate of return the return necessary to compensate an investor for the risk involved in an investment.

required return the rate of return an investor must earn on an investment to be fully compensated for its risk.

residual owners owners/stockholders of a firm, who are entitled to dividend income and a prorated share of the firm's earnings only after all the firm's other obligations have been met.

restricted account a margin account whose equity is less than the initial margin requirement; the investor may not make further margin purchases and must bring the margin back to the initial level when securities are sold.

return the level of profit from an investment—that is, the reward for investing.

returns the rewards from investing, received as current income and/or increased value.

revenue bonds municipal bonds that require payment of principal and interest only if sufficient revenue is generated by the issuer.

rights offering an offer of new shares of stock to existing stockholders on a pro rata basis.

risk the chance that actual investment returns will differ from those expected.

risk premium a return premium that reflects the issue and issuer characteristics associated with a given investment vehicle.

risk-averse describes an investor who requires greater return in exchange for greater risk.

risk-free rate the rate of return that can be earned on a risk-free investment; the sum of the real rate of return and the expected inflation premium.

risk-free rate, R_F the return an investor can earn on a risk-free investment such as a U.S. Treasury bill or an insured money market account.

risk-indifferent describes an investor who does not require a change in return as compensation for greater risk.

risk-return tradeoff the positive relationship between the risk associated with a given investment and its expected return.

risk-return tradeoff the relationship between risk and return, in which investments with more risk should provide higher returns, and vice versa.

risk-seeking describes an investor who will accept a lower return in exchange for greater risk.

round lot 100-share units of stock or multiples thereof.

S

satisfactory investment an investment whose present value of benefits (discounted at the appropriate rate) *equals* or *exceeds* the present value of its costs.

secondary distributions the public sales of large blocks of previously issued securities held by large investors.

secondary market the market in which securities are traded *after they have been issued.*

sector fund a mutual fund that restricts its investments to a particular segment of the market.

sector rotation investing style based on the premise that certain industry sectors perform better during specific stages of the economic cycle.

securities investments that represent evidence of debt or ownership or the legal right to acquire or sell an ownership interest.

Securities and Exchange Commission (SEC) federal agency that regulates securities offerings and markets.

Securities Investor Protection Corporation (SIPC) a nonprofit membership corporation, authorized by the federal government, that insures each brokerage customer's account for up to $500,000, with claims for cash limited to $100,000 per customer.

securities markets forums that allow suppliers and demanders of *securities* to make financial transactions; they include both the *money market* and the *capital market.*

securitization the process of transforming lending vehicles such as mortgages into marketable securities.

security analysis the process of gathering and organizing information and then using it to determine the intrinsic value of a share of common stock.

security market line (SML) the graphical depiction of the capital asset pricing model; reflects the investor's required return for each level of nondiversifiable risk, measured by beta.

security selection the procedures used to select the *specific* securities to be held *within* an asset class.

selling group a large number of brokerage firms that join the originating investment banker(s); each accepts responsibility for selling a certain portion of a new security issue.

semi-strong form (EMH) form of the EMH holding that abnormally large profits cannot be consistently earned using publicly available information.

senior bonds secured debt obligations, backed by a legal claim on specific property of the issuer.

serial bond a bond that has a series of different maturity dates.

series EE savings bonds savings bonds issued by the U.S. Treasury and sold at banks and through payroll deduction plans, in varying denominations, at 50% of face value; pay a variable rate of interest tied to U.S. Treasury security market yields and calculated every six months in May and November.

short interest the number of stocks sold short in the market at any given time; a technical indicator believed to indicate future market demand.

short selling the sale of borrowed securities, their eventual repurchase by the short seller, and their return to the lender.

short-term investments investments that typically mature within one year.

short-term vehicles savings instruments that usually have lives of 1 year or less.

simple interest interest paid only on the initial deposit for the amount of time it is held.

sinking fund a provision that stipulates the amount of principal that will be retired annually over the life of a bond.

small-cap stocks stocks that generally have market values of less than $1 billion but can offer above-average returns.

socially responsible fund a mutual fund that actively and directly incorporates ethics and morality into the investment decision.

specialist stock exchange member who specializes in making transactions in one or more stocks.

speculation the purchase of high-risk investment vehicles that offer highly uncertain returns and future value.

speculative stocks stocks that offer the potential for substantial price appreciation, usually because of some special situation, such as new management or the introduction of a promising new product.

split ratings different ratings given to a bond issue by the two major rating agencies.

Standard & Poor's Corporation (S&P) publisher of a large number of financial reports and services, including *Corporation Records* and *Stock Reports.*

Standard & Poor's indexes true indexes that measure the current price of a group of stocks relative to a base (set in the 1941–1943 period) having an index value of 10.

standard deviation, s a statistic used to measure the dispersion (variation) of returns around an asset's average or expected return.

statement of cash flows a financial summary of a firm's cash flow and other events that caused changes in the company's cash position.

stock dividend payment of a dividend in the form of additional shares of stock.

stock spin-off conversion of one of a firm's subsidiaries to a stand-alone company by distribution of stock in that new company to existing shareholders.

stock split a maneuver in which a company increases the number of shares outstanding by exchanging a specified number of new shares of stock for each outstanding share.

stock valuation the process by which the underlying value of a stock is established on the basis of its forecasted risk and return performance.

stockbrokers individuals licensed by both the SEC and the securities exchanges to facilitate transactions between buyers and sellers of securities.

stockholders' (annual) report a report published yearly by a publicly held corporation; contains a wide range of information, including financial statements for the most recent period of operation.

stop-loss (stop) order an order to sell a stock when its market price reaches or drops below a specified level; can also be used to buy stock when its market price reaches or rises above a specified level.

street name stock certificates issued in the brokerage firm's name but held in trust for its client, who actually owns them.

strong form (EMH) form of the EMH that holds that there is no information, public or private, that allows investors to earn abnormal profits consistently.

subordinated debentures unsecured bonds whose claim is secondary to other debentures.

systematic withdrawal plan a mutual fund service that enables shareholders to automatically receive a predetermined amount of money every month or quarter.

T

tactical asset allocation asset allocation plan that uses stock-index futures and bond futures to change a portfolio's asset allocation based on market behavior.

tangibles investment assets, other than real estate, that can be seen or touched.

tax planning the development of strategies that will defer and minimize an individual's level of taxes over the long run.

tax risk the chance that Congress will make unfavorable changes in tax laws, driving down the after-tax returns and market values of certain investments.

tax swap replacement of a bond that has a capital loss for a similar security; used to offset a gain generated in another part of an investor's portfolio.

taxable equivalent yield the return a fully taxable bond would have to provide to match the after-tax return of a lower-yielding, tax-free municipal bond.

tax-advantaged investments investment vehicles and strategies for legally reducing one's tax liability.

tech stocks stocks that represent the technology, "new-economy" sector of the market.

technical analysis the study of the various forces at work in the marketplace and their effect on stock prices.

term bond a bond that has a single, fairly lengthy maturity date.

term structure of interest rates the relationship between the interest rate or rate of return (yield) on a bond and its time to maturity.

theory of contrary opinion a technical indicator that uses the amount and type of odd-lot trading as an indicator of the current state of the market and pending changes.

third market over-the-counter transactions made in securities listed on the NYSE, the AMEX, or one of the other organized exchanges.

time value of money the fact that as long as an oppurtunity exists to earn interest, the value of money is affected by the point in time when the money is received.

total return the sum of the current income and the capital gain (or loss) earned on an investment over a specified period of time.

total risk the sum of an investment's nondiversifiable risk and diversifiable risk.

traditional portfolio management an approach to portfolio management that emphasizes "balancing" the portfolio by assembling a wide variety of stocks and/or bonds of companies from a broad range of industries.

Treasury bonds U.S. Treasury debt securities that are issued with 30-year maturities.

Treasury inflation-indexed obligations (TIPS) a type of Treasury security that provides protection against inflation by adjusting investor returns for the annual rate of inflation.

Treasury notes U.S. Treasury debt securities that are issued with maturities of 2 to 10 years or less.

treasury stock shares of stock that have been sold and subsequently repurchased by the issuing firm.

Treasury strips (Strip-Ts) zero-coupon bonds created from U.S. Treasury securities.

true rate of interest (return) the actual rate of interest earned.

U

U.S. Treasury bills (T-bills) obligations of the U.S. Treasury, sold on a discount basis, and having varying short-term maturities; regarded as the safest of all investments.

uncorrelated describes two series that lack any relationship or interaction and therefore have a correlation coefficient close to zero.

underwriting the role of the *investment banker* in bearing the risk of reselling, at a profit, the securities purchased from an issuing corporation at an agreed-on price.

underwriting syndicate a group formed by an investment banker to share the financial risk associated with *underwriting* new securities.

unit investment trust (UIT) a type of investment vehicle whereby the trust sponsors put together a fixed/unmanaged portfolio of securities and then sell ownership units in the portfolio to individual investors.

unrealized capital gains (paper profits) a capital gain made only "on paper"-that is, not realized until the fund's holdings are sold.

V

valuation process by which an investor uses risk and return concepts to determine the worth of a security.

value fund a mutual fund that seeks stocks that are undervalued in the market by investing in shares that have low P/E multiples, high dividend yields, and promising futures.

value investing investing in stocks of companies that are out of favor with the market for some reason, as reflected by low price/earnings ratios and low prices compared to their fundamentals.

Value Line composite index stock index that reflects the percentage changes in share price of about 1,700 stocks, relative to a base of 100 set at June 30, 1961.

Value Line Investment Survey one of the most popular subscription services used by individual investors; subscribers receive three basic reports weekly.

W

Wall Street Journal a daily business newspaper, published regionally; the most popular source of financial news.

weak form (EMH) form of the EMH holding that past data on stock prices are of no use in predicting future prices.

Wilshire 5000 index measure of the total dollar value (in billions of dollars) of 5,000 actively traded stocks, including all those on the NYSE and the AMEX in addition to active OTC stocks.

wrap account a brokerage account in which customers with large portfolios pay a flat annual fee that covers the cost of a money manager's services and the commissions on all trades.

Y

Yankee bonds bonds issued by foreign governments or corporations but denominated in dollars and registered with the SEC.

yield (internal rate of return) the compound annual rate of return earned by a long-term investment; the discount rate that produces a present value of the investment's benefits that just equals its cost.

yield curve a graph that represents the relationship between a bond's term to maturity and its yield at a given point in time.

yield pickup swap replacement of a low-coupon bond for a comparable higher-coupon bond in order to realize an increase in current yield and yield-to-maturity.

yield spreads differences in interest rates that exist among various sectors of the market.

yield-to-call (YTC) the yield on a bond if it remains outstanding only until a specified call date.

yield-to-maturity (YTM) the fully compounded rate of return earned by an investor over the life of a bond, including interest income and price appreciation.

Z

zero-coupon bonds bonds with no coupons that are sold at a deep discount from par value.

INDEX

Boldface locators indicate definitions. Locators followed by *f* indicate figures; those followed by *t* indicate tables.